THE FEDERAL VISION

The Federal Vision

Legitimacy and Levels of Governance in the United States and the European Union

edited by

KALYPSO NICOLAIDIS

and

ROBERT HOWSE

OXFORD
UNIVERSITY PRESS

[redacted]

OXFORD
UNIVERSITY PRESS
Great Clarendon Street, Oxford OX2 6DP

Oxford University Press is a department of the University of Oxford.
It furthers the University's objective of excellence in research, scholarship,
and education by publishing worldwide in

Oxford New York
Athens Auckland Bangkok Bogotá Buenos Aires Cape Town
Chennai Dar es Salaam Delhi Florence Hong Kong Istanbul Karachi
Kolkata Kuala Lumpur Madrid Melbourne Mexico City Mumbai Nairobi
Paris São Paulo Shanghai Singapore Taipei Tokyo Toronto Warsaw
and associated companies in Berlin Ibadan

Oxford is a registered trade mark of Oxford University Press
in the UK and in certain other countries

Published in the United States
by Oxford University Press Inc., New York

First published 2001

British Library Cataloguing in Publication Data
Data available

Library of Congress Cataloging in Publication Data
The federal vision: Legitimacy and levels of governance in the United States
and the European Union/edited by Kalypso Nicolaïdis and Robert Howse.

p. cm.
Includes bibliographical references and index.
1. Federal government—United States. 2. Federal government—European Union countries.
3. European Union. I. Nicolaïdis, Kalypso. II. Howse, Robert, 1958–
JK325.F383 2001 320.44x049—dc21 2001034064

ISBN 0–19–924501–0
ISBN 0–19–924500–2 (pbk.)

1 3 5 7 9 10 8 6 4 2

Typeset by Hope Services (Abingdon) Ltd.
Printed in Great Britain
on acid-free paper by
T. J. International Ltd.,
Padstow, Cornwall

[redacted]

To the memory of
***Daniel Elazar** and **Pierre Trudeau**,*
great thinkers and practitioners of federalism,
whom we lost while this book was written

ACKNOWLEDGEMENTS

This book is drawn from a conference held in April 1999, at the Kennedy School of Government, Harvard University, on 'Rethinking Federalism in the EU and US: The Challenge of Legitimacy'. The project was sponsored by the Kennedy School's Project on Visions of Governance for the XXIst Century in collaboration with the European Union Center, at Harvard University, and Notre Europe, Paris. We would like to thank the European Commission for its generous support. This project would not have been possible without Dominic Byatt's firm belief in its merits from the beginning and Amanda Watkins' scrupulous editorial scrutiny and supportive management style all the way to completion. Our thanks to both of them and their support team. Our thanks also to Julie Rooney as well as Kamiliakumari Wankaner and Jenifer Law for their administrative support.

Robert Howse is grateful for the administrative support of the University of Michigan Law School and valuable conversations with his colleagues Eric Stein, Daniel Halberstam, and Rick Hills on comparative federalism. From his teachers of federalism, Deborah Coyne and Kathy Swinton, and from Pierre Trudeau he has learnt more than he can express. Kalypso Nicolaidis is grateful for the financial support of Harvard University in launching this project and the administrative support of the European Studies Centre, St. Antony's College and the Norman Chester Fund, Politics Department, Oxford University, and would also like to thank Simon Saunders for his unwavering support throughout this project.

Kalypso Nicolaidis
Robert Howse
April 2001

CONTENTS

List of Figures xii

List of Tables xiii

Preface xiv
Jacques Delors and Joseph Nye

Introduction: The Federal Vision, Levels of Governance, and Legitimacy 1
Robert Howse and Kalypso Nicolaidis

I: Articulating the Federal Vision

1. The United States and the European Union: Models for Their Epochs 31
Daniel J. Elazar

2. Federalism without Constitutionalism: Europe's *Sonderweg* 54
J. H. H. Weiler

II. Levels of Governance in the United States and the European Union: Facts and Diagnosis

3. Centralization and Its Discontents: The Rhythms of Federalism in the United States and the European Union 73
John D. Donahue and Mark A. Pollack

4. Blueprints for Change: Devolution and Subsidiarity in the United States and the European Union 118
David Lazer and Viktor Mayer-Schoenberger

5. Devolution in the United States: Rhetoric and Reality 144
John Kincaid

6. Federalism in the European Union: Rhetoric and Reality 161
Andrew Moravcsik

III. Legal and Regulatory Instruments of Federal Governance

7. The Role of Law in the Functioning of Federal Systems 191
George A. Bermann

8. Comparative Federalism and the Issue of Commandeering 213
Daniel Halberstam

9. Regulatory Legitimacy in the United States and the European Union 252
Giandomenico Majone

IV. Federalism, Legitimacy, and Governance: Models for Understanding

10. Securing Subsidiarity: The Institutional Design of Federalism in the United States and Europe 277
Cary Coglianese and Kalypso Nicolaidis

11. Federal Governance in the United States and the European Union: A Policy Network Perspective 300
John Peterson and Laurence J. O'Toole, Jr

12. Federalism and State Governance in the European Union and the United States: An Institutional Perspective 335
Vivien Schmidt

13. Democratic Legitimacy under Conditions of Regulatory Competition: Why Europe differs from the United States 355
Fritz W. Scharpf

V. Federalism, Legitimacy, and Identity

14. Citizenship and Federations: Some Preliminary Reflections 377
Sujit Choudhry

15. The Constitutions of Institutions 403
Elizabeth Meehan

16. Beyond Devolution: From Subsidiarily to Mutuality 413
Marc Landy and Steven M. Teles

17. European Citizenship: The Relevance of the American Model 427
Denis Lacorne

Conclusion: The Federal Vision Beyond the Federal State 439
Kalypso Nicolaidis

Appendix: Basic Principles for the Allocation of Competence in the United States and the European Union 483
George A. Bermann and Kalypso Nicolaidis

About the Contributors 505

Index 515

LIST OF FIGURES

3.1. Composition of US government spending, 1962–1998 92
3.2. Composition of US public-sector employment, 1962–1998 93
3.3. Regulatory policies: directives and regulations in force as adopted annually, 1963–1998 114
3.4. Financial framework (EU-21), 2000–2006 115
4.1. The interactions among the President, Office of Management and Budget, and agencies 123
4.2. Numbers of reviews conducted by Office of Information and Regulatory Affairs, 1981–1996 124
4.3. Number of EU Commission proposals 135
4.4. Transposal rate of directives (per cent), 1991–1997 140
11.1. Types of governance structure 307
13.1. National and European problem-solving capabilities 363

LIST OF TABLES

3.1. Issue arenas and levels of authority in Europe 107
3.2. Issue arenas and levels of authority in the United States: selected comparisons with Table 3.1 108
4.1. Procedural changes from Reagan/Bush order to Clinton order 125
4.2. Contrasting premises of Reagan and two Clinton Federalism Executive Orders 127
4.3. The development of subsidiarity and proportionality criteria 134
4.4. Examples of implementation of 'where' criteria 141
4.5. Examples of implementation of 'how' criteria 142
C.1. Paradigm shift and the Federal Vision 443

PREFACE

Jacques Delors and Joseph Nye

Governance is changing in a world characterized by an information revolution, globalization and the emergence of many new voices on the international scene. The type of centralization that was typical of the industrial age no longer fits our post-modern societies and economies. President Clinton and other politicians claimed that the era of big government was over, but they said little about what would take its place. As Daniel Bell has argued, the nation-state is too small for the big problems of life and too big for the small problems. Yet, and for the foreseeable future, the nation-state will not whither away either. This book explores some of the ramifications of such a diagnosis in the context of the current debates about governance in the United States and the European Union.

What is the appropriate level of governmental authority, and for what purposes? What is happening to the uneasy relationship between the States and the Union in the United States and the European Union? How can we make subsidiarity and devolution work better on both sides of the Atlantic? And what do these debates tell us about the new models of governance beyond the state that can sustain the challenge of legitimacy? These are the types of questions that are explored in *The Federal Vision*. Based on a transatlantic dialogue between scholars concerned about modes of governance in both polities, this is a collective attempt at analysing the ramifications of the legitimacy crisis in our multi-layered democracies, drawing from and moving beyond the current policy debates over 'devolution' and 'subsidiarity'. The title is more a metaphor than a description of a unique legal structure. As Robert Howse and Kalypso Nicolaidis point out in the introductory chapter, the very language of federalism in its classic sense is a hotly contested political issue in Europe. While the term and notion of federalism is no longer taboo in Europe, there is still a wide gap between those who ultimately envision a federal state at the European level and those_like the contributors in this volume_who advocate a decentralized, transnational form of federalism, a federation of nation-states. The authors in this book mostly see the European Union as a *sui generis* post-modern polity, rather than an entity modelled on the American federal system, and do not advocate a change in its nature.

So what do the two sides of this trans-Atlantic dialogue have to say to each other if they are not addressing a single federal model? The answer is that both these leading post-modern societies are wrestling with the same set of issues related to appropriate levels of centralization and decentralization and with designing political systems with enduring legitimacy in the eyes of their citizens. Europeans struggle to give operational content to the concept of subsidiarity and are now asking whether such content should be enshrined in a European Constitution. Americans try to understand the shifting economic, political, and legal implications of devolution in their permanent quest to rediscover the spirit of their Constitution. Both are asking Elazar's question, if sovereignty rests in the people, how do the people want functions distributed among institutions? As Nicolaidis and Howse argue, the real federal vision sees political organization as a matrix with larger and smaller arena, not higher and lower, and a flexibility in applying institutions to different functions. Thus, a dialogue between Americans reinterpreting an eighteenth century vision and Europeans inventing new institutions for a new world is a two way street where each side can learn from the other.

We believe with the contributors to *The Federal Vision* that the possibility of mutual learning between Europe and America that was illustrated by Tocqueville and James is still true in the twenty-first century. The 'West'—however we may define it—is not one tradition or canon or ideology, but is itself sustained and revitalized, in part, by its own internal dialogue or conversation, which is often, and perhaps even quintessentially, a conversation between Europe and America. Nevertheless, there is no denying that this also needs to be a global conversation.

Addressing the issues of competence, subsidiarity, and devolution goes to the heart of one of the key problems of governance. Public opinion polls in Europe and in the United States show a decline in expressions of confidence and trust in government, but on both sides, the polls show that confidence in local, sub-regional, and even state government has fared better than the Union level. Can devolution and subsidiarity bring government 'closer to the people?' If so, would this help to restore confidence in government in general? What about the role of the private, non-governmental, and non-profit sectors which make up civil society? Where will they fit in the matrix? Diffusion of power away from central governments may occur at different rates in different societies. There may be several equilibrium points, and the evolution may be slow. As Charles Kindleberger pointed out, 'how the line should be altered at a given time—toward or away from the center—can stay unresolved for long periods, typically fraught with tension.' All the more reason for the type of trans-Atlantic dialogue carried out in this volume.

This is why also we have both felt that it would indeed be a fruitful exercise to associate our respective institutions in the pursuit of such a dialogue. Several years ago, the John F. Kennedy School of Government launched a project on Visions of Governance in the Twenty-first Century which has tried to clarify questions that matter for democracy—and for a multi-disciplinary school devoted to training public leaders—in a new era. The first volume, *Why People Don't Trust Government* (1997) looked into the causes of the decline in confidence in government that has occurred since the late 1960s. *Critical Citizens* (1999), edited by Pippa Norris put the same questions in a more comparative perspective. The next three volumes each explored one of three major trends that were altering the conditions of governance in the current period. The titles tell the story: *democracy.com? Governance in a Networked World?*; *Governance in a Globalizing World* (2000*); Governance Among Bigger, Better Markets* (2001). *The Federal Vision* is a perfect follow on and an important extension of this work. Seven of the twenty three scholars represented in these pages have taught at the School, and Kalypso Nicolaidis was both a distinguished graduate and faculty member there.

Since its establishment in 1996, Notre Europe has provided a continual and thorough analysis of the big question of the Future of Europe. Through its various research activities it has shown how a world characterised by interdependence has forced European states, beyond their fundamental ideal of peace and reconciliation to invent and develop new, unprecedented patterns of co-operation, even in those areas that had traditionally been regarded as forming the hardcore of national sovereignty. On the eve of the reunification of the European continent, this European model, which defies all attempts at categorization along traditional lines, is in need of strengthening. But such a task is made particularly arduous by the wide variety of political cultures that coexist in Europe. As stated above, there is no doubt that the word 'Federalism' has different connotations in France, Germany, and Britain, for example. Hence, then, the importance of the kind of transnational confrontations and debates in which the contributors to this volume have engaged.

This book, we believe, has many virtues. It constitutes an unprecedented attempt at what the editors call 'thinking together' between analysts of the US and EU systems and has actually created a number of new collaborative partnerships which we hope will endure. It also bridges the traditional divide between technical, legal or regulatory discussions of federal governance and philosophical debates over questions of identities and peoplehood. It is highly multidisciplinary, with contributions from history, political science, law, international relations, and political economy. It includes both innovative description and operational prescriptions on how to reshape the federal contract in the US and the EU. It can be read both as a text on federalism, and as a sampling of state of the art scholarly efforts to understand some of the most important issues that will affect our lives as democracies in the age of information and globalization.

As reflected in our respective personal involvement and commitment, we both believe that thinking cannot and should not be divorced from action. Social science is at its best, not when it seeks to soar in abstraction from the real world phenomena, but when it remains close to them, close to political life. The contributors to this volume have been able to engage in an illuminating conversation, to reach across disciplines and indeed methodologies, because they have stayed close to the phenomena, and because they have been able to engage political life on the plane of its own aspirations, anxieties, and ideals, and indeed with the combination of passion and detached observation so well articulated in Raymond Aron's self description as a 'spectateur engage'.

JD and JN
May 2001

Introduction

The Federal Vision, Levels of Governance, and Legitimacy

ROBERT HOWSE AND KALYPSO NICOLAIDIS

There is little doubt that this new century will witness quite dramatic changes in modes of governance, in and among liberal democratic societies. The painful, uneven, and amorphous globalization of societies and economies, changes in prevailing ideas on the role of state and the place of civil society, as well as shifts in patterns and understandings of loyalty and belonging, are, throughout the world, redefining polities and their boundaries. Already, the functions and authority traditionally assumed by the nation-state are being diffused and fragmented among a wide range of actors, both public and private, and at many different levels, from the global to the local. In the long term, the nation-state may prove to be more resilient than many argue, but only if it is able to adapt, evolving or accepting modes of governance that permit both legitimate and effective accommodations with the many entities, both above and below the state, which increasingly shape the public world in our century. We believe that this challenge calls for a federal vision of governance.

This book seeks to contribute towards articulating such a federal vision in the United States and in the European Union. It is about the complex and changing relationship between levels of governance within both polities at a time when they are revisiting the meaning of divided sovereignty. It was born out of a desire on the part of scholars from both sides of the Atlantic to compare notes about issues of multi-level governance in their respective polities that are the focus of their scholarship. Our starting point was to juxtapose and contrast what we may broadly refer to as the 'devolution debates' in the United States and the 'subsidiarity debates' in the European Union. We engaged in this exercise with a keen awareness of all that makes these two political projects terribly hard to compare. Yet, and perhaps not surprisingly to veteran scholars of federalism, we were struck by some of the common themes in the ongoing renegotiation of the federal contract in both polities. Above all, it seemed to us that debates on both sides have often been impeded by implicit and narrow assumptions about what constitutes the ultimate sources of legitimacy and sustainability in times of institutional change. Broadening out from the initial focus, the authors involved in this project came to share the premise that while 'levels of governance' in the US and the EU may differ radically, rethinking federalism on either side requires a self-conscious exploration of what we mean by legitimacy and how it can best be achieved.

The Federal Vision, therefore, is a collective attempt at analysing the ramifications of the legitimacy crisis in our multi-layered democracies, drawing from and moving beyond the current policy debates over devolution and subsidiarity. It is a multi-disciplinary project, bringing together historians, political scientists and theorists, legal scholars, sociologists, and political economists. In bringing such a group of scholars together, we have sought not only to bridge the transatlantic divide on the study of federalism and European integration, but also, and perhaps more importantly, the traditional academic divide between technical, legal, or regulatory discussions of federal governance and philosophical debates over questions of belonging, citizenship, and multiple identities.

1. The Challenge of Legitimacy

Federalism is an old idea, yesterday like today a response to the need for multi-centred governance. It is also, as Tocqueville and many others have said, a complex and even ambiguous idea, for it finesses the question of sovereignty, the question of who ultimately decides, by a myriad of 'federalist formulas', all bound to be contested. What shall we make of the notion of divided sovereignty at the heart of federalism? And what is it supposed to mean on a world stage still made of sovereign states? If a political entity is no more than the sum of its parts, it is really just a confederation or league, with each member having a veto over 'sovereign' acts of the centre, and acting autonomously on the world stage. If the federation is more than the sum of its parts, then a majority of the whole may prevail in sovereignty over the will of any of the parts, which makes federalism often seem like central government with administrative decentralization. In this case, the federation is a federal state: in the end, simply another state. When it has not led to their disintegration, this question has plagued federations throughout their history, sometimes to be resolved through civil wars only to arise anew with the ebb and flow of history.

The largely impossible nature of the task of squaring the federal idea with the modern statist conception of sovereignty has led much scholarship about federalism to retreat from an effort to theorize the federal vision, and rather to address the problem and promise of federalism through the apparently more modest and narrower lens of centralization and decentralization.[1] Merely on the assumption that some kind of divided sovereignty is a given, the question is asked concerning which competences, on some relevant theory of governance, should be allocated centrally and which to lower levels of government. Contemporary social science provides a number of well-known conceptual devices or tools with which to argue that question: principal-agent theory, public choice theory, regulatory competition, and so on. Ultimately, however, all such efforts to generate an ideal allocation of competences end up plagued by radical indeterminacy. Whether in the case of social welfare, economic development policy, or culture, there are good arguments that can be made for centralization, and good ones for decentralization too. And the fact that a given polity at times allocates competences at one level or another does not in and of itself tell us much about its underlying federal character.

The need to situate the debates about decentralization, devolution, and subsidiarity in a broader theoretical context, transcending the notion of divvying up or slicing 'sovereignty', is however perhaps most dramatically illustrated by the empirical reality of essentially all current, viable federal arrangements: the pervasiveness of concurrent or overlapping competences, the coexistence of elements of centralization and decentralization in the same policy field, and the dependence of successful policy outcomes on the ability of different levels of government to interact effectively. Notions of 'cooperative federalism' in the US context and 'pooling of sovereignty' in the EU context have sought to capture the phenomenon; but they seem only to restate the problem: if there are no 'benchmarks' for optimal solutions for distributing sovereignty, how are we to understand and assess change?

For us, in this volume, the broader theoretical context is provided through the optic of legitimacy. The question of legitimacy is more fundamental than that of sovereignty and in fact is presupposed by it. As Daniel Elazar reminds us, federal democracy addresses the fundamental question of jurisdiction and distribution of power by vesting sovereignty in the people who constitute the body politic and requiring them to allocate powers among the governments of their creation. To what level of government is only a secondary question. What matters in a true federal context is that this be done 'within a non-centralized framework whereby all exercise of power is governed by law and related to the rights of the constituents'. What Kymlyka calls 'the federalist revolution' perhaps involves

[1] There are, of course, many notable exceptions, starting with Daniel Elazar's classic *Exploring Federalism* (Tusculoosa, AL: University of Alabama Press, 1987).

above all recognizing the end of the idea that states, including in their federal guise, could somehow appropriate, once and for all, the sovereignty mantle, albeit in order to delegate it upwards or downwards. Instead, the authority vested in different layers of governance is transitory and derivative and it derives above all, at a given moment in time, from the more fundamental and amorphous concept of legitimacy: the notion that it is fair or just in some way that a set of actors accept the influence or say of a particular collectivity exercising power.[2]

Once we see the world of multi-level governance through the optic of legitimacy, the challenge, and promise, of the federal vision come into sharper focus. Surely, the sources of legitimacy are diverse: some are technocratic, and relate to presumed expertise to manage the complexities of policy; others are grounded in conceptions of collective identity and culture; others still in notions of active democratic consent and interest representation. How do we design mechanisms of governance that give all these sources of legitimacy their due, while ensuring that policy outcomes or outputs of governance, which are the product of the action and interaction of multiple levels of governance, themselves enjoy, in the broadest possible sense, legitimacy? This is the key pathos or quandary of public men and women in liberal democracies today: never before have they had to listen, weigh, and attend to so many and varied 'legitimate' voices and influences in the making of policy, and yet the results of such policy-making often leave voters with feelings of disappointment, distance, and distrust. It is precisely through the articulation of a federal vision of governance that we can begin to address this quandary, by asking what it means for policy outcomes to be legitimate when they are produced in a world of multi-level governance, and, then, more concretely, what mechanisms and modes of governance lend themselves to creating or sustaining such legitimacy.

[2] Most authors in this volume present one definition or other of legitimacy. We have not chosen to impose an all-encompassing definition to be used throughout, precisely because we believe that coming up with one's one own is part of the analytical journey. In operating from this stated understanding of legitimacy, we are, of course, well aware of the long-standing debate about whether it is a positive or a normative idea. For purposes of certain kinds of intellectual inquiry or investigation, it can be useful to view legitimacy from either a purely positivistic or a purely normative angle. But from the perspective from which we are writing, namely, the challenges of governance for public men and women of today, such a *dépeçage* is not helpful: those who govern must both consider and understand what, as a matter of fact, leads those over whom they govern to accept as fair or just their decisions, but those who govern must also weigh the sometimes conflicting claims of other collectivities legitimately to influence the decisions. This entails an inherently normative exercise of considering the relative strength of different sources of legitimacy in as much as they ought to influence or shape a given policy decision.

2. Thinking Together'

In some very general sense, this exercise can be called 'comparative', but it is faithful neither to the methodologies nor the goals of the comparative traditions of scholarship, in either law or political science. This project was framed from the outset as a transatlantic dialogue between individuals concerned about patterns and modes of governance on either side. None of us was preoccupied with making scholarly judgements about convergence or divergence between fundamentally different kinds of polity, nor with the naïve notion of transplantation of institutions or mechanisms of governance from one polity to the other. The operating premise was that common to both the EU and the US is a set of challenges to governance, which in both polities are connected to the special nature of the problem of legitimacy in the context of multi-level governance, of federalism in the broadest sense of the term. In thinking together about such challenges, in full awareness of both our differences and our commonalities, we sought to learn from one another. And indeed we consider it an important achievement that a number of transatlantic research partnerships were forged in the context of this project.

The notion of a dialogue or confrontation between Europe and America as a consciousness-raising and horizon-expanding exercise is not new; this is the legacy of Tocqueville and of Henry James, among others. The fundamental premise of Tocqueville's *Democracy in America* was that 'old Europe' could learn from 'young America'. The idea of democratic equality, said Tocqueville, was sweeping the civilized world, and this revolution was farther advanced, better articulated, and more evident in its risks and opportunities in America than in Europe.[3]

The dialogue we propose in this volume appears to depend, in part, on granting equal status to the reverse proposition: 'old America' may also be able to learn something from 'new Europe'. How could an established federal order like that of the United States have anything to learn from an apparently not-quite-yet federal one like the EU? We believe that if one of the key challenges of this twenty-first century is to conceive forms of governance in a world in which sovereignty and the nation-state have become problematic, if still persistent, categories, 'new Europe' may be farther ahead than 'old America'. For, as Joseph Weiler argues in his contribution to this volume, 'new Europe' has already begun the experiment of emancipating the federal idea from statist categories of sovereignty and

[3] De Tocqueville, 'Introduction', *De la démocratie en Amerique*, 2nd edn (Paris: A. Gain, 1951).

constitutional supremacy. Indeed, as will be discussed in this volume, it may be the case that the nation-states in Europe are increasingly using their 'Union' to implement a principle of mutuality and horizontal 'delegation' of competences or authorities from which the 'United' States may have a lot to learn.

That Europe can learn from America's history, or more accurately, the EU learn from the US, has long been taken for granted. But, if today's EU is to be compared with yesterday's US, which US are we talking about? Is it the pre-1787 confederate States engaged in foundational debates pitting federalists and anti-federalists? Or are the Europeans, like the North Americans at the turn of this century, still seeking to implement the lessons of their own great civil war and implement the promise of their own 'Gettysburg address', through a Union without a Federal State—let us not forget that the US federal budget was comparable to the current EU's 2 per cent of GDP at the turn of the twentieth century? Or should today's EU activists look back to the American New Deal when the realization that States alone could not respond to the demands of their residents served as a catalyst for the establishment of a federal government with broad-ranging economic powers and complex mechanisms for allocating authority between the executive branch, Congress, and regulatory agency in the management of regulatory federalism?

Most probably, both all and none of the above. We believe that historically grounded analogies, appealing as they are, can only be unsatisfactory given both historical path dependency and the fact that context matters most: from prevailing ideas to technological and economic structures and international constraints and opportunities. At best, historical parallels can serve as metaphors of 'eternal return' and 'paths not taken'.

Instead, for us, there is an important sense in which, more than a century and a half after Tocqueville, Europe can learn from *today*'s America about the relationship of federalism to democracy. The new European experiment with a federal vision took flight on the ashes of World War II. The pre-war European record of democracy was highly uneven; political democracy in many European states was unstable and aimless, while the social and cultural estate of democracy provided fertile ground for the mass-mobilization exercise of demagogues and tyrants. As has been abundantly noted, despite an implicit democratic teleology from the start—Jean Monnet's 'Nous ne coalisons pas des états, nous unissons des hommes'—the project of a European federal union began as an elite exercise, and still to this day, despite the 'Citizen's Europe' proclaimed in the Amsterdam Treaty, bears the marks of these origins. The project of the common market and ultimate federal union of Europe could not draw on a strong democratic tradition in twentieth-century Europe. So the framers reached back beyond the madness of the 1930s and 1940s to older European traditions: cooperation, tolerance and comity among enlightened rulers; bureaucratic integrity and rationality; the rule of law as a moral and political ideal. The European project did not seek, in the first instance, to modify or challenge the national allegiances and prejudices of the people, but rather to provide a permanent, resilient buffer against their outbreak into zero-sum inter-state competition and conflict. But, for reasons that are well-articulated in a number of contributions to this volume, beginning with that of Mark Pollack and Jack Donahue, the attempt at such a 'buffer' turned into a new level of governance—not simply a check or limit on the nation-state—which could not but end up raising new questions about allegiances and democratic accountability. And, here, there is at least a prima facie case that Europe can learn from today's America, first of all because the institutions, practices, and legal controls of American federalism developed in tandem with consciousness of the democratic ideal, and present a range of options for preserving clarity and integrity of democratic accountability, in situations where more than one level of governance is implicated in the same or overlapping policy fields. Second, and more controversially, America offers a rather different understanding of allegiance and affiliation to the state from that which has predominated in Europe since the nineteenth century, an understanding more congenial to multiple allegiances, mixed identities, and civic forms of patriotism and political commitment—all collective forms of belonging that depend as much on engagement for a common future as on a shared history or, even less, a shared cultural or racial background. Sooner or later, the European polity will have to rise to the challenge of reshaping conceptions of citizenship, allegiance, and identity within Europe, or the majority of Europeans risk becoming alienated, and dangerously so, not just from new realities beyond the nation-state, but from new realities of diversity within it as well.

Hence, our basic proposition that America and Europe, when one considers both where they have come from as federal entities and the challenges of governance they are headed towards, are well situated for learning from one another. We believe that this same kind of proposition underpins a number of important exercises in the parallel or interactive study of European and American federal arrangements over the last few decades. Among the first of these is the two-volume study, *Courts and Free Markets*, which emerged from a meeting of European and American scholars and practitioners of federalism at Bellagio in 1979. In introducing this study, Terrance Sandalow and Eric Stein claim:

The common problems facing the two systems suggest the possibility that, at the appropriate level of analysis, each system may draw on the other's experience. We should not, of course, expect to find that either system has developed 'solutions' to these problems that are readily transferable to the other. But an examination of the manner in which each has responded and the reasons that it has responded as it has may suggest hitherto unseen opportunities for the other. Whether or not such opportunities emerge, the perspective gained from comparing a system with another facing similar issues is likely to provide students of each system with a new insight into its workings. In this light, similarities and differences between the two systems are of equal interest.[4]

In looking in this volume at common issues from the perspective of the challenge of governance in the twenty-first century, our aims and assumptions are both as bold and as modest as those stated by Sandalow and Stein just over 20 years ago.

3. A Caveat on European 'Federalism'

At this point, however, out of concern for political relevance we need to introduce a caveat. Clearly, the fundamentals have not changed since Sandalow and Stein. Today as 20 years ago, it would be an understatement to say that the US and EU do not relate to the notion of federalism in the same way. Ever since the federalist debates, nation-building in the United States has consisted to a great extent in the self-conscious and systematic refining of the federal formula. The EU, on the other hand, does not have a federal 'founding myth', and although most scholars would agree that it has been a federation in the making since the 1960s, the language of federalism, the very term, continues to be highly contested. We may bemoan the gap between the scholarly—or American—understanding of federalism as a decentralizing concept and its pan-European capture as synonymous with central government. The fact remains: today as in 1979, there is little doubt that the EU will never be called a 'federation' *tout court*. This is neither likely nor desirable.

There is an important way, however, in which developments in the intervening 20 years have a bearing on the way in which we may 'think

[4] Terrance Sandalow and Eric Stein, 'Introduction', *Courts and Free Markets—Perspectives from the United States and Europe*, vol. 1, reprinted in E. Stein, *Thoughts from a Bridge: A Retrospective of Writings on New Europe and American Federalism* (Ann Arbor: University of Michigan Press, 2000), 115–16. For subsequent comparative studies see also Mauro Cappelletti, Monica Seccombe, and Joseph H. H. Weiler (eds), *Integration Through Law: Europe and the American Federal Experience* (Berlin and New York: Walter de Gruyter, 1986); Koen Lenaerts (ed.), *Two Hundred Years of U.S. Constitution and Thirty Years of EEC Treaty* (Brussels: Kluwer, 1988); Alberta Sbragia 'Thinking About the European Future: The use of comparison, in Sbragia, A. (ed) *Europolitics*, Brookings, 1992.

together' about the US and the EU experience. That is that not only have both the US and the EU in the last two decades experienced a backlash against centralization or harmonization, if not in practice at least in the prevailing political discourse. It is also that, most recently, the debate in Europe turned, perhaps for the first time on such a scale, from one about subsidiarity in the day-to-day management of the Union to one about the need for a new covenant, a European constitution. Having exhausted most of the potential for policy expansion while contemplating an unprecedented enlargement challenge, the EU polity is rethinking its architecture. Here is the paradox. Most constitution supporters agree on two points: that this should not be the blueprint for a 'federal state' of Europe—in other words, to some extent the discourse of constitutionalism must be liberated from its statist origins; and that a constitution is needed, above all, to make clear and explicit to the citizens who does what in the European Union—the hallmark of democratically accountable federalism. We would seem to want European federalism without the word, with its statist resonances and connotations. Perhaps this is right.[5]

Yet we cannot escape the fact that our own formula, 'Federal Vision', unavoidably has it own normative resonances. Does it refer to the EU as a *federation* of nation states, as Jacques Delors would have it? This is possible, if we believe Joseph Weiler, whether it gives itself a constitution or not. Is it more appropriate then to see it like Daniel Elazar, as a 'post-modern confederation'? Or shall we simply speak of a 'post-federation', a *sui generis* construction of supranational order, predicated on principles of mutual transparency, mutual recognition, and mutual empowerment? Our 'federal vision' is compatible with any of these labels. It is meant as a framework for universal concepts, not as a motto for an ideological crusade. And it is not directly teleological, some vision of an end-state to a socio-political project—although certain substantive norms, such as equality, liberty, the rule of law, and democracy may be inseparable from the realization of the project on its own terms. Instead, and more humbly, it is simply a vision of good governance, in Europe and in the United States.

Finally on the theoretical front—explaining why the polity has evolved in a certain way and what the main factors driving the process are—we

[5] Most commentators still equate 'federal' and 'state'. Thus for instance, Larry Siedentop, in his recent *Democracy in Europe* (London: Allen Lane, The Penguin Press, 2000) argues that Europeans are trying to imitate the US in building a federal state and that this is right—although they are not ready. On the opposite side, Charles Grant argues that the idea of a 'federal state' in Europe is obsolete: *EU 2010: An Optimistic Vision of the Future* (London: Centre for European Reform, September 2000). See Conclusion for a further discussion on this point.

believe, like more and more of our peers, that European studies must now move beyond the stale debate between supranationalism and intergovernmentalism. The study of federalism takes the uneasy relationship between the States, the Union, and the citizens as a starting point. It seeks to understand how conflicts of power and patterns of cooperation between the two evolve over time, in relation to the needs, values, and preferences of citizens. After all, functionalism was the method adopted by the founding fathers precisely to avoid the need for a priori decisions about the type and forms of federal structure Europe should give itself. We hope that this book may contribute in bridging the divide between the study of European integration and comparative federalism.

4. A Roadmap Through the Volume

The book proceeds in five parts. Part I presents two overarching views of what federalism is really about in its US and EU versions. Part II provides an overview of the history and current state of federalism in the US and the EU and a set of diagnoses of devolution and subsidiarity. The rest of the book revisits these developments through a multi-faceted examination of the sources, mechanisms, and challenges of legitimacy in these federal contexts. The contributions in Part III examines the legal and regulatory instruments of mutual control between state and union in each polity. Part IV presents alternative analytical models for understanding the overall relationship between levels of governance and the ways in which legitimacy can be sustained in the US and the EU. Finally, the chapters in Part V discuss the deeper roots of legitimacy in federal systems by asking what determines allegiance to different levels of governance. Most chapters in the book engage in a symmetric fashion with both the US and the EU. A few are asymmetric, focusing particularly on one or the other side. An appendix by George Bermann and Kalypso Nicolaidis lays out the basic legal principles, and variants thereof, on which the federal organization of governance is founded. In some ways, our book measures the distance between this, the theory, and the *praxis* that inspires our vision.

The two chapters in Part I, by Daniel Elazar—who, very regrettably and sadly, has since passed away—and Joseph Weiler, display, respectively, the problem of integrating the federal vision with the modern conception of state sovereignty, and the promise and possibilities that emerge once one liberates that vision from 'statist' conceptions of political organization. They are both interested in the normative values embedded in these polities. Elazar refers to the 'competition between statism and federalism', epitomized by the confrontation in the seventeenth century between

Althusius and Bodin, which unites the modern and what he calls the 'post-modern' epochs. According to Elazar, from the outset federalism in the US was characterized by the choice of a union that would advance comprehensive ends of government—'liberty, justice, and domestic tranquillity'. The creation of a federal system with a central government directly responsible to the people was a reflection of the need to find means that were consistent with both the ideal of democracy and the requirement of a union to advance such comprehensive ends. This ensuing tension between the State and federal elements in the US system calls for a more adequate 'partnership' or cooperation between levels of government, first as a check against the 'State' element overwhelming the 'federal' element, and most recently as a protective device for the States. While the trajectory in the US from confederation or league to 'statist' federalism was already set in motion by the fateful choice for a union with comprehensive political ends, Europeans have, fortunately, not yet made any such choice—although some of the pro-Europe rhetoric implies this kind of choice, which should be made, however, *en pleine connaissance de cause*, as it were. But the promise for realizing the federal vision in Europe remains strong, because, at least, the idea of union began in terms not of comprehensive, but of limited political ends. Europe is well poised to develop a theory of federalism suitable to its confederal tendency and its greater number of 'levels' of governance than any prior federation.

However, according to Elazar, for the EU to remain within the confederative approach that more adequately realizes the federal vision than a statist version of federalism, it actually needs to learn from aspects of the US system that are—ironically, it seems, given what Elazar has already said—less 'statist' than some of what has been developing in Europe. In particular, for Elazar, the notion of 'subsidiarity' has a hierarchical legacy and tint, suggesting a vertical relationship of delegation from the top down, as it was first intended to by the Catholic Church. In contrast, conceptions of partnership between levels of government in the US, albeit not yet well realized, evoke a more horizontal relationship 'within multiple-centred systems in which there is no hierarchy'. As perhaps the most influential writer in the study of federalism, Elazar pointedly reminds us that the real 'federal vision', whether in its confederal European version or its federal US version, must be based on 'covenant-based principles that see the proper political organization as a matrix with larger and smaller arenas but not higher and lower' (p. 42).

In important respects, Joseph Weiler's essay complements that of Elazar, even if its normative foundations are rather different. Weiler describes the EU equally as a mixture of 'federal' and 'confederal' principles:

> Architecturally, the combination of a 'confederal' institutional arrangement and a 'federal' legal arrangement seemed for a time to mark Europe's *Sonderweg*—its special way and identity. It appeared to enable Europe to square a particularly vicious circle: achieving a veritably high level of material integration comparable only to that found in fully fledged federations, while maintaining at the same time—and in contrast with the experience of all such federations—powerful, some would argue strengthened, Member States. (p. 58)

But the great difference between Europe and the US—and for that matter all other federal states—is that the European construct does not presuppose the supreme authority and sovereignty of a single constitutional *demos*. For Weiler what is most humanly valuable about the European federal idea as it has developed so far—despite the 'messy architecture' it has produced—is what he calls 'constitutional tolerance'. Although Europe will always be composed of distinctive peoples and constitutional democracies of which each people is the *pouvoir constituant*, these national states accept to be bound and constrained in their exercise of sovereignty by the claims of others as reflected in the decisions of the Community

For Weiler, then, attempting to transform the European project into one of federal constitutionalism along statist lines is deeply misguided. Instead of providing a healthy self-limit on collective self-determination, the European project would become a competing project of collective self-determination, which would imply, along the lines of statist democratic constitutionalism, the creation of a single European *demos* or people. The parable offered by Weiler may helps the reader reflect on the spiritual meaning of Europe's *Sonderweg*. It suggests that constitutional tolerance reflects the European choice for a 'civilizing strategy' of dealing with the 'other' without seeking to assimilate them, and for making integration an endlessly renewed autonomous, voluntary act of subordination to this European other. This idea of 'emancipation' through internalizing mutual constraints at every level, from the customs duty officer to the prime minister, can be understood as an extreme version of what Elazar and others have called 'federal liberty', or as the constitutional translation of the very European norm of 'mutual recognition'. This idea must be seen in light of some of Weiler's other writings, including those discussed by Denis Lacorne in his contribution to this volume, which suggest the importance of a positive affinity with the European project among European citizens, and therefore that self-identification with the project is required, not simply a sense of the appropriateness of restraint on one's national projects of collective self-realization in recognition of the other. Constitutional tolerance is not a mere grudging toleration: it implies a reaching out across bounded identities 'in recognition of our essential humanity' (p. 66). Thus, it implies human identification and affiliation across national boundaries, but the idea of tolerance signifies that such identification and affiliation does not itself destabilize the boundaries. It is a kind of allegiance that is strong enough to mitigate the totalizing tendencies of bounded communities but weak enough not to threaten their boundaries. This is a promising response to those who denigrate the civic sources of European affiliation as providing very little competition for the identity claims on which the national polity can draw: the aim is not to compete with national state identity politics, but rather to constrain these *enough*. We will have more to say about this in discussing the final part of the volume, on belonging and citizenship.

Each in his own way, Elazar and Weiler provide important conceptual and normative reasons why we should not understand the promise of federalism through the lenses of the modern idea of state sovereignty, that is, as a kind of truce between competing sovereignties, through the division of competence or the hierarchical ordering of authorities. The chapters in Part II explain why, in any event, the day-to-day realities of contemporary democratic politics in the US and the EU preclude any such stable truce between competing sovereignties. These contributions all highlight the dynamic character of federalism, document the process of change, and offer competing diagnosis on trends, past and future. Jack Donahue and Mark Pollack provide a sweeping historical overview of the rhythm of federalism in the US and the EU. They show how, historically in both polities, citizen preferences have tend ed to fluctuate between centralization and decentralization. There *is* no stable federal bargain, understood as a clear settlement over relative power between the States and the Union.

> Citizens perceive more vividly the defects of the recently ascendant theme, and amplify in abstraction the virtues of its opposite. Hence in a reasonably effective democracy—in which popular complaints and yearning have consequences—featuring an ambiguous or unsettled degree of centralization, the norm is fluctuation. Depending on the polity, the issue, and the time, the actors propelling change may include courts, corporations, elected leaders, and appointed officials of central or constituent states, and the electorate itself. The intricate interplay of these actors . . . tends to generate oscillations between the concentration of power in the centre and the reassertion of the individual States in each system. (p. 114)

As a result, as the historical record amply shows, the 'equilibrium' is for ever elusive, and the pattern for Donahue and Pollack is one of lively awareness of what's wrong with the status quo, and a perennial search for ways to accommodate new issues and better resolve old ones.

Since there is no ideal, stable division of sovereignty, or balance of centralization and decentralization, from the perspective of democratic legitimacy, the implication of this analysis is that we will have to search for stability elsewhere—in various norms, institutions, and mechanisms by which citizens bargain on an ongoing basis, and governments bargain on their behalf, for adjustment and re-adjustment of roles in concurrent policy fields. The legitimacy of multi-level governance will depend on the legitimacy of these norms, institutions, and mechanisms. David Lazer and Viktor Mayer-Schoenberger examine the most recent attempts in both the US and EU to respond to attacks on the legitimacy of 'federal' governance by building into the legislative or regulatory processes a federalism or subsidiarity criterion. Not surprisingly, if we believe Donahue and Pollack's argument on indeterminacy, Lazer and Mayer-Schoenberger show that such criteria, when formulated as guidance on 'where' policy should be made, have been largely ineffective and inoperable; 'federalism' criteria have been subsumed and assumed away under either purely political decisions over the scope of devolution or broader cost-benefit analysis in the US, and the EU has not abandoned significant policies under its 'subsidiarity review'. In contrast , we witness the increased use of 'how' criteria which increase accountability of central decision-making by requiring a publicized process of justification for the policies. Gráinne de Búrca's 'procedural subsidiarity' is a concept relevant to governance on both sides, as they each have come to focus on how to provide more discretion to lower levels of governance in implementing or administering federal policies—although that has been achieved in very different ways in the US and the EU, as will be discussed later in Daniel Halberstam's chapter. In short, Lazer and Mayer-Schoenberger make the case that new sources of legitimate governance are not mainly to be found in the recent subsidiarity and devolution pledges appended to the US and EU covenants.

The last two authors in Part II offer somewhat contrarian diagnoses on what has happened to the US and the EU in the last 20 years, highlighting the gap between rhetoric and reality in the devolution and subsidiarity debates. John Kincaid critically examines the fashionable notion that the steady trajectory of US federalism in recent decades has been in the direction of decentralization or devolution, his case resting above all on the pervasiveness of concurrency: 'All public functions are likely to involve intergovernmental power-sharing in one way or another . . . The centralization that has occurred in the United States has rarely involved wholesale federal occupation of policy fields . . . often in a positive-sum manner in which there is a concomitant expansion of State and/or local government powers' (pp. 157–8). In this context, so-called devolution in the US has been far from a wholesale transfer of power but rather a series of halfway measures. More importantly, if legitimacy has not been enhanced through outright devolution—presumably an unachievable first-best in Kinkaid's view—then 'issues of process' are vital. That is the legitimacy of the norms, institutions, and mechanisms that allow constant adjustment of roles and responsibilities between levels of government in response to changing circumstances and changing citizen preferences.

In the next chapter, Andrew Moravcsik brings back our attention from issues of process to issues of competence per se. If, according to Kinkaid, the US is not really decentralizing, according to Moravcsik the EU is not really centralizing. Moravcsik attacks the view, shared by Euro-enthusiasts and Euro-sceptics alike, that current developments in the EU herald the advent of a European federal state. According to him, the EU lacks and is likely to continue to lack the fundamental competences that would make it federal. To make this point, he emphasizes what the EU does *not* do and is unlikely to take on in the foreseeable future, spelling out how the 'EU plays almost no role—at most a weak sort of international coordination—in most of the issue-areas about which European voters care most, such as taxation, social welfare provision, defence, high foreign policy, policing, education, cultural policy, human rights, and small business policy' (p. 163–4). This is not surprising, in Moravcsik's view, since the EU's built-in 'constitutional constraints', from fiscal to legislative and regulatory powers, create a strong bias towards the status quo. His normative conclusion that the 'existing hybrid status quo is sufficiently efficient and adequately legitimate to resist any fundamental institutional reform' (p. 163) seems to echo Weiler's conclusion that the EU 'ain't broke, so don't fix it'. But the two authors get there from opposite premises: Weiler thinks that today's EU founded on constitutional tolerance—bowing to the majority without being one people—is an amazingly ambitious project, while Moravcsik celebrates the EU's character as 'a second-best constitutional compromise designed to cope pragmatically with concrete problems' (p. 169).

Together, the authors in Part II provide a reading of the 'allocative map' that goes beyond mere enumeration of competences, highlighting instead underlying principles and trends. They are all cautious about providing predictions, especially with regard to convergence between the US and the EU. Although he predicts that the centralizing impulse is likely to reassert itself in both polities in the century's early years, Kinkaid is careful to point out that political ideology and the relative weight of the moderates in each polity will have a major role to play in this regard. Donahue and Pollack venture a general argument about what they have identified as the rhythm of federalism, stating that this 'rhythm tends to slow and cycles to lengthen as a polity matures' and as 'first-order ambiguities are settled, and a degree of institutional inertia dampens the effect of discontent with both centralization and decentralization' (p. 117). As a result, the next period of predominant centralization should be somewhat sharper and shorter in Europe than in the US. If they are right, the constraints on centralization identified by Moravcsik will turn out only to be features of this current initial cycle of European integration rather than a structural characteristic of the EU.

If, from the perspective of legitimacy, the federal vision is much more about 'how' than about 'where', to use the Lazer and Mayer-Schoenberger distinction, what are some of the norms, institutions, and mechanisms that allow for legitimate multi-level governance? We explore some of these in Part III and IV.

As we observed at the beginning of this Introduction, in the EU the ideal of the rule of law may historically have been understood as an alternative to democracy among the sources for the Community's legitimacy—law as 'higher law' that *constrains* collective self-determination. And indeed Weiler's essay points out the permanent vitality of the notion that law's normative force cannot simply be reduced to its origins in an act of democratic will. Through providing for judicial as well as political policing of the processes of federal governance, law can be a means for assuring that accountability, transparency, and individual rights are respected in such processes. Promoting federal values in this way is consistent with the focus on legitimate multi-level governance as opposed to division of sovereignty. George Bermann explores the various ways in which the courts can, and choose to, enforce the principles of federalism beyond the classical 'political' and 'procedural' safeguards provided by the institutional structures themselves and the constraints on the deliberative process—including the new 'federalism assessment' discussed earlier by Lazer and Mayer-Schoenberger. Bermann describes the reluctance on the part of courts on both sides to police the borders of enumerated competences, assess the 'necessity' of federal action, or carve out the 'core' of state sovereignty, all of which are ways of 'second-guessing' the political process. Instead, he points to the recent emphasis of the US Supreme Court on what he calls the 'relational' aspects of federalism, whereby courts can identify 'forbidden interfaces' between State and federal governments, even without specific Constitutional grounds. Bermann uses the examples of sovereign immunity and of anti-commandeering to illustrate the manner in which court-enforced constraints on the manner in which different levels of government interact can protect and promote democratic accountability:

> By protecting a State from having to devote its resources to objectives dictated by the federal government, the principle helps ensure that those resources will not be spent in ways that lack the support of that State's population or that otherwise fail to reflect its political priorities. At the same time, it also allows the State electorate to hold State officials democratically accountable in policy and performance terms. (p. 208)

In contrast, European Union law offers no protection against risks to democracy from commandeering, and more broadly relies almost exclusively on the representation of Member States—and now sub-national units—in the Council as—structural—political safeguards. But what happens as Member States progressively lose their veto? Should the EU not devise new types of political safeguards—for example, through the role of national parliaments and sub-national regions? While the European Court of Justice has thus far shown a preference for relying on structural and procedural safeguards, Bermann believes that the latter can still be strengthened and that relational safeguards in the EU context remain to be invented.

The example of commandeering is developed as a case study in Daniel Halberstam's chapter. Halberstam uses commandeering as a window into the differences between EU and the US with respect to the relationship of federalism to democratic accountability. As Halberstam suggests, a directly elected central government in the United States can make law that is directly effective in all the States, and supreme over State law. In the EU, directives which 'commandeer' the Member State governments, and regulations which are directly effective, have traditionally *both* required the consent of the constituent Member States. Thus, there is a check in the EU on non-democratic 'commandeering'—the political community that was being commandeered had to agree. And given that its consent is required, one can understand that a Member State might prefer being commandeered to being directly regulated—since, as Halberstam explains, in the EU context commandeering may well provide greater Member State flexibility to tailor the legislation to local needs and priorities. In any event, commandeering in the EU is the price to pay for refusing to endow the federal level with any resources, administrative or financial. But Halberstam notes two very important reasons why this will not solve the democratic problem in the EU. The first is that, with the innovation of weighted majority voting, each Member State no longer enjoys a veto over being commandeered. We would add that this problem will be greatly exacerbated if the EU is significantly expanded. Second, drawing on Scharpf's earlier work on the 'joint decision trap', Halberstam notes that agreement among elite representatives of polities may well be an inadequate substitute for direct democratic control—an inference that might be mitigated by Moravcsik's point that the current 'insulated' EU process better serves the median voter. While Halberstam is unprepared to draw immediate normative conclusions from his analysis, it does raise the question of whether the problem of supremacy is not intrinsic to the federal vision as such, not merely the statist version of it. Despite the attractive optimism of Elazar and Weiler—to the effect that once federalism is no longer thought in statist terms, it can be conceived as a respectful, non-hierarchical relation between bounded communities—there is the inevitable challenge of dealing with situations where the application of federal law conflicts strongly with a particular unit's conception of collective self-determination. Since we have seen that formal bounds on competences are not a solution to the problem—that is, each is supreme in its own sphere—how can this be resolved without hierarchy? Here again, though he is resistant to drawing out the normative implications, Halberstam's analysis is very rich. He considers the possibility that federal intervention in particular concurrent policy fields could be limited to framework legislation, where the federal level seeks to ensure that the laws and policies reflect a set of legitimate values or norms or do not offend them, but without attempting as it were to fully determine the substance of those laws and policies. The recent trend in the EU towards issuing framework directives, soft laws, and benchmarks for national policies would appear to serve Halberstam's view of legitimate supremacy. But Halberstam also illuminates the difficulties for judicial control of such limits. Perhaps even more subtly, Halberstam introduces the conception of 'viscosity'. Reflecting on differences between international law, the US constitutional system of federalism, and the EU, he hypothesizes that the supremacy of the federal level of law may be qualified or balanced by the greater scope that certain systems offer to constituent federal units with respect to the internal implementation of the commands of superior or supreme law. As long as the measure of disobedience or partial obedience does not threaten the legitimacy of the system as such, it may head off a more zero-sum confrontation between the principle of federal supremacy and that of democratic self-determination within a particular federal unit. Especially where the federal law does not itself draw legitimacy from its being an act of the direct democratic will of a larger *demos*, as in the US system, this 'viscosity' may be crucial to legitimacy.[6]

Giandomenico Majone's chapter returns to themes sounded by Bermann and Halberstam, elaborating them in the context of regulatory federalism. Bermann pointed out that not only did courts lack the means to ensure the effectiveness of political safeguards to vindicate federal values, but regulators by and large escaped the direct effect of these mechanisms altogether. Here, Majone discusses how regulatory independence may nevertheless be reconciled with accountability, in a context where important policy-making powers are delegated to non-majoritarian institutions: an issue the American polity has grappled with for more than a

[6] See Robert Howse and Kalypso Nicolaidis, 'Legitimacy and Global Governance: Why Constitutionalizing the WTO is a Step Too Far', in Pierre Sauve *et al.*, *Efficiency, Equity and Legitimacy of the WTO* (Washington, DC: Brookings Institution, 2001).

century. Joint regulatory action, or regulatory cooperation, is a crucial feature of multi-level governance, where powers are not clearly allocated hierarchically. Majone observes:

> The intertwining of the national and European strands of regulatory policy-making does not correspond to a precise allocation of powers along the vertical dimension. Rather, it prefigures the emergence of a transnational regulatory branch—a 'fourth branch of government', to use the American expression—comprising national, subnational, European, and in some cases—technical standardization, for example—even international regulators. (p. 225–6)

The emergence of transnational regulatory networks is the key development that will help Europe find coordinated rather than vertically distinct solutions to regulatory problems. This also entails important dilemmas of legitimacy. On the one hand, in the context of multi-level governance values of technical competence and political independence argue in favour of governments delegating these joint regulatory activities to bodies of regulators from the various jurisdictions. On the other hand, this poses a very serious challenge to democratic legitimacy since there is no comprehensive democratic body or polity that can apparently effectively control the exercise of these delegated powers. Here, Majone dismisses various philosophies that have been tried in the US and found echoes in the EU, from the traditional 'transmission belt' approach leaving no discretion to regulatory agencies, to the expertise model of the New Deal period or the pluralist proposal to politicize the regulatory process. Instead, he argues that, if one looks imaginatively at some of the control mechanisms that exist in the US system today with respect to delegated federal regulatory powers, the problem may not at all be insuperable:

> The long experience of the American regulatory state indicates that independence and accountability can indeed be reconciled by a combination of control mechanisms rather than by direct oversight exercised by one particular institution: clear and limited statutory objectives to provide unambiguous performance standards; reason-giving and transparency requirements to facilitate judicial review and public scrutiny; due process provisions to ensure fairness among the inevitable winners and losers from regulatory decisions; public participation; and a high level of professionalism to withstand external interference and reduce the risks of an arbitrary use of discretion. (p. 256)

In the EU, these procedural safeguards, designed to strengthen democratic legitimacy in general rather than simply State rights, are all the more necessary since delegation to the Commission—and to a lesser extent to outside bodies—involves wide discretionary powers. In short, the EU should continue to strengthen its multi-level networks as well as to adopt the equivalent of the Federal Administrative Procedure Act and emulate the far-reaching judicialization of regulatory decision-making that has occurred since then in the US.

The chapters in Part IV further elaborate the focus on the legitimacy of the processes and mechanisms of multi-level governance as the key to the federal vision on the basis of more systematic models drawn from political science and political economy. Adopting the conceptual tools of agency theory, Cary Coglianese and Kalypso Nicolaidis attempt to rethink the challenge of federal governance under conditions of broad concurrency in the allocation of competences by examining the relations between States and the union as instances of principal-agent relationships and considering the different kinds of 'mechanisms of control' available to the agents. These mechanisms, or agency ties—delineation, monitoring, sharing, and reversibility—can be read as generalized versions of Bermann's 'political' and 'procedural' safeguards. The principal-agent framework allows us to think of these ties of mutual control as symmetric—both the State and the federal levels can be principals on different issues—and to consider hypothetical trade-offs between them. The importance of these mechanisms to the federal vision is that they offer the possibility of clarifying lines of accountability and, particularly, transparency in the values and interests to which governments are accountable when acting as agents of other governments. At the same time, such agency ties are another way of blunting or finessing the supremacy problem which was put in sharp focus in Halberstam's chapter; as Coglianese and Nicolaidis suggest, 'The structural mechanisms that make up agency ties theoretically constrain the agent at the same time as they reserve some power to the principal' (p. 285), but as long as the agent acts consistently with the specified and limited constraints in the 'contract', it retains a secure zone of autonomy. Thus, agency ties functionally equivalent to those used in other principal-agent situations offer one kind of answer to the supremacy problem posed by the intractability of concurrent powers and the impossibility of a secure allocation of water-tight competences. One can perhaps avert conflicting assertions of power in a concurrent jurisdiction through a constitutionalized supremacy rule, subject to a commitment to resort to alternative agency ties if existing ones are failing. The limits of the principal-agent framework, however, lie in its very premise that levels of governance can be sharply distinguished and identified as either principals or agents.

John Peterson and Laurence O'Toole, as well as Vivien Schmidt, provide richer although less parsimonious models for understanding federalism dilemmas by disaggregating the 'State' or the 'federal' level into the individual or institutional actors that shape their policies. According to Peterson and O'Toole, the characteristic of federalism most relevant to questions of accountability and legitimacy is that it gives rise to 'less formal and intricate structures within which a large number of actors, each wielding a small slice of power, interact' (p. 300). These authors build on the recognition by others, like Majone, of the importance of trans-national or trans-State networks for federal governance. But they move beyond the positivist statement to an analytical stance, namely, that a 'network' perspective is the most effective lens into the strategies, incentives, and constraints of decision-makers in a federal structure. To support a legitimate system of governance, such networks must be open, accessible, and inclusive. Where action in a given policy field does not lend itself to transparent lines of accountability between levels of governance through the kind of mechanisms described by Coglianese and Nicolaidis, ensuring that the network itself is 'representative' of the broadest range of interests may be the only solution. And this is also something of an insurance policy against the risk that bargained 'principal-agent' structures are themselves a product of a closed 'executive federalism'-style policy network. In these respects, Peterson and O'Toole suggest that the EU may have something to learn from what they call the 'hyper-pluralism' of the US system.

Schmidt's institutional perspective is complementary to that of Peterson and O'Toole in that it stresses the constraining impact of Union-wide networks and institutions on the Member States' national institutional structures and decision-making processes. But these networks did not emerge in a vacuum or through simple aggregation; they also entailed a loss of power and autonomy by the executive and legislative branches at the national level. In contrast to those who argue that the EU has strengthened the state, that is, the national executive, Smith takes a differentiated approach, highlighting the disruptive impact of the EU on national structures, especially in those Member States that are unitary rather than federal in nature. At the same time, Schmidt's institutional analysis brings into focus the peculiar characteristics of the centre in the EU, which exhibits a 'dynamic confusion of powers' in contrast with the United State's clear horizontal separation of power. For her, it is in these combined phenomena that the source of the legitimacy deficit lies. But there is little scope for improvement at the centre. In this regard, Schmidt comes to a more nuanced conclusion about pluralism in the US and the EU than Majone or Peterson and O'Toole: 'the EU is somewhat less open to interest influence in formulation; more cooperative in its interrelationships; more delegatory in implementation; and less political or driven by money than the US' (p. 345). Thus in the end, the greatest crisis of legitimacy is felt in those Member States—France, Britain, Italy—who bear the greatest burden of adjustment to the policy changes engendered by the EU. The onus is on national politicians to engage in 'a new political discourse' that recognizes the limits of any government power, at whatever level.

Fritz Scharpf's analysis builds on that of Schmidt in that for him too the source of the so-called 'democratic deficit' in the EU must be sought at the nation-state level. But Scharpf's analytical lens is political economy rather than institutionalism, which leads him to address the challenge of democratic legitimacy in federal governance from the perspective of regulatory competition, and to revisit his recent book in a comparative perspective. According to Scharpf, economic integration in the EU is producing regulatory competition with respect to social policies that is constraining Member State responses to the demands of their citizens for a wide range of distributive policies, while in some cases—for example, subsidies—EU law directly constrains the policies. As Scharpf notes, the response to similar pressures in the US was the constitutional revolution of the New Deal, which permitted the creation of a federal-level progressive regulatory and welfare state. He views this as an unrealistic alternative in the EU, where the welfare state has been shaped by its national scale and where, conversely, the democratic legitimacy of the nation-states is much more closely associated with welfare-state achievements than is true for American States. In light of these constraints and imperatives, Scharpf suggests that regulatory competition itself could be policed at the EU-level, where a rule against improper regulatory competition could constrain tax concessions and deregulation intended to attract foreign businesses at the expense of other countries or domestic competitors. Thus, and perhaps contrary to Schmidt, Sharpf believes that the onus for change lies with the EU level itself through its capacity to design the framework in which Member States operate. For him, a democratic deficit needs not translate into a 'legitimacy deficit' if the EU delivers policies that help rescue and modernize the national welfare state. In this regard, the federal government in the United States may well have a leaf to borrow from the European book.

Contributors to Part V take us from policy analysis to political philosophy, since in the end it is at the individual level, in the different conceptions that people have of their place in a community, that we can find the ultimate determinant of legitimate governance. In asking about identity and citizenship in the US and the EU, we can only start with the contrast initially presented by Weiler in this volume between a European Union wedded to the notion of permanently distinct 'peoplehood' and a United States predicated on the emergence of a single people. But each of the contributors in Part V seeks in his or her own way to move beyond this contrast and to highlight those questions common to all attempts to move beyond single political identities.

As Sujit Choudhry points out at the outset of his chapter, it is puzzling that although federalism is central to any account of our contemporary political practice, it has received so little attention in contemporary political theory. Choudhry sets out to remedy this lacuna by offering an overview of the place of citizenship in a federal context according to alternative schools of thought, including a review of the other authors in this part of the volume. He argues convincingly that none of the three main conceptions of citizenship—civic, ethnocultural, and economic—satisfies what he identifies as the two constraints of liberal democracy, namely, the legitimacy constraint and the stability constraint. Legitimacy requires at least hypothetical consent to a system of law which can exercise coercive power over the individual; while stability requires the existence of a sufficiently strong social bond to ensure the survival of a political community. On these grounds, is it possible to argue that the civic conception of citizenship which prevails in the United States could come to prevail in Europe as a whole? Is the civic conception on its own sufficient to generate the kind of social trust necessary for democratic decision-making, redistribution schemes, and ultimately collective response to acute political crisis? Or is the EU bound to rely mainly on an economic conception of citizenship? Ultimately, the legitimacy of governance at the Union or State level depends on the answer to these questions.

In rehearsing the arguments on all sides, Choudhry demonstrates that the debate cannot be reduced to one between those who would believe in universalistic principles of political morality divorced from specific traditions and associative projects, and those who would simply allow for citizenship in particularistic communities. The key question is that of the relationship between universal values and the particularity of political communities. To be sure, citizenship requires that 'citizens . . . be able to *identify* with a political community as their own—they must be able to claim ownership in the institutions of a political community, in the issues dealt with by those institutions, in the manner in which those issues are debated, and in the decisions of those institutions' (p. 386). Individuals need to know on what grounds they are asked to meet the obligations of citizenship of the Community in which they are part. This may even mean embracing the particularity of political communities. But the fundamental point for liberal democrats is that such particularism ought to possess instrumental rather than intrinsic value. At the same time, we would add to Choudry's account, or perhaps qualify it, by the observation that exclusionary sub-political bonds, such as 'race', ethnicity, and so forth, are not the only kinds of particularity which can create civic bonds: such bonds may be built from common projects informed by universal values, but realized in the context of a singular and distinct political community, whether environmental clean-up or the elimination of child poverty or the building or re-building of a system of public education. Constitution-making itself requires that a people engage in an exercise of self-definition and collective self-realization, albeit *informed* by universal values of liberty and equality. Pierre Trudeau's constitution-building exercise in Canada and Mandela's in South Africa have had that quality to them.

What happens, then, when the search for principles that can provide the cement for social and political solidarity moves from a context of heteregenous polities to one of multi-layered and geographically bounded communities, as is the case in the EU? In discussing the problem of divided or multiple allegiances in federal system, Choudhry astutely blurs the boundaries between apparently distinct positions. He points to the difficulty of simply relying on differing conceptions of citizenship at the federal and sub-federal levels since the identification claims made by citizens by the State and federal communities 'compete in the same political space'. It would thus be warranted to remain sceptical of the Habermasian glue at the Union level, namely 'a shared commitment to liberal democracy.' At the same time, there is little scope either in the EU or in the US for the federal level competing with the sub-federal 'communities of identity'. On the middle ground, one can argue with Habermas himself that it is the history of the community itself that gives universal values their force and significance in a particular polity, the kind of collective self-definition through associative projects and constitution-building we refer to above.

The other authors in Part V all explore in greater depth specific points raised by Choudhry. Marc Landy and Steven Teles do so by taking a strong normative stance in favour of decentralization. Choudhry may have argued that federalism may be more democratic than a unitary state—by allowing for the expression of local majorities that would presumably be federation-wide minorities—but he has not told us why a strong federal centre in itself would be more democratic than a weak one. Indeed, if one can demonstrate the latter, than the trade-off between economic efficiency through greater federal integration and democratic legitimacy through State-level autonomy may remain a real one. But Landy and Teles fall back on their feet, as it were, by echoing a point made on economic grounds by Scharpf, namely, that the role of the federal level should be to allow States to function better as democracy. They call this 'the principle of mutuality.' Accordingly,

> It should be the obligation of each level of government as it participates in joint decision-making to foster the legitimacy and capacity of the other. Local government contributes to central government by taking the brunt of the burden of citizen-demands and of providing a coherent and properly constrained voice for citizen grievances. To do so adequately it must be both responsive and capable.

Central government has the responsibility to facilitate and encourage the ability of lower-level governments to act as sites for deliberation and administration. (p. 414)

This leads Landy and Teles to stress the ways in which EU powers need to be increased precisely and only to the extent to which this facilitative role is called for. In the end, they can see only classic indirect accountability as the way of enhancing the democratic legitimacy of the EU. 'The EU needs democratic legitimacy, but that legitimacy should derive from its ability to protect the possibility for democratic government in its Member States, not from the largely fruitless mission of democratizing itself'.

In her contribution, Elizabeth Meehan directly asks how well the promise of supranational citizenship has been met in the EU. She reminds us that this citizenship is grounded in very diverse notions of 'nationality' across Member States and of the link between nationality and entitlements. Moreover, and unlike Scharpf, she feels that the EU has done well on delivering outcomes and thus it is not its 'social legitimacy' which is most in question. The key question therefore lies with understanding 'European civil society'. On the one hand, it can be argued that the key shared principles for such society at the European level are more likely to include protections against exclusion and discrimination than at the national level. On the other hand, in Europe, contrary to the US, such principled bounds came after long period of pre-democratic national bonding. So the key question becomes whether today there is a strong enough civil society in the EU to transcend the defects of national citizenship. Echoing Choudhry's warning on the trade-offs between democratic practices at different levels of governance, she sees a fundamental problem in the growing mismatches between sets of principled bonds at different levels of governance. Principles of inclusion in Europe, in particular through acquisition of citizenship, are slow to change and civil society at the European level is still too weak to counterbalance this through action at the European level.

Finally, Denis Lacorne draws an analogy between the threats posed by social heterogeneity in the US and the threats posed by differing national allegiances in the EU. He reminds us that core political identities can vary over time and that early conceptions of citizenship in the US focused almost exclusively on State, not federal, citizenship. In his view, within unitary states communities of identity are fine so long as individuals do not conflate these with their core political identity. In a federal system, the problem or challenge is exactly that of belonging to several *political* communities. Lacorne argues against Habermas that pure constitutional patriotism will not suffice, since individuals require a substantial citizenship. What is needed instead are 'common and concrete political experiences' that would give rise to 'a new European ethics of responsibility' (p. 437). Again, as with Choudry, we would respond that this may underplay the autopoetic dimension of European citizenship; as at one point Lacorne himself acknowledges, the building of the Union itself can be understood as a common and concrete political experience, a self-creating civic act. What may simply be required is a broadening of the sense of *ownership* in this project among European publics. In this respect, Lacorne himself might want to take a second look at some of the proposals for a European public space, such as those of Joseph Weiler which he tends to view sceptically taken in and of themselves as substitutes for a 'real' *demos*. Therein may lie the promise for a federal vision shared and carried through by civil societies across Europe.

In closing, our concluding chapter fleshes out some of the common horizontal themes emerging from this volume.

* *

So, dear reader, you are about to embark with us on a quest for a 'federal vision', a federal vision that may successfully address the present-day challenge to legitimacy in governance. As with any such quest, you are not meant to reach the end of the road, but perhaps simply to pass through some inspiring landscapes reflecting your own insights in a new light. No doubt you will chose to select some angles rather than others. We love the landscape image; do you know Lorenzetti's landscape allegories, the effects of good and bad government in the country and the city, in the city hall of Sienna? No doubt also you will quickly figure out that our authors all seem to travel different roads towards the proverbial elephant. Some seek legitimacy in the process, others in outcomes; some in the law, others in institutions; some in people's sense of self, others in peoples' view of others. And they all also provide a different spin on the essence of 'federal' in a federal vision. Some provide definitions, others do not. And when they do, it is on a variety of grounds; on institutional grounds: do the institutions of the Union—'federal' in the US, 'supranational' in the EU—have enough autonomy and direct sources of democratic legitimacy?; on legal grounds: are the laws from the centre directly enforceable by national courts?; on substantive grounds: are core competences such as internal and external security, justice, and money conducted at the federal level?; or on normative-constitutional grounds: is this a single polity with a single constitutional demos? We cannot deny, then, dear reader, the intellectually plural or—dare we say—federal nature of our federal vision.

Nevertheless, by referring to a 'federal vision' the book seeks to move beyond traditional analytical distinctions and exercises in categorization between 'federalism', 'integration', 'confederalism', 'supranationalism', and the like. We do not, of course, deny the critical usefulness of these ideal-types, including for our own debates, as reflected in many of the chapters in this book. But in order to provide a broad paradigmatic umbrella, the kind of federal vision that we refer to can encompass all forms of shared governance which add some degree of legal, institutional, or normative federalism to classical forms of inter-state cooperation. This federal vision may be pluralistic and broad ranging, but it also has a core in that it is grounded on principles of mutual tolerance and empowerment that alone can reconcile our polar political needs, unity of purpose, and diversity of place and belonging. And we believe that, in this broad sense, a federal vision is more necessary than ever, in the US and the EU as well as elsewhere.

I

Articulating the Federal Vision

1

The United States and the European Union: Models for Their Epochs

DANIEL J. ELAZAR

It is easy to draw the contrast between the American and the European experiences of union. The distinctly geographic, demographic, and cultural determinants of the method of unification in each—the differences between a vast undersettled and a circumscribed and bounded settled territory, a generally homogeneous and a highly heterogeneous population, and so forth, shaped the ease with which one found a common cultural denominator as compared with the efforts that had to made by the other to begin to identify a basis for union that transcended their respective national cultures so deeply entrenched and often hostile to one another.[1]

American federal unity was built upon an indigenous American ideology which properly may be termed federal democracy, derived from the synthesis of the Reformed Protestant and Scottish Enlightenment experiences of the colonial period, and the western frontier encounter with American geography and the settlement of an open and extensive territory. Although in American history the move from confederation to federation is treated as a major change, from our broader perspective we can see how both partake of the ideas and practices of federal democracy.[2]

For post-World War II Europe, on the other hand, it soon became apparent that federation was too great a step. Instead, there was a

In the sad circumstance of the author's death before the completion of this manuscript, the editors have, as best they could, attempted to address minor stylistic points and complete the references. However, in a few cases the author did not leave us enough information to do so. In those cases, we have simply left the references in incomplete form.

[1] Daniel J. Elazar and Ilan Greilsammer, 'Federal Democracy: The USA. and Europe Compared', in Mauro Cappellitti, Monica Seccombe, and Joseph Weiler (eds), *Integration Through Law: Europe and the American Federal Experience*, vol. 1, book 1 (Berlin and New York: Walter de Gruyter, 1986).

[2] Donald Lutz, *The Origins of American Constitutionalism* (Baton Rouge: Louisiana State University Press, 1988); Gordon Wood, *The Creation of the American Republic, 1776–1787* (New York: Norton, 1969); Bernard Bailyn, *The Ideological Origins of the American Revolution* (Cambridge, MA: Belknap Press, 1967).

pragmatic withdrawal to 'functionalism', which would avoid explicit expression of the higher purposes of the unification effort. In place of the use of terms like 'federal' or 'confederal', terms like 'supranational' and 'political community' became the relevant political buzzwords.

In many respects the process of European integration has been the very reverse of the American process. European integration has tended to be seen as a valued end in itself, often confusing means with ends. It is only once the process started to produce results, that the question of the form of government and indeed the nature of the political enterprise was raised. In the United States, on the other hand, the federal form of government was conceived to embody the fundamental republican and democratic principles which inhered in American civil society. One of the mistakes of the ideological federalist lobby in interwar and post-war Europe was that it sought to transplant the American understanding where it could not be, at least at the time.[3]

The fact remains, however, that whatever their origins, there exist today two systems which are roughly intended to serve the same purpose: the joining together of identifiable polities in a common enterprise within an embracing authoritative framework. The nature of their respective unions is different, one federal and the other confederal. They share a common status as world models of their kind. How they became models and in what way is the question before us.

1. Two Approaches: Two Epochs

Increasingly the world is coming to recognize that we are living at the cusp of a new epoch. Those of us above 50 years of age were born into the modem epoch which began in the middle of the seventeenth century and came to an end in World War II and the years immediately following. It is being replaced by a post-modern epoch which is only beginning to take form.[4]

One element that has continued from the modern to the post-modern epoch is the competition between statism and federalism, which in turn influences the shape of world affairs in a decisive manner. Statism, whose

[3] *Integration Through Law: Europe and the American Federal Experience*, series under the general editorship of Mauro Cappelletti, Monica Seccombe, and Joseph Weiler, 4 vols (Berlin; New York W. de Gruyter, 1985–88); Derek W. Urwin, *A Community of Europe: A History of European Integration since 1945* (London: Longman, 1991); Nicholas C. Baltas, George Demopoulos, and Joseph Hassid (eds), *Economic Interdependence and Cooperation in Europe* (Berlin, New York: Springer, 1998); *Publius* 26/4 (1996) (issue on the European Union).

[4] Daniel J. Elazar, *Constitutionalizing Globalization: The Postmodern Revival of Confederal Arrangements* (Lanham: Rowman and Littlefield Publishers, 1998).

origins go back to the transformations of the last pre-modern generations in France, Spain, and England in particular, was given its fullest intellectual formulation in the work of Jean Bodin.[5] Statism became the accepted world standard for political organization—that is, the standard in Western Europe—through the Treaty of Westphalia in 1648, as part of the arrangement that ended the Thirty Years War. Following that treaty, statism and the state system became the anchors of the international order in Europe and the European colonies, and, through them, the world. That order held for 300 years.[6]

At the same time that Bodin was presenting his statist ideas, Johannes Althusius was presenting a competing theory of federalism. It was as systematic, comprehensive, and modern as Bodin's theory of statism. An outgrowth of Reformed Protestantism, Althusius developed it with the intention of providing a comprehensive system for the political organization of the Protestant republican polities that he expected to succeed those of medieval Catholicism, to foster a Europe that rejected the authoritarian rule of kings and princes by divine right in favour of power-sharing in communities of different composition and function within a comprehensive framework.[7]

Althusius was one of the Protestant Christian grand designers who straddled the late Reformation and the opening of the modern epoch. He made an effort to synthesize and somewhat secularize Reform Protestant thought on the ideal polity and to push it in concrete, practical directions. His classic work, *Politica Methodice Digesta*, was the first book to present a comprehensive theory of federal republicanism rooted in a covenantal view of human society derived from, but not dependent on, his theological system. It, along with his *Dicaelogicae Libri Tres*, or the *Decalogue*, presented a theory of polity building based on the polity as a compound political association established by its citizens through their primary associations on the basis of consent rather than as a reified state, imposed by a ruler or an elite: the Bodinian model.[8]

[5] Jean Bodin, *Six Books of the Commonwealth*, abridged and translated by M. J. Tooley (New York: Barnes and Noble, 1967).

[6] William Russell, *The History of Modern Europe: with a view of the progress of society from the rise of the modern kingdoms to the peace of Paris, in 1763* (New York: Harper and Brothers, 1839).

[7] Daniel J. Elazar, *The Multi-Faceted Covenant: The Biblical Approach to the Problem of Organizations, Constitutions, and Liberty as Reflected in the Thought of Johannes Althusius* (Ramat-Gan, Israel: Workshop in the Covenant Idea and the Jewish Political Tradition, 5755, 1994); Thomas O. Hueglin, *A Political Economy of Federalism: In Search of a New Comparative Perspective with Critical Intent Throughout* (Kingston, Ontario: Institute of Intergovernmental Relations, Queen's University, 1990).

[8] Johannes Althusius, *Politics*, translated with an introduction by Frederick S. Carney (Boston: Beacon Press, 1964).

The Althusian model directly addressed the complexities of the European situation, taking into consideration families and voluntary associations as well as formal political institutions, corporations, and territorial units. In his *Politica*, he methodically constructed a federal system that was both territorial and consociational. Moreover, it was one that accommodated the European reality of four or five arenas of territorial governance instead of two or three, the accepted number in modern federations.

For a brief time the Althusian model competed with that of Bodin, at least in the German-speaking world. By the later part of the seventeenth century, however, it was clear that the statist model would win and Althusius and his federalist ideas were relegated either to the realm of the antiquarian or the utopian, or simply forgotten.[9] The federalism that did exist in practice survived in two medieval confederations and one early modem one: the Helvetic Confederation in Switzerland, the Holy Roman Empire in Germany, and the United Netherlands, in the Low Countries, all three increasingly governed by oligarchies or princes until the Napoleonic wars.[10]

Statism triumphed overall and sequentially country by country where the issue was raised over those 300 years, with one major exception. Between 1765 and 1795 in the new United States of America, federalism was reinvented, first as modern confederation then as modern federation. Federation as designed by the Americans not only provided a way to divide power territorially in the statist age but turned statism on its head. Statism as defined by Bodin and others provided for a single sovereign in a highly centralized state striving for homogeneity and self-sufficiency. American federalism, by contrast vested sovereignty in the people to prevent the development of a centralized, reified state by making all governments no more than governments of delegated powers whose scope the people could define and change as they pleased through a constitutional system.[11]

[9] Otto von Gierke, *Associations and Law: The Classical and Early Christian Staizes*, edited and translated by George Heiman, with an interpretative introduction to Gierke's thought (Toronto, Buffalo: University of Toronto Press, 1977); *Community in Historical Perspective: A Translation of Selections from* Das Deutsche Genossenschaftsrecht (*The German Law of Fellowship*), translated by Mary Fischer; selected and edited by Antony Black (Cambridge, New York: Cambridge University Press, 1990).

[10] Murray Forsythe, *Union of States* (Leicester: Leicester University Press, 1981); and Frederick K. Lister, *The European Union, the United Nations, and The Revival of Confederal Governance* (Westport, Conn.: Greenwood Press, 1996).

[11] Lutz, *Origins of American Constitutionalism*; Vincent Ostrom, *The Political Theory of a Compound Republic: Designing the American Experiment*, foreword by Daniel J. Elazar, 2nd edn (Lincoln: University of Nebraska Press, 1987); Daniel J. Elazar, *American Constitutional Tradition* (Lincoln: University of Nebraska Press, 1987).

After the fall of Napoleon two of Europe's pre-modern confederations were reconstituted as modern confederations. The Swiss restored their old system on an enlarged and modernized basis and the Germans replaced their old system with a modern version based on the newly consolidated modern German territorial states. Both failed within decades, each in a different way. The Swiss found it necessary to move to modern federation to eliminate the old cantonal oligarchies and introduce liberal regimes. In Germany, confederation fell apart under the pressure of the statist ambitions of its strongest member, Prussia. With their disappearance, conventional wisdom concluded that confederation was no a longer viable form of government and that federalism meant federation only.[12]

Throughout the rest of the epoch, American federalism was the world's model. It had influence, first on the new Latin American republics where it was more influential as an ideal than in practice, then Switzerland when it transformed its confederation into a federation in 1848, and in Canada and Australia. Switzerland, where sovereignty was held to be vested in the people from early confederation days, looked to America primarily for improved institutions and processes. Canada and Australia followed the American lead in developing federal relationships; but because both remained within the British empire, their institutions remained parliamentary and the sovereignty issue was avoided because sovereignty was formally vested in the monarch, or the crown.[13]

Elsewhere, statism continued to flourish, so much so that the handful of federations that survived in the international system did so only by presenting themselves to the outside world as states with a composition similar to all others.[14] The statist system ran into fatal trouble in the twentieth century as the result of World Wars I and II, the latter actually serving as its nemesis. The horrors of Nazism, the bloody extent of the war itself, and the development of nuclear weapons in its course first weakened the commitment to statism in its fullest form and then made the old system of exclusive state sovereignty untenable.

2. Europe: Rejecting Federation

America and Europe emerged from the war and began to erect a framework for a post-war world that, intentionally or not, would replace the

[12] See note 10.

[13] Michael E. Rose (ed.), *The English Poor Law: 1780–1930* (New York: Barnes and Noble, 1971).

[14] Thomas A. Bailey, *A Diplomatic History of the American People*, 9th edn (Englewood Cliffs, NJ: Prentice-Hall, 1974).

modern statist system. While most of its champions believed that the key to this framework was the United Nations, intended to unite the world's states for purposes of collective security and peacekeeping, in fact it was the Bretton Woods agreements, which took the first step toward a globalized economy, that turned out to be more important for globalization. Elsewhere I have discussed the course of globalization from Bretton Woods to the present and how it led to a shift in the paradigm from statism to federalism.[15] While some idealists believed that this would occur on a global scale through the United Nations, cold war rivalries rapidly ended the possibilities for that development. In any case it was unlikely because of the strong commitment on the part of the new states of the third world to developing their newly acquired statehood the old way, something they never had either the power or resources to achieve.

What did emerge from the war, however, was a feeling in Europe, particularly Western Europe, that Europe outside of the Soviet bloc had to move toward greater union of it were to prevent further wars and succeed in rebuilding itself. At first the movers and shakers in this effort sought to replicate American federalism in Europe through a 'United States of Europe', a European federation following the American model. But that was far too radical even for most of those who sought a new European unity in the wake of the two wars. After almost reaching the point of despair they turned to functionalism as a way out and the development of functional solutions to particular facets of the union sought. Thus the European Community (EC) was born. Paradoxically, this new approach was made possible by removing the leading cause for choosing federalism in the past—the search for collective security—from its central role, by removing that use from exclusively European hands and placing it in the hands of NATO. This was a result of the collapse of the effort to deal with Western European defence through Franco-German arrangements and the assumption of responsibility the larger alliance led by the US, the West's superpower.

As a consequence, the new European unity was built on economic union accompanied only by those functional linkages considered necessary to foster economic union. By the late 1960s, observers could discern that the European Community had begun to build what were, in effect, confederal arrangements, based on that functionalism. However, these remained unnoticed in the face of the conventional wisdom that federalism was synonymous with federation and that confederation or confederal arrangements had proved themselves obsolete in the course of the modern epoch.

[15] Elazar, *Constitutionalizing Globalization.*

In fact, in the 1970s, people in Europe were bemoaning the demise of the Community. They were counting the days to its dissolution, waiting for the fist state to pull out. A decade later they were discussing problems of over-centralization, of building a single state of the statist model for Europe. Margaret Thatcher, Jacques Delors, and Wilfrid Martens have, in recent years, very appropriately addressed the question of what approaches will keep a balance when building the European Union. There is a paradox in this; indeed, there are several paradoxes.[16]

It is possible to view confederation in one of two ways: as a union of states, each of which may be constructed in a statist fashion but which together have pooled certain powers for mutual advantage; or as in a union of unions in which sovereignty is vested in the people of each member unit and through them in the whole. In either case, the result could not appear on the world stage as a state since the statist system could not deal with it for purposes of interstate relations, and it could not mobilize and concentrate the requisite force to defend its interests. Not surprisingly, under such conditions, the pre-modern confederations all collapsed in the face of the Napoleonic assault carried out in the name of the French Revolution.

Thus after World War II, the search for a form of federal unity for Europe did not even consider the confederal option. But the process adopted had its own logic and generated its own momentum. The EC developed as a new style confederation in a new way. The union of the states of the Community was based on the union of specific economic functions rather than a general act of confederation establishing an overarching general government, however limited its purpose. This is the essence of the European invention.

Appropriate and substantial if not complete powers for each function were given first to a specific functional authority and then to the EC, which was the multipurpose expression of those functional authorities. Only after the number of functions increased to the point that more general institutions were required were such institutions constituted, in different ways for each class of powers. Adjudication was assigned to a high court which served as the constitutional court of the union within its designated spheres of competence. Administration became the province of the EC bureaucracy, which became the civil service of the union within its functional spheres. Policy is made collegially by councils of ministers of the Member States which function as league-like instruments of the confederation. Budgetary review and approval as well as limited power to set

[16] Lloyd Brown-John, *Centralizing and Decentralizing Trends in Federal States* (Lanham, MD: University Press of America, 1988).

long-term policy guidelines rest in the hands of a party-based European parliament, which functions as a confederation-wide instrument. The high court has shown itself to be a constitutional court with real teeth in the areas of its jurisdiction. The bureaucracy behaves like a classic European state bureaucracy in its areas of jurisdiction. Real power is vested in the Council of Ministers, holding the others in check by this collegial device. The parliament remains the weakest institution but one gaining in scope and powers.

In this way the constitution of common institutions of the new confederation has proceeded in a way designed to minimize the threat to the Member States, which have sought and continue to seek to maintain maximum independence beyond those functions they agreed to transfer when they agreed to unite. The list of functions is growing but still grows function by function. The independence retained is far more than that retained by States in federation, including all the accepted attributes of political sovereignty. At the same time, they have succeeded in the establishment of a sufficiently energetic confederal government in those designated spheres with the means to attain the ends for which it was constituted.

Another critical element in the invention of the EU and EU-style confederation is its asymmetrical character. Modern federation placed great emphasis in symmetry in the relations between the federation as a whole and its government and the constituent units, with even the slightest hint as asymmetry viewed as a violation of the federal bargain. In the EU on the other hand, asymmetry was accepted as one of the necessities for establishing and maintaining union. Consequently it became a confederal reality, involving closer special relations between some states which others did not want to enter into, including the right of some Member States to drop out of particular programmes and have them applied in more limited ways to them or on their territory. In any case, these and other asymmetries have not only been accepted but constitutionalized.[17]

3. The EU as a Confederation

Beginning on a strictly functional basis, the EC has moved forward step by step toward more general institutions culminating to date in the Single Europe Act, the Maastricht Treaty, and the introduction of the Euro as a common currency. Today it may be said that the European Union is essentially complete as a confederation although its Member States and peoples

[17] Michael Keating, 'Asymmetrical Government: Multinational States in an Integrating Europe', *Publius*, 29/1 (1999): [PAGES].

do not necessarily share a sense of that completeness. I would suggest that this is so for essentially psychological reasons, because integration has taken place function by function, conveying little public sense of completeness or development of a mind set for confederation. Most people still see integration as federation; and federation for Europeans all too often means a federal state, that is to say, the construction of an apparatus that allows the complex of state institutions to become fundamentally separated from civil society. These statist expectations are counteracted by the strong pulls for independence on the part of most of the Member States, which in their time were the mothers of statism.

Here we confront two different forms of constitution making, comprehensively, by constitutional convention and by subsequent popular ratification in the States in the case of the United States, and piecemeal through intergovernmental treaties in the Union. While in both the US and the EU the shared powers are delegated, the American redefinition of the locus of sovereignty stands in sharp contrast to the statist approach to sovereignty that animates Europe. In the EU, institutions are always in a struggle between the limited character of delegated powers and the statist ideas that normally accompany the assignment of competences in statist polities. Hence it is relatively easy for the US to remain non-hierarchical and non-centralized. The EU has tried to experiment with the concept of subsidiarity, which accepts a more hierarchical understanding of the system.

Whatever the structural differences between the US and EU, their common federal character is reflected in the relationships that have developed in the intergovernmental entities and populations of the two, albeit each in its own way. These relationships are embodied in the US in the idea of partnership and in the EU in the idea of community. The two may be compared in terms of how each rests on territorial democracy through dual legal systems, federal institutions and purposes, a party system, and private relations that operates in the two major arenas. The difference between partnership American-style and EU community is that the former is based upon a common sense of single nationhood, while the latter is based on the idea that separate countries have many elements in common. For the founders of the US, federalism represented a new political alternative for solving the twin problems of popular government and the political integration of a very large territory. The federalism of the founders was designed to provide substantially new means for the development of (1) a system of government that would be both energetic and responsive to the people; (2) a system of politics that would enhance the possibilities for interaction between the governors and the governed; (3) a reasonable approach to the twin problems of political liberty and political order; and (4) a decent means for securing civil justice and morality. In other words, they saw the federal union under the constitution as having comprehensive political goals. Although in both the US and the EU these four basic elements of the political process combine to ensure working federal relationships, in the EU the relationship between the compact on the one hand and the political institutional processes used on the other is reversed in comparison with the United States. Since the Member States wanted to keep most of their sovereign powers at the beginning and agreed to transfer only limited parts of them in restricted areas of government, the agreements forming the EC and later the EU imparted a limited role to the political and judicial processes; while in the US, since the constitution really established a new, comprehensive frame of government, the political and judicial processes were of utmost importance in maintaining the federation and the Member States.

The founders of the European Community wanted to keep all these questions of regime, philosophy of the state, political culture, and the like within the national framework of each Member State and did not seek to transfer them to the EU. The Community was founded by countries which uniformly accepted the Western parliamentary model of democracy which gave the EC a certain homogeneity of political culture and helped it confront regimes such as Franco's Spain and the Greece of the colonels, ultimately absorbing both after they rid themselves of their anti-democratic regimes as a means to hold them for democracy. But they did not have as a central consideration the problems of administering a large territory in a democratic way; nor does the Community concern itself with the kind of democratic government Member States adopt.

In theory, neither does the US government; but the American States and the US government have all interpreted republicanism within a relatively narrow range of representative and separation-of-power systems, whereas there is a wider diversity within the European Union Member States and between all of them and the EU itself. The EU remains in principle a voluntary union founded on commonly accepted economic liberalism and a restrictive partnership, far less comprehensive than that of the United States. As a result, Europeans seem to be more worried about the 'democratic deficit' in the EU, an aspect of its statist bureaucratic character, than in improving the partnership, which is what concerns Americans.

Connected to this problem are certain issues such as cooperative federalism and citizenship. Cooperative federalism was imported from the United States as an idea. I was connected with the development. of this idea some years ago. It has become a theory. It is not. Cooperative federalism is a technique. It is a mechanism that opens the door to a proper theory. But it is no more than that and it should not be elevated beyond what it is. Cooperative federalism makes it possible for federalism to exist in a highly interdependent world where, if we relied upon earlier notions of federalism as the separation of governments, there would be no function that would not be seized by the larger, stronger government in the course of time. Cooperative federalism is valuable beyond that, since it gives us a vision of human cooperation, which is a good thing, but always within a framework within which real differences are recognized. For example, I have argued that in the United States, cooperative federalism existed in the nineteenth century, even when people talked in a different language. It was a kind of federal relationship in which the primary responsibilities for policy action lay with the States. The federal government provided certain supplementary assistance primarily in the realms of infrastructure and coordination of national policy and no more.

Cooperative federalism, when the term became popular in the US in the 1960s, became an excuse for federal government coercion. It still seemed to involve all governments, and did, but it represented a slogan, a phrase that the federal government could apply against States that did not want to accept some federal policy prescription: States that did not 'toe the line' were denounced as not cooperating. Both kinds of intergovernmental relations fall within the parameters of cooperative federalism, and it was considered better to have that in the 1950s and 1960s in the United States than to have a shifting of powers to the federal government. Why? Because in the 1970s and the 1980s, the power could shift back to the States, within the cooperative framework—as much of it has.

As yet, no proper theory has been developed to explain this new style of confederation. Its initial steps were discussed by the functionalist theorists writing in the 1950s; but since they were engaged in a battle with federalists they limited their theoretical concerns to functional theory.[18] Theorists of federalism, on the other hand, were oriented toward federations and did not include the EC/EU within their optic. Until Europe develops a theory of federalism suitable to its confederal tendency, this tension will not be overcome and a sense of incompleteness can be expected to remain.

One of the innovations of the EU as a new confederation is that it is not confined to two or three arenas of government as in federations, but instead involves four or five. This is partly because several of the Member States of the EC/EU entered as federations, including the German federal republic, the EU's strongest member, and Austria, one of the most recent. Even more significantly, other Member States moved towards reconstituting themselves as federations as part or as a consequence of their

[18] Karl Deutsch, Political Community and the North Atlantic Area: International Organization in the Light of Historical Experience Princeton, NJ: Princeton University Press, 1957).

Community membership, which made such changes possible. These include Belgium, Spain, Italy, and the United Kingdom. While one can see the influence of modern federation on all of them, even more important has been local inventiveness to accommodate the peculiarly European elements in their polities and societies. Thus they have, either knowingly or unknowingly, returned to draw on Althusian ideas even as they were rejecting Bodinian ones.

4. Subsidiarity: Federal or Hierarchical?

At the same time, the principle of power-sharing adopted by the EU as a whole—subsidiarity—has its own problematic elements. Subsidiarity is a concept developed in Catholic Europe, the Europe organized along hierarchical lines, and was and is designed to soften hierarchy by vesting and protecting the powers of its lower levels. Federalism, however, is anti-hierarchical, based on covenant-based principles that see the proper political organization as a matrix with larger and smaller arenas but not higher and lower: a vitally important distinction since larger and smaller do not imply any ranking of degree of importance—for some purposes a larger arena is the most important and for others a smaller arena is.

This distinction takes us back to the struggle between statism and federalism. From the beginning of political science, political scientists have understood that polities have been founded and organized along three models: hierarchically by force or conquest, organically through the aggregation of apparently random events and activities, or federally through pact or covenant. A good summary statement of this can be found in Federalist No. 1. 'It seems . . . to be reserved to the people of this country, by their conduct and example, to decide the important question, whether a society of men are really capable or not, of establishing good government from reflection and choice, or whether they are forever destined to depend, for their political constitutions, on accident and force.' Reflection and choice, accident and force refer to these three traditions of government organization in the most felicitous manner.[19] A proper federal framework involves non-centralization or multiple centres of power. The model that is needed to build the European Union is a matrix or a mosaic and not a power pyramid or a centre-periphery model that is much beloved by many political scientists and sociologists these days. Those

[19] Daniel J. Elazar, 'Federal Models of (Civil) Authority', *Journal of Church and State*, 33/2 (1991), 231–54; and Alexander Hamilton, James Madison, and John Jay, The *Federalist Papers*, Number 1, edited by Clinton Rossiter (New York: New American Library, 1961).

other models suggest that power is naturally concentrated and is decentralized only by the good will of those at the top of the pyramid or those in the centre of the circle.

It is easy to talk about the 'state' as the starting point of discussions because that is what people have known in Europe for so many centuries. Once statist premises are accepted it is very difficult to avoid viewing the European Union as a anomaly; something that has to be turned into a state, even a decentralized state, very soon. This launches Europeans once again on a course that moves them away from their original intent through original confusion and back to what for modernity represents original sin. That is something that needs very close examination since it has a marked effect on how people think about the institutional framework they are building and the consequences of their ideas. For example, to the extent that there is a power pyramid, politics will be the politics of a court: a struggle among those who seek to get close to the ruler or rulers on the top of the pyramid and who jockey for power among themselves as members of that court. Under such conditions, the lower levels, so to speak, no matter how much power is formally decentralized, will remain the lower levels and the most talented people will always strive to get into that court and become part of it.

Beyond that, the nature of power pyramids is that the people are underneath the pyramid; the whole pyramid sits on top of them. That is hardly the model for a democratic order for Europe or for anybody else. Recall that it was pharaonic Egypt that built pyramids as the ultimate monuments to its rulers. It was the best possible symbol they could have selected for the power system they constructed.

The same limitations apply with regard to the centre-periphery model. There the politics in the centre are the politics of a club; somewhat more equal than the politics of a court, but still the closed politics of a club. Those who are admitted to the club can participate in its politics; those who are not remain on the periphery. While the club might be more open than the court, not everybody can be admitted to it. So it is also an inappropriate model if only because what is passed to the peripheries in such a model is always at the mercy of the members of the club.

That model works only when the members of the club spend most of their time in the peripheries and gather at the centre only once in a while to do business. For example, in England before industrialization, the members of the club were the country squires who came to London every so often to take care of their common business and then went back home to sit as justices of the peace in their local parishes. England was still very clubby in its politics and government, but at least there was continuous contact between centre and periphery. But that passed well over a century ago with the rise of cities, professional politicians, and public administrators who sit permanently in Westminster or Whitehall, and it is unlikely in the industrial age or even in the post-industrial age that such clubs will revert to the old model.

So the only appropriate model is a matrix or a mosaic in which the framing institution is the largest arena and itself is comprised of a number of different arenas. The existence of multiple arenas is the real test of a federal organization and distribution of power. Moreover, we need not think only about two or three arenas; quite the contrary. Europe, appropriately, is made up of more than two or three arenas, with a place for the constituent states, *Länder*, provinces, cantons, whatever they are called, and local governments within the European Union framework. One of the most important things that can be done is to have them assert that involvement. They should not wait to ask permission, but they must assert that involvement as part of the overall restructuring of Europe which is taking place. This becomes a possibility because federalism breeds federalism. Once a polity embarks on a course of integration in the federal rather than in the hierarchical or the centre-periphery mode, it is possible to extend the application of the federal principle in many different ways; and that of course is the great possibility and the great hope.[20]

In reality, of course, there are no pure models and most polities represent some combination of all three; but each polity is shaped and guided by one of the root principles. The United States from the first relied more on reflection and choice and with the invention of federalism made the matrix model the basis of its founding, as the authors of *The Federalist* hoped. Europe on the other hand had embraced hierarchy through monarchic government or modified monarchy through parliamentary government, which developed organically. Both were appropriate to, and supported, the emergence of statism as distinct from federalism. Now Europe is forced into a confrontation between the two. All too often the discussions about the future form of the European Union seek to advance federalism in its new style on the basis of statist ideas and practices. In this regard the EU still has much to learn from the American model, or from such indigenous European sources as Althusius rejected over 300 years earlier.

5. The EU's Catholic Cultural Origins

The European Union can be understood as a civil or secular extension of Catholic Europe. In most of the Member States of the European Union,

[20] Daniel J. Elazar, *Exploring Federalism* (Tuscaloosa: University of Alabama Press, 1987).

especially the founding members, one finds that the majority come out of the Catholic cultural tradition and that the Protestant states of Europe, for the most part, have not joined. Therefore the philosophic struggles of the Union are derived principally from the Catholic intellectual experience.

Take subsidiarity, a principle developed inside the Catholic Church to modify and moderate its pronounced hierarchical tendencies. The Catholic Church is the oldest existing power pyramid in the Western world. For 1,600 years or so it has been a power pyramid which has had to accommodate itself to the realities of a more complex world than mere power pyramids alone can handle. So its leaders developed the idea of subsidiarity. But for those who come out of a different tradition, subsidiary is a notion that implies a concession to hierarchy that they are not willing to make. If anything, federalists elsewhere have been struggling with such concepts as noncentralization: within multiple-centred systems in which there is no hierarchy. Therefore, however valuable subsidiarity is to moderate hierarchies, perhaps the European Union has to take the difficult step of breaking out of the philosophic tradition towards which it can gravitate so easily, so as not to think in those hierarchical terms from the beginning.

But even here there is a paradox. What is this Catholic federalism? Is it a civil reformation of the Catholic countries, let us say a breaking down of their hierarchies, by bringing them together to be part of a larger federal structure, or is it the revival of the old dream of a Catholic Europe; of a universal European state within a secularized power pyramid?

This is a question that is worthy of examination: worth addressing directly in order to better understand where Europe is going. Both federal and unitary ideas are expressed in this debate. There is a great deal of statism expressed in the common academic discourse with which European scholars and intellectuals have grown up. For the first time, some of it has begun to creep across the Atlantic, as those of us who have tried to fight against it are so aware.

The EU's seat, Brussels, a predominantly Catholic city, lies on one of the great cultural fault lines of Europe, where Protestants and Catholics divided after the Reformation and also where the Germanic and Latin traditions met centuries earlier. It is a cultural fault line which has played a special role in Europe at least since Roman times.

Earlier expressions of the federal idea—the covenant idea in its original form and the federal idea in its political form—within the European political tradition brings one back repeatedly to that cultural line, that line of development which runs from Switzerland, up the Rhine Valley, through Belgium and the Netherlands, across the North Sea and into Scotland, that marks the region where the covenant idea in theology and political philosophy and the federal idea in practice, whether it was called that or not, have constantly bubbled forth and reasserted themselves whenever and wherever local populations have been allowed to express themselves. Possibly the line continues even further southwards; maybe it even extends into northern Italy.[21] Although we do not entirely know why this is so, one of the reasons clearly must be that where different cultural groups come together and where one cannot conquer or suppress the other, they ultimately must make agreements with each other enabling them to live together. Sooner or later—it may take centuries—they acquire certain habits of negotiated cooperation. They get into the habit of giving up conquest and of trying instead to make their decisions and to organize their lives through peaceful agreements.

It is no accident that these cultural borderlands also have become the heartland of the European Union. We would do well, it seems to me, to explore the history of this heartland and to use that history and the peoples of the heartland to the fullest to build the kind of Europe that will be united, federal, and democratic in the best way.

6. Confederal Arrangements Spread

Meanwhile Europe's new model confederation is already influencing other such arrangements in the post-modern world, as the US federation model did in the modern world, not necessarily in the details of their arrangements but in the possibilities in their systems. The latter reached the peak of its influence in the first half-generation—15 to 20 years—after the end of World War II during the period of decolonization when a number of decolonized countries adopted federation as their basic form of government. A few, such as India, succeeded in their effort. Others, such as Nigeria and Pakistan, while not immediately succeeding, have remained faithful to the attempt and periodically try to reinvigorate their federal systems. Still others such as Ghana and Rhodesia suffered from a failure of federalism as federation and re-emerged as unitary states.[22]

By the mid-1960s, this era of attempted federation-building had come to an end. Since then, the only new federations that have been attempted in the formerly colonized world have been in Ethiopia after the fall of its

[21] Robert D. Putnam with Robert Leonardi and Raffaella Y. Nanetti, *Making Democracy Work: Civic Traditions in Modern Italy* (Princeton, NJ: Princeton University Press, 1993).

[22] Ronald L. Watts, *New Federations: Experiments in the Commonwealth* (Oxford: Clarendon Press, 1966); Thomas M. Franck (ed.), *Why Federations Fail: An Inquiry into the Requisites for Successful Federalism* (New York: New York University Press, 1968).

Marxist regime, and in a modified way in South Africa after apartheid.[23] In Western Europe, on the other hand, Belgium and Spain have become federations and the chances are that Italy and the UK will follow, sooner or later.[24]

Other efforts to use federalism or federal arrangements have all taken place within new frameworks more strongly influenced by the experience of the EU than the US. These arrangements have developed in two ways. The first, dating back to the late 1960s or 1970s, is exemplified by the Caribbean Community; the successor to the failed West Indies Federation. The West Indies Federation, imposed by the British on an area which did not wish to be decolonized, was too 'heavy' an arrangement for islands which by their very nature tend to be insular. Its failure, however, did not reduce the need for inter-island cooperation on a continuing constitutionalized basis. The Caribbean Community is based on certain functional survivals of the federation which form the basis for a new confederal arrangement. These principles of organization are functional, like those of the EU, although economic linkage is the least successful of the Community's functional arrangements.[25]

On the other side of the globe, at approximately the same time, the Association of Southeast Asian Nations (ASEAN) was organized originally by the United States as part of its regional defence structure to contain the Vietnam war. It rapidly shifted from a defensive alliance to a kind of confederal arrangement more along social and economic principles.[26] Finally, the collapse of the Soviet Union in 1991 led to the reconstitution of the Russian Federation and an effort to establish a Commonwealth of Independent States as a league to replace the old USSR.[27] The success of the latter is clearly in question, although its need is not. Both follow the EU pattern of the functional approach, no overarching governing institutions, and new-style separation of powers and arenas.

The second set involves the development of regional economic arrangements. As economic globalization gained in strength and the great economic powers, both governmental and non-governmental, increased their dominance, less powerful states began to organize regional groupings in

[23] Bertus Devilliers.

[24] *Publius*, 27/4 (1997) (issue on Spain); *Publius* issue on Belgium.

[25] William G. Demas, *West Indian Development and the Deepening and Widening of the Caribbean Community* (Kingston, Jamaica: Randle Publishers; Mona, Jamaica: Institute of Social and Economic Research, University of the West Indies, 1997); see also Daniel J. Elazar, *Federal Systems of the World: A Handbook of Federal. Confederal and Autonomy Arrangement* (London: Longman Press, 1991); Lister, *The European Union*.

[26] ASEAN as confederation.

[27] Nicholas J. Lynn and Alexei V. Novikov, 'Refederalizing Russia: Debates on the Idea of Federalism in Russia', *Publius*, 27/2 (1997), [PAGES].

an effort to protect themselves. These economic arrangements were also influenced by the EC, which had demonstrated how confederal arrangements based on economic concerns could enable regions to compete effectively in the world arena without sacrificing the statehood of individual Member States. Groupings from NAFTA to Mercosur reflect this effort with varying degrees but, on balance, increasing success.[28]

In the last analysis we have two 'mother' multi-State federal arrangements. The first, exemplified by the United States of America, led to the establishment of modern federation as an effective way to liberalize the political and social order and to promote democratic republicanism. The other, exemplified by the European Union, is leading to post-modern confederation designed to promote the integration of previously politically sovereign states to better handle the problems of globalization and end devastating inter-state conflicts and to empower ethnic groupings previously submerged by the statism of the nation state. One result of the development of the EC was the emergence of the need to deal with the growing necessity for accommodating ethnic, linguistic, and religious heterogeneity. One of the great discoveries of the post-war world was that these differences, which modern states had sought either to embody in the nation state itself or to entirely repress, had not disappeared. Instead, contrary to earlier predictions, they had intensified. This was as true in Europe, where all of history and high culture for centuries had pointed the elites in the other direction and where for 300 or 400 years it had been the conscious and deliberate state policy to foster suppression of such differences by using both the carrot and the stick.

Finally, the desire to stabilize the world order by permanently fixing state boundaries even while states are losing their exclusive sovereignty makes federal arrangements vitally necessary to handle inter-state or multi-state needs. This has a particular significance for the development of confederation, as distinct from federation, as the preferred form of such relationships. While the states are the building blocks of the new globalization, and peoples that do not have states of their own still seek the state framework, the states themselves must enter into a wide variety of inter-state and multi-state networks for functional reasons. Few states are looking to subordinate themselves to a large comprehensive framework but almost all recognize the necessity of joining these kinds of functional arrangements and so are willing to do so provided they have a share in their governance. Stabilization of the international order requires both states and functional arrangements in proper combination. The results are federal but federal in the confederal manner. Between these two models

[28] Shor.

the world has been given the opportunity to discover and develop several practical ways to move from statism to federalism.

The difficulties with federation, which have so often proved fatal, flow from a basic tension between the comprehensive ends of the constituting polities and the limited ends of the confederation itself. Can this confederal tension be sustained in a polity on a long-term basis and under what conditions? This is a real issue in the European Union today, following the definitions and distinction presented here. The EU is more likely to succeed because it has more limited ends. The Western European states that constituted it deliberately rejected the larger ends of federation and sought the more limited linkages of confederation, whether the term is used or not. Consequently the EU in some respects seems like a league but in fact has real powers in specific spheres which transcend those of even old-style confederations. This has been achieved not as a way station on the road to a United States of Europe but to reach a more confederal end.

Contrast this with the United States and the invention of federation. In the US the principle difference between the Constitution of 1787 and the Articles of Confederation was not a difference in their degree of modernity, since both were modern instruments, but in the adjustment of means to ends. Once Americans were convinced that the ends of union were vital, the question became what means had to be developed to achieve those ends. As the preamble to the 1787 constitution states, what was proposed by that document was the establishment of 'a more perfect union', not a new one; and what was changed over the Articles of Confederation were the means for effectuating that union, which required the expansion of the powers granted to the federal government even to attain to already agreed-upon ends. The nineteenth and twentieth century federations that have followed in the footsteps of the United States were influenced by that first modern federation, and reflect the same intent.

Our examination of the EU in comparison with the US leads us to the conclusion that the integrative trend in Europe is, and is likely to continue to be, confederal rather than federal. The EU is a novel, but nonetheless recognizable and highly-developed, confederation, and as such has perhaps more in common with the American Confederation of the 1780s than with either the modern US federation or the tradition of the pre-modern leagues. There remains to be considered the adequacy and effectiveness of the confederal, when compared with the federal, form of union, in terms of its success both as a form of democratic government—in a civil libertarian tradition—and in furthering the purposes of the union.

Federalism, like constitutionalism, is a rich and complex thing, a matter of formal constitutional divisions, appropriate institutions, patterns of political behaviour, and, ultimately, of political culture.[29] Moreover, federal democracy offers a complete and comprehensive theory of democracy which stands in sharp contrast to the theories of democracy regnant in Europe until now—Jacobin democracy and parliamentary democracy in the Westminster model—not to speak of that monstrous development referred to as totalitarian democracy.[30]

Federal democracy addresses the great questions of sovereignty, jurisdiction, and powers—or competences—the relationships between power and law or right, and the great issues of centralization and decentralization. It does so by vesting sovereignty in the people who constitute the body politic and requiring them to constitutionally allocate competences or powers among the governments of their creation. They must do so in a non-centralized manner that provides for both centralization and decentralization as needed, but always within a non-centralized framework whereby all exercise of powers is governed by law and related to the rights of the constituents.

Even with the federalist revolution in full swing, there will be those states for whom federal structures will remain inappropriate. Federalism is not a catch-all solution for all problems. Nor should it be looked upon in that way. It is certainly not a panacea.

True partisans of liberty, since the beginning of the modern epoch, have consistently emphasized federal liberty, that is to say, the liberty to enter into covenants and to live by them, whether we are talking of Hobbes's limited covenant of peace or John Winthrop's Puritan Christian idea of an all-embracing covenant with God in which federal liberty consists of pursuing the right way to salvation. The range of possibilities between the Hobbesian minimalist covenant and Winthrop's maximalist one is great. It is within that range that we find true liberty. In the last analysis, this may be the greatest contribution of federalism to the development of a peaceful, prosperous, free, and happy world.[31]

[29] Ivo D. Duchacek, *Comparative Federalism: The Territorial Dimension of Politics* (New York: Holt, Rinehart, and Winston, 1970); Ivo D. Duchacek, 'Consociations of Fatherlands: The Revival of Confederal Principles and Practices', *Publius*, 12/4 (1992), 129–77; Ivo D. Duchacek, 'Dyadic Federations and Confederations', *Publius*, 18/2 (1988), 5–31.

[30] Ostrom, *Political Theory of a Compound Republic*; Robert B. Hawkins, Jr, *American Federalism: A New Partnership for the Republic* (San Francisco: Institute for Contemporary Studies, 1982); Elazar, *Exploring Federalism*.

[31] Thomas Hobbes, *Leviathan*, Part 1, ch. 15; on John Winthrop, see Edmund S. Morgan, *The Puritan Dilemma*, ed. Oscar Handlin (Boston: Little, Brown, 1958); and Perry Miller, *The New England Mind: The Seventeenth Century, vol. 2: From Colony to Province* (Cambridge, MA: Harvard University Press, 1953).

7. Federalism and Confederalism as Forms of Democratic Government

All forms of federalism begin with the assumption that government in some form is necessary and that the development of appropriately effective government is a major human task. In this respect federalist theories are realistic. The other 'given' of federalism is that humans are born free and that good government must be grounded in a framework of maximum human liberty. The task of constitution-makers is to develop a regime for each people which secures liberty even while recognizing and allowing for government in its coercive aspects. Thus, the central interest of both federation and confederation and, indeed, of true federalism in all its species, is the issue of liberty.

To say that liberty stands at the centre of federalist striving is to open the door to the questions of what constitutes liberty in the federal context and how federalists deal with the problematics of liberty. On one level, these questions lead us to what may be the decisive difference between confederation and federation. Federations are communities of both polities and individuals and emphasize the liberties of both. The American federation has placed even greater emphasis on the liberty of individuals than on the liberties if its constituent polities, an emphasis which has grown more pronounced over the generations. Confederations, on the other hand, are primarily of polities which place greater emphasis on the liberties of the constituent polities. It is the task of the constituent polities to protect individual liberty, more or less as each defines it, although the constituent polities of confederations of republics must conform to at least minimum standards of individual liberty in order to preserve the republican character of the whole.

Thus to understand a confederation it is necessary to understand, first and foremost, what constitutes the liberties of its constituents and how those constituents see the confederation as protecting those liberties. The Articles of Confederation had as the focus of their concern the federal liberty of the constituent States. Hence they had what was at once a more limited and far broader definition of federal liberty with which to work, restricting the freedom of the constituent States in those few fields where it was deemed necessary for a uniform confederal standard, while allowing each in its own way to determine what constituted federal liberty for its own citizens.

8. The European Union: Some Additional Points of Analysis

First, it is hard not to be struck by the degree to which the European Union was built, in both its positive and negative aspects, by Frenchmen. In a sense, it is the victory of the French federalist tradition over French Jacobinism. In France, Jacobinism won: in Europe, the French federalists have reasserted themselves and struggled hard to rise above the Jacobin tradition and to speak in the name of Montesquieu, de Tocqueville, Proudhon, and others who represent that latter tradition.

This is a very important aspect of the struggle for the European Union because the sense of a philosophy of Europe is being formulated without being 'formulated'. It is bubbling up from the Community-building process. The nature of that philosophy needs to be exposed, in the best sense; it needs to be made visible, made understandable, so that it can be determined whether or not it is an appropriate philosophy.

9. The Challenge for Europe

Every polity is devoted to the attainment of certain ends, to the achievement of justice as it is conceived by those who constitute it. In this respect, the extent to which the general government possesses power, well or crudely related to the defined ends of the polity, is not determinative of those ends.

One of the perceived problems of confederation is that the confederal government was not adequate for the achievement of the ends for which it was instituted. We have already mentioned two elements involved in determining the ends of federal polities, namely liberty, however defined, and good government, however defined. In both cases, federal—that is, composite—polities, because they are constituted in a formal way by a pact or articles of agreement, are likely to be more explicit about their understanding of these and other ends to which they are devoted. These ends are generally stated in the preambles to their constitutions, but many also be stated or explicated in the body of the constitutional document(s).

As a general rule, confederations will have more limited ends than federations. With respect to the United States, the principal difference between the Constitution of 1787 and the Articles of Confederation was one of means rather than ends. In this respect, the preamble to the 1787 Constitution specified that what is proposed in the establishment of 'a more perfect union', not a new one. What was changed were the means for effectuating the union, which required the expansion of the powers granted to the federal government even in order to obtain already agreed upon ends. The major shift with regard to ends was from an emphasis on the liberties of the individual States to the establishment of liberty, justice, and domestic tranquillity for the people of the United States. Article III of the Articles sets forth the ends of the Confederation:

> The said States hereby severally enter into a firm league of friendship with each other, for their common defense, the security of their liberties, and their mutual and general welfare, binding themselves to assist each other, against all force offered to, or attacks made upon them, or any of them, on account of religion, sovereignty, trade, or any other pretense whatever.

Contrast it with the preamble to the Constitution of 1787:

> We the people of the United States, in order to form a more perfect union, establish justice, insure domestic tranquility, provide for the common defense, promote the general welfare, and secure the blessings of liberty to ourselves and our posterity, do ordain and establish this Constitution for the United States of America.

We would not want to minimalize this shift. In a certain sense, it is of the essence, but it is not, as some would have it, the exchange of a loose league for a consolidated union. There is more of a shift in emphasis than in underlying form.

The distinction between the US federal and confederal regimes can be summarized as follows: the Constitution of 1787 provided a government that was partly national and partly federal to replace the Articles of Confederation which established a regime that was partially federal and partially a league. The first combination came to be known as federation and the second came to be known as confederation. The tension built into the former is between the national and the federal elements, while the tension built into the latter is between the federal and the league elements. Since federal arrangements always involve on or another set of built-in tensions, the character of the tension of each particular arrangement is the major clue as to the species of federalism involved.

The difficulties—in the past fatal—of confederation flow from this basic tension. In our consideration of whether confederation can be a viable federal option, we must raise the question as to whether, or under what conditions, the confederal tension can be sustained in a polity on a long-term basis. This is a real issue in the EU today.

2

Federalism Without Constitutionalism: Europe's *Sonderweg*

J. H. H. WEILER

1. Introduction: Europe's Fateful Choice

In the vision of the great thinker and teacher of federalism, the late Dan Elazar, Europe is already a federalism. The federal principle, he rightly explained, should not be confused with its specific manifestation in the federal state.[1] Echoing the same thought, Pescatore, the Marshall of European Law, observes

> [T]he methods of federalism are not only a means of organising states. [F]ederalism is a political and legal philosophy which adapts itself to all political contexts on both the municipal and the international level, wherever and whenever two basic prerequisites are fulfilled: the search for unity, combined with genuine respect for the autonomy and the legitimate interests of the participant entities.[2]

It is, thus, not surprising that comparisons between the distinct federalisms in North America and Europe have constituted a staple feature in the ongoing discussion concerning European integration.[3] Institutional arrangements have attracted a great deal of attention because of the apparent divergence of the European experience from the typical federa-

[1] D. Elazar, 'Options, Problems and Possibilities in Light of the Current Situation', in D. Elazar (ed.), *Self Rule—Shared Rule* (Ramat Gan: Turtledove Publishing, 1979), at 3 and 4.

[2] Pierre Pescatore, 'Preface', in T. Sandalow and E. Stein, *Courts and Free Markets*, i (Oxford: Clarendon Press, 1982), at ix–x.

[3] See, for example, Robert R. Bowie and Carl J. Friedrich (eds), *Studies in Federalism* (Boston: Little, Brown, 1954) and Arthur Whittier Macmahon (ed.), *Federalism Mature and Emergent* (New York: Columbia University Press, 1955) for early comparative analysis in the formative years. For subsequent analyses of the more mature system, see for example Sandalow and Stein (eds.), *Courts and Free Markets*; Mauro Cappelletti, Monica Seccombe, and Joseph H. H. Weiler (eds.), *Integration Through Law: Europe and the American Federal Experience* (Berlin and New York: de Gruyter, 1986); Koen Lenaerts (ed.), *Two Hundred Years of U.S. Constitution and Thirty Years of EEC Treaty* (Brussels: Kluwer, 1988).

tion. In contrast with the classical model of the federal state, and despite considerable refinements, Europe's institutional structure still adheres to the original supranational design of Commission-Council-Parliament and continues to guarantee a decisive voice in European governance to the governments of the Member States. The formal empowerment of, say, the European Parliament over the years has been counterbalanced by informal empowerment of the Medusa-like Council. For its part, the Commission has had to struggle to preserve its own weight in the decisional process. Though superficially—and to some, optimistically—one could compare the Commission to a federal Executive Branch, the Council to a Senate-type State chamber and the Parliament to a popular chamber, the realities of an intergovernmental Europe are still forcefully in place. To use somewhat archaic language of statecraft, institutionally Europe is closer to the confederal than it is to the federal.

Constitutional arrangements, by contrast, have attracted considerable comparative attention because of their apparent convergence with the experience of the federal state. Typically federations allocate certain powers to federal institutions, and typically policies and laws emanating from the exercise of such power are the supreme law of the land, meaning they are the law of the land in the sense of operating without the intermediary of local government and in case of conflict they trump conflicting norms. Federal state constitutions create, always, a vertical hierarchy of a triple nature: a hierarchy of norms which, in turn, is rooted in a vertical hierarchy of normative authority which, in turn, is situated in a hierarchy of real power. Despite many original intentions, federations end up with a concentration of both constitutional and institutional power at the federal level.

As a result of a combination of express Treaty provisions—such as those stipulating that certain types of Community legislation would be directly applicable[4]—of foundational principles of international law—such as the general principle of supremacy of treaties over conflicting domestic law, even domestic constitutional law[5]—and of the interpretations of the

[4] Originally Art. 189 EEC (Treaty of Rome).

[5] The general rule of international law does not allow, except in the narrowest of circumstances, for a state to use its own domestic law, including its own domestic constitutional law, as an excuse for non-performance of a treaty. That is part of the ABC of international law and is reflected in the same Vienna Convention Art. 27. *Oppenheim's International Law* is clear: 'It is firmly established that a state when charged with a breach of its international obligations cannot in international law validly plead as a defense that it was unable to fulfill them because its internal law . . . contained rules in conflict with international law; this applies equally to a state's assertion of its inability to secure the necessary changes in its law by virtue of some legal or constitutional requirement . . .' Sir Robert Jennings and Sir Arthur Watts (eds), *Oppenheim's International Law*, i: *Peace 84–85*, 9th edn (Harlow: Longman, 1992.)

European Court of Justice,[6] a set of constitutional norms regulating the relationship between the Union and its Member States, or the Member States and their Union, has emerged which is very much like similar sets of norms in most federal states. There is an allocation of powers, which as has been the experience in most federal states has often not been respected; there is the principle of the law of the land, in the EU called Direct Effect; and there is the grand principle of supremacy every bit as egregious as that which is found in the American federal constitution itself.

Put differently, the constitutional discipline which Europe demands of its constitutional actors—the Union itself, the Member States and State organs, European citizens, and others—is in most respects indistinguishable from that which you would find in advanced federal states.

But there remains one huge difference: Europe's constitutional principles, even if materially similar, are rooted in a framework which is altogether different. In federations, whether American or Australian, German or Canadian, the institutions of a federal state are situated in a constitutional framework which presupposes the existence of a 'constitutional demos', a single *pouvoir constituant* made of the citizens of the federation in whose sovereignty, as a constituent power, and by whose supreme authority the specific constitutional arrangement is rooted. Thus, although the federal constitution seeks to guarantee State rights and although both constitutional doctrine and historical reality will instruct us that the federation may have been a creature of the constituent units and their respective peoples, the formal sovereignty and authority of the people coming together as a constituent power is greater than any other expression of sovereignty within the polity and hence the supreme authority of the Constitution—including its federal principles.

Of course, one of the great fallacies in the art of 'federation building', as in nation building, is to confuse the juridical presupposition of a constitutional *demos* with political and social reality. In many instances, constitutional doctrine presupposes the existence of that which it creates: the *demos* which is called upon to accept the constitution is constituted, legally, by that very constitution, and often that act of acceptance is among the first steps towards a thicker social and political notion of constitutional *demos*. Thus, the empirical legitimacy of the constitution may lag behind its formal authority—and it may take generations and civil wars to be fully internalized—as the history of the US testifies. Likewise, the juridical presupposition of one *demos* may be contradicted by a persistent social reality of multiple *ethnoi* or *demoi* who do not share, or grow

[6] See generally Joseph Weiler, 'The Transformation of Europe', in *The Constitution of Europe* (Cambridge and New York: Cambridge University Press, 1999).

to share, the sense of mutual belongingness transcending political differences and factions and constituting a political community essential to a constitutional compact of the classical mould. The result will be an unstable compact, as the history of Canada and modern Spain will testify. But, as a matter of empirical observation, I am unaware of any federal state, old or new, which does not presuppose the supreme authority and sovereignty of its federal *demos*.

In Europe, that presupposition does not exist. Simply put, Europe's constitutional architecture has never been validated by a process of constitutional adoption by a European constitutional *demos* and, hence, as a matter of both normative political principles and empirical social observation the European constitutional discipline does not enjoy the same kind of authority as may be found in federal states where their federalism is rooted in a classic constitutional order. It is a constitution without some of the classic conditions of constitutionalism. There is a hierarchy of norms: Community norms trump conflicting Member State norms. But this hierarchy is not rooted in a hierarchy of normative authority or in a hierarchy of real power. Indeed, European federalism is constructed with a top-to-bottom hierarchy of norms, but with a bottom-to-top hierarchy of authority and real power.

You would think that this would result in perennial instability. As we shall see, one of the virtues of the European construct is that it produces not only a surprisingly salutary normative effect but also a surprisingly stable political polity. Member States of the European Union accept their constitutional discipline with far more equanimity than, say, Quebec. There are, surely, many reasons for this, but one of them is the peculiar constitutional arrangement of Europe.

This distinct constitutional arrangement is not accidental. Originally, in a fateful and altogether welcome decision, Europe rejected the federal state model. In the most fundamental statement of its political aspiration, indeed of its very *telos*, articulated in the first line of the Preamble of the Treaty of Rome, the gathering nations of Europe 'Determined to the lay the foundations for an ever closer Union of the peoples of Europe'. Thus, even in the eventual promised land of European integration, the distinct peoplehood of its components was to remain intact—in contrast with the theory of most, and the praxis of all, federal states which predicate the existence of one people. Likewise, with all the vicissitudes from Rome to Amsterdam, the Treaties have not departed from their original blueprint as found, for example, in Art. 2 EC of the Treaty in force, of aspiring to achieve '. . . economic and social cohesion and solidarity among *Member States*' (emphasis added). Not one people, then, nor one State, federal or otherwise.

Europe was re-launched twice in recent times. In the mid-1980s the Single European Act introduced, almost by stealth, the most dramatic development in the institutional evolution of the Community achieved by a Treaty amendment: majority voting in most domains of the Single Market. Maastricht, in the 1990s, introduced the most important material development, EMU. Architecturally, the combination of a 'confederal' institutional arrangement and a 'federal' legal arrangement seemed for a time to mark Europe's *Sonderweg*—its special way and identity. It appeared to enable Europe to square a particularly vicious circle: achieving a veritably high level of material integration comparable only to that found in fully fledged federations, while maintaining at the same time—and in contrast with the experience of all such federations—powerful, some would argue strengthened,[7] Member States.

At the turn of the new century, fuelled, primarily, by the Enlargement project, there is a renewed debate concerning the basic architecture of the Union. Very few dare call the child by its name and only a few stray voices are willing to suggest a fully fledged institutional overhaul and the reconstruction of a federal-type government enjoying direct legitimacy from an all European electorate.[8] Instead, and evidently politically more correct, there has been a swell of political and academic voices[9] calling for a new constitutional settlement which would root the existing discipline in a 'veritable' European constitution to be adopted by a classical constitutional process and resulting in a classical constitutional document. The Charter of Human Rights is considered an important step in that direction. What is special about this discourse is that it is not confined to the federalist

[7] See three classics: Alan S. Milward, George Brenanm and Frederico Romero, *The European Rescue of the Nation State* (Berkeley: University of California Press, 1992); Stanley Hoffmann, 'Reflections on the Nation-State in Western Europe Today', in Loukas Tsoukalis (ed.), *The European Community: Past, Present & Future* (Oxford: Basil Blackwell. 1983); and A. Moravcsik, *The Choice for Europe* (Ithaca, NY: Cornell University Press, 1998).

[8] See for example Giscard d'Estaing and Helmut Schmidt, *International Herald Tribune* (11 April 2000). For a more honest discussion, admitting the statal implications of the new construct, see for example G. Federico Mancini, 'Europe: The Case for Statehood', 4 *European Law Journal* (1998), 29–42, and Harvard Jean Monnet Working Paper 6/98, and, of course, Jürgen Habermas, 'The European Nation-State and the Pressures of Globalization', *New Left Review*, 235 (May 1999), 46–59, and *Die Einbeziehung des Anderen* (Frankfurt: Suhrkamp, 1996), Ch. 3. There is an interesting political-legal paradox here. A 'flexible' Europe with a 'core' at its centre will actually enable that core to retain the present governance system dominated by the Council—the executive branch of the Member States—at the expense of national parliamentary democracy. Constitutionally, the statal structure would in fact enhance even further the democracy deficit.

[9] In the political sphere see for example the over-discussed Berlin speeches of Joschka Fischer and Jacque Chirac. For text and comments on these interventions, see the special symposium on the Harvard Jean Monnet Site: www.law.harvard.programs.JeanMonnet

fringe of European activists, but has become respectable Euro-speak both in academic and political circles.

Four factors seem to drive the renewed interest in a formal constitution rather than the existing 'constitutional arrangement' based on the Treaties. The first factor is political. It is widely assumed, correctly it would seem, that the current institutional arrangements would become dysfunctional in an enlarged Union of, say, 25. A major overhaul seems to be called for. In the same vein, some believe, incorrectly in my view, that the current constitutional arrangements would not work. In particular, the absence of a formal constitution leaves all important constitutional precepts of the Union at the mercy of this or that Member State threatening both the principle of uniformity of, and of equality before, the law as well as an orderly functionality of the polity. One is forever worried: 'What will the German/Italian/Spanish, or whatever, constitutional court say about this or that.' A formal constitution enjoying the legitimacy of an all-European *pouvoir constituant* would, once and for all, settle that issue.

The second factor is 'procedural' or 'processual'.[10] The process of adopting a constitution—the debate it would generate, the alliances it would form, the opposition it would create—would all, it is said, be healthy for the democratic and civic ethos and praxis of the polity.

The third factor is material. In one of its most celebrated cases in the early 1960s, the European Court of Justice described the Community as a '. . . new legal order for the benefit of which the States have limited their sovereign rights, albeit in limited fields'. There is a widespread anxiety that these fields are limited no more. Indeed, not long ago a prominent European scholar and judge wrote that there '. . . simply is no nucleus of sovereignty that the Member States can invoke, as such, against the Community'.[11] A constitution is thought an appropriate means to place limits to the growth of Community competences.

Of greatest interest to me is the final normative and conceptual drive behind the discussion. Normatively, the disturbing absence of formal constitutional legitimization for a polity that makes heavy constitutional demands on its constituent Members is, it may be thought, problematic. If, as is the case, current European constitutional discipline demands constitutional obedience by and within all Member States, their organs and their peoples even when these conflict with constitutional norms of the

[10] Günter Frankenberg, 'The Return of the Contract: Problems and Pitfalls of European Constitutionalism', *European Law Journal*, 3 (2000, forthcoming).

[11] Koen Lenaerts, 'Constitutionalism and the Many Faces of Federalism', 38 A. J.Com. L 205 (1990) at 220. The Court, too, has modified its rhetoric: in its more recent Opinion 1/91 it refers to the Member States as having limited their sovereign rights '. . . in ever wider fields.' Opinion 1/91, [1991]ECR 6079, Recital 21.

Member State, this, it is argued, should be legitimized by a constitution which has the explicit consent of its subjects instead of the current pastiche which, like Topsy, just 'growed'.

Conceptually, the disquiet with the current European constitutional arrangement must be understood against a European constitutional discourse which for years has been dominated by a strange combination of Kelsen[12] and Schmitt.[13] It is Kelsenian in its attempts, under many guises to describe, define and understand the European *Grundnorm*—the source whence the authority of European constitutional disciplines derives. The search for this Kelsenian holy grail, whether or not acknowledged explicitly, underscores the great bulk of the academic literature theorizing European constitutionalism. And this holy grail is, typically, understood in Schmittian terms: the search is for the *ultimate* source of authority, the one that counts in the case of extremity, of conflict.[14] That is the true criteria of the real *Grundnorm*.

Early 'Europeanists' liked to argue that the *Grundnorm*, typically expressed in, say, the principle of supremacy of European law over national law in case of conflict, had shifted to the 'central' or 'general' power: that is, to Europe. That view is less in fashion today and is contested by those who point out that, both in fact and in law, ultimate authority still rests in national constitutional orders which sanction supremacy, define its parameters, and typically place limitations on it.

According to this latter view, the statal *Grundnorm* would shift. Only if one were to take the existing constitutional precepts and enshrine them in a formal constitution adopted by a European 'constitutional *demos*'—the peoples of Europe acting on that occasion as one people—would constitutional authority in fact and in law shift to Europe. For the most part, both for friends and foes of European constitutionalism the debate is conducted on this Kelseno-Schmittian turf.

I am far from certain whether the constitutional discussion will actually result in the adoption of a formal constitution and I am even more doubtful whether we will see in the near future a European state even of a most limited core. My interest in this debate is, thus, that of neither the international relations expert nor the social scientist trying to explain or predict the course that European integration has taken or will take. I am,

[12] Hans Kelsen, 'On the Pure Theory of Law' 1 *Israel Law Review* 3 (1966).

[13] See C. Schmitt, *The Concept of the Political* (Chicago: University of Chicago Press, 1996) at, for example, 35, 43ff.

[14] Whether the *Grundnorm* is internal to the legal order or outside it is a contested matter. Insightful in this genre is Pavlos Eleftheriadis, 'Begging the Constitutional Question', 36 JCMS 255 (1998); 'Aspects of European Constitutionalism' 21 E.L.Rev. 32 (1996).

instead, mostly interested in the normative values of which the constitutional and political discourse is an expression.

I want to explain why the unique brand of European constitutional federalism—the status quo—represents not only its most original political asset but also its deepest set of values. I also do not think that a formal constitution is a useful response to other concerns such as the issue of competences.

2. Authority, Submission and Emancipation: A Parable

Before offering a normative reading of the European constitutional architecture, I want to tweak some of the premises on which the constitutional debate is typically premised. The following parable is offered with this purpose in mind.

There is an inevitable and scary moment in the growing up of an observant Jew and in the raising of religiously observant children. In a religion the constitutive and defining feature of which is Nomos—the Law—and which has no theology, there is no easy answer to the inevitable question: why observe this law? The Pauline antinomian revolution derives from a failure to find a convincing justification for submission to Nomos. To the sceptical reader one may point out that a similar question may be asked regarding submission and loyalty to a constitution.

The simplest, and deepest, answer is rooted in covenant and in the authority—and the Author—whence Nomos derives. But submission and obedience to God surely do not exhaust the significance of a Nomos-based life. One intriguing reply, given by the polymath philosopher Isaiah Leibowitz,[15] is relevant to our current discussions of European constitutionalism.

Take the core set of ritualistic observances: kosher laws, Sabbath laws, and the laws of purity in sexual relations. They are the core set because they affect the three central features of our mundane existence: eating, working, loving. Living by Nomos means a submission to a set of constraints in all these areas. The constraints are designed in such a way that they cannot be explained in rational utilitarian terms. Kosher rules actually exclude some of the healthiest foods; the Sabbath rules have a niggardly quality to them that militates, in some respects, against a vision of rest and spirituality; and the ritualistic laws of purity, involving the messy subject of menstruation and sexual abstention, have arbitrary elements

[15] Y. Leibowitz, *Judaism, Human Values and the Jewish State* (Cambridge, MA: Harvard University Press; 1992).

galore. It is, indeed, as if they were designed to force the observer into pure and mindless obedience and submission. One observes for no other reason than having been commanded. No wonder Paul[16] shrug off this yoke.

There is, however, an interesting paradox in this submission which orthodox Judaism as well as several strands of Islam share. Total obedience and submission are to a transcendent authority which is not of this world. In that very act of submission is encapsulated an emancipation and liberation from any authority of this world. By enslaving oneself to an authority outside of this world, one declares an independence of, and refusal to submit—in the ultimate sense—to, any authority of this world. By abstaining from eating everything that one fancies, one liberates oneself from that powerful part of our physical existence. By arranging life so as not to work on the Sabbath, one subjugates the even more powerful call of career and the workplace. And by refraining from sexual abandon, even if loving, even if within wedlock, one asserts a measure of independence even over that exquisite part of our lives too. Isaiah Berlin, a town mate, friend, and admirer of Isaiah Leibowitz gives the secular equivalent to this insight in his discussion of rational liberty.

There are three relevant lessons to the constitutional and European discourse from this parable.

The first: an act of submission can often be simultaneously an act of emancipation and liberation.

The second: as Aristotle teaches us, virtue is a habit of the soul and habits are instilled by practice.

The third: the purpose of obeying the law is not co-terminous with the consequences of obeying the law. One may obey to submit to the author of the Command. A consequence, not a purpose, may be emancipation.

Let us see now how these play out in the normative understanding of European constitutionalism.

3. Neither Kelsen Nor Schmitt: The Principle of European Constitutional Tolerance—Concept and Praxis

The reason the question of *ultimate* authority and constitutional *Grundnorm* seems so important is that we consider the integrity of our *national* constitutional orders not simply as a matter of legal obedience and political power but of moral commitment and identity. Our national constitutions are perceived by us as doing more than simply structuring the

[16] St Paul needs no citation. But for a somewhat troubling latter-day reincarnation of this aspect of Pauline dogma, cf. R. M. Unger, *What Should Legal Analysis Become?* (London and New York: Verso, 1996) at 186ff.

respective powers of government and the relationships between public authority and individuals or between the state and other agents. Our constitutions are said to encapsulate fundamental values of the polity and this, in turn, is said to be a reflection of our collective identity as a people, as a nation, as a state, as a Community, as a Union. When we are proud and attached to our constitutions we are so for these very reasons. They are about restricting power, not enlarging it; they protect fundamental rights of the individual; and they define a collective identity which does not make us feel queasy the way some forms of ethnic identity might. Thus, in the endless and tiresome debates about the European Union constitutional order, national courts have become in the last decade far more aggressive in their constitutional self-understanding. The case law is well known. National courts are no longer at the vanguard of the 'new European legal order', bringing the rule of law to transnational relations, and empowering, through EC law, individuals *vis-à-vis* Member State authority. Instead they stand at the gate and defend national constitutions against illicit encroachment from Brussels. They have received a sympathetic hearing, since they are perceived as protecting fundamental human rights as well as protecting national identity. To protect national sovereignty is passé; to protect national identity by insisting on constitutional specificity is *à la mode*.

Thus, on this new reading, to submit to the constitutional disciplines of Europe without a proper Kelsenian constitution, which formally vests in Europe Schmittian ultimate authority, is something that not only contradicts an orderly understanding of legal hierarchy but also compromises deep values enshrined in the national constitution as well as a collective identity which is tied up with these values. Indeed, it is to challenge the idea of constitution itself.

Miguel Maduro, one of the most brilliant of the new generation of European constitutional thinkers, gives eloquent expression to this concern:

> European integration not only challenges national constitutions . . . it challenges constitutional law itself. It assumes a constitution without a traditional political community defined and proposed by that constitution . . . European integration also challenges the legal monopoly of States and the hierarchical organisation of the law (in which constitutional law is still conceived of as the 'higher law').[17]

Is this challenge so threatening?

[17] M. Maduro, *We, The Court*. . . (Oxford: Hart Publishing, 1998) at 175. Maduro himself does not advocate a European constitution. I cite him simply for his striking diagnosis of the issue. It is superior to my own clumsy attempt to formulate the dilemma as a 'Constitution without Constitutionalism', as 'doing before hearkening'. J. Weiler, '"We Will Do, And Hearken"—Reflections on a Common Constitutional Law for the European Union', in Roland Bieber and Pierre Widmer (eds.), *The European Constitutional Area* (Zurich: Schulthess, 1995).

In part it is. Modern liberal constitutions are, indeed, about limiting the power of government *vis-à-vis* the individual; they do, too, articulate fundamental human rights in the best neo-Kantian tradition; and they reflect a notion of collective identity as a community of values which is far less threatening than more organic definitions of collective identity. They are a reflection of our better part.

But, like the moon, like much which is good in life, there is here a dark side too.

It is, first, worth listening carefully to the rhetoric of the constitutional discourse. Even when voiced by the greatest humanists, the military overtones are present. We have been invited to develop a *patriotism* around our modern, liberal, constitutions. The constitutional patriot is invited to *defend* the constitution. In some states we have agencies designed to protect the constitution whose very name is similar to our border defences. In other countries, we are invited to *swear allegiance* to the constitution. In a constitutional democracy we have a doctrine of a *fighting* democracy, whereby democratic hospitality is not extended to those who would destroy constitutional democracy itself. To be a good constitutional liberal, it would seem from this idiom, is to be a constitutional nationalist and, it turns out, the constitutional stakes are not only about values and limitations of power but also about its opposite: the power which lurks underneath such values.

Very few constitutionalists and practically no modern constitutional court will make an *overt* appeal to natural law. Thus, unlike the 'constitution' in the parable, the formal normative authority of the constitutions around which our patriotism must form and which we must defend is, from a legal point of view, mostly positivist. This means that it is as deep or shallow as the last constitutional amendment: in some countries, like Switzerland or Germany, not a particularly onerous political process. Consequently, vesting so much in the constitutional integrity of the Member State is an astonishing feat of self-celebration and self-aggrandizement, of bestowing on ourselves, in our capacity of constituent power, a breathtaking normative authority. Just think of the near sacred nature we give today to the constitutions adopted by the morally corrupted societies of the World War II generation in, say, Italy and Germany and elsewhere.

A similar doubt should dampen somewhat any enthusiasm towards the new constitutional posture of national courts which hold themselves out as defending the core constitutional values of their polity, indeed its very identity. The limitation of power imposed on the political branches of government is, as has been widely noticed, accompanied by a huge dose of judicial self-empowerment and no small measure of sanctimonious moralizing. Human rights often provoke the most strident rhetoric. Yet constitutional texts in our different polities, especially when it comes to human rights, are remarkably similar. Defending the constitutional identity of the state and its core values turns out in many cases to a defence of some hermeneutic foible adopted by five judges voting against four. The banana saga, which has taxed the European Court of Justice, the German Constitutional Court, the Appellate Body of the World Trade Organization, and endless lawyers and academics is the perfect symbol of this farce.

Finally, there is also in an exquisite irony in a constitutional ethos which, while appropriately suspicious of older notions of organic and ethnic identity, at the very same time implicitly celebrates a supposed unique moral identity, wisdom, and, yes, superiority, of the authors of the constitution, the people, the constitutional *demos*, when it wears the hat of constituent power and, naturally, of those who interpret it.

It was Samuel Johnson who suggested that patriotism was the last refuge of the scoundrel. Dr Johnson was, of course, only partly right. Patriotism can also be noble. But it is an aphorism worth remembering when we celebrate constitutional patriotism, national or transnational, and rush to its defence from any challenges to it. How, then, do we both respect and uphold all that is good in our constitutional tradition and yet, at the same time, keep it and ourselves under sceptical check?

The advocacy for a European constitution is not what it purports to be. It is not a call for 'a' constitution. It is a call for a different form of European constitution from the constitutional architecture we already have. And yet the current constitutional architecture, which of course can be improved in many of its specifics, encapsulates one of Europe's most important constitutional innovations, the Principle of Constitutional Tolerance.

The Principle of Constitutional Tolerance, which is the normative hall mark of European federalism, must be examined both as a concept and as a praxis. First , then, the concept of European integration has been, historically, one of the principal means with which to consolidate democracy within and among several of the Member States, both old and new, with less than perfect historical democratic credentials. For many, thus, democracy is the objective, the end, of the European construct. This is fallacious. Democracy is not the end. Democracy, too, is a means, even if an indispensable means. The end is to try, and try again, to live a life of decency, to honour our creation in the image of God, or the secular equivalent. A democracy, when all is said and done, is as good or bad as the people who belong to it. The problem of Haider's Austria is not an absence of democracy. The problem is that Austria is a democracy; that Haider *was elected democratically*, and that even the people who did not vote for him are content to see him and his party share in government. A democracy of vile persons will be vile.

Europe was built on the ashes of World War II, which witnessed the most horrific alienation of those thought of as aliens, an alienation which became annihilation. What we should be thinking about is not simply the prevention of another such carnage: that's the easy part and it is unlikely ever to happen again in Western Europe, though events in the Balkans remind us that those demons are still within the continent. More difficult is dealing at a deeper level with the source of these attitudes. In the realm of the social, in the public square, the relationship to the alien is at the core of such decency. It is difficult to imagine something normatively more important to the human condition and to our multicultural societies.

There are, it seems to me, two basic human strategies of dealing with the alien and these two strategies have played a decisive role in Western civilisation. One strategy is to remove the boundaries. It is the spirit of 'come, be one of us'. It is noble since it involves, of course, elimination of prejudice, of the notion that there are boundaries that cannot be eradicated. But the 'be one of us', however well intentioned, is often an invitation to the alien to be one of us, by being us. *Vis-à-vis* the alien, it risks robbing him of his identity. *Vis-à-vis* oneself, it may be a subtle manifestation of both arrogance and belief in my superiority as well as intolerance. If I cannot tolerate the alien, one way of resolving the dilemma is to make him like me, no longer an alien. This is, of course, infinitely better than the opposite: exclusion, repression, and worse. But it is still a form of dangerous internal and external intolerance.

The alternative strategy of dealing with the alien is to acknowledge the validity of certain forms of non-ethnic bounded identity but simultaneously to reach across boundaries. We acknowledge and respect difference, and what is special and unique about ourselves as individuals and groups; and yet we reach across differences in recognition of our essential humanity. What is significant in this are the two elements I have mentioned. On the one hand, the identity of the alien, as such, is maintained. One is not invited to go out and, say, 'save him' by inviting him to be one of you. One is not invited to recast the boundary. On the other hand, despite the boundaries which are maintained, and constitute the I and the Alien, one is commanded to reach over the boundary and accept him, in his alienship, as oneself. The alien is accorded human dignity. The soul of the I is tended to not by eliminating the temptation to oppress but by learning humility and overcoming it.

The European current constitutional architecture represents this alternative, civilizing strategy of dealing with the 'other'. Constitutional

Tolerance is encapsulated in that most basic articulation of its meta-political objective in the preamble to the EC Treaty mentioned earlier in this chapter:

> Determined to lay the foundations of an ever closer union among the peoples of Europe.

No matter how close the Union, it is to remain a union among distinct peoples, distinct political identities, distinct political communities. An ever closer union could be achieved by an amalgam of distinct peoples into one which is both the ideal and/or the de facto experience of most federal and non-federal states. The rejection by Europe of that One Nation ideal or destiny is, as indicated above, usually understood as intended to preserve the rich diversity, cultural and other, of the distinct European peoples as well as to respect their political self-determination. But the European choice has an even deeper spiritual meaning.

An ever closer union is altogether more easy if differences among the components are eliminated, if they come to resemble each other, if they aspire to become one. The more identical the 'Other's' identity is to my own, the easier it is for me to identify with him and accept him. It demands less of me to accept another if he is very much like me. It is altogether more difficult to attain an ever closer Union if the components of that Union preserve their distinct identities, if they retain their 'otherness' *vis-à-vis* each other, if they do not become one flesh, politically speaking. Herein resides the Principle of Tolerance. Inevitably I define my distinct identity by a boundary which differentiates me from those who are unlike me. My continued existence as a distinct identity depends, ontologically, on that boundary and, psychologically and sociologically, on preserving that sentiment of otherness. The call to bond with those very others in an ever closer union demands an internalization—individual and societal—of a very high degree of tolerance. Living the Kantian categorical imperative is most meaningful when it is extended to those who are unlike me.

In political terms, this Principle of Tolerance finds a remarkable expression in the political organization of the Community which defies the normal premise of constitutionalism. Normally in a democracy, we demand democratic discipline, that is, accepting the authority of the majority over the minority only within a polity which understands itself as being constituted of one people, however defined. A majority demanding obedience from a minority which does not regard itself as belonging to the same people is usually regarded as subjugation. This is even more so in relation to constitutional discipline. And yet, in the Community, we subject the European peoples to constitutional discipline even though the European polity is composed of distinct peoples. It is a remarkable instance of civic tolerance to accept to be bound by precepts articulated not by 'my people' but by a community composed of distinct political communities: a people, if you wish, of others. I compromise my self-determination in this fashion as an expression of this kind of internal—towards myself—and external—towards others—tolerance.

Constitutionally, the Principle of Tolerance finds its expression in the very arrangement which has now come under discussion: a federal constitutional discipline which, however, is not rooted in a statist-type constitution.

This is where the first and third lessons of the parable come into play. Constitutional actors in the Member State accept the European constitutional discipline not because as a matter of legal doctrine, as is the case in the federal state, they are subordinate to a higher sovereignty and authority attaching to norms validated by the federal people, the constitutional *demos*. They accept it as an autonomous voluntary act, endlessly renewed on each occasion, of subordination, in the discrete areas governed by Europe to a norm which is the aggregate expression of other wills, other political identities, other political communities. Of course, to do so creates in itself a different type of political community one unique feature of which is that very willingness to accept a binding discipline which is rooted in and derives from a community of others. The Quebecois are told: in the name of the people of Canada, you are obliged to obey. The French or the Italians or the Germans are told: in the name of the peoples of Europe, you are invited to obey. In both, constitutional obedience is demanded. When acceptance and subordination is voluntary, and repeatedly so, it constitutes an act of true liberty and emancipation from collective self-arrogance and constitutional fetishism: a high expression of Constitutional Tolerance.

The Principle of Constitutional Tolerance is not a one way concept: it applies to constitutional actors and constitutional transactions at the Member State level, at the Union level and among the Member States too. This dimension may be clarified by moving from concept to praxis, to an examination of Constitutional Tolerance as a political and social reality.

It is, in my view, most present in the sphere of public administration, in the habits and practices it instils in the purveyors of public power in European polities, from the most mundane to the most august. At the most mundane administrative level, imagine immigration officials overturning practices of decades and centuries and learning to examine the passport of Community nationals in the same form, the same line, with the same scrutiny of their own nationals. And a similar discipline will be practised by customs officials, Housing Officers, educational officials, and many more subject to the disciplines of the European constitutional order.

Likewise, a similar discipline will become routine in policy-setting forums. In myriad areas—whether a local council or a parliament itself—every norm will be subject to an unofficial European impact study. So many policies in the public realm can no longer be adopted without examining their consonance with the interest of others, the interest of Europe.

Think, too, of the judicial function, ranging from the neighbourhood *giudice conciliatore* to the highest jurisdictions: willy nilly, European law, the interest of others, is part of the judicial normative matrix.

I have deliberately chosen examples which are both daily and commonplace but which also overturn what until recently would have been considered important constitutional distinctions. This process operates also at Community level. Think of the European judge or the European public official, who must understand that, in the peculiar constitutional compact of Europe, his decision will take effect only if obeyed by national courts, if executed faithfully by a national public official both of whom belong to a national administration which claims from them a particularly strong form of loyalty and habit. This, too, will instil a measure of caution and tolerance.

It is at this level of praxis that the second and third lessons of the parable come into play. What defines the European constitutional architecture is not the exception, the extreme case which definitively will situate the *Grundnorm* here or there. It is the quotidian, the daily practices, even if done unthinkingly, even if executed because the new staff regulations require that it be done in such a new way. This praxis habituates its myriad practitioners at all levels of public administration to their concealed virtues.

What, then, of the non-Europeans? What of the inevitable boundary created by those within and those without? Does not Constitutional Tolerance implode as an ethos of public mores if it is restricted only to those chosen people with the violet passports? Let us return to the examples mentioned above such as the new immigration procedures which group all Community nationals together. What characterizes this situation is that though national and Community citizens will be grouped together, they will still have distinct passports, with independent national identities, and still speak in their distinct tongues, or in that peculiar Eurospeak that sometimes passes itself off as English. This is critical, because in the daily practices which I am extolling the public official is invited and habituated to deal with a very distinct 'other' but to treat him or her as if he was his own. One should not be starry-eyed or overly naïve; but the hope and expectation is that there will be a spill-over effect: a gradual habituation to various forms of tolerance and with it a gradual change in the ethos of public administration which can be extended to Europeans and non-Europeans alike. The boundary between European and 'non-European' is inevitable, dictated if by nothing else by the discipline of numbers. In too large a polity the specific gravity of the individual is so diminished that democracy except in its most formal sense becomes impossible. But just as at the level of high politics, the Community experience has conditioned a different ethos of intergovernmental interaction, so it can condition a different ethos of public interaction with all aliens.

To extol the extant constitutional arrangement of Europe is not to suggest that many of its specifics cannot be vastly improved. The Treaty can be paired down considerably, competences can be better protected,[18] and vast changes can be introduced into its institutional arrangements. But when it is objected that there is nothing to prevent a European constitution from being drafted in a way which would fully recognize the very concepts and principles I have articulated, my answer is simple: Europe has now such a constitution. Europe has charted its own brand of constitutional federalism. It works. Why fix it?

[18] The issue of competences is particularly acute since there has been a considerable weakening of constitutional guarantees to the limits of Community competences, undermining Constitutional Tolerance itself. See B. Simma, J. H. H. Weiler, and M. Zoeckler, *Kompetenzen und Grundrechte—Beschränkungen der Tabakwerbung aus der Sicht des Europarechts* (Berlin: Dunker and Humblot, 1999). History teaches that formal constitutions tend to strengthen the centre whatever the good intentions of their authors. Any formulation designed to restore constitutional discipline on this issue can be part of a Treaty revision and would not require a constitution for it. For pragmatic proposals on this issue, see J. H. H. Weiler, A. Ballmann, U. Haltern, H. Hofmann, F. Mayer, and S. Schreiner-Linford, *Certain Rectangular Problems of European Integration* (www.iue.it/AEL/EP/index.html) (1996).

II

Levels of Governance in the United States and the European Union: Facts and Diagnosis

3

Centralization and Its Discontents: The Rhythms of Federalism in the United States and the European Union

JOHN D. DONAHUE AND MARK A. POLLACK

The tension between unity and independence ranks among our species' primal themes, figuring centrally in classic myths, fairy tales, and sentimental movies. Human nature is instinctively drawn to the advantages of community, and just as instinctively bridles at the inconvenience of entanglement and the dilution of autonomy. Either principle, of course, is pathological in excess. Floods can be fatal. So can droughts. History affords ample evidence of cultures made miserable by too much unity and by too little. The virtues of each principle tend to be more vivid in its absence; the ills of fragmentation make us yearn for more unity, and the discontents of union breed dreams of independence. Thus the stories of two complex polities—the United States, and the European Union—display oscillations between the poles of unity and autonomy.

While the tone and timing are distinctive to each, comparable rhythms can be discerned on both sides of the Atlantic. The demonstrated disadvantages of fragmentation inspire moves to consolidate authority. Then the costs of centralization arise in unanticipated ways, or simply become more salient as the costs of *de*centralization recede from memory. Discontent with centralization inspires a reaction, and authority is again dispersed. The rhythm is syncopated and often erratic. But cycles of centrifugal and centripetal restructuring, we suggest, are natural in any democratic arrangement that features multiple levels of governance and any indeterminacy in the proper lodging of responsibilities.

This chapter identifies some general themes that typically figure in particular policy debates; traces, in the broadest possible outlines, the historical rhythm of centralization and decentralization in the US and the EU; and offers a few observations, for each polity, on the phase of the cycle at the start of the century. The generic arguments that drive specific debates often concern geography-linked diversity, the advantages and disadvantages that come with governmental scale, the role of autonomous governments as test-beds for innovation, and the alignment of choice and consequence to minimize policy externalities.

1. Themes in the Cycle of Centralization and Decentralization

Diversity

People differ in their circumstances and their values. Sometimes those differences are related in a systematic way to geography; citizens of one region are similar to each other and different from citizens of other locales. Citizens may differ in the values they cherish, in the problems that confront them, in the options at hand for addressing those problems, and so on. What matters is not so much the dimensions of geography-linked diversity, but rather how homogenous regions are internally, and how reliably different from other regions. Economic theorists have long probed the perils of collective choice. The more diverse the group, the lower the odds that a collective decision will gratify the typical member, suggesting that the inherent problems of public spending will be mitigated, to a degree, by pushing decisions down to the smallest and most homogeneous communities possible.[1]

In the American context, Rhode Island's thickly clustered population is as characteristic as Montana's wide open spaces. South Carolina is characteristically genteel and traditional; Massachusetts is sharp-elbowed and progressive. And so on. Even though regions are becoming more ideologically similar over time, State populations still differ measurably on the liberal-conservative spectrum. Empirical work by political scientists has found State-by-State differences in prevailing political sentiment to be

[1] The collective choice literature is vast and demanding; some classic readings include Kenneth Arrow, 'A Difficulty in the Concept of Social Welfare', 1950, reprinted in Edwin Mansfield (ed.), *Microeconomics: Selected Readings*, 3rd edn (New York: W. W. Norton Company, 1979); Knut Wicksell, 'A New Principle of Just Taxation', 1886; translation by James M. Buchanan in Richard A. Musgrave and Alan T. Peacock (eds), *Classics in the Theory of Public Finance* (New York: St Martin's Press, 1967); and Erik Lindahl, 'Just Taxation: A Positive Solution', German original 1919, translation reprinted in Musgrave and Peacock, *Classics in the Theory of Public Finance*; and Anthony Downs, 'Why the Government Budget is Too Small in a Democracy', 1960, reprinted in Edmund S. Phelps (ed.), *Private Wants and Public Needs* (New York: W. W. Norton and Company, 1965). The Framers' perspective was less formal, perhaps, and less purely economic, but they held what constitutional theorist Albert S. Abel termed a 'lively awareness of the need for autonomous solution of special problems not common to all the people . . .', 'The Commerce Clause in the Constitutional Convention and in Contemporary Comment', *Minnesota Law Review*, 25 (1941), 432–94 at 481.

correlated, appropriately, with variations in policy.[2] These differences are magnified in the context of the European Union, composed of 15 sovereign Member States with sharply differing economies, languages, cultures, and political histories.

Even when States vary, of course, there are arguments for uniformity. Institutions and individuals who live or do business in several States face the expense, bother, and confusion of coping with different, and sometimes conflicting, rules. Inconsistencies among laws and regulations can lead to disputes of great complexity and to resolutions of limited appeal. Among the most fervent advocates of regulatory uniformity in both the US and the EU are corporations that would sacrifice scale economies if they had to produce a different product to meet each separate regulatory code.[3]

Experimentation and Learning

Public problems are sufficiently complex, and policy-makers' judgement is sufficiently fallible, that rarely is the one right answer obvious—even in the rare case where a single solution, once discovered, turns out to fit every State. As States or member countries innovate, their experience informs not just their own policy choices but those of the other States as well. The freer regions are to experiment independently, the deeper will be the common well of expertise about what works and what doesn't.[4] The greater the uncertainty about what works and what doesn't, and the greater the ability and willingness of States or Member Countries to share information, the more valuable is a regime protecting autonomous policy innovations and the more costly is any requirement of uniformity.

Scale

The advantages and disadvantages of governmental scale enter into calculations on optimal centralization in several ways. Among the most

[2] Gerald C. Wright, Jr., Robert S. Erikson, and John P. McIver, 'Public Opinion and Policy Liberalism in the American States', *American Journal of Political Science*, 31/4 (1987), 980–1001; see esp. Table 3, p. 991.

[3] For an interesting discussion of the shift towards federal regulation in the 1970s, the resurgence of States amid federal deregulatory efforts in the 1980s, and business's accompanying calls for federal pre-emption, see Susan Bartlett Foote, 'Administrative Preemption: An Experiment in Regulatory Federalism', *Virginia Law Review*, 70 (1984), 1429–66. Another good discussion, specific to a single regulatory issue, can be found in Mark King, 'Federal Preemption of the State Regulation of Nuclear Power: State Law Strikes Back', *Chicago Kent Law Review*, 59 (1984), 989–1018.

[4] In the US context, Justice Louis Brandeis' notion of States as the 'laboratories of democracy' is one of most commonly invoked arguments for weakening central control and giving regions room to manoeuvre.

fundamental arguments is the claim that the emotional bonds of commonwealth simply can't stretch very far, and that only small polities can command popular fealty.[5] The primal psychological argument that only small republics are workable was the core of Montesquieu's politics, which Madison so ingeniously sought to amend through the intellectual architecture of the American Constitution. Nor is this an outdated concern; a contemporary communitarian school celebrates the virtues of the compact community: 'In the age of NAFTA', political philosopher Michael Sandel has written, 'the politics of neighborhood matters more, not less. People will not pledge allegiance to vast and distant entities, whatever their importance, unless those institutions are somehow connected to political arrangements that reflect the identity of the participants'.[6] Similar arguments have been made in the European Union, which has been portrayed as a union of peoples who retain their primary ties to nations based in history, language, and ethnicity. Although the peoples of the European Union may share a sort of 'constitutional patriotism' based on common political values and institutions, the great majority of Europeans feel at best a secondary identification with the EU or Europe as a whole, raising important normative questions about the long-term legitimacy of the Union in the eyes of its citizens.[7]

Modern information technologies may have somewhat eroded the advantages of small-scale government, at the same time, since citizens are no longer reliant on direct observation or word of mouth to keep abreast of public affairs. Indeed, relentless coverage by the news media can mean that Washington or Brussels is *better* understood by the average citizen than regional governments. As the proliferation of new media makes it easier to keep up with regional issues, this factor could fade. On the other hand, if the real constraint is the time citizens can allocate to public affairs, the fragmentation of authority could worsen confusion and alienation.

Slightly subtler than the claim that humans are simply designed for compact commonwealths are arguments about the relative *administrative* efficiency of large-scale and small-scale government. The conceptual case can go either way. On the one hand, some functions of government, like

[5] In a letter to Madison during the Constitutional Convention, Connecticut's Roger Sherman put it bluntly: 'The people are more happy in small than in large States.' Quoted in Martin Diamond, 'What the Framers Meant by Federalism', in Laurence J. O'Toole, Jr., *American Intergovernmental Relations* (Washington, DC: Congressional Quarterly Press, 1993), 39–48, at 44.

[6] Michael J. Sandel, 'America's Search for a New Public Philosophy', *The Atlantic Monthly* (March 1996), 57–74, at 74.

[7] For an illuminating exchange on this question, see the essays by Dieter Grimm, Jurgen Habermas, J. H. H. Weiler, J. G. A. Pocock, and Anthony D. Smith, in Peter Gowan and Perry Anderson (eds), *The Question of Europe* (New York: Verso, 1997).

some industries, can display significant economies of scale. The cost of a car falls substantially as the scale of production rises. The same is not true of haircuts. Where the administrative economics of government looks more like car-making than like barbering, centralization can increase efficiency. Air-traffic control, the maintenance of standard weights and measures, and international diplomacy are areas where economies of scale are plausible, even if not inevitable. If a particular culture generates relatively little top talent in public administration—as is arguably the case in America—centralization may economize on such scarce personnel, while the profusion of talented bureaucrats in Germany, for example, loosens personnel constraints on government decentralization.[8] On the other hand, there are reasons to anticipate that administrative efficiency will erode, not improve, as government grows in scale. Complexity rises, communication becomes garbled, coordination becomes more difficult, and the opportunities for waste and confusion multiply as any organization expands its size and the scope of its responsibilities. Public organizations, chronically more plagued by administrative muddle than their private counterparts, become even more fumble-prone as they grow.

There are some good reasons to predict that smaller-scale governments will do better, all else being equal, at making choices that accord with the public's true values and interests. Homogeneity within a community eases consensus. Political issues tend to be simpler and political procedures more transparent in smaller polities, facilitating the public comprehension that permits effective participation. Small-scale politics may mean superior accountability at the ballot box, if a manageable set of issues and more transparent processes allow voters to reward and punish officials more easily than when they must sort through a larger number of issues, and untangle complex skeins of cause and effect, to fix responsibility and vote accordingly.[9]

[8] On this point see Max Weber, 'Bureaucracy', in H. H. Gerth and C. Wright Mills, *From Max Weber* (New York: Oxford University Press, 1946), 200.

[9] The evidence on this point is quite mixed for the US context. Political scientist John Chubb has found that voters assign State officials little responsibility for the performance of the State's economy: 'Institutions, the Economy, and the Dynamics of State Elections', *American Political Science Review*, 82/1 (1988), 134–54, esp. Table 6, p. 148. Robert Stein, analyzing 1982 exit-poll data from 27 States, reached similar conclusions: 'Economic Voting for Governor and US Senator: The Electoral Consequences of Federalism', *Journal of Politics*, 52/1 (1990), 29–53. Patrick Kenney, in a regression study of gubernatorial elections in 14 States from 1946 through 1980, found no discernible relationship between a State's unemployment and inflation rates and the ballot-box judgment rendered on incumbent governors: 'The Effect of State Economic Conditions on the Vote for Governor', *Social Science Quarterly*, 64/1 (1983), 154–62, esp. Table 1, pp. 158–9.

Externalities

Efficiency requires that an action's full effects be felt by its authors. If there are external consequences, whether positive or negative, then the true tally of costs and benefits will be different from what decision-makers take into account. Misalignment between choice and consequence leads to bad decisions—actions taken that should not be, because some costs are ignored; options passed up that should be seized, because some of the benefits are reaped by others. Fritz Scharpf has noted the tendency, within a federal system, 'for positive or negative externalities to be neglected. Through a decentralized decision-making structure—by the standard of the collective optimum—either too much or too little of a particular sort of activity is undertaken'.[10] Mancur Olson finds 'systematic forces which work against allocative efficiency in any situation where the boundaries of a government and a collective good do not coincide'.[11]

External costs and benefits form much of the justification—at least much of the *economic* justification—for the very existence of government; if our acts had no consequences for others, 'publicness' would have no meaning. But except for the simplest kinds of unitary government, externalities also complicate public policy. The misalignment of costs and benefits presents opportunities for destructive political gamesmanship as politicians burnish their images with voters by claiming credit for benefits while manoeuvring costs onto other jurisdictions.[12]

The surest solution to misaligned authority, of course, is to arrange that communities are of precisely the right scale to capture all the benefits and bear all the costs of communal decisions.[13] Yet the boundaries of cost for some particular undertaking will often differ from the boundaries of benefit; the borders relevant to one activity won't necessarily correspond to

[10] Fritz W. Scharpf, 'Theorie der Politikverflechtung', in Fritz W. Scharpf, Bernd Reissert, and Fritz Schnabel, *Politikverflectung: Theorie und Empirie des kooperativen Foederalismus in der Bundesrepublik* (Kronberg: Scriptor Verlag, 1976), 25.

[11] Mancur Olson, Jr., 'Strategic Theory and Its Applications: The Principle of "Fiscal Equivalence": The Division of Responsibilities Among Different Levels of Government', *American Economic Review*, 59/2 (1969), 479–537, at 483.

[12] The practice is familiar to any newspaper reader. For a sample of the theory, see Alan Williams, 'The Optimal Provision of Public Goods in a System of Local Government', *Journal of Political Economy*, 74/1 (1966), 18–33. Relatedly, Peterson's 'legislative theory' sees externalities as the engine of systematic, not just accidental, misallocation. *The Price of Federalism* (Washington, DC: The Brookings Institution, 1995), 16.

[13] In principle, as Fritz Scharpf explains, 'for each public task a special decision process must be established, encompassing all people who are affected positively or negatively by the undertaking, and only those people'. 'Theorie der Politikverflechtung', 28; free translation by author. On the principle of 'perfect correspondence', see also Albert Breton and Anthony Scott, *The Economic Constitution of Federal States* (Toronto: University of Toronto Press, 1978), 37–9.

the borders relevant to all others—or indeed *any* others; and the perimeters of cost and benefit will seldom correspond to the jurisdictional boundaries that a capricious history has inscribed upon the landscape. The imperatives of efficiency in governmental scale and scope would dictate arrangements very different from the coarse configuration of federal, State, and local authority that we see today.

The gap between the theoretical ideal and actual practice, in the United States and elsewhere, has inspired feverish creativity on the part of theorists. Gordon Tullock suggests that efficiency requires a world in which 'the individual citizen would be a member of a vast collection of governmental units, each of these governmental units being to some respect of a different geographical coverage than the others, and each one dealing with a separate activity'.[14] Conceding the possible inconveniences such an arrangement might entail, Tullock suggests that the respective virtues and defects of unity and autonomy might be best in balance if each individual belonged to 'somewhere between five and eight' governments, differing in their policy portfolios and geographical coverage, bearing no necessary resemblance to the world in which we happen to live.[15] The related theoretical approach known as 'club theory' views government in general as an ill-advised solution to the problem of collective action, and envisages instead an intricate arrangement of private clubs by which individuals will pursue those interests that are difficult to advance in isolation.[16]

Unless we are willing to follow some of the more exuberant theorists into scrapping nation, region, and city in order to start afresh on the puzzle of human community, then a large measure of imprecision is inevitable. If authority must be lodged with a general-purpose government, rather than one custom-tailored to fit the task, then choice and consequence will only with great rarity be in perfect alignment. Getting it a bit closer to right can make a great deal of difference in how faithfully, and how effectively, government works to serve citizens' interests.

An appreciation of the multiple dimensions at play within any concrete choice over centralization and decentralization, and of the complexity layered within each dimension, may aid in understanding why 'equilibrium' is so elusive. The natural pattern is a lively awareness of what's wrong with the status quo, and a perennial search for ways to accommodate new issues

[14] Gordon Tullock, 'Federalism: Problems of Scale', *Public Choice*, 6 (1969), 19–29, at 25.

[15] Tullock, 'Federalism', 21; see also p. 27, esp. Fig. 4, for a sense of Tullock's concept.

[16] For example, see Eitan Berglas, 'On the Theory of Clubs', *American Economic Review* 66 (1976), 116–21, or James Buchanan, 'An Economic Theory of Clubs', *Economica*, 32 (1965), 1–14. Mancur Olson, in a slightly less clean-slate proposal, would not abolish government, but arrange instead for a system of intergovernmental cash payments to compensate for external costs and benefits. See 'Strategic Theory and Its Applications', esp. 486.

and better resolve old ones. And the natural starting point for that search is in the opposite direction from the most recent round of reform, whether that round had a centripetal or centrifugal thrust.

2. The American Experience

The rhythms of federalism have rippled through a longer history in America than in Europe, and the pattern is correspondingly resistant to simple summarization.[17] But the broad contours of that pattern can be discerned. The rhythm follows no steady tempo but rather—to shift metaphors—looks more like what biologists term 'punctuated equilibrium' in natural selection. Episodes of dramatic change are followed by longer intervals of relative stasis, which are eventually disrupted by the next upheaval. Periods of centralization have generally been shorter, sharper, and more obvious; movements in the opposite direction are usually subtler and more diffuse. Key turning points include the years just before and just after the nation's formal founding; the civil war; the New Deal; and, possibly, the Reagan Administration.

From Confederation to Union

America's first try at nationhood hinged on reconciling the need for strength in unity with a jealous embrace, on each State's part, of hard-won independence. It did not go very well. The crucible of the revolutionary war had forged some sense of common identity among colonies that had declared their independence, in the plural, as 'free and independent States.' But the consolidating impulse faltered in peacetime. The Articles of Confederation adopted in 1781 provided for only a feeble form of union, and stipulated at the start that '[e]ach state retains its sovereignty'.[18] The central government's authority was tightly constrained.

The drawbacks of this decentralized starting point were quick to emerge. The most obvious involved money. America's monetary system in the 1780s presented a patchwork of currencies that varied from State to State. Inflation plagued the new nation, but unevenly: some States let their

[17] As one eminent observer puts it, 'American federalism was born in ambiguity, it institutionalizes ambiguity in our form of government, and changes in it tend to be ambiguous too'. Martha Derthick, 'American Federalism: Half-Full or Half-Empty', *Brookings Review*, 18/1 (2000), 24–7, at 24.

[18] Article II, *Articles of Confederation*, drafted 1777, formally adopted 1781, from Samuel Eliot Morison (ed.), *Sources and Documents Illustrating the American Revolution* (London: Oxford University Press, 1923), 178.

currencies plummet in value while other were more cautious. Separate currency systems and the absence of any overarching national authority made both public and private finance chaotic and treacherous. Some States refused to recognize other States' paper money at all. Others passed laws declaring their own questionable currency to be legal tender for all purposes, allowing them to pay off out-of-State creditors at a deep discount while foreclosing court challenges.[19]

Comparably fundamental difficulties arose over repayment of the revolutionary war debt. In 1781 Congress approved a 5 per cent import tax, primarily to service war-related borrowings. But under the Articles, the tax could not be imposed without the unanimous consent of the States. When Rhode Island withheld its approval, the financing plan died.[20] Congress was forced to negotiate for the funds, and the negotiations brought great complications and small success. New York and Rhode Island bluntly refused to help pay off the debt; other States sought to attach onerous conditions to their contributions.[21]

Conflicting economic development policies, in an era when the mercantilist spirit was still strong, also strained relations among the States. States levied taxes on shipping that worked to promote their own ship owners by increasing the cost to merchants of moving goods on vessels registered elsewhere. Tariffs on manufactures, the major source of government revenue, evolved into mercantilist weapons. Massachusetts used trade protection as an industrial development tool to promote its glass, wool, and sugar industries, and all four New England States as well as New York and Pennsylvania had erected tariff protection against other States' goods by 1786.[22]

Perhaps the deepest and most consequential economic divisions among the post-revolutionary American States concerned international trade. 'Gateway' States with the best harbours and rivers—including Maryland, Pennsylvania, New York, and Massachusetts—laid heavy taxes on imported goods destined for inland States, thus financing their

[19] The chaotic currency situation under the Articles is described in Allan Nevins, *The American States During and After the Revolution* (New York: The MacMillan Company, 1927), 568–70.

[20] Curtis P. Nettels, *The Emergence of a National Economy 1775–1815*, The Economic History of the United States, 2 (New York: Holt, Rinehart, and Winston, 1962), 34 and 95.

[21] See Nevins, *The American States During and After the Revolution*, 578, for the specific reference to New York and Rhode Island. Stanley Elkins and Erik McKitrick, *The Age of Federalism* (New York and Oxford: Oxford University Press, 1993), discuss the war debt and related issues in Chapter 3.

[22] See Oscar Handlin and Mary Flug Handlin, *Commonwealth* (Cambridge, MA: Belknap Press, 1969), 63.

governmental operations on the backs of out-of-State consumers.[23] And the struggle for advantage among the separate States dissipated what limited political and economic leverage the new country commanded in its dealings with foreign powers. After the war, Britain barred American ships from trading with its remaining New World colonies, both as a punitive measure against the breakaway nation and as a prophylactic against the emergence of an economic rival. The national government declared a campaign of retaliation, but it had no means of realizing this campaign beyond exhorting the States to form a common front. Several States did ban British ships from their ports. But other States, including Connecticut, South Carolina, and Delaware, openly welcomed British shipping. This had the effect of promoting the development of *their* ports, while rendering pointless the sacrifices of other States and draining all force from the national effort at retaliation.

The economic destructiveness of inter-State division was not the only issue alarming American patriots in the 1780s, or even the most significant. Many were more troubled by the small-minded fractiousness of the period's State politics and the dimming of the republican vision that had been so bright a beacon during wartime. But this set of particularly vivid illustrations of decentralization's downside was one major cause for the movement to 'form a more perfect Union'.[24] As the Framers converged on Philadelphia, America's formative period of centralization commenced.

While few disputed the diagnosis of excessive decentralization, debate raged over the cure—both the specific prescription, and its dosage. Some favoured a continued 'confederation' of States joined only at the top, where the national role would be restricted to foreign affairs, defence against external enemies, and, perhaps, against internal coups. This group aimed for an edited version of the Articles of Confederation, establishing a more durable kind of association among State *governments*, while retaining the Articles' limited scope for direct dealings between citizens and the national government.[25] Others envisioned a diminishing role for the States

[23] Tariffs paid by Connecticut citizens, for example, at one point covered about a third of New York's budget. Nevins, *The American States During and After the Revolution*, 560. See also Abel, 'The Commerce Clause in the Constitutional Convention and in Contemporary Comment', 448–9, 456–7.

[24] For background and commentary on the Framer's era see Samuel H. Beer, 'Federalism, Nationalism and Democracy in America', *The American Political Science Review*, 72/1 (1978), 9–21; Richard B. Morris, *Witnesses at the Creation: Hamilton, Madison, Jay and the Constitution* (New York: New American Library, 1985); and Elkins and McKitrick, *The Age of Federalism*.

[25] Alexander Hamilton, staking out the bluntest version of a growingly shared concern, argued that both other nations' histories and the recent travails of the United States displayed confederal arrangements of this sort as the 'cause of incurable disorder and imbecility': Federalist 9, *The Federalist Papers* (New York: New American Library, 1961), 76;

as American nationhood matured. If Alexander Hamilton was the most avid of the 'nationalists', Pennsylvania's Gouverneur Morris was perhaps the most candid. 'We must have it in view', Morris argued, 'eventually to lessen and destroy the state limits and authorities'.[26]

The outcome fell somewhere in between the goals of those who wanted to strengthen the ties among essentially separate entities and those who sought a new nation to supersede the States as the locus of commonwealth—though precisely *where* it fell remains disputed to this day. The Framers of America's constitution made great use of that timeless political expedient: ambiguity. Article VI declares federal supremacy in ringing terms: 'This Constitution, and the Laws of the United States which shall be made in Pursuance thereof . . . shall be the supreme Law of the Land . . . any Thing in the Constitution or Laws of any State to the Contrary notwithstanding.' The last of the ten original Amendments seems equally clear: 'The powers not delegated to the United States by the Constitution, nor prohibited by it to the States, are reserved to the States respectively, or to the people.'

There may be no strict inconsistency between these declarations—taken together, the two clauses say that national authority is supreme wherever legitimate national laws exist, and not otherwise—but there is a striking discrepancy in tone. The inconsistency arose in large part from the political delicacies of getting the Constitution approved, first by the Convention itself and then by the States. The Supremacy Clause affirms the priorities of the slim majority of nationalists at the Constitutional Convention. The Tenth Amendment was meant to reassure some of the Constitution's more reluctant supporters among the Framers, and to aid in the effort to win ratification by State legislatures.[27] The Constitution thus sets some general parameters for the division of powers between State and national governments. Within those limits, the Framers left it to the wisdom of their successors to find the balance suited to the circumstances and the priorities of future Americans. They bounded the amplitude of subsequent waves of

all Federalist references are to this edition. Leading statements in opposition to the constitution, favouring either separatism or 'a more perfect confederation', are collected in *The Anti-Federalist* (Chicago: University of Chicago Press, 1981), with a thoughtful introduction by editor Herbert J. Storing. Martin Diamond, 'What the Framers Meant by Federalism', in O'Toole, Jr., *American Intergovernmental Relations*, esp. 43–4, gives an interesting account of the subtle shift towards a nationalist perspective in the early days of the Convention.

26 Morris is quoted in Abel, 'The Commerce Clause in the Constitutional Convention and in Contemporary Comment', 436 n. 12.

27 Madison, in particular, saw adding the Bill of Rights as a tactical concession to the constitution's opponents, according to historians Stanley Elkins and Eric McKitrick, providing 'the most convenient possible forum whereby they might change their minds': *The Age of Federalism*, 62.

centralization and decentralization, but quite deliberately left room for the rhythm to play itself out through the history to come.

Secession and Reconstruction

The early decades of America's second attempt at nationhood saw national union haltingly consolidated. The Jefferson administration, in spite of the president's principled distaste for central authority, deployed federal resources to speed westward expansion by subsidizing infrastructure and education. John Marshall, who led the Supreme Court through its formative early decades, played an enormous role in defining the judiciary as a steward of national unity. His experience as a combat commander in the Revolutionary War—including the hardships the underfunded army endured at Valley Forge—informed Justice Marshall's conviction that 'state particularism and national weakness were as deadly as British musket fire'.[28] Ambiguities were settled in favour of national unity by the Marshall Court's key decisions in *McCulloch v. Maryland* (1816) and *Gibbons v. Ogden* (1824).[29]

The centralizing impulse was by no means unchallenged, however. A counterpoint developed to the dominant theme of national consolidation, embodied, for example, in the short-lived but significant doctrine of 'nullification'. Under this notion, States asserted the right to reject federal laws they felt transgressed the perimeters set around national power. The doctrine originated with opposition to the notorious Alien and Sedition Acts of John Adams's government, but came to the test with new tariffs enacted under Andrew Jackson. The trade barriers outraged import-dependent States and led the South Carolina legislature to declare the tariffs null in 1832. But while southern sentiment in favour of the nullification principle remained strong, in practical terms, as Woodrow Wilson wrote, the 'federal government was conceded the power to determine the economic opportunities of the States'.[30]

As the nineteenth century reached its mid-point, the rhythms of American federalism became jumbled and discordant. A growing fraction of Americans considered slavey repugnant. Their willingness to tolerate its practice elsewhere in the name of State discretion eroded. The slave

[28] R. Kent Newmyer, 'John Marshall, Political Parties, and the Origins of Modern Federalism', in Harry N. Scheiber (ed.), *Federalism: Studies in History, Law, and Public Policy* (Berkeley, CA: Institute of Intergovernmental Studies, 1988), 19.

[29] *McCulloch v. Maryland*, 17 US 316 (1819) granted Congress an expansive definition of the 'necessary and proper' clause in Article I. *Gibbons v. Ogden*, 22 US 1 (1824) launched the use of commerce clause as the predicate for federal activism.

[30] Woodrow Wilson, *Constitutional Government in the United States* (New York: Columbia University Press, 1921), 173.

States held that the principles enshrined in the Tenth Amendment left decisions about slavery to the individual States. The south asserted what it declared to be the ultimate right of sovereign States—the right to opt out of the union. State authority, Lincoln countered, did not go so far. The peak of America's decentralizing impulse collided with its opposite—unity repudiated, and unity affirmed with armed force—and the issue was settled by the most searing episode in the country's history.

The civil war and Reconstruction saw a marked shift of authority away from the States and toward the federal government. Prosecuting the war itself accelerated the growth of Washington's power and rendered more concrete the notion of American nationhood. The virtual occupation of the defeated south, and protracted federal monitoring of the former slave States' governments, symbolized the pre-eminence of national authority. And three new amendments etched this post-war spirit into the text of the Constitution. The Thirteenth Amendment, barring slavery, may not in itself impose a strikingly greater restriction on State discretion than, say, the Constitution's prior prohibition of retroactive laws or aristocratic titles. But the accompanying amendments went deeper. The Fourteenth Amendment mandates an ambitious standard of respect for human rights as the obligation of every State, and the Fifteenth extends this guarantee to all citizens, including former slaves. The federal government, crucially, was declared the enforcer of the newly codified rights.[31]

From the New Deal to the Great Society

The rhythms of federalism were more muted in the twentieth century than in the eighteenth or nineteenth, but hardly quiescent. Herbert Croly's influential 1909 book, *The Promise of American Life*, called for a new consolidation of national authority.[32] 'The regulation of commerce, the control of corporations, and the still more radical questions connected with the distribution of wealth and the prevention of poverty—questions of this kind should be left exclusively to the central government', Croly argued. Particularly in the broad economic realm, the States should act essentially

[31] 'We must be careful, when focusing on the events which took place in Philadelphia two centuries ago, that we not overlook the momentous events which followed', Justice Thurgood Marshall went so far as to say 1987. 'While the Union survived the Civil War, the Constitution did not.' Remarks to the Annual Seminar of the San Francisco Patent and Trademark Law Association, Magi, Hawaii, 6 May 1987, quoted in David Beam, Cynthia Colella, and Timothy Conlan, 'Federal Regulation of State and Local Governments: Regulatory Federalism—a Decade Later', draft report for the US. Advisory Commission on Intergovernmental Relations, DC (February 1992), 8.

[32] Herbert Croly, *The Promise of American Life* (New York: Macmillan, 1909).

'as the agents of the central government'.[33] Yet while Croly's book is often credited as the catalyst of the Progressive movement, the first third of the twentieth century witnessed no real surge in centralization. Progressivism had its greatest impact at the *State* level, and this period featured at least as much innovation and reform in the States as in Washington. Justice Louis Brandeis celebrated the States as 'laboratories of democracy', the wellsprings of progressive initiatives that could be adopted more widely if they worked, and otherwise discarded. Felix Frankfurter echoed the theme in a 1930 speech at Yale: 'The states need the amplest scope for energy and individuality in dealing with the myriad problems created by our complex industrial civilization.'[34] As Frankfurter spoke, however, America was on the cusp of the next surge of centralization—the New Deal.

Virtually each initiative in the flurry Franklin Delano Roosevelt launched shifted the balance of power a bit more towards Washington. The Supreme Court initially resisted on constitutional grounds. Legislation barring interstate trade in child labour, for example, was at first struck down. The Court had argued that 'if Congress can thus regulate matters entrusted to local authority by prohibition of the movement of commodities in interstate commerce, all freedom of commerce will be at an end, and the power of the States over local matters may be eliminated . . .'[35] But Roosevelt's ambitions, and the seeming imprudence of disunion in the face of economic peril, contributed to a shift in sentiment. New Deal-era courts dislodged judicial bulwarks of State sovereignty, making way for legislation solidifying the federal government's role. An unprecedented degree of governmental activism on the economy, orchestrated from the centre, meant an unprecedented concentration of authority.

Roosevelt's government was careful to pay obeisance to the principle of balance. As a system of State-run but nationally mandated unemployment insurance was taking shape, Roosevelt's powerful Committee on Economic Security, which spearheaded the effort, was careful to specify that 'all matters in which uniformity is not absolutely essential should be left to the states'.[36] Yet the range in which uniformity, or at least an

[33] Croly, *The Promise of American Life*, 350.

[34] Quoted in Michael E. Parish, 'Felix Frankfurter and American Federalism', in Harry N. Scheiber (ed.), *Federalism: Studies in History, Law, and Public Policy* (Berkeley, CA: Institute of Intergovernmental Studies, 1988), 28. Frankfurter had been a self-described 'hot Hamiltonian' in his younger days; see p. 30.

[35] *Hammer v. Dagenhart*, 247 US 251 (1918), quoted in Philip P. Frickey, 'The Congressional Process and the Constitutionality of Federal Legislation to End the Economic War Among the States', *The Economic War Among the States* (Minneapolis: Federal Reserve Bank of Minneapolis, 1996), 29.

[36] Quoted in Advisory Council on Unemployment Compensation, 'National Interests and Federal Responsibilities in the Unemployment Insurance System' (Washington, DC: US Government Printing Office, April 1995), 4.

unaccustomed degree of national integration, was considered 'absolutely essential' greatly expanded during the New Deal. Roosevelt not only articulated, but also acted upon, what in earlier eras would have seemed a startling proposition: that it is the responsibility of the national government to diminish differences in living standards across States. In response to a 1938 National Emergency Council report on grim conditions in the southern States, Roosevelt declared that 'the South presents right now the nation's No.1 economic problem—the nation's problem, not merely the South's'.[37] That same year Harold Laski, in a famous *New Republic* article, argued that the imperative of a centralized governmental response to centralized modern capitalism meant that 'the epoch of federalism is over'.[38] Even if many disagreed with so sweeping a conclusion there was little appetite in the late 1930s for rolling back the New Deal in the name of States' rights.

The massive national mobilization of World War II, and the Cold War that followed, were a further force for centralization. And the prosperity of the first post-war decades discouraged radical moves in either direction. The decentralizing theme, however, arguably predominated in the early post-war years. A group of governors petitioned the Truman administration for looser strings on federal aid. In 1949 a Presidential commission led by Herbert Hoover proposed a rebalancing of responsibilities and revenue sources across levels of government in ways that would curb the centralizing trend of the 1930s and 1940s. President Eisenhower initiated commissions in 1955 and again in 1957 to revisit the balance.[39] The counterpoint continued, mostly quietly, as well. An early post-war Supreme Court decision, *H. P. Hood and Sons v. Du Mond*, declared explicitly that 'our economic unit is the Nation',[40] and the Interstate Highway Act of 1956 marked a major expansion of the federal government into transportation policy. A more fundamental force for centralization, though, involved civil rights. As the struggle for racial equality escalated in the 1960s, 'States' rights' became an unsavoury code phrase, and recalcitrant southern States faced vigorous assertions of federal authority.

[37] Quoted in Daniel P. Moynihan, 'The Politics and Economics of Regional Growth', *The Public Interest*, 51 (Spring 1978), 3–21, at 4.

[38] Harold J. Laski, 'The Obsolescence of Federalism', *The New Republic* (3 May 1938), 365–9, at 367.

[39] US Treasury Department, Office of State and Local Finance, *Federal-State-Local Fiscal Relations: Report to the President and the Congress* (Washington, DC, September 1985), esp. xx.

[40] 336 US 525, 1949, quoted in Julian N. Eule, 'Laying the Dormant Commerce Clause to Rest', *The Yale Law Journal*, 91/3 (1982) 425–85, n. 47 at 434.

An apt metaphor for this ambiguous period was provided by Morton Grodzins, who compared 1960s American federalism to a marble cake.[41] State and national authority had become intermingled. Just as there were no sharp boundaries on the effects of a policy, so there should be no rigid delineation of which level of government held authority over which set of activities. The architects of Lyndon Johnson's Great Society gave life to the marble-cake metaphor through the surge of targeted intergovernmental transfers that powered most of Johnson's new social initiatives. The Great Society is commonly, but erroneously, seen as an expansion of direct federal activism. Instead, it was an expansion of State and local government activism catalyzed by Washington.

Prior to the New Deal, federal grants had constituted a minor source of revenue for State and local governments. The total of such grants for 1927, the earliest year for which appropriate data are available, was $116 million. This was less than 2 per cent of all State and local income and, as a benchmark for comparison, just a little more than revenues from corporate profits taxes. But in 1934 federal transfers accounted for about 13 per cent of all State and local revenue, and were more than 20 times larger than the contribution of corporate tax revenues.[42] Federal money has never since retreated to the negligible role it once played in State and local finance. But its relative importance has waxed and waned. The years from 1938 through 1958 marked a sort of plateau where federal grants accounted for roughly 10 per cent of State and local revenue, with only minor departures above or below that benchmark. The late 1950s through the mid-1960s saw mild and gradual growth in State and local dependence on federal revenues, as the federal share of sub-national budgets grew close to 15 per cent. But with the Great Society there was another spike in this share. As recently as 1957 only one dollar in every ten spent by the cities and States had been channelled through Washington; by 1973 it was one in five. In 1965 alone, 109 new categorical grant programmes were created, and a total of 240 between 1964 and 1966.[43] State and local reliance on federal grants stayed above 20 per cent of revenues through the 1970s. Significantly, the Great Society intergovernmental programmes treated cities and States similarly, despite the special constitutional status that set States apart.

[41] Morton Grodzins, *The American System: A New View of Government in the United States*, edited by Daniel J. Elazar (Chicago: Rand McNally, 1966).

[42] The discussion of federal grants in the context of overall State and local revenue structure is based on data in Council of Economic Advisers, *Economic Report of the President 2000*, Appendix B, Table B-86, at http://w3.access.gpo.gov/usbudget/fy2000/erp.html, accessed in December 1999.

[43] US Treasury Department, *Federal-State-Local Fiscal Relations*, xxi.

'New Federalism', Old and New

The durable term 'new federalism' surfaced in American political rhetoric at least a century ago, and figured in the title of a much-noted book published in the 1930s.[44] Two modern Republican presidents, Nixon and Reagan, both launched major restructurings flying the 'New Federalism' banner, although they used the same words to mean quite different things—interestingly, the counterpart phrase 'the New Nationalism' was the slogan not of the New Deal, but of Theodore Roosevelt's administration.[45] The logic of Nixon's initiative was to move away from the Great Society's 'categorical' grants, which cast State and local governments as Washington's agents or subcontractors, in favour of spending *funded* by the federal government but *controlled* at lower levels. General revenue sharing surged from less than $500 million in 1970 to over $8.6 billion in 1980.[46] Ronald Reagan's New Federalism was a far more aggressive assertion of the decentralizing theme. Instead of providing resources while ceding control, Reagan sought to renounce the federal government's responsibilities over large areas of policy. At a minimum the Administration aimed to redress the shift towards coordinated social policy that had occurred under Johnson's Great Society, and sought as well to reverse much of the New Deal's centralization of power.

The 1981 Omnibus Budget Reconciliation Act that set the tone for the Reagan era consolidated roughly one-tenth of the 534 existing categorical programmes into nine block grants.[47] States enjoyed more discretion in how they spent money funnelled through Washington, though they had less of it to spend.[48] General revenue sharing, the hallmark of Nixon's New Federalism, dwindled steadily under Reagan until it disappeared in 1986. Overall transfers from Washington to States and cities, which had surged from about 1.5 per cent of the overall economy in the mid-1960s to about 3.5 per cent in the mid-1970s, retreated to around 2.5 per cent of GDP. As a proportion of State and local revenues federal grants dropped

[44] Jane Perry Clark, *The Rise of a New Federalism* (New York: Columbia University Press, 1938).

[45] Samuel H. Beer, 'The Idea of the Nation', in O'Toole, Jr., *American Intergovernmental Relations*, 354.

[46] *Statistical Abstract of the United States 1992*, Table no. 470, at 282.

[47] There are different ways of counting the number of block grants and consolidated programmes. This tally is from the General Accounting Office, in Block Grants: Lessons Learned (Testimony, February 9, 1995, GAO/T-HEHS-95-80).

[48] Reagan's 1982 State of the Union address featured yet bolder, but little-heeded, calls to turn back responsibilities to the States while rearranging the financial burdens of social welfare programmes. On the rise and fall of intergovernmental grants, see Peterson, *The Price of Federalism*, 62–3. See also Richard P. Nathan and Fred C. Doolittle, 'The Untold Story of Reagan's "New Federalism"', *The Public Interest*, 77 (1984), 96–106.

from the 22 per cent level of 1975 through 1980 to around 18 per cent in the early 1980s, and to around 16 per cent in the late 1980s.

The decentralization efforts which Nixon had pursued under the New Federalism label were directed to a substantial degree at bolstering *local* governments, which have no defined constitutional role and, for the most part, a secondary role in the American argument over governmental balance. Nixon's initiatives, in delegating administration to cities and States alike, had at least as much to do with administrative efficiencies as they did with the locus of sovereignty. The Reagan—and, later, Bush—restructuring, conversely, stressed the *States*, and cut closer to the core of the basic argument. Categorical programmes that used to fund city governments and community organizations were replaced by block grants whose allocation was controlled or greatly influenced by governors. The New Federalism in its Reagan–Bush variant, in short, aimed at restoring the States' primacy over much of the public sector's terrain.[49] The results fell well short of the rhetoric, but were significant none the less.

Clinton and Beyond

The rhythm of federalism in the 1990s cannot be cleanly characterized. The Clinton Administration's initial agenda featured a significant reassertion of central-government initiative in major policy areas. But this agenda was largely frustrated, and, whether out of conviction or pragmatism, Clinton never engineered anything that can be characterized as a campaign of centralization. Nor were Clinton's partisan opponents in Congress or the—increasingly Republican—State capitals able to deliver on their sweeping proposals to diminish Washington's authority and bolster State sovereignty. It could be argued that the 1990s were a period of incoherence and ambiguity on questions of federalism, with no trend at all.[50] Yet while the counter examples cannot be dismissed, the best description of the 1990s is as a continuation, in altered form, of the decentralizing impulse that began in the Reagan Administration.

[49] John Shannon coined the evocative term, 'fend-for-yourself-federalism': 'The Return to Fend-for-Yourself Federalism: The Reagan Mark', *Intergovernmental Perspective*, 13/3/4 (1988), 34–7. Another longtime observer of State government judged in 1992 that the United States was 'moving from an era of cooperative federalism to an era of "go-it-alone" federalism . . .'. Thad Beyle, 'New Governors in Hard Economic and Political Times', in Thad Beyle (ed.), *Governors and Hard Times* (Washington, DC: Congressional Quarterly Press, 1992), 8–9.

[50] Derthick, 'American Federalism', makes this case.

Formal Authority

Whether propelled by legislation or court judgments, the balance of formal authority shifted in the States' direction during the 1990s. On the legislative front, the premier example of decentralization was the 1996 welfare reform act that sharply expanded State control over anti-poverty policy. Other legislation passed during the decade augmented State discretion in areas including drinking-water safety, transportation infrastructure investment, and primary and secondary education. States also gained a degree of statutory protection against the imposition of 'unfunded mandates' from Washington. The trend was not unmixed, to be sure. Laws were passed during the decade asserting new federal powers over voter registration and the definition of marriage, for example, and the 'federalization' of criminal law continued or accelerated.[51] But the legislative arena generated, on balance, a centrifugal trend in formal authority.

In the judicial arena the decentralization of governmental authority was considerably less ambiguous. Led by Chief Justice William H. Rehnquist, a narrow but determined majority of Supreme Court justices reversed long-standing precedents to narrow federal powers and affirm State authority across a wide range of issues. The Court blocked Washington from requiring States to develop plans for dealing with nuclear waste—*New York v. United States*—from banning firearms in the vicinity of schools—*United States v. Lopez*—and from requiring States to police hand-gun purchases—*Printz v. United States*. Other decisions curbed citizens' rights to sue States in federal court to demand compliance with federal laws—*Seminole Tribes v. Florida*—undercut the right to redress in *State* courts on matters of federal law—*Alden v. Maine*—and declared that States enjoyed sovereign immunity even on mundane grievances such as patent disputes—*Florida Prepaid Postsecondary Education Expenses Board v. College Savings Bank*. Here, too, there were counter-trends—the Court blocked States from discriminating against new residents in welfare programmes, for instance—and questions about the durability of a judicial campaign waged by a narrow majority of aging Justices. But few disputed Paul Gewirtz's characterization of the judicial trend as 'an across-the-board restriction on national government power on every front, and a bolstering of state sovereignty'.[52]

[51] On this last point, see American Bar Association, *The Federalization of Criminal Law* (Washington, DC, 1998).

[52] Quoted in Joan Diskupic, 'Justices Shift Federal-State Power Balance', *The Washington Post* (30 March 1996).

Resources

At least when measured in budgetary terms, America's public sector has maintained a remarkably steady scale through a generation or two of fervent rhetoric about the merits and evils of big government. From the early 1960s through the end of the century, total public spending was never much less than 25 per cent of the gross domestic product, and never much more than 30 per cent. The *composition* of public spending changed substantially over the 1962–98 period, however, as Fig. 3.1 shows. The big story—and a familiar one—is the shrinkage of defence spending's share of the total as first the Vietnam war and then the cold war wound down, and the explosion in transfer payments, overwhelmingly Social Security and Medicare, as social insurance grew more generous and the population aged. A slightly subtler trend concerns us here—the growing predominance of self-funded State and local spending relative to federal domestic spending other than interest and entitlements. For a tangled complex of reasons, federal discretionary spending has been relatively restrained while State and local spending has grown. The federal share of public spending slipped with the Reagan Administration and for the most part stayed down. Few would guess, from a glance at Fig. 3.2, that an Administration inclined toward central-government activism gained power in the early 1990s.

A similar pattern prevails when the measure is not financial but *human* resources. State and local employees have always outnumbered federal

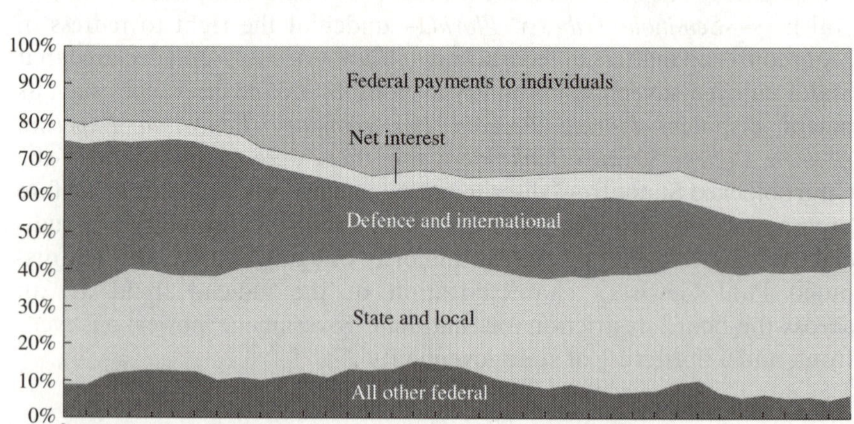

FIGURE 3.1. *Composition of US government spending, 1962–1998*

Source: Office of Management and Budget, Fiscal Year 2000 Budget (Washington, DC, 2000), Historical Table 15.5

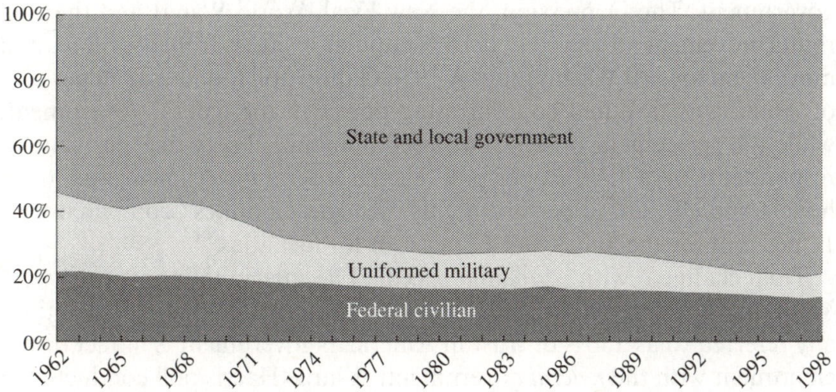

FIGURE 3.2. *Composition of US public sector employment, 1962–1998*
Source: Census Bureau data from office of Management and Budget, Fiscal Year 2000 Budget (Washington, DC, 2000), Historical Table 17.5

employees; their responsibilities involve more street-level service delivery requiring more manpower than the check-writing and rule-making functions more common in Washington. But this imbalance grew in the last third of the twentieth century. Significantly for our present argument, the central government's relative eclipse continued through the 1990s. The erosion of the ranks of military personnel, from just over 2 million in 1990 to just under 1.5 million in 1998, is a familiar and understandable trend. But the *civilian* headcount also fell by about 11 per cent between 1990 and 1998. The State and local payroll grew by eleven per cent over the 1990–7 period.[53] Meanwhile, the quality of State and local personnel—once considered systematically short of the federal standard—held its own or improved, especially in the higher ranks.

Legitimacy

The most important metric for the relative weight of central and regional government, of course, is not formal authority, or spending, or even talented personnel, but rather the citizenry's confidence. By this measure—and to the extent public-opinion data is a valid gauge of legitimacy—the rhythm of federalism has been strongly centrifugal since the early 1970s. To some extent this reflects a return to the American norm after an uncharacteristic dalliance with centralized power. In the country's early years the States tended to enjoy more legitimacy than the distant national

[53] Preliminary estimates show an inexplicably sharp decline in 1998 from the level of the previous several years, making the 1990–8 growth in State and local employment 5 per cent, rather than 11 per cent.

government. The Depression, the New Deal, World War II and the civil rights movement all served to detach popular loyalties from the States and move them toward Washington. A 1936 Gallup poll found that 56 per cent of Americans favoured concentrating power in the federal government, while 44 per cent favoured State predominance. Forty-one per cent of respondents on a 1939 Roper poll felt the federal government was 'most honest and efficient in performing its own special duties', compared with 12 per cent for the States and 17 per cent for localities.[54]

This changed with startling speed. The precipitating events were Vietnam, the energy crisis, and, especially, Watergate. What is conventionally referred to as a loss of trust in American government is in fact disenchantment with the *federal* government. A large Harris poll conducted in 1973 helps pin down the turning point. While the fractions of respondents reporting 'a great deal' of confidence was not radically different for State—24 per cent—than for national government—19 per cent—a follow-on question is telling. Asked how their confidence in government had *changed* since 1968, the majority of respondents said their faith in both State and local government was 'about the same' as it had been five years previously, with roughly similar shares gaining as losing confidence in the cities and States. But a remarkable 58 per cent reported that their faith in the federal government had declined.[55]

For many years the Gallup organization asked a consistently worded set of questions about confidence in various levels of government. In 1972, nearly three-quarters of respondents—73 per cent—had 'a great deal' or 'a fair amount' of confidence in the federal executive branch. State and local governments both had the same confidence of 63 per cent of respondents. Two years later, confidence in the federal executive had plummeted to 40 per cent, while State and local government improved, to 75 per cent and 71 per cent, respectively. Public faith in government has partially recovered from its lows of the 1970s. But the bias against central government has endured. The latest available data from the Gallup series, from 1998, shows 63 per cent reporting high or moderate confidence in the federal government—a respectable improvement, to be sure. But 80 per cent have comparable confidence in their State governments.[56] A separate polling series conducted by Hart and Teeter for the Council for Excellence in Government shows trust in Washington rising during the 1990s. In 1995 15 per cent reported 'a great

[54] The Gallup and Roper polls from the 1930s are summarized in Robert J. Blendon, 'Changing Attitudes in America' (unpublished manuscript, September 1996), Table 6.

[55] The September 1973 Harris poll data are from ftp://vance.irss.unc.edu/pub/search results/POLLtxt , accessed in December 1999.

[56] References in this paragraph are from Gallup archives of polling trends at http://www.pollingreport.com/institut.htm#Federal, accessed December 1999.

deal' or 'quite a lot' of confidence in the federal government; in 1999 that share was 21 per cent. But similarly high confidence in State government rose from 23 per cent to 33 per cent between 1995 and 1999, and the 'confidence gap' between central and regional government increased by half.

In view of the evidence on the balance of formal authority, human and financial resources, and public legitimacy—and without dismissing the imprecision of such measures or the counter-examples within each category—we will risk the generalization that the rhythm of American federalism continued to favour decentralization through the 1990s. The shift away from Washington and toward the States appears to have lasted out the century.

3. The EU Experience: Integration and Subsidiarity

The European Union did not begin life as a federal union, nor, in the view of most analysts, does it constitute a fully developed federation today. Founded in 1951 as a European Coal and Steel Community among six Member States, the EU has grown in fits and starts through a series of Treaty revisions and the adoption of common policies, surviving periodic crises that have threatened to halt or even reverse the tide of European integration. Despite these crises, the process of integration has proceeded to the point where the Union shares numerous characteristics with the United States and other federal states, including a constitutionally defined, yet constantly evolving, separation of powers between a central government and individual Member States. The process of integration—from the early days of the 1950s, through the Gaullist challenge of the 1960s, the relaunching of integration in the 1980s, and the current calls for subsidiarity and retrenchment at the turn of the century—resembles in broad outline the history of American federalism—while differing, to be sure, in timing and important details—and raises many of the same political and constitutional issues.

The Founding of the Union: From Monnet to the EEC

The long process of European integration began, as did the creation of the United States, in the aftermath of a major war. By contrast to the US experience, however, the two major countries in the Union, France and Germany, had been enemies in World War II. To a large extent, therefore, the early history of the Union was dominated by the long and difficult effort by France and (West) Germany to reconcile their past in a common integrationist project.

In the immediate postwar years between 1945 and 1950, the cause of European integration was championed internally by the United Europe Movement, and externally by the United States and its Marshall Plan for the reconstruction of Western Europe. The United Europe Movement was founded by Winston Churchill in 1947, but traced its conceptual heritage back before the war, when intellectuals had argued for a federal or confederal union of European nations. The movement arguably reached its apogee at the May 1948 Congress of Europe and the subsequent creation, in 1949, of the Council of Europe. The Council, however, proved to be a rather weak intergovernmental organization, except in the area of human rights, and disappointed the many members of the movement who had hoped for a genuine United States of Europe. As for the major external impetus to European integration, the United States insisted that recipients of Marshall Plan aid coordinate their economic policies through the Organization for European Economic Cooperation (OEEC). The OEEC, however, also proved to be a weak intergovernmental body.[57] As in the US, therefore, the initial post-war efforts to produce a union of previously independent polities proved disappointing.

Five years after the end of World War II, and in the shadow of a new cold war between the United States and the Soviet Union, a French bureaucrat named Jean Monnet proposed a new and more modest approach to Franco-German reconciliation and European integration. Faced with the imminent revival of the West German economy and the rebuilding of German industrial capacity, Monnet realized that the threat of future aggression from Germany could no longer be suppressed by preventing German economic recovery. A more durable and less wasteful solution lay in channelling and constraining German economic power through a new, supranational authority. In early 1950, Monnet therefore approached Maurice Schuman, the French foreign minister, with a plan for a European Coal and Steel Community (ECSC), which would place the coal and steel industries of France, Germany, and other European countries under a single High Authority. Schuman, a Christian Democrat with a strong personal commitment to Franco-German reconciliation, accepted Monnet's plan, which was formally announced on 9 May 1950 as the Schuman Plan. In his declaration, Schuman called for the coal and steel industries of France and Germany to be placed under a single supranational entity, which would also be open to other European countries. The proposed Coal and Steel Community, Schuman believed, would serve the immediate purpose of reducing the threat of German reindustrializa-

[57] Desmond Dinan, *Ever Closer Union: An Introduction to European Integration* (Boulder: Lynne Rienner, 1999), 11–18.

tion, while at the same time serving as a modest first step in a longer and more gradual process of European political integration:

The organization of Europe in the sense of unification [Schuman later wrote] was indispensable. It could only be achieved within a new political structure. With this in view, the idea of a Federation sprang quite naturally to mind, but we did not think that we had to begin with such an ambitious legal construction. It was better to advance step by step in specific and practical areas.[58]

Supported by the West German government of Konrad Adenauer and by a United States eager to see Western Europe unified in the face of the Soviet threat, the Schuman Plan was followed by extended negotiations among six European countries—France, Germany, Italy, and the Benelux countries—which signed the new treaty creating the European Coal and Steel Community in April 1951. Monnet himself was named the first President of the High Authority, which took up its tasks in August 1952.

At the same time that the Six were negotiating the ECSC Treaty, Europe embarked on a second, and ultimately failed, integration project. In October 1950, following the outbreak of the Korean War and the increasing demands for West German rearmament by the United States, French Prime Minister Rene Pleven proposed to follow the ECSC with a more ambitious European Defence Community (EDC), which would place West German rearmament in the context of a single European army. The logic of the Pleven Plan—embracing a former enemy who could no longer be suppressed—was similar to Monnet's plan for the ECSC, but the 'high politics' area of defence proved more controversial than the coal and steel plan. Although the Six did manage to agree on the text of a treaty creating the proposed EDC, that treaty was ultimately rejected in August 1954 in the French National Assembly, where it was derailed by a coalition of Gaullists opposed to the loss of national sovereignty and Communists opposed to the prospect of German rearmament. The process of European integration, which had begun modestly with the Schuman Plan and the Coal and Steel Community, had suffered its first major setback.[59]

Despite the failure of the European Defence Community, the advocates of European integration soon rallied to a more modest Dutch proposal for economic integration among the Six. The proposed common market would feature free movement of goods, services, labour, and capital, as well as binding European rules for competition and a common external

[58] Quoted in Pierre Gerbet, 'The Origins: Early Attempts and the Emergence of the Six (1945-52)', in Roy Pryce (ed.), *The Dynamics of European Union* (New York: Croom Helm), 35–48, at 45–6.

[59] Daniel Lerner and Raymond Aron (eds), *France Defeats EDC* (New York: Praeger, 1957).

trade policy. On the basis of this proposal, and a related plan for a European Atomic Energy Community proposed by Monnet, the governments of the Six agreed in 1955 to commence yet another intergovernmental conference. This round culminated in March 1957 with the Treaties of Rome, creating the European Economic Community (EEC) and Euratom.

The central element of the Rome Treaties is the common market, which became and remained the shorthand name for the EEC in the English language well into the 1980s. According to the terms of the EEC Treaty, the common market would be an area characterized by the free movement of goods, services, labour, and capital. In addition to this central goal, the Treaty also included several flanking policies, including common policies on external trade, competition, and agriculture. In the area of external trade, the Treaty created a single external tariff and a single trade policy *vis-à-vis* third countries, and authorized the EEC's executive Commission to represent the common market in international trade negotiations. The Treaty provisions on competition, based largely on American antitrust policy and on the cartel-busting powers of the High Authority in the area of coal and steel, grant EEC institutions extensive powers to review state aids to industry—which are more closely regulated in the EU than in the United States—and to police cartels and concentrations. The Treaty provisions on agriculture were inserted at the insistence of France, which demanded Community-level support for French farmers as the political price for agreeing to liberalize trade with its European neighbours.[60]

The Rome Treaties also established a set of four key institutions, including an intergovernmental Council of Ministers, which would adopt new Community legislation; an executive Commission, which was charged with preparing EC legislation, representing the EC in external trade matters, and monitoring Member State compliance with EU law; a Court of Justice to interpret the Treaties and adjudicate disputes; and a Consultative Assembly which would later evolve into the directly elected European Parliament.

Finally, in addition to these specific competences for Community institutions, the EEC Treaty included two more general clauses, Articles 100 and 235 EEC, which would later turn out to play a crucial role in the integration process, comparable to the 'necessary and proper clause' of the US Constitution. Article 100 authorized the Community to adopt binding legislation for the 'approximation' or harmonization of national regula-

[60] On the negotiations of the Treaties of Rome, see e.g. Hans-Jürgen Küsters, 'The Treaties of Rome', in Pryce (ed.), *The Dynamics of European Union*, 78–104; and Andrew Moravcsik, *The Choice for Europe: State Purpose and Social Power from Messina to Maastricht* (Ithaca: Cornell University Press, 1998), 86–158.

tions in order to remove non-tariff barriers to trade. Article 235, the EEC Treaty's own 'elastic clause', was broader still, authorizing the Community to adopt any 'appropriate measures' necessary to obtain one of the core objectives of the Treaty. The effect of these provisions was limited by the requirement of unanimous agreement among the Member States of the Community, which would prove difficult to achieve in practice. The significance of these articles was nevertheless recognized by the scholars of the time, and they would later prove instrumental in the adoption of new sectoral policies in areas such as the environment and consumer protection, on which the Treaties of Rome were silent.[61]

The optimism of this early period, and the incremental nature of the 'Monnet method', were captured in the neo-functionalist theory of Ernst Haas, whose 1958 book *The Uniting of Europe* posited a process of functional 'spillover', in which the initial decision by governments to place a certain sector, such as coal and steel, under the authority of central institutions inevitably creates pressures to expand the authority of those institutions into neighbouring policy sectors. Eventually, Haas predicted, interest groups would gradually transfer their demands, expectations, and loyalties from national governments to a new political centre based in Brussels. Although Haas and his fellow neo-functionalists admitted the possibility that the EEC might encounter crises along the way, they expected these crises to be surmounted through additional integrative steps, and the further centralization of European authority.[62]

De Gaulle's Discontent and the Decade of Europessimism

The progress of centralization was soon challenged, however, by Charles de Gaulle, who held the presidency of France from 1958 until 1969. As a lifelong French nationalist determined to defend French sovereignty

[61] For good discussions of the negotiation and significance of these articles, see John A. Usher, 'The Gradual Widening of European Community Policy on the Basis of Article 100 and 235 of the EEC Treaty', in Jurgen Schwarz and Henry G. Schermers (eds), *Structure and Dimensions of European Community Policy* (Baden-Baden: Nomos, 1988), 25–41; C. Flaesch Mougin, 'Article 235', in Vlad Constantinesco, Jean-Paul Jacqué, Robert Kovar, and Denys Simon, *Traité instituant la CEE: Commentaire article par article* (Paris: Economica, 1992), 1519–21; and Joseph H. H. Weiler, 'The Transformation of Europe', *Yale Law Journal*, 100 (1991): 2438–41.

[62] For the key statements of neofunctionalist theory, see Ernst B. Haas, *The Uniting of Europe* (Stanford: Stanford University Press, 1958); Ernst B. Haas, 'Technocracy, Pluralism and the New Europe', in Stephen R. Graubard (ed.), *A New Europe?* (Boston: Houghton Mifflin, 1964), 62–88; Ernst B. Haas and Philippe C. Schmitter, 'Economics and Differential Patterns of Political Integration: Projections about Unity in Latin America', *International Organization*, 18/4 (1964) [PAGES]; and Leon L. Lindberg and Stuart A. Scheingold, *Europe's Would-Be Polity* (Englewood Cliffs, NJ: Prentice-Hall, 1963).

against the encroachment of European integration, de Gaulle spent much of his decade in office challenging the creeping centralization of power in Brussels, and fighting for his vision of a '*Europe des patries*', or a 'Europe of nations'.

The clearest manifestation of de Gaulle's vision was the 1961 Fouchet Plan, named after de Gaulle's foreign minister Christian Fouchet, which laid out a purely intergovernmental plan for European cooperation in foreign and defence policy, as well as cultural, educational, and scientific matters. Had it been accepted by the other five Member States, the Fouchet Plan would have created a Europe with little or no role for the supranational Commission or Court, dominated by the large powers of France and Germany. Largely for this reason, the plan was resisted by the Netherlands and other Member States, and was buried in committee in 1962.[63] The following year, de Gaulle unilaterally vetoed the United Kingdom's application for membership in the EC, primarily on the grounds that Britain's close relationship with the United States would risk submerging the Community in an American-dominated Atlantic community.

De Gaulle's challenge to supranational integration reached a climax in June of 1965, with the so-called empty-chair crisis. The crisis ostensibly began as a result of the Commission's proposals for the establishment of new EC budgetary resources, over which the supranational Commission and Parliament would exercise considerable control. Perhaps more importantly, the EEC Treaty also stipulated that the Member States in the Council of Ministers would begin to vote by qualified, or weighted, majority on certain issues after January 1966, which de Gaulle interpreted as a violation of French national sovereignty. Faced with the imminent end of the French national veto, de Gaulle responded by recalling France's permanent representative to Brussels and announcing that French officials would no longer participate in the activities of the Council. This state of crisis lasted for over six months, until January 1966, when de Gaulle secured the agreement of the other five to a declaration, the 'Luxembourg Compromise', which called for unanimous decision-making in the Council 'when issues very important to one or more member countries are at stake'. The Luxembourg Compromise, although a political declaration rather than a legally binding change in the Treaties, was widely seen as a turning point in the history of European integration, after which the Community would function less like a political community and more like a traditional international organization, dominated by member govern-

[63] Dinan, *Ever Closer Union*, 42–3. See also Pierre Gerbet, 'In Search of Political Union: The Fouchet Plan Negotiations (1960–62)', in Pryce (ed.), *The Dynamics of European Union*, 105–29.

ments and crippled by the need for unanimous agreement amongst its members—a condition later labelled 'Eurosclerosis' during the difficult years of the 1970s.[64]

Reflecting this shift, a new school of intergovernmentalist theorists argued that member governments would resist the transfer of sovereignty to European institutions, and questioned the teleology of the neo-functionalist model. As William Wallace bluntly argued, 'The success of the neo-functional approach depended upon national governments not noticing—in effect—the gradual draining away of their lifeblood to Brussels'.[65] Indeed, in the view of intergovernmentalists like Paul Taylor, the few decisive political agreements of the 1970s, such as the creation of the European Council in 1974 and the establishment of the European Monetary System of exchange-rate coordination in 1979, had actually taken the Community back to a traditional intergovernmentalist style of decision-making which retained the national veto and minimized the role of supranational actors such as the Commission.[66]

Nevertheless, despite the Gaullist challenge and the apparent reassertion of Member-State dominance during the 1970s, this period can be seen in retrospect as one of significant progress in the development of a European legal system by the European Court of Justice (ECJ). Working in cooperation with national courts, the ECJ established and secured acceptance of the crucial principles of the supremacy of EC law over national law in the case of conflict—*Van Gend en Loos*, 1963—and the 'direct effect' of EC law in national courts—*Costa v. ENEL*, 1964. Gradually, and even during the years of Europessimism of the late 1960s

[64] For good discussions of de Gaulle's European policy, with a special focus on the Empty Chair Crisis, see Lois Pattison de Menil, *Who Speaks for Europe? The Vision of Charles de Gaulle* (New York: St. Martin's Press, 1978), and John Newhouse, *Collision in Brussels* (New York: Norton, 1967). For the text of the Luxembourg Compromise, see Dinan, *Ever Closer Union*, 49.

[65] Quoted by Fritz W. Scharpf, 'The Joint-Decision Trap: Lessons from German Federalism and European Integration', *Public Administration*, 66 (1988): 239–78, at 266.

[66] For key works in the intergovernmentalist tradition, see Stanley Hoffmann, 'Obstinate or Obsolete? The Fate of the Nation-State and the Case of Western Europe', *Daedalus*, 95/3 (1966), 862–915; Paul Taylor, *The Limits of European Integration* (New York: Columbia University Press, 1983); William William, 'Political Cooperation: Integration through Intergovernmentalism', in Helen Wallace, William Wallace, and Carole Webb (eds), *Policy-making in the European Community* (London: John Wiley & Sons, 1983), 373–402; Andrew Moravcsik, 'Negotiating the Single European Act', in Robert O. Keohane and Stanley Hoffmann (eds), *The New European Community* (Boulder: Westview Press, 1991), 41–84; and Andrew Moravcsik, 'Preferences and Power in the European Community: A Liberal Intergovernmentalist Approach', *Journal of Common Market Studies*, 31/4 (1993), 473–524. On the formation of the European Monetary System, see Peter Ludlow, *The Making of the European Monetary System* (London: Butterworth Scientific, 1982).

and 1970s, the Court successfully 'constitutionalized' the Treaties, establishing a new and genuinely supranational system of law, in which EC nationals could claim specific rights in EC law and enforce those rights in their own national courts. Thus, as Joseph Weiler has pointed out, the period of *political* stagnation in European integration coincided with a great leap forward in the *legal* integration of Europe.[67] The relaunching of the political process of integration, however, would have to await a new generation of political crises, and political entrepreneurs, in the 1980s and 1990s.

The Relaunching of European Integration: From the Single European Act to Maastricht

By the early 1980s, European political and economic actors were becoming increasingly aware of the costs of decentralization. Although the EEC Treaty had been agreed with the aim of creating a single internal market among its various Member States, the Luxembourg Compromise and the subsequent turn to unanimous voting meant that the Community's decision-making process remained sluggish by contrast with the rapid growth of national non-tariff barriers to the free movement of goods, services, labour, and capital in the 1970s. By the early 1980s, the goal of a genuine internal market remained an aspiration rather than a reality, and the Community clearly lagged behind both the United States and Japan in terms of employment, business confidence, and competitiveness.[68] By contrast with the decentralizing impulse of the 1960s and 1970s, the arguments of efficiency and scale pointed to the advantages of centralization of certain activities at the European level.

It was against this background of economic crisis and eurosclerosis that Jacques Delors took over as the new president of the European Commission in January of 1985, looking for a key theme or project around which the project of European integration could be relaunched. After rejecting a number of possibilities that might fail to rally the unanimous support of the Member States, Delors settled on the completion of the internal market as the central plank of his relaunching of the European Community, and charged his new internal market Commissioner, Lord Cockfield, with the drafting of a White Paper on *Completing the Internal Market*. In June of 1985, Delors presented the internal market plan—which proposed the adoption by 31 December 1992, of some 300 distinct pieces of legislation to eliminate internal barriers to trade—to

[67] Weiler, 'The Transformation of Europe', 2403.

[68] Jacques Pelkmans and Alan Winters, *Europe's Domestic Market* (London: Routledge, 1988), 6.

member governments at the Milan European Council meeting.[69] Delors argued, however, that in order to adopt such an ambitious agenda in only eight years, the Member States would also have to agree to a revision of the Treaties of Rome, strengthening the power of EC institutions and returning to qualified majority voting for all internal market legislation. Despite the angry protests of Margaret Thatcher, who had replaced de Gaulle as the guardian of national sovereignty within the EC, the European Council agreed to call an intergovernmental conference (IGC) to consider both the completion of the internal market and broader institutional reforms to the Rome Treaties.

In the space of six months, the member governments produced a new Treaty, called the Single European Act (SEA), which codified the goal of completing the internal market by Delors' target date of 1992. The SEA also provided for a series of institutional reforms—most notably, the adoption of qualified majority voting for internal market legislation—to enable EC institutions to meet that deadline. In addition to these central elements, the SEA also created a new 'cooperation procedure' which would grant the European Parliament the right to propose amendments to draft EC legislation in certain areas, and codified EC competence in areas such as foreign policy, the environment, regional development, and scientific research, all of which had previously been the subject of intergovernmental cooperation outside the Treaties or under Art. 235.[70]

A short and modest Treaty, the Single European Act was quickly dismissed by the *Economist* weekly magazine, which argued that Europe had laboured long to produce 'a mouse'. As Delors had anticipated, however, the so-called 1992 project served to revitalize the integration process after two decades of relative stagnation. With a few thorny exceptions like the liberalization of the electricity and gas sectors, where France in particular resisted the dismantling of its state monopolies, Lord Cockfield's programme of internal market legislation was completed largely on time by the end of 1992. European industry responded with a wave of mergers and acquisitions, as firms struggled to reposition themselves to take advantage of the new opportunities in the single market; and the Member States agreed in 1988 to a major increase in the size of the EC budget, including

[69] Commission of the European Communities, *Completing the Internal Market*, COM(85)310 final of 14 June 1985. See also Lord Cockfield, *The European Union: Creating the Single Market* (London: John Wiley & Sons, 1994), 17–75.

[70] For excellent accounts of the negotiations of the intergovernmental conference, see Richard Corbett, 'The 1985 Intergovernmental Conference and the Single European Act', in Pryce (ed.), *The Dynamics of European Union*, 238–72; Jean De Ruyt, *L'Acte unique européen* (Brussels: Éditions de l'Université de Bruxelles, 1986); and Moravcsik, *The Choice for Europe*, 314–78.

a doubling of Structural Fund aid to the poorest regions in the Community.

Nor did the SEA mark the end of the Community's relaunching. Within just a few years of the Single Act, the Community embarked upon the single most ambitious institutional reform in its history, culminating in the Treaty on European Union signed at Maastricht, the Netherlands, in 1992. The initial impetus for a new Treaty came from Member States dissatisfied with the operation of the European Monetary System, which had essentially obliged them to follow the monetary lead of the German Bundesbank. In January 1988, French Prime Minister Edouard Balladur proposed the adoption of a European Economic and Monetary Union, including a single currency and a single central bank. Balladur's proposal met with a mixed reception in Germany, where government and Bundesbank officials expressed scepticism about the prospect of surrendering the D-Mark in favour of an untested European currency, and in the United Kingdom, where Thatcher ruled out any possibility of surrendering the British pound. Nevertheless, the Hanover European Council agreed in June 1988 to support the creation of an expert committee, chaired by Delors, to consider the options. The Delors Committee returned in April 1989 with a report calling for a three-stage transition to Economic and Monetary Union (EMU), with the final stage culminating in the creation of a single currency and a European Central Bank to manage it.

In the autumn of 1989, the EMU proposal was given an unexpected boost by the democratic revolutions in Eastern Europe and by the subsequent unification of Germany in October 1990. The revolutions in the east, according to Delors, created an 'acceleration of history', with Germany, France, and the rest of the EC Member States rushing to 'deepen' their economic and political union and to bind a united Germany firmly into the institutions of a united Western Europe. Accordingly, the Member States agreed in 1990 to convene not one but two new intergovernmental conferences, on economic and monetary union and on a vaguely defined political union. The two intergovernmental conferences were convened in December of 1990, and dragged on for a full year, eventually producing the Treaty on European Union in March of 1992.[71]

[71] For good discussions of the negotiations and contents of the Treaty on European Union, see J. Cloos, G. Reinisch, D. Vignes, and J. Weyland, *Le Traité de Maastricht: Genèse, analyse, commentaires* (Bruxelles: Bruylant 1993); Richard Corbett, *The Treaty of Maastricht* (Harlow: Longman Current Affairs, 1994); Finn Laursen and Sophie Vanhoonacker (eds), *The Intergovernmental Conference on Political Union* (Maastricht: European Institute of Public Administration, 1992); and George Ross, *Jacques Delors and European Integration* (New York: Oxford University Press, 1995).

By and large, the Treaty provisions on EMU mirrored the plans of the Delors Committee, with a three-stage transition to full economic and monetary union, culminating in the creation of a new single currency and a European central bank no later than the deadline date of 1 January 1999. At the insistence of the German delegation, the Treaty also lays down a series of 'convergence criteria' specifying the acceptable rates of inflation, exchange-rate stability, budget deficits, and national debts that every Member State would have to satisfy in order to qualify for membership in EMU. Finally, special provisions were included that would allow Britain and Denmark to 'opt out' of the single currency even if they satisfied all the relevant criteria. In the subsequent years, many Member States encountered substantial difficulties satisfying the criteria for budget deficits and national debt. Nevertheless, the EU observed the Treaty deadline, and the new currency, uninspiringly dubbed the euro, came into being—at least as an electronic unit of account—as the official currency of the eleven Member States of the so-called Euroland.

The Maastricht provisions on political union were at least as complex and ambitious as those on EMU. Encompassing the old European Community, the Treaty created a new legal entity called the European Union, which was in turn divided into three 'pillars.' The existing EC would constitute the first of these pillars, with a series of additions and amendments, most notably the new provisions for EMU, some modest extensions of qualified majority voting to new issue-areas, and the creation of a new 'co-decision procedure' that would make the European Parliament a more equal partner with the Council of Ministers in certain areas of EU legislation. In addition, the Treaty created two new, intergovernmental pillars to encompass cooperation in the areas of Common Foreign and Security Policy, and Justice and Home Affairs, respectively.[72] The pillar structure of the new Union was perhaps the most controversial element of the Maastricht negotiations, since the second and third pillars effectively excluded the Commission, Court, and Parliament from participation in the new areas of cooperation; but the more integrationist Member States managed to secure a clause calling for the pillar structure to be revisited in a subsequent IGC to take place in 1996.[73]

[72] For good discussions of the second and third pillars respectively, see Anthony Forster and William Wallace, 'Common Foreign and Security Policy', in Helen Wallace and William Wallace (eds), *Policy-Making in the European Union* (New York: Oxford University Press, 1996), 411–35; and Monica den Boer, 'Justice and Home Affairs', in Wallace and Wallace (eds), *Policy-Making in the European Union*, 389–410.

[73] The resulting Treaty of Amsterdam, agreed in 1997, did not eliminate the pillared structure of the EU, but it did agree to transfer certain functions from the third pillar to the first, and to strengthen the role of the Court of Justice in the third pillar. For good discussions of these changes, see Andrew Duff, *The Treaty of Amsterdam: Text and Commentary*

Finally, in order to overcome a veto by British Prime Minister John Major, the Treaty created a 'Social Protocol' exempting Britain that would allow the other Member States to make use of EC institutions and procedures to adopt social legislation that would be binding on all the signatories.[74]

Taken as a whole, the Maastricht Treaty was arguably the most ambitious step forward in the process of European integration since the Treaties of Rome. Yet the Treaty's impenetrable prose—reflecting the inevitable compromises required to secure the unanimous agreement of twelve member governments—would later come in for criticism in public debate throughout the Union, as would specific clauses related to EMU, the new pillars, and the Social Protocol. Indeed, some critics suggested that the Maastricht Treaty was the high water-mark of an integration process which is likely to take a pause, or even a step backward, in the near future. We return to this claim in some detail below.

The Development of EU Policies, 1957–1992: A Variation on the American Theme

Thus far, we have concentrated on the key institutional or Treaty developments in the history of European integration, but a parallel story concerns the development of Community policies, which expanded gradually from the relatively narrow mandate of the EEC Treaty of 1957 to embrace almost every conceivable issue-area by the time that the Maastricht Treaty was signed in 1992. This cumulative growth of EU policies can be seen most starkly in Philippe Schmitter's graphic depiction of the growth of centralized EU policy-making (see Table 3.1).

As Schmitter makes clear, the locus of policy-making in the 1950s was overwhelmingly at the national level, with a secondary EU presence in core common-market areas such as the free movement of goods and services, competition, and industry. By the late 1960s and early 1970s, however, the EU had begun to adopt legislation in an increasing number of issue-areas, and by 1992 the EU had established a presence in almost every conceivable issue-area, with the exception of police and public order. Although Schmitter's projections for 2001 seem strained, the most striking development depicted in the table is that by the late 1990s, the EU and

(London: Sweet and Maxwell, 1997), and Michel Petite, 'The Treaty of Amsterdam', Harvard Jean Monnet Working Papers Series No. 2/98, http://www.law.harvard.edu/Programs/JeanMonnet/.

[74] In the 1997 Treaty of Amsterdam, the new Labour government of Tony Blair became a signatory to the Social Protocol, ending this temporary anomaly in the EU legal order. Petite, 'The Treaty of Amsterdam'.

TABLE 3.1. *Issue arenas and levels of authority in Europe*

	1950	1957	1968	1970	1992	2001
I. Economic issue arenas						
1. Goods/services	1	2	3	3	4	4
2. Agriculture	1	1	4	4	4	4
3. Capital flows	1	1	1	1	4	4
4. Persons/workers	1	1	2	2	3	4
5. Transportation	1	2	2	2	2	3
6. Energy	1	2	1	1	2	2
7. Communications	1	1	1	1	2	3
8. Environment	1	2	2	2	3	3
9. Regional development	1	1	1	1	3	3
10. Competition	1	2	2	2	3	3
11. Industry	1	2	2	2	2	3
12. Money/credit	1	1	2	2	2	4
13. Foreign exchange/loans	1	1	2	2	2	4
14. Revenue/taxes	1	1	2	2	2	3
15. Macroeconomic	1	1	2	3	2	4
II. Socio-cultural issue-arenas						
1. Work conditions	1	1	2	2	2	3
2. Health	1	1	1	1	2	2
3. Social welfare	1	2	2	2	2	2
4. Education and research	1	1	2	2	2	3
5. Labour-management relations	1	1	1	1	1	3
III. Politico-constitutional issues						
1. Justice and property rights	1	1	1	2	3	4
2. Citizenship	1	1	1	1	2	3
3. Participation	1	1	1	1	2	2
4. Police and public order	1	1	1	1	1	2
IV. International relations/external security issues						
1. Commercial negotiations	1	1	3	4	5	5
2. Economic-military assistance	1	1	1	1	2	4
3. Diplomacy and IGO membership	1	1	1	1	2	4
4. Defence and war	1	1	1	1	2	3

1: All policy decisions at national level.
2: Only some policy decisions at EC level.
3: Policy decisions at both national and EC level.
4: Mostly policy decisions at EC level.
5: All policy decisions at EC level.
Source: Philippe C. Schmitter, 'Imagining the Future of the Euro-Polity with the Help of New Concepts', in Gary Marks, Fritz W. Scharpf, Philippe C. Schmitter, and Wolfgang Streeck (eds), *Governance in the European Union* (London: Sage Publications, 1996).

the Member States shared competences to a greater or lesser degree in nearly every issue-area.

This result resembles nothing so much as the American conception of 'marble cake federalism', in which there exists no rigid delineation of authority among the federal and state levels of government.[75] Table 3.2 represents a partial and strictly impressionistic effort to compare some of the trends in policy responsibility which Schmitter tracks for the EU to corresponding patterns over the far longer period of US history. The milestones mark the Federal era, the immediate aftermath of the Constitution's ratification, the reconstruction era, the New Deal, and the 1980 high-water mark of centralization in many areas. Although the time scale is considerably longer in the US table, we witness the same general patterns in both cases, with a gradual centralization of authority, culminating in a general sharing of powers between the State and central or federal levels. The similarities among the two cases are most striking in the core economic areas of the internal market, while police and public order—relatively centralized in the US, decentralized in the EU—stands out as the most obvious difference.

TABLE 3.2. *Issue arenas and levels of authority in the United States: selected comparisons with Table 3.1*

	1780	1790	1870	1940	1980	2000
I. Economic issue arenas						
2. Agriculture	1	1	2	4	4	4
5. Transportation	2	2	3	3	4	3
7. Communications	2	2	3	3	4	3
8. Environment	NA	NA	2	3	4	3
9. Regional development	1	1	2	3	4	3
12. Money/credit	2	3	4	4	4	4
14. Revenue/taxes	1	2	2	4	4	3
II. Socio-cultural issue-arenas						
2. Health	1	1	2	3	4	3
3. Social welfare	1	1	1	3	4	3
4. Education and research	1	1	2	2	3	2
III. Politico-constitutional issues						
4. Police and public order	1	2	3	3	3	4

1: All policy decisions at State/local level.
2: Most policy decisions at State/local level.
3: Policy decisions at both State/local and national level.
4: Mostly policy decisions at national level.
NA: few significant policy decisions at any level.

[75] John D. Donahue, *Disunited States* (New York: Basic Books, 1997), 27.

However, if the gradual expansion of EU policy competences resembles the US federal experience in terms of the spread of federal competence to various *issue-areas*, the *types* of policies centralized at the EU level differ substantially from those of the US federal government. In the US context, Theodore Lowi has distinguished three types of policy: redistributive policies, which transfer resources from some individuals or classes to others; regulatory policies, which lay down rules governing individual behaviour; and distributive policies, which dip into the public purse to distribute 'pork barrel' benefits such as army bases or public works projects to various constituencies.[76] For our purposes in this chapter, Lowi's distinctions usefully point to some of the key differences between the United States and the European Union, and in particular the latter's distinctiveness as a 'regulatory state'. In the case of the United States, the federal government's policy role has been characterized primarily in terms of its distributive and redistributive expenditures.[77] By contrast, the European Union's budget is capped at a relatively miserly 1.27 per cent of the Union's GDP, severely limiting its ability to play a similar budgetary role.

In Lowi's terms, the bulk of the EU budget is assigned to redistributive policies which transfer EU funds from mostly wealthy, net contributing Member States, such as Germany, to the primarily poor net recipients, including, most notably, Spain, Portugal, Greece, and Ireland. Historically, these policies have been adopted only as side-payments in major intergovernmental bargains among the richer and poorer Member States, such as the 1988 and 1992 agreements that led to the doubling and re-doubling of Structural Fund expenditures. In addition, the EU has also adopted a series of smaller distributive policies—such as the ESPRIT programme for high-tech R&D collaboration, the SOCRATES programme of student exchanges, and the MEDIA programme to subsidize European television and cinema production—which target EU funds on specific constituencies in each of the Union's 15 Member States.[78] Nevertheless, we should not overstate the significance of these budgetary policies, which are small by comparison with US federal expenditures, and which remain limited by the EU's fixed budgetary ceiling.

In this restrictive fiscal environment, the EU has specialized primarily in the production of regulations, earning it the moniker of a 'regulatory

[76] Theodore J. Lowi, 'American Business, Public Policy, Case Studies and Political Theory', *World Politics*, 16 (1964), 677–715.

[77] Donahue, *Disunited States*, 48.

[78] For extended discussions of EU spending policies, see Mark A. Pollack, 'Creeping Competence: The Expanding Agenda of the European Community', *Journal of Public Policy*, 14/2 (1994), 95–145, and Mark A. Pollack, 'Creeping Competence: The Expanding Agenda of the European Community', Ph.D. thesis (Cambridge, MA: Harvard University, 1995).

state' in the work of Giandomenico Majone.[79] The demand for EU regulation, according to Majone, comes primarily from multinational, export-oriented firms seeking to avoid inconsistent regulations and non-tariff barriers to trade; while the supply comes from an entrepreneurial European Commission eager to expand its mandate within the EU's budgetary envelope. As a result of these pressures, Majone argues, the EU has adopted a wide range of regulations in a more or less steady stream over the past several decades, relatively unaffected by the various political crises that periodically punctuate the history of the Union. Empirically, this gradual pattern of growth in EU regulation began in the late 1960s and the early 1970s, when the institutions of the European Community began to adopt a series of Directives in the areas of environmental and consumer protection, and continued into the 1980s as the Commission proposed, and the Council adopted, new EU regulations as part of the 1992 internal market programme.[80] By the early 1990s, Commission President Jacques Delors confidently, and controversially, predicted that up to 80 per cent of all regulation in Europe would soon take place at the EU level, and the Union seemed well on its way to fitting Majone's description of it as a 'regulatory state'.

The Post-Maastricht Era: Backlash and Devolution?

Thus far we have seen how, in the years between the Treaties of Rome and the Treaty of Maastricht, the policy agenda and competences of the EU expanded, particularly for regulatory policies, so that nearly every conceivable area of policy is now subject to shared national and EU competence. The 1990s, however, have witnessed both a political and an economic backlash against the spread of EU competences, which threaten to bring an end to the previous era of creeping centralization.[81]

The *political* backlash against the growth of centralized EU policies actually pre-dates the Maastricht Treaty, and arose from two distinct sources. In part, the backlash came from member governments which had been outvoted in the adoption of controversial Directives on subjects such as television broadcasting or cigarette labelling, where the Union's competence to legislation was in dispute. A second source of the anti-EU

[79] See Giandomenico Majone, *The European Community as a Regulatory State* (lectures given at the Academy of European Law, European University Institute, 1994); and Giandomenico Majone (ed.), *Regulating Europe* (New York: Routledge, 1996).

[80] Pollack, 'Creeping Competence' (1994); Pollack, 'Creeping Competence' (1995), Ch. 6.

[81] A fuller version of this argument originally appeared in Mark A. Pollack, 'The End of Creeping Competence: EU Policy-Making Since Maastricht', *Journal of Common Market Studies*, 38/3 (2000), 519–38, © Blackwell Publishers.

backlash came from sub-national regions in Member States such as Germany and Belgium, which were concerned about the uncontrolled encroachment of the EU into their constitutionally guaranteed competences. For these Belgian regions and German States—or *Länder*—the most important question in the negotiation of the Maastricht Treaty was how to allocate the shared or concurrent competences that had become commonplace in the EU during the previous two decades.

In response to this question, these regions, and other critics of the Union, seized upon the existing principle of 'subsidiarity', which roughly speaking is the notion that governance should take place as close as possible to the level of the citizen. Largely as a result of lobbying by these regions and by disgruntled member governments like the UK, the Maastricht Treaty includes a legally binding reference in Art. 3B, which states that, outside its areas of exclusive competence, the EU will act only where the proposed action cannot be sufficiently achieved by the individual Member States. In addition, the Treaty also explicitly ruled out harmonization of national regulations in a number of sensitive areas such as education, culture, and health policy, which marked the first explicit denial of EU competence in the history of the Union.

The question of subsidiarity took on even greater importance during the extended debate over the ratification of the Treaty in 1992 and 1993. In June 1992, the Danish electorate shocked Europe by narrowly rejecting the new Treaty in a referendum, and the French electorate nearly did the same, approving the Treaty with a 51 per cent positive vote in the so-called '*petite oui*' the following September. Prior to Maastricht, public opinion was generally perceived to be favourable to the European project, but this 'permissive consensus' can no longer be taken for granted by European elites. Although the Treaty on European Union was later approved by the Danes in a second referendum and entered into force in November of 1993, the weak public support for European integration has subsequently generated an important political and scholarly debate about the democratic legitimacy of the European Union.[82]

The Maastricht Treaty, through its provisions on EMU and the Social Protocol, also introduced into the structure of the Treaty the prospect of cooperation among some subset of EU actors—a notion subsequently referred to under the rubrics of 'flexibility' and 'enhanced cooperation'. Indeed, the subsequent Treaty of Amsterdam, signed in 1997, provides explicitly for further integration among a subset of Member States, subject to specific rules and procedures. These new provisions were

[82] For a good, timely discussion, see Philippe C.Schmitter, *How to Democratize the European Union . . . and Why Bother?* (Lanham, MD: Rowman and Littlefield, 2000).

championed by states such as France and Germany, which want to retain the option of proceeding with further integration even in the absence of unanimous agreement among a growing number of Member States—yet it raises the prospect of a 'Europe à la carte', in which Member States pick and chose those initiatives, beyond the common core of EU policies, in which they elect to participate. These flexibility provisions have no real counterpart in federal systems such as the US, and raise important normative questions for the future of European integration.

Meanwhile, at the same time that the Member States, sub-national governments, and national electorates were challenging EU competence politically, three *economic* developments have coincided to limit the EU's fiscal prospects in the late 1990s and beyond. The first of these developments was the onset of 'donor fatigue' in Germany, which had historically served as the paymaster of the Union, contributing far and away the largest net contribution to the EU budget. By the late 1990s, however, the escalating costs of German unification, together with the dramatic rise in German unemployment and the subsequent increase in the German budget deficit, led successive German governments to demand a limit to Germany's net payment to the Union.

A second and simultaneous development of the mid-1990s was the drive to fiscal austerity among Member States eager to reduce their budget deficits and national debts in order to satisfy the convergence criteria for the new European currency. In most European countries, governments were forced to cut budgetary expenditures, or to raise taxes, in order to meet the Maastricht criterion of a budget deficit under 3 per cent of GDP. As a result, most of the net contributing Member States approached the 1999 round of budgetary negotiations demanding a corresponding fiscal austerity for the EU budget, and eight Member States argued that the EU budget should be frozen in real terms at the level of the 1999 budget. In this context, the Santer Commission proposed in its *Agenda 2000* proposals that the Union budget be capped at 1.27 per cent of GDP, which would allow some incremental growth in line with the growth of the European economy, but which would not dramatically raise the ceiling of EU expenditure as earlier EU budgetary agreements had done.

A third and final source of stress came from the imminent enlargement of the Union to the new democracies of the east, which were significantly less prosperous, and whose accession was likely to result in large net transfers from the existing Member States to the new members as they joined the Union. The implications of this imminent enlargement were particularly ominous for the EU's agricultural and structural policies, the costs of which were set to rise dramatically if the policies were not reformed before the next enlargement. By the late 1990s, therefore, the Union faced the prospect of increasing budgetary demands from new and existing Member States, while the net contributing countries, led by Germany, were insisting on paying less in the future.

In short, the political and economic climate of the European Union in the late 1990s resembled in many respects the picture of the United States in the 1980s, with increasing political and legal demands for States' rights, coupled with a deepening public scepticism about the virtues of centralization. To what extent has the EU responded to these pressures by devolving policy competences and policy-making back to the EU's Member States? In a preliminary effort to measure the continuing centralization, stagnation, or devolution of policy-making in the EU, we examine briefly the most recent available data on the adoption of new EU regulations since 1992, as well as the recently adopted EU financial perspective for the period 2000–6. The results can be found in Figures 3.3 and 3.4.[83]

Let us begin by looking at the record of EU regulation in the 1990s. Figure 3.3 lists all Directives and Regulations in force in the European Union, listed by year of adoption across six broad issue-areas: (1) free movement of workers and social policy; (2) right of establishment and freedom to provide services; (3) economic and monetary union and freedom of capital; (4) industrial policy and the internal market; (5) environment, consumer protection, and health; and (6) science, information, education, and culture. If we look first at the pre-Maastricht period from 1957 until 1992, we see a gradual expansion of EU regulation, concentrated largely in the area of the internal market, and broadening to other areas during the second half of the period, which accords well with Majone's depiction of the EU as a regulatory state. Perhaps more importantly for our purposes here, the figures for the post-Maastricht period on the right demonstrate that the pace of regulation in the core area of the internal market has actually *increased* in the period since 1992, which also features an unprecedented, and intuitively obvious, increase in legislation in the area of economic and monetary union in the run-up to the adoption of the single currency. We should use caution in interpreting these figures, which tell us nothing about the qualitative nature of the regulations adopted before and after Maastricht. It seems likely that much of the current EU legislation lacks the path-breaking quality of the Directives and Regulations of the 1960 and 1970s, which moved the EU into new substantive areas, for the simple reason that the EU is now an active regulator across the full range of issue-areas. Once again, however, these figures indicate that across most issue-areas of EU policy-making, the pace of

[83] Figures 3.3 and 3.4 reproduced from Mark A. Pollack, 'The End of Creeping Competence: EU Policy-Making Since Maastricht', *Journal of Common Market Studies*, 38/3 (2000), 519–38, © Blackwell Publishers.

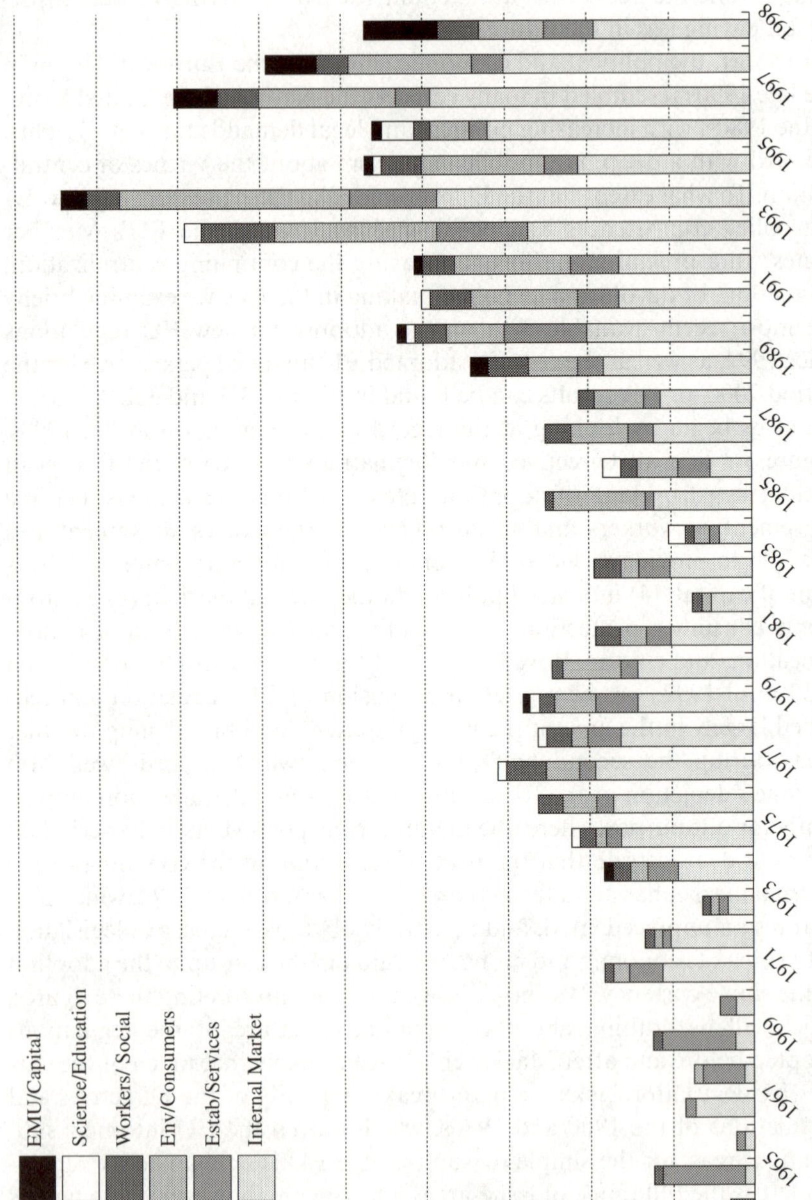

FIGURE 3.3. *Regulatory policies: directives and regulations in force as adopted annually, 1963–1998*

Source: Directory of Community Legislation in Force, December 1998

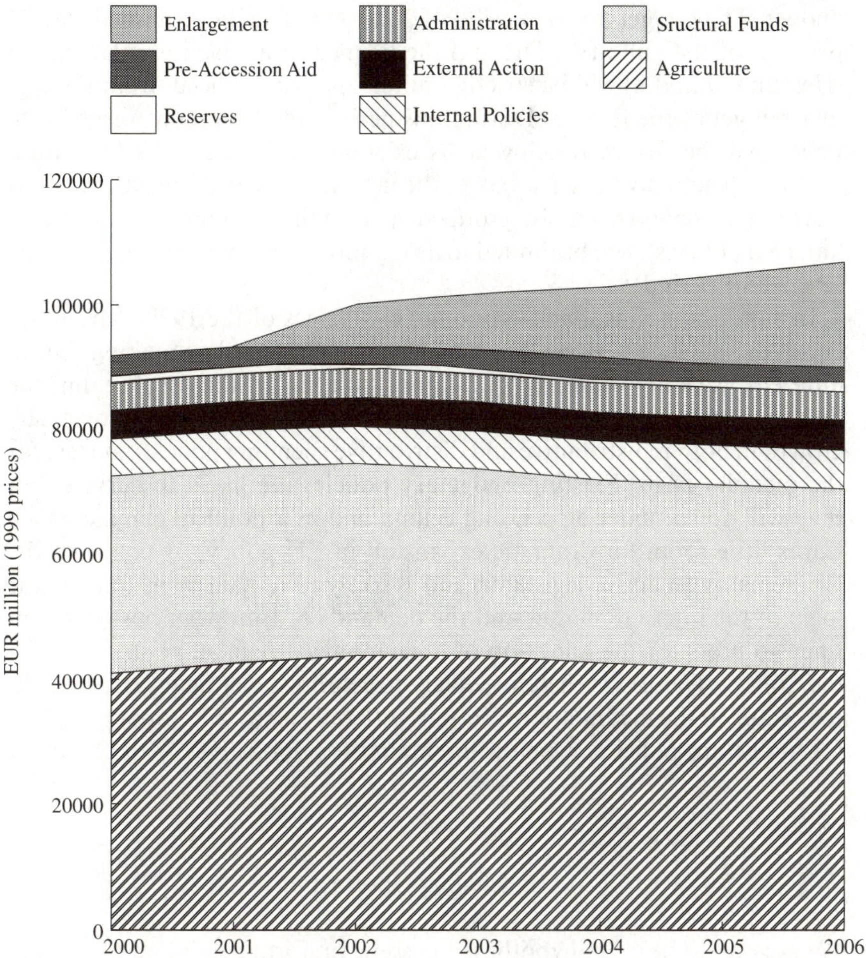

FIGURE 3.4. *Financial framework (EU-21), 2000–2006*
Source: Berlin European Council Presidency Conclusions

regulation has remained steady or even increased in the post-Maastricht period, regardless of both political crisis and economic austerity.

The same, however, cannot be said of EU budgetary policies. Figure 3.4 summarizes the new Financial Perspective adopted by the European Council in March 1999. By contrast with the major financial packages of the 1980s and early 1990s, which increased total EU expenditures drastically while doubling the redistributive Structural Funds, the new Financial Perspective bears the mark of the EU's new fiscal austerity, and of the German determination to limit its own net contribution to the Union's budget. The budget for the period of 2000–6 will again be limited to 1.27 per cent of the Union's GDP, and the finances available for enlargement (Headings 7 and 8) will be strictly limited and 'ring-fenced' from the regular budget of the EU–15. During this period, the Common Agricultural Policy will be frozen roughly at its existing levels, while the Structural Funds will actually be *reduced* over the next seven years. The EU's various distributive policies, finally, grouped in Heading 3 under the rubric of 'internal policies', will be limited to a very modest annual increase over the seven-year period.

In sum, the political and economic challenges of the 1990s *have* influenced the balance between EU and Member-State policy-making, but in different ways for fiscal and regulatory policies. In the fiscal realm, the financial perspective adopted in Berlin marks the end of a period of steady growth in both redistributive and distributive spending policies, at least for the medium term. Existing budgetary policies are likely to survive, but they will do so under a spending ceiling and in a political climate which leaves little room for dramatic expansion in EU policy. By contrast, the EU remains an active legislator, and is likely to remain so as long as the logic of the internal market and the demands of European business continue to press for the adoption of a harmonized regulatory structure for the Union. The EU is therefore likely to retain its character as a 'regulatory state' in the medium-term future, with only a modest, supporting role for budgetary policies, which will remain the prerogatives of the Member States.

4. Concluding Observations

We are not, to be clear, hypothesizing some uniform pendulum of centralization and decentralization, positing any universal equilibrium around which polities pivot, or suggesting a teleology of eventual convergence. It is striking, nonetheless, that two such distinct polities display similar alternations of centripetal and centrifugal impulses. The United States and the European Union are very different political systems—the one a long-established federal arrangement for governing a comparatively homogeneous culture, the other a relatively young international organization with some federal and some intergovernmental characteristics, and with a population that remains culturally, politically, and economically diverse. Yet while we see infinite variation in the timing and details, a few basic themes are seen to recur. The strength and security of coordinated action vies with the flexibility and authenticity of separatism. Each pole represents legitimate aspirations. Each reveals undeniable defects in the transit from aspiration to actuality. Citizens perceive more vividly the defects of the recently ascendant theme, and amplify in abstraction the virtues of its opposite. Hence in a reasonably effective democracy—in which popular complaints and yearning have consequences—featuring an ambiguous or unsettled degree of centralization, the norm is fluctuation. Depending on the polity, the issue, and the time, the actors propelling change may include courts, corporations, elected leaders, and appointed officials of central or constituent states, and the electorate itself. The intricate interplay of these actors, we suggest, tends to generate oscillations between the concentration of power in the centre and the reassertion of the individual States in each system.

So broad an observation hardly supports precise theses, but for the sake of debate we will venture a few stronger generalizations. One is that the rhythms of federalism will be most pronounced where democratic influence is stronger, and more muted where courts, independent authorities, or unelected officials dominate the disposition of an issue. Another is that the rhythm tends to slow and cycles to lengthen as a polity matures; first-order ambiguities are settled, and a degree of institutional inertia dampens the effect of discontent with both centralization and decentralization.

At the moment, the US and the EU seem to be at roughly the same point in the cycle. Starting around 1980, budget pressures in Washington, judicial decisions curbing federal prerogatives, and popular discontent with central government activism have all contributed to a shift toward the separate States. Similarly, the post-Maastricht European Union has witnessed a limited backlash against the centralization of power among both national and sub-national governments, as well as increasing resistance among publics unwilling to surrender further powers to Brussels, leading to a degree of retrenchment in EU resources and authority. If there is something to the story we sketch out here—other than the commonplace that trends tend to end, sooner or later—the centralizing impulse is likely to reassert itself in both polities in the century's early years. The next period of predominant centralization, moreover, should be somewhat sharper and shorter in Europe than in the US, as the asynchronous rhythms of the two polities—one a mature federation, the other not—move out of phase.

4

Blueprints for Change: Devolution and Subsidiarity in the United States and the European Union

DAVID LAZER AND VIKTOR MAYER-SCHOENBERGER

1. Introduction

Where should policy be made in a federal system? When should it be made at the central governmental level, and when should it be made at the State level? When policy is made at the federal level, what are the policy criteria used? In particular, how are the answers to these questions implemented *within central governmental institutions*, which, in principle, have the power to pre-empt the decisions of lower levels of government? This chapter explores how these two dimensions of the regulatory policy process—which we call the 'where' and the 'how' dimensions—are treated in the central governmental institutions of the United States and the European Union. We define the 'how' dimension as how the *benefits and costs* of a potential regulation are weighed, and the 'where' dimension as how the decision to introduce a given policy at a particular level of government—federal versus state, EU versus national—is made.

In neither the EU nor the US have 'where' criteria found a natural home in central institutions. Where subsidiarity/federalism criteria have been in theory implemented, their actual impact has been minimal. In contrast, both settings have significant institutionalization of 'how' criteria.

Finally, in both institutional settings, constituent political units are allowed a fair amount of administrative flexibility in implementing policies set by the centre—although, given their different institutional starting points, far more so in the EU than the US.

Below we examine, in turn, the incorporation of how and why criteria in the US regulatory process, the EU regulatory process, and finally, the similarities and differences between the two processes.

2. The United States

The focus will be on the administrative process within the executive branch, and secondarily on how these issues are addressed in the legislative process. We find a minor increase of technocratic procedures in Congress, with respect to raising awareness of unfunded intergovernmental mandates, and little to no increase of similar procedures with respect to private sector mandates. In the executive branch, there has been greater movement toward 'rational' procedures in weighing the costs and benefits of regulation, while, except for unfunded mandates, attempts to add some technocratic rationality in determining the level at which policy should be introduced have been failures.

Legislative Branch

Typically, Congress has created executive agencies—the Environmental Protection Agency (EPA), the Occupational Safety and Health Administration (OSHA), and so forth—and delegated regulatory authority to them, generally directing them to regulate particular risks without benefit/cost or federalism criteria.[1] We will discuss below how recently debated pieces of legislation would have changed this.

The Unfunded Mandates Reform Act of 1995 (UMRA) marked an incremental change in the legislative process. This act requires Congressional Budget Office (CBO) analysis of legislation that will potentially impose costs on State/local/tribal governments and private sectors. If the CBO states the intergovernmental costs exceed $50 million,[2] the legislation may be ruled out of order and a vote will be required to proceed with consideration of the legislation.[3] While this process does not raise a great hurdle to the passage of legislation, it does generate information and focus attention on significant intergovernmental mandates. During the first three years, legislation that reported from committee contained twelve intergovernmental mandates exceeding the $50 million threshold; of these twelve, six were enacted into law (US Government, General Accounting Office 1998*a*). Of those six, four were amended so that the enacted version

[1] Authorizing legislation sometimes captures part of the benefit-cost or federalism equation. Thus, for example, the act authorizing OSHA specifies action where there is 'significant' workplace risk—capturing, partly, the benefit aspect of the equation; and the Clean Air Act requires the EPA to set nationally uniform air quality standards that are then implemented by States.

[2] In 1996 dollars.

[3] The point of order may be raised only with respect to intergovernmental mandates, not private mandates.

contained mandates below the threshold. While it is impossible to state the counterfactual in this case, it is plausible that these procedures had some impact on Congressional decisions with respect to intergovernmental mandates. Some anecdotal evidence relates that informal consultation with the CBO while legislation is in committee has resulted in greater attention to the costs of intergovernmental mandates (US Government, General Accounting Office 1998*b*).

Notably, Congress does not require any analysis of the rationale for significant legislation at the federal rather than State or local levels. Such information must be brought out in the usual give and take of Congressional—and interest group—bargaining.

In weighing the costs and benefits of potential legislation, UMRA also requires the CBO's assessment of whether private sector mandates exceed $100 million; however, in these cases, no point of order may be raised.[4] Of the 30 private mandates reported by committee, 17 became legislation in some form, 15 of which still exceeded the $100 million threshold.

In what is theoretically a significant retraction of regulatory authority from executive agencies, the Congressional Review Act of 1996 allows Congressional review of agency rule-making, granting Congress 60 days to review a regulation. If Congress passes a joint resolution of disapproval, the rule will not be implemented.

While this marked a potentially important change in the regulatory process, the change has been relatively minor: only the ergonomics rule in 2001 has been disapproved since the act took effect.

In summary, Congress has implemented some technical procedures with respect to unfunded intergovernmental mandates to bring some estimate of the size of mandates into the legislative process. No such technical process exists, however, to examine whether responsibilities should rest at the federal level as compared with State/local/tribal levels. There is also no mandated process to examine costs and benefits of regulatory legislation; however, there is substantial technical support that is provided on an ad hoc basis to Congress from the General Accounting Office (GAO), the Congressional Budget Office, and the Congressional Research Service (CRS). Not surprisingly, the weighing of costs and benefits has been left to the pluralistic process of bargaining among members of Congress, interest groups, and so forth.

[4] Likely because there are more potential private sector mandates.

Executive Branch

The 'How' Dimension

As noted above, in delegating authority to regulatory agencies, Congress gives the executive branch great discretion in delivering policy. As authorized by Congress, agencies go through particular consultative processes dictated by the Administrative Procedures Act. For example, agencies need to post Notices of Proposed Rule Makings (NPRMs) in the Federal Register, outlining the rule and its potential impact, as well as soliciting feedback from affected groups. Agencies also develop informal connections to organizations representing affected groups, especially beneficiaries of a potential regulation (Kerwin 1994).

The explosion of regulatory activity during the 1970s, combined with stagnation and inflation, caused pressure to mount on the government to reduce cost pressures on business, and on the Presidency to assert some control over this massive volume of technical policy. President Ford and then President Carter created ad hoc regulatory review processes that reviewed a select subset of rules. However, this mechanism proved ineffective for a number of reasons. First, the lack of institutionalized review did not allow the executive office to organize a staff experienced in particular areas of regulation; second, its size was inadequate to handle the massive quantity of policy involved.

In 1981, President Reagan created a larger scale, institutionalized regulatory review process with Executive Order 12291. This executive order specified that, where permitted by statute, regulations/proposed regulations with an economic impact of greater than $100 million should develop a 'Regulatory Impact Analysis', and that agencies should apply strict benefit-cost criteria to potential regulations. The order also required the Office of Management and Budget (OMB) to check new or proposed rules for consistency with the executive order. The review responsibility was placed within the OMB in the newly created Office of Information and Regulatory Affairs (OIRA).

The executive order was purely an executive branch procedural innovation and did not create legally enforceable criteria for regulation—that is, outside parties could not sue based on EO 12291.

Executive Order 12291 thus squarely addressed the 'how' of regulation; as we will discuss, the 'where' was added later.

The placement of review responsibilities in the OMB was important because of the OMB's insulation from many agencies' internal and external political pressures. Historically, the responsibility of the OMB, formerly the Bureau of the Budget, was to provide a reservoir of neutral policy expertise to the President. The OMB deals with high-volume, very technical minutiae common to policy in the executive branch—for example, budget requests, management of programmes, and, since 1981, regulatory policy. As executive agencies make budgetary or regulatory proposals that are then reviewed by the OMB, the agencies are placed in opposition to the OMB in a number of important ways. First, while other agencies attempt to expand their responsibilities and power, and thus tend to support greater government intervention and expenditure, the OMB does not benefit from government expansion. Second, the OMB is insulated from the constituencies affected by agency actions. This singular isolation of the OMB creates an inherent tension in OMB-agency relations. As one long-time member of OIRA stated:

> I think that we're not in the business per se of putting a lot of rules on the books . . . [W]e are interested in making sure as we implement the programs we do it . . . no more than the statute requires, because if you go [beyond] the statute, you usually impose an additional burden, so that's costly, it's got to show up somewhere. So we are more in the role of being skeptics. The agency's more in the role of promoting its programs. It gets money from the Congress to promote those programs, to put those programs in place, and get regulations in place to implement those programs. And that's really what they should be about. So there's . . . tension between what they see as their objective function, and what we see as our objective function. (As quoted in Lazer 1999: 17)

The review process therefore produces shared power in rule making between the OMB and regulatory agencies. The OMB, in reviewing regulatory proposals and analyses submitted by the agency, either accepts the agency's proposal without making any significant change, or proposes changes. In practice, the OMB review will examine whether the benefits of the rule given its costs are consistent with other federal rules, and whether the benefits of components of a rule given their costs are consistent with other federal rules.[5] If the costs of the rule seem balanced by its benefits, both aggregated and disaggregated, the OMB will typically accept the rule. If the OMB feels that the costs are not balanced by the benefits, or that the evidence is ambiguous, it either negotiates with the agency to make the rule more cost effective or pushes the agency to further research the rule's costs and benefits. If the agency resists OMB's changes, deadlock results, and the conflict can escalate to political appointees in the agency and potentially up to the White House.

The conflict generated by the institutionally opposed viewpoints of the agencies and the OMB ultimately permits the President some influence over the bureaucracy. Only if an agency anticipates political support from above—the President, for example—will the conflict escalate. This process

[5] In this process, the OMB will sometimes ask for additional data from the agency.

guarantees the President a steady stream of useful policy signals regarding the regulatory output of agencies, and has proven a powerful tool for the Presidency to assert control over regulatory policy (Lazer 1999). Figure 4.1 summarizes this process.

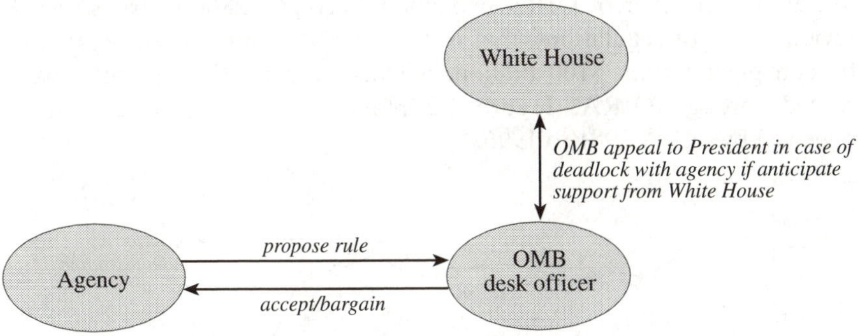

FIGURE 4.1. *The interactions among the President, Office of Management and Budget, and agencies*

The regulatory review process was a cornerstone of the Reagan deregulatory efforts during the 1980s, and, not surprisingly, was greatly criticized by Democrats, environmentalists, consumer advocates, unions, and so forth, on both the process and the substance of decisions. There were myriad substantive criticisms of the particular rules involved; the overarching criticism held that the executive order was inherently anti-regulatory and resulted in too much attention to the costs of regulation. The procedural criticisms were twofold: first, Congress had delegated regulatory authority to particular agencies and OMB involvement subverted Congressional intent; second, the process was invisible: no records existed of contact between OMB and affected parties, or of OMB-agency negotiations that resulted in any rule changes.

These criticisms were redoubled when Reagan supplemented EO 12291 with EO 12498, which mandated the publication of an annual Regulatory Program, in which, subject to OMB approval, regulatory agencies outlined their major regulatory initiatives for the upcoming year. As critics saw it, EO 12498 allowed unprecedented OMB intrusion in internal agency deliberations.

Clinton replaced EO 12291 and EO 12498 with EO 12886 in 1993.[6] Notably, given the strong Democratic criticisms of the Reagan regulatory

[6] For an insightful discussion of the differences between 12886 and 12291, see Shane (1995).

review process, President Clinton, while making significant changes to the order, retained the review process. The Clinton order contains three important modifications of the Reagan order. First, whereas EO 12291 did not specify a timetable for OIRA to review regulations, 12866 states that OIRA must complete its review within 90 days, 'to put some pressure on us', as one member of OIRA explained. Second, 12866 restricts OIRA review to major regulations, that is, those with an anticipated regulatory burden greater than $100 million; whereas under 12291 all rules were routed through OIRA. Figure 4.2 plots the number of regulations reviewed by OIRA 1981 to 1996.

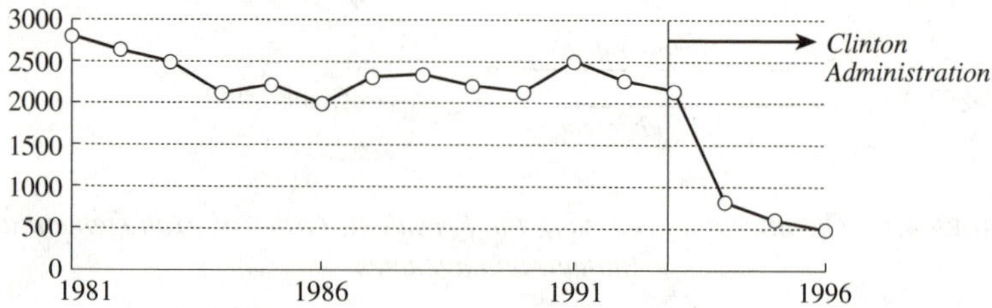

FIGURE 4.2. *Numbers of reviews conducted by Office of Information and Regulatory Affairs, 1981–1996*

Sources: 1981–9 data: US Government (1990); 1990 data: US Government (1991); 1991 data: US Government (1992). The data from the Clinton administration are available at the OIRA docket library, and from the author upon request.

As Fig. 4.2 highlights, the number of regulations seen by OIRA dropped more than 70 per cent. While this overstates the impact on OIRA, since it still reviewed the most important rules, it does, as one member of OIRA stated, reflect 'more trust of agency actions under the Clinton administration' (as quoted in Lazer 1999: 24).

Finally, EO 12866 contains sunshine provisions requiring a log of all communications between members of OIRA and non-federal employees, as well as a record of all changes to rules resulting from OMB review.

Table 4.1 summarizes the key procedural differences between the two executive orders.

The Clinton executive order also modified the key benefit-cost criteria that OMB used in its review. The Reagan executive order dictated that 'regulatory action shall not be undertaken unless the potential benefits to society for the regulation *outweigh* the potential costs to society'. In contrast, 12866 requires that 'each agency assess both the costs and the benefits of the intended regulation and, recognizing that some costs and benefits are difficult to quantify, propose or adopt a regulation only upon a reasoned

TABLE 4.1. *Procedural changes from Reagan/Bush order to Clinton order*

Clinton (12866)	Reagan (12291)
90-day timetable for review.	No timetable.
Only major (>$100 million economic impact) regulations subject to review.	All regulations subject to review; more thorough review requires of major regulations.
Sunshine provisions.	No sunshine provisions.

determination that the benefits of the intended regulation *justify* its costs'. These clauses highlight two notable differences between the two executive orders. First, the 'outweigh' criterion is a clearer, and more stringent, test of a regulation than a 'justify' criterion. As one interviewee stated,

> The decisional criteria are different under 12866, it's benefits justify costs, as opposed to benefits outweigh costs. And that's a major difference . . . In a justify scenario, the costs could outweigh the benefits by a factor of 10 before political reasons [intervene] . . . and we would go ahead with the rule. In an outweigh scenario, that presumably wouldn't happen. So that also increases the hand of the agencies, who are generally representing the intended beneficiaries of the rule more than we are. (As quoted in Lazer 1999: 23)

The second significant difference is Clinton's stipulation that regulatory impact analyses look at costs and benefits that may not easily be quantified. This reflects, as one informant stated, 'less emphasis on rigid quantitative analysis on the course of regulatory review'.

The 'Where' Dimension

The second dimension of 'rational regulation' proposed in the beginning of this paper is the issue of whether regulation occurs at the State or at the federal level. This was not part of the review process until 1987, when Reagan signed EO 12612. This order asserted the general superiority of policy-making at the state level, mandating very high thresholds for federal intervention. It required extensive review of federalism issues connected to the review process specified in EO 12291, and commanded a Federalism Assessment where potential federalism issues were involved.

The review mechanism established by Clinton has, in part, incorporated federalism criteria by requiring an analysis of unfunded intergovernmental mandates.[7] The Clinton regulatory review executive order specifically incorporates the economic impact on 'State, local or tribal governments or communities' as part of the overall cost calculation of a potential rule. It

[7] Note that the Reagan/Bush review process did not exclude unfunded mandates.

also requires, where possible, that an agency 'seek views of appropriate [s]tate, local, and tribal officials before imposing regulatory requirements that might significantly or uniquely affect those governmental entities'. This was then supplemented by EO 12875, which required consultative procedures where there were unfunded mandates.

In 1998 Clinton signed an executive order to replace the Reagan federalism executive order, EO 13083. It was suspended by Clinton within days of his signature, because of vociferous protests from State and local government representatives and their allies in Congress, none of whom had been consulted regarding the executive order. In 1999, Clinton signed a new federalism executive order, 13132, this time produced with extensive consultation with representatives of State and local governments.

The three executive orders embody substantially different approaches to federalism issues. While 12612 claimed a very limited role for the federal government, 13083 promoted a much more positive vision of its role. Finally, EO 13132 is really 12612 'lite': taking the very pro-federalist language of 12612 and toning it down, resulting in a document that has a broader view of federal action.

The contrast is immediately apparent in viewing the preambles to the three executive orders. Whereas 12612 repeatedly asserts that '[i]n most areas of government concern, the States uniquely possess' the capacity to govern, 13083 asserts the necessity to 'balance' federal and State power. Order 12612 thus suggests that states should do most of the governing, whereas 13083 suggests that there is a general need for the federal government to counterbalance the States. Order 13132, borrowing some of the language of 12612, proclaims that States possess 'unique' qualifications in governing, but does not say that States are 'uniquely' qualified, and is generally silent on how much governing should take place at the state versus the federal level (see Table 4.2 for a sample of excerpts contrasting the premises of the three executive orders).

Order 12612 therefore establishes a clear presumption in favour of State authority:

> In the absence of clear constitutional or statutory authority, the presumption of sovereignty should rest with the individual States. *Uncertainties regarding the legitimate authority of the national government should be resolved against regulation at the national level.* (emphasis added)

It also contains a special section on pre-emption, again establishing a strong presumption against the interpretation that Congress intends to pre-empt State law:

> To the extent permitted by law, Executive departments and agencies shall construe, in regulations and otherwise, *a Federal statute to preempt State law only*

TABLE 4.2. *Contrasting premises of Reagan and two Clinton Federalism Executive Orders*

EO 13083 (Clinton I)	EO 13132 (Clinton II)	EO 12612 (Reagan)
Federalism reflects the principle that dividing power between the federal government and the States serves to protect individual liberty. Preserving State authority provides an essential balance to the power of the federal government, while preserving the supremacy of federal law provides an essential balance to the power of the States.	Federalism is rooted in the belief that issues that are not national in scope or significance are most appropriately addressed by the level of government closest to the people. The Framers recognized that the States possess unique authorities, qualities, and abilities to meet the needs of the people, and should function as laboratories of democracy.	Federalism is rooted in the knowledge that our political liberties are best assured by limiting the size and scope of the national government. In most areas of government concern, the States uniquely possess the constitutional authority, the resources, and the competence to discern the sentiments of the people, and to govern accordingly.

when the statute contains an express preemption provision or there is some other firm and palpable evidence compelling the conclusion that the Congress intended preemption of State law, or when the exercise of State authority directly conflicts with the exercise of Federal authority under the Federal statute . . .

When a federal statute does not preempt State law . . . Executive departments and agencies *shall construe any authorization in the statute for the issuance of regulations as authorizing preemption of State law by rule-making only when the statute expressly authorizes issuance of preemptive regulations or there is some other firm and palpable evidence* compelling the conclusion that the Congress intended to delegate to the department or agency the authority to issue regulations preempting State law . . . (emphasis added)

Further, where 12612 asserts that regulation may be justified only for issues of 'national scope'—and does not define 'national scope'—and *not* for issues 'merely common to the States', 13083 makes the same distinction, but turns 12612 on its head, stating that problems that are 'merely common to the States' may not justify federal action, and further lists nine criteria for matters of national scope that might justify federal action:

(1) when the matter to be addressed by federal action occurs interstate as opposed to being contained within one State's boundaries;
(2) when the source of the matter to be addressed occurs in a State different from the State (or States) where significant amount of harm occurs;

(3) when there is a need for uniform national standards;
(4) when decentralization increases the costs of government thus imposing additional burdens on the taxpayer;
(5) when States have not adequately protected individual rights and liberties;
(6) when States would be reluctant to impose necessary regulations because of fears that regulated business activity will relocate to other States;
(7) when placing regulatory authority at the State or local level would undermine regulatory goals because high costs or demands for specialized expertise will effectively place the regulatory matter beyond the resources of State authorities;
(8) when the matter relates to federally owned or managed property or natural resources, trust obligations, or international obligations; and
(9) when the matter to be regulated significantly or uniquely affects Indian tribal governments.

This list of conditions evoked considerable controversy after 13083 was signed, and, unsurprisingly, EO 13132 does not enumerate affirmative justifications for federal actions. Instead, it again takes some of the profederalist language of 12612 and moderates it. For example, where 12612 says that 'uncertainties' in the authority of national government should be resolved against federal action, 13132 says that where there are 'uncertainties' the federal government should act with the 'greatest caution':

> The national government should be deferential to the States when taking action that affects the policymaking discretion of the States and should act only with the greatest caution where State or local governments have identified uncertainties regarding the constitutional or statutory authority of the national government.

Executive Order 13132 copies the language from 12612 regarding preemption, but modifies the language on prohibiting preemption. For example, 13132 removes 12612's admonishment to agencies not to pre-empt states 'To the extent permitted by law.'

Another example: where 12612 requires 'firm and palpable' evidence of Congressional intent to pre-empt, 13132 merely requires 'clear' evidence:

> Agencies shall construe in regulations and otherwise, a Federal statute to preempt State law only where the statute contains an express preemption provision or there is some other clear evidence that the Congress intended preemption of State law, or where the exercise of State authority conflicts with the exercise of Federal authority under the Federal statute.

> Where a Federal statute does not preempt State law . . . agencies shall construe any authorization in the statute for the issuance of regulations as authorizing preemption of State law by rulemaking only when the exercise of State authority

directly conflicts with the exercise of Federal authority under the Federal statute or there is clear evidence to conclude that the Congress intended the agency to have the authority to preempt State law.

Order 13132 also adds a passage on pre-emption that mirrors the EU proportionality criterion:

Any regulatory preemption of State law shall be restricted to the minimum level necessary to achieve the objectives of the statute pursuant to which the regulations are promulgated.

Federalism review. Where EO 12612 required an extensive review process routed through the OMB, and required designated officials at every department and agency to address implementation, 13083 removed these requirements—although 13083 does repeat the language of another executive order it was replacing, 12875, signed in 1993, noting that unfunded mandates on State and local governments required that evidence be submitted to the OMB on state and local government consultations. Order 13132 reaffirms the review process, requiring a 'federalism summary impact statement' for any regulation not required by statute that 'has federalism implications' or 'imposes compliance costs on State and local governments'. It also requires extensive consultation processes with State and local government, and maintains 12612's requirement of designated officials at every department and agency to address implementation.[8]

Waivers of statutory and regulatory requirements. Both Clinton executive orders incorporate the language of an earlier Clinton executive order, 12875, which addressed granting waivers to State and local government for the implementation of federal programmes—this language is identical in all three executive orders:

Increasing Flexibility for State and Local Waivers.
(a) Agencies shall review the processes under which States and local governments apply for waivers of statutory and regulatory requirements and take appropriate steps to streamline those processes.
(b) Each agency shall, to the extent practicable and permitted by law, consider any application by a State or local government for a waiver of statutory or regulatory requirements in connection with any program administered by that agency with a general view toward increasing opportunities for utilizing flexible policy approaches at the State or local level in cases in which the proposed waiver is consistent with applicable Federal policy objectives and is otherwise appropriate.

[8] Note that UMRA requires similar consultative procedures. Since 12875 preceded UMRA, the incremental impact of UMRA was small; however, it did provide a statutory basis for the review of unfunded mandates by OMB.

(c) Each agency shall, to the extent practicable and permitted by law, render a decision upon a complete application for a waiver within 120 days of receipt of such application by the agency. If the application for a waiver is not granted, the agency shall provide the applicant with timely written notice of the decision and the reasons therefor.
(d) This section applies only to statutory or regulatory requirements that are discretionary and subject to waiver by the agency.

The Reagan executive order did not address these issues. Executive order 12875 was aimed at programmes for which the federal government provided much of the funds, but that were administered by the States. Traditionally, the States were highly constrained in their administration of federal programmes, but under EO 12875, the States have much more discretion in administering these programmes, most notably in the case of welfare.

Three approaches to federalism. The three executive orders are thus a study in contrasts: EO 12612, in principle, establishes a very high threshold for federal regulation as well as an ostensibly powerful review process. It does *not* establish a prescriptive basis for federal regulation except in statutory requirements. That is, it does not attempt to delineate when federal action is best and when State action is best. Rather, it begins with the assumption that State governance is innately superior to federal governance.

Executive order 13083 does establish a prescriptive basis for federal regulation, as well as for State and local regulation over federal regulation, where 'diversity', healthy 'competition', and experimentation are especially important. It does not, however, attempt to establish a method for weighing the benefits of federal regulation as compared with the benefits of State regulation, and it fails to establish any review mechanism that would create such a method.

Finally, 13132 adopts somewhat more positive language than 12612 regarding federal action, retains at least the outlines of a review process, but again does not establish a prescriptive criterion for federal action. In fact, it removes what is the clearest criterion in 12612—which was simply that if the federal government does not *have to* act, it should not act.

Thus, strikingly, none of the orders attempts to establish some administrative review mechanism to prescribe the level at which a policy should be made.

Implementation of the 'How' and the 'Where' Criteria

There has been a dramatic disjuncture in the treatment by the executive branch of the two dimensions of rational rule making. The presidency's institutional need to gain some control over regulatory policy flow created regulatory review. Given the integrative nature of the Presidency, this creates a natural brake on regulation, relative to leaving it in the agencies' hands, although how often that brake is applied depends on the president—Reagan and Bush were more inclined to apply that brake than Clinton. The review process, however, with its focus on weighing benefits and costs, complements the OMB's inherent objectives. Federalism does not fit into the OMB's agenda, except, to a limited extent, with respect to unfunded mandates and to the reduction of the regulation of federal programmes administered by the States. Thus, for example, a GAO study of the impact of 12612 shows that agencies prepared federalism assessments for only five out of 11,000 final rules, and that regulatory agencies adopted very high thresholds at which to require a federalism review.[9]

This lack of impact by 12612 is unsurprising. Federalism criteria, like benefit-cost, do not have a natural home in agencies. Further, unlike benefit-cost analysis, they do not have a natural home in the OMB. This, combined with a lack of attention by the Reagan, Bush, and Clinton administrations, made 12612 a non-priority.

Unsurprisingly, there is no evidence that EO 13137 resulted in a re-energized implementation of federalism criteria at the end of the Clinton administration.

Summary

There has been some movement towards adding technocratic review procedures in the legislative processes for unfunded intergovernmental mandates, and somewhat less in unfunded private sector mandates. However, the process is still predominantly pluralistic—and always will be.

In executive administrative processes there has been significant movement towards adding technocratic review procedures with respect to weighing benefits and costs. There has been little movement towards adding effective mechanisms with respect to federalism issues, except for unfunded mandates and for granting more flexibility in administering certain federal programmes. While there has been no rigorous analysis of whether review processes have made a difference, anecdotally it appears that the regulatory review process does put pressure on agencies to maintain some consistency between the benefits and costs of a rule, and to examine what parts of a rule do not add benefits commensurate to their costs.

[9] GAO/T-GGD-99-93

3. The 'Where' and 'How' of Regulation Within the European Union

For decades, the 'where' of regulation within the European Union was assessed by reference to primary Community law, namely the amended treaties of the European communities and the rules of Community competence they included.

The Community's decision to legislate a particular matter was its prerogative, and needed no justification based on efficiency or appropriateness. Once duly enacted it could be nullified only if the European Court of Justice declared that the Community had overstepped its authority. Given the generally extensive interpretation of Community authority by the Court, the threat of invalidating Community legislation was limited.

Member States were willing to accept this centralized set-up because in practice, with the exception of competition legislation enacted directly by the Commission, all Community legislation had to be agreed on unanimously by the European Council. If a Member State felt that the Community was taking on a regulatory matter better handled by national Member States' legislation, passage of the questionable Community regulation could easily be blocked in the Council. In this sense, the European Council functioned as a parliamentary 'upper house', reminiscent of the original structure of the US Senate, when Senators were not elected by popular vote but by State legislatures. Because such a direct representation of Member States' governments was coupled with the important requirement of unanimity, the chance of Member States facing Community legislation on matters that they thought should have been nationally regulated was minimal (see Schilling 1995; Weiler 1991).

The introduction of quality majority voting (QMV) in the Council changed this: Community legislation could be passed despite individual Member States' opposition, which especially concerned nations with strong national agendas like Britain, and with elaborate federal structures, like Germany (Follesdal 1999).

Introducing 'Subsidiarity' to the EU

The Community also faced opposition from the public. The problem was the perceived 'distance' between the citizens and 'Brussels', shorthand for the European institutions. This feeling of powerlessness by the population as well as by Member States with national agendas was to be cured by introducing into Community law the principle of 'subsidiarity'.

'Subsidiarity' in its most general meaning describes 'the allocation or the use of authority within a political order where there is no unitary sovereign' (Follesdal 1999). It mandates that a legislative action should not be taken at a higher level within a system unless this higher level is more effective in achieving the legislative goal (Trachtman 1997; Follesdal 1999). While it centres on the essence of the question of 'where' to regulate in a multi-tiered system, the term 'subsidiarity' itself has different connotations and meanings for different constituencies.

In untangling subsidiarity's strands, de Búrca (1999) labelled the attempt to bring legislative decision making as close to the citizen as possible 'democratic' subsidiarity. In contrast, he describes 'executive' subsidiarity as the issue of whether Community law-makers or national legislatures retain the authority to regulate a matter. Both of these dimensions of subsidiarity were advocated in the debates leading up to its formal incorporation into Community law.

'Subsidiarity' was introduced at the Community level first by the Single European Act (SEA) with reference to environmental policy (Art. 130), then prominently by the Maastricht Treaty, through its amendments to the Treaty of the European Community (TEC).[10] According to Art. 5 TEC, the Community shall take action only 'if and insofar as the objectives of the proposed action cannot be sufficiently achieved by the Member States and can therefore, by reason of the scale or effects of the proposed action, be better achieved by the Community'. This notion of 'subsidiarity' was combined with the principle of 'proportionality', the rule that any Community action must not go beyond what is necessary to achieve the objectives of the TEC (Art. 5 para. 2 TEC). In sum, Art. 5 TEC forces the EU institutions, particularly the Commission, to examine Community competency not from a purely formal-legal, but also substantive viewpoint, with goal-oriented proportionality and regulatory efficiency.

The Maastricht Treaty's emphatic endorsement of this conception of subsidiarity left many questions unanswered. Some of them were addressed by the Amsterdam Treaty of 1997, which further defined the use of subsidiarity embodied in Art. 5 TEC through the Protocol on the Application of the Principles of Subsidiarity and Proportionality (see Table 4.3).[11]

The Protocol aims at specifying the process by which subsidiarity and proportionality are to be achieved. It does not, however, define subsidiarity. Rather, para. 5 of the Protocol lists two 'aspects' of the subsidiarity

[10] The principle of subsidiarity was introduced into the TEC through Art. 3b, which because of a subsequent renumbering of the TEC is now Art. 5. While still sometimes referred to as Art. 3b, in this article we will refer to the subsidiarity principle as Art. 5 TEC.

[11] Protocol (No 30) on the application of the principle of subsidiarity and proportionality, OJ C 340, 10/11/1997, p. 0105; see also the Declaration relating to the Protocol on the application of the principles of subsidiarity and proportionality, OJ C 340, 10/11/1997, p. 0140.

TABLE 4.3. *The development of subsidiarity and proportionality criteria*

Single European Act	Maastricht Treaty	Amsterdam Treaty
Subsidiarity introduced to Community level with reference to environmental regulations.	Art. 3b (now Art. 5) enshrines subsidiarity and proportionality as guiding principles for Community legislation.	Protocol No. 30 details process by which planned Community legislation needs to be assessed *vis-à-vis* subsidiarity and proportionality. Necessity and effectiveness criteria are introduced. Procedural subsidiarity reiterated.

principle, which need to be met to justify Community action. The first of these aspects, the 'necessity criterion' (EU Commission 1999), requires for Community action that the objectives of the proposed action cannot be sufficiently achieved by Member States' action. The second aspect, the 'effectiveness criterion' (EU Commission 1999), demands that the objectives can be better achieved by action on the part of the Community. These two criteria must be substantiated by the Community 'by qualitative or, wherever possible, quantitative indicators'.[12] A few guidelines—transnational aspects, possible conflict with Treaty requirements, and Community action as clear benefits by reason of scale or effect—are added in the Protocol to help in the decision making. The Protocol also dictates that Community action shall be 'as simple as possible'[13] and favours national implementation wherever possible.[14]

When this understanding of subsidiarity is compared with its original, more general mandate of seeking the appropriate 'where' of regulation across all layers of rule-making—not only between Community and Member States—the limitations of the EU's subsidiarity approach become apparent (Follesdal 1999). The fundamental supremacy of Community law remains largely untouched. Subsidiarity is to guide the Community only in its legislative activities. Member States may appeal to the Court where they feel the Community disregarded subsidiarity, but national legislatures cannot override Community legislation in cases where they feel subsidiarity would warrant it.[15] Furthermore, sub-

[12] Para. 5 of the Protocol. [13] Para. 6 of the Protocol.

[14] Para. 7 of the Protocol.

[15] See also the Declaration relating to the Protocol on the application of the principles of subsidiarity and proportionality, OJ C 340, 10/11/1997, p. 0140

national entities cannot secure from the EU's principle of subsidiarity a mandate to have regulatory authority transferred to them from national legislatures.

Publicly, the new principle of subsidiarity was portrayed almost as the saviour of the Union (Schilling 1995). Member States hailed the fact that substantive competence issues now played a more important role in the assessment of Community legislation. However, and less visible, questioning the appropriate level of legislation—Community versus national—Member States who objected to substantive issues in proposed Community legislation were able to frame their opposition in more formal, neutral terms of subsidiarity.

Implementing Subsidiarity

The Commission was requested to report once a year on the implementation of the subsidiarity and proportionality principles in the drafting process of its legislative proposals. Much talked about, the Commission promised to review all of its legislative proposals and later declared it would abandon several of them in light of subsidiarity. Indeed, the total number of commission proposals has dropped from 787 in 1990 to 667 in 1993 to 491 in 1998. Further substantial reductions have been announced since then (see Fig. 4.3).

Impressive as these numbers may seem, they present only part of the picture. As the Commission itself conceded in its 1998 report (EU Commission 1999), roughly a third of all legislative proposals were necessary implementations of international agreements the EU had concluded.

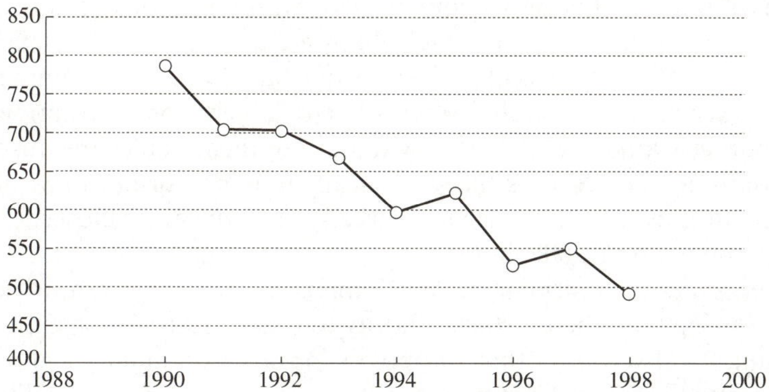

FIGURE 4.3. *Number of EU Commission proposals*

Source: EU Commission (1999)

A further 25 per cent of legislative proposals concerned amendments to existing Community law. Thus only about 40 per cent of all proposals considered by the EU can be termed new initiatives and thus subject to full-blown subsidiarity review. This 40 per cent was cut by another 10 per cent for legislative actions mandated by existing Community law—that is, annual price fixings—which brings subsidiarity review to roughly only a third of the total proposals considered. Consequently, the very application of subsidiarity—since Maastricht a prime principle in EU law, second only to the principle of anti-discrimination—is already limited to fewer than one in three of the Community's legislative proposals.

One should not, however, overlook the fact that the question of subsidiarity need not be limited to just 'new' legislative initiatives. Implementation of international agreements could arguably take place at national levels, and amendments to existing community law could restrict the scope of community regulations in favour of national legislative action. Therefore, the restriction of the scope of subsidiarity review is by deliberate choice, rather than by an independent external factor.

Other important aspects of the Community proposal decline are also sometimes neglected. The reason for the large number of Community proposals in the early 1990s was the EU's push to complete the legal framework for the common market by 1992. Once the common market framework was in place, the number of proposals decreased. Furthermore, the Commission's reason for abandoning proposals often was not that the proposal violated subsidiarity. On a number of occasions, in order to prove its support of subsidiarity, the Commission abandoned what it viewed as less important proposals, while keeping alive the momentum for proposals it considered strategic, regardless of the proposal's impact on subsidiarity.

The withdrawal of proposed directives for harmonization of frequencies for commercial aircraft and train telephony are cases in point.[16] Ironically, these are exactly the type of matters better handled at the Community level to ensure inter-operability for what is largely communications in cross-border traffic. Nevertheless, withdrawing them, under the auspices of subsidiarity, helped pass the strategically more important draft directives that opened national telecom markets—an issue much closer to subsidiarity than aircraft telephony.

In reporting on subsidiarity, the Commission further downplayed its role of seizing the 'where'—the authority to initiate legislative action—by reporting that two out of three proposals for new Community legislation are suggested by other Community institutions. It took responsibility for

[16] Interview with DG IV source by author.

initiating only 10 per cent of all Community proposals under consideration in 1998 (EU Commission 1999).[17]

Adding 'How' to 'Where': The New 'Commission Mix'

The Commission has attempted to deflect potential criticism of its insensitivity towards even the limited principle of subsidiarity enshrined in the Maastricht Treaty by pointing at other Community institutions. In addition, it has recently combined the issue of 'where' to regulate—subsidiarity and proportionality—with the issue of 'how' to regulate. The Commission's 'how' focuses on enhancing the quality of legislative drafting, simplifying, and consolidating proposals, and in general offering a process of continuous information and consultation of law-making to the interested public. Prime evidence for this shift are the annual Commission reports on subsidiarity implementation. Originally called 'Report on the Application of the Principle of Subsidiarity' (COM(93) 545 and COM(94) 533), in later years it has been expanded to include legislative quality and was renamed 'Better Lawmaking'. Over only a handful of years, the once treasured buzzword of 'subsidiarity' has been completely dropped from the title. To be sure, the report still talks about subsidiarity, but primarily by defining what it does *not* mean and to which areas it does *not* apply.

This blending together of subsidiarity and the more process-oriented issue of legislative quality further dilutes any residual prominence subsidiarity might have had. While after Maastricht it had enjoyed only very limited importance in daily Community affairs, it now seems to have lost much of its publicity value as well. A much foggier concept of 'better law-making'—an eclectic mix of issues on 'where' and 'how' to regulate—has taken its place in the official debate.

Why has Europe permitted the once revered principle of subsidiarity to play such a minimal role in the actual Community law-making?

A number of reasons can be suggested, focusing mainly on shifts in the agenda of the various players involved. Public opinion and media attention in Europe have drifted away from post-Maastricht fatigue associated with the desire for subsidiarity to more acute topics, like the ambitiously centralizing monetary union, the challenging drive for widening the EU eastward, or the agonizing issues of EU's stance on security exemplified by the break-up of former Yugoslavia.

The Commission, which always feared subsidiarity might lead to loss of power, greatly supported diluting its value. The European Parliament,

[17] Reductions have also been caused by consolidating planned regulations informally and as part of the Single Market Initiative programme; it continued this line of argument in EU Commission (1999).

long a supporter of subsidiarity—in part because it saw subsidiarity as supporting its own quest for more power—lost interest in it after it discovered the more powerful political weapon of a vote of no-confidence in the Commission.

The Member States had lost much interest in subsidiarity as well. As the Commission never failed to point out, the European Council proposed by far the highest number of legislative initiatives.[18] Thus Member States started to fear that pushing for more subsidiarity might backfire by restricting not so much the Commission's regulatory agenda but the Council's own. Recent changes in the governments of Britain and Germany, the two Member States most adamantly in support of subsidiarity—albeit for very different reasons—resulted in a substantially diminished push by them towards subsidiarity. In addition, shifting public opinion also changed the issue's landscape among the Member States' governments. Overall, the Council and the Member States willingly took the Commission's bait that much of subsidiarity's mission had already been achieved.

Implicit 'Procedural' Subsidiarity: Structurally Combining 'Where' and 'How'

However, there may be another reason for the rather quick demise of subsidiarity as it was framed by the Maastricht Treaty. While most explanations focus on the changing agendas of the players involved, subsidiarity may have been short-lived because a different, more viable variant of it had been embodied by the Community treaties from the outset: 'procedural' subsidiarity (de Búrca 1999)

The principle of subsidiarity embodied in Art. 5 TEC requires Community institutions, primarily the Commission, to evaluate whether a matter should be regulated on the Community level or left to Member States. It holds that regulatory competence rests exclusively within either the Community or the Member States. Framed this way, the question of 'where' can be answered only in a simple either/or.

However, this is rarely the law-making approach applied by the Community. Most Community legislation is enacted not in the form of directly applicable regulations, but in the form of directives that need to be transposed into Member States' laws by national legislatures. In doing so, Member States enjoy a certain flexibility to adapt Community rules to national circumstances. Furthermore, since the early 1980s, Community law in more sensitive areas has often been passed in the form of so-called

[18] See for example EU Commission (1999); aptly, the Commission subtitled its report on 'better law making' a *shared* responsibility.

'framework directives' that in effect provide national law-makers even more freedom in implementation.

By employing legislative methods with such a 'built-in' subsidiarity, the Community has, over time, incorporated the principle of subsidiarity in its law-making process. In stark contrast to 'executive' subsidiarity—the main principle enshrined in Art. 5 TEC—the procedural strand does not exclusively distribute regulatory authority. Instead, authority is shared between the Community and the national law-making bodies. The 'where' of Community law-making then occurs at both levels of the Community/Member States system.

To be sure, procedural subsidiarity cannot substitute for democratic subsidiarity. Law-making is confined to national and Community institutions. Sub-national law-making units in federal Member States will perhaps feel overlooked. But they are not worse off than with the executive subsidiarity approach of Art. 5 TEC. The inclusiveness of procedural subsidiarity gives it an advantage over Art. 5 TEC's executive subsidiarity. As competence is not exclusive, there are no obvious winners or losers. Taking the threat of losing power out of the regulatory process drastically reduces the stakes from a pure power perspective, which has arguably blocked any substantial changes in the system of executive subsidiarity.

Procedural subsidiarity fosters a legislative centre in which the Community prescribes the goals and, with some flexibility, the means to achieve them. National law-makers find themselves in a Community-wide 'regulatory competition'. This is a very limited 'market of regulations'—restricted by the outer limits outlined in each Community directive—but a market nevertheless.[19]

Defining these outer limits appropriately is difficult but necessary for the overall system to work. Given too much flexibility, national legislatures may enact implementation regulations too varied to achieve the directive's goal of harmonization. Given too little flexibility, national law-makers might feel disempowered and the Community might lose the benefit of regulatory competition. Measures taken by the Community, such as the 'mutual recognition' approach to harmonization since the early 1980s (Reich 1992), and intensified action against Member States that fail to correctly implement—'transpose'—directives into national law (EU Commission 1999), have contributed to the creation of enough centripetal forces to permit continued use of procedural subsidiarity.

Procedural subsidiarity may also play a positive role in the willingness of national law-makers to transpose Community directives. Transposal

[19] For more detailed analysis and implications see Reich (1992); Joerges (1997); critically Sun and Pelkmans (1995); in a broader context Genschel and Plümper (1997).

rates have consistently been very high, with well over 90 per cent of directives implemented in Member States. Thus, while the importance of executive subsidiarity decreased after 1992, the transposal rate steadily increased from below 90 per cent in 1990 to a record 95.7 per cent in 1998—in 1997 it was 94 per cent (see Fig. 4.4).

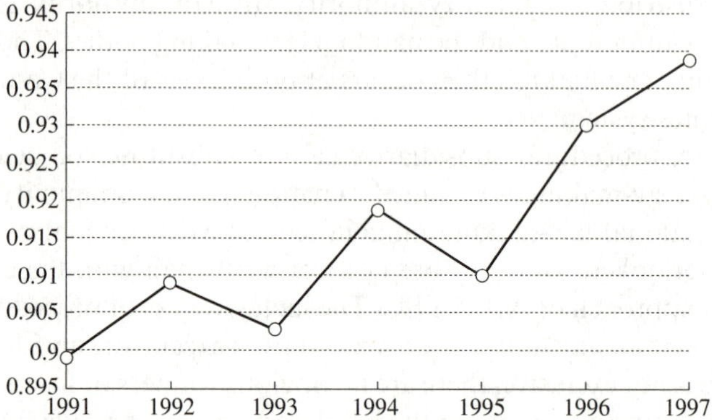

FIGURE 4.4. *Transposal rate of directives (per cent), 1991–1997*
Source: EU Commission (1999)

This does not suggest a causal link between the demise of executive subsidiarity and transposal rates. Rather, the increase in transposal rates—overall and for each of the Member States—is indicative of the relative success of procedural subsidiarity: national law-makers seem to accept their role as substantive implementers of more general Community directives in a system of shared legislative power across layers.

De Búrca (1999), in his eloquent analysis of procedural subsidiarity, points to the 'Protocol on the Application of the Principle of Subsidiarity' in the 1997 Amsterdam Treaty as a driving force behind this new concept. Indeed, the protocol includes explicit guidelines stipulating, among others, that, all else being equal, directives should be preferred to regulations and framework directives to directives (para. 6) and 'Community measures should leave as much scope for national decisions as possible' (para. 7). But the protocol's impact on Community rule making—the 'how' of regulations—is difficult to measure, especially given the fact that for decades the preferred law-making method of the Community has been the directive. The protocol then just restates what has always been informal Community policy. And it is precisely this tradition of preferring directives that has ensured procedural subsidiarity a central place in the Community's legislative process.

In a very real sense then, the issue of subsidiarity—the 'where' of regulation—is linked with the question of 'how' to regulate. The European Union's attempt to structure the 'where' in the form of executive subsidiarity has been much reported and debated. Its outcome is meagre. But a different form of the principle—procedural subsidiarity—has fared much better, not only because of the diminishing exclusivity of the 'where', but also because it links to the appropriate method of 'how'.

4. Conclusion

Comparing the 'how' and the 'where' of regulation in the US and EU produces insight into both the structural similarity and dissimilarities of the two entities. First, it is striking that the processes to address the 'where' dimension have not found a natural home in the executive branches of either the EU or the US (Table 4.4). In the US, efforts to require a relatively modest federalism review have had essentially no impact on the regulatory process. No bureaucratic actor was willing to invest significant energy in pursuing a federalism agenda, and no political actor—neither the President nor Congress—has imposed that agenda. In the EU, where one might have expected subsidiarity to have stronger political backing, the Commission has not energetically pursued subsidiarity, and external political pressures on it to do so have now subsided.

TABLE 4.4. *Examples of implementation of 'where' criteria*

	Examples of 'where' criteria	Implementation impact
European Union	Single European Act	None
	Maastricht Treaty	Minor
	Amsterdam Treaty Protocol No. 30	Unknown
United States	Federalism executive orders 12612, 13083, and 13132	None
	Unfunded mandates reform act	Minor

In contrast, institutional processes addressing the 'how' dimension have found a much more natural home in both the US and the EU (Table 4.5). In the EU the procedures set up to implement subsidiarity—the 'where' dimension—have gradually evolved into processes to deal with the 'how' dimension. In the US, procedures set up to implement the 'how' dimension have effectively rejected efforts to graft 'where' standards in the process as well.

TABLE 4.5. *Examples of implementation of 'how' criteria*

	Examples of 'how' criteria	Implementation impact
European Union	Directive as pre-eminent legislative tool	Moderate to substantial
United States	Regulatory review executive orders 12291 and 12866	Moderate to substantial

However, in both the US and the EU, where the central government needs the cooperation of lower governments, there are significant efforts to give lower-level governments discretion in implementing federal/EU policies. Thus, in Europe, the EU sets the overall policy through directives, but gives constituent states substantial discretion in implementation. In the US, in recent years, flexibility granted to state governments in implementing federal programs, such as welfare, has greatly increased. Thus we see a convergence of approaches in the US and the EU.

This parallel, however, also illustrates the fundamental dissimilarity of the two federal systems. The EU has very limited capacity to actually implement any policies, but instead must rely mostly on Member States to implement its policies. Law-making through directives and related approaches thus encompass much of what the EU does. In contrast, the US federal government has considerable capacity to directly implement its policies. Thus—in dramatic contrast to the EU—federal policies regulating health, safety, environment, and so forth, are carried out to a large extent by the federal government.

References

De Búrca, G. (1999). *Reappraising Subsidiarity's Significance after Amsterdam* (Jean Monnet Working Paper Series, WP N7/99). Cambridge, MA: Harvard University Law School.

EU Commission (1999).1999 Commission Report to the European Council on Better Lawmaking, CM (1999) 562 final. Brussels.

Follesdal, A. (1999). *Subsidiarity and Democratic Deliberation* (ARENA Working Paper, No. 99-21). Oslo: Research Council of Norway.

Genschel, P. and Plümper, T. (1997). *Regulatory Competition and International Cooperation* (Working Paper No. 97-4). Cologne: Max Planck Institute for the Study of Societies.

Joerges, C. (1997). 'The Market without the State? The "Economic Constitution" of the European Community and the Rebirth of Regulatory Politics' (*European Integration Online Papers* 1/19). European Community Studies Association Austria.

Kerwin, C. (1994). *Rulemaking: How Government Agencies Write Law and Make Policy*. Washington, DC: Congressional Quarterly Press.

Lazer, D. (1999) *Regulatory Review: Presidential Control through Selective Communication and Institutionalized Conflict* (Working Paper No. 98-21). Cambridge, MA: Kennedy School of Government Politics Research Group.

Reich, N. (1992). 'Competition Between Legal Orders: A New Paradigm of EC Law?'. *CML Rev* 29: 861–96.

Schilling, T. (1995). *Subsidiarity as a Rule and a Principle or: Taking Subsidiarity Seriously* (Jean Monnet Working Paper). Cambridge, MA: Harvard University Law School

Shane, P. (1995). 'Political Accountability in a System of Checks and Balances: The Case of Presidential Review of Rulemaking'. *Arkansas Law Review*, 48/1: 161–214.

Sun, J. and Pelkmans, J. (1995). 'Why Liberalisation Needs Centralisation: Subsidiarity and EU Telecoms'. *World Economy*, 18, 5: 635–65.

Trachtman, J. (1997). *Trade and . . . Problems, Cost-Benefit Analysis and Subsidiarity* (Jean Monnet Working Paper). Cambridge, MA: Harvard University Law School.

US Government (1990). *Regulatory Program of the United States Government*. Washington: Government Printing Office.

——(1991). *Regulatory Program of the United States Government*. Washington: Government Printing Office.

——(1992). *Regulatory Program of the United States Government*. Washington: Government Printing Office.

US Government, General Accounting Office (1998*a*). *Unfunded Mandates: Reform Act Has Little Effect on Agencies' Rulemaking Actions*. Letter Report, 02/04/98, GAO/GGD-98-30. Washington: Government Printing Office.

——(1998*b*). *Federalism: Implementation of Executive Order 12612 in the Rulemaking Process*, Statement, 05/05/99, GAO/T-GGD-99-93. Washington: Government Printing Office.

Weiler, J. (1991). 'The Transformation of Europe', *Yale Law Journal* 100: 2438–41.

5

Devolution in the United States: Rhetoric and Reality

JOHN KINCAID

While debates about subsidiarity have waxed and waned in the European Union, there has been much talk in recent years of a 'devolution revolution' (Nathan 1996; Kingsley 1996; Conlan, 1998) in the American federal system. One observer even declares that authority has been 'cascading' from Washington, DC 'to lower levels of government' (Donahue 1997: 7). The Republican majority elected to the Congress in 1994 championed devolution as part of its plan to 'renew America' (Gingrich 1995) while Democrats in their 1996 presidential party platform claimed that 'Republicans talked about shifting power back to the states and communities—Democrats are doing it'. Yet, when one examines the academic and journalistic literature as well as political rhetoric, one finds only two commonly cited examples of devolution: congressional repeal of the national 55/65mph speed limit and welfare reform (Kincaid 1998; 1999*b*).

Both occurred in 1996; neither conforms to any customary definition of 'revolution'; and neither is, strictly speaking, an example of devolution. The repeal of the national speed limit was simply the repeal of a regulatory condition that had been attached to federal highway aid as part of the Emergency Highway Energy Conservation Act of 1973. Welfare reform, embodied in the Personal Responsibility and Work Opportunity Act of 1996, abolished the 61-year-old Aid to Families with Dependent Children categorical grant—along with the entitlement status of this type of welfare—and created a block grant called Temporary Assistance for Needy Families (TANF). The block grant gives States more administrative flexibility than they possessed in the past over various aspects of welfare provision, but only within the boundaries of onerous conditions which, among other things, obligate the States to ensure that, by 2002, 50 per cent of all recipients from all welfare families are working at least 30 hours a week and that 90 per cent of all recipients from two-parent welfare families are working at least 35 hours a week. Failure to meet this condition results in reductions of federal funding. Temporary Assistance for Needy Families is, therefore, as conservatives have put it, a block grant with moral principles enforced by fiscal hammers, not devolution.

Similarly, a recent book titled *Medicaid and Devolution: A View from the States* (Thompson and DiIulio 1998) argues that federal steps toward devolving more Medicaid authority to the States have been accompanied by as many, or more, steps toward centralization. Much of the book is devoted to a hypothetical question: what if there were significant Medicaid devolution to the States? The book takes this tack, perhaps, because the editors began their project in 1996, when it appeared that a Republican Congress might devolve Medicaid. However, devolution proposals were soundly defeated in Congress, in part because of President Clinton's veto threats.

The Intermodal Surface Transportation Act of 1991 (ISTEA) was also cited by many observers as a significant harbinger of devolution. Indeed, since completion of the interstate highway system, the federal-aid highway programme has been viewed by many economists and transportation experts as a prime candidate for virtually total devolution, including a turnover of the federal motor-fuels tax to the States (US Advisory Commission on Intergovernmental Relations 1987). The Intermodal Surface Transportation Act did delegate significant administrative discretion to the States and local governments, particularly the country's 339 metropolitan planning organizations; however, the 1998 reauthorization of the highway programme, the Transportation Equity Act for the 21st Century (TEA-21), neither broadened nor deepened 'devolution' in this field (Dilger 1998).

It is not surprising, therefore, that a recent survey of chief administrative officers of all US cities with populations over 100,000 found majorities of city officials detecting no devolution or being quite uncertain about devolution (Cole, Hissong, and Arvidson 1999). For example, when asked if devolution had produced more flexibility and discretion for city officials, 9 per cent said 'definitely yes', 29 per cent said 'probably yes', 24 per cent answered 'uncertain', 32 per cent said 'probably no', and 5 per cent said 'definitely no'. When asked if, overall, devolution policies had had an effect on their cities, 10 per cent said 'definitely yes', 30 per cent said 'probably yes', 25 per cent answered 'uncertain', 32 per cent said 'probably no', and 3 per cent said 'definitely no'. It is surprising that more respondents did not answer affirmatively because the survey's authors simply assumed the existence of devolution. The authors did not ask the respondents if devolution actually exists or to identify any specific devolution policies, and their survey questions suggested a very broad definition of devolution.

Consequently, there is a considerable disjunction between the rhetoric of devolution and the reality of devolution.

1. Devolution Definitions

A key problem with the devolution debate is that there is no consensually accepted definition of 'devolution'. In addition, the term is often confused with, or used interchangeably with, 'delegation', 'deregulation', and 'decentralization'. Devolution is often implicitly defined as political, fiscal, and/or administrative transfers of functional responsibilities from a large areal government to smaller areal governments. In the United States, this means devolution of responsibilities from the federal government to State and/or local governments, or devolution of responsibilities from States to local governments. However, this is a very broad definition that encompasses any delegation of flexibility or discretion, no matter how small, to State and local governments.

Devolution could more appropriately be defined as a transfer of specific powers or functions from a superordinate government to a subordinate government. The transfer is of constitutional magnitude, even if not effected through a written constitution—for example, devolution in the United Kingdom; it is ordinarily intended to be permanent; it surrenders all the powers associated with the devolved functions—that is, political, administrative, and fiscal; and it leaves the functional field vacant for occupancy by subordinate governments. Devolution, therefore, occurs in the context of a vertical relationship between governments. Hence, devolution can occur within the United Kingdom's parliamentary union, for instance. It can also be said to occur within the 50 American States where, constitutionally, local governments are creatures of their States.

Strictly speaking, however, devolution cannot occur between the United States government and the 50 States without constitutional change. There are three principal reasons for this. First, the United States and the 50 States are co-sovereign constitutional polities; the States are not creatures of, or subordinate to, the United States government. Second, the United States government is one of limited, delegated powers; all powers not delegated to the federal government remain constitutionally reserved to the States or to the people (Tenth Amendment). Third, the Congress is not a supreme legislative body. Federal law is supreme only within its realm of constitutionally delegated authority; otherwise, State law is supreme. Furthermore, although the United States government cannot exercise powers not delegated to it, the States can exercise many powers delegated to the federal government but not exercised by the United States government. These are among the reasons, therefore, as to why the term 'devolution' has no lineage in American political discourse prior to the mid-1980s.

Of course, as a practical matter, liberal interpretations of the US Constitution by the US Supreme Court, the Congress, and presidents have allowed the United States government to pre-empt, regulate, and otherwise intrude upon the entire range of powers constitutionally reserved to the States. Consequently, the federal system is vastly more centralized today than it was even 30 years ago (Kincaid 1993). In this context, therefore, virtually any gesture of flexibility and discretion by the federal government toward State and local governments might be mistaken for devolution. In reality, though, every conceivable example of devolution one can find in academic or political rhetoric is actually a 'turnback' of authority previously reserved to the States. The repeal of the national highway speed limit, for example, simply restored to the States a power they had exercised for 184 years. Indeed, strictly speaking, the federal government never pre-empted—that is, displaced under the supremacy clause—this power. The Congress simply enacted a crossover sanction providing that any State failing to comply with the national speed limit would lose significant portions of its federal-aid highway money.

However, given that 'devolution' is the currently predominant term, it will be employed here in order to avoid confusion about the current debate.

2. Explanations for the Rhetoric-Reality Disjunction

There are, perhaps, three sets of explanations for the disjunction between devolution rhetoric and devolution reality in the United States.

First, devolution has been limited in the United States because (1) political interests cannot translate generalized support for devolution into agreements on specific devolutions, and (2) functional responsibilities cannot, in any event, be sorted out neatly between the federal, State, and local governments.

The first part of this explanation relates to a now general political phenomenon in which citizens hold contradictory sentiments. For example, generalized support for cutting government budgets cannot be translated easily into agreements on specific cuts because vested interests protect their own budget benefits while supporting reductions of benefits to other interests. Similarly, opinion polls show that citizens simultaneously support lower taxes and higher spending, along with reductions in the size of the federal government and increases in federal programmatic responsibilities. Consequently, when congressional Republicans proposed major and significant quasi-devolutions through block grants of such programmes as Medicaid, which accounts for about 42 per cent of all federal aid to State and local governments, these proposals were all defeated by a combination of pressures from opponents in Congress, presidential veto threats, and vested interests. Likewise, congressional Republicans pledged to terminate more than 20 domestic programmes funded at $75.3 billion in 1995. Only several small programmes were terminated; the remaining set of programmes was funded at $77 billion in 1999.

The second part of this explanation acknowledges what has long been recognized by most observers of the federal system, namely, that all public functions are shared intergovernmental—that is, federal, State, and local—responsibilities (Elazar 1984). Consider policing, for example. There is no convincing rationale, let alone political support, for establishing a federal police force to perform local police functions nationwide. There are, however, rationales for State and federal fiscal support of policing in fiscally distressed communities, State rules governing police personnel and training, State and federal prohibitions on racial profiling, federal requirements that police officers inform suspects of their Miranda rights, and so on. Policing was intergovernmentalized in the twentieth century, as were all other government functions. Even in foreign affairs, for example, the issue of reparations to Holocaust victims from Swiss banks was forced on to the international agenda by US State banking and insurance commissioners and attorneys-general, not by US government officials.

There is some evidence, moreover, that citizens prefer federal–State–local power-sharing in most functional policy areas. A recent survey of Michigan residents found that, overall, they embrace 'marble cake' federalism in which functions are intergovernmentalized rather than 'layer cake' federalism in which functions are neatly sorted out among the federal, State, and local governments (Thompson and Elling 1999).

The second general explanation is more complex and less firm because relevant research is virtually non-existent. Put simply, devolution rhetoric appears to be inflated out of proportion to reality because (1) President Reagan's popularity and President Clinton's popularity made devolution a fashionable political trope and (2) both proponents and opponents of devolution have vested interests in inflating the rhetoric and/or reality of devolution, thereby making 'devolution' a broad and variably defined buzz word.

Devolution-like language entered academic and journalistic discourse because of Reagan's New Federalism proposals of the early 1980s. As Reagan said in his first inaugural address: 'It is my intention to curb the size and influence of the Federal establishment and to demand recognition of the distinction between the powers granted to the Federal government and those reserved to the states' (US Senate 1989: 33). Although Reagan's proposals barely resonated with voters, the far-reaching implications of redistributing power in the federal system did register with political actors, interest groups, State and local officials, and academics who study these matters. Consequently, even though the reality of devolution during the Reagan years fell far short of Reagan's rhetoric, Reagan's proposals generated intense and continuing debate about devolution among academics and political actors in the intergovernmental arena.

Devolution came to the fore again during the Clinton administration, as reflected, for instance, in Clinton's 1996 declaration of 'the end of the era of big government' and in his reinventing government programme (National Performance Review 1993). To the extent there has been some devolution in terms of increasing State and local administrative discretion, it has occurred under Clinton. For example, the Clinton administration issued more waivers of federal law for States to experiment with welfare and Medicaid reform than any previous administration. There is disagreement about why this is so, but one corollary hypothesis is that Democrats in Congress resisted waivers during the Reagan years because they believed that Reagan would misuse waiver authority to the detriment of social welfare, much as President Nixon had misused the impoundment power in an effort to gut President Johnson's Great Society programmes. Congressional Democrats have expressed more trust in Clinton's use of waivers, while the Republican majority swept into Congress by the 1994 elections has generally supported Clinton's waiver activity because that activity has not been radically liberal. This 'devolution', however, involves waivers of federal law by the executive branch, not changes in federal law by the Congress. Waivers, moreover, are granted only after federal agencies approve plans submitted by the States. As such, waivers produce asymmetric devolution rather than uniform devolution across the States.

Both Reagan and Clinton enjoyed unusually strong and sustained public support, and both have been the only full two-term presidents since Dwight D. Eisenhower—who also campaigned unsuccessfully against centralization. Both also delivered a strikingly similar message, albeit from different political perspectives: namely, that they would help the people take power back from the corrupt politicians in Washington. This is the popular political rhetoric of devolution. Neither president used the word 'devolution' for popular consumption, however, because it would not resonate with the voters. Instead, the preferred rhetoric employs such terms as 'power to the people', 'community empowerment'—one of Clinton's favourite terms—and 'individual empowerment—a Republican favourite. Although this rhetoric is, in part, 'mere rhetoric', it is not frivolous because policy proposals do flow from it. This rhetoric also acknowledges that public trust and confidence in the federal government had already plummeted by the time of Reagan's election in 1980 and has not yet recovered its previous highs, while public trust and confidence in local and State governments has increased since the mid-1980s (Cole and Kincaid 2000).

Regarding the second part of this explanation, proponents of devolution appear to inflate both the rhetoric and the reality of devolution for the obvious purpose of promoting devolution. Opponents indirectly inflate the rhetoric of devolution by seeking to deflate that rhetoric. In turn, they seem to inflate the reality of devolution in an effort to demonstrate that devolution has already gone too far and that further devolution will have horrendous consequences. For example, one critic of devolution argues that power is, in fact, 'cascading' down to States and localities and that such 'wholesale devolution invites the balkanization of America' (Donahue 1997: 14). Likewise, in the preface to a series of publications by the liberal Century Foundation titled 'The Devolution Revolution', the series editor, Carol Kellerman, makes the absurd claim that: 'Under Reagan, more than 500 categorical programs were consolidated into nine block grants' (Donahue 1999: viii). In reality, Reagan's nine block grants consolidated 77 categorical grants and terminated only 62 additional categorical grants (Conlan 1998: 96). Overall, there were 534 categorical grants when Reagan entered office in 1981. This number dropped to 392 in 1984, but then increased to 478 when Reagan left office in early 1989. By 1995, there were 618 categorical grants, plus 15 block grants (US Advisory Commission on Intergovernmental Relations 1995: 14). The series preface makes other incorrect and misleading statements, all for the purpose of sounding 'a clear warning of the dangers we face if the balance of power shifts too heavily in the prevailing [devolution] direction' (Donahue 1999).

A third possible explanation for the disjunction between devolution rhetoric and devolution reality is that support for selective devolution exists on both the left and right—liberal and conservative, respectively, in the United States—ends of the political spectrum because (1) politically, during the era of mostly divided government—that is, different party control of the three branches of the US government—that the nation has experienced since 1968, interests at each end of the political spectrum fear that forces at the other end will gain sufficient control of federal institutions to centralize their policy preferences and devolve their policy aversions, thereby encouraging forum shopping; (2) ideologically, both the left and the right have long had elements sympathetic to State and local autonomy; and (3) extremists are more likely than moderates to prefer devolution.

Conservative Republicans champion devolution in certain policy fields because they believe that the Democrats' New Deal and Great Society policies created an excessively powerful and intrusive federal government that sucked power out of the States and local communities, thereby enervating civil society, destroying traditional values, and undermining liberty. At the same time, though, conservative Republicans support centralization in certain policy fields because they wish to impose their policy preferences nationwide: for example, the Defense of Marriage Act of 1996. Liberal Democrats oppose devolution in certain policy fields because they believe that Republicans wish to gut many New Deal and Great Society policies by devolving them to the States. At the same time, liberal Democrats support devolution and oppose centralization in policy fields where they believe that Republican centralization has destroyed or weakened—or will do so—more liberal State and local policy-making. For example, most liberal Democrats have opposed Republican efforts to pre-empt—that is, displace—State product-liability laws so as to enact a federal product-liability statute that would limit damages and otherwise reduce corporate exposure to liability. Liberal Democrats wish to devolve more consumer-protection authority to the States because they believe that the States, most of whose attorneys-general have been Democrats, are more aggressive consumer advocates than Presidents Reagan and Bush, the Republican Congress, and the predominantly Republican federal judiciary. Similarly, conservative Republicans will be more likely than liberal Democrats to support the National Rifle Association's current effort to secure federal legislation to prohibit local governments from suing gun manufacturers for gun-related violence.

Divided government, therefore, along with greater party competition in most States, seem to have encouraged more intergovernmental forum shopping in which parties and interest groups seek to lodge policy-making authority in the government most friendly to their interests. Liberals, for whom the federal government was the preferred forum for the past 60 years, now find States and localities to be more friendly forums for some of their interests. The Republican success in capturing the legislative branch of the federal forum has given conservatives a taste for exercising federal power to achieve their policy objectives nationally.

Regarding the second part of the explanation, sectors of the political right have long had a well-recognized aversion to—and, on the extreme right, an implacable hostility toward—federal power. A thread of decentralized communitarianism has also run through the American left, beginning at least with Thomas Jefferson's romantic vision of a confederation of ward republics. This thread was almost broken during the 1960s when it became clear to the left that individual civil rights could not be secured without federal power overriding States' rights: for example, to eliminate race segregation in the southern States. Nevertheless, sectors of the New Left committed to neighbourhood organizing and communitarianism sustained the notion that 'power to the people' is best secured locally rather than nationally. The rise of Republican power in the federal establishment appears to have reinforced this thread as more individuals on the left have sought to revive a liberal vision of local communitarianism in the face of Reagan/Gingrich-style nationalism.

Sectors of both the left and the right also tend to be enamoured of the democratic potential of modern technology to 'flatten hierarchies' and empower individuals and local communities. The telecommunications revolution has, in their view, rendered old urban-industrial models of command-and-control organization obsolete in both the private and the public sectors. Instead, democracy should be refashioned electronically into non-centralized, interactive, and interdependent networks of individuals, communities, and voluntary associations operating with less and less reliance on a large 'central' government. Thus, as Kirkpatrick Sale (1998: 23) put it recently, 'you have the antiauthoritarians, the decentralists of all stripes, anti-big government, antistatist, communitarian, the anarchocommunalists and communitarians and communards and anarchists on the Left, and the libertarians and Jeffersonians and individualists on the Right, and they're really not so far apart'.

Regarding the third part of the explanation, recent game-theoretic research suggests that extremist voters tend to prefer the decentralization that would flow from devolution, while moderate voters tend to prefer centralization (Crémer and Palfrey 1999). All other things being equal, retaining or locating power in the federal government is more likely to produce decisions that lie closer to the ideal point of the median voter. This theory is plausible in part because extremist voters are more likely than median voters to turn out for primary elections to nominate party candidates for Congress and the presidency; however, it is also divorced from empirical reality, and it may not account for voter perceptions of excessive centralization that might shift the median voter's ideal preference point toward devolution. The religious right, for example, consists mostly of previously moderate and politically quiescent voters who were galvanized into political action by what they regard as concerted federal assaults on their values, especially the US Supreme Court's *Roe v. Wade* (1973) abortion ruling.

3. Devolution Politics

Politics can be defined as 'the authoritative allocation of values' (Easton 1965). Every federal arrangement, particularly the distribution or redistribution of powers, involves significant value tradeoffs (Kincaid 1995). Shifting the locus of decision-making authority in a federal system can dramatically alter decision-making outcomes. Consequently, the nationalization or the devolution of various powers in the American federal system is of tremendous political importance as well as personal significance for citizens. To take an obvious, heated example, a devolution of abortion policy-making to the States would be as much a revolution as was the US Supreme Court's centralization of abortion policy-making in 1973.

As such, the devolution debate is one facet of the cultural warfare evident in American political life since the 1960s. Although the general public pays virtually no attention to this debate per se, and has little understanding of federalism, interest-group action is triggered from all relevant sectors of the public when interest groups become aware of the consequences of specific devolution proposals.

In addition, even though there has been little devolution to date, there is fiscal pressure for devolution in the federal system because, despite the current federal budget surplus, there continues to be less budgetary room for discretionary spending. Entitlement spending and other payments to individuals now consume about 70 per cent of the federal budget and could consume a larger portion of the budget in the future. Consequently, the federal government will likely be compelled to off-load to the States fiscal responsibility, if not also administrative and political responsibility, for some domestic functions. De facto fiscal devolution, therefore, is probable in the long run.

It is partly this fiscal prospect that led Alice M. Rivlin (1992) to argue that the federal government should assume responsibility for all redistributive welfare programmes and devolve all developmental—for example, highways, education, economic development—programmes to the States. Rivlin has been an important figure in the devolution debate because she is a liberal Democrat who served as director of Clinton's Office of Management and Budget, and now serves on the Board of Governors of the Federal Reserve Bank.

Rivlin's argument reflects another important dimension of the devolution debate, namely, attempts to formulate a rational, purposeful approach to devolution. Advocates of devolution argue principally that devolution will produce greater efficiency, effectiveness, and accountability in governance. Efficiency would be promoted primarily by tying public functions more closely to their territorial economies of scale. Effectiveness would be promoted because centralized bureaucracies have limited knowledge of, and limited ability to respond to, localized diversities. Democratic accountability would be promoted because functional responsibilities would be moved 'closer to the people'.

Opponents often concede the efficiency argument, but counter that efficiency gains would be offset by equity losses under devolution because (1) poor jurisdictions—for example, the State of Mississippi and the city of Camden, New Jersey—lack the fiscal capacity and human capital to manage devolved responsibilities, and (2) the poor and minorities would bear the brunt of inequities induced by devolution. Inequities would be aggravated by heightened interjurisdictional competition (Kenyon and Kincaid 1991), especially 'races to the bottom' whereby States would drive down social welfare spending so as not to become 'welfare magnets', reduce environmental protection in order to promote economic development, lower progressive taxes in order to attract the rich, and so forth—although, to date, there is no evidence of racing to the bottom. Opponents also argue that many States lack the ability to improve the effectiveness of devolved policies and that devolution does not necessarily enhance democratic accountability because it often moves policy-making closer to politicians in the State capital or city hall than to the people themselves. Indeed, former US House Speaker Newt Gingrich (1995) has argued that devolution should really bypass State and local officials so as to empower citizens directly.

The devolution debate in the United States is also a reflection of the worldwide debate about devolution, decentralization, deregulation, denationalization, and dereservation of State enterprises and lands, and decriminalization of market and voluntary sector activities in the face of widespread perceptions of the economic and political failures of the centralized state (Wunsch and Olowu 1995), especially since the fall of the Berlin Wall in 1989. These 'de' words are invariably linked to democratization, even though, again, reality often falls short of the rhetoric.

Arguably, however, the most potent force for altering the balance of federal-State power at the turn of the century is the non-elected US Supreme Court. While the European Court of Justice has been playing an important role in constitutionalizing the treaties that underlie the EU and in enhancing the powers of the EU (Starr-Deelen and Deelen 1996)—a role similar to that played by the US Supreme in the American federal system for much of the twentieth century—the US Supreme Court has changed direction by issuing a series of rulings since the early 1990s in which the Court has not devolved power to the States *per se* but rather, for the first time since 1937, limited and rolled back the reach of federal power by using the Tenth and Eleventh Amendments to the federal Constitution, the republican guarantee clause of the Constitution (Art. IV, Sec. 4), and various judicial doctrines to shield State powers from federal encroachment (Kincaid 1999*b*). Nevertheless, nearly all of the Court's federalism rulings have been 5-4 decisions; hence, a change of only one justice on the Court could halt this line of State-friendly rulings.

4. Implications for the European Union

The relevance of devolution debates in the United States for the European Union is difficult to discern because the US and the EU are vastly different. Furthermore, subsidiarity, the related Catholic term in Western Europe, has no base or history in the largely Protestant American federal tradition. Historically, subsidiarity has assumed that there is a centre of power that rules over an organic or quasi-organic polity in which the local extremities need protection and support in order to function as vital organs within the body politic. Historically, the American federal tradition has assumed that there is not, and should not be, a single centre of power. The States are not peripheries, and local governments are not extremities; they are constituent elements of what James Madison called a 'compound republic'.

Devolution debates in the United States also occur in the context of relatively limited conceptions of government. Americans generally view government as performing more limited functions than is ordinarily the case in continental Europe's social welfare states. As Carl J. Friedrich pointed out many years ago, the average American has no conception of the European notion of 'the state', let alone the French notion of *dirigisme*. Furthermore, given that many public functions are performed non-governmentally in the United States and that notions of free enterprise are deeply embedded in American culture, the current debate about devolution is only one part, and not the biggest part, of larger balance-of-power debates in the American system, especially debates about the balance of power between the public sector—that is, the state—and the private sector—that is, civil society. Consequently, subsidiarity debates in the more statist-oriented European Union have, perhaps, more urgency than in the United States.

There are different perceptions of federalism as well. In the United States, 'federalism' is now usually associated with decentralization and States' rights. This is a major reason why the Clinton Administration generally shunned the word 'federalism' in favour of the adjective 'intergovernmental', whereas the Reagan Administration preferred 'federalism' over 'intergovernmental'. In the EU, federalism is often associated with centralization. The federalists usually want 'ever closer union'; the anti-federalists usually want 'never closer union'. These perspectives on federalism make some sense because the EU is a union still in the making while the United States is a 211-year-old union remaking itself in the aftermath of twentieth-century centralization. The EU's anti-federalists, therefore, can point to the United States as an example of what can go wrong with 'ever closer union'. A major implication of the US devolution debate for EU advocates of subsidiarity, then, is that a failure to entrench subsidiarity in Community law and practices now might allow more and more power to gravitate toward the EU, recapitulating the American experience.

Structurally, however, the EU is hybrid. It is neither international nor national and neither wholly confederal nor wholly federal (Kincaid 1999*a*), nor is there consensus on these matters. Intergovernmental relations in the EU may often look like intergovernmental relations in the United States or other federal polities, but all relations between governments, intranationally and internationally, have certain similar bargaining and negotiating characteristics. Such relations in the EU, moreover, run on two tracks: (1) intergovernmental relations characteristic of international relations and (2) intergovernmental relations characteristic of domestic intragovernmental relations. The most important EU policy decisions are made on the former track, the international/confederal track, but the execution of those decisions must try to switch on to the latter track, the national/federal track. The American federal system operates entirely on the latter track.

Two intergovernmental consequences flow from this difference. For one, unlike US citizens, EU citizens are essentially passengers on the trains that run on these intergovernmental tracks. Only the EU Parliament is elected by citizens of the EU, but the Parliament's powers are extraordinarily limited compared with the powers of the legislative bodies of the Member States and of the US Congress. This 'democratic deficit' limits the ability of EU citizens to influence the subsidiarity debate. There is no comparable 'democratic deficit' in the US federal system; hence, the balance of federal-State power is shaped partly by citizen preferences. United States intergovernmental relations, moreover, are shaped primarily by elected officials, especially the Congress and the president, as well as governors and mayors, who are accountable to their constituents. The US Supreme Court sets certain limits on the scope of federal and State powers, but otherwise stays out of the game of intergovernmental relations. Bureaucrats shape the daily administrative dynamics of federal-State-local relations, but they are constrained by constitutional, statutory, and regulatory limits set by their respective legislative, executive, and judicial superiors. In the American system, elected officials, especially legislators, also intervene in specific and detailed bureaucratic matters much more than is usually the case in Western Europe.

Second, given that intergovernmental relations in the United States operate on the national/federal track within common cultural, linguistic, and legal frameworks, there is less need for formal intergovernmental institutions and mechanisms than is the case in the EU. Federal, State, and local officials are accustomed to working together and communicating with each other, and the common English-language framework alone, for instance, allows all actors, including street-level bureaucrats like police officers and firefighters, to engage directly in intergovernmental relations spontaneously and as necessary. Consequently, there is nothing comparable in the United States to the elaborate commitology system that has emerged in the European Union. Instead, intergovernmental relations are fluid; organized mechanisms tend to be ad hoc; and there is no command centre or coordinator for intergovernmental relations. Furthermore, the ongoing institutions that address intergovernmental issues are mostly non-governmental associations of government officials, such as the National Governors' Association and National League of Cities, and associations of professionals, scientists, and citizens sharing certain interests. These associations also promote considerable uniformity throughout the federal system, not by directives, but by consensus-building processes in which federal, State, and local members across the country come to share common ideas and to agree on standards of performance. Such fluidity may not be possible in the EU because intergovernmental relations operate on two tracks that connect Member States which have different cultures, languages, and legal systems. Consequently, advocates of union may perceive a greater need for the EU to impose uniformity and harmonization from above than is the case in the United States, while advocates of subsidiarity may be alarmed about looming centralization. Furthermore, there are many more turf-protection concerns in the EU than in the United States. National and regional rules governing programme content and language on television and radio, for example, are virtually non-existent in the United States but extremely important and volatile in most of Western Europe.

Another implication, especially of the US difficulty in actually devolving powers, is that in a complex, interdependent world, it is extremely difficult to sort out public functions among different governments in any neat, rational fashion. All public functions are likely to involve intergovernmental power-sharing in one way or another. Indeed, power-sharing is part of the essence of federalism, and in so far as federalism legitimizes power-sharing among multiple centres of power in a multi-centric, rather than multi-layer or multi-tier, arrangement, it necessarily fosters intergovernmental cooperation, collusion, conflict, coercion, and competition that encourage all governments to seek pieces of the action in all fields, thus rendering functional distributions of power dynamic rather than static. The centralization that has occurred in the United States has rarely involved wholesale federal occupation of policy fields that deprives States of powers in a zero-sum manner; instead, it has usually involved a growing federal fiscal and regulatory role in policy fields, often in a positive-sum manner in which there is a concomitant expansion of State and/or local government powers. After World War II, moreover, the federal government engaged in many capacity-building exercises to help State and local governments become stronger intergovernmental partners.

Hence, issues of process are vital, and, in the final analysis, these issues are primarily political and secondarily constitutional. In the United States, devolution debates occur within a highly legitimized and constitutionalized process in which citizens have many points of direct authoritative voice and representation, as well as virtually unfettered interjurisdictional mobility. In the European Union, the subsidiarity debate occurs within the context of a partially legitimized and only quasi-constitutionalized process in which citizens have little direct authoritative voice and representation, as well as limited cross-national mobility. Consequently, there may be limits to federalization and power-sharing in the EU, limits that might be very acceptable to EU citizens and limits that will become all the more apparent with enlargement into central and eastern Europe and possibly Turkey. The EU is a unique experiment, and there is no reason to believe that it will or should become a United States of Europe or Federal Republic of Europe. On the contrary, it could become a complex, multifaceted, asymmetric confederation of confederations, federations, and unitary systems in which centralization, power-sharing, and subsidiarity will vary among policy fields and in which core Member States will be more highly integrated than peripheral Member States.

References

Cole, Richard, and Kincaid, John (2000). 'Public Opinion and American Federalism: Perspectives on Taxes, Spending, and Trust—An ACIR Update'. *Publius: The Journal of Federalism*, 30: 189–201.

——, Hissong, Rodney V., and Arvidson, Enid (1999) 'Devolution: Where's the Revolution?', *Publius: The Journal of Federalism*, 29/Fall: 97–111.

Conlan, Timothy (1998). *From New Federalism to Devolution: Twenty-Five Years of Intergovernmental Reform*. Washington, DC: Brookings Institution Press.

Crémer, Jacques and Palfrey, Thomas R. (1999). 'Political Confederation', *American Political Science Review*, 93: 69–83.

Dilger, Robert Jay (1998). 'TEA-21: Transportation Policy, Pork Barrel Politics, and American Federalism', *Publius: The Journal of Federalism*, 28/Winter: 49–69.

Donahue, John D. (1997). *Disunited States*. New York: Basic Books.

——(1999). *Hazardous Crosscurrents: Confronting Inequality in an Era of Devolution*. New York: The Century Foundation Press.

Easton, David (1965). *A Systems Analysis of Political Life*. New York: John Wiley.

Elazar, Daniel J. (1984). *American Federalism: A View from the States* (3rd edn). New York: Harper and Row.

Gingrich, Newt. (1995). *To Renew America*. New York: HarperCollins.

Kenyon, Daphne A. and Kincaid, John (eds) (1991). *Competition among States and Local Governments: Efficiency and Equity in American Federalism*. Washington, DC: Urban Institute Press.

Kincaid, John (1993). 'From Cooperation to Coercion in American Federalism: Housing, Fragmentation, and Preemption'. *Journal of Law and Politics*, 9: 333–433.

——(1995). 'Values and Value Tradeoffs in Federalism'. *Publius: The Journal of Federalism* 25/Winter: 29–44.

——(1998). 'The Devolution Tortoise and the Centralization Hare'. *New England Economic Review* (May/June): 13–40.

——(1999*a*). 'Confederal Federalism and Citizen Representation in the European Union'. *West European Politics* 22/April: 34–58.

——(1999*b*). 'De Facto Devolution and Urban Defunding: The Priority of Persons Over Places'. *Journal of Urban Affairs*, 21: 135–67.

Kingsley, G. Thomas (1996). 'Perspectives on Devolution'. *Journal of the American Planning Association*, 62: 419–25.

Nathan, Richard P. (1996). 'The Devolution Revolution: An Overview'. *Rockefeller Institute Bulletin 1996*. Albany: Nelson A. Rockefeller Institute of Government, State University of New York: 5–13.

National Performance Review (1993). *Creating a Government that Works Better and Costs Less: Report of the National Performance Review*. Washington, DC: US Government Printing Office.

Rivlin, Alice M. (1992). *Reviving the American Dream: The Economy, the States and the Federal Government*. Washington, DC: Brookings Institution.

Sale, Kirkpatrick (1998). 'An Overview of Decentralism'. *The Good Society* 8/2: 23–5.

Starr-Deelen, Donna and Deelen, Bart (1996). 'The European Court of Justice as a Federator'. *Publius: The Journal of Federalism* 26/Fall: 81–97.

Thompson, Frank J. and DiIulio Jr, John J. (eds) (1998). *Medicaid and Devolution: A View from the States*. Washington, DC: The Brookings Institution Press.

Thompson, Lyke and Elling, Richard C. (1999). 'Let Them Eat Marblecake: The Preferences of Michigan Citizens for Devolution and Intergovernmental Service-Provision'. *Publius: The Journal of Federalism*, 29/Winter: 139–53.

US Advisory Commission on Intergovernmental Relations (1987). *Devolving Selected Federal-Aid Highway Programs and Revenue Bases: A Critical Appraisal.* Washington, DC: ACIR.

——(1995). *Characteristics of Federal Grant-in-Aid Programs to State and Local Governments.* Washington, DC: ACIR.

US Senate, 101st Congress, 1st Session (1989). *Inaugural Addresses of the Presidents of the United States.* Washington, DC: US Government Printing Service.

Wunsch, James S. and Olowu, Dele (eds) (1995). *The Failure of the Centralized State: Institutions and Self-Governance in Africa.* San Francisco: ICS Press.

6

Federalism in the European Union: Rhetoric and Reality

ANDREW MORAVCSIK

It is an appropriate moment to take stock of the European Union (EU). Over the past half-century, the EU successfully expanded its substantive scope and institutional mandate until it now stands without parallel among international institutions. These institutions are so significant that political innovation in contemporary Europe is as likely to come from Brussels as the national capitals.

Consider first the substance of European Union policies. Tariffs, quotas, and most customs barriers within Europe have been all but eliminated. In regulatory areas such as environmental policy, competition—that is, anti-trust—policy, agricultural policy, and various types of industrial standardization, the EU is a dominant regional and global force. Today close to 80 per cent of new economic regulation of productive activity in Western Europe comes from Brussels. European Union spending on agriculture and regional policy totals 5–10 per cent of the GDP of smaller Member States. The EU is a bone fide superpower in the area of global trade negotiations. It is hardly an exaggeration to say that, at least until recently, what the US and EU decide under the General Agreement on Tariffs and Trade (GATT) and the World Trade Organization (WTO) is what happens. Thirteen of the 15 Member States of the EU have agreed to a common currency and a monetary policy centralized in Frankfurt. Discussions are under way concerning common social, transport, immigration, police, foreign, and defence policies.

For suggestions and comments in response to presentations of variants of this argument, I am indebted to David Cameron, Geoffrey Garrett, Robert Howse, Robert Keohane, Charles Maier, Kalypso Nicolaidis, Joseph Nye, George Ross, Andrea Sangiovanni, Cindy Skach, Anne-Marie Slaughter, Helen Wallace, and participants in meetings at Yale University, Duke University, the Delegation of the Commission of the European Communities (New York), the annual meeting of the European Community Studies Association (Canada), the Kennedy School of Government, and the European Union Center at Harvard University.

Consider next the EU's uniquely stable and powerful institutions. The European Court of Justice (ECJ) has established the supremacy of EU law, the right of individuals to file suits on this basis—direct effect—and overall constitutional review for consistency with the Treaty of Rome, which is binding through the near-uniform acceptance of its decisions by domestic courts.[1] The powers of the directly elected European Parliament (EP) have steadily increased over the past decade.[2] The European Commission enjoys exceptional autonomy among international secretariats. It holds a unique power of proposal in core legislative procedures, considerable responsibilities to implement regulations, and unique prosecutorial powers in areas like anti-trust. The European Council is a forum for permanent meetings. Under its aegis, thousands of meetings among national officials, ministers, and heads of state and government are held annually, resulting in hundreds of pieces of legislation.

This spectacular record of growth and achievement has sparked controversy. Euro-enthusiasts favour an emergent European federal state. The success of the EU, they argue, clearly demonstrates not only that European integration has been successful, but that integration breeds more integration through myriad spillovers. Moreover, many Euro-federalists maintain, the status quo is unstable. This is the so-called 'bicycle theory': should integration cease, the 'rider' will fall off and progress to date will be lost. Euro-sceptics, led by British and American conservatives, by contrast, evaluate federalism negatively.[3] They warn of the rise of a 'superstate' in Brussels run by democratically illegitimate technocrats—a 'bureaucratic despotism' recalling the *ancien régime* in France and, in a few more extreme formulations, the Nazi dictatorship in Germany.[4] In this view those who would defend democracy and freedom, as well as the existing accomplishments of European integration, should band together globally—even if this means effective withdrawal from all or part of the EU—to fight the creation of a European superstate.[5] If

[1] Anne-Marie Burley and Walter Mattli, 'Europe before the Court: A Political Theory of Legal Integration', *International Organization*, 47/1 (1993), 41–76.

[2] Richard Corbett, Francis Jacobs, and Michael Shackleton, *The European Parliament*, 4th edn (London: Cartermill, 2000).

[3] For discussions of the bicycle theory, see George Ross, *Jacques Delors and European Integration* (Oxford: Polity Press, 1995); Andrew Moravcsik and Kalypso Nicolaidis, 'Keynote Article: Federal Ideals and Constitutional Realities in the Treaty of Amsterdam', *Journal of Common Market Studies*, 36 (1998, Annual Review), 13–38.

[4] For an intelligent but inflated comparison to the *ancien* regime, by way of de Tocqueville, stressing the threat of 'bureaucratic despotism', see Larry Siedentop, *Democracy in Europe* (London: Penguin, 2000). Numerous Tory politicians have obliquely raised the parallel to Nazi Germany.

[5] Bill Cash (Conservative MP), 'Is the EU a Threat to U.S. Sovereignty?', remarks presented at the American Enterprise Institute, Washington DC (4 April 2000). For a response

determined opposition fails, efforts to establish European federalism will surely lead the EU to overreach, thereby undermining not just new projects, but progress to date—a sort of 'reverse bicycle theory'.

The battle between Euro-enthusiasts and Euro-sceptics grabs the headlines and tempts political entrepreneurs, but it disguises broad agreement on shared assumptions. Journalistic commentaries, politicians' speeches, and scholarly articles agree on two main points. First, something akin to a federal nation-state is the natural outgrowth of current developments in Europe. Second, in order to be legitimate such a federal state must be substantially more democratic—that is, more accountable to popular majorities than the EU is today.

As is so often the case in ideological debates, the middle is missing. The current debate between Euro-enthusiasts and Euro-sceptics overlooks a plausible position, one that is distinctive in both a positive and a normative sense. Perhaps Europe is not headed for a substantially more federal and democratic future. Perhaps, instead, we already glimpse the constitutional compromise that is the logical endpoint of European integration, at least for the foreseeable future. The current position of the EU is likely to remain unchanged for some time. Perhaps the major functional tasks that could optimally be carried out at a regional level—liberalization of movements in goods, services, and factors, monetary stabilization, and economic regulation closely connected with trans-border externalities or non-tariff barriers to competitiveness—are already launched. Perhaps, moreover, the functional pressure for cooperation that has powered European integration for two generations is lessening and nothing comparable will replace it. The EU may expand geographically, reform institutionally, and deepen substantively, but all this will take place largely within existing contours of European institutions. Perhaps the existing hybrid status quo is sufficiently efficient and adequately legitimate to resist any fundamental institutional reform.

If we accept the premise—the line of argument I shall explore in this chapter—two conclusions follow, one positive and one normative.

The positive conclusion: *the EU is not a superstate in the making*. The contemporary EU is far narrower and weaker a federation than any extant national federation—so weak, indeed, that we might question whether it is a federation at all. The EU plays almost no role—at most a weak sort of international coordination—in most of the issue-areas about which European voters care most, such as taxation, social welfare provision, defence, high foreign policy, policing, education, cultural policy, human

to this 'conservative idealist' line of reasoning, see Andrew Moravcsik, 'Conservative Idealism and International Cooperation', *Chicago Journal of International Law* (forthcoming).

rights, and small business policy. European Union institutions are tightly constrained, moreover, by supermajoritarian decision rules, a tiny administration, radical openness, stringent provisions for subsidiarity, a distinct professional ethos, and the near-total absence of the power to tax and coerce. The EU was designed as, and remains primarily, a limited international institution to coordinate national regulation of trade in goods and services, and the resulting flows of economic factors. Its substantive scope and institutional prerogatives are limited accordingly. The EU constitutional order is not only barely a federal state; it is barely recognizable as a state at all. To term it a 'superstate' is absurd.

The normative conclusion: *the current institutional form of the EU may well be democratically legitimate, despite the absence of many institutional opportunities for direct participation in majoritarian decision-making.* Current critics judge the EU against an abstract standard of democratic participation rather than assessing it as a second-best constitutional compromise designed to cope pragmatically with concrete problems. Constitutional checks and balances and indirect democratic control appear adequate to avoid abuse. The insulation of decision-makers, moreover, can be justified as a second-best means to empower median voters against powerful but particularistic interests—such as protectionist economic sectors, concentrated recipients of government assistance, and oligopolistic producers. It is striking, in this regard, that the political functions that the EU carries out—constitutional adjudication, trade negotiations, technical administration, central banking, and criminal prosecution—are rarely subject to highly participatory and majoritarian decision-making in the Member States of the EU, or in other advanced industrial democracies. This suggests that the insulated policy-making style of the EU is a function of the particular activities delegated to it, not—as many claim—unfair advantages enjoyed by multinational capital, the scale and scope of transnational politics, or the happenstance particularities of EU institutions. If such arrangements are common within national polities, should they be controversial in Europe? Perhaps, then, the existing institutions in Brussels, Strasbourg, and Luxembourg are not just stable, but just and fair as well.

This chapter explores this line of argument in detail. The first section describes existing EU institutions, focusing on the substantive narrowness and institutional weakness of its mandate. The second section examines the causes of this narrow and weak institutional mandate. The third section assesses its consequences of our normative assessment of the democratic legitimacy of the EU.

1. The Confederal Structure of the European Union

Viewed in comparative perspective, the EU is an exceptionally weak political structure. The range of issues it handles is narrow and the institutional authority it enjoys to handle them is modest compared with any advanced industrial democracy.[6] Such constraints are deeply embedded in the constitutional structure of the EU and are unlikely to change significantly in coming decades. Indeed, the last decade of the EU is best interpreted as a simultaneous movement in two directions: towards deepening and widening of cooperation in an established core of economic issues, and towards the imposition of looser, less centralized arrangements on cooperation outside of these core areas.[7] Let us consider in detail just how narrow and weak the EU really is.

The Narrowness of the EU: Substantive Constraints

Compared with existing domestic federations, the EU is substantively narrow. Its core functions are restricted almost entirely to the regulation of policy externalities resulting from the direct regulation of economic production. European Union regulation focuses on trade in goods and services, the movement of factors of production, the production and trade in agricultural commodities, exchange rates and monetary policy, money, foreign aid, and trade-related economic regulation of other externalities, such as certain environmental, consumer, competition, and workplace policies. In addition, there is a smattering of policies that emerged as side-payments for the acceptance of core policies by recalcitrant States, notably regional and structural funding.

[6] Some, most recently German Foreign Minister Joschka Fischer, have treated the EU as the analogue of the US under the Articles of Confederation, thereby suggesting an optimistic future trajectory. The two institutions look similar, yet it is unclear how useful it is to draw an analogy between a confederation of limited eighteenth-century States and a confederation of modern nation states. The difficulty is clear: most of the activities of the twenty-first century state were not carried out by any government in the eighteenth century, hence their absence is of little significance. Today, the failure of the EU to carry out many of these activities, and the corresponding success of national governments, is far more significant.

[7] Though space does not permit a full exploration of the history of the EU, there exists substantial evidence that the Member States *deliberately* created a weak polity because it suited their interests to do so; it is not an unintended consequence or an unfortunate happenstance. For an extended argument, see Andrew Moravcsik, *The Choice for Europe: Social Purpose and State Power from Messina to Maastricht* (Ithaca: Cornell University Press, and London: UCI/Routledge, 1988).

Impressed by this wide range of activity, analysts of the EU rarely stop to consider what is missing.[8] Consider the following.

First, the EU is almost entirely uninvolved in the major activity of advanced industrial democracies, namely, the provision of social welfare. National welfare systems provide direct income support, unemployment insurance, various forms of medical care, retirement and pension benefits, assistance for children—hardly any of which is directly regulated by the EU.[9] The only exceptions involve a narrow set of trans-border problems, such as the right of individuals to receive benefits abroad or invest pensions abroad—and even these rights are limited. In the related area of labour regulation, the EU has provided weak labour standards at something close to the lowest common denominator of national political aspirations.

Second, the EU lacks significant defence, military, and police policies.[10] As we have seen, this is perhaps the oldest and most fundamental activity of the modern state and it remains one of the largest elements in state spending in advanced industrial democracies. Even if the ambitious plans currently on the table for European defence coordination were realized, NATO would remain the preeminent international institution in European defence. The EU does not have, and does not envisage having, control over the details of military spending. It is hard to see why current proposals for defence industrial rationalization should be more successful than those of years past or, if they are successful, why they should take a 'European' form.[11] Through its third pillar, the EU is coordinating efforts to combat international crime, but the basic structure of national police, criminal justice, and punishment systems remains unchanged.

[8] Few of the issues I mention are found on Mark Pollack's elegant tables elsewhere in this volume. Pollack's admirable work is typical of the tendency of scholars studying the EU to focus on policies that are present rather than policies that are absent. The result is to inflate the importance of modest inroads into large policy areas.

[9] For a nuanced, maximally optimistic, yet nonetheless sceptical view of European social policy, see Stephan Leibfried and Paul Pierson, 'Social Policy: Left to Courts and Markets?', in Helen and William Wallace (eds), *Policy-Making in the European Union*, 4th edn (Oxford: Oxford University Press, 2000), 267–92. For an argument that the CAP should be seen as an indirect form of social policy closely related to the rise of the post-war social welfare state, see Elmar Rieger, 'The Common Agricultural Policy: Politics against Markets', in Wallace and Wallace (eds), *Policy-Making*.

[10] Jan Zielonka, *Explaining Euro-Paralysis: Why Europe Is Unable to Act in International Politics* (New York: St Martin's, 1998); Anthony Forster and William Wallace, 'Common Foreign and Security Policy', and Monica den Boer and William Wallace, 'Justice and Home Affairs', in Wallace and Wallace (eds), *Policy-Making*.

[11] The most informed prognoses predict that European defence industries will link up with US champions.

Third, the EU lacks a significant education policy.[12] With the exception of admirable but sporadic efforts to assure mutual recognition of advanced degrees and the free movement of students for semesters abroad, education policy in Europe remains national and local. All issues of primary and secondary education, as well as nearly all the educational issues that spark true public controversy in advanced industrial societies—the level of financing, the quality of education, the substance of the curriculum, admissions, and preferential access, the role of religion, multiculturalism, the proper role of unionized labour, the status of private schools, and so on—are almost entirely outside EU competence.

Fourth, EU policies aimed at the provision of civilian infrastructure—material structures like transport, energy, telecom networks, and other public works—are limited.[13] To be sure, the EU seeks to provide equal market access for external producers and funds particular infrastructure in poorer regions. Yet these programmes remain far smaller than national programmes, except in the poorest Member States, and are geographically restricted. They emerged, as we shall see in the next section, largely as side-payments to larger bargains and are unlikely to be expanded in the new, more 'flexible' EU that is emerging today. David Allen concludes: 'Consolidation would appear to be the name of the game for the next decade.'[14]

Fifth, the EU lacks a significant cultural policy.[15] European governments have relatively extensive policies to protect and propagate national cultural traditions. Though globalization, backed by EU regulations, has of course expanded access to media in Europe, EU regulations have little direct impact on media content.

Sixth, the EU has only a peripheral impact on national legal systems and civil litigation. To be sure, the EU enforces trans-border economic rights and, by virtue of an explicit clause in the Treaty of Rome, influences gender equality in the workplace. International protection of any other civil and political rights, in so far as it exists at all, occurs not through the EU, but rather the European Convention on Human Rights or the Council of Europe. Specific definitions of domestic economic discrimination, economic rights, and positive policies—'affirmative action'—

[12] For an optimistic scenario, in which national governments remain dominant, see Wiltold Tulasiewicz with Colin Brock, 'The Place of Education in a United Europe', in Colin Brock and Wiltold Tulasiewicz (eds), *Education in a Single Europe* (London: Routledge, 2000).

[13] David Allen, 'Cohesion and the Structural Funds', in Wallace and Wallace (eds), *Policy-Making*.

[14] David Allen, 'Cohesion and the Structural Funds', in Wallace and Wallace (eds), *Policy-Making*.

[15] Major overviews of EU policy rarely make any mention of cultural affairs.

towards racial and ethnic minorities, women, and the elderly, is dictated almost entirely by domestic law. The EU has little impact on policy towards religion and family. Similarly, electoral systems, the definition of political parties, and the regulation of other forms of political competition are defined domestically.

Seventh, isolated exceptions inherited from the 1970s aside, EU environmental policy is limited to those policy instruments directly related to cross-border economic or environmental externalities. Product regulation of the industries with high economies of scale, such as the chemical and automotive industries, and process regulations on levels of water and air pollution constitute the bulk of recent EU activity. This leaves to the Member States policies involving conservation, land management, natural resources, commons, noise pollution, and many other forms of environmental degradation. There is increasing scepticism about further deepening in this area.[16]

Eighth, direct support for industry and small business remains largely national. To be sure, the EU increasingly regulates industrial subsidies that might distort international competition, and construes that task increasingly broadly. Yet national industrial subsidies and tax advantages remain significant. Positive EU activities are limited to R&D policies, which mostly, though not exclusively, coordinate existing national subsidies. Small-business policy, in so far as it does not discriminate against foreign businesses, is relatively untouched by the EU.

Let us not exaggerate. European policy specialists will rightly object that the EU has made modest inroads in this or that policy area. Social scientists may justly point out that some large national federations—notably Germany, Canada, and the US—decentralize some of these functions, most often education, policing, some types of civil law, and support for small business. Still, there remains a difference so great as to be a difference in kind. *No* national federation relegates all of these policies—those regulating social welfare, pensions, unemployment, children, national defence, policing, education, civilian infrastructure, culture, human rights, industry, small business, *and* many environmental externalities—to subnational authorities. The decentralization of European policies is particularly surprising, given the traditionally centralized character of many West European states.[17]

[16] Alberta Sbragia, 'Environmental Policy: Economic Constraints and External Pressures', in Wallace and Wallace (eds), *Policy-Making*.

[17] Comparisons with the eighteenth century US under the Articles of Confederation, as we have seen, are unhelpful.

The Weakness of the EU: Constitutional Constraints

Substantive limitations on EU policy are not just happenstance. They are related to underlying constitutional structure. Lacunae in EU policy reflect limitations on EU policy-making institutions. Not only are EU policies narrow, but EU institutions are weak. What characteristics of EU institutions perpetuate its substantively limited policy role?

Fiscal Constraints

One institutional weakness is the EU's insignificant fiscal capacity. Since the early modern era, much of the centralization, and perhaps also the democratization, of the modern state has been connected with the need to strengthen its power to extract revenue.[18] In the twentieth century, tax revenues and state spending increased, often initially in connection with war but generally longer-term in connection with social welfare, until they totalled 25–50 per cent of GDP across advanced industrial nations. This trend is often cited as a measure of the power of the state.

Yet the EU remains an exception. It lacks the common fiscal base of a modern state. Its fiscal resources, derived through agricultural levies and a portion of national value-added taxation, remain capped at 1.27 per cent of GDP—roughly 3 per cent of national and local government spending in its Member States, which totals 30–55 per cent of GDP. Most of these financial resources are explicitly dedicated, moreover, to a small range of policies: the common agricultural policy, structural funding, and development aid. This leaves little discretionary funding. Even in its areas of the EU's greatest activity, the bulk of public funding remains national and local.

Though creative accounting, economic growth, and enlargement may create temporary slack of interest to EU policy analysts, there is no medium-term prospect of significantly lifting the formal fiscal ceiling—the overall 1.27 per cent constraint. EU budgetary policy is subject to unanimity and thus remains tightly controlled domestically by finance ministers, foreign ministers, and heads of state and government.[19] To be sure, the accession of poorer countries in central and eastern Europe will create demands for a more robust fiscal system. Yet such demands are unlikely to lead to increased EU spending. In the past, enlargement to include such countries—Britain, Ireland, Spain, Portugal, and Greece—new financial

[18] John Brewer, *The Sinews of Power: War, Money and the English State, 1688–1783* (Cambridge: Harvard University Press, 1990); Margaret Levi, *Of Rule and Revenue* (Berkeley and Los Angeles: University of California Press, 1989).

[19] Brigid Laffan and Michael Shackleton, 'The Budget', in Wallace and Wallace (eds), *Policy-Making*.

demands were backed by threats to veto common policies, resulting in a series of significant financial side payments. Current candidates face a radically different situation, however. Few new policies loom on the horizon and those that do are likely to be established with 'flexibility' provisions designed precisely to permit 'core' member countries to circumvent a veto and thereby avoid burdensome financial transfers. As Brigid Laffan and Michael Shackleton observe, 'Funds are unlikely to approach the level of transfers found in traditional federal systems. The Union . . . does not conform to the principles of fiscal federalism and is unlikely to do so in the future, notwithstanding the arrival of EMU'.[20]

The overall result, as Giandomenico Majone has written, is that the EU remains a 'regulatory polity'—a polity with administrative instruments but little fiscal capacity.[21] It is surely not coincidental that most of the policies listed in the preceding section as absent from the EU's policy portfolio—notably social welfare, defence, education, and infrastructure—require significant direct government expenditure. The institutions of the EU are most authoritative and autonomous, by contrast, in areas that do not involve the disbursement of tax revenues, notably constitutional adjudication, technical regulation, state prosecution, and legislative agenda-setting.

Administrative Incapacity and the Absence of Coercive Force

Not only is the EU a regulatory state; it is a regulatory state that does not implement its own regulations. Policy analysts often observe that the real politics of regulation lies in implementation. Yet while the Commission oversees implementation of EU policies, it actually implements almost none of them. Let us start with the obvious. In contrast to all existing national federations, the EU has no police powers, no army, and no realistic prospect of obtaining either one.[22] Even if successful, recent efforts to create a modest intergovernmental capacity to cooperate militarily would not change this. The EU does not rely on its own means either to resolve disputes among levels of government or even simply to enforce the law. When the ECJ—often cited as the critical element in the EU's enforcement apparatus—issues a decision, it generally takes the form of an advisory opinion to national courts under Art. 177 of the original Treaty of Rome,

[20] 'The Budget', in Wallace and Wallace (eds), *Policy-Making*, 240.

[21] Giandomenico Majone, *Regulating Europe* (London: Routledge, 1996).

[22] Even the most ambitious among recent proposals for a European rapid deployment force foresee a small unit designed for ad hoc intervention, with NATO approval, in cases of peace-keeping and peace-making.

which then orders, if it so chooses, enforcement of that opinion using national legal and coercive means.

With the exception of competition policy, where the Commission has independent prosecutorial powers—though even there we are dealing with only a handful of important cases—and the conduct of, though not the ultimate control over, external trade negotiations, the administrative and implementation powers of the Commission are extraordinarily weak. Policies are typically implemented by national or perhaps sub-national governments. It could hardly be otherwise, for the EU bureaucracy in Brussels is extraordinarily small. Setting aside secretarial and logistical positions, the entire Commission employs no more than 5,000–7,000 top officials—about the size of a European city government or a single moderately-sized Washington agency. These officials tend to have generic skills rather than specific technical and legal knowledge—a situation the Commission is currently seeking to correct—and are often at a disadvantage in areas like agricultural and environmental policy when facing larger and more permanent national bureaucracies. The core of the EU legislative process lies therefore in the complex subcommittees of the Committee of Permanent Representatives (COREPER)—the heart of the Council of Ministers—which structures the constant participation of national officials in ongoing meetings on specific legislative items. These officials, along with their permanent staffs in Brussels, far outnumber Commission officials. Indeed, the legislative system of the EU can be thought of as a network of specialized regulatory officials from national governments, centred on COREPER and the Council of Ministers, engaged in the dissemination of information about national positions, technical possibilities, and legal details. The process of policy-making is as much diplomatic as it is technocratic.

Even these relatively modest agenda-setting enforcement powers of the Commission, Court, and Parliament are constrained by the institutionalization over the past decade of a 'three pillar' structure within the EU. Since the Maastricht Treaty, the EU has been moving consistently towards a structure in which core economic policies remain subject to the 'Community method' of legislation, which accords a prominent role to the Commission and Court—the 'first pillar'—but many issues of defence, foreign policy, policing, and immigration policy—the second and third 'pillars'—as well as monetary policy, remain outside of this traditional legal order. With the exception of monetary policy, which has been assigned to an independent agency, these policies remain under classic intergovernmental control, quite similar to what is found in most international organizations.

Subsidiarity, Flexibility, and Unilateralism

To a greater extent than in most federations, member governments of the EU can avail themselves of alternatives to strict multilateralism that, in practice, permit them to opt out of particular policies. Three separate forms of unilateralism can be distinguished. The first and simplest form of unilateralism is to act alone. In recent years EU Member States have begun to define the concept of 'subsidiarity'—the notion that policy tasks adequately carried out at a lower level of government should best be addressed there—so as to explicitly discourage the expansion of the EU into certain new areas such as education, culture, and some sorts of social policy.

The second form of cooperation is unilateral action in areas of mixed competence. While in the core areas of tariff and subsidy policy EU rules are relatively strict and inflexible, there are numerous areas in which governments can act unilaterally inside or outside of the EU. This is true of most policies in foreign policy, home and internal affairs, non-tariff trade barriers, and many policies regarding service provision. In many areas, such as human rights, defence, and border controls, this has led to the formation of alternative international organizations. In other areas, it has encouraged unilateralism, as when the US was recently able to forge bilateral air transport agreements with a half dozen smaller west European countries. In other areas, such as environmental and social policy, special exceptions have been made permitting richer countries to adopt regulatory standards higher than the EU standard, even if trade is thereby diverted. The EU standard becomes little more than a floor.

More interesting and unique to the EU, as compared with national federations, is a third type of divergence from strict multilateral policy-making whereby a 'core' of governments can move ahead collectively inside the institutions. This is commonly termed a 'multi-speed Europe' or a 'Europe of concentric circles'.[23] Some governments can opt out of any policy. Currently outsiders have a *de jure* veto over the formation of any such core—though if the veto provokes even less desirable forms of institutional cooperation outside of the EU, it may not be of *de facto* importance. As recently as 1988, this sort of arrangement was viewed as 'anti-European' and championed only by Margaret Thatcher. Yet European federalists soon came to realize that progress can be made only

[23] For a fuller discussion along these lines, see Andrew Moravcsik, 'Europe's Future at Century's End', in Andrew Moravcsik (ed.), *Centralization or Fragmentation? Europe Facing the Challenges of Deepening, Diversity, and Democracy* (Washington, DC: Brookings Institution Press, 1998).

on this basis. Provisions for 'flexibility' or 'enhanced cooperation' have become part of the Brussels orthodoxy.

We see such provisions in many policy areas. It is employed in the initial decision at Maastricht to move ahead in social policy with 14 of the 15 Member States and to move ahead later to a single currency with eleven—soon to be twelve—of the 15 members. Foreign policy and defence policy coordination is focused on 'coalitions of the willing', in which those governments that wish to pursue a particular policy may move ahead without fully committing the others. In transport, R&D and structural fund policies, similar ad hoc arrangements have long existed. The Schengen Agreement establishing a zone free of customs checks has increasingly been integrated into the EU, though it does not include all EU members and not all participants belong to the EU. There will very likely be long transition periods in extending the Common Agricultural Policy (CAP) to eastern Europe. The primary purpose of such arrangements is to avoid a veto by, compromise with, or side-payment to smaller and weaker states. This sort of organized fragmentation is found in no national federation, though ad hoc collaborative arrangements sometimes do arise among subnational governments in the US, Canada, and elsewhere.

Consensual Decision-Making and Transparency

Political decisions in the EU are taken under rules that require unanimity or super-majoritarian support in order to reach a decision. This level of consensus, namely, support of representatives of between 70 per cent and 100 per cent of the weighted votes of territorial representatives, depending on the particular issue, is far higher than in any existing national polity. The resulting bias in favour of the status quo imposes narrow constraints on legislative activism.

The creation of single market, agricultural policy, single currency, parliamentary reform, and other major new policies required unanimous amendment of the Treaty of Rome. Today this requires consent by all 15 governments, followed by subsequent parliamentary or administrative ratification.[24] This high level of consensus is difficult to achieve. It has emerged in the past two decades only by focusing on core areas of broad consensus, by watering down specific proposals to near insignificance, or by providing financial side-payments.

Even everyday EU legislation must secure approximately 70 per cent of the weighted votes of national ministers sitting in the Council of Ministers.

[24] The creation of the Common Agricultural Policy in the 1960s, which took place within the existing Treaty of Rome, required unanimous support but not separate domestic ratification.

This is a comparatively high standard, which severely limits potential legislative activity. Many veto players are thereby empowered. Though supermajorities are sometimes required in existing federal polities to close debate—for example, the US Senate—or to pass legislation in certain circumstances—for example, Canada and Germany—no existing federal state requires such a high level of consensus for all legislation. Statistically speaking, it is harder to pass an everyday piece of legislation in the EU than to amend the American or German constitution. An exceptionally broad consensus of European leaders is required to initiate change.

The ECJ, it is important to note, is a significant exception to this rule. The European Court decides, it appears, by majority vote. In the EU context, where its decisions cannot easily be overridden by legislation—a characteristic due, ironically, to precisely the decision-making rules designed to constrain the EU's autonomy—its power to legislate judicially is further enhanced.[25] In the context of supermajoritarian decision-making and judicial independence, it is not surprising that the ECJ has been, in comparative perspective, an exceptionally strong branch of government.

In addition to impeding new policies, this cumbersome decision-making process has another implication, seldom noted. It renders EU politics—contrary to its reputation—exceptionally transparent. With a score of commissioners, 15 national representatives, more than 600 parliamentarians, and constant participation by national officials, there can be no monopoly of information in the EU. In contrast to the widespread impression of a cadre of secretive Brussels-based gnomes, supranational officials in fact work under public scrutiny far more intense than that prevailing under most national governments. Take it from me as an active scholar: it is far easier to get information from the Commission than the British or French government! The recent scandals, often cited as evidence of the lack of control over the corruption of Brussels bureaucrats, in fact prove the opposite. In this much-publicized scandal, parliamentary investigation uncovered only one case of corruption in the Commission, that involving the former French Prime Minister and then Commissioner, Edit Cresson, who had awarded a contract to her home-town dentist. During a long and successful political career in France, Cresson—who, to put it charitably, had never had the reputation of having particularly clean hands—had never been called to account for such activities. Shortly after her arrival in Brussels, the intense multinational and multi-institutional scrutiny characteristic of the EU had led to her resignation. The press reports of these

[25] Joseph H. H. Weiler, 'The Transformation of Europe', *Yale Law Review*, 100 (1991), 2403–83.

scandals, not to mention the use made of them in certain political circles in Europe, are quite misleading. The EU is, without a doubt, more transparent than all, or nearly all, of its Member States.

Territorial Representation

In most EU contexts, the most critical decision-making institutions represent established territorial interests. This is true in two senses. The first is that representatives to the most critical forums for legislation and treaty amendment, the Council of Ministers—national ministers—and the European Council—heads of state and government—are under the direct instruction of existing national governments or states. In other words, the Councils represent territorial governments rather than territorial electorates. A hypothetical analogy with the US is instructive. Imagine a system in which US senators were not only selected by national legislatures, as was once the case, but rather served at the pleasure and under the direct instruction of State governors. They could be recalled and reinstructed at any time. Whereas this is true of some legislative bodies in existing national federations—for example, the German *Bundesrat*—the regional loyalty of such representatives is typically tempered by party discipline. Yet party discipline is—and this is the second sense in which EU representation is territorial—all but absent in the EU. Individual representatives in the Council tend to directly represent particularistic territorial interests. Compromises on specific issues are generally reached ad hoc or by supermajority vote, rather as a function of partisan discipline and institutional hierarchy. This system of decision-making tends to privilege defenders of existing institutional prerogatives, who enjoy a formal veto over institutional changes. The axes of influence and responsibility in the EU tend to run vertically from national governments to their supranational representatives, rather than horizontally through transnational party structures or interest groups.

The Commission and European Parliament constitute only partial exceptions to the EU's extreme tendency towards direct representation of national governments. The Commission is able to act relatively independently in proposing and, in conjunction with the ECJ, enforcing everyday legislation. Yet national representatives and interests still play an important role, since the need for Council of Ministers agreement tightly constrains the set of viable proposals. The EP is directly elected, generally by proportional representation within governments, and it does have a working system of party cooperation and votes often split along party lines. But the EP's influence is limited by three factors. First, though there is cooperation among parties, there tends to be little sense of a transnational electoral process.[26] The mandate for European parties to act is correspondingly weak. Second, while its power has increased over the past decade, it remains able to amend or reject legislation only once it has been proposed by the Commission and approved by the Council. Voting rules make it difficult for the EP to act decisively. Its ability to shape the agenda of European politics remains modest. As a result, most sober cross-issue studies of decision-making in the EU still give pride of place to the territorial interests of member governments.[27]

This analysis confirms Daniel Elazar's conclusion, elsewhere in this volume, that in comparative perspective the EU polity appears more confederal than federal. The EU, we have seen, is a political institution incomparably weaker, narrower, and more decentralized in most respects than any existing national federation. It is substantively limited largely to the tasks of international economic liberalization and stabilization. It lacks the powers to tax, to coerce, to police, to administer, and to mandate uniform application of the law. Its cumbersome decision-making process is constrained by super-majoritarian and unanimous decision-making, as well as direct representation of national and sub-national governments. To the extent that these five conditions obtain, the EU should be thought of a polity so much weaker and narrower than any national federation that a difference in quantity becomes a difference in kind. Yet determining on which side of this abstract dichotomy the EU falls is a far less important task than addressing its causes and consequences—to which I now turn.

2. The Causes of the European Constitutional Settlement

Why did the EU evolve as a multi-level political body narrower, weaker and more diffuse than anything found at the national level? Three circumstances account for these differences: the essential irrelevance of military force, the absence of a common identity, and the prior existence of comprehensive national bureaucracies. In each of these respects, the history of the EU differs from that of modern nation-states. Let us consider each in turn.

[26] Jean Blondel, Richard Sinnott, and Palle Svensson, *People and Parliament in the European Union: Participation, Democracy and Legitimacy* (Oxford: Clarendon Press, 1998).

[27] See, for example, Jonathan Golub, *Europeanization and Domestic Structural Change: The Case of EU Environmental Policy* (Fiesole: European University Institute, 1996); Adrienne Héritier, Susanne Mingers, Christoph Knill, and Martina Becka, *Die Veränderung von Staatlichkeit in Europa. Ein regulativer Wettbewerb: Deutschland, Grosbrittanien, Frankreich* (Opladen: Leske+Budrich, 1994), 386, passim.

The Essential Irrelevance of Military Force

The functions and borders of existing nation-states, if not their very sovereign status, were often created to meet external or internal military threats.[28] The evolution of the EU has had little to do with such considerations. Traditional geopolitical considerations—matters of power, order, and war—play at most a secondary and sporadic role in EU history.

The EU as we know it is the result of many incremental decisions punctuated once a decade by major intergovernmental bargains. Five or six major decisions, depending on how one counts, stand out: the negotiation of the Treaty of Rome in the 1950s, the terms of the CAP in the 1960s, the European Monetary System (EMS) in the 1970s, the Single European Act in the 1980s, and the Maastricht and Amsterdam Treaties in the 1990s.[29] Consistently the most important national purposes underlying these bargains were commercial and the most important force underlying European integration was therefore globalization. The establishment of a common market and a common currency served to promote the long-standing economic interests of European states faced with unprecedented opportunities to profit from rising trade and factor flows. Beginning in the late 1940s Europe witnessed the epochal expansion in export-led growth among advanced industrial democracies, followed in the 1980s and 1990s by a similar expansion in flows of investment and information. These global forces were irresistible, and they influenced countries' national policies whether they were members of the EU or not. Yet those governments that accommodated them through policies of trade liberalization, openness to factor flows, and monetary stability tended to profit most. If such policies were pursued more thoroughly in Europe than elsewhere, it has been primarily because Europe was far more interdependent economically.[30]

The story of post-war European integration is of course more complex than can be captured in this simple account of functional adaptation. Two exceptions deserve mention. First, geopolitical considerations such as the rehabilitation and reintegration of West Germany, the relative decline of Britain and France *vis-à-vis* the superpowers, and the Soviet threat, not to mention the attractiveness of European ideology as a centrist alternative to proletarian internationalism, played significant, though clearly

[28] The literature is extensive. For one effort to link the literature on Western state formation to that on the EU, see Gary Marks, 'The Third Lens: European Integration and State Building Compared' (Chapel Hill: University of North Carolina, n.d. [1990s]).

[29] Moravcsik, *Choice for Europe*; Alan S. Milward, *The European Rescue of the Nation-State*, 2nd edn (London: Routledge, 2000).

[30] For comparative data, see Moravcsik, *Choice for Europe*, 495.

secondary, roles.[31] Second, the ECJ, in a process described in detail elsewhere, established the important constitutional principles of supremacy and direct effect, which in turn contributed to the effectiveness of European governance.[32] Still, for 50 years European integration has been, above all else, a functional adaptation to economic interdependence.

Still, geopolitics played a relatively minor role in European integration. Indeed, recent historiography reveals that considerations such as the prevention of future Franco-German war, the maintenance of the cold war balance, and the desire for independence from the superpowers—the geopolitical factors most often cited by clever politicians and conventional diplomatic historians to justify European integration—are of decidedly secondary importance in explaining major EU decisions.[33] The result: in modern nation-states the waging of war has led inexorably to the monopolization of coercive force and the centralization of fiscal extraction, whereas in Europe, as a whole, neither has occurred.

The Absence of a Common Identity

Citizens in the Member States of the EU share little underlying sense of distinct 'European' national identity, derived from a common history, culture, or philosophy. There is, as many have noted, no *demos* underlying European integration and, as fewer have noted, no common educational system aimed at bolstering such a sense.[34] To only a very limited extent, therefore, do Europeans view one another as part of a common polity to which all members are, as a matter of principle, assured equal consideration. Leaving aside basic civil rights—guaranteed, in the first instance, by the Council of Europe, not the European Union, and nearly universally enforced in the developed world—any rights have had to be justified functionally—as an adjunct to economic liberalization—or judicially—as the result of decade-long incrementalism by the courts—rather than on the basis of fundamental 'constitutional moments' similar to those that drove cooperation forward in the United States.[35] The result: the EU has achieved some progress in the areas of civil and political rights, even if this lags behind Strasbourg, but almost none in the areas of socioeconomic rights, despite the similarities among European national norms in this area.

31 One estimate of the precise role is set forth in Moravcsik, *Choice for Europe*, 473–9.
32 Weiler, 'Transformation of Europe'.
33 Moravcsik, *Choice for Europe*; Milward, *European Rescue of the Nation-State*.
34 Joseph Weiler, *The Constitution of Europe* (London: Oxford University Press, 1999).
35 Bruce Ackenman, *We the People* (Cambridge, MA: Harvard University Press, 1991).

The Prior Existence of Strong Nation-States

The EU emerged late in the process of European state formation, after post-World War II constitutional revisions and policy innovations had established nearly all the broad functions of the modern nation-state. Any new European functions had to be justified, therefore, as an improvement on existing national policies, which already functioned on a relatively large scale. In the lack of any external crisis—depression or war—any such effort at centralization faced entrenched opposition from existing social and bureaucratic interests. The EU has therefore evolved within the constraint of a constant presumption in favour of national, rather than federal, policies—a presumption formalized through the rule of unanimity for any revision to the Treaty of Rome. It is striking, in this regard, that in the few remaining areas in which new issue-areas emerged after 1957, such as environmental and anti-trust policy, the EU has been relatively active—to the extent that it is sometimes criticized for going beyond the regulation of economic externalities. The result: the 'path dependence' of previous national choices privileges national solutions.[36] Member-State governments have tended to pursue national policies until clear policy failures ensued—as in the trade deficits of the 1950s, unilateral devaluation of the 1970s, industrial subsidization of the early 1980s, and upheavals in the Balkans more recently—before moving forward to common action.

3. The Normative Consequences of the European State Structure

Is the unique state structure of the EU democratically legitimate? What does it mean to say, as many do today, that the EU suffers from a 'democratic deficit'?[37]

Current political and scholarly debates focus our attention on the need to justify the EU through greater reliance on electoral or legislative institutions—institutions that provide so-called 'input legitimacy'. From this perspective, the EU appears presumptively illegitimate, because it provides

[36] This argument differs from the claims found in leading historical institutionalist accounts, such as Paul Pierson, 'The Path to European Integration: A Historical Institutionalist Account', *Comparative Political Studies*, 29/2 (1996), 123–64. I disagree with Pierson's specific empirical conclusions about European integration—see Moravcsik, *Choice for Europe*, 489–94—but his microfoundational analysis offers the most coherent and persuasive theoretical starting point.

[37] This section draws on and extends two earlier analyses. See Moravcsik, 'Conservative Idealism and International Institutions', *Chicago Journal of International Law* (forthcoming) and 'Democracy and Constitutionalism in the European Union', *ECSA Review* (Spring 2000).

relatively few opportunities for direct public participation or for majoritarian decision-making by directly elected representatives. This can be remedied, so the argument goes, only if European citizens are granted a greater formal role in selecting its policies or, at the very least, in selecting those who select its policies. The more direct the representation and the more numerous the citizens involved are, the more democratically legitimate the institution is.

Critics of the EU's democratic deficit are, to be sure, ideologically varied and thus differ in their assessment of the ultimate consequences. Euro-federalists believe that much must be done to increase democratic accountability lest the EU stagnate or even collapse. Social democrats seek a generous European social policy to balance trade liberalization and monetary discipline. Eurosceptics—most notably those on the extreme right of the British, French, Italian, and Austrian political spectrums, but not absent from parties of the left—fear the creation of a 'superstate' in Brussels. They cite recent scandals and the Commission's efforts to promote certain sorts of regulation as evidence that EU officials wield their bureaucratic discretion in an arbitrary manner. All agree that European decision-makers are distant, technocratic, and ultimately unaccountable.

The lack of consensus as to the concrete implications of the 'democratic deficit' should immediately alert us as to the lack of precision in many such criticisms. Indeed, when we examine the arguments more precisely, they still fail to convince, for at least four independent reasons related to our discussion thus far. In contrast to the view of an autonomous, technocratic superstate, the EU is a weak state structure, it functions under direct and indirect democratic control, its departures from majoritarian decision-making fall into normatively justifiable categories, and there is little evidence of an overall policy bias. Let us briefly consider the normative implications of these facts.

The EU is an Exceptionally Weak and Dependent State Structure

Eurosceptical fears of a corrupt and arbitrary superstate run by an all-powerful Brussels-based technocracy are strikingly at odds with a simple factual description of the organization. As a first approximation, we have seen, the EU lacks nearly all the instruments required to establish such a despotism: a police force and standing army, powers to tax and spend, a large administrative bureaucracy, independent legal authority, broad administrative discretion, responsibility for policy implementation, and control over information. Nearly all the fears that give rise to classical arguments for liberal controls on the state are absent in the case of the EU. In sum, there are many ways to constrain and control a political institution, of which widespread participation in majoritarian decision-making is only one.[38] In comparative perspective, the EU is perhaps the least likely of all federations in history to establish despotic rule.

EU Institutions Remain under Indirect Democratic Control

The notion that the EU functions without democratic support is quite misleading. The most obvious democratic controls are those imposed on the European Parliament, which is composed of directly elected representatives. The EP is increasingly usurping the role of the Commission as the primary interlocutor to the Council of Ministers in the EU legislative process. While the Commission still initiates legislation, it is now the EP that, in the final instance, controls the agenda—that is, the EP can reject legislation or make proposals for amendment to the Council that are more difficult to amend than to accept. To be sure, European citizens do not cast votes for the EP on the basis of 'European' issues, but there are many reasons why this might be so, not least of which is the lack of an EU mandate in areas of public interest—a point to which I shall return below.

Yet the EP is, in the end, secondary. The Council of Ministers is far more important, and is itself also democratically accountable. The permanent representative of each country receives instructions from a national executive elected directly or through a parliamentary vote. Parliaments consider and comment on many EU policies. Even Commissioners and ECJ judges, though clearly more insulated, are named by directly elected national governments. But the Commission has relatively little discretion, compared with the Council and Parliament.

To be sure, national governments conduct EU policy through traditionally secret, non-participatory foreign-policy apparatus and networks of technocratic officials. This tends to strengthen national executives *vis-à-vis* powerful minorities within legislatures—much like many domestic mechanisms, such as 'fast track' provisions do so in the United States.[39] Yet the national governments represented in the Council are directly elected, clearly responsible for policy outputs, and maintain close super-majoritarian control over decision-making. Many insiders view even the Commission or Council as highly representative of citizen concerns—perhaps more so than the European Parliament. As British Prime Minister Tony Blair recently observed:

[38] For a related argument, see Majone, *Regulating Europe*.

[39] Andrew Moravcsik, 'Why the European Community Strengthens the State', Center for European Studies Working Paper (Cambridge: Harvard University, 1994).

The European Parliament is more directly democratic but it is more remote from people than their National Parliaments or their elected governments. The Council of Ministers is closer to people in the sense that the British Prime Minister is directly accountable to the British electorate in a very obvious way and yet, in terms of the European decisions we take, [the Council] is less directly democratic. That's the dilemma.[40]

So the EU does not lack democratic checks per se. The question is instead whether these checks are significantly weaker—dangerously so—than those common in national systems. And the answer to that question is, at the very least, unclear and uneven. Moreover, where the EU does afford less direct democratic control, we are about to see, insulated policy-making may be normatively justified.

Limits on Direct Participation in EU Politics Fall into Normatively Justifiable Categories

Though the EU remains under indirect and sometimes even direct democratic control, there is good reason to believe that the scope of the EU, as well as its distance from individual voters, serves to insulate national and supranational officials from a measure of immediate accountability to legislative and electoral pressure. The scale of the EU is larger, and its institutions disproportionately involves not just a modest delegation of power to supranational judges and bureaucrats, but a significant empowerment of networks of national ministers, executives, and officials. The EU thereby 'strengthens the state' in the sense of increasing the domestic influence of national executives, ministers, and perhaps even ministerial officials *vis-à-vis* other social groups.[41]

Before we condemn such practices, however, we must recall that departures from direct majoritarian control by citizens are hardly unique to EU politics. National political institutions in advanced industrial democracies are far from perfectly majoritarian or participatory. No modern liberal democracy governs primarily by referendum or direct parliamentary activity, let alone collective deliberation among the citizenry. Instead, all modern governments delegate power to elected and non-elected representatives of various sorts: coalitions of parties, legislative representatives, judges, prosecutors, expert officials, central bankers, and so on.[42] The reason is simple: it is intolerably costly—in time, money, information, and education—for all citizens to be involved in all decisions. A modern state

[40] Cited in Moravcsik, 'Conservative Idealism' (manuscript version), 21.

[41] Moravcsik, 'Why the European Community Strengthens the State'.

[42] Robert Dahl and Edward Tufte, *Size and Democracy* (New Haven: Yale University Press, 1970).

that sought to maximize popular participation in government would soon become ungovernable. The essence of modern constitutional design lies, therefore, in the designation of different processes of indirect representation and control—some tighter, some looser—for different functions. Though all functions of government are *ultimately* under control by voters or their immediate representatives, there is no expectation, in either the theory or in practice of democratic governance, that all such functions be immanently under such control. Constitutional architects regularly design strong non-participatory, non-majoritarian institutions, such as courts, independent technical agencies, diplomatic and military establishments, central banks, independent national executives, and complex arrangements for the separation of powers.

The trend toward non-majoritarian institutions has gained force in European domestic polities over the past generation, giving rise to an extensive literature on the 'decline of parliaments'.[43] Most of this decline in the influence of parliaments is generally believed to have little or nothing to do with European integration, but instead with the increasing technical, political, and logistical complexity of modern governance, as well as the constellations of interests in modern polities.

Individual and group participation in majoritarian decision-making is not, therefore, either the unique or the primary standard against which the legitimacy of modern democratic political institutions is to be judged. Democratic institutions should surely seek to address the core interests of major groups in society, but majoritarian participation is only one way to achieve induce representative policy-making. Limitations on majoritarian decision-making may be normatively justifiable, broadly speaking, if they increase the efficiency and technical competence of decision-making; guarantee political, cultural or socioeconomic equality—rights—against majority decisions; or offset imperfections in representative institutions.

Is this the case in Europe? There is good reason to believe so. There is a striking correlation between the use of non-majoritarian institutions at the EU level *among* Member States and their use in domestic politics *within* Member States. *The most autonomous EU institutions are found precisely in those areas—constitutional adjudication, foreign economic*

[43] On the decline of parliaments, see Sue Pryce, *Presidentializing the Premiership* (London: Macmillan, 1997), Patrick Weller, Herman Bakvis, and R. A.W. Rhodes (eds), *The Hollow Crown: Countervailing Trends in Core Executives* (London: Macmillan, 1997); R.A.W. Rhodes and Patrick Dunleavy (eds), *Prime Minister, Cabinet and Core Executive* (New York: St Martin's, 1995); Otto Kirchheimer, 'The Transformation of Western European Party Systems', in Joseph LaPalombara and Myron Weiner (eds), *Political Parties and Political Development* (Princeton: Princeton University Press, 1966); Herbert Kitschelt, *The Transformation of European Social Democracy* (Cambridge: Cambridge University Press, 1993).

diplomacy, technical regulatory administration, central banking, and criminal prosecution—where non-majoritarian decision-making is most widespread and legitimate in the domestic polities of the Member States. This suggests that the reasons for the relatively insulated quality of EU policy-making have more to do with the functional imperatives of modern democratic governance than with either the imperatives of globalization or the specific character of the European institutional construction

Indeed, these areas of non-majoritarian decision-making arise primarily in areas where persistent imperfections in representative institutions create long-term threats to weak political groups. While we need not go so far as has Giandomenico Majone, who sees non-majoritarian institutions as legitimate where pure 'efficiency' considerations dominate, we can safely say that these are all areas in which insulated national executives and supranational officials act in the interest of diffuse majorities of consumers, citizens, and victims of uncompetitive behaviour and environmental degradation to overturn policies set to the advantage of powerful, particularistic interest groups.[44] On this reading, non-majoritarian decision-making is justified in democratic theory not simply because it may be efficient, but because, ironically, it may better represent the long-term interests of the median voter than does a more participatory system—in distributive conflicts as well as matters of efficiency. In other words, the EU performs much the same political function for European governments as a strong executive and 'fast-track' legislation has for post-war America: a function that could be argued to have a democratic result—that is, one favourable to the median citizen—precisely because it is non-majoritarian.

Why is this indirect procedure of overcoming powerful particularistic interests accepted by European citizens? In large part it is because the issues handled by the EU—agricultural subsidies excepted—are not those about which significant number of voters care most. The policies most salient in the minds of European voters—overall levels of taxation, social protection and pensions, education, and major military commitments—remain firmly in the hands of national governments. Widespread apathy and non-participation in European elections is often taken to be a clear sign of the illegitimacy of the EU, but it may instead reflect the lack of salience accorded by voters to the issues it handles.[45]

[44] Majone, *Regulating Europe*.

[45] Jean Blondel, Richard Sinnott, and Palle Svensson demonstrate that European voters doubt neither the efficacy of the European Parliament nor their ability to influence them. Nonetheless, they shun elections to the European Parliament. One plausible explanation would be the low salience of the issues that the EP handles. See Blondel *et al.*, *People and Parliament*.

In sum, the lack of participation in majoritarian decision-making does not in itself render the EU democratically illegitimate.[46] The existence of indirect democratic control, the lack of direct democracy in domestic institutions, the tendency of the EU to accrue functions that are already non-majoritarian in domestic polities—and, most fundamentally, the apparent legitimacy of insulated, non-majoritarian and non-participatory institutions—undermines any such critical conclusion.

There Is Little Evidence of an Overall Policy Bias in European Governance

Some critics of the EU, like critics of the strong US executive, insist that the EU's reliance on delegated power—whatever arguments might be made for its efficiency—imparts an illegitimate bias into European policy. Super-majoritarian decision-making, the strong judiciary and Commission, and the strengthening of national executives, along with the Treaty of Rome mandate for trade liberalization and the subsequent rise in economic interdependence, mean that the EU liberalizes trade and tightens monetary discipline but discourages labour organization and social spending. Fritz Scharpf and others have argued that tight controls on EU decision-making create 'joint-decision traps' that favour particularistic interest groups—notably industrial and agricultural exporters—at the expense of workers, consumers, and other broader groups in society.[47] In short, non-majoritarian EU institutions overrepresent neo-liberal interests.

This is indeed a curious claim for, if we consider national and EU policies as a whole, it is very difficult to conclude that European policy is radically at odds with underlying popular sentiment.[48] Scharpf's critique implies that there exists majority support, both within and across EU Member States, for different policies—for example, lower agricultural subsidies and higher social spending, which would prevail absent a joint-decision trap. There is little evidence for this. In the case of agricultural spending, as Elmar Rieger has shown, the claim is demonstrably false.[49]

[46] This also calls into question the standard of input legitimacy altogether, which appears circular absent a strong theory of the cost-effectiveness of participation at achieving some normative or positive goal—but full consideration of this issue takes us beyond the scope of this paper.

[47] Fritz Scharpf, *Governing in Europe: Effective and Democratic?* (Oxford: Oxford University Press, 1999); Fritz Scharpf, 'The Joint-Decision Trap: Lessons from German Federalism and European Integration', *Public Administration*, 66 (1988), 239–78.

[48] For a response more firmly grounded in historical institutionalist theories of path dependence, see Moravcsik, *Choice for Europe*, 489–94.

[49] See Elmar Rieger, 'Agrarpolitik: Integration durch Gemeinschaftspolitik?', in Markus Jachtenfuchs and Beate Kohler-Koch (eds), *Europäische Integration* (Opladen: Leske+Budrich, 1996), 401–28.

High price subsidies for major agricultural commodities were not created by the EU, they pre-dated it. Prominent non-member states with similar economic structures, most notably and Switzerland, have long maintained *higher* agricultural subsidies than governments within the EU. As for social policy, most European governments realize the need to control government spending, often for reasons having little to do with interdependence.[50] If any majority emerged in the EU, Paul Pierson and Stefan Leibfried conclude in what is surely the most authoritative study of EU social policy-making, it would most likely support lower rather than higher social expenditures. There is, in sum, every reason to believe that the current structure of the EU serves primarily to strengthen, rather than obstruct, underlying tendencies in Member State policy.

4. Conclusion

I have argued that the EU is an exceptionally weak federation. So weak, indeed, that the difference in degree between it and national federations amounts to a difference in kind. The EU's narrow substantive range, modest budgetary resources, lack of coercive force, minuscule bureaucracy, constraining decision-rules within a multi-level system, and far more powerful competitors mean that it might well be thought of something qualitatively different from existing federal systems. The existence of these constraints on EU decision-making, along with the existence of indirect democratic control and normative justifications for delegating power, undermine criticisms of the EU as having a severe 'democratic deficit'.

This is not, of course, to deflect all criticism of the democratic legitimacy of EU institutions.[51] Closer inspection may well reveal deep, unintended, or illegitimate biases in the multi-level EU system of governance. Yet any such critique must begin from two premises. First, the EU is not a 'superstate' in the making. It best understood as one level in a complex multi-level decision-making system or, more precisely, a severely limited international organization for bureaucratic and judicial coordination among democratic governments. At the very least, we need to ask whether the EU is more or less representative than the national systems it replaces, and whether its particular biases are legitimate.

Second, there is no necessary correlation on the margin between participation in majoritarian decision-making and influence over policy

[50] Stefan Leibfried and Paul Pierson (eds), *European Social Policy: Between Fragmentation and Integration* (Washington, DC: Brookings Institution, 1995).

[51] Nor is it to deny that insights from theories of federal systems, or domestic politics more generally, may be useful in explaining EU policies.

outcomes—that is, between democracy and representation. It is far from presumptively obvious that simply because a political institution involves delegated power, it is unrepresentative of broad majorities—whether judged by the standards of democratic theory or by existing domestic practices. The European constitutional order, like any other constitutional order, inhabits the world of the second-best. In the second-best world of constitutional construction, there is no necessary correspondence between procedural equity, equal influence, fair policy outputs, responsiveness to the median voter, and normatively justified governance. Many forms of constitutional control may, under certain practical circumstances, prove responsive to broadly inclusive sets of public interests rather than to encapsulated constituencies with special interests—the ultimate goal of any democratic system.

This is a quite a different starting point from that taken by most participants—Euro-federalist or Euro-sceptical—in contemporary scholarly or public debates about the 'democratic deficit'. They argue almost entirely at the level of abstract democratic theory: Most European citizens neither deliberate nor participate in EU activities: therefore the EU is undemocratic. This sort of reasoning will not do. The EU must be judged not in terms of its adherence to some ideal of national democracy but instead as a particular sort of *limited, multi-level constitutional polity* designed within a specific social and historical context. It follows that any legitimate normative criticism of a European 'democratic deficit' must be grounded in a sophisticated analysis of how the EU system has emerged, how it actually works, and whose concrete interests it represents under specific circumstances. Moreover, if biased representation of interests can be properly identified and evaluated only after detailed analysis of the real-world institutional constraints imposed on EU institutions and policies by a complex multi-level system, the actual nature of governance in the Member States, and the varying patterns of politics in distinct issue areas, we must turn more of our primary attention to the social science and history of the EU before returning to a discussion of ideal political philosophy. Yet beyond a handful of prominent but isolated contributions, one looks in vain in the contemporary debate for such arguments spanning positive and normative theory.[52] One can only conclude that controversy over the true extent of the European 'democratic deficit', and over the desirability of alternative constitutional orders for an integrated Europe, has only just begun.

[52] Giandomenico Majone, 'Europe's "Democratic Deficit": The Question of Standards', *European Law Journal*, 4/1 (1998), 5–28; Scharpf, *Governing in Europe*. In a recent book, Joseph Weiler hints at the need for a more differentiated analysis by issue area. See Weiler, *Constitution of Europe*, 270ff.

III

Legal and Regulatory Instruments of Federal Governance

7

The Role of Law in the Functioning of Federal Systems

GEORGE A. BERMANN

1. Introduction

Federal systems are about the distribution of legal and political power. But law is not only one of the currencies of federalism; it is also one of federalism's most important supports. In this chapter, I consider the role that law plays in establishing and enforcing the system by which both legal and political power are distributed within the United States and the European Union.

I begin with three basic assumptions about federalism. First, I assume that federalism—by which I mean the allocation of power among different vertically-situated levels of government[1]—is strongly capable of promoting a range of values that occupy a high rank within modern liberal democracies. These values include liberty, diversity, self-determination, accountability, and the various efficiencies associated with regulatory competition.[2] I further assume that, even as the United States embarks on a widening array of cooperative international regimes in which concern over the allocation of government authority within the US has no obvious place, we nevertheless remain interested in protecting and promoting federalism principles.

Third, I assume for present purposes that the allocation of power with which federalism is concerned is essentially a subject matter rather than a functional allocation. This is a major assumption, since there are federal systems whose vertical allocations of power run along functional lines—for example, who legislates? who executes? who adjudicates? who taxes?

[1] On a basic ambiguity in the term 'federalism', and the fact that, as currently used, the term sometimes denotes centralization and sometimes decentralization, see William Safire, 'Federalism: The Political Word that Means its Opposite', *New York Times Magazine*, 30 January (2000), 20.

[2] George A. Bermann, 'Taking Subsidiarity Seriously: Federalism in the European Community and the United States', *Columbia Law Review*, 94 (1994), 331, 339–43.

who spends?—rather than subject matter lines. Focusing on subject matter allocations means essentially asking: Who gets to address what substantive issues? What general principles, if any, determine this allocation? What presumptions, if any, about the allocation may be at play? Are powers at a given level enumerated only? Do any particular rules of construction govern the exercise of power allocations? Are powers exclusively allocated to one level and one level only, or are they shared? If powers are shared, what if any principles of sharing—for example, subsidiarity[3]—govern the sharing? Under what circumstances does the exercise of authority on a given subject at one level pre-empt the prior or subsequent exercise of power at another? And so on.

2. Law and Federalism

It should be obvious that law has a role to play in drawing the allocative map to which I have referred. For all practical purposes, drawing such a map is an exercise in constitution-making, albeit on only one of the issues—division of powers—that interest constitution-makers. But law also plays a longer-term role in promoting federalism values. Certainly in both the EU and the US, it also seeks to ensure that sub-constitutional law and policy faithfully reflect the allocative map, as well as to ensure that the map is enforced by courts when sub-constitutional law and policy fail to do so. In other words, allocations of rule-making authority are determined not only by constitutional design but also by patterns of legislative implementation and judicial enforcement.

Law supports allocations of legislative authority in basically three ways. First, law may require that decisional authorities at the federal level be

[3] Article 5 [ex Art. 3b] of the EC Treaty provides that 'In areas which do not fall within its exclusive competence, the Community shall take action . . . only if and in so far as the objectives of the proposed action cannot be sufficiently achieved by the Member States and can therefore, by reason of the scale or effects of the proposed action, be better achieved by the Community'. As worded, subsidiarity is not so much a principle of power allocation as a principle that prescribes when powers, once allocated, should or should not be exercised. The protocol on the application of the principles of subsidiarity and proportionality, attached to the Treaty of Amsterdam, clarifies (in para. 4) that subsidiarity has two aspects. In order for Community action to be justified, subsidiarity requires both that the Member States cannot sufficiently achieve the objectives at hand and that the Community can better achieve them. Put simply, Member State alternatives must be both 'ineffective' and 'inefficient'. The protocol builds upon previous instruments, notably the European Council's 'Guidelines for Application of the Subsidiarity Principle', 25 E.C. Bull. No. 12 (1992), 15, and the 'Interinstitutional Agreement on Democracy, Transparency and Subsidiarity', O.J. C. 32/132 (6 December 1993). For the text of the protocol, see O.J. C 340/92 (10 November 1997).

structured and composed in such a way as to ensure that the interests of sub-national communities are represented in the federal legislative process. Second, law may impose specific procedural requirements to help ensure that the interests thus represented are also actually considered in the deliberative process. Third, law may formulate certain more or less well-defined principles of federalism by which the output of the federal political process—in short, legislation or regulation—may be judged, not only politically but also legally. Each of these legal strategies has a distinctive methodology and distinctively implicates public and private institutions, including of course the courts.

Law and the Political Safeguards of Federalism

As a first means of influence, law may seek to enforce established power allocations by governing the structure and composition of the federal political—chiefly legislative—institutions, such as the US Senate or the EU Council of Ministers. The notion is that law enhances respect for federalism values by requiring that federal institutions be structured and composed in ways that specifically cause the interests of sub-national units of governments and their constituencies to be taken into account in the policy-making process. The US States and the EU Member States thus enjoy the right to be heard, and presumably have their interests taken into account, as the Senate and the Council, respectively, make their political determinations. Mandatory consultation of various committees, both in the US and the EU, afford analogous opportunities for influence in the 'federal' legislative and administrative process. Whether or not these organic norms are formally expressed in the constitution or the constitutive treaties, as the case may be, they are assumed to affect importantly whether and to what extent the established allocations of power will in fact be respected.

It would be a mistake to think of these safeguards in static terms, as if, once consecrated by the constitution, they automatically have their effect. The utility of entrenched rules about the structure and composition of federal institutions depends, by the very nature of such rules, not only on their legal effectiveness but also on their political effectiveness. It is for good reason that the literature describes them as '*political* safeguards of federalism'.[4] Their effectiveness is accordingly no less a political than a legal issue, and it is in these terms that the theory of safeguards has been widely

[4] See Herbert Wechsler, 'The Political Safeguards of Federalism: The Role of the States in the Composition and Selection of the National Government', *Columbia Law Review*, 54 (1954), 543.

called into question, at least in the US.[5] In order to enhance the strength of these political safeguards of federalism, the bodies that are designed to incorporate them may need to take further steps to make them operational. In recent years we have seen scattered examples of federal institutions putting further safeguard mechanisms into motion. For example, Congress has placed legislative limitations on the use of *unfunded mandates*,[6] by which I mean requirements that State and local governments implement federal policies even when they are not given the federal funding with which to do so. For its part, the Executive Branch has imposed its own requirement of a 'federalism assessment'—including but not limited to the financial impact on State and local governments—as part of its more general federal regulatory review process.[7]

The operation of the political safeguards of federalism in the EU, on the other hand, has not been sufficiently studied. The founders may have originally structured and composed the European institutions so as to ensure respect for the autonomy and interests of the Member States, but it is open to question whether over time they have succeeded. Viewed structurally, the Commission and Parliament do not have very many natural incentives to vindicate Member State interests. The Council, being composed of Member State representatives, may be their more natural guardian. But even then, as prospects for the casting of Member State vetoes diminish with each successive intergovernmental conference and each revision of the constitutive treaties, the Council's ability to function in this way is weakened. One consequence is that the Member States have felt constrained to devise alternative treaty safeguards,[8] not only to protect their own interests but on occasion the interests of sub-national units.[9]

At the end of the day, if the problem with the political safeguards of federalism is basically more political than legal, then there are necessarily

[5] See Carol F. Lee, 'The Political Safeguards of Federalism? Congressional Responses to Supreme Court Decisions on State and Local Liability', *Urban Lawyer*, 20 (1988), 301, 333; Lewis B. Kaden, 'Politics, Money and State Sovereignty', *Columbia Law Review*, 79 (1979), 847, 897; Andrzej Rapaczynski, 'From Sovereignty to Process: The Jurisprudence of Federalism after *Garcia*', *Supreme Court Review*, 1985 (1985), 341, 419.

[6] The Unfunded Mandates Reform Act of 1995, Pub. L. 104-4, 109 Stat. 48, 2 U.S.C. sec. 658d et seq.

[7] Executive Order 12612, 3 CFR, sec. 252, 52 Fed. Reg. 41685, replaced by Executive Order 12875, 3 CFR sec. 669, 58 Fed. Reg. 58093, reprinted in 5 U.S.C. Sec. 601. See the chapter by David Lazer and Viktor Mayer-Schoenberger in this volume.

[8] Examples include creation of the Committee of the Regions in EC Treaty art. 263 [ex art. 198a], and attachment to the Treaty of Amsterdam of a protocol on the role of national parliaments in the European Union (establishing a Conference of European Affairs Committees, or COSAC). O.J. C 340/113 (10 November 1997).

[9] See, for example, Art. 23 of the German Basic Law—*Grundgesetz*—vesting certain of Germany's decision-making rights in the Council of the European Union in the hands of the German *Länder*.

limits on the extent to which the law can strengthen them. To the extent that we rely on political safeguards to vindicate federalism values, we are relying first and foremost on constitution-makers, and secondarily on the drafters of the organic legislation that organizes the basic political institutions. Courts have the means to enforce such safeguard mechanisms, but no way of ensuring that they work, and regulators by and large escape the direct effect of these mechanisms altogether.[10]

Procedural Reinforcements of Federalism

If institutional law can achieve only so much by determining the way in which federal bodies are structured and composed, we have reason to explore alternative avenues of legal influence. Among the most prominent, and presumably legitimate, strategies that law may pursue is to mandate certain aspects of the deliberative process by which federal institutions reach their decisions. To this extent, the law's intervention becomes predominantly procedural.

Procedural mandates in the interest of federalism take a variety of forms. The most obvious, and I suppose time-honoured, are requirements that decision-makers consult certain public or private bodies which, by virtue of their own composition or mission, may be expected to express either the institutional interests of sub-national governments or the policy preferences that those governments, or their constituencies, are likely to harbour.[11] To the dismay of the Committee of Regions, consultation on specific legislative matters is about all that that Committee can legally demand of the political institutions at the EU level. Mandatory consultation of bodies representing sub-national interests is even less embedded in US law, perhaps the best example being the role of the US Advisory Commission on Intergovernmental Relations under the Unfunded Mandates Reform Act of 1995.[12]

Legally imposed consultation requirements proceed on the basis of a succession of assumptions: namely (1) that there are identifiable institutional interests and policy preferences of sub-national governments; (2) that the mandatorily consulted body in fact adequately reflects those interests and preferences; (3) that that body will effectively express them; and (4) that, in reaching their decisions, the political branches will give due attention and consideration to such expressions. These are assumptions

[10] See the chapter by Giandomenico Majone in this volume.

[11] Paragraph 6 of the Subsidiarity Protocol to the Amsterdam Treaty (see note 3 above) instructs the Commission to 'consult widely' and 'publish [its] consultation documents' on the subsidiarity aspects of its proposals.

[12] See note 6 above.

that it may seem reasonable to make, but they are large assumptions nonetheless.

Perhaps fuelled by doubts that the political branches 'listen' meaningfully to the bodies that they are required to consult, legislatures have recently shown a fondness for requiring that the political branches themselves conduct the relevant inquiries and/or make the relevant findings. To be sure, federalism is not the only set of values that prescribed 'regulatory analyses', 'impact statements', 'requirements of reasons', or 'findings requirements' are designed to advance. Such devices may promote, for example, environmental values—as in the case of environmental impact analyses—or solicitude for small and medium-sized businesses—as in the case of small and medium-size business impact statements. But federalism does figure among the ostensibly protected values, both in the US[13] and in the EU.[14] The requirement of a federalism inquiry of one sort or another, much like a consultation requirement, is based on an assumption that conducting such exercises increases the likelihood that the relevant political considerations—in this case federalism values—will be taken into account in the deliberative process.[15] However, unlike required consultation of outside bodies, the requirement that the decision-maker itself address the federalism issues, such as they are, offers greater hope of amounting to more than a pure procedural formality.

In the EU, matters have been taken yet a step further. The European Commission in particular has been asked to account on a regular basis for its contributions as an institution to implementation of the principle of subsidiarity.[16] Through a series of annual reports, it now documents both its withdrawals of legislative proposals and its proposals for the with-

[13] For examples, see George A. Bermann, *Regulatory Federalism: European Union and United States*, The Hague Academy of International Law Recueil des cours, 263 (The Hague: Martinus Nijhoff, 1997), 94–6.

[14] The Subsidiarity Protocol to the Amsterdam Treaty (see note 3 above) is most explicit (in para. 4) about the Commission's role: 'For any proposed Community legislation, the reasons on which it is based shall be stated with a view to justifying that it complies with the principle of subsidiarity. These reasons must be substantiated by qualitative and, wherever possible, quantitative indications.' As for the Council and Parliament, the Protocol (paras 11, 12) enjoins them specifically to consider the question of a measure's compliance with the principle of subsidiarity. The Council is further required to inform the Parliament of its position and the reasons for it.

[15] See the chapter by David Lazer and Viktor Mayer-Schoenberger in this volume.

[16] Paragraph 9 of the Subsidiarity Protocol (see note 3 above) calls upon the Commission in effect to give an 'accounting' of its subsidiarity efforts, in the form of an annual report setting out both the proposals for legislation that are being withdrawn on account of subsidiarity and the existing measures whose legislative repeal is being proposed on that account. This device operates in part on a principle of 'embarrassment'. Were the Commission's annual report devoid of any content, the Commission would have some explaining to do.

drawal of legislation in accordance with the principle. The institution is thus compelled not only to justify in subsidiarity terms the specific proposals that it from time to time advances for adoption, but also its overall record as the EU's 'legislative engine'.

Procedural reinforcements of federalism have the merit of not depriving, or at least not appearing to deprive, the political branches of their policy-making responsibilities. Put in simple terms, the political branches can be made to take federalism considerations into account without necessarily having to favour or disfavour certain substantive outcomes and without having to assign these considerations any particular weight, much less make them outcome-determinative. But having said this, on what basis are we to suppose that procedural mandates make any difference at all in the deliberative process, other than by ensuring that decision-makers are not wholly ignorant of a proposed measure's federalism implications? Observers have found neither the reports of the EU Commission on subsidiarity[17] nor the 'federalism analyses' by the US government[18] to be terribly convincing elements of proof that federalism considerations enter meaningfully into the deliberative rule-making process. At the end of the day, procedural reinforcements can be no more than *potentially* protective of federalism values. A court can certainly police whether the required exercises have been conducted—and possibly even whether they have been honestly and truly conducted—but, given the nature of procedural controls, it can realistically do little more.

Direct Judicial Policing of Boundaries

We have seen that a system that operates chiefly on the basis of political safeguards of federalism cannot realistically assign to the courts a major policing role; their role in this respect is to supervise structure. A system that operates chiefly on the basis of procedural safeguards of federalism may give courts a better defined role to play, but it is limited to supervising adherence to procedures. If courts wish to play a more central part in the protection of federalism values, they must look elsewhere, and they from time to time do so.

Among the most obvious means by which courts may do more is through direct review of the 'competence' question, by which I mean the question whether national or sub-national authorities, in acting as they have, have respected the constitutional or quasi-constitutional limits on

[17] To a very large extent, the Commission's annual reports describe a simplification and consolidation of existing legislation in the interest of better order, rather than a significant curtailment of it in the interest of subsidiarity. See Bermann, 'Regulatory Federalism', 81.

[18] See Bermann, 'Taking Subsidiarity Seriously', 442–5.

their power. With any luck, the courts will not be the first to ask this question. In the case of federal action, the federal authorities, and all entities that these authorities are called upon to consult prior to acting, should have considered the competence question independently. But at some point, when a litigant with standing to raise the question does so, the courts will also address it, and presumably do so with some degree of independence.

For all the reasons that have historically favoured reliance on political and procedural rather than judicial safeguards of federalism, direct federalism review by the courts may be problematic. Such review assumes that there are indeed objective standards by which the conformity of secondary legislation with federalism principles may be judged, and that the courts are capable of applying those standards without interfering with the policy judgements that, in a democracy, are the political branches' to make. It is consequently small wonder that courts approach direct judicial review of federalism with some hesitation and with a degree of experimentalism. In section 3, I turn to both some of the established and some of the newer patterns of judicial intervention.

3. Courts and Legislative Federalism

In purporting to enforce constitutional principles of federalism, courts naturally take their cues from the federalism formulae that constitutions themselves supply. A court's task, at least in the first instance, is to construe the constitutional language that describes the allocation of lawmaking authority and to determine whether the political branches have respected it.

Enforcing 'Catalogues' of Competence

To the extent that allocations of authority are drawn in subject matter terms, the judicial exercise consists basically of determining whether or not an exercise of legislative power properly falls within the scope of the relevant subject matter attribution. At the extreme, one can imagine a 'menu' or 'catalogue' of enumerated competences within which an exercise of legislative authority either falls or does not fall, depending on how the court defines the competence and/or characterizes the exercise. At the other extreme, constitutions contain general formulae, in the form of statements of principle about the allocation. Subsidiarity is an example.[19]

[19] See note 3 above.

In truth, both the US Constitution and the EC Treaty fall well short of a catalogue of competences. The great majority of federal legislative interventions in the US are justified not on the ground that their subject matter is one that the Constitution has specifically entrusted to federal authorities, but on the ground that the problem addressed 'implicates' interstate commerce.[20] To a lesser extent, the same may be said of the EU, most of whose legislative activity has been predicated on general 'harmonization' provisions in the interest of a better functioning internal market.[21]

Even so, neither the US Supreme Court nor the European Court of Justice has traditionally shown a great deal of interest in closely examining the question whether a given exercise of legislative authority is or is not constitutionally justified by reference to the commerce clause or the EC Treaty's harmonization provisions, respectively. This has almost certainly not been due to a conviction that doing so would be constitutionally out of bounds, but rather that it would be politically dangerous. Thus, even when striking down the Gun-Free School Zone Act in the case of *United States v. Lopez*,[22] as outside the boundaries of the inter state commerce clause, the Supreme Court appeared to lay down an essentially deferential test. Under *Lopez*, Congress basically needs only to conclude—and be able plausibly to do so—that the requirements of interstate commerce justify the legislation in question.[23] On the other hand, still more recent decisions of the Court do demonstrate that even express congressional findings of an effect upon interstate commerce will not necessarily support use of the interstate commerce clause.[24]

For its part, the European Court of Justice has never taken the opportunity to define restrictively the Treaty's competence-conferring provisions, nor has it seriously questioned whether a Community law measure

[20] 'The Congress shall have the power to . . . regulate commerce with foreign nations, and among the several states.' US Constitution, Art. I, sec. 8.

[21] 'The Council shall . . . adopt the measures for the approximation of the provisions laid down by law, regulation or administrative action in Member States which have as their object the establishment and functioning of the internal market.' EC Treaty, art. 95 [ex 100a].

[22] 514 U.S. 549 (1995).

[23] See also *Reno v. Condon*, ___ U.S. ___, 120 S. Ct. 666 (2000). On the other hand, for reasons explored below, the Supreme Court has recently taken a considerably harder look at the justification, in terms of 'proportionality', for legislation that Congress enacts on the basis of section five—the enforcement clause—of the Fourteenth Amendment. See notes 48–52 below and accompanying text.

[24] See *United States v. Morrison*, ___U.S.___, 120 S. Ct. 1740 (2000). There, the Court, in a 5-4 opinion, ruled that the inter-State commerce clause could not support enactment of the federal Violence Against Women Act of 1994, since Congress may not regulate non-economic violent criminal conduct merely on the basis of the conduct's aggregate effect on inter-State commerce.

bears a sufficient connection to the internal market to justify its adoption pursuant to the Treaty's internal market harmonization provisions. The closest the Court has come to doing so is deciding, in cases where a measure has more than one plausible legal basis in the Treaty, which is the measure's 'proper' legal basis.[25] Even then, the inquiry is made not to determine whether the Community institutions are competent to enact the measure, but rather to determine which legislative procedure they needed to follow in doing so. In none of these legal basis cases was the measure claimed to fall outside of Community competence altogether.

'Necessity' for Federal Intervention

Distinct from the question whether or not a measure falls within a recognized category of subject matter competence is the question whether, assuming it does, the measure may be regarded as actually 'necessary' for achieving its stated objective. By this I refer to whether the objective being pursued could or could not reasonably be attained without taking the measure that is being questioned. The US Supreme Court has traditionally avoided inquiring into the necessity of federal legislation in this particular sense; arguably even when Congress uses the Constitution's 'necessary and proper' clause, rather than a specifically enumerated power, as the basis for legislation, necessity has not been the subject of close judicial scrutiny. It is fair to say that Congress's determination that legislation enacted under Art. I of the Constitution is required for achieving a legitimate federal objective is virtually unreviewable judicially. A fortiori, US courts have not asked the precise question that subsidiarity poses, namely, whether the States were in a position to effectively and efficiently achieve the objective underlying a piece of federal legislation.[26] This of course is different from the question whether Congress may permissibly 'find' that interstate commerce is implicated, a matter into which the courts evidently may now look.[27]

[25] See George A. Bermann, Roger J. Goebel, William J. Davey, and Eleanor M. Fox, *Cases and Materials on European Community Law* (St Paul, MN: West Publishing, 1993) and cases cited therein, along with the 1998 Supplement.

[26] Reviewing Congress's determination that action at the State level would be ineffective in achieving a federal objective, or that action at the federal level would be more efficient, would be considered illegitimate 'second-guessing' on policy matters that the courts lack the political legitimacy to decide and that are properly left to the political branches.

[27] See *United States v. Morrison*, note 24 above. Moreover, a majority of the Court has recently shown a willingness to review the 'proportionality' of federal legislation enacted pursuant to section five—the enforcement clause—of the Fourteenth Amendment. See notes 48–52 below and accompanying text.

By contrast, the language of the subsidiarity clause of the EC Treaty[28] would suggest that necessity is very much a legal condition for Community action, at least in areas of concurrent competence. From the point of view of language alone, the Treaty drafters could scarcely have been clearer in declaring that the Community institutions may not legally act in such areas unless the inability of the Member States adequately to address the problem at hand renders it necessary that the Community take action. The EU's political branches have repeatedly acknowledged that they are bound by this understanding of the subsidiarity doctrine, and the Member States solemnly endorsed it in the 'Subsidiarity Protocol' to the Amsterdam Treaty.[29]

Still, even in the presence of constitutional language of necessity, the Court of Justice has thus far shown a great reluctance to grapple with that issue. In neither of the two relevant judgments rendered thus far—*United Kingdom v. Council*[30] and *Germany v. Parliament and Council*[31]—did the Court require more than a conclusory statement of reasons by the Council—or Council and Parliament—for believing that Community-level action was required;[32] it certainly did not demand that such a finding be supported either by evidence or by detailed or elaborate reasoning. Put differently, the political institutions may need to show that they took a look at the subsidiarity question, but not necessarily that they took a 'hard look' at it.[33] The Court itself is clearly not taking a 'hard look' at that question, nor should we expect that it would. Thus, the Court has not only proceduralized the subsidiarity inquiry, but done so in terms which ensure that the Court will in the end be rather easily satisfied. Arguably, the Court

[28] See note 3 above.

[29] See note 3 above.

[30] Case C-94/94 (Working Time Directive), [1996] ECR I-793. In this case, the UK challenged the Council's use of the EC Treaty article, then 118a, on social policy, rather than articles that would have required unanimity in the Council, in adopting a directive regulating hours of employment. The Court ruled that the Council could reasonably conclude that improving the health and safety of workers required harmonization of national law, and that harmonization in turn necessitated Community-wide action.

[31] Case C-233/94 (Deposit Guarantee Schemes), [1997] ECR I–2405. Here, Germany challenged a directive requiring the Member States to establish a system for guaranteeing bank deposits. Germany faulted the Parliament and Council for failing to support the directive with a statement of reasons that demonstrated the measure's compatibility with the principle of subsidiarity. The Court found the institutions' statements in this regard to be sufficient.

[32] The Subsidiarity Protocol to the Amsterdam Treaty—see note 3 above—does not require that the Council, or Council and Parliament, give any statement of reasons as such. To this extent, the Court's judgements go procedurally further.

[33] In the *Working Time Directive* case, the Court implied that once the institutions find that harmonization of national laws is necessary, action at the Community level automatically becomes necessary. This makes the requirement of a statement of reasons quite easy to satisfy. In the *Deposit Guarantee Scheme* case, the Court seemingly accepted at face value the official statement of reasons that Community-level action was necessary.

should in the future not content itself with a purely procedural requirement of a statement of reasons, but rather also review, if only deferentially, the subsidiarity determination itself, that is, the determination whether the criteria of subsidiarity are met.[34]

To the extent that subsidiarity is proving to be at bottom a political rather than a judicial instrument, the onus necessarily shifts back to the political institutions of the Community, and their constituencies, to ensure that the capacities and interests of the Member States are duly taken into account when legislative measures come up for consideration. This in turn suggests the need for new or improved political safeguards of federalism within the EU context. These may include such measures as strengthening the participation of the national parliaments, giving a larger role to the Committee of the Regions, or indeed inventing new safeguard mechanisms altogether.[35]

Protecting the 'Core' of State Sovereignty

Even if the courts are not positioned to police effectively the frontiers of the 'federal' institutions' enumerated powers or to review the necessity of their interventions, they may nevertheless seek to protect what they regard as the vital aspects, or 'core,' of state sovereignty which these institutions are not permitted to invade even when making an otherwise valid use of their powers, as for instance Congress under Article I of the Constitution. This is a strategy that at one point appealed to a majority of the Supreme Court,[36] but that, with a change in the Court's composition, subsequently fell out of favour. In the case of *Garcia v. San Antonio Housing Authority*,[37] the majority, essentially subscribing to the theory of political safeguards of federalism, ruled that the states, acting through the federal political institutions—including notably Congress—should be deemed capable of protecting their essential 'sovereign' interests, and that the federal courts should not be asked to perform this function for them. This judgement rests at least in part on the difficulty of arriving, through notions of 'tra-

[34] This may be the import of para. 13 of the Subsidiarity Protocol to the Amsterdam Treaty—see note 3 above. If such 'substantive' review, like the procedural review, is destined to be deferential, the question naturally arises whether it is worth conducting. I conclude that it is.

[35] See notes 8 and 9 above and accompanying text.

[36] *National League of Cities v. Usery*, 426 U.S. 833 (1976). In *National League of Cities*, the Court upheld a challenge to the application of federal minimum wage standards to State and local public officials on the ground that State employment policies are matters that have 'traditionally' been left to the States, and that lay beyond the proper scope of Congress's powers under the Tenth Amendment, because federalizing them would hamper the States in the performance of their essential functions.

[37] 469 U.S. 528 (1985).

ditional' or 'essential' state functions, at the core of sovereignty insulated by the Tenth Amendment in the first place, not to mention determining the extent to which a legislative measure impairs them. However, given the slimness of the Supreme Court majority in *Garcia*, the subsequent changes in the Court's composition, and the Court's recent heightened sensitivity to questions of federalism, it cannot be assumed that the Court's position will not change again.

Interestingly, the European Court of Justice has not shown much inclination to carve out specific matters in which the Member States of the EU have 'core' sovereignty interests that deserve to be sheltered from Community governance. Perhaps the Court shares the Supreme Court's discomfort with such an approach. More likely, it operates on the assumption that if the Member States are capable of doing anything as they gather around the table at their periodic intergovernmental conferences, it is to identify what they consider to be the areas of vital national interest and to protect them through appropriate means—the most obvious examples being eliminating the Community competence altogether, subjecting Community action to unanimous voting or preserving the right to 'opt out'. So long as the Member States do convene at intervals to reshape the constitutive treaties, as well as to decide upon the specific means by which action in various sectors may be taken at the Community level, there is little reason to suppose that they cannot adequately protect themselves. In any event, the case for judicial intervention to protect the Member States from themselves is correspondingly weaker when, by its very nature, the Treaty enables the Member States to express their sovereignty concerns and to do so in ways that will thereafter limit the freedom of action of the Community's political branches.[38]

4. Federalism as a 'Relational' Problem

In place of the fairly obvious strategies just canvassed—policing the borders of enumerated powers, reviewing the necessity for federal intervention, and protecting certain 'core' sovereign interests of the states—the Supreme Court has focused lately on a variety of what I call, for lack of a

[38] The case law of the Court of Justice on 'the correct legal basis' of legislation—see note 25 above and accompanying text—rests on the premise that when Member States consider sovereignty concerns important enough, they include appropriate voting formula language in the relevant treaty articles. On this reasoning, it is enough for the Court to enforce the requirement that for each Community law measure the 'correct' treaty basis must be used and to ensure that the procedures and voting formulae associated with that legal basis are actually followed.

better term, 'relational' aspects of federalism. By this I mean to suggest that the Court has identified certain forbidden 'interfaces' between the federal and State governments. The question then arises whether these, or any other, specific interfaces could be said to fall foul of the EU constitutional system and, more particularly, the relation between the EU and the Member States.

State Immunity to Suit

On occasion, the Court finds an explicit basis for its relational claims in the constitutional text itself. Perhaps the best example is the notion of state sovereign immunity to suit in federal court. The Eleventh Amendment expressly provides that 'The Judicial Power of the United States shall not be construed to extend to any suit in law or equity, commenced or prosecuted against one of the United States by Citizens of another State, or by Citizens or Subjects of any Foreign State'—a provision that has been construed by extension to protect the States from federal court suit by their own citizens as well. In recent years, the Supreme Court has ruled that Congress may not 'abrogate' Eleventh Amendment immunity by using the interstate commerce clause of Art. I to pass legislation that expressly subjects the states to litigation in the federal courts.[39] As for circumventing the Eleventh Amendment by authorizing suits against State officials, rather than against the States themselves, the Court has severely narrowed this possibility too, by confining it to suits that are brought against State officials to restrain future violations, thus barring any possibility of suing state officials for damages or other remedial relief for past violations.[40]

Still more recent decisions of the Court teach us, however, that sovereign immunity to suit is not merely a product of the Eleventh Amendment and its more or less specific language. In the case of *Alden v. Maine*, the Court ruled that Congress lacked constitutional power to subject the states to unconsented suits in State as well as federal courts, even though the Eleventh Amendment by its terms exclusively addresses suits in federal court. Rather, the notion of State sovereign immunity flows from a 'principle so well established that no one conceived it would be altered by the . . . Constitution';[41] that principle, according to the Court, protects States from unconsented suits in their own courts as well.

However robust the principle of State immunity to suit may lately have become in US Supreme Court doctrine, it does not hold out much promise

[39] Seminole Tribe of Florida, 517 U.S. 44 (1996).
[40] Idaho v. Coeur d'Alene Tribe of Idaho, 521 U.S. 261 (1997).
[41] 527 U.S. 706 (1999).

as a limitation on Community power within the EU. Far from prohibiting actions against Member States in the Community courts, the EC Treaty specifically authorizes them, at least at the instance of the Commission or other Member States.[42] While the Treaty does not subject the Member States to suits in the Community courts brought by private parties, Court of Justice case law now requires that the Member States open the doors of their own courts to private liability actions against themselves for the damage caused by their own failures or infringements under Community law.[43] Such private liability actions in national courts have become a conventional means of enforcing Community law obligations against the Member States. The contrast with *Alden v. Maine* in the US could scarcely be more striking.

Uses and Abuses of the Fourteenth Amendment

In a highly interesting development, Eleventh Amendment jurisprudence has further led indirectly to a substantial narrowing of the scope of the Fourteenth Amendment: the amendment that essentially affords protection of due process and equal protection against the States[44] and that, through its section five, specifically authorizes Congress to enact legislation to 'enforce' the Amendment's guarantees.[45] The context of this development is the notion that Congress may choose to 'abrogate' the States' Eleventh Amendment immunity from suit by enacting appropriate legislation action on the basis of a constitutional provision, such as section five of the Fourteenth Amendment, which post-dates the Eleventh Amendment. This has opened up the possibility for courts to determine whether a given legislative use of the Fourteenth Amendment is a valid one or not.[46] For example, according to a leading decision of the Court, Congress misuses its Fourteenth Amendment power to abrogate State sovereign immunity when it enacts legislation whose purpose is to define the

[42] EC Treaty, Arts. 226, 227 [ex Arts. 169, 170].

[43] Brasserie du Pecheur SA v. Germany, and The Queen v. Secretary of State for Transport ex parte Factortame Ltd., Joined Cases C-46, 48, [1996] ECR I-1029; Francovich v. Italy, Cases C-6, 9/90, [1991] ECR 5357.

[44] 'No State shall make or enforce any law which shall abridge the privileges or immunities of citizens of the United States; nor shall any State deprive any person of life, liberty, or property, without due process of law; nor deny to any person within its jurisdiction the equal protection of the laws.'

[45] 'The Congress shall have the power to enforce, by appropriate legislation, the provisions of this article.'

[46] Thus, limits on Congress' use of the Fourteenth Amendment are relevant not only to the enactment of legislation abrogating Eleventh Amendment immunity, but also more broadly to the enactment of legislation establishing a remedy against private persons. See *United States v. Morrison*, note 24 above.

scope or meaning of the Fourteenth Amendment through primary legislation, rather than to 'enforce' it as such by means of remedial legislation.[47]

The Court's case law on the scope of Congress's enforcement power under the Fourteenth Amendment is still more far-reaching. According to the Court, even when Congress is truly enforcing the Fourteenth Amendment, it does not have free rein in deciding how to do so. Rather, any such legislative enforcement must be appropriate in the sense that 'there must be a congruence and proportionality between the injury to be prevented or remedied and the means adopted to that end'.[48] In other words, as to each statute that is questioned, the Court considers its proportionality as a preventive or remedial measure. A thin majority of the Supreme Court has only recently struck down several pieces of federal legislation as exceeding in this respect the limits of section five of the Fourteenth Amendment.[49] The inquiry evidently to be conducted is not very different in principle from the inquiry mandated by the principle of proportionality, as set out in the EC Treaty[50] and the jurisprudence of the Court of Justice.[51] Quite clearly, by defining what it means for Congress to 'enforce' the Fourteenth Amendment by statute, and even more by reviewing the 'proportionality' of any such statute, the current Supreme Court majority is taking a rather close look at whether Congress has an adequate basis for depriving the States of their immunity from suit or otherwise using the Fourteenth Amendment.

One may legitimately question this recent Fourteenth Amendment jurisprudence. First, section five of the amendment authorizes Congress 'to enforce' the Fourteenth Amendment's guarantees, without specific reference to any requirement that the legislation be necessary, useful or proportional. Second, if the Court is not prepared to scrutinize the necessity

[47] *City of Boerne v. Flores*, 521 U.S. 507 (1997). In *City of Boerne*, the Supreme Court declared that Congress exceeded the bounds of section five of the Fourteenth Amendment in enacting the Religious Freedom Restoration Act (RFRA) of 1993, which sought to prohibit any unnecessary burdening of freedom of religion by requiring the States, whenever burdening it, to prove both a compelling State interest in doing so and the unavailability of a less restrictive alternative. The Court ruled that enforcing the Fourteenth Amendment's guarantees means essentially acting to remedy past violations or to prevent future ones. According to the Court, the RFRA did not do either of these things, but instead impermissibly sought to define what the Fourteenth Amendment means.

[48] *City of Boerne*, 521 U.S. at 520.

[49] *United States v. Morrison*, note 24 above; *Kimel v. Florida Bd. of Regents*, ___ U.S. ___, 120 S. Ct. 631 (2000); *College Savings Bank v. Florida Prepaid Post-Secondary Educ. Expense Bd.*, 527 U.S. 666 (1999); *Florida Prepaid Post-Secondary Educ. Expense Bd. v. College Savings Bank and United States*, 527 U.S. 627 (1999).

[50] EC Treaty, Art. 5 [ex Art. 3b]: 'Any action by the Community shall not go beyond what is necessary to achieve the objectives of this Treaty.'

[51] See, for example, Case 11/70, *Internationale Handelsgesellschaft GmbH v. Einfuhr- und Vorratsstelle für Getreide und Futtermittel*, [1970] ECR 1125.

for federal legislation enacted pursuant to the interstate commerce clause of Art. I—I assume this to be a fair reading of the *Lopez* case[52]—then it is not apparent, except for the fact that the Fourteenth Amendment targets State action, why the Court should scrutinize the necessity for legislation enacted pursuant to section five of the Fourteenth Amendment. Legislative exercises under both constitutional bases can importantly compromise the States' freedom of action. If the Court persists in this line of decision, the judiciary stands to perform, with respect to Congress's use of its legislative authority under the Fourteenth Amendment, precisely the kind of second-guessing that the Court seemingly sought to avoid in *Lopez* regarding Congress's interstate commerce powers.

The 'Anti-commandeering' Principle

The relational principle for which the Court has, in my view, had the greatest difficulty finding a specific textual basis in the Constitution is the principle according to which Congress may not compel the States to assist in the furtherance of federal policies. As articulated in the decisions in *New York v. United States*[53] and *Printz v. United States*,[54] the 'anti-commandeering' principle protects States from having to enact legislation or administer policies to which they are opposed. Thus, while Congress has broad authority to legislate under the interstate commerce clause, it may not 'conscript' State legislatures or administrative officers into the business of implementing that legislation or its underlying policies if the relevant State authorities refuse to do so. From a practical point of view, unless Congress can prevail on a State to lend its support to the achievement of a federal policy—for example, by offering it federal funds or other adequate incentives—Congress has no choice, if it wants the policies to be effective within that state, but to make federal legislative or administrative resources—for example, personnel, materiel, or funds—available in its place.

Although commandeering of scarce state resources has been described as a virtual 'way of life' within the European Union,[55] the anti-commandeering

[52] See notes 22 and 23 above and accompanying text. But see note 25 above and accompanying text, referring to the Court's recent opinion in *United States v. Morrison*.

[53] 505 U.S. 144 (1992). In *New York*, the Court ruled that Congress could not compel the States to enact legislation that either provided for disposal of all radioactive waste by a certain date or subjected the States to all liability for that waste as its owner.

[54] 521 U.S. 98 (1997). In *Printz*, the Court ruled that Congress could not compel local sheriffs to conduct background checks on purchasers of handguns as a feature of federal gun control policy.

[55] George A. Bermann, 'Judicial Enforcement of Federalism Principles', in Michael Kloepfer and Ingolf Poernice (eds), *Entwicklungsperspektiven der europaischen Verfassung im Lichte des Vertrags von Amsterdam* (Baden-Baden: Nomos Verlagsgesellachaft, 1999), 64, 74.

principle does have a basis in democratic theory. By protecting a State from having to devote its resources to objectives dictated by the federal government, the principle helps ensure that those resources will not be spent in ways that lack the support of that State's population or that otherwise fail to reflect its political priorities. At the same time, it also allows the State's electorate to hold State officials democratically accountable in policy and performance terms. For its part, the federal government ends up bearing not only the administrative and financial costs of the policy regimes that it prescribes, but also the political costs, including the political responsibility. The contrast with the EU is striking. EU Member State authorities are required to devote the necessary personnel and resources to the enforcement of EU law, regardless of the political preferences of a Member State's population. At the same time, they effectively bear political responsibility for policies that have basically been determined in Brussels.

The Supreme Court's anti-commandeering jurisprudence exemplifies its readiness to construct federalism principles unsupported by constitutional text.[56] While the Court ultimately invoked the Tenth Amendment in support of this jurisprudence, the language of the Amendment expresses at most the principle of enumerated powers and its corollary, a principle of reserved powers:[57] principles whose meaning and effectiveness do not logically require that the States enjoy freedom from commandeering. Although the full import of the anti-commandeering jurisprudence remains to be seen, it has great potential for ensuring that, in the face of State opposition, the federal government will have to bear the full financial and political costs of its policies, and that the States will consequently have more ample opportunity to pursue their own policies if they are truly determined to do so.

What is the potential role of relational principles in the EU? The question arises because the EU's traditional safeguard mechanisms—for example, defining the structure and composition of the Council and other EU bodies, requiring the conduct of subsidiarity analyses—may prove to be inadequate, and at the same time traditional judicial approaches, such as policing competences, reviewing necessity, and identifying 'core' aspects of state sovereignty, may prove unattractive. It is not simply a question of translating relational rules from the US to Europe, or between

[56] See, for example, Saikrishna Prakash, 'Field Office Federalism', *Virginia Law Review*, 79 (1993), 1957; Richard Levy, 'New York v. United States: An Essay on the Uses and Misuses of Precedent, History and Policy in Determining the Scope of Federal Power', *Kansas Law Review*, 41 (1993), 493. Congress can, of course, make its own legislative contribution to the anti-commandeering effort. Consider the Unfunded Mandates Act of 1995, note 6 above.

[57] 'The powers not delegated to the United States by the Constitution, nor prohibited by it to the States, are reserved to the States respectively, or to the people.'

any two federal or federal-type systems. By their very nature, such rules reflect basic assumptions about the relationship between levels of government and about the importance of various aspects of that relationship, like being commandeered or being sued, in overall calculations of power and influence: assumptions in respect of which systems in fact differ widely. For example, in contrast to the US, the EU system extends a broad invitation to commandeering of the Member States, through directives or otherwise. Any relational rules devised by the Court of Justice would have to be appropriate to the EU's own particular historical and political environment.

The truth is that, even in federal or federal-type systems, courts have other, and arguably more compelling, things to do than to enforce allocative maps. This is particularly apparent in polities that have a programmatic mission, which is what the EU has historically had, in the form of commitment to a fully integrated internal market. A court that feels called upon to champion certain fundamental policies—whether market integration, human rights, or anything else—may act in ways that profoundly affect the polity's allocations of power. Arguably, the Fourteenth Amendment has had a far greater effect on federalism in the US than the amendment—the Tenth—that ostensibly addresses the allocation question, and the same may be said of the EC Treaty's provisions on harmonization in furtherance of the internal market. Similarly, a determination to pursue transatlantic regulatory cooperation—or any form of international regulatory cooperation, for that matter—inevitably has strong federalism implications for the nations that participate.[58] If we fix our attention too closely on federalism decisions of the courts as such, we risk missing the collateral federalism effects of other decisions, political and judicial alike.

5. Conclusion

Although at the end of the day politics, more than anything else, determines the real allocative map of power in vertically-divided systems, the law has found ways to shape and enforce that map. Law—more precisely, constitutional law—lays down the fundamentals, in the form of principles intended to guide both the political institutions in their exercises of power and the courts in reviewing the legality of those exercises. No matter what

[58] George A. Bermann, 'International Regulatory Cooperation and US Federalism', in G. Bermann, M. Herdegen, P. Lindseth (eds), *Transatlantic Regulatory Cooperation* (Oxford: Oxford University Press, 2000), 373–84.

the favoured strategy of legal control happens to be, these principles serve as the primary points of constitutional reference.

Because formulae, however, are not self-enforcing, both the US and EU are also engaged in the process of devising mechanisms of enforcement. Curiously, not only the youthful EU but also the centuries-old American Republic finds itself in an essentially experimental mode regarding the design and operation of such mechanisms. A traditional way of enforcing the prescribed allocation of authority is to structure and compose federal institutions so as to bring the voice of sub-national communities into the federal legislative process. Taking this strategy a step further, the law may require decision-makers actually to conduct certain inquiries and analyses, or to make certain findings, about matters such as the necessity for federal-level intervention or the impact of such intervention on the interests of State and local governments. In other words, federalism may be made a procedural part of the deliberative process.

Strategies based on structural or procedural safeguards have inherent limitations flowing from the fact that they are based on questionable assumptions about how institutions work and about how structures and procedures affect outcomes. Consequently, consideration inevitably turns to the further possibility of examining the output of the federal political process more directly, by measuring its conformity with whatever principles of federalism are expressed or implied in the constitutive documents. The political actors may, and hopefully will, ask the relevant questions; indeed the structural and procedural strategies that I have discussed presume that they will. But courts can also be expected to have something to say.

The most obvious way for courts to intervene—apart, of course, from enforcing the structural and procedural requirements to which I have alluded—is to enforce directly the limitations of competence—subject matter or otherwise—that are provided for by the constitutive documents, by invalidating any measures that exceed them. Doing so necessarily entails construing the relevant constitutional provisions and then determining how much deference the political branches are owed in their application. A somewhat less obvious way for courts to intervene is to review the question whether the measures at issue are truly 'necessary' for achieving a legitimate objective—with special reference, perhaps, to the constituent States' capacity to achieve that objective through their own action. Doing so likewise entails construing a legal notion—'necessity'—and again determining the deference owed to the political branches in applying this criterion. Under a third approach, the courts might seek to identify independently what attributes constitute the vital 'core' of state sovereignty and then to ensure that those attributes are safeguarded. Here, too, there arises the question whether the courts owe deference to Congress's assessment of the States' sovereignty claims, or of the extent of damage that particular federal interventions do to them.

For the reasons I have stated, each of these strategies in its own way places the courts in the position of second-guessing the political branches on what are essentially political judgements. This is manifestly the case when courts take it upon themselves to review the 'necessity' for action at a certain level of government. But it also arises when courts substitute their definition of a constitutional competence for that of the political branches, or purport to elevate certain matters to the level of 'core' sovereign interests, even though the political branches have in fact failed to accord them that particular status.

It is perhaps because these three strategies—policing the borders of enumerated powers, reviewing the necessity for federal intervention, and protecting certain core sovereign interests of the States—are so potentially problematic that the Supreme Court has lately shown a preference for seemingly more objective principles which I describe as 'relational' in nature. These are principles which identify certain forbidden 'interfaces' between levels of government. The clearest example is the 'anti-commandeering' principle, a principle whose basic purpose is to entitle the States to determine freely the political priorities to which their human, administrative, and financial resources will be devoted. Immunity from unconsented suit in federal court—and, since *Alden v. Maine*, in State court as well—can also be understood in this light. Unfortunately, the Supreme Court's very recent jurisprudence examining whether Congress has validly 'abrogated' this immunity by enacting a particular piece of legislation under the Fourteenth Amendment—and making the result depend on a court's assessment of the legislation's proportionality—takes the courts off this path and back in the direction of second-guessing political judgements by the political branches.

Assuming the Court maintains its preference for relational rules, as exemplified by sovereign immunity and the anti-commandeering principle, the preference is an intriguing one. While relational rules are rarely 'bright-line' in nature, they arguably also lend themselves to easier application than do rules of a more plainly political character. On the one hand, such rules do look more objective in the sense that their application avoids the appearance of second-guessing determinations on matters of policy that the political branches have presumably already made.[59] To the extent

[59] It should be easier for federal courts to recognize 'commandeering' or 'conscription', when they see it, than to determine whether a piece of federal legislation genuinely implicates inter-State commerce, whether an activity represents a sufficiently 'traditional' or 'essential' attribute of State sovereignty to insulate it from federal regulation, or whether the federal intervention is 'necessary' or 'proportionate.'

that relational rules raise questions that the political branches have not themselves raised, they also avert the delicate matter of determining the degree of deference, if any, that the courts owe to the political branches upon the occasion of judicial review. All of this makes relational rules distinctly advantageous from the Court's point of view.

On the other hand, the relationship between relational rules and the constitutional text can be quite tenuous. Indeed the very foundation of such rules in constitutional thought may be open to serious doubt, as shown by the 5–4 division within the opinions of the Court that have announced them. Though, in operation, they may be highly effective tools of federalism, relational rules generate fundamental questions about their own legitimacy: questions that the thinness of their margin of support in the Supreme Court strongly echoes. The creativity shown by the Court in crafting instruments of federalism and the legitimacy of the reasoning by which it crafts them do not necessarily go hand in hand.

While there are accordingly risks present in all judicial strategies for enforcing federalism principles, the European Court of Justice has thus far shown a preference for largely structural and procedural approaches to judicial review. By contrast, direct judicial review of the Community's determinations of legislative competence are thought to raise real risks of second-guessing, risks illustrated by the US Supreme Court's recent Fourteenth Amendment jurisprudence. As for 'relational' approaches to federalism, the specific choices that the Supreme Court has made—sovereign immunity, anti-commandeering—are not ones that the European Court of Justice is likely to embrace. Liability of Member States for infringement of EU law on the one hand, and enlistment of national administrative and judicial machinery for the enforcement of EU law on the other, have become central to the EU system. This does not mean, however, that there are no relational principles that would be suitable to the EU system and that would support an appropriate balance between national and European authority. Given the EU's great potential for effective political safeguards of federalism, efforts would seem best directed at strengthening them and then enlisting the Court of Justice in their support.

8

Comparative Federalism and the Issue of Commandeering

DANIEL HALBERSTAM

Divided power systems, such as the United States, the European Union, and the Federal Republic of Germany, confront a common question: whether the central government may 'commandeer' its component States, that is, whether the central government may issue binding commands that force its component States to take regulatory action with respect to private parties. This chapter explores what may initially appear as a puzzling difference in the answers given. Whereas US constitutional jurisprudence currently prohibits commandeering, the founding charters of the EU and Germany permit such action. And all do so in the name of protecting the integrity and importance of their respective component States.

The Supreme Court of the United States recently held in *New York v. United States* and *Printz v. United States* that the federal government may regulate private parties directly, request State assistance in regulating private parties, or bargain with the States for such assistance, but that it generally may not commandeer the States.[1] Although State courts must

I would like to thank Bruce Ackerman, David Barron, George Bermann, Michael Halberstam, Don Herzog, Rick Hills, Rob Howse, Ellen Katz, Larry Kramer, Kalypso Nicolaidis, Richard Pildes, Mathias Reimann, Terry Sandalow, Bruno Simma, Mark Tushnet, and Ernest Young for reading and commenting on previous drafts, Gráinne de Búrca, Gert von Helden, Meinhard Hilf, and Peter Kalbe for discussions about some of the issues raised in this piece, Nancy Vettorello for excellent library support, and Rob Mikos and Tom Meehrpohl for helpful research assistance. I would like to thank especially Eric Stein for his comments and our many wide-ranging discussions about the EU. I borrow the term 'divided power systems' from him. See for example Eric Stein, 'On Divided-Power Systems: Adventures in Comparative Law', *Legal Issues of European Integration* 1983(1): 27 (1983). Finally, I would like to express my gratitude to the University of Michigan Law School for providing generous research support from the Cook Endowment.

[1] See *Printz v. United States*, 521 U.S. 898 (1997); *New York v. United States*, 505 U.S. 144 (1992). For examples of two kinds of permissible 'bargaining' in the US system, see *South Dakota v. Dole*, 483 U.S. 203 (1987), upholding federal statute withholding federal funds from States with drinking ages under 21; and *FERC v. Mississippi*, 456 U.S. 742 (1982), upholding federal law requiring State utility commissions, which are subject to federal pre-emption, to consider adopting federal standards.

adjudicate federal laws when such courts exist and are competent to adjudicate similar State laws,[2] the federal government may not commandeer the executive or legislative branches of State governments. The arguments in support of such a rule have been varied. Justice Sandra Day O'Connor has declared on behalf of the Supreme Court that commandeering confuses lines of responsibility and accountability in a federal system because it makes it difficult for citizens to identify the level of government that is responsible for a particular action.[3] Some scholars have argued that the anti-commandeering rule preserves the autonomy of State officials and legislators and thereby ensures the proper incentives for participation in State government.[4] Others have noted that the Supreme Court's decisions in this area may be concerned about commandeering as an impermissible expression of disrespect for the States and their officials.[5] And finally, Justice David H. Souter, who has dissented from the Court's anti-commandeering rule where State executive officials were subject to federal commands, has argued that federal commandeering of State legislative officials undermines the basic task of a legislator: to exercise discretion in voting for any given legislative proposal.[6]

In the European Union, by contrast, the subject of concern is not Union action that 'commandeers' Member State legislative or administrative bodies, but EU legislative activity that has direct effect in the legal systems of the Member States. Member States tend not to welcome Community regulations, which have immediate legal force for individuals within a Member State, and instead prefer that the Community pass directives, which command a Member State to regulate in a particular area and thus require further Member State legislative action to become fully effective within that State.[7] So, too, 'commandeering' is a basic feature of German

[2] See generally *Testa v. Katt*, 330 U.S. 386 (1947); *Printz v. United States*, at 928–9; *New York v. United States*, at 178–9.

[3] *New York v. United States*, at 182–3.

[4] Roderick M. Hills, Jr., 'The Political Economy of Cooperative Federalism: Why State Autonomy Makes Sense and "Dual Sovereignty" Doesn't', *Mich. L. Rev.* 96: 813 (1998); H. Jefferson Powell, 'The Oldest Question of Constitutional Law', *Va. L. Rev.* 79: 633 (1993).

[5] See Elizabeth Anderson and Richard H. Pildes, 'Expressive Theories of Law: A General Restatement', *University of Pennsylvania L. Rev.* 148: 1503, 1559 (2000); cf. Adam B. Cox, 'Expressivism in Federalism: A New Defense of the *Printz* Anticommandeering Rule', *Loyola L.A. L. Rev.* (forthcoming 2001). For criticism of this view of the Court's federalism decisions, see Matthew D. Adler and Seth F. Kreimer, 'The New Etiquette of Federalism: New York, Printz, and Yeskey', *Supreme Court Rev.* 1998: 71, 133–42.

[6] *Printz v. United States*, at 975 (Souter, J., dissenting).

[7] To be sure, regardless of the particular form that EU legislation takes, Member States may object on federalism grounds by arguing, for example, that the provision violates the principle of subsidiarity. See generally, George A. Bermann, 'Taking Subsidiarity Seriously: Federalism in the European Community and the United States', *Colum. L. Rev.*

federalism, where the *Länder* implement federal legislation by taking administrative or legislative action.[8] Enshrined in the German *Grundgesetz*—hereinafter 'Basic Law', 'GG' or 'German constitution'—this vertical division of powers is not considered to threaten the autonomy of the German *Länder*. Indeed, the founders of the modern German constitution, with considerable prodding from the Allies, promoted this division of powers in order to provide the *Länder* with a forceful role in the governance of the nation.[9]

This chapter examines the difference between the European and the American perceptions of the effects and desirability of commandeering as a mechanism of central-component system interaction. Justice Stephen G. Breyer noted this difference in a rare comparative investigation[10] in his dissenting opinion in *Printz*:

94: 331 (1994). Nonetheless, where these more specific objections are absent, Member States have expressly stated their preference that EU legislation take the form of regulations rather than directives. See European Council, 'Birmingham Declaration' at par. 5, adopted 16 October 1992, reprinted in Richard Corbett, *The Treaty of Maastricht* (Essex: Longman Group, 1993); European Council, 'Conclusions of the Edinburgh meeting' at Part II, Third Paragraph, (v), issued 11–12 December 1992, reprinted in Corbett, *The Treaty of Maastricht*, at 493, 498; Single European Act, Declaration on Art. 100A of the EEC Treaty, OJ 1987 L169/24. See generally Treaty Establishing the European Community art. 249 (ex art. 189), hereinafter 'EC Treaty' or 'EC', describing Community forms of legislation. Although even directives have certain direct effects within Member State legal systems, these effects are somewhat more limited than those deriving from the full immediate effectiveness of regulations. See generally Sacha Prechal, *Directives in European Community Law* (Oxford: Clarendon Press, 1995).

[8] See Art. 83 GG, providing for administration of federal law by *Länder*; Art. 75 GG, authorizing federal framework legislation requiring *Länder* implementing legislation; see generally David P. Currie, *The Constitution of the Federal Republic of Germany* (Chicago: University of Chicago Press, 1994), 50–2; Theodore Maunz and Günther Dürig *et al.*, *Grundgesetz: Kommentar* Art. 75 (C.H. Beck, 1996) (Looseleaf), hereinafter *Maunz/Dürig*. For an example of framework legislation, see *Hochschulrahmengesetz*, *Bundesgesetzblatt (BGBl)* 1976(I): 85, setting forth guidelines for governance of universities. The term 'Federation' is used here for the German *Bund* to denote the governing structure at the federal level, which would correspond to the term 'federal government' in the United States. Although 'federation' and 'federal government' will be used interchangeably, when discussing the German system 'Federation' will be used predominantly, simply because the German term *Bundesregierung*, which would translate directly as 'federal government', is taken to refer only to the federal executive. See for example Currie, *The Constitution of the Federal Republic of Germany*, at 139.

[9] See generally Peter H. Merkl, *The Origin of the West German Republic* (New York: Oxford University Press, 1963), 66–73.

[10] For a critical review of the US Supreme Court's tendency to refrain from comparative investigations, see Christopher McCrudden, 'A Common Law of Human Rights?: Transnational Judicial Conversations on Constitutional Rights', *Oxford J. of Leg. Stud.* 20: 499 (2000); Vicki C. Jackson, 'Ambivalent Resistance and Comparative Constitutionalism: Opening up the Conversation on "Proportionality," Rights and Federalism', *Univ. of Pennsylvania J. Const. L.* 1: 583 (1999).

At least some other countries, facing the same basic problem, have found that local control is better maintained through application of a principle that is the direct opposite of the principle the majority derives today from the silence of our Constitution. The federal systems of Switzerland, Germany, and the European Union, for example, all provide that constituent states, not federal bureaucracies, will themselves implement many of the laws, rules, and regulation, or decrees enacted by the central 'federal' body . . . They do so in part because they believe that such a system interferes less, not more, with the independent authority of the 'state', member nation, or other subsidiary government, and helps to safeguard individual liberty as well.[11]

Acknowledging that 'we are interpreting our own Constitution, and not those of other nations, and there may be relevant political and structural differences between their systems and our own', Justice Breyer noted that 'their experience may nonetheless cast an empirical light on the consequences of different solutions to a common legal problem: in this case reconciling central authority with the need to preserve the liberty-enhancing autonomy of a smaller constituent governmental entity'.[12] Rejecting this foray into comparative law, Justice Antonin Scalia responded on behalf of the majority: 'We think such comparative analysis inappropriate to the task of interpreting a constitution, though it was of course quite relevant to writing one.'[13] Noting that the Founders had specifically reviewed the Swiss experience and rejected it as a model for the United States, he concluded: 'The fact is that our federalism is not Europe's. It is the unique contribution of the Framers to political science and political theory.'[14]

Without attempting to assess whether the Europeans have gotten it right, whether commandeering makes sense as a matter of policy, or whether the current anti-commandeering rule in US constitutional doctrine is justified as a matter of constitutional interpretation, this chapter sets out to take up Justice Breyer's comparative inquiry with two goals in mind: first, to illustrate that comparative investigations into foreign constitutional systems may assist in developing a richer understanding of one's own; and second, to demonstrate that any conclusion derived from such comparisons must be highly attentive to the broader institutional and political context in which the studied phenomenon, such as commandeering, occurs. Thus, as a general matter this chapter seeks to illustrate that even though US federalism is distinct from its European counterparts, a sensible comparison may nevertheless shed empirical light on common problems confronted by each. More specifically, the chapter concludes that by not adequately developing the comparison between the US and European systems, Justice Breyer's dissent did not consider countervailing

[11] *Printz v. United States*, 521 U.S. at 976–7.
[12] Ibid. at 977.
[13] Ibid. at 921 note 11.
[14] Ibid.

institutional dynamics that complicate any reliance on the European example as a ready argument against the US anti-commandeering rule.

In successive sections, this chapter explores the relevant political and institutional background against which commandeering takes place in the US, the EU, and Germany. It describes (1) the history of the European Union as an international treaty organization; (2) the formal supremacy of central law within component legal systems; (3) the 'viscosity' of the central legal system, that is, the intensity of the obligation to adhere to the central legal system's norms; (4) the specificity of commands issued by central to component units of government; (5) the corporate representation of component systems within the lawmaking bodies of central systems; and (6) the relative completeness and effectiveness of the levels of governance and the prominent alternatives to commandeering in each system.

After rejecting the significance of the first three features for purposes of the present inquiry, and after raising some questions about the fourth as a stable means for distinguishing between different forms of commandeering, the piece submits that a key difference between the systems lies in the features identified in sections 5 and 6. The piece does not draw on these differences in any attempt to explain why commandeering exists in the EU and in Germany or why it is currently held to be unconstitutional in the United States.[15] Instead, it suggests that under a simplified conception of the component State as a unified actor,[16] these key features—that is, the corporate representation of the component State within the central lawmaking bodies, the relative completeness and effectiveness of the central and component State systems, and the prominent alternatives to commandeering—may account for differing component State preferences regarding commandeering in the various systems. Section 7 then briefly discusses recent German developments that strikingly illustrate the interplay of the key factors described in sections 5 and 6. Finally, section 8 touches on some general considerations regarding the relative merits of the distribution of power in the various systems and suggest avenues for further research.

This chapter concludes, albeit on idealized assumptions, that the roles that commandeering plays in the EU and in Germany, and that it would play in the United States, differ significantly in light of the institutional

[15] This piece, then, does not seek to provide a functional explanation of the existence *vel non* of commandeering in the various systems. For a critique such functional explanations, see Jon Elster, *Nuts and Bolts for the Social Sciences* (Cambridge: Cambridge University Press, 1989), 99–100, 123.

[16] The problematic nature of this and other simplifying assumptions of the piece are briefly noted in the conclusion.

differences between these systems. The radically different views regarding commandeering in the various systems may be somewhat less puzzling after the more searching examination of the institutional dynamics presented in this piece.

1. Commandeering in International Law and the Apparent Paradox in American Views

Under traditional international law, treaties pronounce norms that bind sovereign states but leave the translation of those norms into domestic law to the good faith exercise of the domestic lawmaking processes of the signatory states.[17] Traditional international law thus employs something like 'commandeering', as opposed to directly effective legislation, as the mechanism for translating 'central' legal norms into 'component' legal systems. To be sure, international law can reach directly into a domestic legal system when a nation state's constitutional regime allows for the immediate effectiveness of international law.[18] This is the case, for example, with self-executing treaties in the United States and in the European Union.[19] But even in such 'component' systems that allow for self-executing treaties, the political branches that must ratify treaties often appear to prefer passage of non-self-executing treaties, which require domestic implementing legislation before becoming fully effective within the domestic legal system. As Professor Lori Damrosch has observed with respect to the US, for example, there is 'a pattern in treaty actions of the US Senate which tends to weaken the domestic legal effect of treaties . . . by qualif[ying] its consent to US ratification of the treaty with a declaration or other condition to the effect that the treaty shall be non-self-executing . . . [and] not be used as a direct source of law in US courts'.[20] Indeed, both houses of Congress sought to mitigate the domestic legal effect of the NAFTA and the GATT (WTO) by passing provisions limiting the domestic effects of these agree-

[17] See Eric Stein, 'International Law in Internal Law: Toward Internationalization of Central-Eastern European Constitutions?', *Am. J. Int'l L.* 88: 427, 431 (1994).

[18] See generally Francis G. Jacobs and Shelley Roberts (eds), *The Effect of Treaties in Domestic Law* (London: Sweet and Maxwell, 1987). For additional discussion of this concept regarding US law, see generally Carlos M. Vazquez, 'The Four Doctrines of Self-Executing Treaties', *Am. J. Int'l L.* 89: 695 (1995); Yuji Iwasawa, 'The Doctrine of Self-Executing Treaties in the United States: A Critical Analysis', *Va. J. Int'l L.* 26: 627 (1986).

[19] See for example Ronald A. Brand, 'Direct Effect of International Economic Law in the United States and the European Union', *J. Int'l L. & Bus* 17: 556 (Winter 1996/Spring 1997).

[20] Lori F. Damrosch, 'The Role of the United States Senate Concerning "Self-Executing" and "Non-Self-Executing" Treaties', *Chi.-Kent L. Rev.* 67: 515 (1991).

ments.[21] So, too, did the Council of the EU when it adopted the GATT (WTO).[22]

In the realm of international law, the ratifying political branches' aversion to self-executing or directly effective treaties is simple to understand. Whether viewed in terms of dignity or actual legal impact, the greater compromise of state sovereignty is the loss of control over one's domestic legal order, not the requirement to pass legislation in order to comply with international law. By retaining control over the implementation of international agreements, the domestic legislative branches regain some of the voice lost in the drafting, and indeed also ratification, of the treaty, which typically involves the executive branch more heavily than does ordinary legislation. Directly effective treaties, which are enforced by the judiciary without further input from the legislative branch, bypass the legislative branches of nation states without this opportunity for further use of their voice.[23]

When it comes to translating 'central' international law into the domestic legal order of the 'component' nation state, then, the EU and US have similar views on commandeering versus circumvention. Both systems or, more precisely, the ratifying political branches in both systems, opt for 'commandeering' where possible.

[21] See 19 USC. § 3512 (1994) (GATT), declaring that GATT shall not pre-empt any federal laws and may not be invoked by private individuals in court to challenge the action of any federal or State governmental actor or the validity of any federal or State law; 19 USC. § 3312 (NAFTA) (same).

[22] Council Decision 94/800/EC OJ 1994 L336/1, 2: 'whereas, by its nature, the Agreement establishing the World Trade Organization, including the Annexes thereto, is not susceptible to being directly invoked in Community or Member State courts'. The question surrounding the invocability of the trade agreements in domestic courts was the subject of the intense litigation in the famous banana saga. See for example Meinhard Hilf, 'The Role of National Courts in International Trade Relations', *Mich. J. Int'l L.* 18: 321 (1997).

[23] Indeed, by circumventing the elected branches of government, directly effective treaties, and directly effective central law more generally, tap into the judiciary, which comprises a cadre of expert professionals who are charged with upholding the law. Component State judges tend to share this characteristic with the judges that inhabit the judiciary at the central/international level. See Evan H. Caminker, 'State Sovereignty and Subordinacy: May Congress Commandeer State Officers to Implement Federal Law?', *Columbia L. Rev.* 95: 1001, 1050 (1995). Accordingly, Joseph Weiler has suggested that the 'compliance pull of a dialogue conducted between courts in legalese' has made the alliance between national courts and the European Court of Justice in the dissemination and implementation of Community law so successful.' J. H. H. Weiler, 'A Quiet Revolution: The European Court of Justice and Its Interlocutors', *Comparative Political Studies*, 26: 510, 521 (1994); see also Laurence R. Helfer and Anne-Marie Slaughter, 'Toward a Theory of Effective Supranational Adjudication', *Yale Law Journal* 107: 273 (1997), discussing this and other factors contributing to the effectiveness of EU law. For a critical view of the receptivity of judges to international law, see Eyal Benvenisti, 'Judicial Misgivings Regarding the Application of International Law: An Analysis of Attitudes of National Courts', *Eur. J. Int'l L.* 4: 159 (1993).

The EU's attitude toward international law is in harmony with the approach taken by the Member States with regard to internal EU law itself. Within the EU system itself, both 'commandeering'—that is, directives—and directly effective laws—that is, regulations—are permitted forms of EU legislation. And indeed here, the Member States of the European Union prefer that the EU act within the Community legal system through directives rather than regulations, much as the EU prefers international law that is non-self-executing to international law that has immediate domestic effect. In the United States, in contrast, current Supreme Court doctrine forbids the use of commandeering as a method of federal regulation. And the Court did so, of course, at the behest of component States within the US federal system bringing suit to challenge such federal commands. In other words, the preference for the command mechanism is embraced by the US acting internationally, but rejected by the States when it comes to commandeering within the domestic federal system. This presents an apparent paradox. As a sovereign participant within the system of international law, the United States appears to prefer commands over self-executing treaties, whereas within the federal domestic system commandeering is seen to violate the residuary sovereignty of the States. The next section examines whether adoption of the US Constitution explains these two attitudes in the United States and distinguishes the US legal order sufficiently from that of the EU.

2. The Supremacy of Central Law

The US Supreme Court has repeatedly invoked the formal unification of the US legal system under the Supremacy Clause of Art. VI as justification for the anti-commandeering rule.[24] As described below, the Court sees this unification as pivotal in the move away from the confederal mode of congressional action through the States to a constitutional mode of federal legislation with immediate effectiveness within the States.

The pre-constitutional Articles of Confederation largely resembled an international treaty organization with unreliable signatory states. Congress 'could not directly tax or legislate upon individuals', since it 'it had no explicit "legislative" or "governmental" power to make binding "law" enforceable as such'.[25] As Alexander Hamilton famously lamented in *The Federalist* No. 15: 'The great and radical vice in the construction of

[24] See for example *Printz*, 521 U.S. at 919–920; *New York*, 505 U.S. at 161–66.
[25] Akhil R. Amar, 'Of Sovereignty and Federalism', *Yale L.J.* 96:1425, 1447 (1987).

the existing Confederation is in the principle of LEGISLATION for STATES or GOVERNMENTS, in their CORPORATE or COLLECTIVE CAPACITIES, and as contra-distinguished from the INDIVIDUALS of whom they consist.'[26] Acts of the existing confederation, he further noted, 'in theory . . . are laws, constitutionally binding on the members of the Union, yet in practice they are mere recommendations, which the States observe or disregard at their option'.[27] As one scholar observes, there was widespread agreement 'that rampant state non-compliance [with Congressional enactments] rendered this structural arrangement ineffectual'.[28] To remedy this problem, the Founders included the Supremacy Clause of Art. VI in their draft of the Constitution to ensure the immediate effectiveness of federal law within the States. No longer would State legislative action be required to translate Congressional enactments into the law of the several States. As James Madison explained after the Constitutional Convention:

> It was generally agreed that the objects of the Union could not be secured by any system founded on the principle of a confederation of Sovereign States. A *voluntary* observance of the federal law by all the members could never be hoped for. A *compulsive* one could evidently never be reduced to practice, and if it could, involved equal calamities to the innocent and the guilty, the necessity of a military, both obnoxious and dangerous, and, in general, a scene resembling much more a civil war than the administration of a regular Government. . . . Hence was embraced the alternative of a Government which, instead of operating on the States, should operate without their intervention on the individuals composing them. . . .[29]

According to the Supreme Court, acceptance of the Supremacy Clause also implied a rejection of commandeering. The federal government's ability to regulate individuals directly, so a majority of the Court recently held in *New York* and *Printz*, meant that the federal government could no longer employ the State legislatures or executives to do so on its behalf.

The Court's holding has been sharply criticized for its lack of historical foundation, but scholars otherwise sympathetic to the ruling have made functional arguments that also rely on the Supremacy Clause and the

[26] *The Federalist* 89, 93 (Jacob E. Cooke, ed., Middletown, Connecticut: Wesleyan University Press, 1961).

[27] Ibid.

[28] Caminker, 'State Sovereignty and Subordinacy', at 1020 n. 76 (1995); *See also* Powell, 'The Oldest Question of Constitutional Law', at 653.

[29] Letter from James Madison to Thomas Jefferson, 24 October 1787, in *Letters and Other Writings of James Madison* 1: 343, 344 (Philadelphia: J. B. Lippincott, 1865).

federal government's ability to regulate individuals directly.[30] Professors Roderick Hills and Jefferson Powell, for example, have argued on policy grounds that where a central government has the power to pass legal norms that are directly applicable in its component systems, it should not be allowed to use the commandeering route because the cost that commandeering imposes on the State political systems is no longer justified. In particular, Professor Hills argues that the federal government should bargain with the States for their services in transposing or administering federal law whenever it is cost-justified to have the States provide such services.[31]

Arguments based on the immediate effectiveness of federal law in the States, however, do not distinguish between federal law and international treaties and thus do not help to explain the apparent paradox in US views identified in the last section. Under the Supremacy Clause, not only federal law but also 'all Treaties made, or which shall be made, under the Authority of the United States' are 'the supreme Law of the Land'.[32] This means that treaties enjoy at least the same status as federal laws within the US constitutional hierarchy of norms. As a formal matter, then, international treaties may regulate within the United States with the same immediacy with which federal law regulates within the States.[33] In this sense, 'commandeering' the United States by treaty is as unnecessary as commandeering the States by federal statute. Yet the preference in the United States for commandeering at the international level persists.

[30] See for example Vicki C. Jackson, 'Federalism and the Uses and Limits of Law: Printz and Principle?', *Yale L.J.* 111: 2180 (1998); Hills, 'The Political Economy of Cooperative Federalism'; Evan H. Caminker, 'Printz, State Sovereignty, and the Limits of Formalism', *Supreme Court Review* 1997: 199; Caminker, 'State Sovereignty and Subordinacy'; Powell, 'The Oldest Question of Constitutional Law'. Others have criticized the Court on functional grounds as well. See for example Adler and Kreimer, 'The New Etiquette of Federalism'.

[31] Hills, 'The Political Economy of Cooperative Federalism', at 938–44. Hills adds that, as a consequence, commandeering does not fall within the scope of the constitution's Necessary and Proper Clause. As a matter of US Constitutional interpretation, however, such an argument is in considerable tension with Chief Justice Marshall's broad interpretation of the Necessary and Proper Clause in *McCulloch v. Maryland*, 4 Wheat.(17 U.S.) 316, 324–5 (1819): 'These words, "necessary and proper," in such an instrument, are probably to be considered as synonymous. Necessarily, powers must here intend such powers as are suitable and fitted to the object; such as are best and most useful in relation to the end proposed. If this be not so, and if congress could use no means but such as were absolutely indispensable to the existence of a granted power, the government would hardly exist.'

[32] US Const. art. VI, cl. 2.

[33] See for example Vazquez, 'The Four Doctrines of Self-Executing Treaties'. But cf. John C. Yoo, 'Globalism and the Constitution: Treaties, Non-Self-Execution, and the Original Understanding', *Colum. L. Rev.* 99: 1955 (1999), taking a critical view of the presumption that treaties should be given a self-executing interpretation.

Moreover, the Supremacy Clause does not distinguish the United States from Germany or the EU. The German comparison on this score is plain, since Germany has clear supremacy provisions in its constitution. Article 31 of the German Basic Law provides categorically that 'Federal law shall override *Land* law', and Art. 72(1) GG emphasizes that in the sphere of concurrent powers, the *Länder* have legislative power only to the extent that the Federation has not acted.[34] Although the European Union lacks a similar statement in its founding documents, the European Court of Justice has prominently established its version of these principles in the landmark series of cases beginning with *van Gend and Loos*, which established the direct effect of Community law within Member State legal systems.[35] Here the Court laid the groundwork for the constitutionalization of the Community's legal order by moving beyond the conception of the Community as a conventional international treaty organization. In language that is probably as well known in Europe as the Supremacy Clause is in the United States, the Court held: 'The Community constitutes a new legal order of international law for the benefit of which the states have limited their sovereign rights, albeit within limited fields, and the subjects of which comprise not only Member States but also their nationals.'[36] Only one year after *van Gend*, the Court established the supremacy of Community law in *Costa* v. *ENEL*,[37] which held that a Member State could not affect the validity of existing Community law by subsequently adopting a contrary rule of national law. Finally, in *Simmenthal*[38] and *Internationale Handelsgesellschaft*[39] the ECJ expanded on the idea of

[34] See *Maunz/Dürig*, at Art. 31 (1960); ibid. at Art. 72 (1996); Currie, *The Constitution of the Federal Republic of Germany*, at 49.

[35] Case 26/62, *N.V. Algemene Transport-en Expeditie Onderneming van Gend & Loos v. Nederlandse Administratie der Belastingen*, [1963] European Court Reports [ECR] 1, 16, holding that Art. 12 of the European Economic Community Treaty, which prohibits the introduction of new duties on imports from other Member States, 'produces direct effects and creates individual rights which national courts must protect'. For the classic accounts of these decisions, see Eric Stein, 'Lawyers, Judges, and the Making of a Transnational Constitution', reprinted as updated in *Thoughts from a Bridge* (University of Michigan Press, 2000), 15; J. H. H. Weiler, 'The Transformation of Europe', *Yale L.J.* 100: 2403 (1991); G. Federico Mancini, 'The Making of a Constitution for Europe', *CMLR* 26: 595 (1989).

[36] Case 26/62, at 12.

[37] Case 6/64, *Flaminion Costa v. ENEL*, [1964] ECR 585, 599, holding that Italian law nationalizing electric power industry 'cannot take precedence over Community law' even though national law was enacted subsequent to the effective date of the Treaty.

[38] Case 106/77, *Amministrazione delle Finanze dello Stato v. Simmenthal SpA*, [1978] ECR 629, holding national law regarding the jurisdiction of its constitutional court 'automatically inapplicable' whenever in conflict with Community law.

[39] Case 11/70, *Internationale Handelsgesellschaft mbH v. Einfuhr- und Vorratsstelle für Getreide und Futtermittel*, [1970] ECR 1125, holding that respect for fundamental rights 'whilst inspired by the constitutional traditions common to the Member States, must be ensured within the framework of the structure and objectives of the Community'.

supremacy, indicating that even constitutionally based principles of Member State law could not compromise the validity of Community law. Thus, the ECJ's twin holdings of direct effect and supremacy establish that Member States acting contrary to Community law no longer violate the law of a separate legal order, but their own. The Court essentially determined that the very distinction between a national legal order and a Community legal order, much like the distinction between a State and federal legal order in the United States, was no longer apt.

In short, since the Supremacy Clause allows Treaties to regulate directly within the US legal system, and since the United States, Germany, and the EU are all based on the principle that central law is both supreme and directly applicable within their component States, the Supremacy Clause alone does not help us understand the different appreciation of commandeering in the various systems.

3. The Viscosity of Legal Systems

A state's willingness to incur legal obligations and hence its view on commandeering may depend on the degree to which the state is not only normatively but also practically bound to obey the law. Put simply, a state may be more sanguine about incurring legal obligations it can disregard than ones it must heed. Thus, even when a given rule or principle is properly interpreted as a binding norm, something like the 'viscosity' of the legal system within which such normatively binding rules or principles are issued may be relevant. Just as the 'viscosity' of a liquid reflects the forces of adhesion and friction that act on a body moving through the fluid substance, so, too, the viscosity of a legal system may be viewed as a combination of the adhesive force of its norms, that is, the compliance pull that its norms exert on legal actors, and the friction caused by non-compliant action, that is, the real costs that actors incur by non-compliance.[40] The greater these forces are—the greater a system's 'viscosity' is—the greater is the constraint that the system places on actors' freedom of movement within that system. In a related vein, though perhaps less intuitive, the greater a system's viscosity, the less able it is to survive the strain of non-

[40] Cf., for example, Thomas M. Franck, *The Power of Legitimacy Among Nations* (1990), developing idea of 'compliance pull'; Harold H. Koh, How Is International Human Rights Law Enforced?, Indiana L. J. 74: 1397(1999), discussing elements of compliance. Because individual norms within a system will invariably differ in the compliance pull and costs associated with them, it may be better to speak of a system's 'specific' viscosity, which may be seen as an indication of the general, average, or unit forces of adhesion and friction of the system. The text will use the term 'viscosity' as referring to this general, average, or unit notion of viscosity.

compliant actors. Where both the compliance pull and the non-compliance costs are immense, successful non-compliance poses a far greater challenge to the system's survival than when these forces are weak. Thus, without questioning that the relevant actors in any given legal system are under an obligation to comply with applicable law, the viscosity of the system reflects the inability of legal actors, as a matter of pure practical reality, to move autonomously within the system in disregard of their formal legal obligations and to do so without destroying the system itself.

In a low-viscosity system, where unilateral exit is formally prohibited, norms exert some pull on legal actors and actual defectors sometimes incur modest costs by virtue of their non-compliance.[41] At the same time, actual non-compliance in such a system may take place and, indeed, takes place without irreparably tearing the fabric of the governing legal order. In a high-viscosity system, in contrast, where exit is also prohibited, the compliance pull preventing exit is quite high, and the costs of non-compliance are both certain and great. Here, non-compliance is less of a practical possibility, and any instance of open, unrepentant, and successful non-compliance will pose a severe challenge to the continued viability of the system. Determined neither by the formal 'paper' rules governing the interaction of legal actors, nor by the question of legal or illegal exit, viscosity provides a very practical indicator of the constraints placed on autonomous action within any given normative system and the relation of such action to the fundamental survival of the system itself.[42]

One might speculate that the viscosity of the particular legal system involved could explain the difference in US views regarding commandeering within the international and US constitutional systems, as well as the different component State attitudes towards commandeering in the US, the EU, and Germany. This view would draw, for example, on a perceived practical difference between constitutional and international legal systems. Although as a normative matter legal actors must heed their obligations under both constitutional and international law, defection may be a practical possibility in the latter system to an extent to which it is not in the former. To be sure, within the system of international law, compliance with legal obligations is required, as illustrated in the bedrock treaty

[41] The term 'exit' is used here in the sense described in Albert O. Hirschman, *Exit, Voice, and Loyalty* (Cambridge, MA: Harvard University Press, 1970).

[42] The viscosity of a legal system is thus related to, but different from, the characteristics of 'hardness' or 'softness' of legal rules, which refer principally to the degree to which legal rules are binding as a normative matter as opposed to the degree to which they are observed as a practical matter. For a discussion of soft law, see C. M. Chinkin, 'The Challenge of Soft Law: Development and Change in International Law', *Int'l & Comp. L. Q.* 38: 850 (1989).

principle *pacta sunt servanda*.[43] And indeed, adherence to international law tends to be the general rule, as Professor Henkin noted in his famous observation that 'it is probably the case that almost all nations observe almost all principles of international law and almost all of their obligations almost all of the time'.[44] Nonetheless, even deliberate and considered violations of international law continue to be a practical possibility.[45] A State within a constitutional system, such as that of the United States, in contrast, might have less practical ability to violate central—here, federal—law. Although both systems have enforcement mechanisms, the certainty and severity with which they are deployed and the compliance pull felt by the relevant legal actors might differ as between the two systems.[46]

Thus, insofar as international law is a low-viscosity system, incurring obligations to translate international legal norms into one's domestic system arguably provides a substantial degree of control over whether international law in fact infiltrates domestic law. Because defection in such a case would be a practical, even if rarely used, possibility, the component state could increase its control over the domestic legal landscape by

[43] See for example Abram Chayes and Antonia Chayes, 'On Compliance', *Int'l Org.* 47: 175, 185 (1993)—'the fundamental norm of international law is pacta sunt servanda'; Burns H. Weston, Richard A. Falk, Anthony D'Amato, *International Law and World Order* (St Paul, Minn.: West Pub. Co., 1990), 44, describing *pacta sunt servanda* as 'one of the most basic principles of international law'.

[44] Louis Henkin, *How Nations Behave*, 2nd edn (New York: Columbia University Press, 1979) 47 (emphasis omitted); See also Harold Hongju Koh, 'Why Do Nations Obey International Law?', *Yale L.J.* 106: 2599 (1997), noting that empirical surveys have borne out this statement.

[45] See Henkin, *How Nations Behave*, at 43, discussing some of the 'many instances where a state is admittedly in violation [of international law]'; ibid. at 68–87, discussing reasons for the persistence of violations; George W. Downs and David M. Rocke, *Optimal Imperfection?* (Princeton: Princeton University Press, 1995), 77, arguing that in order to cope with 'uncertain interest group demands', GATT 'establish[es] sanctions for non-compliance that are low enough to allow politicians to break the agreement when interest group benefits are great, but high enough to encourage states to obey the agreement most of the time and thereby prevent trade wars'; Eyal Benvenisti, 'Exit and Voice in the Age of Globalization', *Mich. L. Rev.* 98: 167, 192–6 (1999), discussing same.

[46] For example, although a study of GATT dispute resolutions through the 1980s found 100% compliance with known rulings in favour of complainants until 1980, it found that this figure had dropped during the 1980s to 87%. See Robert E. Hudec, *Enforcing International Trade Law: The Evolution of the Modern GATT Legal System* (Salem, NH: Butterworth Leg. Pub., 1993), 290. Examining the potential of the new WTO procedures to bring the figure back up to full or near-full compliance, Robert Hudec takes the somewhat sceptical view that 'the new WTO legal system will have to learn to cope with legal failure'. See Robert E. Hudec, 'The New WTO Dispute Settlement Procedure: An Overview of the First Three Years', *Minn. J. Global Trade* 8: 1, 14 (1999). For one suggestion that the WTO is currently still as weak as the US Supreme Court was in the early nineteenth century, see Mark L. Movsesian, 'Sovereignty, Compliance, and the World Trade Organization: Lessons from the History of Supreme Court Review', *Michigan Journal of International Law* 20: 775 (1999).

including a non-self-execution clause, even though the international agreement may require the component state to pass domestic implementing legislation. Perhaps, then, the low viscosity of the international legal system helps explain why Congress preferred being commandeered by NAFTA than circumvented by NAFTA.[47]

Insofar as the constitutional system of the United States is a relatively high-viscosity system, a State has less freedom to ignore a command by the federal government to enact certain legislation than the Congress does in deciding whether to ignore an international command. To the extent this difference exists, it stems not simply from the supremacy of federal law, but from the strong compliance pull of US constitutional norms, the greater and more certain punishment brought to bear on non-compliant actors, and the danger of a breakdown of the entire system in the event of open and successful non-compliance. In such a system, one might argue, a State would rather not incur the cost of implementing federal norms, because it does not gain much control over the integrity of its State legal order in return. Because State compliance is a foregone conclusion, central commandeering in a high-viscosity legal system imposes a burden on the component State to exercise its regulatory powers on behalf of the central authority without the corresponding benefit of being able to make the ultimate decision of whether to heed the central command.

And yet, the viscosity of the international, US, and EU legal systems fails to explain the different component state appreciation of commandeering. Even in a high-viscosity legal system, a component state may choose a central command if the alternative is to allow directly effective central law to penetrate the component legal system. Even in such a system, a component state may exploit the inevitable 'play in the joints' or drag its feet in a manner that is not easily detectable and punishable, as has been the case in the United States, for example, with the implementation of federally prescribed speed limits by some States,[48] or with States' disregard of their obligations to notify the consulates of foreign citizens who are arrested.[49] Thus, as the viscosity of a legal system rises, a component state

[47] This attitude is not limited to trade agreements. See for example David P. Stewart, 'United States Ratification of the Covenant on Civil and Political Rights: The Significance of the Reservations, Understandings, and Declarations', *Depaul L. Rev*. 42: 1183 (1993).

[48] See Ashutosh Bhagwat, 'Three Branch Monte', *Notre Dame L. Rev.* 72: 157, 175–6 n. 100 (1996), noting California and Montana's failure to enforce federal speed laws; see also Hills, 'The Political Economy of Cooperative Federalism', at 868–9, discussing States' failure to comply with federal requirements under the Social Security Act and Clean Air Act.

[49] The most prominent case has been that of Angel Francisco Breard, a citizen of Paraguay, whose consulate was not notified by the State of Virginia. See *Breard v. Greene*, 523 U.S. 371 (1998) (*per curiam*).

may develop an even stronger preference for affirmative commands if the alternative is to invite pre-emption or other directly effective central law.

In the European Union, we indeed witness an increased preference for commandeering as the viscosity of the system rises. In Professor Joseph Weiler's compelling analysis of the transformation of the European legal order, he explains how strong intergovernmentalism facilitated the ECJ's incremental construction of legal restraints proscribing exit, that is, its decisions establishing the direct effect and supremacy of Community law.[50] As Weiler notes, Member States remained sanguine about the ECJ's decisions foreclosing exit options because Member States enjoyed full voice—that is, a veto—in the decision-making process that produced the Community norms. Now that unanimous decision making has largely given way to majority rule in the Council, Member States are caught in the legal architecture built by the ECJ when the Member States were less concerned about preserving their option to exit from Community norms.

In addition to a decrease in formal exit options and in the ability of individual Member States to block the emergence of EC norms to which they object, the EU has also experienced a rise in the viscosity of its legal system, as more effective rules for the enforcement of Community law have been created and European Union law increasingly becomes the subject of litigation. For example, the Court has established that an individual may sue a Member State directly for money damages when the latter's substantial failure to transpose a Community directive has caused the individual harm.[51] Similarly, since the Maastricht Treaty amended Art. 228 (ex Art. 171) EC, the ECJ may impose, and recently has imposed, monetary penalties against Member States for non-compliance with its judgements.[52] As a practical matter, Member State non-compliance with Community norms has become increasingly difficult. Indeed, over the past decade the percentage of directives transposed by the Member States has increased each year.[53]

[50] See Weiler, 'The Transformation of Europe'.

[51] Cases C-6 & 9/90, *Frankovich and Bonifaci v. Italy*, [1991] ECR I-5357; C-46 & 48/93, *Brasserie du Pêcheur SA v. Germany, and R. v. Secretary for Transport, ex parte Factortame Ltd.*, [1996] ECR I-1029. For a critical evaluation of these developments from the perspective of subsidiarity, see Edward T. Swaine, 'Subsidiarity and Self-Interest: Federalism at the European Court of Justice', *Harv. Int'l L. J.* 41: 1 (2000). For a comparative evaluation of the effectiveness of supranational adjudication, see Helfer and Slaughter, 'Toward a Theory of Effective Supranational Adjudication'.

[52] For the first imposition of such a fine, see C-387/97, *Commission* v. *Greece* (4 July 2000) (toxic waste directive) [not yet reported].

[53] See the chapter in this collection by Professors David Lazer and Viktor Mayer-Schoenberger, which notes that 'the transposal rate [of directives] steadily increased from below 90 per cent in 1990 to a record 95.7 per cent in 1998'.

Despite these developments, however, the EU Member States continue to prefer directives to direct action by the Community-level institutions.[54] Even in what now seems to be a high-viscosity system, Member States adhere to the belief that regulations are more destructive of component State autonomy than directives. Member States thus appear to take the view that even if State cooperation is a foregone conclusion, requiring the central government to work through component States rather than around them promotes both the voice of component States and the idea of subsidiarity, that is, the decentralization of decision making.[55]

Without a more rigorous examination of the level of adherence to law and infliction of sanctions in international law, the EU, and the United States, comparisons among the different systems with regard to their viscosity[56] and conclusions about the relationship between viscosity and the penchant for commandeering within each must await further inquiry. Even so, bringing Germany into the comparison provides an example of a high-viscosity system that nonetheless adheres to commandeering as a mode of central-component system interaction. The next three sections therefore explore certain shared aspects of the European and German

[54] See for example European Council, 'Birmingham Declaration'.

[55] Thus, when the European Court of Justice holds that directives can have direct effect, it undermines this particular function of directives. See Francis Jacobs and Kenneth Karst, 'The "Federal" Legal Order: The USA and Europe Compared—A Jurisdictional Perspective', in Mauro Cappelletti *et al.* (eds), *Integration Through Law* (New York: W. de Gruyter, 1986), 169, 235. But since as a general matter directives still rely more upon the Member States for transposition than do regulations, Member States still play a greater role in the fine-tuning of the former than the latter.

[56] Perhaps one indication that the viscosity of the EU system is in some respects still lower than that of the US system is the German 'Maastricht' decision, in which the German Constitutional Court defied the ECJ and claimed to be the final arbiter of whether the Community institutions' actions remain within the confines of the powers conferred upon the Community in the Treaty. See *BVerfGE* 89: 155 (1993) (Maastricht Decision), reported in [1994] 1 *CMLR* 57. Although in this case the German court did not strike down any Community action, it is difficult to imagine any State supreme court in the US issuing a similar ruling today. In the US the adherence of a State to the view that it is the final umpire of the scope of central authority was the subject of battles waged long ago. See *Martin v. Hunter's Lessee*, 1 Wheat. (14 U.S.) 304 (1816); *Cohens v. Virginia*, 6 Wheat. (19 U.S.) 264 (1821). In addition, one scholar, after evaluating the degree of compliance in the EU, maintains: 'The degree to which non-implementation has taxed, and continues to tax the energies, credibility, and success of the Community is hard to overstate'. Swaine, 'Subsidiarity and Self-Interest', at 89. But see Weiler, 'The Transformation of Europe', at 2464, noting that although there is some non-compliance with ECJ judgments, 'In this respect the Community is no different (in principle) than, for example, any state of equivalent size and complexity'; Daniel A. Farber, 'Taking Slippage Seriously: Non-compliance and Creative Compliance in Environmental Law', *Harv. Env. L. Rev.* 23: 297, 298 (1999), noting that in certain areas of US law, particularly in the area of environmental regulation, 'Slippage between regulatory standards and the actual conduct of regulated parties is far from being a peripheral element of the legal regime'.

systems that may help explain component States' acceptance of commandeering even in high-viscosity systems.

4. The Directive as a Limited Tool of Commandeering

The discussion has assumed so far that all commands are created equal. The calculus might, however, be affected by a distinction between two types of commands: those that do not leave the recipient of the order any discretion, such as an order to carry out a particular task using specified means to achieve precisely defined results; and those that do allow the recipient some sphere of discretion, such as an order to achieve a roughly defined result, leaving the further specification of the means and the more precise contours of the particular result to the recipient of the order. With regard to the former type of command, a government has only the 'discretion' either to act lawfully and obey the command or to act unlawfully and ignore the command. Where such an element of choice exists, the difference between specific and general commands may not be as crucial, since the ability to disregard the law provides a certain measure of decisional autonomy. In the case of a background normative system that both legally and as matter of practical reality severely curtails disobedience, however, the element of choice in carrying out a highly specific command would be negligible.

A command to achieve a general goal thus allows for some degree of discretion even in a high-viscosity legal system. Although this kind of discretion differs from the discretion to obey or disobey the command entirely, it preserves the relevance of the addressee's political process and gives some voice to the addressee in the shaping of this secondary sphere of law. The US Supreme Court in *Printz* recognized this. After recounting the government's argument that the Brady Gun Control Act did not unconstitutionally commandeer the States because it only required them to perform ministerial acts and not to make policy, the majority opinion stated: 'Preservation of the States as independent and autonomous political entities is arguably less undermined by requiring them to make policy in certain fields than . . . by reduc[ing] [them] to puppets of a ventriloquist Congress.'[57]

The form of command that maintains a policy-making role for the component government charged with implementing the command corresponds to the directive in the EU and the *Rahmengesetz*—'framework law'—of Art. 75 GG. If the choice is between issuance of such a guideline

[57] 521 U.S. at 928; internal quotation marks and citation omitted.

to be carried out by the component units of government and passage of a comprehensive law instead, the responsible evolution of the law and component State autonomy may indeed both be furthered by choosing the limited command over the complete circumvention of the component State. As Professor Robert Howse puts it: '[A] directive does not involve supplanting sub-unit regulation by a fully uniform community-wide scheme. Rather, directives serve to guide governments to an adequately harmonious result, while permitting regulatory divergence and diversity where these do not jeopardize the requirements of economic union.'[58] This may be especially valuable where the legal systems of the component States differ significantly, so that the modes of implementation and possibly even substantive elements of the legislation may be calibrated to local conditions.[59]

When component States exercise such discretion, they not only gain power but must also take responsibility for their part in implementing or shaping the central programme. The US Supreme Court fears that such sharing of duties will only obscure the lines of political accountability and thus undermine the ability of voters to determine which level of government is to praise or blame for any given program or policy.[60] As several scholars, both critical and supportive of the anti-commandeering rule, have argued, however, the danger of blurring lines of accountability in the case of commandeering is not categorically different from what happens in the case of federal pre-emption, which the Court accepts. In both cases, the component State's actions or inactions are only partially determined by State politicians, yet citizens are likely to view the component State officials as fully responsible whenever the latter are the most salient agents involved. In both cases proper lines of accountability can be preserved when component States are vigilant in publicizing the respective roles of the federal and State policy-makers on any given issue. Given proper information, citizens should find the lines of accountability reasonably clear.[61]

A more serious question raised by framework laws and directives, however, is how to preserve the proper amount of discretion to be

[58] Robert Howse, *Economic Union, Social Justice, and Constitutional Reform: Towards a High but Level Playing Field* (North York, Ontario: York University Center for Public Law and Public Policy, 1992), 98.

[59] See for example Stephen Weatherill, 'Beyond Preemption? Shared Competence and Constitutional Change in the European Community', in David O'Keefe and Patrick Twomey (eds), *Legal Issues of the Maastricht Treaty* (London: Chancery Law Pub, 1994), 21.

[60] See *New York*, 505 U.S., at 168–9; Cf. *FERC*, 456 U.S. at 787 (O'Connor, J., concurring in the judgement in part and dissenting in part).

[61] See generally, Caminker, 'State Sovereignty and Subordinacy', at 1060–74; Hills, 'The Political Economy of Cooperative Federalism', at 828; Adler and Kreimer, 'The New Etiquette of Federalism', at 83–102.

exercised by the central government on the one hand, and the component States on the other. First, it may be difficult to prevent the central government from abdicating its policy-making responsibilities and the component States from interpreting the scope of their implementing discretion in an expansive manner. Similar issues have surfaced prominently in the United States in the case of federal agencies, which have come to exercise enormous discretion in the implementation of federal laws.[62] Second, and more important from the point of view of the component States, it is questionable whether component State discretion is reliably preserved solely by defining the central government's commandeering power narrowly and hoping for judicial protection of component State autonomy within this scheme. Even if the central government is expressly authorized to issue only 'framework commands', those commands may not maintain any significant realm of discretion for the component States. For example, framework laws that specify only the legislation's goals, while leaving the means or methods of achieving these goals to the implementing State may still be quite detailed. Indeed, the quest for any enduring distinction between means and ends has been criticized as elusive. Insofar as the distinction is a formal one based on the relationship between various components of an

[62] See for example Lisa Schultz Bressman, 'Schechter Poultry at the Millennium: A Delegation Doctrine for the Administrative State', *Yale L.J.* 109: 1399 (2000); Cass R. Sunstein, 'Nondelegation Canons', *University of Chicago L. Rev.* 67: 315 (2000); Cass R. Sunstein, 'Law And Administration After Chevron', *Columbia L. Rev.* 90: 2071 (1990).

[63] See for example Prechal, *Directives in European Community Law*, at 16–17; John Dewey, 'Means and Ends', in JoAnn Boydston, *John Dewey: The Later Works* (Carbondale and Edwardsville: Southern Illinois University Press, 1988), 349. Prechal's charming example illustrates the problem best: 'A sending person B to buy some dinner . . . could simply say: "Buy something for dinner". On the other hand, A could also say: "Buy some pasta, sauce and wine" or "Buy tagliatelle, pesto and red wine" or "Buy fresh spinach tagliatelle, Buitoni pesto and Chianti". A could also send B to the Italian shop on the corner for the tagliatelle and pesto, and to the wine merchant on the other corner for the Chianti, etc. Finally, it may happen that B has nothing to do other than to get there. And even in this respect it is conceivable that A says: "Take the car". In other words, one situation may involve a distinction between the result on the one hand and the means to realize it on the other, while in another situation both these facets become the result.' Ibid. A means/ends distinction therefore becomes intelligible only if certain acts are considered illegitimate when engaged in for their own sake; for example, if A may organize dinner but has no independent authority to dispose of the car, then A cannot claim that use of the car is a result, and would have to argue that use of the car is necessary to get dinner. This, indeed, is the basis of the ubiquitous means/ends analysis in US constitutional law, and proportionality review in the EU and in Germany. Acts that place burdens on individuals are viewed as illegitimate unless justified, with a varying degrees of stringency, as a means to pursue other, legitimate ends. See for example *United States v. O'Brien*, 391 U.S 367 (1968), upholding prohibition on burning draft card despite incidental effects on expressive conduct; Günter Hirsch, 'Das Verhältnismäßigkeitsprinzip im Gemeinschaftsrecht', in *Scritti in Onore Di Giuseppe Federico Mancini*, ii (Milano: A. Giuffrè, 1998), 459, comparative discussion of proportionality review in the ECJ and Member State courts.

activity, it offers little promise as a rule of decision, because means can easily be recharacterized as part of the ends that are sought to be achieved.[63] Similar decisional, or enforcement, problems arise if, instead, a framework law must be 'general' in nature, or leave some 'sufficient' degree of discretion in the implementation of the command.

Many EC directives have been extremely detailed without leaving much discretion in the fine tuning during the implementation phase.[64] The Council issued many such directives during the 1970s, at a time when the Community still sought to harmonize the common market by promulgating specific standards for countless industry products and practices, such as safety features for automobiles.[65] Nonetheless, the ECJ upheld these detailed directives as long as they were necessary to the achievement of legitimate Community goals.[66] And as Professor Bermann notes, ECJ review of the 'necessity' of Community action has never been too strict.[67] To be sure, the Commission did shift in the mid-1980s 'away from the concept of harmonisation towards that of mutual recognition and equivalence' and adopted a general preference for less detailed 'framework directives'.[68] But given the ECJ's jurisprudence, this shift was not the product of ECJ decisions declaring that detailed directives were incompatible with the Treaty. Pressures other than the formal definition of 'directives' in the Treaty led to the Community's new programme of preserving greater flexibility in implementation for the Member States.[69]

[64] See for example Prechal, *Directives in European Community Law*, at 15–18, 88–9, 109–13.

[65] See for example Council Directive 78/932/EEC: head restraints of seats of motor vehicles, OJ 1978, L 325/1.

[66] See Case 38/77, *Enka BV v. Inspecteur der Invoerrechten en Accijnzen Arnhe*, [1977] ECR 2203 , upholding Council Directive 69/74, OJ Sp. Eng. Ed. 1969 I/82 regarding customs warehousing procedure, noting that 'in order to bring about the uniform application of the common customs tariff it may prove necessary to ensure the absolute identity [of national measures on the subject]'.

[67] See George Bermann's chapter in this volume.

[68] COM(85)310 (par. 13). This new practice of requiring only that products and practices of one Member State be recognized as adequate to fulfil the regulatory requirements of another was foreshadowed by the Commission in its Communication of January 1980, Bull. EC1-1980, 12. It had also been the Court's rule that controlled in the absence of active Community harmonization. See Case 120/78, *Rewe-Zentrale AG v. Bundesmonopolverwaltung für Branntwein* (Cassis de Dijon), [1979] ECR 649, striking down national law that prohibited import of certain alcoholic beverages, and finding 'no valid reason why, provided that they have been lawfully produced and marketed in one of the Member States, [they] should not be introduced into any other Member States' (par. 14).

[69] For an example of this latter type of measure, see Directive 88/378/EEC, OJ 1988 L 187/1: safety of toys. For a discussion on flexibility in the implementation of the Directive on Integrated Pollution Prevention and Control, see Joanne Scott, 'Flexibility, "Proceduralization", and Environmental Governance in the EU, in Gráinne dę Búrca and Joanne Scott, *Constitutional Change in the EU: From Uniformity to Flexibility?* (Oxford: Hart, 2000). See also the discussions of the shift toward mutual recognition and the

In Germany, the Constitutional Court has declared that a framework law must be 'capable of, and in need of, completion', leave the *Länder* a regulatory task of 'substantial weight', allow for *Länder* 'discretion in the material development of the law', and not simply 'limit *Länder* legislators to a choice between prescribed legal options'.[70] Although the Constitutional Court has occasionally held that the Federation overstepped the bounds of its authority to issue framework laws, the criteria the Court has offered have been criticized as a rather vague rule of decision that insufficiently protects *Länder* autonomy.[71] Finally, in the US context, the Court in *Printz* has deemed the distinction between 'policy-making' and mere 'implementation' of the law an elusive one that has not served to produce a coherent jurisprudence regarding the unconstitutional delegation of legislative power to the executive.[72]

To summarize: the more limited form of commandeering represented by framework legislation promises to preserve the voice of the component units of government even when they are subject to commands within a high-viscosity legal system. Component States may fear, however, that defining the central government's powers in this limited manner will not sufficiently protect their autonomy given the difficult nature of policing the distinction between framework laws and more comprehensive laws.[73] Indeed, as a further examination of the German and EU contexts reveals, these systems place central lawmaking powers within an institutional context that appears to have other safeguards against overreaching by the central government.

issuance of framework directives in David Lazer and Viktor Mayer-Schoenberger's, and Cary Coglianese and Kalypso Nicolaidis's, contributions to this volume.

[70] North Rhine Westphalia Civil Service Salaries Case, 4 BVerfGE 115,129–30 (1954) (author's translation).

[71] *Ingo v. Münch, Grundgesetzkommentar* (München: C. H. Beck, 1978), 131; Hans D. Jarass, 'Regelungsspielräume des Landesgesetzgebers im Bereich der konkurrierenden Gesetzgebung und in anderen Bereichen', *Neue Zeitschrift für Verwaltungsrecht* 15/11: 1041, 1047 (1996); Cf. Manfred Welan, 'Grundsatzgesetzgebung und Ausführungsgesetzgebung', in E. C. Hellbling *et al.* (eds), *Theorie und Praxis des Bundesstaates* (Salzburg: Univ. Verlag Anton Pustet: 1974), 11, 51, noting difficulty of defining the limits of framework laws based on Austrian Constitutional Court decisions. But cf. Peter Saladin, 'Rahmengesetzgebung im Bundesstaat', *Zeitschrift des Bernischen Juristenvereins* 114: 505, 528 (1978), concluding in the Swiss context that limitation of scope of framework laws is in principle possible.

[72] *Printz*, 521 U.S., at 927.

[73] Such a definition of limited authority may serve, however, as the basis for political debate about the necessary detail of central legislation.

5. Corporate Representation of Component States at the Central Level of Governance

Unlike the United States, the European Union is still formally a creation of the corporate structures of the Member States. The authors of the various treaties that form the basis for the EU are the governments of the Member States, not the people themselves as was the case when the United States Constitution was adopted. When the original treaties governing the Union were passed and when amendments to them have been proposed, the decision whether to submit the measure to popular ratification has been one of Member State constitutional law, not European Union law. Thus, even instances of popular ratification take place within existing Member State constitutional structures, and the results of such plebiscites are mediated through the Member States in their corporate capacities.[74]

This corporate constitution of the Union continues to be reflected in the representation of the Member States in the Council. While a Member State may now be outvoted in the Council, the Member State government is still directly represented in the deliberations. Ministers meeting in the Council represent their governments: they are members of their respective State governments, subject to recall by their government, and required to cast an undivided vote on behalf of their State. Member States thus have a voice in the decision making process of the EU from which central norms, including directives, emerge.

The German Federation is not formally a creation of the *Länder* in their corporate capacities,[75] but the *Länder* directly participate in the federal lawmaking process through their representatives in the *Bundesrat*. Much like the Council of the EU, the *Bundesrat* is composed of members of the executive branches of the *Länder*.[76] While each *Land* government appoints a delegation, as opposed to a single representative, to the *Bundesrat*, each

[74] To be sure, under the United States Constitution, the legislatures of the several States may also be involved in the ratification of constitutional amendments, but their involvement is an alternative that Congress may, but need not, choose. See US Const. art. V.

[75] The Preamble to the German Constitution notes that the 'German People' have given themselves this Basic Law, and makes further reference to the fact that the 'Germans *in* [the various *Länder*]' have freely engaged in this act of self-determination. Präambel GG; emphasis added. Ratification of the Basic Law, however, is in slight tension with the idea that the German people created the Federal Republic directly, since the existing *Länder* parliaments, not popular conventions especially elected for the purpose of ratification, ultimately approved the founding document. See Peter H. Merkl, *The Origin of the West German Republic*, at 51–4, 159–60.

[76] See Art. 51 GG. Others have commented on this similarity between the German and EU systems. See for example Simon J. Bulmer, 'The European Council and the Council of the European Union: Shapers of a European Confederation', *Publius* 26/4: 17, 38 (1996).

delegation must vote as a bloc.[77] This means that in the case of coalition governments at the *Länder* level, a delegation must either agree upon a unified view of the interests of their *Land* or abstain from casting a vote.[78] And while the *Bundesrat* does not participate in all federal matters, and is considerably less powerful than the Council of the European Union, the *Länder* are specifically empowered to veto collectively federal laws whenever such laws have a significant impact on the *Länder*.[79] Thus, federal laws that would command the *Länder* to assist in the implementation of a federal regulatory programme emerge from the federal legislative process only with the collective consent of the *Länder*.

In Germany, we further observe an additional correlation between corporate representation of the component *Länder* and the federal government's ability to issue commands. Under the German Basic Law, Art. 83 expressly authorizes 'executive commandeering', that is, commands that the *Länder* administer a federal programme regulating private parties: 'The Länder shall execute federal statutes as matters of their own concern insofar as this Basic Law does not otherwise provide or permit.' Until recently, the Basic Law less clearly authorized 'legislative commandeering', that is, commands that the *Länder* pass legislation to implement a federal regulatory programme. Prior to recent amendments,[80] Art. 75 GG simply authorized the Federation to 'enact framework legislation' without specifying any *Länder* duty to pass actual implementing legislation,[81] leaving doubt as to whether Art. 75 GG merely authorized the Federation to set forth a framework that the *Länder* could choose to fill in, or whether the *Länder* were under a constitutional obligation to do so. The Constitutional Court never resolved the disagreement among scholars.[82]

[77] See Art. 51 GG; *Maunz/Dürig*, at Art. 51, §§ 26–7 (1996); Uwe Leonardy, 'The Working Relationships between *Bund* and *Länder* in the Federal Republic of Germany', in Charlie Jeffery and Peter Savigear (eds), *German Federalism Today* (New York: St Martin's Press, 1991), 40.

[78] For an analysis of party competition within this structure, see Roland Sturm, 'Party Competition and the Federal System: The Lehmbruch Hypothesis Revisited', in Charlie Jeffery (ed.), *Recasting German Federalism* (London: Pinter, 1999).

[79] Indeed, although the *Länder* did not formally create the Federation, as the Member States did the Union, the German Basic Law was nonetheless ratified by the *Länder* parliaments, as opposed to conventions composed of delegates chosen for the particular purpose of ratification. See Merkl, *The Origin of the West German Republic*, at 51–4, 159–60.

[80] The amendments will be discussed in section 7.

[81] See Art. 75 GG (version effective prior to 14.11.94), reprinted in, *Maunz/Dürig* Art. 75 (1996).

[82] Compare *Maunz/Dürig* Art. 75, pp. 9–11 (1986), claiming that *Länder* duty to legislate cannot be derived from the Basic Law, with Fritz Otten, 'Wird vorkonstitutionelles Recht, das Gegenstände der Rahmengesetzgebung des Bundes betrifft, Bundes- oder Landesrecht?', (Inaugural Dissertation: Westfälische Wilhelms-Universität Münster, 1965), 24–5, arguing that federal framework legislation would be pointless absent duty on the part of the *Länder* to pass implementing legislation, and Hans-Otto Heeger, 'Die

What is interesting to note for present purposes is that the different treatment of executive and legislative commandeering under the Basic Law corresponds to the different representation of the *Länder* executives and *Länder* parliaments in the federal lawmaking process. While the *Länder* executives, who are clearly subject to a constitutional requirement to heed federal commands, are represented in the *Bundesrat*, the *Länder* parliaments, upon whom the old version of Art. 75 GG did not clearly impose an obligation of assistance, are not.[83]

In the United States, by contrast, neither the governments nor the legislatures of the several States in their corporate capacities are represented in the federal decision-making bodies.[84] Even prior to the Seventeenth Amendment, when US senators were appointed by the State legislatures, senators were less closely linked to their respective State governments than are the members of the Council of the EU or of the German *Bundesrat*. For example, senators were not subject to recall by the State legislatures that appointed them, did not have to develop a joint position on behalf of their State, and were not officially members of State governments when they came to Washington.[85] Since the adoption of the Seventeenth Amendment introduced the popular election of US senators, these differences between the EU and Germany on the one hand, and the US on the other, have become even more pronounced. Senators are now formally independent of their State governments, and need not have the particular interests of their respective State governments in mind when deliberating or voting in the Senate. This means that if the Congress were to pass a command instructing the States to carry out federal regulatory tasks, it would emerge from a legislative process that had no input from the component States in their corporate capacities.

Rahmengesetzordnung, ihr Inhalt und ihre Auswirkung' (Inaugural Dissertation: Westfälische Wilhelms-Universität, 1962), 73–8, arguing that fidelity to federalism requires *Länder* to implement federal framework legislation.

83 To be sure, given the relatively close connection between legislative and executive branches in parliamentary systems, the relevance of parliamentary representation in addition to executive representation is not as great as in a system with an independently elected executive branch. The exclusion of the parliament, however, is nonetheless meaningful. Cf. European Council, 'Birmingham Declaration', at 491 par. 4, underscoring the importance of involving Member State parliaments at the European level.

84 See generally C. M. Hoebeke, *The Road to Mass Democracy* (New Brunswick, NJ: Transaction Pub. 1995).

85 For a discussion of early State legislature's unsuccessful efforts to instruct their senators, see William H. Riker, 'The Senate and American Federalism', *Am. Pol. Science Rev.* 49: 452 (1955). As Professor Larry Kramer has noted after reviewing the history of the Senate, together with that of State control of qualifications for federal elections, federal districting, and the electoral college: 'These are, on their face, rather flimsy devices for safeguarding the institutional interests of state governments *vis-à-vis* the federal government.' Larry Kramer, 'Understanding Federalism', *Vanderbilt L. Rev.* 47: 1485, 1506 (1994).

Thus, one significant difference between the United States on the one hand and the EU and Germany on the other is the lack of corporate representation of component States at the central level of governance. As a consequence, in the EU and in Germany commandeering is subject to some control and allows for some voice on the part of the governmental units that are ultimately being commandeered. The United States, in contrast, both in its creation and modern government, bypasses the corporate State entities in its lawmaking power, with no direct involvement in the federal legislative process of the governmental units that would be carrying out the federal commands.

6. Central Government Dependence on Component States Resources

Another significant institutional difference between the EU and Germany on the one hand and the United States on the other is the ability of the central government to carry out its policies without the help from the component units of government. In the United States, the federal government has not only the general legal authority to pass laws with immediate effect on the citizens within the 50 States, but it may also draw on a fully developed federal bureaucracy and judiciary for the implementation of federal laws. The federal government has both the constitutional authority and, since the passage of the Sixteenth Amendment authorizing a federal income tax, the financial resources to create new bureaucracies whenever necessary and to do so without the consent of the States.[86] In the European Union, in contrast, the Community's legislative powers do not universally include the power to issue immediately effective regulations as well as directives. And even though the power to issue regulations has increasingly been added to the legislative repertoire of the Community legislature,[87] as a practical matter the EU must still rely on the Member States for administrative services. The EU has a minuscule judiciary, only very limited powers of taxation, which do not include the power to tax income,[88] and, partly as a consequence, a fledgling bureaucracy that generally cannot carry out the task of implementing Community policies. In

[86] See Douglas Laycock, 'Notes on the Role of Judicial Review, the Expansion of Federal Power, and the Structure of Constitutional Rights', *Yale L.J.* 99: 1711, 1737–8 (1990): 'The Sixteenth Amendment worked as profound a change in American federalism as the Fourteenth.'

[87] One of the most prominent changes has been the introduction by the Single European Act of Art. 95 (ex 100a) EC, which provides generally for majority voting in the Council regarding measures to harmonize the common market.

[88] See Koen Lenaerts and Piet Van Nuffel, *Constitutional Law of the European Union* (London: Sweet and Maxwell, 1999), 361–3.

this sense, then, despite the strength of the EU legal system, the Community institutions are practically dependent on the cooperation of the Member States for the success of Community policies. Germany is, again, similar to the European Union in this regard. The Basic Law provides for virtually no federal judiciary at the lower level,[89] and generally assigns the task of executing federal law to the *Länder*.[90] Moreover, the federal ministries generally lack any administrative apparatus of their own, which has led some scholars to describe them as rather elaborate policy offices.[91] And although the Federation possesses the exclusive power of taxation in Germany, the constitution contains revenue-sharing provisions that guarantee fiscal equalization among the *Länder*.[92] Moreover, the *Bundesrat*, once again, has full input into the decision-making process by which revenue is distributed within the federal system.[93]

At first it may seem ironic that the US Supreme Court has come to champion commandeering on behalf of the States just as the federal government's power, bureaucracy, and independence have grown so as to make reliance on the States seem unnecessary. As noted above, however, Professor Hills has argued as a matter of constitutional interpretation that the ability of the federal government to execute the laws renders the power to commandeer less 'necessary' and therefore not worth the political cost or within the scope of federal power under the Necessary and Proper Clause.[94]

As a practical matter, one might view the anti-commandeering rule as simply another way of limiting the power of the central government. As Professors Coglianese and Nicolaidis explain in their contribution to this volume, where the central government enjoys broad powers that are difficult to keep in check by 'delineation', mechanisms other than substantive review of enumerated powers may be used to curb the central government's sphere of influence. In the United States, the Supreme Court has had considerable difficulty imposing limits on the scope of Congress's enumerated powers, especially Congress's power to make all laws necessary and proper for the regulation of inter-State commerce. As Professor Fritz Scharpf aptly puts it:

[89] See Currie, *The Constitution of the Federal Republic of Germany*, at 75–6.

[90] For a brief overview, see ibid. at 66–74.

[91] See Renate Mayntz and Fritz W. Scharpf, *Policy-Making in the German Federal Bureaucracy* (Amsterdam: Elsevier, 1975), 45–6.

[92] See Art. 104a–107 GG.

[93] See ibid.; see generally, Stefan Korioth, *Der Finanzausgleich zwischen Bund und Ländern* (Tübingen: Mohr Siebeck, 1997); Clifford Larsen, 'States Federal, Financial, Sovereign, and Social: A Critical Inquiry into an Alternative to American Financial Federalism', *Am. J. Comp. L.* 47: 429 (1999).

[94] See discussion in section 2.

The reason [for the expansion of central governments with enumerated powers] is succinctly contained in the old poker rule that 'you cannot beat something with nothing'. In the present context this means that even the weakest argument creating a link to one of the enumerated powers of the central government will prevail—in court as well as in political debate—against unspecified appeals to the residual competence of Member States.[95]

For over half a century since the Supreme Court's now widely discredited attempts to curb the expansion of the federal government in the era leading up to the New Deal, judicial control over the substantive scope of Congress's enumerated powers was virtually non-existent. Indeed, at one point Professor Andrzej Rapaczynski observed that 'even a moderately searching scrutiny of the powers of the federal government shows that the alleged existence of a residual category of exclusive state powers over any private, nongovernmental activity is in fact illusory'.[96]

To be sure, the Supreme Court recently reclaimed some control over the substantive scope of Congress's Commerce Clause powers by striking down a federal ban on the possession of guns near schools[97] and portions of the federal Violence Against Women Act[98] as lacking the requisite connection to inter-State commerce.[99] But despite these claims of tighter control, even Congress's core Commerce Clause powers continue to provide a ready basis for federal takeovers of vast policy arenas long occupied by the States.[100] In addition to being difficult to conduct, review of the substantive scope of federal powers as a means of limiting Congress's sphere of influence implies that, once a given area of activity is indeed found to be beyond Congress's reach, there are no other avenues for the federal government to regulate the activity absent the States' voluntary cooperation. As Professor Ernest Young has noted: 'Because the remedy is so drastic . . . the Court has been most reluctant to impose these sorts of limits (at least in the post-New Deal era).'[101]

95 Fritz W. Scharpf, 'Can there be a Stable Federal Balance in Europe?', in J. J. Hesse and V. Wright (eds), *Federalizing Europe* (Oxford University Press, 1996), 361, 368.

96 Andrzej Rapaczynski, 'From Sovereignty to Process: The Jurisprudence of Federalism after Garcia', *Sup. Ct. Rev.* 1985: 341, 351.

97 *United States v. Lopez*, 514 U.S. 549 (1995). This was the first time in 60 years that the Court struck down a federal law on the grounds that it exceeded Congress's powers under the Commerce Clause. See ibid. at 584 (Souter, J., dissenting).

98 *United States v. Morrison*, 120 S. Ct. 1740 (2000).

99 The Supreme Court has also reasserted control over Congress's exercise of powers under Section 5 of the Fourteenth Amendment. See, for example, *City of Boerne v. Flores*, 521 U.S. 507 (1997), holding that in enacting Religious Freedom Restoration Act of 1993 Congress exceeded its powers under Section 5 of the Fourteenth Amendment.

100 *AT&T Corp. v. Iowa Utilities Board* (1999), upholding federal pre-emption of State regulation of local telephone service.

101 Ernest A. Young, 'State Sovereign Immunity and The Future of Federalism, *Supreme Court Rev.* 1999: 1, 29.

Put differently, when the federal government is not significantly constrained by the enumeration of powers, has the practical ability to legislate comprehensively for the entire nation, has the power to impose and collect taxes, and has created a large bureaucracy to administer its laws, a rule against commandeering might be viewed as a potential limitation on the federal government's powers. The ability to commandeer a State is surely an added tool in the kit of governance. And the quick judgement by the current majority on the US Supreme Court seems to be that depriving Congress of this tool will aid in restraining the federal government's powers.[102] Indeed, the thought may be that, in any event, the States have little to lose by depriving the federal government of the power to commandeer.[103]

Although judicial enforcement of the 'delineation' of central powers has been weak in the EU[104] and Germany[105] as well, here the central bureaucracies are far smaller as a proportion of component State bureaucracies than their counterpart in the United States. Indeed, even Germany's fully developed federal government is relatively modest compared with that of the United States.[106] Thus, in the EU and Germany commandeering may be seen as a mechanism to prevent the creation of a large central bureaucracy, appreciably avert—or, at a minimum, shape—the general intrusion

[102] In support of this argument, see, for example, D. Bruce La Pierre, 'The Political Safeguards of Federalism Redux: Intergovernmental Immunity and the States as Agents of the Nation', *Wash. U. L. Q.* 60(3): 779, 988–9 (1982). This empirical judgement is, of course, debatable, as is the more general question whether the US Supreme Court has the institutional capacity to make such an empirical assessment with the confidence necessary to justify a court-enforced anti-commandeering rule.

[103] For this calculus to appear meaningful, the Supreme Court must place further faith in the ability of the States to act as autonomous bargaining partners in negotiations with the federal government. Otherwise, the federal government's ability to control State action by conditional spending and conditional pre-emption would simply undermine any value of the anti-commandeering rule.

[104] See Bermann's chapter in this volume. On the underlying concept of subsidiarity generally, see Bermann, 'Taking Subsidiarity Seriously'.

[105] See generally Karl-Peter Sommermann, 'Die Stärkung der Gesetzgebungskompetenzen der Länder durch die Grundgesetzreform von 1994', *Juristische Ausbildung* 1995/8: 393.

[106] The ratio of central government to component State and local employees in the United States (1:6) is vastly greater than in Germany (1:12) and the EU, where the ratio of EU to German government employees alone is 1:132. Compare US Census Bureau, *Statistical Abstract of the United States: 1999*, 119th edn (Washington, DC, 1999), Table 535: 2,807,000 federal civilian employees, 16,733,000 State and local employees; Statistisches Bundesamt, 'Personalbestand der Bundesverwaltung im Jahr 1999', http://www.statistik-bund.de/presse/deutsch/pm/p0018062.htm: 320,000 federal civilian employees; Statistisches Bundesamt, 'Beschäftigtenzahlen bei Bund, Ländern und Kommunen 1999 weiter rückläufig', http://www.statistik-bund.de/presse/deutsch/pm/p0066062.htm: 3,800,000 State and local employees; *Eurostat Yearbook* 98/99 441: 31,000 total permanent staff.

of central law into the component State legal system, and, thereby, broadly sustain component State control over its 'internal' legal order.

In summary, commandeering may be viewed as empowering or disempowering component States depending on the context in which it occurs. In the EU and in Germany the central government that issues commands is structurally dependent on the component governments' administrative services such that centralization might be seen as less of a threat and commandeering as being routinely necessary. Indeed, this is, perhaps, why both in Germany and in the European Union the concept of 'faithfulness' to the common enterprise plays such a prominent role.[107] In the United States, in contrast, the federal government is considerably less dependent on the States to carry out federal regulatory programmes. This has arguably led the Court, at the behest of the States, to develop a strategy of containment of federal powers, not State cooptation of the federal decision-making process. Each level of government is 'complete' and independent, such that States may take on a competitive relationship with the federal government and reject cooperation.[108]

7. Corporate Representation and Central Government Dependence: A German Case in Point

The significance of the factors identified in the last two sections to the issue of commandeering is further highlighted in the German example by the story surrounding the participation of the *Länder* in EU affairs. We see here the direct interplay between the availability of commandeering, the corporate representation of the addressee of the command in the central lawmaking system, and the central government's dependence on the component State for the implementation of law.

While the *Länder* have a voice in the *Bundesrat*, until recently they lacked any similar input into the decision-making process at the European level, where the federal executive had been the sole negotiator on Germany's behalf. This was changed significantly over the course of the past decade, due in large part to the Federation's dependence on the cooperation of the *Länder* in the implementation of Community law. After Germany had experienced serious difficulty with the implementation of

[107] See Currie, *The Constitution of the Federal Republic of Germany*, at 77–80; Lenaerts and Van Nuffel, *Constitutional Law of the European Union*, at 419–26.

[108] See for example Albert Breton, *Competitive Governments* (Cambridge University Press, 1996), 189–90; William W. Buzbee, 'Brownfields, Environmental Federalism, and Institutional Determinism', *W. & M. Envtl L. & Pol'y Rev.* 21: 1 (1997), describing vertical competition in environmental context.

EU directives in areas in which the Federation was dependent on *Länder* collaboration,[109] the *Länder* won two major concessions in return for improving their cooperation in EU affairs.[110] First, the *Länder* received a commitment from the federal executive to increase the flow of information to the *Länder* about EU affairs and to allow for the establishment of *Länder* missions in Brussels. Second, and more important, the *Länder* won a constitutional amendment that provided for a direct role of the *Länder* in the representation of Germany in the Union Council.[111] According to the new Art. 23 GG, the *Länder* are not only consulted prior to developing any EU policy on matters reaching into the *Länder*'s exclusive competences, but they take part in and, moreover, lead the delegation in the Council of the EU on that particular issue.

This amendment was soon followed by another that removed the ambiguity regarding the *Länder's* obligation to pass implementing legislation for federal framework laws.[112] Article 75 GG was changed to make clear, or establish for the first time, depending on one's view of the prior state of affairs, that the *Länder* are under a duty to implement federal framework laws.[113] Thus, as the *Länder* have come to play a diplomatic role in the representation of the Federation in the Council, they have accepted a duty to legislate whenever necessary to comply with the commands of the EU.

Professor Charlie Jeffery has observed that as EU law reaches more deeply into the regional and local spheres of Member State governance, we may expect more aggressive demands for inclusion in EU affairs by other sub-national units as well.[114] This is especially likely to be the case where Member States must rely on the cooperation of their sub-national units of government for the implementation of EU law. In the United States, we

[109] On account of the *Länder*, Germany had particular difficulty heeding its Community obligations in the environmental area. See for example Case C-361/88, *Commission v. Germany*, [1991] ECR I-2567 (air pollution directive); Case C-59/89, *Commission v. Germany*, [1991] ECR I-2607 (air pollution directive); Case C-58/89, *Commission v. Germany*, [1991] ECR I-4983 (surface water directive); Case C-131/88, *Commission v. Germany*, [1991] ECR I-825 (groundwater directive); Case C-288/88 *Commission v. Germany*, [1990] ECR I-2721 (wild bird directive). For a discussion of Germany's difficulties in this area, see for example Susan Rose-Ackerman, *Controlling Environmental Policy: The Limits of Public Law in Germany and the United States* (New Haven: Yale University Press, 1995), 115–16.

[110] See generally, for example, Martin A. Rogoff, 'The European Union, Germany, and the Länder: New Patterns of Political Relations in Europe', *Colum. J. Eur. L.* 5: 415–430 (1999); Juliane Kokott, 'Federal States in Federal Europe: The German Länder and Problems of European Integration', in Antero Jyränki (ed.), *National Constitutions in the Era of Integration* 175 (The Hague: Kluwer, 1999).

[111] Art. 23 GG; see for example *Maunz/Dürig* Art. 23 (1999).

[112] On the ambiguity, see the discussion of Art. 75 in section 4.

[113] Art. 75(3) GG.

[114] See Charlie Jeffery, 'Sub-National Mobilization and European Integration: Does it Make Any Difference?,' *J. Comm. M. Stud.* 38: 1 (2000).

have witnessed a similar phenomenon in the negotiation of NAFTA and the Uruguay Round agreements of GATT (WTO).[115] Here, too, apparently in response to the increased importance of recent international trade law for matters of traditional concern to the States, the latter have successfully pressured Congress into including them in the formulation of US external trade policy.[116] Although in this respect the US States have not achieved the status that the German *Länder* have with regard to European affairs, the inclusion of States in this manner is nonetheless remarkable and may indicate that a similar dynamic was at work in both situations.

8. Consensus Government and the Twin Dangers of Joint and Separate Administration

In his well-known comparative study on majoritarian and consensus tendencies of various democratic structures, Professor Arendt Lijphart notes that 'The consensus model is characterized by *non*-concentration of power, which can take the two basic forms of sharing of power and division of power'.[117] Applying this basic insight to the present comparison of the role of central commands in component governments in the United States, the EU, and Germany, the various constitutional rules surrounding commandeering in each system can be seen as part of a consensus mode of governance.[118] Both the European Union and Germany present a similar combination of sharing and dividing power to achieve consensus. In both systems, the central decision-making structures are instances of collective power-sharing among the different levels of government: the EU's Council as well as the German *Bundesrat* both push for vertical

[115] See 19 USC. § 3512 (1994), providing for a federal-State consultation process for addressing GATT-related issues 'that directly relate to, or will potentially have a direct effect on, the States', and ensuring that 'the Trade Representative will take into account the information and advice received from the States . . . when formulating United States positions regarding matters [that directly relate to, or will potentially have a direct impact on, the States]'; 19 USC. § 3312 (same for NAFTA).

[116] See Stephen Zamora, 'Allocating Legislative Competence in the Americas: The Early Experience under NAFTA and the Challenge of Hemispheric Integration', *Houston J. Int'l L.* 19: 615, 638–9 (1997).

[117] Arend Lijphart, *Patterns of Democracy* (New Haven: Yale University Press, 1999), 185.

[118] More generally, the degree of 'consensus governance' differs significantly among the US, EU, and German systems by virtue of their respective electoral structures and parliamentary versus executive or presidential systems. See generally Lijphart, *Patterns of Democracy*; cf. Samuel Issacharoff, Pamela S. Karlan, and Richard H. Pildes, *The Law of Democracy* (New York: Foundation Press 1998), 773–84. The claim made in the text is not that the three systems are the same in the level of 'consensus governance' generally, but simply that the commandeering structure of each system can be viewed as a feature of 'consensus governance.'

agreement among the central and component institutions of governance during the creation of central norms. In addition, both systems generally divide the powers of legislation and implementation vertically among the different levels of government: the Member States in the EU and the *Länder* in Germany generally retain what amounts to a practical, if not legal, monopoly over implementation. This division of power ensures the central government's dependence on the component States, preserves component States' control over their 'internal' legal sphere, and thus further pushes for consensus among the different levels of governance before any policy is ultimately implemented.

Similarly, the separation of governmental spheres in the United States might be thought to push for consensus. Lijphart observes:

> Majoritarian government is . . . both unitary (nonfederal) and centralized. The consensus model is inspired by the opposite aim. Its methods are federalism and decentralization—that is, not only a guaranteed division of power between the central and noncentral levels of government but also, in practice, strong noncentral governments that exercise a substantial portion of the total power available at both levels.[119]

In the United States, then, the maintenance of separate governmental structures at the federal and State levels together with the current anti-commandeering rule can also be viewed as a mechanism of consensus governance. Under the Court's implicit theory, the anti-commandeering rule ensures that when the central and component governments come together to cooperate they do so voluntarily.

If forcing consensus is indeed a significant aspect of these different institutional rules surrounding commandeering, further inquiry is needed to assess the merits of consensus governance generally and the relative merits of each consensus approach in particular. And while an evaluation of the relative virtues and vices of these different structures of governance is beyond the scope of this study, it may be useful to note briefly some of the concerns raised by each.

Most important, in raising these concerns here, as well as in the broader evaluative inquiry that lies ahead, the perspective from which this chapter has approached the comparison so far must be expanded. Apart from determining, as this chapter has done, what self-interested States conceived of as corporate actors would choose—that is, why component States would remain sanguine about commandeering in one system but oppose it in another—the inquiry must be expanded to ask about such things as the relative efficiency of the various structures and the democratic legitimacy of each.

[119] Lijphart, *Patterns of Democracy*, at 186.

For example, the intertwining of decisional structures that lies at the heart of the German and European consensus mechanisms has been famously criticized by Professor Fritz Scharpf as creating a 'joint decision trap'.[120] Scharpf argues that joint decision-making, which he terms *Politikverflechtung*,[121] threatens to be undemocratic. He explains that if two decision makers are required to share the burden of a given government programme, each actor will view the programme as being cheaper than other programmes that the actor would have to finance or carry out alone. According to Scharpf, by so reducing opportunity costs at each level of government, joint decision-making creates 'the tendency to "overspend" on joint programs . . . distor[ts] . . . "real" political preferences at the local and *Land* levels [and] . . . increase[s] the salience of "federal" issues in *Länder* elections at the expense of regional issues'.[122] Moreover, Scharpf notes, existing programmes in Germany that depended on the close cooperation of the federal and *Land* governments have proven inflexible due, for example, to the Federation's inability to lower expenditures for such programmes unilaterally.[123] Similarly, the Federation's inability to act unilaterally may retard action due to the necessity of convincing the *Länder* to go along where the latter are reluctant to do so.[124] Scharpf thus takes a critical view of the ability of intertwined decisional structures to solve policy problems effectively.

Scharpf also speculates about the reasons why joint administration may have persisted in Germany despite these drawbacks, and notes some of the benefits that policy-makers may see in such a system. First, the reduction in opportunity cost is welcomed by policy specialists seeking to promote their particular programmes, since the programmes may be more easily adopted by each level of government.[125] Second, the intertwining of decisional structures allows such policy specialists to resist interest-group demands for other government programmes by diffusing the blame for the rejection of these demands.[126] Finally, policy generalists at the State and federal levels, according to Scharpf, also prefer intertwined decisional

[120] Fritz W. Scharpf, 'The Joint-Decision Trap: Lessons from German Federalism and European Integration', *Law and State* 36: 1 (1987). Scharpf's criticism is directed specifically at the 'joint tasks'—*Gemeinschaftsaufgaben*—which require the federal and *Länder* governments to cooperate closely in carrying out certain governmental tasks, such as the financing of hospitals.

[121] See generally Fritz W. Scharpf, 'Theorie der Politikverflechtung', in Scharpf *et al.*, *Politikverflechtung: Theorie und Empirie des kooperativen Föderalismus in der Bundesrepublik* (Kronberg, Taunus: Scriptor,1976), 13–70.

[122] Scharpf, 'The Joint-Decision Trap', at 17–18.

[123] Ibid. at 18.

[124] Scharpf, 'Theorie der Politikverflechtung', at 42.

[125] Fritz W. Scharpf, 'Nachwort: Der politisch-bürokratische Nutzen der Politikverflechtung', in Scharpf *et al.*, *Politikverflechtung*, at 237–8.

[126] Ibid. at 38–9.

structures. For them, these structures facilitate horizontal agreements among the *Länder*, vertically supported in Germany by a fiscally conscious federation, to ward off policy demands by interest groups.[127] Linking the governing structures of the *Länder* and the Federation together in this manner essentially allows for the emergence of a cartel formed by the various government actors to prevent what is viewed as ruinous competition among the States to make public expenditures for the sake of satisfying policy demands of interest groups.[128]

The decisional structure of bargaining in the United States, in contrast, might not lead into a joint decision trap if, indeed, the federal government can exit by implementing federal regulatory programmes on its own. As noted above,[129] this exit was crafted as a specific response to the failure of the States, under the Articles of Confederation, to cooperate with the Continental Congress in the execution of federal policy. Further investigation is needed, however, to determine whether such cooperation might not sometimes be necessary, as it may be in the case of maintaining speed limits throughout the nation or notifying the consulates of foreign citizens who are arrested by State authorities.[130] Conversely, further review is needed to examine whether States realistically may decline participation in so-called 'voluntary' federal programmes, which is a central assumption of the bargaining hypothesis.[131]

Even if the central government can act alone whenever it needs, and the component States can bargain from a position of strength whenever they want, providing the central government with the legal tools and practical powers to take independent action might nonetheless introduce a bias in favour of centralization. Central-component system relations might atrophy and the central government might come to rely increasingly on its own resources. This centralization bias might thus be viewed as the Scylla to the joint-decision trap's Charybdis. In this sense, the anti-commandeering rule might have perverse effects, by prodding the central government to develop the bureaucracy necessary to implement its policy without involving the component States.[132] Where the central government has the capacity to do this and expands central functions, the central infrastructure

[127] Ibid. at 240–2. [128] Ibid. [129] See section 2.

[130] It would seem highly impractical, for example, for Congress to employ a vast corps of officers to police speeding on the nations roads or to monitor State arrests and prosecutions.

[131] See Richard A. Epstein, *Bargaining with the State* (Princeton: Princeton University Press, 1993), 150–7.

[132] See *Printz*, 521 U.S. at 959 (Stevens, J., dissenting): 'In the name of State's rights, the majority would have the Federal Government create vast national bureaucracies to implement its policies.'

might short-circuit what would have otherwise have become a productive cooperative relationship with component States.

Where to chart a course between combination and separation will also be influenced, quite prominently, by an assessment of the value of the component State's political institution that is to be given voice or ignored in the central decision-making process. For example, after the American experience with State governments under the Articles of Confederation, the Founders of the constitutional republic had lost faith in the State legislative processes and set out to create a powerful federal government. The States became the object of further distrust or weakness, and the federal government the locus of progressive force, during Reconstruction, the New Deal, and the Civil Rights era of the 1950s and 1960s. In the current era of globalization, in contrast, the salient role of the federal government may have turned more to managing the coexistence of overlapping jurisdictional spheres than to galvanizing national moral consensus.[133] Under these circumstances, the revival of 'States' rights' in the jurisprudence of the Supreme Court, and the apparent effectiveness of the States' call for inclusion in the debate about foreign policy and trade commitments, is perhaps unsurprising. Modern Germany, in turn, was created in the aftermath of the Weimar Republic's devastating failure to prevent the centralization of power during the Nazi era. As a consequence, in Germany the *Länder* were hailed as the principal safeguard of democracy. The founders of modern Germany, and especially the American occupying forces with notable support from Bavaria, accordingly created a strong and enduring role for the *Länder* in the governance of the nation. Finally, in the EU, the Member State legislatures are still considered to be very much at the heart of democratic governance within the Member States, yet here it is some version of 'centralization', that is, the integration of the Member States into a common supranational organization, that has long been the beacon of lasting peace and prosperity in Europe.[134]

Of all three systems, the European Union has settled least on where it fits into the spectrum between separate and joint administration. As a practical matter the Community is currently still dependent on the Member States to carry out Community law, especially because it does not possess the power of direct taxation that would support a large central

[133] Cf. Daniel J. Elazar, 'The State System + Globalization (Economic Plus Human Rights) = Federalism (State Federations Plus Regional Confederations)', *South Tex. L. Rev.* 40: 555 (1999).

[134] Shortly after World War I, Jean Monnet was already contemplating multinational institutional frameworks to help contain a defeated Germany and prevent it from menacing the world again. See François Duchêne, *Jean Monnet: The First Statesman of Interdependence* (New York: Norton, 1994), 39.

bureaucracy. As a matter of Treaty law, however, the Community has the power of direct legislation and is not generally required to hand implementation of the law over to the Member States. At the same time, its primary lawmaking institution, the Council, is still composed of representatives of the component States. Fritz Scharpf has noted that intertwined systems of governance tend to perpetuate themselves,[135] and despite frequent intergovernmental conferences one might therefore expect the corporate representation of the Member States to endure. On the other hand, however, a diminution of such representation would not be the first time that European integration has progressed dramatically by diminishing intergovernmental aspects of decision making within its central structure of governance.

9. Conclusion

What initially may have looked like diametrically opposite approaches to the issue of commandeering in the United States on the one hand and in the EU and Germany on the other reveal some similar characteristics when considered in the light of the broader institutional context of each system. The US anti-commandeering rule exists in the context of a federal system marked by independently constituted, independently competent levels of governance that coexist in a high-viscosity legal system with a powerful federal government whose sphere of influence has proven difficult to contain by other means. Here, the anti-commandeering rule may be viewed as a consensus-forcing device by separating independent tiers of governance and requiring federal and State decision makers to reach agreement before working together. Although the EU has progressed beyond its low-viscosity origins and Germany is presumably not marked by any more State defiance of legal obligations than the United States, the EU and Germany have both preserved other limitations on central government expansion and mechanisms of component State control over central government norms. Constitutional provisions and practical realities in both the EU and Germany make the central governing structure in both systems dependent on the component States for administrative services. And in both systems, component States are represented in their corporate capacities in the central governing institutions. Thus, in the EU and in Germany, commandeering is embedded within a system of consensus-forcing governance with structural limitations on the expansion of the

[135] Scharpf *et al.*, *Politikverflechtung*, 62.

central government.[136] Under these circumstances, commandeering may be viewed as a further mechanism to maintain the dependence of the central government on the component States and to preserve a sphere for additional component State input while carrying out central commands.

This does not mean that the US Supreme Court's establishment of the anti-commandeering rule is justified as a matter of policy or right as a matter of US constitutional interpretation. These questions depend on a host of factors not considered in this chapter. First, additional relevant features of the EU and German systems merit further comparative exploration. To what degree do individual component States have any practical control over the creation of central commands? To what extent do the majority-voting rules in the Council and the *Bundesrat* infringe on component State's autonomy interests? And to what extent may this infringement be mitigated by equality norms such as fiscal equalization in Germany and faithfulness to the Community in the EU? Second, this investigation has not pierced the veil of governmental structures to examine the extent to which various competing actors that are formally within or outside government may have stakes in one or the other form of central-component system interaction.[137] More generally, it has not considered the extensive literature in EU scholarship on the relevant debates surrounding multi-level governance theory and its alternatives.[138] Third, the description of US federalism provided in this chapter is also still an

[136] Indeed, in the light of this analysis the difference in US attitude regarding commandeering within the domestic federal system and within the international legal system may not seem as paradoxical at it did at the outset. Even putting aside the question regarding the viscosity of international law, which may give the US Congress a certain degree of freedom in implementing international law that a State legislature would not have in implementing a federal command, international legal institutions, unlike the federal government, have only fledgling bureaucracies and are largely dependent on 'component States' for administrative resources, and at least in theory international rule making is, as Professor Henkin has explained, based on structural assumptions of consensus among the 'component' nation states. See Henkin, *How Nations Behave*, 33.

[137] On the incentives that bureaucrats may have within federal systems, see for example Paul E. Peterson, Barry G. Rabe, and Kenneth K. Wong, *When Federalism Works* (Washington, DC: Brookings Inst., 1986); Scharpf *et al.*, *Politikverflechtung*. On the role of political parties in US federalism, see Larry Kramer, 'Putting the Politics Back into the Political Safeguards of Federalism', *Colum. L. Rev.* 100: 215 (2000).

[138] See for example Gary Marks, Liesbet Hooghe, and Kermit Blank, 'European Integration from the 1980s: State-Centric v. Multi-Level Governance', *Journal of Common Market Studies* 34: 341 (1996); A. Moravcsik, 'Liberal Intergovernmentalism and Integration: A Rejoinder', *Journal of Common Market Studies* 33: 611 (1995); Andrew Moravcsik, 'Preferences and Power in the European Community: A Liberal Intergovernmentalist Approach', *Journal of Common Market Studies* 31: 473 (1993). The debates and the literature about the relevance of the various actors are, of course, too extensive to cite here even in abbreviated form. See Paul Craig, 'The Nature of the Community: Integration, Democracy, and Legitimacy', in Paul Craig and Gráinne de Búrca (eds), *The Evolution of EU Law* (Oxford: Oxford University Press: 1999).

idealized one. For example, as noted earlier, the view that States possess the kind of power and autonomy to engage in 'voluntary bargaining' with the federal government is subject to debate. And the view that the federal government can always effectively implement federal policies without the help of the States requires a more nuanced evaluation as well.

Finally, this chapter has not grappled with the difficult questions surrounding the normative implications of comparative constitutional law. It has not, for example, discussed the basic canons of constitutional interpretation or where in these there may be room for input from comparative analysis.[139] By focusing on some of the most salient differences between the US, EU, and German systems, however, I do hope to have illustrated that a context-sensitive account of the comparison of these systems on the issue of commandeering 'may . . . cast an empirical light on the consequences of different solutions to a common legal problem: in this case the problem of reconciling central authority with the need to preserve the liberty-enhancing autonomy of a smaller constituent governmental entity'.[140] In short, I hope to have shown how analyzing federal systems promises to deepen the understanding of one's own.

[139] For a classic statement of the different modes of constitutional interpretation, see Phillip Bobbit, 'The Modalities of Constitutional Argument', *Constitutional Interpretation* 1991: 12. For an examination of the usefulness of comparative constitutional law as a discipline, see generally Vicki C. Jackson and Mark Tushnet (eds), *Comparative Constitutional Law* (New York: Foundation Press, 1999), 144–89. For differing views on the values of comparative constitutional law, see Donald P. Kommers, 'The Value of Comparative Constitutional Law', *J. Marshall J. of Practice and Procedure* 9: 685 (1976), and Günter Frankenberg, 'Critical Comparisons: Re-thinking Comparative Law', *Harv. Int'l L. J.* 26: 411 (1985). For recent prominent exercises in comparative constitutional law, see Bruce Ackerman, 'The New Separation of Powers', *Harv. L. Rev.*113: 633 (2000), and Mark Tushnet, 'The Possibilities of Comparative Constitutional Law', *Yale L. J.* 108: 1225 (1999).

[140] *Printz v. United States*, 521 U.S., at 977 (Breyer, dissenting).

9

Regulatory Legitimacy in the United States and the European Union

GIANDOMENICO MAJONE

1. Introduction

Two decades ago a distinguished member of the European Court of Justice (ECJ) urged Europeans 'to recognize that on many issues arising in a federal context the United States have the advantage of some 150 years of a highly diversified judicial development from which many useful lessons may be learned' (Pescatore 1982: x). Judge Pescatore had in mind the role of the US Supreme Court in the creation and maintenance of the American common market, but his suggestion to take note of the experiences accumulated on the other side of the Atlantic is more generally relevant today. For if it is true that there are striking similarities between the Supreme Court and the ECJ, the development of the American regulatory state—a process profoundly affected by the federal courts—also deserves careful comparative analysis: not to draw superficial and possibly misleading analogies, but for the deeper insight that such analysis may offer into the problems of the regulatory regimes now emerging in the European Union and in its Member States. In fact, since statutory regulation has only recently become a significant element of national policy-making in European countries, on issues of regulatory legitimacy the EU has more to learn from the century-old experience of the US than from individual Member States.

At the time Judge Pescatore was writing the lines quoted above, few European scholars were familiar with the expression 'regulatory state', and even those few considered it a neologism of American origin and of dubious practical or conceptual relevance on this side of the Atlantic. In fact, statutory regulation played a very minor role in the political economy of the Keynesian welfare state. Public ownership of utilities and of other key industries was supposed to make economic regulation superfluous, while social regulation—of the environment, consumer protection, and health and safety—was politically insignificant by comparison with the central role of redistributive social policy.

That yesterday's neologism is used more and more frequently today, not only by scholars but also by policy-makers and the media, is a clear indication of the growing importance of regulatory policies at both national and European levels. Of the several factors which explain the rise of the regulatory state in Europe, two are particularly relevant to our discussion. First, the failure of public ownership as a method of guiding and controlling the national economy led to a mode of regulation which has been used in America for more than a century. Under this mode of regulation, utilities and other industries deemed to affect the public interest are left in private hands, but are subject to rules developed and enforced by specialized agencies. Such bodies are usually established by statute as independent administrative authorities: independent in the sense that they operate outside the line of hierarchical control by the central departments of government, but also in the sense that they are insulated from the electoral cycle and party politics. At the same time, the newly privatized companies lose their pre-existing immunity from national and European competition law. In fact, the power of the former monopolists is often so great that competitors owe their existence to the regulatory constraints imposed on their larger rivals. Thus, the new regulatory regime following privatization includes both sectoral and general economic regulation, and in some cases—the water industry, for example—also environmental regulation.

The Europeanization of policy-making—that is, the increasing interdependence of domestic and supranational policies within the European Community/European Union (EC/EU)—is the second important factor in the growth of the regulatory state in the old continent. Regulation is by far the most important type of policy-making in the EC, the 'first pillar' of the EU. Because the Community budget is too small to allow large-scale initiatives in the core areas of welfare-state activities—redistributive social policy and macroeconomic stabilization—EC policy-makers could increase their influence primarily by expanding the scope of supranational regulation. Rule making puts a good deal of power in the hands of the Brussels authorities in spite of the tight budgetary constraints imposed by the Member States. Thus, lacking an independent power to tax and spend, the Community had no other way to grow than as an almost pure type of regulatory state (Majone 1996).

Now, the expansion of European regulations could not fail to affect the development of regulatory policies and institutions at national level. For example, when the Treaty of Rome was signed in 1957 only Germany, among the founding members, had a modern competition law and a forceful regulatory body, the Federal Cartel Office, to implement it. Forty years later, all members of the EU have competition laws, which substantially resemble EC competition law, and increasingly expert and independent competition regulators. Similar developments may be observed in most other areas of regulation, so that the extensive delegation of regulatory powers to the European level has not reduced but actually increased the importance of national regulators. This apparent paradox is easily explained. In the policy-making system created by the Treaty of Rome, implementation of most European rules is the responsibility of the Member States, which often have to create new bodies, or at least to expand existing ones, for that purpose. In addition, national experts play an active role in European rule making through their membership in advisory, scientific, and 'comitology' committees. Hence, in order to influence the substance of European regulations and then to implement them domestically, Member States have been forced to expand their regulatory capacities on an unprecedented scale.

What is even more important, national and European regulators have learned to work closely with each other, with the result that a new pattern of regulatory federalism is now emerging, based on partnership and networking rather than on the traditional separation of responsibilities along the vertical dimension.

2. Regulatory Federalism in the EU: From Pre-emption to Partnership

The central issue of regulatory federalism is traditionally stated as the optimal allocation of regulatory responsibilities among the different levels of government forming the federal polity.

This formulation, with its emphasis on the vertical dimension of the distribution of powers, never matched the constitutional reality of the EC/EU: a mixed polity where rule making through directives leaves ample margins of discretion to the Member States in the choice of means for achieving the common regulatory objectives; where national experts and administrators play a large role in Community rule making; and where rule enforcement is firmly in the hands of the national bureaucracies.

The traditional view of regulatory federalism had a certain plausibility in the early days of the EC, when it was thought that market integration requires the total harmonization of the rules and regulations of the Member States. Under total harmonization, once Community rules have been put in place, national regulations no longer apply. Hence, the effect of total harmonization is analogous to federal pre-emption in the US constitutional system.

As shown in section 7, however, by the 1970s the practical and political limits of total harmonization had become clear. The emphasis shifted from total to 'optional' and 'minimum' harmonization, while the scope of pre-emption was eventually reduced to basic regulatory objectives of health, safety, and prudential supervision. Today, most regulatory competences of the Community are shared with the Member States, and as a general rule 'the more competences the Community is acquiring, the less exclusive [is] its jurisdiction' (Norbert Reich, cited in Weatherill 1995: 156).

Even in areas of exclusive Community competence the tendency is to move toward a system of cooperative partnership with the national regulatory authorities. The most striking example of this tendency is the recent Commission White Paper on Modernization of the Rules Implementing Articles 85 and 86 of the EC Treaty (European Commission 1999). Regulation 17, implementing Arts 85 and 86 of the Rome Treaty, laid down the system of supervision and enforcement procedures which the Commission has applied for over 35 years without any significant change.

Under this regulation, the Commission, national courts, and national competition authorities can all apply Art. 85(1), prohibiting anti-competitive agreements and concerted practices between firms, but the power to grant exemptions under the third section of the article was given exclusively to the Commission. Now, the White Paper proposes the abolition of the present notification and exemption system and its replacement by a Council Resolution which would render the exemption rule of Art. 85(3) directly applicable, without prior decision by the Commission, by national courts and competition authorities. In the words of the White Paper, '[A]fter 35 years of application of the Community competition rules, the time has come to make better use of the complementarity that exists between the national authorities and the Commission, and to facilitate the application of the rules by a *network of authorities* operating on common principles and in close co-operation' (European Commission 1999: 32; emphasis in the original).

Transnational regulatory networks already exist, in more or less well developed form, in a number of regulatory areas (see section 7). The convergence of national regulatory philosophies—a convergence aided by the common framework provided by European law—the emphasis on subsidiarity which has characterized the constitutional development of the Union in the 1990s, and the mismatch between an ever expanding set of regulatory tasks and the limited resources of the Commission are thus leading to original forms of coordinated partnership between European and national regulators.

This intertwining of the national and European strands of regulatory policy-making does not correspond to a precise allocation of powers along the vertical dimension. Rather, it prefigures the emergence of a transnational regulatory branch—a 'fourth branch of government', to use the American expression—comprising national, subnational, European, and in some cases—technical standardization, for example—even international regulators. This is in striking contrast to other policy types, such as distributive and redistributive policies, where the distinction between the national and the EU levels continues to remain important.

The normative implications of these developments are far-reaching. On the one hand, the active participation of national authorities increases the legitimacy of European regulatory networks. On the other hand, political independence, at both national and European levels, is essential to the viability of such networks. Politically motivated behaviour by a regulator would compromise his or her reputation in the eyes of other members of the network and make cooperation more difficult to achieve in the future. The problem, then, is how to make independence and accountability complementary and mutually reinforcing rather than antithetical values. The long experience of the American regulatory state indicates that independence and accountability can indeed be reconciled by a combination of control mechanisms rather than by direct oversight exercised by one particular institution: clear and limited statutory objectives to provide unambiguous performance standards; reason-giving and transparency requirements to facilitate judicial review and public scrutiny; due process provisions to ensure fairness among the inevitable winners and losers from regulatory decisions; public participation; and a high level of professionalism to withstand external interference and reduce the risks of an arbitrary use of discretion.

Normative discourse in the EU has focused on the issue of the 'democratic deficit' as a peculiar problem of European policies and institutions. The emergence of a transnational 'fourth branch of government' in Europe shows that problems of regulatory legitimacy are not limited to any one level of governance (Majone 1998). Although the following pages usually make reference to the EU, this is only for simplicity of exposition. The key issues discussed here are as relevant to the national and subnational levels as to the supranational and, in the future, to the international level of regulation.

3. Regulatory Legitimacy: Early American Views

The developments briefly reviewed in the preceding sections raise institutional and normative problems which have been largely neglected by political, legal, and economic theories of the European welfare state, but which are well known to students of the American regulatory state. The welfare state was characterized by a high level of centralization in administration and policy-making. This meant that all important governmental decisions were under the direct control of elected politicians, at least in theory. Even nationalized companies were supposed to be under the political control of a cabinet-level minister.

By contrast, the regulatory state relies on extensive delegation of powers to politically independent institutions: agencies, commissions, boards, but also the courts which, as the American experience shows, are key players in the regulatory game. The issue of regulatory legitimacy arises from the delegation of important policy-making powers to such non-majoritarian institutions. Both in Europe and in America, the key normative problem of the regulatory state is, in Richard Stewart's words, 'to control and validate the exercise of essentially legislative powers by administrative agencies that do not enjoy the formal legitimation of one-person, one-vote election' (Stewart 1975: 1688).

The American polity has grappled with this issue for more than a century. In its successes as well as in its failures, the long struggle to find an acceptable normative foundation for institutions that lack direct democratic legitimacy has much to teach Europeans concerned about the 'democratic deficit' of their regulatory institutions.

The 'non-delegation doctrine' was the first attempt to resolve the normative problems raised by the emergence of a modern system of administrative regulation. For several decades the doctrine enjoyed such widespread acceptance that it came to be regarded as the traditional model of administrative law. The model conceives of the regulatory agency as a mere transmission belt for implementing legislative directives in particular cases. Vague, general, or ambiguous statutes create discretion and thus threaten the legitimacy of agency action. Hence, when passing statutes Congress should decide all questions of policy and frame its decisions in such specific terms that administrative regulation will not entail the exercise of broad discretion by the regulators (Stewart 1975: 1675–6).

The non-delegation doctrine had already found widespread acceptance when the first institutionalization of the American regulatory state, the Interstate Commerce Commission, was established by the 1887 Interstate Commerce Act. The Act, with its detailed grant of authority, seemed to exemplify the transmission-belt model of administrative regulation. However, the subsequent experience of railroad regulation revealed the difficulty of deriving operational guidelines from general standards. By the time the Federal Trade Commission was established in 1914, the agency received essentially a blank check authorizing it to eliminate unfair competition.

The New Deal agencies received even broader grants of power to regulate particular sectors of the economy 'in the public interest'. The last time the Supreme Court used the non-delegation doctrine was in 1935, when in *Schechter Poultry* it held the delegation in the National Industrial Recovery Act unconstitutional (Horwitz 1992: 216–17).

The doctrine against delegation unravelled because the practical case for allowing regulatory discretion is overwhelming, but also because the conceptual distinction between policy and administration is far from being clear-cut. It is not the case that policy settles everything down to a certain point while administration deals with everything below that point. Policy and administration do not occupy two separate spheres of action, nor are they the responsibility of two completely separate groups of people. Rather, policy and administration interact throughout the entire regulatory process (Majone 1989).

New Deal advocates of regulation rejected every attempt to fit regulatory agencies into the policy-administration dichotomy and, more generally, into traditional separation-of-powers thinking. For James Landis, for example, the novelty of the Interstate Commerce Commission consisted primarily in the delegation of legislative, executive, and judicial functions: 'In the grant to it of that full ambit of authority necessary for it in order to plan, to promote, and to police, it presents an assemblage of rights normally exercisable by government as a whole' (Landis 1966 [1938]: 16).

But how could agency discretion be disciplined? The New Deal's answer was: through expertise. For if agency decisions are simply a function of the goal to be achieved and of the objective constraints of the situation, then the discretion that the regulator enjoys is more apparent than real. To be sure, the New Deal advocates of regulation knew that the expertise of the regulatory bureaucracy is not always above suspicion. Still, they insisted that issues of fact should be handled by experts, using whatever methods appeared to be most appropriate. Judicial review of the evidence used in reaching a decision would be a serious threat to 'the very virtue of specialized knowledge which constitutes one of the chief justifications for the establishment of [regulatory] commissions' (Fainsod 1940: 318).

It is interesting to note that the New Deal's belief in the power of expertise influenced functionalist and neo-functionalist theorists of regional integration. For functionalists like Mitrany regional institutions grow out of the need for technocratic management of economic and social policy, which leads to the formation of international agencies. Such agencies gain legitimacy by promoting economic welfare. Like the functionalists, Ernst Haas assumed that in modern welfare states rational economic management requires expert, apolitical administration. Effective management of closely interdependent economies leads to economic integration. The expectations and values of economic and social actors eventually adapt to integration, creating a transnational community which in the end legitimizes centralized supranational governance (Moravcsik 1998: 13–16).

Expertise has been viewed as an important source of legitimacy also by some European legal scholars, who conceive of the Community as a purposive association (*Zweckverband*) of countries pursuing specific economic goals, having limited competences, and disposing of mere technical-administrative means. Thus, Ipsen characterized EC policy-making as being 'oriented towards expertise and independent from the political balancing of interests' (Winter 1996: 19).

By the time functionalist scholars were extending the New Deal's technocratic model to the international level, confidence in expert policy-making had largely disappeared in the United States. Expertise was increasingly seen as a myth concealing the inevitability of hard value choices. According to the critics, vague statutory language was the main cause of the capture of the agencies by the very interests they are supposed to regulate. One proposed remedy was statutes that have clear goals, set fixed deadlines for achieving them, and empower citizen groups to take slow-moving agencies to court. Thus legislatures and courts were called upon to fill the legitimacy gap created by the fall of the myth of expertise (Ackerman and Hassler 1981: 7–9).

Agency capture is also facilitated by the difficulty of objectively determining the public interest. Actually, pluralist thinkers, whose writings began to exert a strong influence on American courts in the 1960s, taught that the public interest is a will-o'-the wisp: the only objective reality is the clash of competing interests. Pluralists would improve regulatory legitimacy by transforming the regulatory process into a surrogate political process. Once the function of regulatory agencies is conceptualized as adjusting competing private interests, it is no longer possible to legitimize agency action by either the traditional 'transmission belt' theory or by the expertise model of the New Deal period. 'Participation' becomes the key normative concept. However, the balancing of interests is an inherently discretionary, ultimately political process, and it is difficult to see how non-elected officials could legitimately assume responsibility for adjusting the competing claims of various private interests. Thus, the pluralist proposal to politicize the regulatory process would actually aggravate the legitimacy problem. Analogous proposals to reduce Europe's democratic deficit by politicizing EC policy-making are open to the same objection.

4. Delegation and Commitment

Before considering more recent American thinking on the delegation problem, we should examine how this problem arises in the EU context. Here, two different types of delegation should be distinguished: external and internal. The first type denotes the transfer of rule-making powers from the Member States to the European institutions, or from the European institutions to outside bodies, including Member States. Internal delegation is the transfer of executive powers from the Council of Ministers to the Commission. I shall discuss the two types separately since each gives rise to rather different legitimacy issues.

Traditionally, the transfer of powers to the European institutions has been legitimized by a theory vaguely reminiscent of the American transmission-belt model. The traditional theory derives the legitimacy of the European institutions from the democratic character of the Member States. National parliaments ratify the treaties; democratically accountable heads of state or government meeting in the European Council set strategic priorities; the Council of Ministers, composed of people who are normally elected members of the national executives, must approve the Commission's proposals before they become European law. Thus the entire process of European integration is guided and controlled by sovereign democratic states.

This scheme of indirect legitimization was considered to be sufficient as long as the Community dealt mainly with such matters as tariff reductions and agricultural quotas. In fact, the scheme makes perfect sense from an intergovernmentalist perspective: we do not usually worry about the legitimacy of international treaties freely signed by democratic states. As recently as 1993, the German Constitutional Court, in the *Brunner* case, based the constitutionality and legitimacy of the Treaty on European Union (TEU) on the democratic legitimacy of the Member States which signed it. The Court argued that the TEU, like the previous European treaties, is nothing more than an international agreement among sovereign states. The members of the Union, the Court said, remain the 'lords of the Treaty' (*Herren der Verträge*) and never surrendered their power to secede.

State-based standards of legitimacy imply that the veto power of the Member States is the most legitimizing element of the integration process, so that the shift to majority voting can only aggravate the democratic deficit. However, even if it is true that the democratic character of the Member States and the possibility of vetoing legislative proposals are sufficient to legitimize the intergovernmental component of the Union, such indirect legitimization cannot provide an adequate normative foundation for its supranational component and, in particular, for the regulatory functions of the Community.

It is therefore not surprising that other legitimacy arguments have been used since the extension of qualified majority voting and the growth in Community competences under the Single European Act. A recurrent theme in the debate about democracy in the Union is the need to increase the powers of the European Parliament (EP). Although the idea of reducing the democratic deficit of the EC/EU by assigning a larger role to the EP is not new, the procedure introduced by the Treaty of Amsterdam for the appointment of the Commission (Art. 214 of the Consolidated Treaties) contains a number of radical changes not only with respect to previous practices, but also with respect to the new Art. 158 of the Maastricht Treaty. If under Art. 158 the national governments could nominate a new Commission President only after consulting the EP, now their nomination must be approved by the parliament. Moreover, the president and the other members of the Commission are subject to a vote of approval by the EP, as in classical parliamentary systems.

Not surprisingly, influential MEPs openly advocate a 'Parliamentary Commission', in which the composition and programme of the European executive would reflect the will of the parliamentary majority. As Dehousse (1997) points out, these developments amount to a deep transformation of the relationship between the EP and the Commission. The Commission will be fully responsible to the parliament in all its activities, whether administrative, regulatory, or legislative. It appears that the signatories of the Maastricht and Amsterdam Treaties, in their desire to reduce the Union's democratic deficit, have radically modified the balance of power between the Commission and the EP.

An increasing level of politicization of EU policy-making becomes unavoidable as more and more tasks involving the use of political discretion are shifted to the European level. Thus, new competences in the area of immigration, the Schengen arrangements, and the problems connected with the next enlargement of the Union not only increase the administrative tasks of the Commission but also emphasize the Commission's political responsibilities. Against this background, the demand for a greater role of the European Parliament becomes understandable. At the same time, one should not be blind to the risks which politicization entails for the credibility, and hence ultimately the legitimacy, of European regulatory policies.

In a democracy, the policies of the current majority can be legitimately subverted by a new majority with different and perhaps opposing interests. The fact that democratic politicians lack the means of credibly committing themselves to long-term policies explains why in areas where credibility is essential to success, such as monetary policy and regulation, delegation to non-majoritarian institutions is increasingly seen as the most effective means of achieving policy credibility. Today most European countries delegate regulatory policy-making to agencies operating at arm's length from government. As was mentioned above, delegation of rule making, adjudication, and enforcement to independent agencies and commissions is a century-old tradition in the United States.

A less technocratic, more political Commission may enjoy greater democratic legitimacy, but eventually it will have to face the same commitment problem of all democratic governments. The delegation of powers to regulatory agencies distinct from the Commission itself may provide a feasible solution to the credibility problem under the new political conditions prevailing in the Union. Some first steps in this direction are discussed in section 7.

5. Internal Delegation: Legitimization through Committees?

The only provision in the original Rome Treaty expressly concerned with internal delegation is Art. 155. This article merely requires the Commission to exercise the powers delegated to it by the Council, but contains no express authorization for such delegation. Explicit authority is provided by Art. 145 of the Treaty, as amended by Art. 10 of the Single European Act (now Art. 202 of the Consolidated Treaties). According to this article, the Council *must* delegate implementing powers to the Commission. The range of implementing measures covers rule making of a general type, such as making directives to complete a framework directive or regulation, as well as merely executive activities.

The limits of permissible delegation depend on how the Court interprets the term 'implementation'. In *Rey Soda* (Case 23/75) the Court said that the concept of implementation is to be interpreted widely, in light of the overall context of the treaty. Particularly in the sphere of the Common Agriculture Policy, the Council may confer on the Commission 'wide powers of discretion and action'.

In *Köster* (Case 25/70) the Court was asked whether there were any limits to the delegation of powers from the Council to the Commission. It answered that only general principles of Community policy cannot be delegated. Extensive discretionary powers may be delegated to the Commission, provided the enabling provision lays down the basic principles governing the matter in question (Hartley 1988: 113).

More recent cases, such as *Germany v. Commission* (Case C 240/90), confirm the general impression that the Court is prepared to accept a large measure of discretion in the case of internal delegation. The situation is quite different in the case of delegation to bodies other than Community institutions. Here the leading case is *Meroni v. High Authority* (Case 9/56). In this old case, which arose under the European Coal and Steel Community Treaty, the Court ruled that the High Authority possessed only very limited power to delegate to outside bodies. Clearly defined executive powers may be delegated provided their exercise is subject to strict rules based on objective criteria; discretionary powers involving extensive freedom of judgment may not be delegated (Hartley 1988: 115).

An important reason for the distinction between delegation to the Commission, which may involve wide discretionary powers, and delegation to outside bodies—including Member States and independent agencies—which may be only of a very limited nature, is the widespread system of committees of national representatives through which the Council can control the exercise of the delegated powers by the Commission. Recall that under Art. 145 (3) of the Rome Treaty, the Council must delegate implementing powers to the Commission, and may reserve such powers to itself only in special cases. This was part of the same effort to streamline EC decision-making which also introduced qualified majority voting for harmonizing measures needed for the completion of the internal market. However, in order to re-establish the institutional balance, Art. 145 (3) adds that in delegating implementing powers the Council may impose certain requirements on the exercise of such powers. These requirements were spelt out by a Council Decision of 13 July 1987, the so-called Comitology Decision. According to this Decision, which to a large extent codifies existing practices, the Commission must submit the draft of a proposed measure to a committee made up of representatives of national governments and chaired by a Commission representative who does not vote. There are three types of committees: advisory, management—introduced in 1962 for the implementation of the Common Agriculture Policy—and regulatory—introduced in 1968 for delegating powers in areas other than agriculture, especially for adapting directives and regulations to technical progress: hence the name.

The Commission is not bound by the opinion of an advisory committee; it must only take the opinion into account. The most constraining procedure is that of the regulatory committee. While under the management committee procedure the Commission has only to avoid a qualified majority being formed against its proposal, under the regulatory-committee procedure it can implement a proposed measure only if it has the explicit approval of the committee.

It should be noted that the Comitology Decision does not specify the cases in which a particular procedure, or a particular variant of a given procedure, should be adopted. It is therefore up to the Commission to propose the procedure to be followed, and up to the Council to accept or reject, by unanimity, the proposal. While the Commission and the European Parliament favour advisory committees, particularly for internal market legislation, the Council generally favours regulatory committees. In spite of such disagreements, the Commission seems to feel that the advantages of the comitology system outweigh its disadvantages. The main advantages are the obligation imposed on the Council by Art. 145 (3) to delegate implementing powers, and greater efficiency in decision-making, since now the Council does not have to concern itself with technical matters which in the past have seriously retarded the adoption of regulations needed for completing the internal market.

The Court of Justice agrees with the Commission's overall assessment. In *Köster* it concluded that the management-committee procedure allows the Council to delegate more while retaining control over the powers it delegates. In *Rey Soda* the Court pointed out that under the comitology system the Council can delegate exceptionally wide powers of implementation, while reserving the right to intervene where necessary. Nor does the Court share the opinion that the regulatory-committee procedure could paralyze Community decision-making. In *Tedeschi v. Denkavit Commerciale* (Case 5/77) it argued that even the strictest variant of this procedure does not necessarily lead to a deadlock since the Commission is always free to submit a new proposal (Vos 1997).

We cannot conclude, however, that, because the Council retains control over the powers it delegates, no legitimacy problem arises. For all its value, the comitology system has not satisfied public demands that administration be made politically accountable. Notwithstanding the widespread committee practice of publishing their agendas and reports, commentators continue to bemoan their opacity. The variety of committees and procedures makes it very difficult immediately to identify and assess the dominant rationality—scientific, administrative, or political—behind each individual decision. Such concerns were brought to a head by the Bovine Spongiform Encephalopathy (BSE) crisis, where public suspicion of the motives of some national representatives within the committee system was augmented by the lack of transparency of the decision-making processes. Thus, the main deficiencies of comitology are of a procedural nature, but procedures have important legitimizing functions (Luhmann 1975). The American experience is particularly instructive in this respect.

6. Procedural legitimacy: Towards a European Administrative Procedure Act?

As was indicated in section 3, the New Deal's emphasis on expertise as a source of regulatory legitimization resulted in the elimination of elaborate procedural protections. Before the enactment of the Federal Administrative Procedure Act (APA) in 1946, many agencies used to pay scant attention to procedural matters at all, while others followed ad hoc schemes that departed widely from judicial-type procedures (Freedman 1978).

As claims to scientific expertise grew weaker, courts reverted to procedural protections, and reacting in part to the APA developed a number of techniques to control the exercise of regulatory discretion. Since passage of the APA, followed in the 1970s by the Freedom of Information and the Government in the Sunshine Acts, regulatory decision-making has undergone a far-reaching process of judicialization. Under APA, agency adjudication was made to look like court adjudication, including the adversarial process for obtaining evidence through presentations by the contending parties, and the requirement of a written record as a basis of agency decisions.

Administrative Procedure Act requirements for rule making were less demanding: before promulgating a rule, the agency must provide notice and opportunity for comments; when it promulgates the rule, it must supply a concise statement of the rule's 'basis and purpose'; the rule can be set aside by a court only if it is 'arbitrary, capricious, or an abuse of discretion'. Such differences in requirements for adjudication and rule making did not matter much as long as most regulation was of the rate-setting and permit-allocation type and hence relied largely on adjudication. However, with the growth of social regulation in the 1970s, rule making—standard setting, for example—became much more important (Shapiro 1988). Thus, the courts began to develop a large body of new procedural rules and strict standards of judicial review for rule-making proceedings.

First, they undertook a more searching scrutiny of the quality of the evidence supporting agency fact finding. Both the essential factual data on which a rule is based and the methodology used in reasoning from the data to the proposed standard should be disclosed for comment at the time the rule is proposed. Second, the courts demanded consistency in agency decision-making. Third, they began to demand a clear statement of legislative intent as a means of restraining the range of agency choice when fundamental individual liberties were at risk. As Richard Stewart (1975: 1679) notes, these various techniques, which matured in the 20 years after the enactment of the APA, are well adapted to discipline agency discretion without excessively intruding upon the delegated authority implicit in an enabling statute.

It is important to realize that these procedural innovations have been achieved by elaborating the general and apparently innocuous giving-reasons requirement of the APA. This proves that the simplest and most effective way of improving transparency and accountability is to require regulators to give reasons for their decisions: 'giving reasons is a device for enhancing democratic influences on administration by making government more transparent. The reason-giving administrator is likely to make more reasonable decisions than he or she otherwise might and is more subject to general public surveillance' (Shapiro 1992: 183).

The importance of the giving-reasons requirements did not escape the framers of the Treaty of Rome. According to Art. 190 of the Treaty, 'Regulations, directives and decisions of the Council and the Commission shall state the reasons on which they are based'. Similarly, Art. 15 of the European Coal and Steel Community Treaty provides that 'Decisions, recommendations and opinions of the High Authority shall state the reasons on which they are based', while Art. 5 of the same treaty states that 'the Community shall . . . publish the reasons for its actions'. At the time the founding treaties were drafted there was no general requirement to give reasons in the law of the Member States, so that these Community provisions were, and largely still are, not only different from, but in advance of, national laws (Hartley 1988).

However, the ECJ is quite prepared to impose the obligation of giving reasons upon national authorities so that individuals are able to protect their rights under Community law. In the *Heylens* case (Case 222/86), the Court reasoned that effective protection requires that the individual be able to defend his or her right under the best possible conditions. This would involve judicial review of the national authority's decision restricting that right—in *Heylens*, the right of free movement of workers. For judicial review to be effective, however, the national court must be able to call upon the authority to provide its reasons (Thomas 1997).

A question still debated by legal scholars is whether Art. 190 of the Rome Treaty—according to Martin Shapiro (1992: 220) 'one of the world's central devices for judicial enforcement of bureaucratic transparency'—will be used by the ECJ to move beyond formal requirements toward substantive judicial review of regulatory decision-making. At any rate, the enactment of a European APA would provide the EU with a unique opportunity to decide what kind of rules is more likely to rationalize decision-making, to what extent and in which form interest groups should be given access to the regulatory process, or how judicial review could be facilitated.

The need for greater transparency and accountability in regulatory decision making exists also—indeed, is even more urgent in some respects—in the Member States. If the problem of regulatory legitimacy seems to be more acute at the European level, this is because, relative to other functions of government, the regulatory function is much more important here than at the national level. Thus, a European APA would not only contribute to the legitimacy of the Community policy-making system but also serve as a useful model for the Member States. Indeed, a common body of procedural rules for agency decision-making would be the natural consequence of the tendency of European and national regulatory institutions to merge into transnational networks (see section 2).

7. Subsidiarity

Since preferences vary locally and local conditions often affect both the costs and benefits of regulation, decentralized rule making and/or enforcement can provide a better match between local public goods and citizen preferences. Hence subsidiarity is an important source of regulatory legitimacy.

In the EC the notion of subsidiarity was first introduced by the Single European Act in connection with environmental policy, and later extended by the Treaty on European Union to all areas of regulation which do not fall within the exclusive competence of the Community. As a result the Commission now exercises self-restraint in drafting new rules, and the Council submits all drafts to the subsidiarity test. Some drafts have even been withdrawn, although there has been no large-scale 'repatriation' of European regulatory law, as some governments had hoped.

Even before subsidiarity was given constitutional status by Art. 3 B of the TEU, the EC was moving in the direction of greater decentralization. From the early 1960s to about 1973, the date of the first enlargement of the Community, the Commission's approach to the harmonization of the laws and regulations of the Member States was characterized by a distinctive preference for detailed measures designed to regulate exhaustively the problem in question, to the exclusion of previously existing national regulations: the approach known as total harmonization. In those years, and even later, the ECJ supported total harmonization as necessary for the construction of the common market. In a number of important cases the Court determined that where the Community had legislated, that area had been transferred into the exclusive competence of the EC.

By the late 1970s, however, it had become clear that harmonization as then practised had been ineffective, and had seriously compromised the legitimacy of European regulations. Mounting opposition of the national governments and of public opinion to excessive centralization convinced the Commission that the powers granted to it by the treaties had to be used so as to interfere as little as possible with the regulatory autonomy of the Member States. The emphasis shifted from total to optional and minimum harmonization.

Optional harmonization aims to guarantee the right of free movement of goods in the common market, while allowing the Member States to retain their traditional forms of regulation. Thus, a food specialty, such as cheese made from non-pasteurized milk, not conforming to European standards may still be produced for the domestic market. Under minimum harmonization the national governments must secure the level of regulation set out in a directive but are allowed to set higher levels, provided that the stricter national rules are justified under primary Community law. Like optional harmonization, minimum harmonization liberalizes trade without suppressing legitimate regulatory diversity. The main objection to this approach lies in the risk that it may lead to a segmentation of the internal market. However, the areas where minimum harmonization is the rule—environment, consumer protection, and occupational safety and health—are not at the core of market building. Stricter national standards mainly affect production processes located in the regulating state, or methods of marketing products rather than the products themselves. By contrast, measures dealing with the safety and other aspects of traded goods directly affect market integration and hence must follow the traditional approach whereby Community rules preempt national rules (Weatherill 1995).

The new regulatory philosophy found expression in the Commission's 1985 White Paper on the completion of the internal market. This document introduced a strategy based on the following key elements: mutual recognition of national regulations and standards; total harmonization to be restricted to essential requirements binding on all Member States; delegation of responsibility for setting technical standards to the European standardization bodies. In essence, the White Paper proposed a conceptual distinction between matters where harmonization is essential and those where it is sufficient for there to be mutual recognition of the equivalence of the various requirements laid down under national law. Unlike total harmonization, mutual recognition does not involve the transfer of regulatory powers to the Community, except for the regulation of essential health and safety requirements, but only restricts the regulatory sovereignty of the Member States (Majone 1996).

Interestingly, in the United States also the demand for subsidiarity—for cooperative rather than pre-emptive federalism—has grown significantly since the late 1970s. Particularly in the Reagan and Bush administrations there was an emphasis on transferring some of the control over rule making and enforcement to the States. In 1988 the Office of Management and Budget issued a regulatory policy guideline which could satisfy the most intransigent advocates of subsidiarity in Europe: 'Federal regulations should not preempt State laws or regulations, except to guarantee rights of national citizenship or to avoid burdens on interstate commerce' (US Office of Management and Budget 1990: 20).

In the field of social regulation, the recognition that there are legitimate differences among States had already emerged in the 1970s. Thus, the 1972 Clean Water Act Amendments replaced a federal permitting scheme with the National Pollutant Discharge Elimination Scheme (NPDES) programme. This programme establishes the water-pollution permits that serve as the firm's regulatory standard for its water pollution discharges, and many States have assumed authority for the enforcement of these environmental regulations. The evolution from federal pre-emption to the philosophy of the NPDES programme reflected a Congressional judgement that the federal discharge-permitting scheme had been ineffective, and that the States were best situated to carry out the permit process (Mott 1990).

As well, the 1970 Occupational Safety and Health Act (OSH Act) incorporates special mechanisms for utilizing State resources. The most important of these are the provisions for State Implementation Plans (SIPs) in Section 18 (b)–(g). While the Act generally pre-empts State enforcement once the federal government regulates, Section 18 (b) provides that States desiring to regain responsibility for the development and enforcement of safety and health standards may do so by obtaining federal approval of an SIP that meets the technical, administrative, and financial requirements set forth in Section 18 (c). The approach of the OSH Act represents an interesting attempt to reconcile the desire to have labour standards applied uniformly throughout the country and the desire of the States to retain their responsibility in this as in other areas of regulation.

In the EU decentralized administration tends to be the rule rather than the exception, as in the US. Yet to require the Member States to draw up the equivalent of a SIP would force them to address the implementation issue more systematically than is currently the case. Community resources, from the structural funds for example, could be used to assist those Member States lacking sufficient resources to develop the requisite regulatory and enforcement structures. Such a scheme would be in line with the subsidiarity principle: Member States would retain their primary regulatory responsibilities, while the Community's main task would be to assist and supplement their action.

As this discussion indicates, policy-makers in both the US and the EU increasingly realize that there are legitimate differences among states, and good economic as well as normative reasons for preserving such differences and for making sure that federal or supranational intervention is truly needed.

The rise of the new European agencies—the Environment Agency, the Agency for the Evaluation of Medicinal Products (EMEA), the Agency for Health and Safety at Work, and the proposed Agency for Food Safety, to mention only a few—is another interesting development, particularly in a comparative perspective. The new agencies do not have the powers normally granted to the corresponding American institutions or to many regulatory bodies in the Member States. Even the EMEA, which comes closest to being a full-fledged regulatory agency, does not take decisions concerning the safety and efficacy of new medical drugs, but submits opinions concerning the approval of such products to the Commission. One reason for this reluctance to give formal powers of decision-making to the new agencies is the 'Meroni doctrine' against the delegation of rule-making authority to bodies not envisaged by the founding treaties (see section 5). Nevertheless, the creation of European agencies is an important stage in the development of a European regulatory state, for at least two reasons. First, it is an explicit acknowledgement that legislative harmonization is not sufficient to create and sustain a truly integrated European market. Regulation is not achieved simply by passing a law or by harmonizing national laws, but also requires, in the words of an outstanding American student and practitioner of regulation, 'the pursuit of energetic measures upon the appearance of an emergency, and the power through enforcement to realize conclusions as to policy' (Landis 1966: 25).

Second—and this is particularly interesting from the point of view of subsidiarity—the European agencies have been designed not as self-contained organizations but as transnational networks where national regulatory authorities, independent scientific committees, Member States, Commission, and European Parliament each have a role to play. For example, a central role in EMEA's work is played by two committees of national experts, the Committee for Proprietary Medicinal Products (CPMP) and the Committee for Veterinary Medicinal Products (CVMP). These committees are entrusted with the tasks of formulating the scientific opinions of the agency, and of arbitrating disputes between pharmaceutical firms and national authorities which may be unwilling to approve an application authorized in another Member State.

The CPMP, like the CVMP, consists of two members nominated from each Member State, while the Commission is not represented in the committees. The committee members represent the national regulatory authorities, and serve for renewable three-year terms. However, it would be wrong to assume that through their power of appointment the national governments control the drug authorization process. In fact, since the creation of the EMEA both committees have become not only more important than when they assisted the Commission, but also more independent. This is because it is in their interest to establish an international reputation for good scientific work, and for this purpose the degree to which they reflect the views of the national governments is irrelevant.

The complex structure of EMEA and of the other European agencies was largely dictated by the political realities of European policy-making, but could provide, as a more or less unintended by-product, a favorable environment for the development of the two most important qualities of credible regulation: independence and expertise. When agencies see themselves as part of a transnational network of institutions pursuing similar objectives, rather than as part of a national bureaucracy with multiple and often conflicting objectives, they are more motivated to defend their independence and to enhance their expertise. Agency executives have a strong incentive to maintain their reputation in the eyes of the other members of the network since, as noted in section 2, unprofessional or politically motivated behaviour would compromise their international reputation and make cooperation more difficult to achieve in the future. In this way, the network becomes an intangible asset carrying a reputation that is beneficial for efficient information exchange and division of labour, and conferring that reputation upon the agencies in good standing (Majone 1997).

8. Conclusion

The central normative problem of the regulatory state is essentially the same on the two sides of the Atlantic, namely, how to control and validate the exercise of legislative powers by administrative agencies that do not enjoy the democratic legitimacy provided by the electoral process. This explains why, in spite of all historical, institutional, and political differences, the debate on regulatory legitimacy has evolved along surprisingly similar lines in the US and the EU. Normative discourse in both jurisdictions relies on the same evaluative criteria—expertise, proceduralization, subsidiarity—although the relative importance attached to these criteria may vary.

Differences become more pronounced at the level of practical implementation of conceptually similar solutions. In Europe, as in America, the delegation of powers to independent agencies is viewed as an important means whereby governments can commit themselves to regulatory strategies that would not be credible in the absence of such delegation. In America the value of agency independence is ingrained in the political culture of the country, and political principals rely to a large extent on indirect procedural controls in order to discipline agency discretion without excessively intruding upon the agency's delegated authority. European governments are also aware of the importance of policy credibility in an increasingly interdependent world, and are thus prepared to accept in principle the independence of national and European regulators; but in practice they are often driven, by considerations of political expediency as well as by a long tradition of direct intervention in the economy, to interfere with the regulators' decisions.

The limits of the political independence of regulators remain uncertain not only at the national but also at the EU level. This is even more worrying since the credibility and the coherence of European regulatory law depends crucially on the perception that the Commission is able and willing to enforce the common rules in an objective and even-handed way. In spite of the independence proclaimed by Art. 213(2) of the Consolidated Treaties—'The Members of the Commission shall, in the general interest of the Community, be completely independent in the performance of their duties'—the Commissioners are not immune from political influences from the Member States and from within the Commission itself. The Commission is a collegial body and the need to achieve a majority within the *collegium* has on several occasions produced flawed and politically motivated decisions.

An even more serious threat to the credibility of European regulatory policies is the progressive parliamentarization of the Commission. As already noted, the growing influence of the European Parliament is not only unavoidable in view of the expanding competences of the Union, but also positive for the overall legitimacy of the integration process. From the point of view of regulatory policy-making, however, the new powers of the EP raise issues of commitment and consistency that are very similar to those already discussed in the national context.

This chapter has argued that the dual problem of independence and accountability should be tackled simultaneously at national and European levels. The future of regulation in Europe depends crucially on the ability to find coordinated, rather than vertically distinct, solutions. The emergence of transnational regulatory networks is an important step in this direction, and may prefigure the shape of transatlantic regulatory cooperation in the coming years.

References

Ackerman, Bruce A. and William T. Hassler (1981). *Clean Coal/Dirty Air*. New Haven: Yale University Press.

Dehousse, Renaud (1997). 'Regulation by Networks in the European Community: The Role of European Agencies'. *Journal of European Public Policy*, 4/2: 246–61.

European Commission (1999). *White Paper on Modernization of the Rules Implementing Articles 85 and 86 of the EC Treaty*. Brussels: Commission Programme No. 99/027.

Fainsod, Merle (1940). 'Some Reflections on the Nature of the Regulatory Process', in K. Friedrich and J. Mason (eds), *Public Policy*. Cambridge, MA: Harvard University Press.

Freedman, James O. (1978). *Crisis and Legitimacy*. Cambridge: Cambridge University Press.

Hartley, T. C. (1988). *The Foundations of European Community Law* (2nd edn). Oxford: Clarendon Press.

Horwitz, Morton J. (1992). *The Transformation of American Law, 1870–1960*. New York: Oxford University Press.

Landis, James L. (1966 [1938]). *The Administrative Process*. New Haven: Yale University Press.

Luhmann, Niklas (1975). *Legitimation durch Verfahren*. Neuwied, Germany: Luchterhand.

Majone, Giandomenico (1989). *Evidence, Argument and Persuasion in the Policy Process*. New Haven: Yale University Press.

——(1996). *Regulating Europe*. London: Routledge.

——(1997). 'The New European Agencies: Regulation by Information'. *Journal of European Public Policy*, 4/2: 262–75.

——(1998). 'Europe's "Democratic Deficit": The Question of Standards'. *European Law Journal*, 4/1: 5–28.

Moravcsik, Andrew (1998). *The Choice for Europe*. Ithaca, NY: Cornell University Press.

Mott, Richard N. (1990). *Federal-State Relations in US Environmental Law: Implications for the European Community*. Florence: EUI (Working Paper EPU No. 90/2).

Pescatore, Pierre (1982). 'Foreword', in T. Sandalow and E. Stein (eds), *Courts and Free Markets*. Oxford: Clarendon Press.

Shapiro, Martin (1988), *Who Guards the Guardians?* Athens, GA: University of Georgia Press.

——(1992). 'The Giving-Reasons Requirement'. Chicago: *The University of Chicago Legal Forum*, 180–220.

Stewart, Richard B. (1975), 'The Reformation of American Administrative Law'. *Harvard Law Review*, 88: 1667–813.

Thomas, Robert (1997). 'Reason-giving in English and European Community Administrative Law'. *European Public Law*, 3/2: 213–22.

US Office of Management and Budget (1990). *Regulatory Program of the United States Government, April 1, 1990–March 31, 1991*. Washington, DC: US Government Printing Office.

Vos, Ellen (1997). 'The Rise of Committees'. *European Law Journal*, 3/3: 210–29.

Weatherill, Stephen (1995). *Law and Integration in the European Union*. Oxford: Clarendon Press.

Winter, Gerd (1996). 'Reforming the Sources and Categories of European Union Law: A Summary', in G. Winter (ed.), *Sources and Categories of European Union Law*. Baden-Baden: Nomos.

IV

Federalism, Legitimacy, and Governance: Models for Understanding

10

Securing Subsidiarity: The Institutional Design of Federalism in the United States and Europe

CARY COGLIANESE AND KALYPSO NICOLAIDIS

The way governmental authority is allocated between centralized and decentralized institutions can affect the performance and legitimacy of a governing regime. Concern for the proper allocation of governmental authority has a long history in the United States, but has recently emerged with renewed vigour in the wake of a changed political climate and recent decisions of the US Supreme Court. In Europe, the trend has been towards centralization at the EU but the European legal and policy community has focused much attention of late on the subsidiarity provision of the Maastricht Treaty. Elsewhere around the globe—in recently divided or unified nations, in older federal polities, and in international trade institutions—policy actors are giving increasing attention to whether policy authority should be centralized or decentralized.

Current debates over federalism, devolution, and subsidiarity almost always centre on whether centralization is 'better than' decentralization.[1] Economic theories of federalism, particularly in the context of the United States, traditionally have sought to determine the 'optimal' distribution of public economic functions between different levels of government and the appropriateness of their possible transfer.[2] Debate over the federal-State

[1] Susan A. MacManus, 'Federalism and Intergovernmental Relations', in William Crotty (ed.), *Political Science: Looking to the Future*, iv. (Evanston, Ill.: Northwestern University Press, 1991), 204.

[2] These theories, which seek to provide a functional rationale for the division of federal versus State power to intervene in the economy, are usually constructed as *decentralization* issues for mature federations. As presented, for instance, by Oates, 'the determination of the appropriate degree of decentralization for a particular government sector . . . requires matching public functions with their appropriate levels of application'. Wallace Oates, 'An Economic Approach to Federalism', in Wallace E. Oates, *Fiscal Federalism* (New York: Harcourt Javanovich, 1972), 3. For recent work debating decentralization, see Richard L. Revesz, 'Rehabilitating Interstate Competition: Rethinking the "Race-to-the-Bottom" Rationale for Federal Environmental Regulation', *New York University Law Review* 67: 1210–54 (1992); Daniel C. Esty, 'Revitalizing Environmental Federalism', *Michigan Law Review* 95: 570–653 (1996); Richard L. Revesz, 'The Race to the Bottom and Federal

division of policy authority in the US tends to focus on whether States or the federal government are better suited to governing on matters ranging from social welfare to environmental protection to drug usage. Similar questions arise in the European context over the subsidiarity provision of the Maastricht Treaty, which expressly calls for a consideration of the level at which policy decisions can be 'better achieved'.[3] While the precise terms of debate in the US, Europe, and, more recently, international trade community may vary to some extent, the core issue remains the same: what is the optimal way to allocate authority between upper- and lower-level institutions?[4]

In principle, both centralization and decentralization have certain advantages.[5] Decentralization can allow government to respond more effectively to variations in local needs and preferences; reduce costs of planning and administration; provide opportunities and incentives for policy innovation; and give citizens greater choice and voice in policy-making. Centralization, on the other hand, can permit government to address problems having cross-border—or spillover—effects; protect consumers against product risks; exploit any available economies of scale; coordinate policies more effectively; and promote equality and political homogeneity across a larger domain to reflect 'shared values'. Centralization may also secure a level playing field for fair trade, as States seek to limit 'regulatory

Environmental Regulation: A Response to Critics', *Minnesota Law Review* 82: 535–64 (1997); John D. Donahue, *Disunited States* (New York: Basic Books, 1997).

[3] Treaty on the European Union, Art. 3b, reads in full: 'In areas which are not under its exclusive power, the Community shall act in conformity with the principle of subsidiarity, only if and in so far as the objectives of the proposed action cannot be sufficiently achieved by the member states and can therefore, by reason of the scale and efforts of the proposed action be better achieved by the Community.' A similar test of where policy can be best attained is found in the Single European Act's provision with respect to environmental policy: 'The Community shall take action relating to the environment to the extent to which the objectives referred to in paragraph 1 can be attained better at the Community level than at the level of individual member states' (Art. 130R).

[4] The terms 'devolution', 'decentralization', 'delegation', 'federalism', and 'subsidiarity' share a common concern with the proper allocation of authority in what we call 'tiered regimes'. We use 'tiered regimes' deliberately to include both *nations* organized along federal lines, such as the US or Germany, and *inter- or supra-national institutions* comprised of nation-states as members, such as the European Union. Because we mean to encompass both kinds of tiered regimes, we use the terms 'lower-level' and 'upper-level' governments as the generic terms for units in either kind of regime. In using these terms, we do not intend to imply any normative superiority for the 'upper level' or inferiority for the 'lower level'. We also recognize that governance can be organized or understood spatially and functionally as well as hierarchically. Indeed, our claim would be that the issues we address in connection with tiered regimes also arise in allocating authority along other dimensions.

[5] For a summary of the advantages of decentralization and centralization, on which this paragraph draws, see Reiner Eichenberger, 'The Benefits of Federalism and the Risk of Overcentralization', *Kyklos* 47: 403–20 (1994).

competition'.[6] It should be apparent, however, that the theoretical advantages of centralization and decentralization appear to counterbalance each other, suggesting that the precise nature of an optimal allocation of authority may prove to be highly context-dependent. It may also suggest that optimality would be better conceived in a dynamic sense, allowing for changes in governing allocations over time.

Such changes in allocations do occur. In order to exploit the advantages of centralization, decentralized units of what we call a 'tiered regime'[7] may delegate authority to a centralized unit. Similarly, the centralized unit in such a regime may at some point devolve authority back to the member states when decentralization seems advantageous. In either case, the governmental level that possesses authority in a particular policy domain may seek to shift that authority to a different level. An allocational shift may arise for several reasons. The original allocation could have been mistaken, with the advantages anticipated from that allocation never materializing or with other unintended consequences arising. In addition, circumstances may change in such a way as to justify a change in the allocation. For example, as long as air pollution remains a limited and localized problem, decentralized policy units may be able to address it adequately. As pollution increases and spills over into other states, the issue may become more appropriate for attention by centralized institutions.[8] Changes in technologies, governmental capacities, information, and ideology may all prompt changes in authoritative allocations.

In what manner are allocational shifts carried out? How can these shifts be designed in such a way to ensure that the transfer of authority from one unit to another will be used in the way it was intended? Can units of governance retain some degree of control or oversight of those units to which they delegate authority? These are the central questions motivating

[6] Of course, as David Vogel has noted, it is certainly possible for regulatory convergence to occur even in the absence of centralization. David Vogel, *Trading Up: Consumer and Environmental Regulation in a Global Economy* (Cambridge, MA: Harvard University Press, 1995).

[7] Our use of the word 'regime' may seem a bit unconventional in the federalism context, but it is intended to include federal and quasi-federal systems, as well as international institutions such as the EU and WTO. In hoping to convey certain analytic similarities between the different kinds of governance structures, we do not mean to deny that important differences exist in these structures.

[8] Sometimes actual changes in the conditions of the world do not drive allocational shifts, but rather changed *knowledge* about prevailing circumstances does. The case of transboundary sulfur dioxide pollution appears to be one such case. See William C. Clark, Jill Jäger, Josee van Eijndhoven, and Nancy M. Dickson (Social Learning Group) (eds)., *Learning to Manage Global Environmental Risks: A Comparative History of Social Responses to Climate Change, Ozone Depletion and Acid Rain* (Cambridge: MIT Press, forthcoming 2001).

this chapter. Instead of asking whether centralization is 'better than' decentralization, we consider how changes in governing allocations can be structured to enhance their overall legitimacy. We seek to identify specific mechanisms that may help ensure the legitimacy of shifts from decentralization to centralization, or vice versa. We argue that shifts in governing allocations can be viewed basically as delegations of policy-making authority from one governing level to another, and thus our ideas about the legitimacy of such allocations draw on the insights of principal-agent theory. We argue that shifts in governing allocations will be accompanied by mechanisms which seek to ensure that any transferred authority is used for appropriate and intended purposes. After exploring the implications of principal-agent theory for issues of intergovernmental structures, we examine two different tiered regimes—the United States and the European Union—for evidence of the mechanisms suggested by our theoretical analysis. We argue that these tiered regimes feature several characteristic mechanisms which may help sustain the legitimacy of allocations of authority between different levels. Policy debate surrounding federalism should include attention to these mechanisms along with the discussion of the appropriateness of centralization or decentralization.[9]

1. Allocation and Legitimacy from a Principal-Agent Perspective

A decision to shift the allocation of governing authority from one level to another is similar to any decision to make a delegation of authority. As with any delegation, there is a risk that the entity receiving the delegated authority will take it and use it for its own purposes, to the neglect or even harm of the entity that gave it the authority in the first place. Scholars have long noted that when one individual relies on the action of another, an agency relationship arises with common characteristics across issue areas. The individual taking the action, under delegated authority, is called the

[9] In Europe, the principle of subsidiarity takes on at least two dimensions. The first involves the level at which authority should be vested for specific policy areas, and it mirrors the long-standing debate over centralization and decentralization. The second dimension arises once a decision is made to delegate authority to the centre. This second dimension raises the question of how intrusive policy-making by the centre should be, and is often referred to as the principle of proportionality or intensity of action. Commission of the European Communities, 'The principle of subsidiarity. Communication of the Commission to the Council and the European Parliament', Services of the European Commission (92), Brussels, 27 October 1992. Our approach encompasses these two dimensions, but also seeks to address a much broader question of how member states can retain some of their control over a policy area even after making a delegation to the centre.

agent while the one affected by these actions is called the principal.[10] To protect his interests, the principal finds it necessary to define, monitor, and reward the actions of his agent. The challenge in the principal-agent relationship arises from two sources: (1) differences in interests between agents and principals which lead them to prefer different goals and strategies; and (2) information asymmetries which come from the fact that 'agents typically know more about their task than their principals do, though principals may know more about what they want accomplished'.[11] As a result, the agent may be able to perform tasks in ways which do not conform to the goals of the principal while the latter might not easily be able to do much about it.

While the principal-agent problem originally emerged as a way of understanding economic actors and organizations, it shares much in common with the problem of centralization and decentralization in governing authority. As William Riker noted, centralized governments tend to keep acquiring more power, creating 'the tendency, as time passes, for the rulers of the federation to overawe the "rules" of the constituent governments'.[12] A similar tendency can occur in what Riker termed 'peripheralized federalisms', where rulers of the lower-level governments tend to acquire more power and overawe the central government. These tendencies in tiered governance regimes are similar to the tendencies in non-governmental principal-agent relationships. Yet in the context of governing, the principals—and by this we mean simply those governing units transferring authority to other units—are themselves only agents of a larger public. In the absence of resounding democratic support to abandon completely all control over a policy issue, such as at the level of 'high politics',[13] shifts of governing authority need to address the principal-agent problems inherent in any delegation of authority to another level.

What, then, are the prescriptive implications of principal-agent theory? While agency can be viewed as a *problem* of minimizing agency costs, it can also be viewed as a *solution*, or 'a neat kind of social plumbing', to address the need for specialization, decentralization, and delegation.[14] Whether viewed as a problem or a solution, the principal-agent lens helps identify mechanisms to regulate the relationship between the two types of

[10] For the seminal overview, see John Pratt and Richard Zeckhauser, 'Principals and Agents: An Overview', in John Pratt and Richard Zeckhauser (eds), *Principals and Agents: The Structure of Business* (Boston: Harvard Business School Press, 1985).

[11] Ibid., 3.

[12] William H. Riker, *Federalism: Origin, Operation, Significance* (Boston: Little, Brown, 1964), p. 7.

[13] Bruce Ackerman, *We the People* (Cambridge: Harvard University Press, 1991).

[14] See Harrison C. White, 'Agency as Control', in Pratt and Zeckhauser, *Principals and Agents*, 188.

actors. In order to minimize agency loss, principals typically resort to a mix of inducement and enforcement methods, creating both systems of control, or monitoring, and systems of incentives. Systems of control allow the principal to devise ways to obtain information on the agent's actions in addition to the observed outcome, as well as to shape the agent's actions through the types of mandates the agent is given. Incentives are meant to do away with the need to gather full information and constrain the agent by aligning the agent's interests better with those of the principal. These mechanisms can be described most generically as different types of 'agency ties', which form the ongoing web of connection between principals and their agents.[15] More broadly and ultimately, as one author argues, 'agency is more than a tie: it is a context for ties that cast shadow over commitment'.[16] Principals and agents are in a symbiotic relationship where the action of the agent commits the principal in ways that are supposed to have been shaped by that principal in the first place.

One of the core problems that the principal must face in engineering these relationships is that of the reversal of control where he comes under the control of the agent after the latter becomes what is termed a specialized purveyor.[17] Among the challenges associated with the design of agency relationships is the avoidance of such reversal. The theoretical potential for reversal means that for some purposes it may be analytically more appropriate to treat an actor who originally or formally was designated the agent as in fact the principal.

How can the principal-agent conceptual framework be applied to the relationship between different levels of governance? And what are the specific insights that can be drawn from this framework regarding the mechanisms governing allocational control in tiered regimes? If we are to apply the principal-agent framework to explore the design of relationships between different jurisdictional levels, we first need to conceptualize the principal and agent in this context. In so doing, we readily acknowledge that the terms 'principal' and 'agent' will be construed by some as having normative overtones and that even when understood as positive, analytical concepts—as we mean them here—they greatly simplify the relationships between different levels of spheres of governance. We certainly do not mean to suggest that one level is *the* principal and another is *the* agent for all purposes, for the reality is that jurisdictional relationships are often complicated and interdependent and vary across policy fields and over time. We recognize that governmental levels are not unitary actors, but

[15] The spectrum of agency ties has been thoroughly explored in the business context, from the analysis of merchant networks to the running of large corporations. See Harrison C. White, 'Agency as Control', 187–209.

[16] Ibid., 189.

[17] Ibid., 205.

rather that they consist themselves of conflicts, coalitions, and multi-level games. However, we plead the need of modellers everywhere to make simplifying assumptions for the larger cause of analytical clarity, which we believe the insights from principal-agent theory can bring to our understanding of federalism.

We start from the premise that the principal is the governmental level which holds political legitimacy and has been entrusted with the authority to act in a given sphere. This we term the 'endowed level' of government, which then may transfer authority to the 'delegated level' in making a shift in the allocation of authority. To identify the initial endowment of authority, it is often helpful to refer to the relevant legal delineation of powers or attribution of competence. Constitutions, whether written or unwritten, can be viewed as sources for identifying the endowment of authority, though they may also represent contracts that shift the endowment from one level to another. In the US, for example, the federal constitution represents an effort to shift some authority originally held by the States to the national government. Many State constitutions in the US shift authority in the opposite direction, explicitly delegating authority originally endowed in the States to city or county governments acting as agents of the State. That the functions of principals can be split between levels is a core characteristic of federal systems, as reflected in Wheare's widely accepted definition:

> [In a federal system] powers are divided between a general level of government which in certain matters . . . is independent of the governments of the associated states, and, on the other hand, state governments which in certain matters are, in their turn, independent of the general government. This involves, as a necessary consequence, that general and regional governments both operate directly on the people; each citizen is subject to two governments.[18]

As a result, in cases where the upper level government acts in a given area, we need to specify whether, for the purpose of analysis, (1) authority has become reversed and the upper level is now de facto acting as a principal, even though powers were originally delegated to it as an agent; or (2) the upper level is still acting as an agent on the basis of authority delegated to it by lower-level units which continue to hold jurisdiction and define the upper level's mandate. Similarly, when we see States acting in an area, we need to ask whether they act because they have exclusive competence as principals or because they have been mandated to act by the higher level.

Up to now, we have spoken of agency ties in general to describe the relationships between the principals and their agents. More specifically, a

[18] K .C. Wheare, *Federal Government*, 4th edn (New York: Oxford University Press, 1964), 2.

number of insights can be drawn from the principal-agent framework to analyze the actual mechanisms governing allocational control in the context of tiered governance regimes. First, agency studies highlight the importance of strategic control, that is, control connected with the formulation of the agent's task and overall objectives. The specificity of this formulation constitutes the initial constraint on the agent's margin of manoeuvre. A sales agent can be asked to act 'in the best interest' of its firm, or it can be told to maximize the number of widgets sold in a given day. Similarly, as we will discuss below, the scope of an agent's delegated authority in inter-governmental contexts can be more or less specifically delineated by prevailing norms and specific legal acts.

Second, agency theories examine mechanisms of operational control, that is, control connected to the ongoing implementation of the task delegated to the agent. These consist above all in monitoring techniques. Such techniques range from obligations of reporting regularly to the principals to the standardization of task descriptions and assessments according to specified categories. There may be a trade-off between such monitoring mechanisms and the first strategic aspect of control, in that the principal can afford to be flexible at the broad strategic level if he can devise reliable modes of monitoring his agent's action. Similarly, in tiered systems of governance, principals may more readily delegate tasks to agents if they can subsequently monitor the implementation of the commonly agreed objectives by the latter.

There is a third, more radical, way for the principal to control the actions of the agent, namely, by reducing its autonomy to the point where the principal shares in the activities of the agent. Thus, a joint venture with former suppliers strengthens agency ties by allowing the principal to become a party to the agent's operations. Conversely, we can also ask whether the agent has a say in shaping the mandate given to it. In other words, does the agent sit in the boardroom? In all cases, the question is the degree to which the principal and the agent actually share their respective functions or participate in each other's deliberation and actions. This issue of power sharing is obviously crucial in governance contexts, where the degree of States' participation in federal structures reflects their level of influence or subordination. This is true whether we are concerned with the level of States' control in their capacity as principals or as agents.

A final insight we extract from the agency framework is the question of the mechanisms by which the agency ties can be suspended or severed at any future time. Students of agency focus on the duration of the agency relationship and the degree of entanglement implied. They also ask about the extent to which the actions or pronouncements of the agent commit the principal—does he act 'in the name' or 'in the person' of the principal?—and therefore the extent to which the principal can dissociate himself if he chooses to from his agent. As we will argue, the possibility of reversibility is the ultimate if blunt measure of control in inter-state arrangements.

Taking account of these various mechanisms, agency relationships in the business world can be arrayed along a spectrum from employee relationships—the strongest ties—to contracting out—the least strong. Similarly, we will now analyze how relationships between different levels of governance can be arrayed along a spectrum defining the strength of agency ties between these levels according to the attributes of principal-agent relationships as outlined above.

2. Mechanisms for Securing Allocational Legitimacy

In making allocational shifts, one level of government gives up authority to another level. Agency ties seek to provide some assurance to the principal that the authority it transfers to its agent will not be used contrary to the purposes of the delegation. The strength of the agency ties in this sense defines the power of both the principal and the agent. The structural mechanisms that make up agency ties theoretically constrain the agent at the same time as they reserve some power to the principal. In the context of tiered governance regimes, this means that attention to these mechanisms is necessary in order to analyze fully the allocation of authority between centralized and decentralized institutions.

We now turn to considering the specific agency ties that characterize agency-like relationships in tiered governance regimes. We show how the four characteristic mechanisms thought to resolve principal-agent problems also find their way into the established US federal system and in the EU's emerging federation. We cannot obviously cover in a single chapter all or even most aspects of policy-making in tiered governance regimes.[19] Rather, we concentrate on some of the salient aspects of the US and EU allocational debates which illuminate the conceptual categories that we introduce.

[19] The issue of optimal assignment obviously applies to the whole array of economic policy-making functions that, according to Musgrave, can be categorized under a triptych encompassing allocation, stabilization, and distribution functions. R. Musgrave and P. Musgrave, *Public Finance, Theory and Practice*, 3rd edn (New York: McGraw-Hill, 1980). Musgrave's functional classification is widely used in the EC context. See, for instance, the Padoa Schopa Report, *Commission of the European Communities* (Luxembourg, 1987). Note that we use the term 'allocation' differently from Musgrave to refer to the assignment of policy authority to different levels of government.

Delineation

Delineation mechanisms provide for the determination of standards or guidelines that mark the scope of activity, functions, task, or jurisdiction of the agent. These standards can be either jurisdictional or substantive; they can be more or less specific and more or less binding; they can circumscribe the domain of the agent through criteria for balancing different principles—for example, trade versus regulatory objectives—or through policy area—for example, trade policy, defence, food standards. They can also delineate the functional powers to be exercised by the agent, such as standard-setting authority versus enforcement.[20] While the respective powers of different levels are usually delineated in constitutions or treaties, residual powers—not explicitly enumerated—may rest with (1) the constituent units, as in the US, under amendment 9; (2) the federal level, as in Canada, under section 91; or (3) the constituent units but with open-ended criteria for centralization, as in the EU, under Art. 235 of the Treaty of Rome. Such provisions are obviously subject to great margin of interpretation. A main rationale behind the current call for a European constitution has been to render such delineation more transparent in the eyes of European citizens.

One of the core powers traditionally delegated from the lower level to upper level has been that of regulating inter-State trade by policing the ways in which individual States at the lower level apply their own regulations to incoming goods, services, and firms.[21] If power to regulate products and firms remains at the lower level, the question that arises in this realm is what the guidelines are for delineating the powers transferred to the upper level in order to ensure that such regulation is compatible with freedom of movement between regulatory jurisdictions. This issue has engendered much debate in the context of the application of the dormant

[20] One of the recent trends in the EU is to retain centrally defined standards but interpret subsidiarity as a mandate to decentralize their enforcement. For instance, in the autumn of 1996, the Commission proposed to increase its powers to vet mergers under the shared Community jurisdiction over competition law, while at the same time decentralizing enforcement of EU law to national authorities in the areas of price fixing and market-sharing cartels. The outcome in this instance will result from a bargain between the Commission and the national competition authorities, where concerns over resources, or lack thereof, will play as much a role as that over authority. Similarly, under the so-called 'global approach' of 1990, the EU took one step further to decentralize enforcement in the area of product conformity assessment, not only to the national level but also by delegating some enforcement functions to private bodies. There is thus a complex division of labour between the EU Commission supervising standard setting, the private organizations that ultimately enforce European standards, and the Member States who retain the power to accredit the latter.

[21] See US Constitution, Art. 1, section 8, clause 3 (the 'commerce clause'); EU Treaty of Rome, Arts 30 and 59; GATT Articles.

commerce clause by the US Supreme Court[22] and the completion of a single market in Europe. The guiding principle for delineation, most often enforced by courts at the upper level, has frequently been that of proportionality, or roughly balancing the burdens of intervention against the benefits.[23]

The lower levels can also decide that laws and regulations themselves need to be centralized, that is, designed and enforced at the upper level. In these cases, the scope of power of the upper level can still be limited by the extent to which it is allowed to constrain the lower level. These two can be combined through a mix of horizontal and vertical delegation. One of the more intriguing examples of such combination in the EU context has been the adoption of what one of us has called 'managed mutual recognition' as the core principle for completing the single market.[24] This has meant that the upper level of governance, through the Council of Ministers along the lines suggested by the European Court of Justice, has mandated and organized the delegation of authority by the lower level, but done so horizontally—that is, from one Member State to another—through so-called home country control, home country certification, or home country licensing.[25] This is not simply an injunction to waive host country regulation as the judicial application of proportionality suggests, since the careful delineation of jurisdictional authority between the home and host State has most often been accompanied by provisions for regulatory cooperation between them in order to monitor each other's regulations and has often required a minimum of centralized setting of standards.

Another way in which the EU has sought to apply the principle of subsidiarity in its approach to delineation has been through the increased resort to 'government by objectives' rather than laws, and, to the extent that laws are adopted, resort to generic standards rather than specific rules at the upper level.[26] For instance, framework directives are adopted as a

22 See, for example, *Pike v. Bruce Church, Inc.*, 397 U.S. 137 (1970); *Hunt v. Washington State Apple Advertising Commission*, 432 U.S. 333 (1977); *Raymond Motor Transportation, Inc. v. Rice*, 434 U.S. 429 (1978); *New Energy Co. of Indiana v. Limbach*, 486 U.S. 269 (1988); C *& A Carbone, Inc. v. Town of Clarkstown, N.Y.*, 511 U.S. 383 (1994).

23 The US Supreme Court's balancing test was most notably articulated in the Pike case, in which the Court held invalid nondiscriminatory burdens on interstate commerce that were 'clearly excessive in relation to the putative local benefits.' 397 U.S. at 142.

24 On vertical and horizontal delegation see Kalypso Nicolaidis 'Regulatory Cooperation and Managed Mutual Recognition: Developing a Strategic Model', in George Bermann *et al.* (eds), *Transatlantic Regulatory Cooperation* (Oxford: Oxford University Press, 2000).

25 For a discussion see Kalypso Nicolaïdis, 'Mutual Recognition of Regulatory Regimes: Some Lessons and Prospects', in *Regulatory Reform and International Market Openness* (Paris: OECD Publications, 1996).

26 For a discussion of rules vs standards at the international level see for instance Kalypso Nicolaidis and Joel P. Trachtman, 'From Policed Regulation to Managed

basis for voluntary agreements in the environmental field and political declarations set common objectives in the field of labour market reforms enforceable through transparent reporting.[27] More generally, in the hierarchy of norms that characterize the EU legal systems, the least constraining norms—white papers, recommendations—are increasingly preferred to the most constraining ones—regulations and directives.

As already noted, in some instances the upper level of government in a federal system may be viewed as endowed with authority, at least for analytic purposes, either de facto through a reversal or by exercising its delegated powers legitimately.[28] When the upper level returns authority back to the States, it makes controlled or delineated delegations as well. For example, for many years the federal welfare law in the US allowed States to depart from national standards in order to experiment with new approaches by conducting demonstration projects. In order to undertake a demonstration project, however, the States needed to submit detailed plans to the US Department of Health and Human Services (HHS). These plans were reviewed by HHS under a set of substantive guidelines designed to ensure that the demonstration projects shared the national aims of helping the poor and had appropriate evaluation methods in place in order to assess their success. Guidelines like these—and they are found in US environmental law as well[29]—serve to delineate the power being shifted from one level to another.

The use of governing authority by the delegated level can be subject to review either by a different branch of the delegated level or by some branch of the endowed level, based on the pre-determined delineation. So, for example, in the US the general constitutional structure historically began with States as the endowed level delegating power to the national level through explicit grants of authority in Art. 1 of the US constitu-

Recognition: Mapping the Boundary in GATS', in Pierre Sauvé and Robert M. Stern (eds), *GATS 2000: New Directions in Services Trade Liberalization* (Washington, DC: Brookings Institution Press, 2000), 241–82.

[27] See, for instance, the review of the fifth environmental programme. See also discussion in the Commission's Simpler Legislation for the Internal Market (SLIM) initiative of 1995 to help simplify community directives, especially in the areas of construction and recognition of diplomas.

[28] Indeed, one of the only other works we know of which analyses US federalism in principal-agent terms explicitly and only treats the federal government as the principal *vis-à-vis* the States. See John Chubb, 'The Political Economy of Federalism', *American Political Science Review* 79: 994 (1985). The US Supreme Court has recognized that 'the sovereignty of the States is limited by the Constitution'. *Garcia v. San Antonio Metropolitan Transit Authority*, 469 U.S. 528 (1985). But cf. *New York v. U.S.*, 112 S. Ct. 2408 (1992) and *U.S. v. Lopez*, 115 S.Ct. 1624 (1995).

[29] See, for example, the Clean Air Act's provisions for state implementation plans. 42 U.S.C. § 7407, 7410.

tion—inter-State commerce, 'tax and spend', and so forth. These jurisdictional limits are enforced in large part through review by the federal Supreme Court.

One critical issue is that of the balance between the judicial and the political branches in assessing and mandating delineation. In the case of the EU, where there was great uncertainty about the extent to which the Treaty of Rome actually constrains States' domestic policies, the role of the ECJ shifted over time, in part as a function of the overall political context.[30] The ECJ has been engaged in determining both the latitude of the lower levels to determine what criteria can justify their independent action and the extent to which it itself as the upper level court can scrutinize these justifications. Its jurisprudence has progressively shifted in this regard, from the bold *Cassis de Dijon* jurisprudence in the early 1980s to the more cautious *Keck* and *Mithouard* jurisprudence after 1993.[31] To some extent, the Court has reflected the prevailing political mood on appropriate distribution of jurisdiction as reflected by debates at the intergovernmental level. Whether the ECJ should leave further fine tuning of the principle of subsidiarity to the political realm itself is a question open to debate, one which raises issues of power sharing discussed in some detail below.

Monitoring

While one level may decide to delegate authority to another, it may also retain some control by monitoring the other level's activities. Since a principal is unable by definition to monitor its agent completely, it may use proxies for such monitoring or require that the agent itself report in predetermined ways. It may, to borrow from McCubbins and Schwartz, decide to engage in 'police patrols' or 'fire alarms' depending on the burdens and effectiveness of the different methods of monitoring.[32]

[30] For alternative analysis of the role of the ECJ in European integration see Joseph Weiler (1981) 'The Transformation of Europe', *Yale Law Journal*, 100/8: 2403–83; Anne Marie Burley and Walter Mattli (1993) 'Europe Before the Courts: A Political Theory of Legal Integration', *International Organization*, 47/1: 47–76; Karen Alter (1998), 'Who are the "Masters of the Treaty?": European Governments and the European Court of Justice', *International Organization*, 52/1: 121–47.

[31] Case 120/78, *Cassis de Dijon, Rewe-Zentral AG v. Bundesmonopolverwaltung fur Branntwein*, 1979 E.C.R. 649, [1979] 3 C.M.L.R. 494 (1979); Joined Cases C-267 & C-268/91, *Keck and Mithouard*, 1993 E.C.R. I-6097, I-6131, [1995] 1 C.M.L.R. 101, 124 (1995).

[32] McCubbins and Schwartz articulate the distinction between 'police patrols' and 'fire alarms' in their analysis of congressional oversight of administrative agencies. Police patrols refer to proactive, ongoing, and direct efforts to oversee a delegated authority. Fire alarms refer to reactive responses to complaints presented by third parties, such as interest groups. Fire alarms allow a principal to externalize some monitoring costs, but at the risk

Much monitoring occurs through democratic political processes. Open debate, 'government-in-sunshine' laws, and freedom of information laws all serve a larger purpose of making government accessible to the public—the ultimate principal in a democratic system—but these practices and laws also have the effect of facilitating monitoring of the delegated level of government by the endowed level. State governments have organized collectively in the US to create institutions designed, among other things, to monitor and influence the activities of the federal government as they affect the States. The Council of State Governments, National Conference of State Legislatures, and National Governors' Association have been instrumental, for example, in documenting the extent to which State governments have been burdened with complying with federal laws and regulations.

These State organizations were instrumental in securing congressional passage of the federal Unfunded Mandate Reform Act of 1995,[33] an act designed to increase the amount of information about proposed federal legislation or agency regulations that would mandate compliance by State and local governments without accompanying appropriations to fund that compliance. Over the years, the federal government has adopted extensive environmental, civil rights, and labour regulations that apply to both State governments and the private sector. Although the private sector has borne most of the overall financial impact of such laws, it has become burdensome for State governments, especially in times of shrinking tax bases, to comply with federal standards. The Unfunded Mandate Reform Act requires the Congressional Budget Office to estimate the costs of proposed national legislation that would place costly burdens on State, local, or tribal governments and requires Congress to take a special vote before adopting such unfunded mandates.[34] The act serves to place some constraint on the federal government's use of delegated authority by infusing the legislative and regulatory process with information about the impacts of proposed mandates.

In the EU context, Member States have devised a host of procedures to monitor their supranational agent starting with the use of some supranational institutions—such as the Parliament and the Court—to monitor others—like the Commission. To a great extent, the complex system of committees where Commission and State representatives sit together serves as a system for mutual monitoring—although its primary function

of truncating (and biasing) the issues that get monitored. See for example Matthew McCubbins and Thomas Schwartz, 'Congressional Oversight Overlooked: Police Patrols Versus Fire Alarms', in Matthew McCubbins and Terry Sullivan (eds), *Congress: Structure and Policy* (New York: Cambridge University Press, 1987), 426–40.

[33] Pub. L. 104-4, 109 Stat. 63 (Mar. 22, 1995).

[34] Ibid.

is one of power sharing, as discussed below. The greater decentralization of the implementation of EU directives has also been accompanied by a greater emphasis on inspection by the EU Commission, such as monitoring by the federal level of functions it has delegated. Some monitoring has occurred in environment and social policy—inspection of factories, for example—although some observers argue it is still inadequate. In 1996, a group of experts recommended the establishment of audits of national enforcement procedures in order to increase mutual confidence between enforcement agencies, as well as to promote the exchange of information about enforcement procedures and problems.[35]

Monitoring is also relevant between States themselves whether or not it is facilitated by federal-level authorities. Thus, the application of mutual recognition in the EU has been accompanied by rather stringent provisions for mutual monitoring. By doing so, individual States are supposed to constrain their delegation of regulatory authority and ensure it is based on regulations in the home country equivalent to those in the host country. This may require more resources than currently assumed, as the health and safety inspectorates of importing countries often have difficulties determining the validity of proofs of conformity with home country regulations. Information networks need to be set up between regulators as well as conformity assessment bodies, and are still at an embryonic stage. In the same context, monitoring is also key to ensuring that host States do not abuse their residual regulatory prerogatives. A mutual information procedure first set up in the EU in 1983, Dir 83/189, has recently been strengthened to offer Member States and the Commission the opportunity to review any new national law and regulation for its potential trade-impeding effect in order to preempt a later need for centralized regulation. Member States of the EU are also required to provide notice of all products from which they withhold the benefits of mutual recognition to allow for a collective assessment as to whether the measure is 'objectively' supported. Thus, experience in the implementation of the single market has shown that monitoring through central notification is a necessary corollary to the decentralized determination of equivalence between national standards.

Sharing

Sharing mechanisms involve representation or involvement by both levels of government in each other's affairs. They designate the extent to which

[35] See for example Economic Advisory Group, 'The Impact and Effectiveness of the Single Market, 30 October 1996', Communication from the Commission to the European Parliament and Council, European Commission, DGIII; and accompanying background information in The 1996 Single Market Review, 15 November 1996.

the endowed units participate in the delegated level's decisions that will in turn affect them. This is different from allocations where the endowed level monitors, reviews, or approves the decisions of the delegated level according to some delineated standard. In certain areas there is no jurisdictional or substantive standard by which review should be made. Indeed, it is not delineation of power or review per se at all, but rather the design of structures at the delegated level that ensures that the endowed level retains some control over its actions. In addition to the issue of representation, sharing mechanisms include decision-making rules—majority versus unanimity—as well as the division of authority between the legislative and the judicial branches in determining the standards for delineation of authority and the ways in which they should be interpreted and applied.

In the US context, the federal legislative representatives are drawn from the States; presidential elections are based on the outcomes of State races; and States can prompt changes to the federal constitution. Under the basic allocational contract—the US constitution—the representational ties to the States were more direct than they are today. Prior to the Seventeenth Amendment in 1913, senators were chosen by State legislatures instead of the voters of the States. As the US Supreme Court has reasoned, 'the principal means chosen by the Framers to ensure the role of the States in the federal system lies in the structure of the Federal Government itself. It is no novelty to observe that the composition of the Federal Government was designed in large part to protect the States from overreaching by Congress. The Framers thus gave the States a role in the selection both of the Executive and the Legislative Branches of the Federal Government'.[36]

The participation of individual States in upper-level decision making is obviously much more pronounced in the EU context. The EU, with its two-headed executive—the Council of Ministers and the Commission—and its two-headed legislative branch—the Council and the Parliament—has one component of pure intergovernmentalism and one of supranationalism in each of the two branches. The only branch which is purely supranational in the EU context is the judicial branch—the European Court of Justice—although even it is dependent on the national courts. Most important is the complex system of committees associated with the Council, dubbed 'comitology', whereby advisory, management, and regulatory committees made up of representatives of Member States review and issue more or less binding opinions on Commission proposals and actions. Their influence is paramount both directly and indirectly, as

[36] *Garcia v. San Antonio Metropolitan Transit Authority*, 469 U.S. 528 (1985).

the Commission not only responds to but anticipates the preferences of Member States expressed through these channels. But it can also be argued that the more the Commission as an agent can exploit conflicts of interests between Member States, the less control these States will have over the Commission in spite of their collective oversight.[37] Recently, however, with the increase of competences granted to the EU as a whole, the trend has been towards a greater degree of 'sharing' in the EU, at the expense of the Commission. As a result, the need to reform the functioning of the Council in particular to better ensure horizontal integration between issues has become paramount.[38]

Even if they are represented at the upper level, States as principals may retain control collectively but not necessarily individually. Voting procedures at the delegated level therefore constitute a key feature of control mechanisms. The issue has always been at the heart of debates on State sovereignty in the EU context. For this reason, Art. 100a constituted the central and most controversial element of the Single European Act negotiations in 1985. While it did not replace the original Art. 100, which had been the object of the infamous Luxembourg compromise on unanimity voting in 1965, it served to extend majority voting to all issues related to the internal market, 'unless provided otherwise by the present Treaty', and with an explicit exception for fiscal harmonization, the movement of persons, and salaried workers.[39]

Reversibility

When an endowment of authority remains at a given level within an allocational regime, a delegation of authority from the endowed level to the delegated level will usually be reversible to some extent. Any allocation will likely satisfy two apparently contradictory requirements: legitimacy and reversibility. Legitimacy demands both a sound justification for initial

[37] Even without specific conflicts of interest, monitoring may pose collective action problems, as any State has some incentive to free-ride on the monitoring performed by other States. For a related discussion, see Mark Pollack, 'Obedient Servant or Runaway Bureaucracy? Delegation, Agency and Agenda Setting in the European Community' (Cambridge, MA: Center for Foreign and International Affairs Working Paper No. 95-10, Harvard University, 1995).

[38] For a detailed discussion see 'Operation of the Council with an enlarged Union in Prospect' (Report by the Working Party set up by the Secretary-General of the Council, Trumpf/Piris Report), Brussels (10-03-1999), 2139/99.

[39] The exclusion of the movement of people (Art. 100a.2) constituted a political compromise with Britain which consistently argued that a common immigration policy ought to be a prerequisite to free movement of persons and refused to see immigration rules fall under a majority voting procedure, for fear of having to adopt Germany's more lenient rules of entry.

allocations of authority and a degree of permanence or 'stickiness' to these allocations to ensure respect for allocational choices. Reversibility, in contrast, implies that initial allocational choices may need to change due to unintended consequences or subsequent changes in technologies, ideology, or circumstances.

With regard to reversibility, two issues need to be kept in mind. First, is there any reversibility left? If not, then the endowed level has given up all its authority and ceases to hold an endowment. Second, how easy is it to reverse an allocational delegation? Here we distinguish between the reversibility inherent in any endowment—which we might call a reserved or implicit reversibility—and express or explicitly-stated reversibility. Even among express mechanisms of reversibility, however, it is best to think of these along a continuum of easier or harder reversibility.

Sunset provisions are among the clearest examples of reversible mechanisms. Here the delegation expires at a certain date when the authority automatically reverts back to the endowed level upon the tolling of the deadline. We find frequent examples of sunset provisions in the US, where the national government possesses a secondary endowment over issues such as welfare or environment. Welfare waivers granted by the federal government to the States to allow them to experiment with welfare reform expressly stated a time limit for the duration of the waivers.[40] Similarly, the national approvals of State implementation plans for environmental laws require States to revise these plans and resubmit them for federal review on a regular basis.[41]

Revocability provisions are another example of reversibility mechanisms. These are 'escape' clauses that permit the endowed level to step in to revoke the delegation under certain circumstances. Environmental laws in the US, for example, permit the federal government—acting as principal—to override delegations made to States in public health emergencies.[42] Many of the directives implementing the single market in Europe and involving some degree of mutual recognition include rather broad allowance for escape when States need to 'protect the public interest'. In the EU, the powers of the Court and even more those of the Commission can obviously be revoked through Treaty revisions, such as the IG 1996 exercise. Most importantly, some powers have been delegated to the Commission through Council regulations with a fixed expiration date, as with the framework R&D programme, RACE, or the structural fund regulations. The requirement of unanimity for renewal ensures a high likelihood of reversibility in case of discontent on the part of principals.

[40] See Department of Health and Human Services, 59 Federal Register 49,249 (1994).

[41] Clean Air Act, 42 U.S.C. sect. 7410.

[42] Clean Air Act, 42 U.S.C. sect. 7603; Clean Water Act, 33 U.S.C. sect. 1364.

At another level altogether, the Amsterdam Treaty adopted in 1997 introduced a new clause in the EU Treaties—Arts 6 and 7—that allows for the withdrawal of the rights associated with membership for States in breach of basic human right standards, even though it has increasingly been considered impossible to do so in practice. Similarly, if States in the US remain the ultimate endowed level as they were at the founding of the constitution, we should therefore expect them still to have the theoretical ability to revoke any delegations of authority given in Art. 1 to the federal government. The amendment provisions in Art. 5 of the constitution do give States the theoretical, but heretofore unused, option of calling for a constitutional convention on the vote of two-thirds of the State legislatures, which preserves an extreme option for States to control the federal government.

The EU has resorted to escape clauses to buy off States' adherence to increased constraints put on their capacity to regulate domestically. A prime example is that of the Single European Act where the introduction of a safeguard clause constituted a clear quid pro quo for the extension of majority voting in Art. 100a.4. This provision allowed a Member State to opt out—that is to say, to continue to apply its national provisions to imported products—if it felt that its interest was overruled by a Council vote. This was a clear departure from the principle of 'preemption of harmonization' established by the Court's jurisprudence, under which host country requirements could be justified only 'in the absence of Community measures'.[43] This clause led some prominent observers of the Community to regard the Single European Act as a set-back in community integration.[44] To be sure, the scope of the safeguard clause was itself limited since it could not be used against a unanimity decision by the Council and needed to be justified 'on ground of major needs', as provided for in Art. 36 of the Rome Treaty, or relating to protection of the environment or the working environment. Ultimately, however, political pressures would be the strongest limit against the systematic use of the safeguard clause.

3. Federalism and Allocational Legitimacy

We have examined four mechanisms—delineation, monitoring, sharing, and reversibility—that accompany transfers of policy authority in tiered

[43] Under the Court's jurisprudence, after harmonization has been completed a Member State cannot invoke Arts 36 for goods and 56 for services in order to avoid having to comply with a Council's decision.

[44] See Pierre Pescatore, 'Some Critical Remarks on the 'Single European Act'', in *Common Market Law Review* 24: 9–18 (1987).

regimes such at the US and EU and that we suggest will be central to allocational legitimacy in any tiered regime. At the outset of this chapter, we stated that our aim was to move beyond the long-standing debate over the appropriateness of centralization or decentralization. Any inquiry into the proper allocation of policy authority, we have argued, needs to give attention to allocational mechanisms and how they are crafted, combined, and traded off against each other. Allocational mechanisms may help prevent unintended consequences resulting from a shift in authority and in doing so help can make those same shifts more legitimate by providing assurance to the governance level making a delegation of power and to the citizenry which it serves.

Within each type of mechanism, it is important to consider how much control the principal has left after authority has been transferred. As we have suggested, agency ties vary in their strength. Delineations can be narrow or broad; monitoring regularized or happenstance; sharing direct or indirect; and reversibility implicit or explicit. The variation in the strength of these mechanisms means that trade-offs can be made between them. Narrowness in delineation, for example, might be sacrificed if sharing is high or reversibility easy and clear. George Bermann has argued that this is essentially the trade-off made in the US, where a delineating principle of subsidiarity is not as necessary because of the institutional linkages that define US federalism.[45] He argues that Europe, in contrast, needs to take the principle of subsidiarity much more seriously because other institutional mechanisms in Europe offer 'weaker assurances' of respect for State interests.[46]

In a sense, how an allocational shift is secured is not unrelated to the overarching question of whether it should be made in the first place. Yet the degree to which power is centralized or decentralized depends on more than simply a static decision about the appropriate level for exercising policy authority. It also depends on how that authority gets transferred, and what mechanisms exist for modifying, constraining, and abandoning the transfer if necessary. If States make up the endowed level, and authority is being transferred to a central institution, then tightly constraining mechanisms may preserve at least the latent advantages of decentralization. The principle of subsidiarity, for example, can be used as a delineating norm if it is inscribed in a treaty or constitution, and if used in conjunction with monitoring, sharing, and reversibility can entrench a preference for decentralization, even in a regime where authority gets transferred to a centralized institution.

[45] George Bermann, 'Taking Subsidiarity Seriously: Federalism in the European Community and the United States', *Columbia Law Review* 94: 331–456 (1994).

[46] Ibid. at 337.

The allocational mechanisms described here can be thought of as complementary and interconnected components of the overall degree of decentralization in a given tiered regime. Together, they cover the different facets of subsidiarity as generally understood in the European context, including the limits and constraints put on the delegation of authority from the lower to the higher jurisdictional level;[47] the requirements to decentralize the implementation and enforcement of tasks formulated at the higher level; and the formulation, monitoring and enforcing of the delegation of jurisdictional authority horizontally from one unit at the lower level to another unit.[48] A focus on these allocational mechanisms constitute a more generic framework of analysis than simply asking what powers are delegated to whom and provides a basis for thinking about allocational issues in more dynamic and process-oriented ways.[49]

Several sets of questions follow from our analysis. First, under what conditions are we likely to see different kinds of allocational mechanisms in place? Are endowed upper levels likely to act differently from endowed lower levels? We might think that sharing mechanisms are more likely with State-endowed levels delegating to some higher level, where representatives from the States can serve on the decision-making body of the higher, delegated level. But do we ever see the reverse?

Second, under what conditions are some mechanisms more appropriate than others? Does the strength of constraint depend on trust, shared cultural understandings, importance of the policy issue at stake, or the likelihood of error in making the allocation? We can venture that, for instance, the explicit reliance on all-out reversibility becomes less attractive the greater the trust developed between constituent units. Similarly,

[47] In the EU context, and in areas of mixed competence, subsidiarity requires that action at the EU level must be based on an appraisal of how necessary the proposed measures are—can the objective be satisfactorily attained by Member States?—and how effective they will be—can the objective be better attained by action at the Community level?

[48] It is worth noting that, in the spirit of subsidiarity, mutual recognition had served to limit the transfer of sovereignty to supranational European authority. But mutual recognition is not actually a straightforward example of subsidiarity in that it consists itself in a delegation of authority between States.

[49] In some cases, these mechanisms can be applied asymmetrically in order to maintain a federal order when the willingness and capacity for delegation varies among sub-units. Canada, for instance, considered setting up a mechanism, dubbed 'interdelegation', in the early Confederation debates in the 1860s whereby power is resident at one level of government in the constitution but a non-constitutional mechanism is provided where the power is transferred, usually irreversibly, to another level of government. Thus, for instance, a threshold can be set for the number of provinces needed for power to flow to them irreversibly and without a formal constitutional change. Those not party to the agreement would continue to see Ottawa exercise the power. This approach retains the appearance of a symmetrical division of powers but provides a mechanism where a mere legislative agreement can trigger an irreversible transfer of that power. We would like to thank Graham Flack for pointing us to this idea.

the sharing of power at the centre is more likely to serve as a mechanism of control in the early phase of federation rather than at a more mature stage where monitoring short of participation and even simple delineation may be considered as sufficient safeguards.

Third, in analyzing efforts to centralize policy authority, when do some States—say, larger or more powerful ones—need stronger allocational constraints than other States? When is it optimal to have differentiated degrees of constraints, such as the vetoes reserved to permanent members of the UN security council? Under what conditions are constraints better made equal across States or unequal? In the US Senate, for example, there is a disproportionate influence of small States relative to their size. Perhaps big States need smaller States more and will give them greater constraints. Of course, one could look at the disproportionate involvement of larger States in the House and their disproportionate impact on presidential elections and make the reverse claim: namely, that larger States have the disproportionate power. In any event, the key question here is whether the constraints need to be, or should be, equally shared when the endowed level consists of multiple, independent units—and if not, then what is the optimal arrangement.

Finally, the concern arises that in allowing endowed levels to rein in their delegations when serious mistakes become evident, these same governmental levels are also permitted the ability to change the delegation when the nature or seriousness of a mistake is not so clear. We may, after all, be mistaken about mistakes. More worrying, the various control mechanisms, including reversibility, which we praise in the name of flexibility may be exploited for reasons that have little to do with their original purpose. Allocations might be changed for reasons having nothing to do with perceived mistakes, but rather with capture or rent-seeking behaviour at the endowed level. Although we have treated lower-level units most often as the principals in tiered governance regimes, they are themselves actually but agents of the public, and the risk may remain that these levels could shirk their responsibility to the public interest.

In this way, our comparative discussion of the US and EU holds immediate relevance to the debates over global trade institutions. The problems raised by the jurisdiction of the World Trade Organization are analytically the same as in the US and European federal systems, though perhaps in a much earlier stage in the deliberation. As Migué has written: 'The title "federalism" can be applied to any political structure in which the power of political authorities extends to less than the size of the economy in which resource movement is free of trade barriers. Its competitive action works within national economies in decentralized federal states or among countries associated in common-market arrangements with only limited central power.'[50] While there are obvious limits to drawing parallels between such divergent regimes, in each the institutions which issue rules for free trade and regulate goods and services often do not operate at the same level. Free trade places national governments in a similar position *vis-à-vis* the WTO as individual States find themselves *vis-à-vis* a national US government or supranational EU structure. In each case, the federal institutions represent the collective action of member States and may take decisions which become binding on those States.

The legitimacy concerns that give rise to mechanisms for securing allocational shifts will probably prove especially important in the WTO context. Concerns about centralization should be at least as pronounced in multilateral as in formal federal structures, especially since the latter exhibit closer cultural, territorial, and economic ties that may lessen the need for controls by one level of government on another.[51] International institutions also have much less direct democratic accountability to the global citizenry on whose behalf they ultimately should serve. Thus, to the extent that the US and EU rely on mechanisms to address legitimacy concerns, these mechanisms should be all the more relevant to the multilateral level.

The debate over federalism has had at its core the question of centralization versus decentralization. As important as this question is, it leaves open the question of how to design the institutional mechanisms that will transfer policy authority to the appropriate level of government. Our aim here has been to shift the debate beyond just 'up or down' and draw attention to the ways institutions can be designed to accompany shifts of authority from one level of government to another. We have raised the question of what institutional arrangements will best secure the effectiveness and legitimacy that underlie the principle of subsidiarity. These institutional arrangements need to help ensure that policy allocations remain at the levels most appropriate for the relevant issues and yet are also capable of modification when new circumstances or knowledge arises. We have drawn attention to four mechanisms for institutionalizing allocational changes and have shown how these mechanisms have accompanied allocational decisions in the US and EU. Arrangements such as these appear to play a valuable role in sustaining the legitimacy of governmental institutions in times of allocational change and are deserving of more attention from students of federalism.

[50] Jean-Luc Migué, *Federalism and Free Trade*, Hobart Paper 122 (London: The Institute of Economic Affairs, 1993), 27. See also Daniel J. Elazar, *Constitutionalizing Globalization: The Postmodern Revival of Confederal Arrangements* (Lanham: Rowman and Littlefield Publishers, 1998).

[51] For a discussion of the importance of shared cultural and territorial domains for federal structures, see Daniel J. Elazar, 'International and Comparative Federalism', *PS: Political Science & Politics* 26: 190–5 (1993).

11

Federal Governance in the United States and the European Union: A Policy Network Perspective

JOHN PETERSON AND LAURENCE J. O'TOOLE, JR

Federalism, by nature, means complex institutional settings for governance. Federal systems must accommodate 'mutuality, not hierarchy, multiple rather than single causation, a sharing rather than a monopoly of power' (Wildavsky 1979: 142–3). More than in unitary systems, outcomes are negotiated instead of imposed, bargained rather than dictated. Actors are interdependent, not independent. Even when formal institutions exist to facilitate bargaining between different levels of government, federalism usually gives rise to less formal and intricate structures within which a large number of actors, each wielding a small slice of power, interact. Governance within such complex, informal structures naturally gives rise to legitimacy concerns: who can tell who decides what when? A number of conceptual lenses provide insights into federal prospects and problems in dealing with the legitimacy challenge. However, we argue here that a network perspective is particularly apposite.

'Network' is probably the single most widely used metaphor in the analysis of modern governance. The variants are almost limitless: information networks, policy networks, value networks, transgovernmental networks, networks of civic engagement, issue networks, the 'network society', and so forth. Much of the academic literature on networks is either vague or abstract—or both. But there is widespread agreement that society, culture and economy, especially in federal systems, are increasingly products of relations involving mutuality and interdependence as opposed to hierarchy and independence. In short, 'networks are the fundamental stuff of which new organizations are and will be made' (Castells 1996: 168).

In this chapter we consider the role of networks in modern governance in the United States (US) and European Union[1] (EU). Our analysis is

[1] In our treatment of 'Europe' as a comparative case, we generally mean the EU itself as a system of governance in its own right. However, the quasi-federal nature of the EU makes

deliberately comparative and highlights a series of similarities and contrasts between network structures on either side of the Atlantic. It is also normative: we use the research literature to analyze problems of legitimacy that seem endemic to governance by network. We offer some suggestions for enhancing legitimacy in both systems over the longer term. However, our thrust is conceptual and exploratory: we raise far more questions than we answer and offer suggestions for future research, while recognizing that our knowledge of network governance remains primitive.

Our basic premise is that network structures have become something like the default institutional form in many western policy sectors, for two basic reasons. First, the US (see O'Toole 2000) and the EU (see Hooghe and Marks 1997; Scharpf 1997; 1999) are both deliberately and normatively 'multi-level' systems of government. Yet US federalism reserves more powers to the individual States than do other variants of federalism. Meanwhile, one of the most fundamental principles underpinning EU governance is subsidiarity: the notion that decisions should be taken at the lowest possible tier of government (see Peterson 1994; Van Kersbergen and Verbeek 1994; Peterson and Bomberg 1999: 57). Thus, both exhibit a constitutional preference for individual State action in the absence of overarching national—in the US case—or 'European'—in the EU case—interests. Each depends fundamentally on the concertation of multiple layers of governance between which powers are separated, but face collective action problems that cannot be solved simply by resort to the prerogatives of strong central authority.

Moreover, in both systems more than most others, powers held by different levels of government are implied, tacit, or contested, and not plainly granted by constitution or treaty. One upshot is that most policy outcomes are products of negotiation and mutual adjustment between different—and nominally independent, but clearly interdependent—levels of government. Network analysis offers leverage for understanding multi-level governance because actors that represent different levels, between which powers are divided in ways that are disputable, must cooperate and share resources to achieve common goals. Legislation at any level is unlikely to achieve its stated goals unless it is shaped, moulded, and scrutinized by actors interacting across different levels.

Second, the US and the EU have both been touched by similar reformist political imperatives: to 'reinvent government' in the US (Osborne and

hard distinctions between the EU *qua* EU and its constituent national parts difficult to draw. One upshot is that a wide variety of different kinds of network are involved in EU governance. For example, the implementation of EU policy is mainly a national concern which gives rise to networks with nodes in national capitals, while the pre-legislative formulation or 'shaping' of EU policy occurs within networks centred in Brussels.

Gaebler 1992) and 'do less but do it better' in Europe (Peterson 1999*a*). Concerns about the substance of policy have been elevated at the same time as it has become *de rigeur* to reduce, or at least hold constant, the size of the state, and to avoid the creation of new public institutions. Consequently, an increasingly diverse range of organisations—private, non-governmental or para-governmental—have become involved in formulating or delivering public policy through government contracting, various types of consultancy, and public-private partnerships.

Our argument may be stated simply, and by means of two related points. First, more 'real life' governance in federal systems occurs from interactions within networks than occurs within formal institutions in which different levels of government are represented. Second, scholars, but probably also practitioners, have neglected the fundamental importance of legitimizing network forms of governance. Perhaps understandably, given the complexity of both network structures and the policy tasks they often seek to achieve, both academics and practitioners have mainly concerned themselves with the *management* of networks.[2] To the extent that this focus addresses the question of whether networks effectively deliver what citizens want, management and legitimacy are not mutually exclusive concerns: a point clear in work which focuses on 'output' legitimacy (see Fritz Scharpf's chapter in this volume). The focus on management is by no means an unproductive one: when managed effectively, networked arrangements for governance offer considerable advantages in a number of respects. In almost all cases, networks are more pliable and flexible than hierarchies. Their memberships, goals, and structures may be adapted to suit shifting loyalties or economic patterns. Those operating within them may be able to seize opportunities for both 'negative' and 'positive coordination' (Scharpf 1993, 1996; see also Mayntz and Scharpf 1975), particularly by connecting or disconnecting nodes[3] to maximize problem solving capacity for the purposes at hand. More generally, 'networks can both enhance and reduce the efficiency and legitimacy of policy-making' (Börzel 1998: 254).

Yet, as institutional forms for the governance of polities on a massive scale in the US and the EU, networks face particularly serious and poten-

[2] As a caveat, we note Klijn's (1996: 96) contention that 'One of the remarkable characteristics of at least part of the network literature . . . is the lack of attention to the management aspect . . . If the reader finds prescriptions, they are usually aimed at repairing what researchers consider the democratic deficits of policy making in communities'. We would concede that the European networks literature, particularly works on corporatist settings, show far more concern for issues of legitimacy. However, we also believe that, on balance, management easily trumps legitimacy as a concern across the networks literature.

[3] Nodes are points at which subsidiary actors within networks 'centre' or connect. Of course hierarchies or portions thereof may themselves be linked by networks.

tially disabling challenges in terms of legitimacy. Network forms of governance tend to advantage experts or sophisticated actors who are familiar with all levels of government in federal systems, as opposed to ordinary citizens. To ignore the normative questions about input legitimacy to which network governance gives rise risks weakening the democratic foundations of the federalist contracts that bind together levels of governance, public, quasi-public, and private actors, and states and citizens in Europe and America.

We present our argument in four sections. First, we explain why network forms of governance have proliferated and consider the legitimacy issues that arise. This section yields a set of assessment criteria to be applied in framing analyses of legitimacy in different, real-world political systems. Second, we examine networks in the EU. Third, we offer an assessment of network structures in American governance. Fourth, we compare and contrast network structures in the two polities, highlighting both critical issues and network features with implications for legitimacy, as well as ways in which the democratic deficit that plagues network forms of governance might be closed.

1. Networks and Modern Governance

Modern governance is shaped fundamentally by shifts in both loyalties and power. Changes in the way that modern citizens identify themselves combined with the transfer of powers previously monopolized by nation-states create a sort of 'new medievalism': a proliferation of systems of overlapping authority and multiple loyalty.[4] Globalization encourages shifts of power 'upwards', even if few citizens seem very loyal to the idea of global governance—or, in the EU's case, regional governance. The proliferation of information technologies (IT) facilitates, perhaps above all, sideways shifts because modern IT makes the performance of non-governmental bodies tasked with providing public goods easier for public administrations to monitor (see, for instance, O'Toole 1998). The re-emergence of strong local attachments promotes devolution of power to smaller units of government. Together these trends encourage a fundamental change in the way that organizations are structured. Increasingly,

[4] In some cases, the 'new medievalism' is not new at all (see Bull 1977): many nineteenth-century Glaswegians owed a 'slice' of loyalty to the British empire, the United Kingdom, Great Britain, Scotland, and Edinburgh—and often even New York, Boston, or Hong Kong. What *is* new is the rapid pace of shifts of power away from the state 'up, down and sideways—to supra-state, sub-state, and above all, nonstate [private or non-governmental] actors' (Slaughter 1997: 138; see also Peterson 1999*b*).

networks that span the sub-national, national, transnational, and international levels are replacing traditional Weberian hierarchies found at the state level (Hanf 1994).

For our purposes, networks are:

> structures of interdependence involving multiple organizations or parts thereof, where one unit is not merely the formal subordinate of the others in some larger hierarchical arrangement. Networks exhibit some structural stability but extend beyond formally established linkages and policy-legitimated ties. The notion of network excludes mere formal hierarchies and perfect markets, but it includes a very wide range of structures in between. (O'Toole 1997*c*: 45)

A variety of kinds of 'glue' may hold networks together: authority bonds, resource exchange, or common interests. However, what most distinguishes networks from more traditional forms of governance is their lack of hierarchy across nodes: 'administrators cannot be expected to exercise decisive leverage by virtue of their formal position' (O'Toole 1997*c*: 45).

Adopting a network perspective is only a starting point for an analysis, not a substitute for it. The analyst must cope with tremendous variety in terms of structure and other characteristics,[5] making it difficult to generalize about the nature of network governance, and its virtues and vices. In the public policy literature, *policy networks* are usually portrayed as being characterised by interdependence between actors, patterned resource exchange, and informal rules or norms in specific policy sectors—agriculture, defence, social policy, and so forth. This literature highlights both the 'division of labour between different policy domains and an enlargement of the set of consequential actors beyond office-holders in government' (Pappi and Henning 1998: 553). It paints a picture of highly 'differentiated polities' (Rhodes 1998): both the problem-solving capacity of network structures (Scharpf 1997) and the politics of policy-making within them (Lowi 1985) vary considerably between different policy sectors.

Networking dynamics are visible in multiple policy arenas—distributive, redistributive, and regulatory—and in numerous stages of the policy process. Hard evidence about where and when networks are most powerful is thin on the ground. We require far more and more systematic research that puts networks at the centre of policy analysis (see Börzel 1998). However, logic would suggest that network governance is particularly prominent in redistributive policy-making—when resources are extracted from one region or group to benefit another—because programmatic decisions to redistribute usually leave the actual spoils to be divided later

[5] Among the many structural dimensions typically used in analyses of networks are size, degrees of stability, formalisation, complexity, concentration, and density.

through a process of bargaining. We also could expect networks to emerge, often quite naturally, in regulatory policy-making because specialist expertise about regulatory cause and effect is essential. Moreover, in line with the imperative to employ the lightest possible bureaucratic 'tackle' in enforcement, regulation increasingly involves forms of oversight which pit very few public regulators against a large number of regulated actors, giving rise to voluntaristic or self-policing networks to ensure compliance.

In sequential terms, a plausible hypothesis is that the input of networks into the policy process is most common and significant *before* and *after* the 'policy decision point', or the point when legislation is actually chosen or policies are set—usually by way of public votes by legislators. Networks are obviously active in agenda setting (Rhodes 1998), but their role is also indisputable in implementation (Milward, Provan, and Else 1993). In other words, and crucially from the point of view of legitimacy, networks may be most powerful during the least visible, transparent, and rules-based stages of the policy process.

Allegations of a newly 'networked world' set alight three burning questions. First, how do we really know that networks have become so pervasive? Second, so what? Do they matter? Third, should we evaluate their increasing prominence positively or negatively? We tackle each question in turn below.

How Do We Know Networks Exist?

In important respects, 'argument by anecdote' has dominated debates about the emergence of an increasingly networked world (Hall and O'Toole 2000: 671). The assumptions that public programmes are increasingly intergovernmental, spanning multiple structures and delegating policy tasks to actors *other* than public agencies have not gone unchallenged (Kettl 1990; 1993). Yet two recent and broad changes suggest that modern governance increasingly involves 'making a mesh of things' (Appleby 1949). First, the nature of *issues* has changed: increasingly more public management is concerned with complex or 'wicked problems' (Rittel and Weber 1973), or ones that 'cannot be handled by dividing them up into simple pieces in near isolation from each other' (O'Toole 1997*c*: 46). No public authority, or combination of them, has either the ways or the means to impose solutions to wicked problems. Consider redistributive proposals for reforming US health care or regulatory EU efforts to protect cultural diversity in the European media. In both cases, a vast number of public agencies at different levels of government and private or non-governmental actors must be mobilized in the pursuit of collective action. Network solutions are often the only solution, if any exist at all, to 'wicked problems'.

Second, the way in which *power* is exercised has changed. Perhaps counterintuitively, pooling sovereignty at the level of the European Union may strengthen states in important ways by making possible outcomes—above all, wealth and prosperity which spring from the world's largest capitalist market—that would be impossible if the EU did not exist.[6] In Europe, more than elsewhere, 'the state is not disappearing, it is disaggregating into its separate, functionally separate parts' (Slaughter 1997: 184). These parts often re-aggregate in the form of Brussels-based, sector-specific EU policy networks. Meanwhile, even under Democratic presidential administrations in the 1990s, the United States has relentlessly shed responsibilities to private and voluntary associations (O'Toole 2000). One recent study of all substantive legislation passed by Congress during two very different eras in American governance[7] concludes that most—86 per cent—new legislation involves multiple actors. A majority of new or substantively modified programmes are clearly intergovernmental. Business and non-profit actors are each assigned explicit roles in around one-third of all federal programmes (Hall and O'Toole 2000). Firm evidence also exists of a proliferation in the number of inter-agency committees and advisory commissions in US government (Light 1995). Many types of new policy instruments such as cross-cutting regulations—applying civil rights or environmental rules to many programmes—increase the need for network types of coordination (O'Toole 1997*c*: 47).

Thus far, we lack comparable, systematic data to validate the view that the EU is a system of governance by network. However, three prominent features of EU governance suggest that policy networks are an 'indispensable part of any toolkit' for understanding the EU (Rhodes, Bache, and George 1996: 385). First, and most simply, the EU itself is constructed as a kind of network. As Keohane and Hoffmann (1991: 13) observe, 'individual units are defined not by themselves but in relation to other units' and 'formal and informal institutions at different levels in the formal structure, if in the formal structure at all, are linked by a variety of networks'. Second, adding complexity to this web of relationships, around one-third of the EU's common budget is spent on 'cohesion', or narrowing disparities between rich and poor sub-national regions. A firmly ingrained principle of EU cohesion policy is 'partnership', or the idea that multiple kinds of stakeholders from the EU, national and sub-national level, as well as the private or non-governmental sectors, should be involved in programme design and implementation (see Peterson and Bomberg 1999: 147–54). Third, the 'directive' is the most common form of

[6] This argument is convincingly made, in different ways and for different purposes, above all by Alan Milward (1992) and Andrew Moravcsik (1998).

[7] The study compares the 89th (1965–6) and the 103rd (1993–4) Congresses.

legislating in the EU. Directives usually set out general—often *very* general—agreed objectives of EU policy, but leave it to Member States to specify the means by which they are achieved. The effect is virtually to guarantee both continuing discussion and review of EU policies, especially their implementation, while also institutionalizing a kind of networked interdependence across nodes. The precise content and modalities of EU policies often remain subject to negotiation between a range of different governments and levels of government *after* they have been agreed in Brussels or Strasbourg.

So What?

This question deserves a far more extended treatment than we can offer here (see O'Toole 1997c). Yet four responses are immediately obvious. The first is that governance by network is different from traditional forms of governance in crucial respects. Mayntz and Scharpf (1995) argue that policy networks are a 'fifth form' of governance in the middle of a traditional fourfold classification of governing arrangements (Heinz *et al* 1993; see also Pappi and Henning 1998). In the face of similar forces of globalization and devolution, the US and the EU could both be seen to be converging at the middle of Fig. 11.1, with the US moving further towards the left side, and Europe moving from different loci on the right side.

Second, viewing US and EU governance through the lens of a network perspective offers insights, especially comparative ones, that other approaches do not. In the American case, the analysis of intergovernmental arrangements has been notable for its descriptive richness; but the

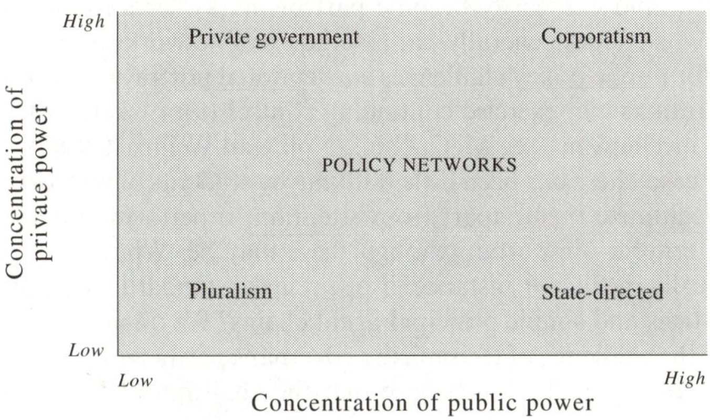

FIGURE 11.1. *Types of governance structure*
Source: Mayntz and Scharpf (1995); Pappi and Henning (1998: 557)

literature still lacks a core of solid theoretical work that can aid in explanation, and thus institutional design (Beam, Conlan, and Walker 1983). Much the same could be said for scholarship on the EU: intergovernmentalist or institutionalist treatments which focus on quasi-constitutional or 'history-making' decisions do not tell us much about how or why policy outcomes are determined in day-to-day negotiations between a variety of policy stakeholders before and after rounds of 'grand bargaining'. Moreover, conducting comparative analyses of systems like the EU and the US requires a conceptual apparatus that offers dimensions and precision appropriate to the task and the opportunity to develop insights from both cognitive and normative streams of institutional analysis, as well as a freedom from context-specific biases. We are unable to utilize fully all of these elements in the study at hand, but we believe that a network perspective offers considerable promise on these grounds.

A third answer to the 'so what' question has to do with implementation failures: a major pathology of government in both the US and—especially—the EU. Such gaps in performance can weaken legitimacy (Pressman and Wildavsky 1984). If we are right that network forms of government are proliferating, then specifying the conditions under which networks facilitate or debilitate effective implementation emerges as an important, and socially useful, expenditure of academic energy (see O'Toole and Montjoy 1984).

A fourth reason to study networks is simply that 'standard nostrums of public administration probably do not apply' to them (O'Toole 1997*c*: 47). Specifically, it is not easy to subject governance by network to democratic controls. For example, oversight by legislatures becomes problematic when most oversight committees and legislators themselves are policy-specialized, and can easily become part of murky, unaccountable 'subgovernments'. More generally, the emergence of networks as institutional settings for public policy challenges conventional portrayals of how political institutions can exercise continuing control (for a sketch of the oft-assumed mechanisms, see McCubbins, Noll, and Weingast 1987).

In any case, there has been little thinking by students of networks about how to legitimize them, apart from attention to performance and management criteria—important though these may be. What can 'accountability' really mean, for instance, if one relaxes standard assumptions of unitary states and simple principal-agent chains? We do not deny the difficulty of the challenge of legitimizing governance by network, either practically or conceptually, but believe that the challenge can no longer be avoided.

Legitimacy and Networks: Friends or Foes?

As an aid to comparing networks in the EU and the US, we simplify somewhat and develop below a short list of assessment criteria. However, a prior analytical task is to consider the specific characteristics of network forms of governance that raise concerns about legitimacy when viewed from the perspective of classic, rational-legal standards of democracy (Weber 1946), which include clarity, consistency, accountability, competent and neutral execution, and instrumental rationality. Three tendencies are readily observable.

First, a common drawback of network governance is ambiguity in terms of both policy process and policy results. The result is often insufficient transparency: stakeholders who are not direct participants in network deliberations have difficulty determining when and by whom important decisions are made. Moreover, networks often bring together actors who share general interests—in environmental protection—but have separate specific goals—regulation versus market incentives. Thus, the effectiveness of policies formulated or implemented by networks often cannot be judged using the yardstick of a schedule of goals mediated through a common authoritative set of institutions (Klijn 1996: 95), making it particularly difficult to assess policy success or failure. In traditional Weberian structures, even in the absence of clear and consensual output and outcome criteria and goals, interested parties can look to clear and open decision processes as sources of legitimacy. In networks, however, clarity and transparency of process are often difficult to generate and sustain.

Second, networks often exhibit a tendency toward 'drift' and therefore a relative lack of authoritativeness. Indecisiveness and lack of leadership within networks (see below) can have direct policy consequences, leading to destabilized understandings, reduced trust, and institutional inconstancy (LaPorte and Metlay 1996). Governance by networks may leave governments unable to provide clear direction or firm leadership in a specified area of policy. Networks that are populated by a very large number of stakeholders whose interests are diverse and difficult to reconcile introduce a bias towards incrementalism, and may even preclude any policy change at all. Perhaps the single most influential study of networks in American governance highlights how relatively heterogeneous and unstructured networks 'complicate calculations, decrease predictability, and impose considerable strains on those charged with governmental leadership' (Heclo 1978: 102). Drift and indecisiveness can be accommodated under relatively stable conditions, when political understandings, economic patterns, and basic policy choices are constant. But when these dimensions are subject to increased complexity and dynamism—arising from pressures for devolution, increased globalization, or the clear failure of past policy choices—legitimacy crises can easily occur. The concomitant reduction in trust, escalation in unpredictability, and associated decline in efficacy can weaken network systems.

Third, networks often are plagued by systemic problems of accountability. Generally, '[public] managers in networked settings do not supervise most of those on whom their own performance relies, monitoring channels are typically diffuse and unreliable, and a common organizational culture exercises a limited and indirect influence' (O'Toole 1997*c*: 47). Specifically, governance by network may privilege private power in a way that ostensibly, and contrary to democratic principles, substitutes it for state power (Slaughter 1997 : 184). Increasingly 'hollow states', which emerge when power shifts from public to private governance and central to sub-central levels (see Milward, Provan, and Else 1993), may become paper tigers in terms of policing compliance. In networks, as opposed to traditional hierarchical agencies, administrators lack the means to steer policy formulation or implementation without cooperation from other kinds of actor. Public actors must practice a form of judo, and make the weight of their—non-public—counterparts work to the benefit of the collective—public—interest. Doing so is rarely easy.

The positive side of the ledger is not blank. First, networks may foster more innovative policies. In particular, wicked policy problems usually require the 'management' of innovation. As one of us has argued, 'innovations are often priorities in sectors or niches where the accretion of structural complexity threatens to overwhelm public performance, so some networked pattern is a common starting place for innovation' (O'Toole 1997*a*: 117).

Second, perhaps counter-intuitively, networks may foster more effective implementation. Because networks facilitate bargaining and exchange between government and the governed, they can help avoid zero-sum relationships between the two. More specifically, networks can ensure that interest groups which are important to proper implementation are not 'unable to significantly alter the costs of implementing a policy' (Hindmoor 1998: 40).[8]

[8] Moreover, at least in theory, the chance of proper implementation may actually *increase* with the number of units involved in implementation (O'Toole and Montjoy 1984). Adding actors can result in increasing the system's capacity for performance and can also expand the supportive coalition, thus potentially enhancing legitimacy. Yet increasing the size of the network often adds constraints, limits the freedom of action available, and multiplies veto points. The key determining factor is patterns of interdependence between the units implementing a policy. For example, when a single granting unit of administration has many potential recipients of funding and is not obliged to interact with all of them, we

Third, networks frequently, although not inevitably, help forge consensus between social actors with different values, identities, and orientations through dialogue and exchange. Networks may raise the level of information or expertise available to decision-makers, particularly by linking public and non-public actors. This process can curb the potential excesses or arbitrariness of unchallenged public power. The result may be to 'legitimize outcomes by allowing affected interests to participate directly in policy formulation' (Peterson 1995*a*: 88).

Accordingly, a short list of criteria can be offered—some of them broad and all with paired, related values—for use in assessing EU and US, as well as other, network arrays in the face of their legitimacy challenges:

- adaptability and capacity for innovation;
- transparency and accessibility;
- representativeness and consensus-building capacity; and
- accountability and authoritativeness.[9]

We are unable here to apply these criteria in a thoroughgoing and serial fashion to network arrangements in the EU and the US. Still, we offer them as a guide to analysis for any general, legitimacy-sensitive review of networks.

2. Networks and EU Governance

Governance by network is visible in Brussels on a daily basis. An enormously diverse range of actors is brought together for dialogue, exchange, and negotiation each business day. The process does not always produce common policies, but it inevitably promotes mutual understanding.[10]

European Union networks score well on the criteria of *adaptability and capacity for innovation*, an oft-cited advantage of federal arrangements.

'could expect the high total number of actors to be an aid, not a hindrance, to implementation since not all the actors need to be simultaneously coordinated or in agreement' (O'Toole and Montjoy 1984: 494).

[9] For an early effort to develop guidelines for assessing networks in terms of the features of democratic theory, along with expectations about likely consequences, see O'Toole (1997*b*).

[10] EU policy-making is a fundamentally inter-institutional process. But even leaving aside the need for inter-institutional networking to forge policy agreement, the Council of Ministers—the EU's main legislative institution—is itself a sort of umbrella for a very extensive series of networks between national ministers, officials, and experts. Every working day an average of around 1,000 officials or experts attend 20 different Council 'working group' meetings in Brussels. Each brings together officials from all 15 Member States plus the European Commission to negotiate policy details. About 70 per cent of the EU's legislative output is actually 'decided' at the working-group level (Hayes-Renshaw and Wallace 1997: 15).

One of the EU's clearest virtues is its capacity for improvisation: '[w]ithout the benefit of any grand design, the EU has developed a flexible, and often surprisingly effective, set of mechanisms for the resolution of very complex conflicts' (Peterson and Bomberg 1999: 59). The EU is by no means always a source of innovative policy, but the role of ideas—especially new, creative, experimental ones—is more prominent in the EU than in most systems of governance (see Cram 1997; McNamara 1998; cf. O'Toole 1997*a*).

More specifically, 'policy transfer' is frequent and increasingly systematic at the EU level. Policy transfer is what happens when governments learn from one another by sharing information about how policies have been constructed, and how and why they have succeeded or failed. Best practices are mimicked and thus 'transferred'. The exhaustion, after more than 40 years, of the so-called Monnet method[11] of promoting European integration means that policy transfer—agreeing policy targets, benchmarking, and peer review—has become the new, preferred method of decision-making in a wide range of sectors (see Begg and Peterson 1999). By nature, policy transfer promotes the diffusion of solutions that are embraced 'voluntarily' and thus may be viewed as more legitimate than those that are seen to be 'imposed by Brussels'.

In some EU policy sectors, policies do not transfer well. For instance, rates of EU policy implementation vary considerably among Member States in environmental and social policy. However, the Union has succeeded against great odds in transferring the principles of sound money and public finance in the process of creating the Euro. The European Commission's (1997) *Action Plan for the Single Market* provoked a particularly effective form of policy transfer in terms of implementation, leading to remarkable reductions in the number of internal market rules not fully implemented across the EU. In both of these cases, what mattered most in terms of outcome was the creation of *processes* by which Member States scrutinized each other's methods and progress towards an agreed set of goals. These goals looked clearly defined but, as is so often the case in the EU, were accompanied by escape clauses and scope for political

[11] One of the founding fathers of European integration, Jean Monnet (1978: 93), himself described the method as 'starting with limited achievements, establishing de facto solidarity, from which a federation would gradually emerge'. For Milward (1992: 336) the method was essentially technocratic, relying on 'small and powerful committee(s) able to make far-reaching decisions'. The British Prime Minister who took the UK into the European Community described the method as 'giving a mandate to experts and leaving them to get on with it' (quoted in Peterson and Bomberg 1999: 232). See also Wallace (1996).

fudge.[12] The point is that the EU works on the basis of knowledge transfer by means of networks, as opposed to clear blueprints.

It is difficult to argue that most EU networks are very *transparent or accessible*. The problem arises from the enormous complexity that has resulted from the construction of the EU's institutions according to a delegative model, with Member States acting as principals and the Union's institutions as agents. Profound tensions between the two have frequently produced 'institutional stalemate as states layer controls on EU institutions . . . The result is often precisely the opposite of what was intended: non-transparent forms of governance that work through elaborate policy networks' (Ansell and Weber 1999: 87). When rules and controls are so rigid as to produce deadlock, such networks almost naturally arise to prevent outright impasse and atrophy.

To be fair, the EU has made considerable strides in recent years towards making its deliberations easier to follow, understand, and influence (see Peterson 1995*b*; Lord 1998; Grønbech-Jensen 1998). The EU also has systematized interest representation and developed new codes to regulate the occupation by private actors of public space (Greenwood 1997: 80–100). Interestingly, it also has embraced more formalized network structures, such as the Bangemann Group on telecommunications, the Social Dialogue—between employers and trades unions representatives—on social policy, and the European Science and Technology Assembly (ESTA) on research policy (see Peterson and Bomberg 1999). Usually, the memberships and deliberations of such networks are made public.

Yet the explosive 1999 report by a Committee of Independent Experts into 'Allegations of Fraud, Mismanagement and Nepotism' in the European Commission painted a picture of unaccountable, backroom decision-making concerning the distribution of EU funding and jobs within tightly-sealed networks (European Parliament 1999).[13] Majone (1999: 22) argues that the 'proliferation of committees, working

[12] For example, the Maastricht Treaty of 1992 set out five 'convergence criteria' which all member states wishing to join the single currency had, in principle, to meet. However, the Treaty explicitly stated that all decisions about which states would become 'ins' or 'outs' would be political decisions taken by the European Council, with the criteria providing no guarantees or automaticity.

[13] Consider, for example, the Committee's investigation of the 'Med' programmes—to promote decentralized cooperation with Mediterranean countries. It found 'a network of firms controlling the implementation of a policy, which was set up by external consultants on the initiative of the Commission', and allowed for 'no competitive tendering at all' (European Parliament 1999: 39). In effect, 'what the Commission had actually done was to delegate its powers *de facto* to a third body, rather than sign mere service agreements' (European Parliament 1999: 48). In the case of the Leonardo programme—to promote pan-European educational exchanges—a consultant was paid €2,677 a day as a consultant for his 'networking know-how' (European Parliament 1999: 75).

groups, and agencies, the overlap of their activities, and divergences between the rules governing their functioning create a real lack of transparency'. The transparency deficit is exacerbated by the difficulty of judging the success of many EU policies. Inevitably, crafting one EU policy for 15 different Member States frequently produces lowest common-denominator policies with goals that are hazy or sometimes even contradictory.

The transparency and accessibility of EU networks are crucial because a striking amount of policy content is determined *before* formal EU initiatives are tabled: a rough guess is that about 80 per cent of the content of most EU policies is cast before the Commission even tables a proposal (see Hull 1993; Peterson and Bomberg 1999). Under these conditions, first mover advantages clearly matter in EU policy-making. Yet it is often impossible to know who the first movers are or when or by whom decisions were taken which earned them this status.

In terms of *representativeness and consensus-building capacity*, we find a mixed picture. The struggle for control of the EU's agenda often encourages a reliance on networks that are not broadly representative. Neither state nor a classic international organization, the EU is not easily subject to control by majoritarian democratic institutions. It is thus uniquely difficult to aggregate interests by means of political parties or broadly representative interest groups, such as trades unions, in EU governance. We do find some cases, such as that of women's groups and social policy (see Mazey 1998; Pollack 1997), where the Commission and/or EP have made concerted, sustained efforts to expand representation in the EU's policy process and empowered broad social interests or citizen groups. Yet the access extended to relatively broad social groups—women's, environmental, or consumer groups—by EU institutions has taken place mostly in sectors where the EU's competence is recent, underdeveloped, or weak—audiovisual policy, social policy, environmental policy. Where the EU's competence is clearest, its ethos is generally a neo-liberal one that pursues, above all, free trade. This ethos does not encourage the broad representation of societal interests in EU networks.

On the other hand, EU networks are often remarkably proficient in building consensus. The EU is a massive polity that incorporates 15 sovereign Member States, eleven languages, 370 million citizens, and a diverse range of political, administrative, and economic traditions. In structural terms, the EU is a radically differentiated polity. Even leaving aside its multi-level configuration, 'fire walls' between finely divided and often hermetic policy sectors are high in Brussels. The Commission's Directorates-General or 'services'—the Brussels equivalents of ministries or departments—are sub-divided into far narrower policy fields than are most national administrations,[14] with each usually allotted its own dedicated Commissioners, Council of Ministers and EP committee. Again, an important effect is to dilute the power of relatively broad social interests, which usually are most effective in mobilizing support within broad institutions that span multiple policy 'villages'.

Yet the Commission's formal rules of procedure require more inter-agency coordination than occurs in most national systems. Anything besides the most trivial EU legislative proposal is scrutinized by a dizzying array of services, including some whose actual interest in a proposal is tangential.[15] Thus the EU policy process cannot even start until agreement has been negotiated within a cluster of networked organizational units.

Even after the formal policy process begins, the EU continues to lack formal institutions which can adequately 'manag[e] the policy dialogue' (Wallace 1997: 10). Yet inter-institutional consensus is needed between an extremely wide variety of decision-makers before policies may be set. The EU is usually unable to produce policy without the agreement of all three of its major legislative institutions: the Council, the Commission, and the EP. Thus EU policy formulation is a process of bargaining between agents representing both its Member States and institutions within network structures. Most set-piece occasions in EU decision-making—meetings of the Council, the EP's plenary sessions, 'conciliation committees' to settle Council-EP disputes—are overly formal and do not permit much meaningful bargaining to take place. 'As a result they have come to be supported by a vast network of informal and unstructured channels between EU actors' (Nugent 1999: 298). When the EU legislates effectively, it usually is a direct result of effective consensus building within informal networks.

In terms of *accountability and authoritativeness*, a range of EU policies—the Common Agricultural Policy, above all—give rise to networks that seem immune to political control. The EU is unique in its lack of

[14] For example, even after a 1999 consolidation of the Commission's Directorates, which reduced the total number by six to 36, the Commission still maintained separate services for fisheries, 'information society'—as well as research—and two separate Directorates for external relations and trade along with a 'common service for external relations'.

[15] A good example is the 1994 directive on packaging waste, which harmonized national policies on waste management of product packaging (see Nunan 1999): no fewer than 16 different Commission services were involved in formulating the proposal. In the interest of encouraging less combative exchanges between Commission Directorates, most of which operate dogmatic 'anti-poaching' policies in their policy domains, the Santer Commission (1994–9) created the equivalent of cabinet sub-committees—'*Groupes des Commissaires*'—as well as aptly named 'networks' of managers of Commission services—'*réseaux de Directeurs-Générales*'.

hierarchy. It has no government and no opposition.[16] Its policy agenda itself is subject to negotiation since the EU lacks any agreed political programme, such as a manifesto or a Queen's speech.

If the European Commission has some of the characteristics of a government, the analogy is easily overstretched. The Commission retains a monopoly right of initiative: no legislative proposal—leaving aside foreign and justice and home affairs policies—may be agreed unless the college of Commissioners votes, by a simple majority if necessary, to table it. Yet, even before its dramatic fall from grace in March 1999,[17] it was clear that the Commission under the 1995–9 presidency of Jacques Santer was fundamentally weaker and less dynamic than it had been under the 1985–94 presidency of Jacques Delors. During the Delors era, the EU was, at least for a time, subject to firm political control by something like a 'government': the European Council with Delors as a trusted and principal member (see Grant 1994; Ross 1995). Santer's far weaker authority and the general drift of European integration—leaving aside EMU—allowed EU policy networks to operate with far more autonomy and less political direction than during the Delors years (see Peterson 1999*a*).[18]

More generally, the Commission remains extremely resource-poor. It must negotiate both a policy agenda and substantive legislative proposals with a diverse array of groups and national actors. Unless it tables proposals which already satisfy a critical mass of affected policy stakeholders, the Commission has little chance of having its initiatives become legislation. Despite exceptions, most EU networks appear to be loosely constituted and densely populated equivalents of Heclo's (1978) 'issue networks'. Most look capable of collective action, let alone responsiveness to political direction, only with great difficulty.

[16] The European Council, or summits of Heads of State and Government, acts as a sort of 'board of directors' for the EU (see Bulmer and Wessels forthcoming). However, it meets for the equivalent of around one working week in any year and is usually more preoccupied with questions of 'high politics'—enlargement, the budget, the Kosovo crisis, and so forth—than with EU legislation *per se*.

[17] An EP-instigated report into Commission management of the EU's budget produced many serious allegations of mismanagement, thus triggering the college of Commissioners' mass resignation (see European Parliament 1999). Ironically, a range of initiatives under the presidency of Jacques Santer had actually improved the management of the Commission since the early 1990s. Moreover, relatively speaking, the Commission remains a clean, high-performance bureaucracy when compared with other administrations in Europe. See Heywood (1997); Peterson (1997; 1999a).

[18] Santer was succeeded by Romano Prodi, the former Italian prime minister. Prodi enjoyed impressive early results in initiating reform of the Commission and accelerating the pace of EU enlargement. However, his proposals for an ambitious round of Treaty reforms in the 2000 intergovernmental conference to prepare the EU for enlargement were essentially rebuffed by European leaders at the December 1999 Helsinki summit.

In particular, many EU networks seem to privilege powerful private or non-governmental actors to an extent that defies accepted notions of democratic accountability and authoritativeness (see Greenwood 1997; Greenwood and Aspinwall 1998). Much EU regulation is highly technical and requires expertise that the Union's institutions lack. We thus find a rather classic case of valued expert knowledge in the hands of private actors which is bargained for control of the policy agenda, which remains, in principle, under the control of public actors. This pattern of exchange relations is usually seen in the literature as characteristic of pluralist systems (see Pappi and Henning 1998: 559).

Yet the EU is hardly a kind of Jeffersonian system of democracy. For one thing, EU governance often features a relatively small number of anointed private—or at least non-governmental—actors occupying a great deal of ostensibly public space. The result is

> political distortion which follows from the very privileged access of these special interests to the E[U] policy process and a lack of balance between public interest and private interests . . . It is significant that some 20 per cent of Commission staff are 'irregulars', [and] far removed from the Weberian model [that] many of these irregulars are being drawn from the private sector. (Wallace 1993: 300)

This distortion, in terms of the classic division of labour between public administration and private agents, is particularly visible in public-private EU partnerships. Prime examples include: aid to non-EU Europe—the PHARE programme; research policy—the Framework programme; and, most notoriously, education and training.[19] The Commission's resource constraints force it to rely very heavily on non-governmental organizations (NGOs) for policy delivery. This dependence is reflected, for example, in the dispersal of more than €1 billion per year in EU funding to NGOs for development and human rights in the less-developed world. The problems of insufficient accountability were highlighted in 1998 in a successful challenge by the United Kingdom of the legal bases for a large number of EU social and development programmes managed by NGOs. In these programmes, as in many others funded by the EU, problems of public control are endemic.

To summarize: the European Union is a remarkably adaptable polity, not least because it relies far more on relatively flexible network structures than on rigid hierarchies. Yet it is built on 'particularly weak forms of broader political accountability' and employs a 'peculiarly obscure

[19] The Leonardo programme, designed to promote cross-border training and educational exchanges, was singled out as the worst case of mismanagement uncovered in the Independent Expert's Report which led to the Santer Commission's resignation in March 1998 (see European Parliament 1999).

process of decision-making' (Wallace 1993: 299). Hyper-pluralism at the systemic level, where a dizzying variety of relatively narrowly-organized interests must be satisfied, or at least appeased, before policy is set, invites meso-corporatism—a policy dialogue with a limited circle of participants—at the sub-systemic level where policies are shaped (see Peterson and Bomberg 1999). In other words, policy networks may play an important role in aggregating interests and identifying clear policy alternatives, thus preventing EU decision-making from seizing up altogether. The downside is that EU networks often lack legitimacy because they are usually engaged in informal, backroom bargaining that is difficult to scrutinize.

Returning to the 'so what?' question, it might be argued that EU policy networks can only set the table. They cannot impose outcomes because the EU is subject to control by democratically elected agents—ministers and members of the EP—who make actual legislative decisions. Veto points are abundant and widely distributed. So why bother about the power of networks?

We should bother because the EU is a remarkably active system of governance. It is often forced to act, quickly and in unison, in the face of the powerful market forces unleashed within the world's largest single capitalist market. When collective action is needed quickly, the natural tendency is to cut deals informally and away from democratic scrutiny within policy networks. Moreover, agreement in and of itself is highly prized in a system where disagreement is viewed as damaging to the European 'project' to create a politically and economically united Europe. Yet the project itself does not command deep public support, nor is it subject to majoritarian democratic controls. To simplify in one phrase the dizzying complexity of EU governance, and the problems of legitimacy to which it gives rise, the Union's Member States have pooled sovereignty but divided accountability (Peterson 1997). The result is governance by networks of actors that must somehow act collectively while remaining accountable only to a narrow 'slice' of the EU body politic. Under these circumstances, many networks face incentives to skirt formal controls, avoid close scrutiny, and present negotiated outcomes as *faits accompli*.

3. Networks and US Governance

Increasingly, governance in the United States is inadequately captured by the basic federal principle. Indeed, networks and their role in US governance encompass far more than the constitutionally designated actors, today more than ever.[20] But the choice of an explicit federal design principle deserves attention, not least because of the purported advantages and disadvantages of networked arrays as a form of 'compound republic' (V. Ostrom 1987).

The US federal arrangement has benefited from the simultaneous authorization of both governmental levels, the design of representative units nationally and regionally—with more representation authorized over time: for instance in the case of the US Senate—and in any given unit considerable transparency of operations. There have been times in the evolution of federalism, US-style, when the costs have seemed unacceptable. Leaving aside issues of slavery, sectionalism, and the civil war, one of the most significant challenges to the design principle occurred in the Progressive Era. Reformers explicitly sought to embrace a blend of accountability, expertise, and transparency by centralizing political institutions and endorsing the superficially attractive notion of a politics-administration dichotomy. The reform effort certainly offered a fundamental challenge to the conventional wisdom regarding the Madisonian logic of checked and limited authority:

> [L]et me say that large powers and unhampered discretion seem to me the indispensable conditions of responsibility . . . There is no danger in power, if only it be not irresponsible. If it be divided, dealt out in shares to many, it is obscured; and if it be obscured, it is made irresponsible. (Wilson 1887: 498)

The founder's principle thus was countered with another. And for the past century, both notions have had their adherents, both designs their partial victories. One result, despite substantial support for decentralization, devolution, and grass-roots institutions, is that the US has seen the development of a kind of 'idea of the nation' (Beer 1982).

Yet the United States at beginning of a new century constitutes a kind of schizophrenic polity, with pressures for substantial decentralization coexisting with strong forces for centralization. A system, or non-system, of 85,000 governments remains extraordinarily decentralized, with waves of rhetoric and reformist efforts to devolve still more. Opinion polls reflect and support such moves. Fiscal projections for the coming decades indicate that, absent major policy changes, and excepting a couple of major national transfer payment programmes like social security, State and local authorities will experience the great bulk of revenue and programmatic growth (see the chapter by Pollack and Donahue in this volume). Indeed,

[20] The point applies equally to the EU, particularly in light of the fact that an enormous amount of the work of the Commission, designated by the EU's Treaties as responsible for ensuring the 'proper functioning and development' of the single market, is now contracted out to private actors.

in this regard the formal array tells only a tiny part of the story. The governing system has broadened greatly to include a huge and growing number of additional actors. By virtually any measure, the further development of network relations outside the sphere of government has rendered governing in the US a mixed, complex, and thoroughly networked affair.

Moreover, the pluralistic American system offers few loci and few visible incentives for consensus formation centrally. Handling regional and local agendas at sub-national levels reduces the decision load and the challenges to legitimacy that could be aimed at Washington. In particular, as sketched in the classic essay by Morton Grodzins, the 'marble cake' allows for considerable adaptation and innovation. It offers innumerable opportunities for access by the many parties at contest. Above all, perhaps, it serves as glue for legitimacy rather than as challenge to it.

But central institutions are hardly insignificant. Pressures for further shifts of influence upward remain intense, in a variety of policy sectors, as a consequence of business regulation, numerous social welfare issues involving questions of equity and redistribution, and environmental issues for which States do not encompass the full impacts. Democratic and Republican administrations both have found it difficult to hold to a devolutionary agenda in the face of pressure from function-based interests to standardise and centralize operations, reduce transaction costs, and solve a series of short-term problems by moving power to Washington. And all this omits mention of the forces of globalization which tend to encourage centralization, especially in sectors where policies are increasingly agreed or shaped internationally.

Similarly, in the development and dynamics of intergovernmental grant programmes over time, a kind of pendulum effect can be seen: pressures toward State or local autonomy and a minimum of red tape being replaced at periodic intervals by efforts to recentralize, impose stringent conditions, establish more explicitly redistributive criteria on the distribution of aid, and focus the impact of centrally established programmes on centrally authorized goals (see Kettl 1988). It is unlikely that even the most recent pressures toward devolution—welfare 'reform', proposals to shift Medicaid to the States, and so forth—will be exempt from reactions aimed at recentralizing some significant aspects of policy. The continuing forces shaping and encouraging both horizontal and vertical interdependence simultaneously, then, enhance the influence of networks of policy-relevant actors. Further, and just as significantly, a set of legitimacy concerns continues to raise questions about the costs of decentralized federalism, US-style. The rest of this section offers a brief assessment, employing the criteria designated in section 2.

It has long been argued that one of the clearest advantages of the networked US setting has been its capacity for *adaptability and innovation*. Scholarship on the diffusion of innovation among the States, for instance, shows how vibrant such processes have often been (Rogers 1995). In this sense, the expansive governance apparatus has withstood innumerable challenges and unforeseen problems with resilience. Today's evidence is clearer than ever that the States have been laboratories of innovation in a wide variety of policy sectors (see, for instance, Anton 1997). These results surely enhance the system's legitimacy.

Nonetheless, even here, on one of US federalism's strongest grounds, a cautionary note must be entered. Networked constellations of actors that foster innovation are often less impressive in institutionalizing action over the longer haul. Long-term authoritative action that is also consistently effective, therefore, is often in short supply. Both theory and evidence suggest that the US version of networked action resembles laboratories, but not factories, of innovation (O'Toole 1997*a*). Institutionalizing adaptive action and attending to the unglamorous follow-up so necessary after the entrepreneurs and reinventers move on to yet another issue is critical but relatively ill-addressed in the US drive to reform and devolve.

As we have suggested, *transparency and accessibility* are other oft-vaunted virtues of American intergovernmental networks. Unlike the EU, the networks of governance in the US offer sets of visible and relatively open decision forums in most of the States and in the nation's capital. Certainly the operations in these settings meet the usual requisites for democratic governance in this regard, even if the States, in particular, exhibit a range of styles and degrees of performance. Meanwhile the expansion of the networked apparatus into the third sector and the world of for-profit corporations in a sense increases access even more. At a minimum, the number of venues at which some stakeholders can have some voice has always been large and is now multiplied further. An attraction of the kind of pluralism, or hyperpluralism, so characteristic of the US system is the opportunities afforded to nearly anyone to find a forum and seek influence. Arguably, governance by networks in the US offers Jeffersonian democracy in full form: the sheer multiplicity of decision points creates plenty of settings at which stakeholders who have not got their way elsewhere can fight on another day.

In another important respect, then, the US version of the network offers an advantage for enhancing legitimacy: nearly endless participation, or cooptation, possibilities. But here too there are negative externalities. As has often been observed, this particular kind of network pattern provides many chances for stopping action but reduces opportunities for accomplishing dramatic new initiatives that can be sustained. The institutional bias in many US networks, that is, favours the status quo on critical issues, especially those that would involve fundamental redistributive and non-incremental matters. While it may be true that in the US issues of class and redistribution are often dispersed through the predominantly liberal political assumptions and cultural norms, nevertheless the arrangement does find itself subject to challenge for its policy bias towards only small changes system-wide.

Furthermore it is clear that as contracting and other forms of privatization and involvement of not-for-profit entities have emerged, the transparency of programme operations has declined (O'Toole 1989). The issue is even more serious in the intergovernmental realm when additional partners are involved. The standard barriers to openness that can be expected to be present when operations cross governmental lines are magnified considerably when additional, non-governmental, actors are added to the mix.

As for *representativeness and consensus-building capacity*, networks can be more or less reflective of core constituencies, depending on their politics and the institutional rules for selecting participants. In the US design, of course, one of the virtues of the structure initially chosen was to head off the effects of faction by requiring large-scale action to be premised upon the crafting of majorities in multiple loci. Republican governance systems that are also networked can thus offer considerable advantage. Yet, as Riker has famously argued, the US federal array permitted locally oppressive majorities to exert domination for extended periods. Federalism, US-style, has therefore operated in the service of racism (Riker 1975), as the policy tilt toward small changes system-wide operated in *de facto* support of oppressive majorities decentrally.

Still, there is clearly no inherent relationship. The chance that networks will support such untoward objectives is dependent on the ability of unrepresentative nodes to operate with longevity and insulation from democratic standards. Thanks to the eventual increase in the salience of racial discrimination among a national majority, the Voting Rights Act of 1965, along with associated successes of the civil rights era, imposed major changes on US federalism. The legislation worked precisely by increasing the odds that regional nodes of governance would develop a strongly representative character. The networked link to national standards made possible an eventually decisive shift. Federalism *per se* seems largely supportive of representativeness in this context and can be seen to entail elements supportive of legitimacy.

A more critical perspective emerges, however, once one moves beyond governmental nodes to the other participants and relations in the expanded network, including firms, not-for-profits, and the like. To put the matter too simply, the core scores reasonably well on representativeness, but in an era of a 'hollow state' it is the periphery that bears watching. There are few reliable data on representativeness in broader networks: another cost arising from insufficient transparency and accessibility. However, the empirical evidence that is available raises serious questions. Privatization, for instance, would seem to include likely sacrifices on ground of representativeness (for one such study, see O'Toole 1989), with potentially important costs in terms of the legitimacy of the network, even if operational performance as well as efficiency criteria are impressively met. Similarly, the networked governance arrangements are mostly devoid of consensus-building capacity, even if one concentrates primarily on intergovernmental arrangements.

And what of *accountability and authoritativeness*? Two significant qualifications need to be kept in mind regarding any assessment on these criteria: the increasingly private and non-profit character of parts of US networks, and the accountability—and transparency—of the system overall when it operates between or among the nodes. More and more, as suggested above, aspects of the US intergovernmental network are being moved or expanded outward to encompass additional parties. Unlike the situation common in the European Union, the forms that these networking arrangements have usually taken do not typically involve private parties operating directly, in effect, as policy-making actors. For the most part, decision makers at policy formation stages are officially designated and explicitly public officials in the US network. There are, it can be added, some exceptions (Heilman and Johnson 1992), and there are likely to be more as increasingly significant segments of several policy actors are more or less permanently contracted out. Among other consequences, the deskilling of the public sector in some core functions renders government gradually dependent on the private actors who have gained the policy-relevant knowledge and operate with a virtual monopoly of context-specific information in dynamic sectors.

The main realm in which the characteristics of the 'hollow state' have appeared in the US system, however, is with regard to programme administration and implementation. With the challenge to openness mentioned earlier comes also a challenge to accountability. Empirical experience in the US system suggests that, unless great care is paid to nuanced accountability questions at the time of contracting, for instance, the involvement of the third sector and businesses in the performance of federal programmes creates confusion and reduces accountability to individual citizens and the polity, as well as to political overseers. There are good reasons, in short, to be concerned about performance on these criteria in the US federal system, particularly when additional parties are involved in programme operations.

In addition, a matter of longstanding concern in the American federal system is the question of accountability and authoritativeness—as well as transparency—when operations cross governmental lines. In her classic study, published decades ago, of intergovernmental influence in the operation of one venerable grant programme between Washington and a State, Martha Derthick (1970: 214) offered the following unsettling observation:

> In addition to the defenses that administrators normally have against legislators, the grant system offers special ones, a result of the diffusion of responsibility it entails. When called to account for controversial actions, administrative agencies at both federal and state levels can escape responsibility *vis-à-vis* their own legislatures by attributing responsibility to a counterpart at the other level. In parallel fashion, each legislature can escape responsibility *vis-à-vis* its own constituents. The ability of all major official actors to deny responsibility very much reduces the chances of successful opposition.

This diffusion of responsibility remains a systemic feature of intergovernmental programme negotiations, revision, and management in the US. Derthick's case is a relatively simple one. Even in that instance, the patterns of influence among the web of actors were so intricate that the participants themselves were often uncertain as to the original stimulus for their own actions or formal initiatives. The issue becomes multiplied substantially in programmes now, since additional parties are frequently added to an implementation chain or an intergovernmental bargaining forum. These networked arrays operate over years, involve complicated and technocratic issues, and are largely shielded from oversight by politically responsible actors and the media. Similarly, with the advent of additional policy instruments during the 1980s and 1990s—including cross-cutting mandates, unfunded mandates, and the accompanying veto-point institutions as narrow overseers—obligations have multiplied without a corresponding expansion of system-wide responsibility or attention to the broader interest. The result is a system that scores relatively low on these important grounds.

4. Comparing US and EU Networks

It should be clear that the requisites of robust legitimacy in the EU as well as the US are partially, but only partially, in place in either system. Rather than reviewing the full set of our assessments, we offer some selected cross-cutting observations. It is helpful to begin with consensus formation, or the ability of networks to aggregate interests and preserve a public space for civic discourse.

The effective aggregation of interests, as a balance to broad representation and access, is a particularly salient feature that can help legitimize networks in governance. The EU networks that 'work' are those able to arrive at something like the 'European interest': a vision of what brings the greatest good to the greatest number of EU citizens. Often, the collective EU interest—in policing the internal market, negotiating on trade with non-EU states, or managing the single currency—is quite different from the sum total of national interests (for the significance of a US version, see Beer 1982). Yet networks which can formulate a vision of what is 'best for Europe' are relatively rare. An important effect of the EU's distinctively multi-level structure is that powers are distributed[21] or 'separated' between horizontal levels. Thus, effective networks must link different layers—the supranational, national and sub-national—in a way that, for example, compensates for the resource-poverty of the EU's supranational institutions, which might themselves perform this function if Member States let them. Yet, as we have seen, powers are also, in practice, divided vertically and quite narrowly between EU policy sectors.

The crucial point is that *only* the EU's Member States are powerful at every horizontal level of decision-making: from the high political level where quasi-constitutional changes are negotiated to the deepest reaches of the sub-systemic level where committees of national officials scrutinize every micro-move the Commission makes (Grande 1996). Only they are powerful in every policy sector. Casting our gaze across the full range of the EU's vertical divisions, we find only a few sectors, such as research or cohesion policy, where the Commission has enough resources to 'buy its own constituency' from a range of non-public actors to support its agenda (see Peterson and Sharp 1998). In all EU policy sectors, scope for the expression and pursuit of national interests is formidable.

Yet the Commission frequently exploits one of the few freedoms it *does* enjoy: its 'virtually free hand in creating new networks' (Marks, Hooghe, and Blank 1996: 359). To be clear, the power of national agents and ubiquity of distinct national interests are palpable at all levels and sectors of EU decision making. But the EU survives, and sometimes thrives, when it spawns networks that transcend its horizontal and vertical divisions and build consensus in support of supranational policy solutions.

If anything, concerns about consensus-building are even stronger in the US, where there are few consensus forming institutions and processes in place. American pluralism in a normative sense typically embraces the notion that the public interest is the vector sum of functional and geographic—not to mention individual—interests. There are few political

[21] Ansell and Weber (1999: 88) argue that national sovereignty in the EU is not, in fact, pooled but rather 'distributed' between multiple levels of governance in a way that naturally invites network governance: 'Each member of the network acts quasi-independently . . . but with the understanding that they are part of a broader enterprise'.

incentives to encourage leaders to adopt another form of collective decision making. The operational force of this lack of coherent aggregation is visible in many features of the intergovernmental system. Consider, for example, the explicitly distributional focus of most grant-in-aid debates, at the expense of substantive problem solving, and the tendency toward coordination deficits (see Scharpf, Reissert, and Schnabel 1976) that often plague US policy sectors. In terms of system design, it may well be that the US can learn valuable lessons from the EU about how to build consensus in the face of enormous diversity.

Similarly, it would seem that protection of public space, or the problem of balancing public and private interests, is a very real one in large networks on both sides of the Atlantic. In the case of the EU, the problem arises from two specific factors: the EU's relatively narrow neo-liberal policy agenda, and the refusal of Member States to give the EU's institutions, particularly the Commission, sufficient resources to carry out their assigned tasks. A similarly liberal agenda has framed the intertwining of private parties in public policy in the US.

These problems arise more generally from what broadly could be termed 'devolution'—specifically, the renationalization of politics in Western Europe and regionalization of politics in the US—together with the denationalization of economies under pressures from globalization. The result is disjunction: economic actors that are politically rootless, but political actors that remain primarily national—in the case of the US, often sub-national—including in terms of economic issues. Given this disjunction, traditional notions of, for example, authoritativeness—the notion that democratically-elected governments should be able to impose direction on policy—seem rather meaningless.

In the absence of authoritativeness, the natural result is often informal bargaining between federal and State agents, along with non-political—often private—actors, over the terms of a policy agenda that cuts across traditional political divisions. Such bargaining is essential for governance to occur at all given the shifts in loyalties and power that we have highlighted. The problem is that it is difficult to see how basic standards of majoritarian democracy can be applied to multi-level governance (Majone 1999; but see also Keohane 1998).

Clearly, we cannot easily legitimize governance by informal networks with formal rules. It is not just formal intergovernmental agendas that matter: so much is handled informally within networks that no amount of regulation or formal institutional design can really solve the legitimacy challenge. Instead, it seems that less conventional methods are more promising: developing monitoring (Nicolaidis 1996) and trust within networks, encouraging the development of a transnational 'civil society'

(Reinicke 1999–2000), creating independent agencies which must explain their actions (Majone 1999), safeguarding against the 'privatization of public space', and so forth. In particular, it seems intuitively clear that trust is a critical element of network governance in both the US and EU, given how it 'lubricates' exchanges within networks and lowers transactions costs (O'Toole 1995; Hindmoor 1998). The challenges to trust, already formidable in both settings, are becoming increasingly daunting as networks disperse ever more: in the US in response to apparently relentless pressures for devolution and in the EU as a consequence of both enlargement and the unending fetish for subsidiarity.

Finally, we should consider the interests of central institutions—European in EU, national in US—in fostering some of the conditions that legitimize network governance. It is impossible not to suspect that such an effort could work against the narrow, short-term, agenda of central institutions—to act quickly, decisively, or authoritatively—in some cases. The most important variables in determining whether governance embraces a long-term policy perspective seem to be network size—the smaller the better—and stability—less disruption, and thus a longer shadow of the future into the present, the better (E. Ostrom 1990). It may be difficult to reconcile small, stable, forward-looking networks with accountability. On the other hand, it may seem naïve to urge those at the centre to pay special attention to legitimacy, or to recommend avoiding the enactment of a central agenda *per se* too quickly or frequently. But in an increasingly networked world, it seems even more naive to cling to the traditional view of 'democracy as largely extraneous to administration' (O'Toole 1997*b*: 444).

5. Conclusion

The central point of our analysis is that both scholars and practitioners face hard choices. In both Europe and America, some of the most important choices are between competing values: 'to choose or prioritize one value over another is not a technical judgement, merely: it is also a judgement requiring moral reasoning, and for this reason, policy analysis represents a form of applied ethics' (Dunn 1994: 4). Federalism by nature is a method for reconciling competing values: strong yet small government, minimum 'federal standards' alongside local discretion, and private sector autonomy with the provision of public goods. Network governance can help reconcile such dilemmas, but often gives rise to new ones about legitimacy, accountability, and transparency.

We have highlighted the many trade-offs involved in governance by networks. Particularly in the complex networks which federalism encourages, the central problem is that 'administrators often must balance technical needs for clear and concentrated program authority with political demands for inclusion and broader influence' (O'Toole 1997*c*: 47). This trade-off, along with others endemic to network governance, is a classic one in some senses. It arises naturally in American federalism, since the 'national interest' must be defined and pursued amidst undying pressures for devolution. The same goes for the quasi-federal EU, in which the 'European interest' must be defined and pursued while respecting subsidiarity. But in balancing these trade-offs, the problems of legitimacy that we have highlighted must be confronted. Particularly in federal systems, output legitimacy is not enough: policies must be judged not *only* according to their results, which may be difficult in any case, for reasons we have explained, to assess. They must be judged on the basis of how many different voices have been heard and heeded as they have been formulated.

There are few simple solutions to the legitimacy problems of network governance, and we have none to offer here. However, our comparative analysis at least highlights the following lines of investigation.

1. On some of our criteria networks in Europe and America clearly differ, and these differences can be instructive for enhancing their legitimacy. For example, EU networks may bear observation and even emulation on grounds of effective consensus formation. By the same token, the features of US networks that promote transparency and accessibility may be worth study by European institutional designers.[22]
2. On other criteria, there are roughly comparable weaknesses in both systems. Both score poorly in terms of accountability and authoritativeness. More specifically, the trend in both polities is towards the broadening and complexifying of networks, leading to the usurping of public space by private actors. These defects are serious ones which are likely to be perennial. They deserve attention from normative theorists and institutional specialists and, in this context, pooled efforts on the part of experts on both sides of the Atlantic.
3. The changed character of public space in the EU and US bears particularly close attention for legitimacy concerns. We know far too little about how to craft and protect such space, how to nurture strong civil societies, and how to shape political discourse—and institutions—that can deal effectively with powerful economic forces given the disjunction between polities and economies that we have noted.

[22] In this context, we note Majone's (1999: 22) call for the EU to adopt the equivalent of the US Administrative Procedure Act, which defines the remit of US agencies and is, in his view, an important source of their procedural and substantive legitimacy.

4. Clearly, part of the effort to ensure that network forms of governance do not suffer from a legitimacy deficit involves focusing on the concept of trust—and possibly social capital—in institutionally large, networked, and complex systems. In particular, these values act to safeguard against the privatization of public space, with its negative implications for legitimacy. The work of a variety of analysts—institutional specialists, game theorists, students of social movements, and others—could be usefully directed to identifying how trust can be nurtured and sustained within network settings.

As our analysis makes clear, governance by network is neither a good nor a bad thing. It may produce either drift or mastery (Lippmann 1914). Perhaps it is to be expected that the focus of academics and practitioners thus far has been with efforts to manage networks to minimise drift and master the problems of modern governance. But it is now time also to master the problem of inadequate accountability.

References

Ansell, C. K. and Weber, S. (1999). 'Organizing International Politics: Sovereignty and Open Systems'. *International Political Science Review*, 20/1: 73–93.

Anton, T. J. (1997). 'New Federalism and Intergovernmental Fiscal Relationships: The Implications for Health Policy'. *Journal of Health Politics, Policy and Law*, 22: 691–720.

Appleby, P. (1949). *Big Democracy*. New York: Knopf.

Beam, D. R., Conlan, T. J., and Walker, D. B. (1983). 'Federalism: The Challenge of Conflicting Theories and Contemporary Practice', in A. W. Finifter (ed.), *Political Science: The State of the Discipline*, Washington, DC: APSA.

Beer, S. H. (1982). 'The Idea of the Nation'. *The New Republic*, 19 and 26 July: 23–9.

Begg, I. and Peterson, J. (1999), 'Editorial Statement', *Journal of Common Market Studies*, 37/2: 1–12.

Börzel, T. (1998). 'Organizing Babylon—On the Different Conceptions of Policy Networks'. *Public Administration*, 76/Summer: 253–73.

Bull, H. (1977). *The Anarchical Society: A Study of Order in World Politics*. New York: Columbia University Press.

Bulmer, S. and Wessels, W. (forthcoming). *The European Council*. London and New York: Palgrave.

Castells, M. (1996). *The Rise of the Network Society*. Oxford and Malden, MA: Blackwell.

Cram, L. (1997). *Policy-making in the EU: Conceptual Lenses and the Integration Process*. London and New York: Routledge.

Derthick, M. (1970). *The Influence of Federal Grants*. Cambridge, MA: Harvard University Press.

Dunn, W. M. (1994). *Public Policy Analysis* (2nd edn). Englewood Cliffs, NJ: Prentice Hall.

European Commission (1997). *Action Plan for the Single Market*. Communication of the Commission to the European Council, CSE (97) 1 final, Brussels, 4 June.

European Parliament (1999). 'Committee of Independent Experts—First Report on Allegations Concerning Fraud, Mismanagement and Nepotism in the European Commission'. Brussels, 15 March.

Grande, E. (1996). 'The State and Interest Groups in a Framework of Multi-Level Decision-Making: The Case of the European Union'. *Journal of European Public Policy*, 3: 318–38.

Grant, C. (1994). *Delors: Inside the House that Jacques Built*. London: Nicholas Brealey.

Greenwood, J. (1997). *Representing Interests in the European Union*. Basingstoke and New York: Macmillan and St Martin's Press.

—— and Aspinwall, M. (eds) (1998). *Collective Action in the European Union*. London: Routledge.

Grønbech-Jensen, C. (1998). 'The Scandinavian Tradition of Open Government and the European Union: Problems of Accountability?'. *Journal of European Public Policy*, 5/1: 185–99.

Hall, T. E. and O'Toole, L. J. Jr. (2000). 'Structures for Policy Implementation: An Analysis of National Legislation, 1965–1966 and 1993–1994'. *Administration and Society* 31: 667–86.

Hanf, K. I. (1994). *The International Context of Environmental Management: From the Negotiating Table to the Shop Floor*. Breukelen, The Netherlands: Nijenrode University Press.

Hayes-Renshaw, F. and Wallace, H. (1997). *The Council of Ministers*. Basingstoke and New York: Macmillan and St Martin's Press.

Heclo, H. (1978). 'Issue Networks and the Executive Establishment', in A. King (ed.), *The New American Political System*. Washington, DC: American Enterprise Institute.

Heilman, J. G. and Johnson, G. W. (1992). *The Politics and Economics of Privatization*. Tuscaloosa: University of Alabama Press.

Heinz, J. P., Laumann, E. O., Nelson, R. L., and Salisbury, R. H. (1993). *The Hollow Core: Private Interests in National Policy Making*. Cambridge, MA, and London: Harvard University Press.

Heywood, P. (ed.) (1997). *Political Corruption*. Oxford and Malden, MA: Blackwell.

Hindmoor, A. (1998). 'Transactions Costs and Policy Network Theory: The Importance of Being Trusted'. *Public Administration*, 76/Spring: 25–43.

Hooghe, L. and Marks, G. (1997). 'Contending Models of Governance in the European Union', in A. W. Cafruny and C. Lankowski (eds), *Europe's Ambiguous Unity*. Boulder and London: Lynne Rienner.

Hull, R. (1993). 'Lobbying Brussels: A View from Within', in S. Mazey and J. Richardson (eds), *Lobbying in the European Community*. Oxford and New York: Oxford University Press.

Keohane, R. (1998). 'International Institutions: Can Interdependence Work?'. *Foreign Policy*, 110/Spring: 82–96.

——and Hoffmann, S. (1991). 'Institutional Change in Europe in the 1980s', in R. O. Keohane and S. Hoffmann (eds), *The New European Community: Decisionmaking and Institutional Change*. Boulder: Westview Press.

Kettl, D. F. (1988). *Government by Proxy: Managing Federal Programs*. Washington, DC: CQ Press.

——(1990). 'The Perils—and Prospects—of Public Administration'. *Public Administration Review*, 50/4: 411–19.

——(1993). 'Searching for Clues About Public Management: Slicing the Onion in Different Ways', in B. Bozeman (ed.), *Public Management: The State of the Art*. San Francisco: Jossey-Bass.

Klijn, E.-H. (1996). 'Analyzing and Managing Policy Processes in Complex Networks: A Theoretical Examination of the Concept Policy Network and its Problems'. *Administration and Society*, 28/1: 90–119.

LaPorte, T. R. and Metlay, D. S. (1996). 'Hazards and Institutional Trustworthiness: Facing a Deficit of Trust'. *Public Administration Review*, 56: 341–7.

Light, P. C. (1995). *Thickening Government: Federal Hierarchy and the Diffusion of Accountability*. Washington, DC: Brookings Institution.

Lippmann, W. (1914). *Drift and Mastery*. New York: Mitchell Kennerley.

Lord, C. (1998). *Democracy in the European Union*. Sheffield: Sheffield Academic Press.

Lowi, T. (1985). 'The State in Politics: The Relation Between Policy and Administration', in R. G. Noll (ed.), *Regulatory Policy and the Social Sciences*. Berkeley and Los Angeles: University of California Press.

McCubbins, M., Noll, R. G., and Weingast, B. R. (1987). 'Administrative Procedures as Instruments of Political Control'. *Journal of Law, Economics, and Organization*, 3: 243–77.

McNamara, K. R. (1998). *The Currency of Ideas: Monetary Politics in the European Union*. Ithaca, NY: Cornell University Press.

Majone, G. (1999). 'The Regulatory State and its Legitimacy Problems'. *West European Politics*, 22/1: 1–24.

Marks, G., Hooghe, L., and Blank, K. (1996). 'European Integration from the 1980s: State-Centric v. Multi-Level Governance'. *Journal of Common Market Studies*, 34: 341–78.

Mayntz, R., and Scharpf, F. W. (1975). *Policy-making in the German Federal Bureaucracy*. Amsterdam: Elsevier.

——(1995). 'Steuerung und Selbstorganisation in staatsnahen Sektoren', in R. Mayntz and F. W. Scharpf (eds), *Gesellschaftliche Selbstregulierung und politische Steuerung*. Frankfurt and New York: Campus.

Mazey, S. (1998). 'The European Union and Women's Rights: From the Europeanization of National Agendas to the Nationalization of a European Agenda?'. *Journal of European Public Policy*, 5/1: 131–52.

Milward, A. (1992). *The European Rescue of the Nation-State*. London: Routledge.

Milward, H. B., Provan, K. G., and Else, B. A. (1993). 'What Does the "Hollow

State" Look Like?', in B. Bozeman (ed.), *Public Management: The State of the Art*. San Francisco: Jossey-Bass.

Monnet, J. (1978). *Memoirs*. London: Collins.

Moravcsik, A. (1998). *The Choice for Europe*. Ithaca, NY: Cornell University Press.

Nicolaidis, K. (1996). 'Mutual Recognition of Regulatory Regimes: Some Lessons and Prospects', in *Regulatory Reform and International Market Openness*. OECD Publications. Also in Harvard Jean Monnet Working Paper Series, 1997: http://www.eiop.or.at/erpa/harvard.htm.

Nugent, N. (1999). *The Government and Politics of the European Union* (4th edn). Basingstoke and New York: Macmillan and St Martins' Press.

Nunan, F. (1999). 'Policy Network Transformation: The Implementation of the EC Directive on Packaging and Packaging Waste'. *Public Administration*, 77/3: 621–38.

Osborne, D. and Gaebler, T. (1992). *Reinventing Government: How the Entrepreneurial Spirit is Transforming the Public Sector*. Reading, MA: Addison-Wesley.

Ostrom, E. (1990). *Governing the Commons*. Cambridge: Cambridge University Press.

Ostrom, V. (1987). *The Political Theory of a Compound Republic: Designing the American Experiment*. Lincoln: University of Nebraska Press.

O'Toole, L. J. (1989). 'Goal Multiplicity in the Implementation Setting: Subtle Impacts and the Case of Wastewater Treatment Privatization'. *Policy Studies Journal*, 18/1: 3–22.

——(1995). 'Rational Choice and Policy Implementation: Implications for Interorganizational Network Management'. *American Review of Public Administration*, 25/1: 43–57.

——(1997*a*). 'Implementing Public Innovations in Network Settings'. *Administration and Society*, 29/2: 115–38.

——(1997*b*). 'The Implications for Democracy in a Networked Bureaucratic World'. *Journal of Public Administration Research and Theory*, 7: 443–59.

——(1997*c*). 'Treating Networks Seriously: Practical and Research-Based Agendas in Public Administration'. *Public Administration Review*, 57/1: 45–52.

——(1998). *Institutions, Policy and Outputs for Acidification: The Case of Hungary*. Aldershot, UK: Ashgate.

——(ed.) (2000). *American Integovernmental Relations: Foundations, Perspectives and Issues* (3rd edn). Washington, DC: CQ Press.

——and Montjoy, R. S. (1984). 'Interorganizational Policy Implementation: A Theoretical Perspective'. *Public Administration Review*, 44: 491–503.

Pappi, F. U. and Henning, H. C. A. (1998). 'Policy Networks: More than a Metaphor?'. *Journal of Theoretical Politics*, 10: 553–75.

Peterson, J. (1994). 'Subsidiarity: A Definition to Suit Any Vision?'. *Parliamentary Affairs*, 47/1: 116–32.

——(1995*a*). 'Decision-Making in the European Union: Towards a Framework for Analysis'. *Journal of European Public Policy*, 2/1: 69–93.

——(1995*b*). 'Playing the Transparency Game: Policy-making and Consultation in the European Commission'. *Public Administration*, 73/3: 473–92.
——(1997). 'The European Union: Pooled Sovereignty, Divided Accountability', in P. Heywood (ed.), *Political Corruption*. Oxford and Malden, MA: Blackwell.
——(1999*a*). 'The Santer Era: The European Commission in Historical, Theoretical and Normative Perspective'. *Journal of European Public Policy*, 6/1: 46–65.
——(1999*b*). 'Sovereignty and Interdependence', in A. Gamble, I. Holliday and G. Parry (eds), *Fundamentals in British Politics*, Basingstoke and New York: Macmillan and St Martin's Press.
——and Bomberg, E. (1999). *Decision-Making in the European Union*. London and New York: Macmillan and St Martin's Press.
——and Sharp, M. (1998). *Technology Policy in the European Union*. London and New York: Macmillan and St Martin's Press.
Pollack, M. (1997). 'Representing Diffuse Interests in EC Policy-Making'. *Journal of European Public Policy*, 4: 572–90.
Pressman, J. and Wildavsky, A. (1984). *Implementation* (3rd edn). Berkeley: University of California Press.
Reinicke, W. H. (1999–2000). 'The Other World Wide Web: Global Public Policy Networks'. *Foreign Policy*, Winter: 44–57.
Rhodes, R. A. W. (1998). *Understanding Governance: Policy Networks, Governance, Reflexivity and Accountability*. Buckingham: Open University Press.
——, Bache, I., and George, S. (1996). 'Policy Networks and Policy Making in the EU: A Critical Appraisal', in L. Hooghe (ed.), *Cohesion Policy and European Integration*. Oxford: Oxford University Press.
Riker, W. H. (1975). 'Federalism', in F. I. Greenstein and N. W. Polsby (eds), *Handbook of Political Science Volume 5: Governmental Institutions and Processes*. Reading, MA: Addison-Wesley.
Rittel, H. W. J. and Weber, M. (1973). 'Dilemmas in a General Theory of Planning'. *Policy Sciences*, 4/June: 155–69.
Rogers, E. M. (1995). *Diffusion of Innovations* (4th edn). New York: Free Press.
Ross, G. (1995). *Jacques Delors and European Integration*. New York and London: Polity Press.
Scharpf, F. W. (1993). 'Coordination in Hierarchies and Networks', in F. Scharpf (ed.), *Games in Hierarchies and Networks*. Frankfurt am Main: Campus Verlag.
——(1996). *Games Real Actors Can Play*. London: Westview.
——(1997). 'Introduction: The Problem-Solving Capacity of Multi-level Governance'. *Journal of European Public Policy*, 4/4: 520–38.
——(1999). *Governing in Europe: Effective and Democratic?* Oxford and New York: Oxford University Press.
——, Reissert, B., and Schnabel, F. (1976). *Politikverflechtung: Theorie und Empirie des kooperativen Föderalismus in der Bundesrepublik*. Kronberg: Scriptor.
Slaughter, A. M. (1997). 'The Real New World Order'. *Foreign Affairs*, 76/5: 183–97.

Van Kersbergen, K. and Verbeek, B. (1994). 'The Politics of Subsidiarity in the European Union'. *Journal of Common Market Studies*, 32/2: 215–36.

Wallace, H. (1993). 'European Governance in Turbulent Times'. *Journal of Common Market Studies*, 31/3: 293–303.

——(1996). 'The Institutions of the EU: Experience and Experiments', in H. Wallace and W. Wallace (eds), *Policy Making in the European Union* (3rd edn). Oxford and New York: Oxford University Press.

——(1997). 'Introduction', in H. Wallace and A. Young (eds), *Participation and Policy-Making in the European Union*. Oxford: Clarendon Press.

Weber, M. (1946). 'Bureaucracy', in H. H. Gerth and C.W. Mills (eds), *Max Weber: Essays in Sociology*. Oxford and New York: Oxford University Press.

Wildavsky, A. (1979). *The Art and Craft of Policy Analysis*. Basingstoke: Macmillan.

Wilson, W. (1887). 'The Study of Administration'. *Political Science Quarterly*, 2/2: 197–222 (reprinted in 1941: *Political Science Quarterly*, 56/4: 481–506).

12

Federalism and State Governance in the European Union and the United States: An Institutional Perspective

VIVIEN SCHMIDT

The European Union is by no means a federal state like the United States of America. And yet in its institutional structures and policy-making processes it bears more resemblance to the United States than to any other political system, let alone to any of its Member States. Like the US, its institutional structures exhibit both a vertical division of powers between central and sub-national units and a horizontal division of powers between executive, legislature, and judiciary. But there is much less vertical division in the EU than in the US, given the greater independent powers of the EU's Member States and their greater control over the central governing apparatus. There is also less horizontal division, given the 'dynamic confusion of powers' between the Council of Ministers, the European Parliament, the European Union Commission, and the European Court of Justice (ECJ) in the EU. Similarly, moreover, as in the US, the EU's policy-making processes are pluralist in their openness to interest groups in the formulation process and regulatory in their implementation. But the EU is somewhat less open to interest influence in formulation, given the gate-keeping role of its civil servants, and more delegatory in implementation, given the role of Member States in transposing and administering EU directives.

Whatever the differences between the EU and the US, these pale by comparison with the differences between the EU and its Member States. These differences are more than simply academic, since the emerging

This chapter offers a theoretical discussion which expands on arguments made in Vivien A. Schmidt, 'European Integration and Democracy: The Differences among Member States', *Journal of European Public Policy*, 4/1 (1997), 128–45; Vivien A. Schmidt, 'National Patterns of Governance under Siege: The Impact of European Integration', in Beate Kohler-Koch (ed.), *The Transformation of Governance in the European Union* (London: Routledge, 1998); and Vivien A. Schmidt, 'European "Federalism" and its Encroachments on National Institutions', *Publius*, 29/1 (1999), 19–44.

European governance system, with its quasi-federal institutional structures and quasi-pluralist policy-making processes, has required institutional adaptation by all Member States, although more so for some Member States than for others. This is because of differences among Member States' institutional structures that affect which branches or units of government have what sorts of power over which kinds of decisions and in policy-making processes that allow access and influence to different actors at different stages of the process and enforce decisions in different ways. As such, the EU's quasi-federal institutional structures have had a greater impact on Member States with unitary institutional structures, by altering the traditional balance of powers among branches and levels of government, than on those with federal institutional structures, where the traditional balance of powers has been largely maintained. Moreover, the EU's quasi-pluralist policy-making processes have impinged more on Member States with statist policy-making processes, by diminishing state autonomy in formulation and flexibility in implementation, than those with corporatist ones, because they have been more able to maintain their flexibility in implementation. And this has in turn raised greater questions for democratic legitimacy and accountability in unitary, statist polities than in federal, corporatist ones.

Thus, this chapter has two interrelated arguments: (1) that the EU has quasi-federal institutional structures and quasi-pluralist policy-making processes which in many ways resemble those of the United States; and (2) that although the EU imposes general adaptational pressures on all Member States' institutions, it nevertheless has a differential impact on Member States depending upon whether they are unitary or federal in structure and whether they are statist or corporatist in processes.

1. The Institutional Structures of the European Union

The EU's governance structure is difficult to define, since it conforms to neither of the traditional forms of national institutional structures, whether unitary or federal, although it is closer to the latter.[1] Like most

[1] There is a growing literature on the federal characteristics of the European Community/European Union and its similarities with other federal systems. See, for example, Fritz Scharpf, 'The Joint Decision Trap: Lessons from German Federalism and European Integration', *Public Administration*, 66 (1988), 239–78; Alberta Sbragia, 'The European Community: A Balancing Act', *Publius*, 23 (Summer 1993), 23–38; Arthur B. Gunlicks (ed.), 'Federalism and Intergovernmental Relations in West Germany: A Fortieth Year Appraisal', *Publius*, 19/4 (1989); Fritz Scharpf, 'Community and Autonomy: Multi-Level Policy-making in the European Union', *Journal of European Public Policy*, 1 (1994), 219–42; and Daniel Wincott, 'Federalism and the European Union: The Scope and Limits of the Treaty of Maastricht', *International Political Science Review*, 17 (1996), 403–15.

federal systems, the EU's institutional structures exhibit both a vertical division of powers between central and lower level units and a horizontal division of powers between executive, legislature, and judiciary. In the EU, however, there is much less vertical division given the greater independent powers of the EU's Member States and their greater control over the central governing apparatus; and there is also less horizontal division, given the 'dynamic confusion of powers' between the Council of Ministers, the European Parliament, the European Union Commission, and the ECJ in the EU. To understand the differences fully, however, it is first necessary to consider national institutional structures, both federal and unitary.

Federalism is ordinarily defined as a system with a formally established, vertical division of power such that the central governing body incorporates sub-national units in its decision procedures on a constitutionally entrenched basis.[2] The unitary state, by contrast, typically has no constitutionally guaranteed, vertical division of power, and the centre has formal control over the periphery of sub-national units which have at best limited legislative powers, even though they may have substantial autonomy based on national legislation or informal practice. Given these definitions, the EU clearly has nothing in common with the unitary state. It is weak in central control, with the 'periphery' of Member States also the ultimate central authority in the EU through the Council of Ministers and the European Council. At best, therefore, the EU could be described as a collection of unitary states acting in supranational concert, and which therefore more closely resembles a confederacy, as 'state-centric', intergovernmentalist international relations theorists argue. [3] However, to depict EU decision-making as a confederacy in which 'States', represented by State executives, are the primary movers in the EU does little to account for the multifarious ways in which institutional and other actors at EU, national, and sub-national levels interrelate, and which make the institutional structure of the EU more akin to a federal system[4]

[2] Preston King, *Federalism and Federation* (London: Croom Helm, 1982), 77.

[3] 'State-centric' approaches include those of Stanley Hoffmann, 'Obstinate or Obsolete? The Fate of the Nation State and the Case of Western Europe', *Daedalus*, 95 (1966), 892–908; Paul Taylor, 'The European Community and the State: Assumptions, Theories and Propositions', *Review of International Studies*, 17 (1991), 109–25; Andrew Moravscik, 'Negotiating the Single European Act: National Interests and Conventional Statecraft in the European Community', *International Organization*, 45 (1991), 651–88; Alan Milward, *The European Rescue of the Nation-State* (Berkeley: University of California Press, 1992).

[4] The EU has been variously described as a 'federal union': J. Pinder, *European Community: The Building of a Union* (Oxford: Oxford University Press, 1994); a quasi-state: William Wallace, 'Government without Statehood', in H. Wallace and W. Wallace (eds), *Policy-making in the European Union* (Oxford: Oxford University Press, 1996); 'co-operative federalism': Wolfgang Wessels, 'Administrative Interaction', in William Wallace (ed.), *The Dynamics of European Integration* (London: Pinter, 1990); 'cooperative federalism without

characterized by 'multi-level governance'[5] than any supranational confederation of States—except when it comes to the negotiation of the major EU treaties.

But although most akin to a federal system, the EU is its own particular brand of federalism, and not as close as one might assume to the federalism of the United States. Germany is perhaps a more apt comparison.[6] In Germany as in Europe, policy-making effectiveness depends upon negotiations among politically autonomous governments. But in Germany, the federal government has political and fiscal resources to impose its will in ways that the European Commission does not, and can depend upon a shared national politics and public opinion; viable political parties to balance out state power; and a high degree of economic and cultural homogeneity, none of which exists in Europe at large.[7] For Europe, in fact, democratic legitimacy remains at issue in a way it does not in national federal systems because of the heterogeneity of populations with little common sense of European identity, let alone a European 'politics', a European party system, or a European public opinion.[8]

Although not part of the definition of federalism, which limits itself to the vertical division of power, the horizontal division of power, commonly known as the 'separation of powers', is also a characteristic of most federal systems, whether the United States, Canada, or Germany. What this means is that the federal executive has relatively little autonomy given a legislature and judiciary each with its own independent authority. This is in contrast to unitary states such as France and Britain, where the centralization of power at the national level also gives the executive a great deal of autonomy, with the legislature and judiciary largely subordinated to it. But it is also in contrast to the EU, where instead of the clearly defined, constitutionally-fixed and formally unchanging separation of

a state': Yves Mény, Pierre Muller, and Jean-Louis Quermonne, 'Introduction', in *Adjusting to Europe: The Impact of the European Union on National Institutions and Policies* (London: Routledge, 1996).

[5] On multi-level governance, see G. Marks, L. Hooghe, K. Blank, 'European Integration since the 1980s: State-Centric versus Multi-Level Governance', *Journal of Common Market Studies*, 34 (1996), 341–78; on governance networks, see Beate Kohler-Koch, 'Catching up with Change: The Transformation of Governance in the European Union', *Journal of European Public Policy*, 3/3 (1996), [PAGES].

[6] See Alberta Sbragia, 'Thinking about the European Future: The Uses of Comparison', in A. Sbragia (ed.), *Europolitics: Institutions and Policymaking in the 'New' European Community* (Washington, DC: Brookings Institution), 1992; Gunlicks (ed.), 'Federalism and Intergovernmental Relations in West Germany: A Fortieth Year Appraisal'; Scharpf, 'Community and Autonomy'.

[7] Scharpf, 'Community and Autonomy', 221–2.

[8] Dieter Grimm, 'Does Europe need a Constitution?', in Peter Gowan and Perry Anderson (eds), *The Question of Europe* (London: Verso, 1997).

powers between executive, legislative, and judicial branches of government, as found in the US or German federal systems, the EU exhibits a 'dynamic confusion of powers'. This confusion involves not only the lack of traditional separation among the various EU institutions but also the mixing up of their very roles. The legislative function is more the domain of the Council of Ministers—which could be taken for the executive given that it is made up of national executives—than of the directly-elected legislature, the European Parliament, although it been increasing in legislative powers in recent years. The executive function is more the purview of the bureaucracy, the EU Commission, which has powers of initiation and implementation, than of the seeming executive, the Council of Ministers, to which it reports; and the judicial function, although the only one performed by the expected institution, the ECJ, encroaches on the executive and the legislative functions through the judiciary's activism.[9]

This confusion of powers in the EU causes problems with regard to traditional understandings of democratic accountability that go way beyond the problems of national federal or unitary systems. Compared with other federal systems, where the balance of powers generally serves as a check on different branches of government and a guarantee of democratic accountability, the confusion of powers in the EU means that it has fewer checks on its different institutions or guarantees of accountability. And these only add to the problems of democratic legitimacy typically referred to as the EU's 'democratic deficit', given a directly elected parliament which, unlike in most federal systems, is the weakest of the three branches.

Although the increasing powers of the European Parliament with regard to budgetary matters, co-decision, and most recently veto over appointments to the Commission have gone some way to enabling it to become the locus of democratic accountability, the institutional structure which gives the unelected members of the Commission powers of initiation and formulation and the nationally-elected members of the Council of Ministers powers of approval ensures that, short of major institutional restructuring, the problems of democratic legitimacy will remain. Moreover, even if one were to argue that the Council of Ministers, as the representative of the nationally elected executive and also involved in a variety of ways in the legislative process, provides some modicum of intergovernmental democratic legitimacy, it adds to the problems of democratic accountability. These result not only from the lack of transparency of the Council of Ministers, given secrecy rules, but also the lack of significant democratic control of the Council from either the European

[9] See Schmidt, 'European Integration and Democracy.'

Parliament or national parliaments.[10] The Commission also suffers from problems of accountability, although here the issues are related more to questions of corruption and cronyism, as the report from the Parliamentary Commission which led to the resignation of the Commission attests.

One way out of these problems, of course, is institutional reform. But how? Any solution short of instituting a truly federal system, which does not seem to be on the cards, would be likely to create other problems of legitimacy or accountability of one sort or another. For example, if the European Parliament were to gain approval powers beyond its current co-decision ones, this would decrease Member-State power as represented in the Council of Ministers, and thereby undermine the traditional intergovernmental bases of EU legitimacy. If on top of this the Commission were to be directly elected, or even only elected by Parliament from among its members, this would even further reduce the powers of the Council of Ministers and the traditional grounds of legitimacy. This would be acceptable, of course, if the European Parliament concomitantly gained in representative legitimacy, that is, if it were generally accepted as speaking for European citizens. This, however, is still a long way away, given nationally based EP elections that often focus on national rather than European issues, and the still-national basis of citizens' views of democratic representation and legitimacy.

Most importantly, however, any such increases in the powers of the European Parliament, or other institutional structures, would also serve to reduce the powers of national institutional structures. And whatever the problems for legitimacy and accountability at the EU level, they are nothing compared with the problems generated at the national level by the increasing encroachment of EU powers on national decision-making institutions.

2. The Impact of EU Institutional Structures on Member States

In the course of European integration, the EEC/EC/EU's institutional structures have increasingly taken precedence over the national, diminishing national executives' autonomy in national policy-making; usurping national parliamentary powers of initiative and/or review; subordinating national judicial authority to the ECJ; and reducing sub-national units' often newly-gained autonomy. In this, however, the European Union's

[10] See Juliet Lodge, 'Transparency and Democratic Legitimacy', *Journal of Common Market Studies*, 32/3 (1994), [PAGES].

quasi-federal institutional structure has been more disruptive to unitary Member States, where the EU has served to undermine traditional executive autonomy and to diminish legislative power while promoting national court independence and sub-national autonomy, than to federal Member States, which have largely maintained the balance between executive, legislature, and judiciary as well as between centre and periphery. As a result, unitary Member States have had to confront greater problems with regard to democratic accountability and legitimacy than federal Member States.

In the exercise of its powers, the quasi-federal EU has not only reduced the powers of national level institutions generally, it has also generally affected the balance of powers between executive, legislature, and judiciary and diminished central control over sub-national units. The EU has, above all else, reduced the traditional powers of Member States' legislatures, as EU institutions have increasingly taken these over in a wide variety of areas. National legislatures' relative powers next to national executives have also concomitantly diminished, given the executives' role in transnational policy-making and the parliaments' lack of authoritative power over national executives' policy decisions made in the Council of Ministers.[11] This loss in relative power to the executive is only increased by the fact that in domains covered by EU decision-making, their contribution to government is less and less one of initiation and deliberation and more and more solely one of translating into national law EU directives elaborated in the EU Commission and approved by national executives in the Council.

While national parliaments have lost power in consequence of the EU, some have argued that national executives have gained with respect not just to the national legislature but also societal interests through the 'strengthening of the state'.[12] But although one might be able to claim this for the most heroic of policies, such as Treaty negotiations, one cannot for most other cases, which is the bulk of EU decision-making. This is because what the state—meaning the executive—may gain in power over national legislatures and some national actors, it loses in autonomy with respect to supranational actors—not only other governmental actors, as one of 15 in the Council of Ministers, but also non-governmental actors that have increasing access to EU decision-making—and in control over domestic institutional actors—given the growing powers of the judiciary and independence of sub-national actors—as well as over the aggregation of

[11] Philip Norton (ed.), *National Parliaments and the European Union* (London: Frank Cass, 1996).

[12] Milward, *The European Rescue of the Nation State*; Andrew Moravcsik, 'Preferences and Power in the European Community: A Liberal Intergovernmentalist Approach', *Journal of Common Market Studies*, 31 (1993), 473–524.

domestic interests, in particular those domestic actors with access to the EU policy-making process.[13]

The loss of control by the executive over other governmental actors as a result of EU institutional structures is most apparent with regard to the judiciary. The development of the ECJ in particular has contributed to the courts' growing powers even as it has subordinated national court systems generally to itself. For in expanding its own powers, the ECJ has also served to expand those of national courts, especially the lower courts through their ability to seek 'authoritative guidance' from the ECJ and thereby to change national law while circumventing their own national judicial hierarchy.[14] Sub-national authorities, too, have gained in independence with respect to the executive, although this is probably more related to internal, decentralizing reforms that diminished central control over the periphery than to increasing European access, through the Committee of the Regions, and resources, through the structural funds and other programmes. But at the same time that European integration has added to sub-national authorities' growing independence, it has also diminished their autonomy, in particular with regard to EU rules governing a whole range of areas that regions must implement.

What is more, the significance of such gains and losses in autonomy, power, independence, or control differ in unitary states from federal states. In federal states, where the executive has never had much autonomy while the legislature and judiciary already benefit from a constitutionally-fixed separation of powers and sub-national units enjoy constitutionally-guaranteed autonomy, EU incursions on national powers have not significantly altered the balance of powers, and therefore the relative strength or weakness of the executive, although this did demand some internal readjustments. By contrast, in unitary states, where power is mostly concentrated in the executive which predominates over legislature and judiciary as well as over sub-national units, the traditional balance of power has been altered in consequence of the loss of executive autonomy and the increasing separation of powers, thereby actually weakening the executive. Not only does the EU not generally strengthen the state, then, it actually reduces the relative 'strength' of the state much more in unitary states than in federal states.

[13] For more detailed arguments, see Schmidt, 'European "Federalism" and its Encroachments'.

[14] Anne-Marie Burley and Walter Mattli, 'Europe before the Court: A Political Theory of Legal Integration', *International Organization*, 47 (1993), 41–76; J. H. H.Weiler, 'A Quiet Revolution: The European Court of Justice and its Interlocutors', *Comparative Political Studies*, 26/4 (1994): 510–34.

For a unitary state such as France, the notion of the strengthening of the state is an especially hollow concept. There is no doubt that the traditionally weak legislature, which never had much independent power as long as the government had a solid majority, has become even weaker. But to call this a strengthening of the state carries little weight, given how all-powerful—at least with regard to the legislature—the executive has traditionally been. More to the point is the fact that the formerly seemingly all-powerful executive has lost its virtual monopoly in policy-making, given not only the increasing importance of the EU level in policy formulation but also the growing independence at the national level of the traditionally subordinated judiciary and sub-national authorities.[15] In fact, this only adds to internal processes related to the rise of judicial powers and sub-national governments.

The strengthening of the state is also a hollow concept for Britain. The traditionally strong British executive has lost autonomy with regard to EU level policy-making, although comparatively less than in France because of its opt-outs from various EU policies under Prime Ministers Thatcher and Major. At the national level, moreover, the executive's gains over a Parliament which it has always controlled as long it maintained a solid majority and party discipline are no more significant than in France, even though the British Parliament has always had a more powerful role than the French in terms of oversight and representation of public concerns. What is more, the traditionally more independent British judiciary has simply become more so. Only over sub-national authorities has the executive substantially increased its control—in the Thatcher years, although devolution is now beginning under Prime Minister Blair.

Finally, the strengthening of the state is an equally hollow concept for federal states such as Germany, albeit for different reasons. Not only has the federal state never had much autonomy to begin with, given the separate powers of the judiciary, legislature, and sub-national units, but the increases in executive power as a result of the EU have been countered by Parliament-led adjustments that served to reinforce its own powers and concomitantly those of the *Länder*, which had eroded as a result of European integration.[16]

The differential effects of the EU on unitary as opposed to federal states also have differing consequences for questions of democratic legitimacy

[15] See Vivien Schmidt, 'Loosening the Ties that Bind: The Impact of European Integration on French Government and Its Relationship to Business', *Journal of Common Market Studies*, 34 (1996), 223–54.

[16] See Thomas Saalfeld, 'The German Houses of Parliament and European Legislation', in Philip Norton (ed.), *National Parliaments and the European Union* (London: Frank Cass, 1996).

and accountability. It stands to reason that federal states have had fewer lasting problems with democratic legitimacy and accountability than unitary states as a result of the expansion in the powers of the EU, since they have readjusted the relative powers of the executive and legislature to ensure against any permanent shift in power balance. But this is only part of the explanation. Because federal states such as Germany operate with notions of 'compounded representation' similar to those of the EU,[17] where no one institutional body has control over the decision-making process and different bodies share responsibility for its outcome, they are likely to adjust more readily to having an added level of shared decision-making with no clear lines of responsibility—once they have accepted the legitimacy of that added level, of course.

By contrast, the adjustment is likely to be much harder for unitary states such as France and Britain, which operate with more simple notions of representation, where the executive is expected to be in control over the decision-making process and solely responsible for its outcome, whether it is the French Jacobin notion of the executive as representative of the French nation, one and indivisible, or the British notion of parliamentary sovereignty as embodied in the executive. Add to this the fact that the executive has lost significant control, whether because of its loss of autonomy with respect to the EU or the changes in the balance of power regarding the judiciary and sub-national units, and the legitimacy and accountability problems for unitary states can be seen as much more significant than for federal states. Here, even if the legitimacy of the EU level has been accepted, individual EU level decisions which challenge the national executive's assumed control can always lead to questions about the executive's representation of the nation and, therefore, national democratic legitimacy.

Complicating this even further, however, are the differing patterns of policy-making between the EU level and the national. And here, although EU policy-making processes in some cases alleviate problems of legitimacy resulting from the EU institutional structure, they also add to the legitimacy problems at the national level.

[17] On compounded representation, see Joanne Brzinski, Thomas D. Lancaster, and Christian Tuschhoff, 'Federalism and Compounded Representation in Western Europe', paper prepared for presentation at the First Workshop of the 'Federalism and Compounded Representation' project, Emory University, Atlanta GA., 3–6 October 1997.

3. EU Policy-making Processes

European integration has generated change not only in Member-State institutional structures but also in their policy-making processes. And just as European institutions do not fit any national model of institutional arrangement, although they are closest to the federal, so European policy-making processes do not fit any national model of policy-making.[18] They do generally come closest to the pluralism of the federal United States, however, and have been called a model of 'transnational pluralism'.[19] Like the US, the EU's pluralist policy-making processes tend to be open to interest group influence in the formulation process and regulatory in their implementation, where the rules are to be applied without exception. But the EU is somewhat less open to interest influence in formulation; more cooperative in its interrelationships; more delegatory in implementation; and less political or driven by money than the US.

To begin with, the EU policy formulation process is more insulated from the pressures of undue influence and less vulnerable to the politics of party or money, given an EU Commission with apolitical EU civil servants rather than partisan legislators and their staffs, and with a greater emphasis on the technical than the political in decision-making.[20] For national politicians and civil servants, whether American or European, by contrast, the policy along with its justification may often sacrifice efficiency for more political goals. The EU Commission also suffers less from the problems of agency capture or 'iron triangles' that are found in the US pluralist process, given the wide range of interests and actors involved in any given policy initiative which enable it to refuse interest groups' unwanted or unrealizable claims.[21] This doesn't entirely guard against the undue influence of industry experts, of course, and the dangers of quasi-clientelistic relationships.[22] But since Commission officials are not elected

[18] See Sonia Mazey and Jeremy Richardson, 'EU Policy-making: A Garbage Can or an Anticipatory and Consensual Policy Style?', in Mény *et al.* (eds), *Adjusting to Europe*, 53.

[19] Wolfgang Streeck and Philippe Schmitter, 'From National Corporatism to Transnational Pluralism: Organized Interests in the Single European Market', *Politics and Society*, 19 (1991), 133–64. In the social policy arena, however, one could argue that the model is closer to corporatism. See Gerda Falkner, 'Social Policy in the EU', in Kohler-Koch (ed.), *The Transformation of Governance in the European Union*.

[20] Giandomenico Majone, 'When does Policy Deliberation Matter?', *Politische Veirteljahresstiftung* (Autumn 1993), 1.

[21] Edgar Grande, 'The State and Interest Groups in a Framework of Multi-Level Decision-Making: The Case of the European Union', *Journal of European Public Policy*, 3 (1996), at 329; Sonia Mazey and Jeremy Richardson, 'Introduction', in Sonia Mazey and Jeremy Richardson (eds), *Lobbying in the European Community* (Oxford: Oxford University Press, 1993).

[22] Mazey and Richardson, 'Introduction', 21–2.

politicians who have electoral coffers to fill, the dangers are lesser—although cronyism and favouritism remain a problem, albeit on a lesser scale, given that highest-level Commission officials are often former national elected politicians with debts to repay.

Politics, of course, does play a role in the EU. This is most evident in the Council of Ministers. But in the Council it is generally the politics of national interest rather than party or money per se. And the arguments themselves are more often than not couched in technical terms, even if they serve as a cover for more political motivations. Only in the European Parliament could one talk about the politics of party. But here, the parties are still so underdeveloped and the Parliament itself so lacking in power by comparison with the Council or Commission that party politics are barely at play. Instead, another kind of interest politics is at work, that of public interest politics focused around groups representing environmental, consumer, and human rights concerns.[23] This is not so much because all members of Parliament are necessarily sympathetic to such issues but because these issues generally have a broader public appeal and are less well represented in the Commission, and therefore serve to increase MEPs' political weight and to gain public attention.[24]

But at the same time as the EU's pluralism may be less politicized than that of the US, it is less 'pluralistic' in the kinds of interests represented as well as in their access and potential influence. The EU Commission has much greater control over the entire process of interest representation than the US, where any interest that organizes itself is regarded as legitimate so long as it can make itself heard. In the EU, only those interests the EU Commission chooses to legitimize, and thus allow into the process, will be heard. This was actually a problem in earlier years with regard to the access and influence of environmental groups and others—by contrast with business, which for the most part had ready access. But in more recent years, it is the Commission itself which has sought to overcome the problem by expanding its openness to a wide range of interests along with its transparency. Even so, the Commission remains in control. This is a by-product of its strategy of gaining information and political support through the development of networks of advisory committees and working groups made up of experts, representatives of

[23] On the environment and biotechnology, see David Judge, David Earnshaw, and Ngaire Cowan, 'Ripples or Waves: The European Parliament in the European Community Policy Process', *Journal of European Public Policy*, 1/1 (1994), 28–51.

[24] Beate Kohler-Koch, 'Organized Interests in European Integration: The Evolution of a New Type of Governance?', in A Young and H. Wallace (eds), *Participation and Policy-making in the European Union* (Oxford: Oxford University Press, 1997), 85–6.

Member States at national and sub-national levels, and societal interest groups.[25]

The EU's pluralism is also much more closed to citizen participation than that of the US. Whereas in the United States, grass-roots campaigns focused on Congress have become a preferred tool of special interest as well as public interest groups, this has little prospect in the EU. This results in large measure from the comparative paucity of Europe-wide non-business organizations but also from the fact that the most likely recipients of such campaigns, EU members of Parliament, have themselves little direct influence on the policy formulation process—although they can cause problems once a dossier is well on its way. Protests, moreover, and the relatively new 'Eurostrikes'[26] are likely to have an increasing impact, although for the moment their effect is mainly indirect, as national governments have tended to be the ones having to deal with their consequences—although this has been changing as protest increasingly moves to Brussels, in particular in the case of agriculture.

Finally, whereas the EU's pluralist policy formulation process may avoid some of the worst problems of the US, even admitting its own problems with regard to access and representativeness, in the EU's policy implementation process it courts many more than the US. This is because in the US, the federal civil servants' implementation of the rules—whether alone, in tandem with, or in addition to State-level civil servants—are for the most part done according to the same procedures, and therefore ensure great relative uniformity in application—the major exception being the new welfare reform of 1996. By contrast, in the EU, the process is more complex, given that Member States themselves implement regulations as well as transpose directives into national law and then implement them according to national procedures. This allows Member States much greater latitude in the interpretation and application of the rules—which naturally raises questions about the equal application of the rules, given different regulatory cultures and practices.[27]

But whatever the differences between the EU's model and the ideal-typical pluralist model of the United States, they are nothing compared

[25] Les Metcalfe, 'Après 1992: 'Can the Commission Manage Europe?', *Australian Journal of Public Administration* 51, 1 (1992), 117–30.

[26] Doug Imig and Sidney Tarrow, 'From Strike to Eurostrike: The Europeanization of Social Movements and the Development of a Euro-Polity', Working Paper No. 97-10 (Cambridge, MA: Weatherhead Centre for International Affairs, Harvard University, December 1997). See also Uwe K. H. Reising, 'Domestic and Supranational Political Opportunities: European Protest in Selected Countries 1980–1995' (European Integration Online Papers [EIOP], ii, 1998).

[27] See Renaud Dehousse, 'Integration v. Regulation? On the Dynamics of Regulation in the European Community', *Journal of Common Market Studies*, 30 (1992), 389–92.

with those between the EU's quasi-pluralist model and the corporatist or statist models of Member States. And here, the impact of the EU on national policy-making processes is as significant for questions of democratic accountability and legitimacy as it is with regard to the clash of institutional structures.

4. The Impact of EU Policy-making Processes on Member States

European policy-making processes have increasingly impinged on national ones generally, diminishing Member States' autonomy in policy formulation by allowing access and influence to a wider range of actors and their flexibility in policy implementation by promoting regulatory or legalistic enforcement patterns. But this has been experienced differently by Member States, given differences in national policy-making processes which tend to be either statist or corporatist. By comparison with EU quasi-pluralist policy-making processes, statist policy-making processes tend ideal-typically to be more closed to interest influence in policy formulation; more open to interest accommodation through either administrative discretion or self-regulatory arrangements; and more conflictual in interactive style, with decisions often political and generally taken at the top. By contrast with EU quasi-pluralist policy-making processes, corporatist policy-making processes tend ideal-typically to be more open to certain 'privileged' interests in policy formulation; more flexible in implementation, by being open to interest accommodation through joint self-governing arrangements; and more consensual in style, with decisions less clearly political and rarely taken at the top. In consequence of these differences, the EU's quasi-pluralist policy-making processes have tended to impose greater adjustment burdens on statist polities than on corporatist ones.[28] This is because whereas in statist polities the EU's 'pluralism' has served to diminish the state's autonomy in policy formulation and the EU's regulatory model has reduced its flexibility in implementation, it has had less effect on corporatist polities, in which the state has never had as much autonomy in formulation and which have been for the most part allowed to continue with corporatist implementation processes.

In the statist pattern of state-society relations characteristic of France—the model for this ideal-type—Britain, and to a much less extent Italy, societal interests tend to have comparatively little input into a policy

[28] For a theoretical discussion of the differences between pluralist, statist, and corporatist policy-making processes, see Vivien A. Schmidt, *From State to Market? The Transformation of French Business and Government* (Cambridge: Cambridge University Press, 1996), Chs 1 and 2.

formulation process where the state has great autonomy. The executive in this context ordinarily has the capacity to act unilaterally or even 'heroically'. But whereas societal interests are generally kept out of statist policy formulation, they are for the most part allowed into the policy implementation process, which is generally flexible in application. Such flexibility may be the result of administrative discretion, where derogation of the rules is accepted practice, and where the state generally accommodates societal interests or risks confrontation—in France and even more so in Italy—or it may be the result of state-sanctioned, self-governing arrangements by societal interests—more the case in Britain.[29] Given the pattern of unilateral government action in policy formulation, the style of state-society interaction is generally conflictual, although more obviously so in some countries, where protest seems the only way to be heard—as in France and even more so Italy—than in others, which have a less confrontational tradition—as in Britain. Because of the style, where a policy finds high levels of opposition which the state cannot or will not accommodate, societal mobilization can occur. And in the face of confrontation, the state often backs down—the pattern in France and Italy. Even where this does not occur, however, the state may be censured, if only at the ballot box—typically the pattern in Great Britain.

By contrast, in the corporatist pattern characteristic of the Netherlands, the Scandinavian countries, Austria, and Germany—a more complicated model given its federal structure—certain 'privileged' societal interests, mainly business and labour, are brought into both policy formulation and policy implementation processes. Here, the state generally does not have the capacity to impose, mainly because however highly organized it may be—that is, even if it is unitary in structure—it faces equally highly organized or at least mobilized societal interests. Where it is federal or decentralized in structure, moreover, the executive's lack of autonomy ensures its inability to impose. Rather than acting unilaterally, therefore, the state generally seeks to act in coordination with societal interests. Such coordination allows interests to influence policy formulation from the inside, by co-devising the policies, and not just, as in the pluralist relationship, to exert influence from the outside. Agreement, moreover, is generally reached through a more consensual style of interaction among state and societal actors, whether it is more 'solidaristic', as in some of the smaller European countries such as the Netherlands or Austria, or more rational self-interested, as in Germany.[30] Conflict is always possible here too, but it tends to be preliminary to the reaching of a consensus at the formulation

[29] For more detail, see Schmidt, 'National Patterns of Governance.'

[30] See Fritz W. Scharpf, *Games Real Actors Play: Actor-Centered Institutionalism in Policy Research* (Boulder, CO: Westview, 1997).

stage rather than leading to confrontation at the implementation stage, as in statist systems.

In corporatist state-society relations, moreover, as in statist relations, implementation is flexible in application. But here, the rules formulated by the 'social partners' are applied by them through joint self-governing arrangements. The processes by which such implementation patterns arise are incorporated into the structures of political organization, for example, through social partners' participation in parliamentary committees, the decisions of which are then rubber-stamped by the parliament—as in Austria—or they may be sanctioned by law and not even seen as part of public policy—as in Germany.

In both statist and corporatist polities, however, policy implementation is not always flexible. For where the judiciary has some modicum of independence, implementation can resemble the regulatory or legalistic model of the pluralist pattern of state-society relations. This means that alongside the administrative discretion of civil servants or the self-governing arrangements of societal interests, strongly legalistic patterns of implementation may impose themselves, proscribing any kind of flexibility. This has a long tradition in those statist and corporatist polities where the judiciary has always been independent to some degree—for example, Britain and Germany. In such polities, it is often very hard to predict which implementation process will be operative, the legalist or the flexible. Generally, this is the result of tradition, and of whether the courts or the bureaucracy got to the issue first. But the legalistic approach to implementation has been gaining in recent years in all polities, including in those statist polities which had traditionally had a highly subordinated judiciary and a strong administrative tradition—France, for example. This stems from reforms that have increased the powers of the judiciary and/or have established independent regulatory agencies, whether in response to internal dynamics or external pressures, in particular those from the European Union, where its regulatory/legalistic model has been imposed in an ever-growing number of sectors.

The EU, in fact, whether in policy formulation, policy implementation, or decision-making culture, has affected its Member States' policy-making processes, but more so for statist than for corporatist polities.[31] For one, the EU's pluralist policy formulation process has engendered a loss of autonomy—discussed above more generally when considering the impact of EU institutional structures—which has been felt more keenly in statist polities, where the executive has lost its virtual monopoly on policy formulation, than in corporatist polities, where the executive never had the

[31] See: Schmidt, 'National Patterns of Governance.'

same kind of autonomy given the social partnership. For statist France, where the loss of autonomy was accepted under the assumption that the 'heroism' lost at the national level would be replaced by a French-led 'heroism' at the European level, the failure to exercise such leadership in all but the most 'heroic' of areas—that is, the Treaties including the Single Market Act and Maastricht—has been a source of national dissatisfaction. This has even occasionally led to mainly symbolic attempts to demonstrate leadership: for example, in the demands for a French head of the NATO southern command or of the European Central Bank. But this only prolongs the popular illusion that the government somehow has sole responsibility for policies that are in fact made jointly in Brussels, or that it is therefore accountable for actions taken in Brussels over which it in fact has little or no control. Both are detrimental to French democratic legitimacy.

For statist Britain, the threat to governmental autonomy has been even more keenly felt than in France, but more successfully resisted—as the initial opt-outs from the Social Chapter of the Maastricht Treaty and European Monetary Union attest. Where the French response has been to seek a greater EU 'heroism' in exchange for its loss at the national level, the British response, at least under Thatcher and Major, has been to resist 'heroically' what it sees as European incursions on national sovereignty. But although this may have increased government popularity, it has at the same time eroded democratic legitimacy, given that as often as not the government incorporated into national law the very EU measures it had so vociferously opposed.

For corporatist Germany, by contrast, the loss of autonomy and, concomitantly, legitimacy have not been felt nearly as much as in France or Britain. This is because of complex decision-making processes which assume joint responsibility for any policies, whether formulated in Germany or Brussels. The problem for Germany, by contrast with France or Britain, is that its institutional structures together with its policy-making processes make it difficult for it to exercise leadership when it comes to grand strategy, where France excels, or forcefully to resist policy initiatives of which it disapproves, where Britain is past master.[32]

Second, the EU's regulatory approach to implementation has produced a loss of flexibility which has been more pronounced in statist polities, where it has closed off traditional means of accommodation involving administrative discretion or self-regulatory arrangements, than in corporatist polities, where joint regulatory arrangements have been allowed to continue. The loss of the possibility of making exceptions to the rules

[32] Ibid.

where EU rules and regulations are concerned has been particularly problematic for France, given that citizens who have never had much access to decision-making in policy formulation and now have even less accommodation in policy implementation are more likely to resort to confrontation when their concerns are not met.[33] And this represents a threat not just to French societal stability but also to democratic legitimacy, given that French democracy has always been predicated on the state's administrative discretion, that is, on its ability to adapt the rules to accommodate affected constituencies—which is no longer possible. One answer for the French, of course, would be to allow greater access to citizens at the policy formulation stage, so that there would no longer be the need to adapt the rules in the implementation, and to encourage greater citizen interest organization and participation in EU policy-making. But this is not easy to accomplish in a country where the state tends to act and society to react, although the Jospin Government does seems to be attempting to do some of this.

For Britain, by comparison, the major problem has been the increasing rigidification of public life related to the dramatic increase in EU, as well as national, regulations, which have replaced the informal, voluntary arrangements with formal rules administered by independent regulatory agencies or enforced by the courts. And this represents a threat not only to British societal autonomy, given the expansion of public powers over a wide range of areas traditionally left to private actors, but ultimately to traditional notions of democratic legitimacy, given that British democracy has always been predicated on leaving as much room as possible to private self-governing arrangements. And there is no answer for the British on this score, other than perhaps to seek to keep Brussels from enacting more rules and regulations.

For Germany, by contrast, which has not only always codified more laws than Britain but has also applied them without exception, unlike France or even more so Italy, the EU rules and regulations have not been nearly as problematic. But this is mainly because those areas traditionally outside the more legalistic domain, those jointly administered by social partners, have largely been able to continue to operate as they have traditionally. In consequence, German policy-making processes, which entail shared responsibility for policy implementation as much as for formulation have not been challenged nearly as much as the French or British.

Finally, even the EU's cooperative, 'bottom-up', and less political decision-making culture has engendered greater adaptational problems for statist polities when it comes to exerting influence in the EU, given a more

[33] Schmidt, 'Loosening the Ties', and Schmidt, *From State to Market?*, Ch. 7.

conflictual, 'top-down', and political culture, than for corporatist countries, where their more consensual, more horizontal, and less political decision-making culture is closer to that of the EU. However, although the French in particular were at a disadvantage early on by comparison with those countries with long-standing, well developed lobbies, as in the case of the British, or with cohesive peak associations, as in the case of the Germans, the differences in country capability in EU lobbying has been diminishing, as national actors learn a more EU style of interaction.

All in all, though, the EU's quasi-pluralist policy-making process has tended to impose greater adjustment burdens on statist systems such as the French and the British, by undermining government autonomy in policy formulation, reducing flexibility in implementation, and expecting greater cooperation in EU policy-making, than on corporatist systems such as the German, which has never had the same kind of governmental autonomy, has lost less flexibility given an implementation process that has for the most part been deemed compatible with the regulatory, and has a consensual culture that better matches the EU's cooperative one.[34] Because the 'fit' between pluralist and statist processes is less close than between pluralist and corporatist processes in such areas as societal actors' interest organization and access and in governing bodies' interactive style and adaptability, statist polities have had a more difficult time than corporatist ones in adjusting to EU level policy formulation, a more difficult task in implementing the policy changes engendered by the EU, and a greater challenge in adapting their national interactive styles to the new realities. And in consequence, the EU has posed greater problems with regard to democratic legitimacy for statist polities than for corporatist ones.

5. Conclusion

Thus, the EU, with its quasi-federal institutional structures and its quasi-pluralist policy-making processes, has had a significant impact on Member States' national institutional structures and policy-making processes. It has generally affected the traditional balance of power in both unitary and federal states, albeit more in the former than in the latter, by reducing executive autonomy and control, diminishing legislative power, and increasing judicial power and sub-national independence. And it has altered traditional patterns of policy-making in both statist and

[34] See Schmidt, 'European Integration and Democracy' and Schmidt, 'National Patterns of Governance'.

corporatist systems, albeit again more in the former than in the latter, by reducing government autonomy in policy formulation and flexibility in implementation.

As such, the EU has generated problems with regard to democratic representation, accountability, and legitimacy for all of its Member States, albeit again more for unitary and statist polities than federal and corporatist polities. This is mainly because the traditional concentration of power and authority in the executive in unitary, statist systems such as France and Britain has made it harder for them to legitimize actions that they no longer entirely control, but for which they are assumed accountable, than in federal, corporatist systems such as Germany, where the traditional dispersion of power entails that the executive generally must oversee the carrying out of policies for which it has never in any case been held entirely accountable.

The differences, in other words, come from the greater difficulty for the French and British in accepting that democratic representation and accountability need not be concentrated in a single, all-powerful authority but can be situated in a multiplicity of authorities and emerge through the plural points of access of a more open policy-making process. But for this, they would have to redefine their notions of democratic legitimacy and accountability, and even promote a move towards greater 'federal' separation or sharing of power for national institutional structures which have traditionally focused power and authority primarily in the executive and towards greater 'pluralistic' openness to interest representation for national policy-making processes which have traditionally tended to limit interest access in policy formulation. And to succeed in this, national politicians would themselves not only have to recognize and embrace such change. They would also need to engage in a new political discourse capable of convincing the public not only that this is a necessary change in national understandings of democratic representation and accountability but also an appropriate one, despite the fact that it may violate long-held notions of state authority and responsibility. And although such a change in discourse is not easy, it may certainly be better than continuing to mislead the public by creating expectations about national government power and capabilities that they are bound to disappoint.

13

Democratic Legitimacy under Conditions of Regulatory Competition: Why Europe Differs from the United States

FRITZ W. SCHARPF

1. Introduction: Is There a European Democratic Deficit?

Unlike the United States, the European Community was not, and could not have been, founded as a democratic nation state. Originally, the legitimacy of its limited governing functions was solidly based on *intergovernmental* agreement. Among the—democratically legitimized—governments and parliaments of the Six, the political commitment to create a common market was unequivocal, and the *supranational* actions of the European Commission and the European Court of Justice to promote market integration were justified by that fundamental commitment even where they went against the preferences of individual governments in the given case (Garrett 1992; Moravcsik 1998).

Ostensibly, that was also true of the Single-Market programme of 1986, even though the intergovernmental basis of legitimacy was weaker because of the more active role of the Delors Commission in designing the agreement, and the less complete understanding of its far-reaching implications among some governments and ratifying parliaments. Even the move toward monetary union and the establishment of a *supranational* European Central Bank was an *intergovernmental* project promoted by France when it was realized that its commitment to a hard currency had made French monetary policy dependent on choices that were made by the *Bundesbank* with a view to the state of the *German* economy rather than to the European economy that was in fact governed by it (Verdun 1996; Moravcsik 1998; Dyson and Featherstone 1999).

So why is it that the legitimacy of the supranational institutions that were created through intergovernmental agreements ratified by democratically legitimized national parliaments is now under challenge? Why is it

This contribution is based on my recent book (Scharpf 1999).

that seemingly academic concerns about a 'European democratic deficit' (Williams 1991) were raised to the status of a serious constitutional issue in the Maastricht decision of the German Constitutional Court? Why have they motivated the Amsterdam Summit to greatly enlarge the competencies of the European Parliament? And why did the Cologne Summit put the issue of a European constitution on the agenda of the next Intergovernmental Conference? In my view, there are two explanations for the remarkable political salience of the alleged democratic deficit of the European Union: one pragmatic, the other more fundamental.

Pragmatic Reasons

The pragmatic reason is that the European Union's institutions, designed to organize a mere customs union among six Member States, are considered inadequate for a union with 15 members and a vastly expanded range of competencies, and will become totally unworkable when Eastern enlargement further increases the number of governments represented in the Council and the number of Commissioners among whom the Union's portfolio must be subdivided. It is also realized, however, that even the changes which everybody considers minimally necessary for the continued performance of the Union's present functions—fewer Commissioners and a general move to majority decisions in the Council—will reduce the control of individual national governments over European policy choices to an extent that would finally destroy the plausibility of the intergovernmental legitimization arguments that still must support the exercise of European powers.

The European Trilemma of the Democratic Welfare State

If these pragmatic concerns explain the current search for institutional fixes that might convey independent legitimacy on Union decisions that can no longer be said to be under the control of democratically legitimized national governments, the second argument sees the democratic deficit arising from a more fundamental political-economic trilemma of European integration. It exists because of characteristics of the European constellation that are quite different from the situation in American federalism.

The first part of the trilemma arises from the fact that the democratic legitimacy of European nation states is much more closely associated with welfare-state achievements than is true of American States. There, the creation of a nationwide 'internal market' had preceded efforts to build a welfare state. At the State level, these efforts were largely impeded by economic and legal constraints. On the one hand, economic competition among producers in different States created conditions of 'regulatory competition' among State governments which practically prevented all of them from adopting regulations—for example, regarding the employment of child labour—that would have reduced the competitiveness of local production. On the other hand, the 'negative commerce clause' doctrine of the Supreme Court prevented States from protecting local producers against imports from other States that were produced under less stringent regulations. As a consequence, even in States with 'progressive' majorities welfare-state provisions remained at a minimal level (Skocpol and Amenta 1986).

In Europe, by contrast, national welfare states had reached their full development in the early post-war decades, when advanced industrial democracies were still in full control of their national economic boundaries. In the absence of regulatory competition, the solutions could be much more generous than in the US, and they could also differ from one country to another in the type of functions assumed by the state, the level of generosity of the benefits provided, and the institutional structures through which benefits were provided. But regardless of fundamental differences between universalistic Scandinavian welfare states, Continental varieties of 'social-market economies', or the Beveridge model of Anglo-Saxon countries (Esping-Andersen 1990), citizens have come to base their life plans on the expectation that certain functions, but not others, would be provided by the welfare state—with the consequence that their fate and that of their families would in fact depend on the stability of these expectations. If these expectations were massively disappointed, the fundamental 'social contract' and hence democratic legitimacy would indeed be in question.

The second part of the trilemma arises from the fact that the Member States of the European Union have become irreversibly committed to a pervasive programme of European economic integration whose very success is now confronting national welfare states with the same kind of regulatory competition that had impeded the development of social policies in the American States. There, however, a solution became available after the New Deal constitutional revolution, when the Supreme Court finally allowed political responsibility for welfare state functions to be exercised at the federal level. In Europe, by contrast, the transfer of welfare state functions to the EU level is effectively ruled out for pragmatic and normative reasons. The trilemma, in short, exists because EU Member States cannot want to shed their welfare-state obligations without jeopardizing the bases of their legitimacy; they cannot want to reverse the process of economic integration which exposes national welfare states to regulatory competition; and they cannot want to avoid regulatory competition by shifting welfare-state responsibilities upward to the European level.

It is the third part of the European trilemma which I will primarily discuss here. In doing so, I will begin with a brief theoretical discussion of the preconditions of democratic legitimacy; then I will explore how these are affected by European integration. I will conclude with an examination of European policies that could strengthen national efforts to cope with the constraints of regulatory competition.

2. Legitimacy: Effective Problem Solving and Democratic Accountability

Legitimacy is here understood as a widely shared belief that it is my moral duty to comply with requirements imposed by state authorities even if those requirements violate my own preferences or interests, and even if I could evade them at low cost. In the absence of such beliefs, compliance would depend exclusively on the effectiveness of controls and the anticipation of sanctions—which, as the decline and fall of the socialist dictatorships demonstrated once again, greatly reduces the efficiency of governing.

As Max Weber has shown, there is—theoretically and historically—a considerable variety of beliefs on which the legitimacy of government may be based. Yet in this day and age, and in Western societies, 'democratic' legitimization has come to be seen as the only game in town—which of course does not rule out disagreement about the specific conditions that could support claims to this type of legitimization. In my view, it is useful here to distinguish between two types of legitimizing arguments. On the one hand, 'input-oriented' claims presuppose that in a democratic polity the powers of government must be exercised in response to the articulated preferences of the governed—which, in the language of Abraham Lincoln's Gettysburg Address, refers to 'government *by the people*'. On the other hand, 'output-oriented' legitimization arguments demand that democratic government should advance the common good by dealing effectively with those problems that are beyond the reach of individual action, market exchanges, and voluntary cooperation among individuals and groups in civil society—which, in Lincoln's terms, emphasizes the dimension of 'government *for the people*'.

In constitutional democracies, the capability for *effective* action is thought to be assured by the potentially comprehensive authority of the territorial state over the resources and action choices of its subjects, exercised through powers of legislation and taxation whose enforcement is backed by the monopoly of legitimate coercion. To assure the responsive and public-interest oriented exercise of these powers, democratic constitutions rely on free media of communication, public debate and political parties, and the electoral accountability of key office holders, as well as on institutionalized checks and balances. But while democratic constitutions vary greatly in the way, and in the extent, to which the exercise of public power is circumscribed by the institutionalization of judicial, legislative, and federal veto positions, no polity would be considered democratic that does not make office holders invested with authority to exercise public power directly or indirectly dependent on, and hence responsive to, the—anticipated—preferences and the subsequent judgement of constituents, expressed in free and general elections.

The Problem: Loss of Effective Control at the National Level

The 'European democratic deficit' is usually discussed with reference to institutions and policy processes at the European level, where the preconditions for direct democratic accountability are clearly not realized. Its primary effect, however, is felt at the national level, where European integration is weakening the problem-solving effectiveness as well as the accountability of governments with seemingly impeccable democratic credentials.

Economic Constraints and Regulatory Competition

The main impact of European integration is economic. With the completion of the internal market, and now with monetary union, national boundaries have lost their effectiveness as obstacles to the free movement of goods, services, and capital. As a consequence, the nation state has lost the power to protect national producers against foreign competitors producing under more business-friendly regulatory and tax regimes. By the same token, producers and investors are now free to chose the most attractive location in Europe without jeopardizing their access to the home market. Since governments depend on producers and investors to assure the employment and incomes of their citizens, economic integration creates conditions of regulatory competition which reduces the effective capacity of all Member States to tax mobile factors of production and capital profits or to impose market-correcting regulations that are considered a burden on business. To the extent that such policies had responded to the political aspirations of constituencies, the new constraints are also experienced as a loss of responsiveness and democratic accountability.

Legal Constraints of 'Negative Integration'

In order to bring about economic integration, the European Community had to develop legal prohibitions—corresponding to the 'negative commerce clause' doctrines of US constitutional law—that abolished not only national tariffs and quantitative restrictions on imports, but also all other measures that had the effect of restricting or distorting free international competition in the European markets for goods and services, or the free movement of capital across national borders.

In fact, however, the 'negative integration' of European markets has gone much further, requiring the abolition of national subsidies to declining regions or industries and the liberalization—and, in practical effect, the privatization and deregulation—of a wide range of infrastructure services and facilities, such as telecommunications and postal services, airports and airlines, railroads and road haulage, electricity and natural gas, or job placement services, which in most European countries had been provided directly by the state, by licensed monopolies, or by highly regulated cartels. In addition, monetary union has eliminated national control over interest rates and exchange rates, and has severely constrained the capacity of national governments to employ the remaining instruments of macroeconomic policy for employment-increasing strategies.

In the judgement of most economists, these changes did increase economic efficiency, and many of them have clearly benefited European consumers—usually at the expense of employment in hitherto protected and hence less efficient branches. But there is also no question that the range of available policy choices, and hence the capacity of governments to respond to the preferences of their citizens—which may emphasize values that cannot be reduced to measures of economic efficiency—have been significantly constrained. This is true not only of macroeconomic, industrial, and regional policies but also of the capacity to tax mobile factors of production and capital incomes, and of the capacity to regulate employment conditions with a view to strengthening workers' rights or to equalize primary incomes. Intense competition and high capital mobility rule out cross-subsidization, so that in principle each job must be able to earn its own cost plus adequate profits in competitive markets. If governments and unions should still try to intervene through minimum-wage laws or solidaristic wage policies, the outcome would not be greater equality but the loss of those jobs which are priced out of the market.

In short, European integration has significantly reduced the range of policy instruments available, and the range of policy goals achievable, at the national level. To that extent, the effectiveness as well as the responsiveness of government, and hence democratic legitimacy, are seen to have been weakened—at least in those countries which, in contrast to Britain, have not completely converted to neo-liberal preferences.

European Solutions?

There is a hope—certainly among unions and left-of-centre political parties, but also among the members and staff of the Commission and the European Parliament—that the American experience of the New Deal period (Skocpol 1995) could be repeated in Europe: namely, that the regulatory capacity that was being lost at the national level might be regained through regulations at the European level. Economically, the parallel is of course not perfect because the US in the 1930s was practically decoupled from the world market, whereas the EU is part of the WTO free-trade regime and completely integrated into worldwide capital markets. Nevertheless, the EU internal market is so much larger than the national markets of Member States that regulatory options which are economically unfeasible at the national level could indeed be realized by European legislation.

Status Quo: A Problem-Solving Gap

Under the present institutional conditions of the European polity, however, such hopes are mostly disappointed. The Community started out as an intergovernmental negotiation system whose decisions, under the Luxembourg compromise, depended on unanimous agreement of member governments in the Council of Ministers, and hence were easily blocked by conflicts of interest among these governments. Nevertheless, the Commission and the European Court of Justice were able to advance European integration through direct legal action against the violation of—extensively interpreted—Treaty provisions which, under the doctrines of 'supremacy' and 'direct effect', were able to override national legislation. But these legal strategies were mainly effective in expanding the reach of 'negative integration' in order to remove national barriers to trade and free competition. Market-correcting policies of 'positive integration', by contrast, continued to depend on political agreement in the Council of Ministers.

There, however, European problem-solving capacity is severely constrained by multiple vetoes since decisions must be taken either unanimously or by qualified majorities—a condition that was in no way improved by the expansion of co-decision rights of the European Parliament, which mainly had the effect of strengthening another veto position and weakening the agenda-setting power of the Commission (Tsebelis 1994). That is not meant to say that positive integration must generally end in a 'joint-decision trap' (Scharpf 1988) where divergent national interests lead to blockage or will at best allow solutions at the lowest common denominator. There are indeed policy areas where national interests converge sufficiently to allow even very demanding European regulations. This is particularly true for the harmonization of safety and environmental standards for industrial products, where governments were often willing to accept the demands of countries with high national standards in order to assure uniform conditions and free access throughout the internal market (Eichener 1997; Pollack 1997). Similarly, once some countries were forced by judgements of the European Court of Justice to allow foreign competitors in their protected public-service branches, their governments tended to support Council directives requiring the general liberalization of these services (S. Schmidt 1998). By contrast, in policy areas where national interests do in fact diverge, as was true for the European regulation of industrial relations (Streeck 1997), decisions at the lowest common denominator are indeed the best that can be expected.

It is possible to state with some precision the policy areas in which national problem-solving capabilities are most severely affected by the economic and legal constraints of European integration, and in which policy areas European problem-solving is most likely to be blocked by conflicts of interest among national governments (Scharpf 1997). In effect, both of these constraints tend to overlap in a limited range of policy areas which, however, includes precisely those instruments of market-correcting policy that have been of critical importance for the legitimization of democratic welfare states: social policy, industrial-relations policy, and the taxation of business profits and capital incomes. In these policy areas, located in the lower-left quadrant of Fig. 13.1, European integration does create a problem-solving gap. Here the nation state is most constrained by the economic pressures of international competition and capital mobility as well as by the legal prohibitions of negative integration. At the same time, however, it is also in these policy areas that agreement on the European level is most constrained by conflicts of interest and of ideological preferences among member governments.

The reasons are easy to see: EU Member States differ in their level of economic development, with the consequence that the level of social protection offered by, say, Denmark would be completely unaffordable in Greece or Portugal. Moreover, even countries at the same level of economic development differ greatly in the levels and the structures of social provision. For British citizens, who have made private arrangements to complement very lean public benefits, the Swedish 'full-service' welfare state would be as unacceptable as British industrial-relations rules would be for workers and unions accustomed to German co-determination rights. In short, there is no chance that common, Europe-wide solutions can replace national welfare and employment regimes under institutional

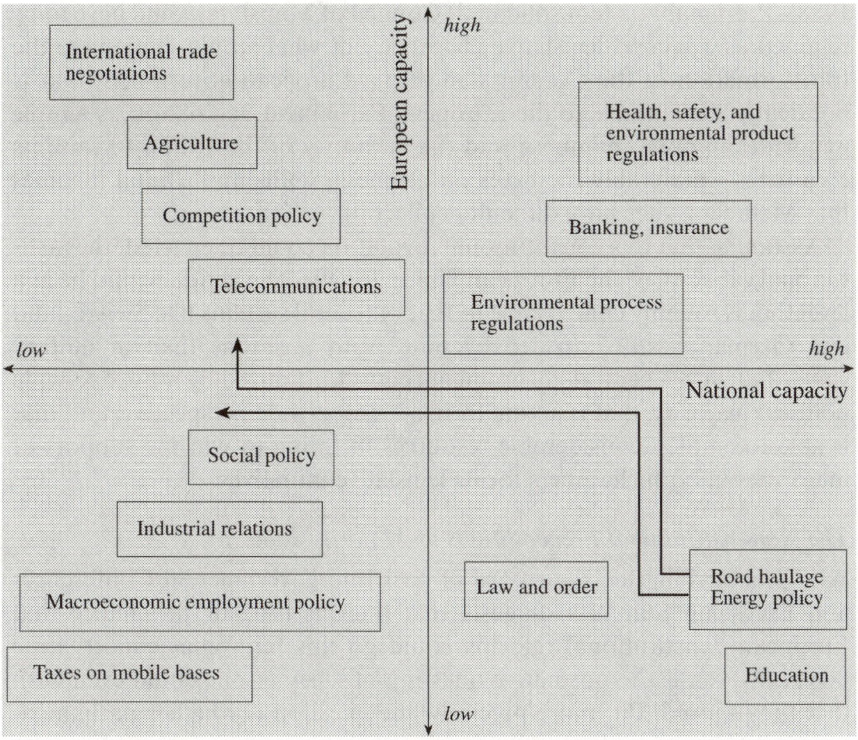

FIGURE 13.1. *National and European problem-solving capabilities*
Source: Scharpf (1999: 117)

conditions where these would depend on the agreement of national governments.

The Institutional Preconditions of Effective European Action

Under these circumstances, it is tempting to think that the European problem-solving gap might be closed through constitutional changes that would simultaneously increase the capacity for, and the democratic legitimacy of, effective action at the European level. In order to realize this hope, so it is thought, Europe would need to transform its present constitution—which, essentially, is still that of a confederacy governed by negotiations among Member States—to that of a federal state whose decisions cannot be blocked by the opposition of a few member governments. In other words, the European Union would have to become more like the United States—or at least more like the German federal state (Scharpf

1988). Presumably, a (consolidated) Council of Ministers would have to be retained as a second legislative chamber, but what would matter are the transformation of the Commission into a European government that is politically accountable to the European Parliament, legislation by simple majorities in both chambers, and the authority of the Union to raise its own taxes—preferably the taxes on business profits and capital incomes that Member States have difficulty collecting.

Assuming that this constitutional revolution could be enacted, the institutional capacity of the European Union for effective action would be at a level that is roughly comparable to that of federal systems like Switzerland and Germany—still impeded by more veto positions than in unitary states, but with a central government that is legitimized by a Europe-wide political majority, that is acting from a Europe-wide perspective, and that is able to employ considerable resources in trying to win the support of majorities in both chambers for its legislative initiatives.

The Non-institutional Preconditions of Majority Rule

As a practical matter, the record of past Intergovernmental Conferences and European Summits suggests that there is little or no chance that European constitutional reforms could go this far. What concerns me here, however, is the normative question of whether one could even wish that they should. Put more precisely, the question is whether parliamentary majorities could actually legitimize decisive action in those areas where European policy is presently blocked by major conflicts of interest or preferences among member governments.

That question presupposes that decisions by majority, which allow dissenting minorities to be overruled, may not be normatively acceptable under all conditions, and that their capacity to create a moral duty of voluntary compliance depends on non-institutional preconditions that legitimize the majority rule itself. In Lincoln's Gettysburg triad, these precondition are addressed in the reference to 'government *of the people*'. I interpret this to mean that majoritarian democracy presupposes the 'we-identity' of a *demos*—a collectivity in which the identification of members with the group is sufficiently strong to override the divisive interests of subgroups in cases of conflict. If that were not true, secession or civil war would be an ever-present danger; and in polities where that sense of a collective identity is in fact weak or lacking—think of Northern Ireland, Bosnia, the former Czechoslovakia, or even Belgium and Canada—the mere counting of votes was never considered sufficient to create a moral duty to comply among outvoted minorities. Instead, it would set off disintegrative and even explosive dynamics of resistance and repression.

As of now, nobody seems ready to claim that the multi-ethnic, multi-lingual, multi-cultural and multi-institutional peoples of the European Union have yet achieved a robust we-identity that is more salient than existing cleavages and conflicts of interest. This is of course not meant to say that a common *ethnic* identity should be considered an indispensable prerequisite of democratic majority rule: the United States and Switzerland show that this is not so. But in its place, these multi-ethnic polities have developed a fierce national patriotism, based on a strong historical sense of common fate and common destiny: conditions which surely are also not yet realized among the 15 nations of the present Union, and that will take even longer to develop after eastern enlargement. And even if common identity were considered less essential, it must matter for the input-oriented legitimization of European policy choices that the peoples of Europe do not yet constitute a common European public: that there are as yet no Europe-wide media of communications, no Europe-wide political parties, no Europe-wide candidates for political office, and no Europe-wide political debates and controversies.

Under these conditions, the most that one could hope for in a revised European constitution are institutions, decision rules, and practices of mutual accommodation that surely must be even more protective of minority interests than is true in 'consociational democracies' in those nation states like Canada or Belgium, which must also deal with deep cleavages through accommodation rather than through straightforward majority rule. But if that is so, the potential gain, in terms of majoritarian capacity for decisive action, of any normatively defensible constitutional reform will be quite limited. That is not meant to suggest that such reforms are undesirable or could not help to facilitate the slow progress toward greater public attention to and participation in election campaigns for the European Parliament, debates about European issues, and the selection of European office holders. But these are hopes for the longer term.

2. National Democracy: Coping with the Loss of Boundary Control

These, however, are hopes for the longer term. In the immediate future, Europe will have to make do with its present constitution, and thus with its dependence on broad agreement among national governments for any major policy initiatives. As a consequence, it is also unrealistic to hope that control over the economy that was lost at the national level could soon be regained through market-correcting European policies. But does that mean that the erosion of democratic legitimacy at the national level is inevitable, as governments must either accept the continuing decline of their economies or accept retrenchments of the welfare state, of worker rights, and of social equality, which neither they nor their constituents would have freely chosen? I think not.

In order to support this conclusion, I must once more turn to the normative foundations of democratic legitimacy discussed above. In public debates, and under fair-weather conditions, governments as well as opposition parties often tend to equate input-oriented responsiveness with wish fulfillment, and output-oriented effectiveness with omnipotence. But these are populist misunderstandings (Riker 1982). Instead, democratic legitimacy is about good reasons that should persuade me to comply with policies that do not conform to my own wishes. Its true test comes when the going gets tough. What matters then are the institutional conditions that allow citizens to trust that governments will choose among *feasible* options in such a way that the policies adopted will, *under the circumstances*, be responsive to expressed citizen preferences and effective in pursuing the common interest.

If circumstances no longer allow the state to control its economic boundaries, and if regulatory competition increases, that is not the end of politically salient and legitimacy-enhancing choices in national economic, employment, and social policy, even though the overall set of feasible choices may be narrower and less attractive than before. There is no question that the adjustment may be painful, especially for those countries—Sweden, for instance—where the state had in the past been very effective in steering the national economy by exercising control over interest rates and the allocation of credit, over wages and working conditions, or over the direction of industrial research and development. In a thoroughly Europeanized economy, most of these opportunities for political steering and control are gone. They have been replaced by international capital markets and by the dominant orientation of managers to the benchmarks of shareholder value. Moreover, the welfare-state policy legacies in some states are considerably more vulnerable to international competition and capital mobility than is true of others (Scharpf 2000).

But to say that there are tighter legal constraints and stronger competitive pressures is not the same as denying the existence of politically salient policy choices that do make a difference in the economic fate of the country and in the incomes, employment opportunities, or material inequality of their citizens. Thus, small open economies have long learned to pursue very ambitious social policy goals while coping successfully with international product markets they could never hope to control. In the crisis period of the late 1970s and early 1980s, moreover, Britain and the Netherlands had competed for the title of being 'the sickest man in Europe'. By the 1990s, however, both of these countries were held out as models of successful adjustment. Yet they have achieved their turnaround by pursuing very different strategies—neo-liberal versus neo-corporatist—and they have succeeded in reducing unemployment through very different methods and with different distributional consequences. Even more important for present purposes is the fact that although Dutch and British reform strategies had initially been extremely controversial in national discourses, these controversies and their outcomes have strengthened rather than weakened democratic legitimacy in both countries (V. Schmidt 2000). The same could be said of Denmark, Switzerland, Australia, or even Italy. By contrast, countries like Belgium, France, Germany, or Sweden, that had not yet found strategies in which political aspirations are matched to the economic options and constraints of the 1990s, seemed to be more affected by political uncertainty, self-doubt, discontent, alienation, or radicalization: in short, by a sense of malaise that threatened to erode public confidence in the responsiveness and problem-solving effectiveness of democratic government (Scharpf and Schmidt 2000).

3. European Regime for Regulatory Competition

The implication is that if economic internationalization creates a challenge to democratic legitimacy, that challenge must primarily be met by responses at the national and subnational levels of European polities. But since, as I have argued, Europe is part of the problem, European policies can also help to alleviate it—provided that measures can be identified that will not be blocked by massive conflicts of interest among the member governments. Essentially these would need to moderate the intensity of regulatory competition among Member States. This could be achieved, first, by allowing national policy makers greater freedom to pursue policies serving non-economic goals even if these have some limiting effect of market competition; second, by adopting a form of 'proportional minimum standards' for total welfare spending; third, by providing institutional support for coordinated reforms among subsets of Member States; and fourth, by allowing the Commission and the Court to develop a European case law of 'unfair regulatory and tax competition'.

Softening the Constraints of Negative Integration

Most important would be a selective softening of the legal constraints of negative integration. Since these have been created and extended primarily by legal actions of the Commission, reinforced by judicial activism during the period when Council decisions were still blocked by the unanimity rule, they have been guided by a single-minded commitment to achieve economic integration and to maximize free competition against the protectionist machinations of recalcitrant Member States. In many areas, negative integration in the European Union has gone much further than the legal constraints imposed on the American States by Congressional legislation or by the decisions of the US Supreme Court under the 'negative commerce clause' doctrine.

Yet now, when the single European market has become a reality that no Member State would want to dismantle, the perfectionist application of the syllogisms of undistorted competition should give way to a more balanced approach that weighs the seriousness of an alleged infringement of market freedoms against the importance and normative validity of the purposes served by a given instance of market-correcting national regulations. In fact, recent decisions of the European Court of Justice are already moving in that direction. Moreover, it is also appropriate that in the application of this balancing test, the political judgement of the Council of Ministers or the European Council should have a legitimate role, examples of which can be found in several resolutions adopted at the Amsterdam Summit.[1]

Proportional Minimum Standards

Since the Member States of the Union are locked in a constellation of regulatory competition with each other, reforms in one country are likely to be read as beggar-my-neighbour stratagems by others, inducing them to respond in kind, which in turn will persuade others to do likewise in order to avoid capital outflows and job losses. This is how Sweden and other Scandinavian countries ended up with a 'dual income tax', greatly favouring capital incomes in comparison with income from work, even though Denmark, which had first tried out the idea, soon had second thoughts about it. Tax harmonization, which would avoid such 'races to the bottom' is, however, among the EU policy areas in which agreement has so far been notoriously difficult to achieve (Dehejia and Genschel 1999), and the same is even more true for the Europe-wide harmonization of highly diverse social-welfare systems.

As pointed above, there are two reasons for this: differences among Member States in levels of economic development, and differences in welfare-state structures. The first would allow at best the adoption of very low minimum standards that would not strain the ability to pay of the less advanced Member States—which, however, would in no way reduce the much more important pressures of regulatory competition among the

[1] Examples are discussed in Scharpf (1999: 160–9).

richer welfare states. Neither would it help to adopt two levels of regulations, since the enormous institutional and structural diversity among the more advanced welfare states would prevent these from agreeing on common and more demanding solutions, even if these applied only among the group of rich countries.

Empirically, however, it is also true that the Member States of the European Union are remarkably similar with regard to *total social expenditures relative to their wealth.*[2] While countries differ greatly in the structure of social expenditures—that is, in the shares that are spent on pensions, health care, unemployment benefits, or social services[3]—their total social expenditures happen to be almost directly proportional to their per-capita GDP expressed in a common currency. Thus there seems to be a *de facto* consensus that richer countries should spend proportionately more on social welfare than less well-to-do countries. It seems not impossible, therefore, that this latent consensus might be translated into an explicit EU agreement on a lower proportional threshold of total social spending, defined for each country relative to its wealth position. If such an agreement were in place, all countries could engage in structural and institutional reforms of their welfare systems without setting loose a chain reaction of competitive welfare retrenchment. Since all countries, including the United Kingdom and Luxembourg, are presently close to the regression line on social spending, an agreement to maintain that relative position should be more easily reached than any attempt at harmonizing institutionally incompatible national welfare systems. Conceivable, a similar quantitative agreement might also be achieved with regard to the share of GDP collected from all types of taxes on business and capital incomes.

Coordinated Reforms

Coordination could become an even more effective way of taking the pressures of regulatory competition out of the reform processes which are necessary to adjust existing national policy legacies to the new economic environment. Given the differences among these legacies, however, no useful purpose would be served by attempts at Europe-wide coordination. But there are subgroups of countries belonging to the same welfare-state 'family'—Scandinavian, Anglo-Saxon, Continental, Southern (Esping-Andersen 1990)—that have similar institutions and similar structures of financing and benefits and that are facing basically similar problems (Esping-Andersen 1999; Scharpf 2000). Given these similarities, policy

[2] Data are presented in Scharpf (1999: 175–80).

[3] For more comprehensive comparative statistics, see OECD (1999).

changes in one country are most closely monitored, and most likely to trigger a chain reaction of competitive responses, in countries belonging to the same group.

At the same time, however, these countries could benefit most from analyzing each others' experiences and from developing common reform strategies on that basis. Doing so could create complete-information conditions that would not only improve the quality of policy design but would also offer the best protection against suspicions that might trigger beggar-my-neighbour strategies.[4] Such coordination would be greatly facilitated if it could make use of the organizational resources and good services of the European Commission in providing trustworthy comparative information and analyses and in monitoring the reform efforts of all parties involved. Unfortunately, however, the very restrictive rules for 'closer cooperation and flexibility' adopted at the Amsterdam Summit seem designed to foreclose this option. It is to be hoped that the next Intergovernmental Conference will enlarge the opportunities for closer cooperation among subgroups of EU Member States.

Toward a European Law of 'Unfair Regulatory Competition'

Finally, it seems also possible to instrumentalize the legal instruments of negative integration and competition policy to create a European regime for controlling excesses of regulatory competition.

With the support of the Court, the Commission has made extensive use of the tools provided by the Treaty (Arts 90, 92 and 93) for scrutinizing state aids and other national measures that could be construed as a distortion of competition within the common market. At the same time, the Court has developed a body of case law that distinguishes subsidies serving legitimate purposes from illegitimate ones. Admittedly, it is not always easy to discern the dividing line between subsidies to Volkswagen in Saxony and subsidies to Rover in England, but there is no question that the monitoring and policing functions of the Commission and the Court have a considerable effect in disciplining the otherwise massive incentives for competitive subsidization.

If that is accepted, there is no logical reason why Commission and Court could not also be empowered to monitor and police deregulation and tax concessions when these are employed in improper competitive

[4] Somewhat similar monitoring and trust-building functions may be performed by the national representatives in the hundreds of EU committees that are involved in the preparation and implementation of Council directives (Joerges and Vos 1999). Similarly, unions in Germany and some neighbouring countries are now exchanging observers who are allowed to attend each others' collective bargaining negotiations.

strategies. Again, there will be legitimate reasons for both, but as in the field of subsidies there are also important instances where tax concessions and deregulation are precisely targeted to attract foreign businesses, company headquarters, or financial operations to the disadvantage of other countries or domestic competitors. That the dividing line is unlikely to be a simple, hard-and-fast rule is not a major objection. The same is true in the private sector, where the dividing line between the anti-trust law of free competition and the law of unfair competition must also be worked out on a case-by-case basis by the courts. If an abstract guideline seems necessary, it could well be a variant of the Kantian 'categorical imperative': competitive strategies involving deregulation and tax concessions are improper if, even in the eyes of their initiators, they would be self-defeating if they were applied by all other countries as well.

From newspaper reports it appears, moreover, that during the Finnish presidency the ECOFIN ministers had come close to an agreement on some code of conduct governing discriminatory tax concessions before negotiations failed altogether after the British veto against common rules on interest taxation. I take this incident, first, as demonstrating that it is indeed possible to formulate plausible and practicable rules distinguishing proper and improper practices of tax competition; and second, I take it, as providing strong support for an active role of the Commission and the Court in a field where competitive incentives are preventing political agreement in the Council. If there are good reasons to use legal rather than political processes for the control of state aids, these would also support the use of the same kinds of procedures for controlling the temptations of unfair regulatory and tax competition.

4. Conclusions

What does all this imply for the European democratic deficit? My first conclusion is that there is no lack of legitimacy for what the Union has actually been able to do. This legitimacy is based on the norm-based authority of the Court and on intergovernmental agreement, and the area of effective European action may still continue to expand as agreement is reached on additional purposes and means of European action. However, the democratic deficit would surely become a major and potentially explosive issue if the European constitution were now changed in ways that would allow the Union to act more effectively by simple majority vote in the face of strong objections from more than a very few member governments. That also implies, unfortunately, that Europe still will be unable to deal with the wide range of social problems—among them mass unemployment and the crisis of the welfare state—that are caused by economic integration but for which European solutions are blocked by major conflicts of interest or ideology among member governments. By necessity, therefore, dealing with these problems will be left to the Member States, where the failure of governments to come up with normatively defensible and pragmatically effective solutions may indeed erode input-oriented as well as output-oriented democratic legitimacy.

In principle solutions must be found and implemented at the national level. Nevertheless, Europe should and could have a role in enabling, facilitating, and protecting national coping strategies, instead of single-mindedly maximizing the one goal—market integration and free competition—which the Union is able to pursue without the political agreement of member governments. This role would depend on the acknowledgment that regulatory competition is not the unmitigated good that neo-liberal economists claim it to be, and that there may be social values and political purposes that are more important than weeding out the last remaining national regulation that competition lawyers could construe to be a distortion of free competition. In this regard, the Commission and the European Court of Justice could learn much from the United States, where anti-trust law is applied much more vigorously against private monopolies than is true in Europe, but where, after the post-1937 decline of the 'negative commerce clause' doctrine, State legislation is generally not challenged by the anti-trust division or the federal courts unless it is in direct conflict with federal legislation.

In most other regards, however, the American situation is too different to allow direct lessons to be drawn for the European predicament. On the one hand, welfare-state functions have a much lower political salience in the American States than in European nation states, and the structural and institutional diversity in existing state functions is considerably lower than is true in Europe. On the other hand, the democratic legitimacy of decisions at the federal level is clear and strong, and the most important welfare-state functions—social security, Medicaid, or the earned income tax credit—are shaped by federal law rather than by the States. And even in those areas where the States have a role—unemployment insurance, social assistance, and active labour market policies—their choices are strongly conditioned by federal subsidies. Hence the incentives as well as the opportunities to engage in regulatory competition are relatively unimportant for the American States. The same is true for tax competition, which is dampened by the partial offset of State taxes against the federal income tax. None of these devices is available in Europe. In this regard, in short, transatlantic comparison serves primarily to highlight differences rather than to provide lessons that could be put into practice on the other shore.

References

Dehejia, Vivek H. and Genschel, Philipp (1999). 'Tax Competition in the European Union'. *Politics and Society*, 27: 403–30.

Dyson, Kenneth and Featherstone, Kevin (1999). *The Road to Maastricht. Negotiating Economic and Monetary Union*. Oxford: Oxford University Press.

Eichener, Volker (1997). 'Effective European Problem Solving: Lessons from the Regulation of Occupational Safety and Environmental Protection'. *Journal of European Public Policy*, 4: 591–608.

Esping-Andersen, Gøsta (1990). *The Three Worlds of Welfare Capitalism*. Cambridge: Polity Press.

——(1999). *Social Foundations of Postindustrial Economies*. Oxford: Oxford University Press.

Garrett, Geoffrey (1992). 'International Cooperation and Institutional Choice: The European Community's Internal Market'. *International Organization*, 46: 533–60.

Joerges, Christian and Vos, Ellen (eds) (1999). *EU Committees: Social Regulation, Law and Politics*. Oxford: Hart Publishing.

Moravcsik, Andrew (1998). *The Choice for Europe. Social Purpose and State Power from Messina to Maastricht*. Ithaca: Cornell University Press.

OECD (1999). *Social Expenditure Database 1980–1996*. Paris: OECD.

Pollack, Mark A. (1997). 'Representing Diffuse Interests in EC Policy-Making'. *Journal of European Public Policy*, 4: 572–90.

Riker, William H. (1982). *Liberalism against Populism: A Confrontation between the Theory of Democracy and the Theory of Social Choice*. San Francisco: W. H. Freeman.

Scharpf, Fritz W. (1988). 'The Joint Decision Trap: Lessons from German Federalism and European Integration'. *Public Administration*, 88: 239–78.

——(1997). 'Introduction: The Problem-Solving Capacity of Multilevel Governance'. *Journal of European Public Policy*, 4: 520–38.

——(1999). *Governing in Europe. Effective and Democratic?* Oxford: Oxford University Press.

——(2000). 'The Viability of Advanced Welfare States in the International Economy: Vulnerabilities and Options'. *Journal of European Public Policy*, 7/2: 190–228.

——and Vivien A. Schmidt (eds) (2000). *Welfare and Work in the Open Economy. Volume II: Diverse Responses to Common Challenges*. Oxford: Oxford University Press.

Schmidt, Susanne K. (1998). 'Commission Activism: Subsuming Telecommunications and Eelectricity under European Competition Law'. *Journal of European Public Policy*, 5: 128–45.

Schmidt, Vivien A. (2000). 'The Role of Values and Discourse in Welfare State Reform: The Politics of Successful Adjustment', in Fritz W. Scharpf and Vivien A. Schmidt (eds), *Welfare and Work in the Open Economy. Volume I: From Vulnerability to Competitiveness*. Oxford: Oxford University Press.

Skocpol, Theda (1995). *Social Policy in the United States: Future Possibilities in Historical Perspective*. Princeton: Princeton University Press.

—— and Amenta, Edwin (1986). 'The States and Social Policies'. *Annual Review of Sociology*, 12: 131–57.

Streeck, Wolfgang (1997). 'Industrial Citizenship under Regime Competition: The Case of the European Works Council'. *Journal of European Public Policy*, 4: 643–64.

Tsebelis, George (1994). 'The Power of the European Parliament as a Conditional Agenda Setter'. *American Political Science Review*, 88: 128–42.

Verdun, Amy (1996). 'An "Asymmetrical" Economic and Monetary Union in the EU: Perceptions of Monetary Authorities and Social Partners'. *Journal of European Integration*, 20: 59–81.

Williams, Shirley (1991). 'Sovereignty and Accountability in the European Community', in Robert O. Keohane and Stanley Hoffmann (eds), *The New European Community: Decision Making and Institutional Change*. Boulder: Westview.

V

Federalism, Legitimacy, and Identity

14

Citizenship and Federations: Some Preliminary Reflections

SUJIT CHOUDHRY

1. Federalism and Political Theory

Is federalism the future? To some, federalism is emerging as the defining constitutional arrangement of the twenty-first century. Will Kymlicka, for example, has gone so far as to proclaim that a 'federalist revolution' is sweeping the world.[1] To be sure, similar claims have been heard before; William Riker argued in 1964 that we lived in 'an Age of Federalism'.[2] Indeed, federalism is far from a recent innovation in constitutional design. In the post-war wave of constitutional engineering, countries as disparate as Germany, Austria, India, Nigeria, and Malaysia opted for federal arrangements, building upon the long experience of nations such as the United States, Canada, Australia, Switzerland, and Mexico with federal systems of government. What is startling, though, is that well-established liberal democracies hitherto organized as unitary states—notably the United Kingdom—are now in the process of refashioning themselves along federal lines to ensure their survival into the twenty-first century. Moreover, after a half century, the US Supreme Court has rediscovered the federalism-based limits on the authority of the federal government.[3]

I thank the Harvard University Center for Ethics and the Professions for financial support, Kalypso Nicolaidis for her kind invitation to speak at the conference, and Kalypso Nicolaidis and Robert Howse for their generous comments.

[1] Will Kymlicka, *Finding Our Way: Rethinking Ethnocultural Relations in Canada* (Toronto: Oxford University Press, 1998), 2.

[2] William H. Riker, *Federalism: Origin, Operation, Significance* (Boston: Little Brown, 1964), 1.

[3] For example, the United States Supreme Court has (a) developed the principle that the federal government cannot 'commandeer' State governments into implementing federal policy (*Printz v. United States*, 521 U.S. 898 (1997); *New York v. United States*, 505 U.S. 144 (1992)), and (b) begun to articulate limits to federal authority under the Commerce Clause (*United States v. Lopez*, 514 U.S. 549 (1995); *United States v. Morrison*, 120 S. Ct. 1740). For a detailed discussion of these cases, see George Bermann's contribution to this volume.

And these two trends *within* nation-states are occurring alongside the self-conscious and deliberate transformation of the European Union from a purely economic arrangement *among* nation-states into a nascent federal entity. Within nation-states, federalism is lauded for the values it promotes: the accommodation of territorially concentrated ethnocultural minorities, democratic self-government, policy experimentation, and the facilitation of a closer fit between people's preferences and public policies. In the EU, the move toward federalism is understood as providing a measure of political—and democratic—integration commensurate with the high degree of economic integration already achieved among Member States. It would seem that federalism's hour has arrived.

To others, though, the prospect that federalism is humanity's destiny is a cause not for celebration, but for circumspection and even trepidation. Far from being an unqualified success, federalism has had its failures; witness the dissolution of Czechoslovakia and the Soviet Union. In the US, federalism has been synonymous with the devolution of responsibility for welfare from the federal government to the States, and a corresponding rise in economic inequality.[4] In Canada, some argue that the institutions of federalism, rather than simply recognizing and accommodating pre-existing diversity, have also nurtured a sense of provincialism that now threatens to break up the country. During the South African constitutional negotiations, federalism was identified with ethnic nationalism and hence with the racist past. Even worse, federalism was unable to prevent the tragedy of Yugoslavia. Almost 30 years ago, Thomas Franck argued that, without a shared sense of political community, federations, no matter how well designed, are doomed to fail.[5] Federalism, then, captures both the hopes for and the fears of the new millennium.

It is readily apparent that federalism is central to any account of our contemporary political practice. It is accordingly a source of considerable embarrassment that federalism has received relatively scant attention from contemporary political theory. By comparison, most other features of contemporary liberal democracies—distributive justice and the welfare state, democracy, constitutionalism, and the rule of law, and more recently multiculturalism, citizenship, and immigration—have received sustained and probing examination from the likes of John Rawls, Jürgen Habermas, Judith Shklar, and Charles Taylor. This is not to say that federalism has not attracted academic attention. Political scientists and economists have produced a vast and illuminating literature on the origins and characteris-

[4] Paul E. Peterson, *The Price of Federalism* (Washington: Brookings Institution, 1995).

[5] Thomas M. Frank, 'Why Federations Fail', in Thomas M. Frank (ed.), *Why Federations Fail: An Inquiry into the Requisites for Successful Federalism* (New York: New York University Press, 1968).

tics of federal systems. But, as Wayne Norman argues, federalism still awaits the attention of political theory, in the manner that the welfare state did before Rawls.[6]

But why should political theorists take up Norman's invitation? Political theory is valuable in practice because it can provide just or fair solutions to political conflicts that would otherwise be resolved on the basis of brute power and political bargaining. A normative theory of federalism, for example, would be of practical assistance in designing just federal institutions, or in the judicial interpretation of open-textured constitutional language that aspires to divide jurisdiction between a federal government and the governments of federal sub-units in a principled fashion, such as the principle of subsidiarity in Art. 5 of the EC Treaty. But the benefits flow the other way as well, because an engagement with concrete political issues can furnish the occasion to reassess the basic principles of political theory. For example, reflection on the practice of federalism might lead us to revisit and reinterpret basic concepts such as democratic legitimacy and distributive justice.[7]

In this chapter, I offer some preliminary reflections on the place of citizenship in a theory of federalism. Citizenship is one of central concepts in political theory. An account of citizenship, at the very least, defines the criteria for, and the method for the acquisition of, membership in a political community. More importantly, it also lays down the rights and responsibilities which attach to membership. I have two points. First, I argue that the papers in this section further the debate on citizenship and federalism by invoking three different conceptions of citizenship—civic, ethnocultural, and economic—which in turn express different underlying conceptions of political community. Second, I argue that the papers do not fully

[6] Wayne Norman, 'Towards a Philosophy of Federalism', in Judith Baker (ed.), *Group Rights* (Toronto: University of Toronto Press, 1994), 79–100, at 97. Norman himself offers the outline of a theory of federalism in this article. For other recent attempts, see Mark Tushnet, 'Federalism and Liberalism' (1996) 4 *Cardozo Journal of International and Comparative Law* 329–44, 'Federalism as a Cure for Democracy's Discontent?', in Anita L. Allen and Milton C. Regan (eds), *Debating Democracy's Discontent: Essays on American Politics, Law, and Public Philosophy* (New York: Oxford University Press, 1998). Will Kymlicka also discusses federalism in *Multicultural Citizenship* (Oxford: Oxford University Press, 1995), 116–20, 181–91, as does Charles Taylor, 'Shared and Divergent Values', in Ronald L. Watts and Douglas M. Brown (eds), *Options for a New Canada* (Toronto: University of Toronto Press, 1991), and James Tully, *Strange Multiplicity: Constitutionalism in an Age of Diversity* (Cambridge: Cambridge University Press, 1996), 140–82. By contrast, the term 'federalism' does not appear in the index to John Rawls's *A Theory of Justice* (Cambridge: Harvard University Press, 1971), widely regarded as the most significant work of political philosophy written in the twentieth century.

[7] I discuss the correct relationship of the facts of political sociology to normative political theory in 'National Minorities and Ethnic Immigrants: Liberalism's Political Sociology', *Journal of Political Philosophy* (forthcoming).

address the complication that federalism poses for citizenship, which I term the problem of divided or multiple allegiances.

2. Identifying the Issues

Three Conceptions of Citizenship and Two Constraints for Liberal Democracies

The chapters that follow articulate three different conceptions of citizenship. Since these conceptions have been developed at length elsewhere, I will introduce them briefly. As well, in order to situate the work of the authors, I will briefly describe the debate raging among political theorists about the appropriate conception of citizenship for liberal democracies.

First, citizenship can be understood in *ethnocultural* terms. Political communities are imagined as emerging from peoples or nations that are united by a common bond that exists independent of and prior to the creation of a political community, and which is the object of loyalty, belonging, or identification.[8] In its extreme formulations, the ethnocultural conception of citizenship is defined by descent—that is, race or ethnicity—and thus precludes the possibility of the acquisition of membership by outsiders. More moderate formulations, however, define the nation in terms of a shared language, history, religion, cultural traditions, or some combination thereof, thereby maintaining the possibility of the acquisition of membership by persons who lack these characteristics but who choose to embrace them. An individual is a member of a people or nation because she possesses the nation's defining characteristics. Crucially, these sociological or anthropological criteria possess normative significance. Political communities, generally nation-states, exist or ought to exist in a one-to-one relationship with nations or peoples, such that only nations or peoples should constitute political communities. Citizenship in the political community tracks membership in the underlying nation or people. Moreover, political communities are valued because they are the means whereby a people or nation ensures its survival and flourishing, through the instrument of the state. Citizens have an obligation to participate in this collective enterprise; moreover, on extreme versions of nationalism, the rights they have are limited to the extent that they conflict with the collective project that gives the political community its *raison d'être*.

[8] For the moment, I put to one side 'liberal' nationalists such as Yael Tamir, *Liberal Nationalism* (Princeton: Princeton University Press, 1993), who sharply distinguish nationality from ethnicity.

Elsewhere, Robert Howse calls this the 'community of identity'; Habermas's *Schicksalsgemeinschaft* captures the same idea.[9]

A second conception of citizenship can be termed the *civic* conception of citizenship.[10] In its strongest form, the political community is based not on a pre-political bond, but rather on an allegiance to shared principles of political justice flowing from a liberal political morality, and to a common set of political institutions through which those principles are realized. A political community is imagined as a voluntary association of citizens considered free and equal, who constitute a political community because of a shared belief that they should associate for political ends. In Ernest Renan's famous phrase, the nation is a daily plebiscite whose existence depends on the will of its members.[11] The key point is that citizenship can be held by any person willing to affirm and uphold the principles of political justice and the political institutions that lie at the foundation of a political community. In principle, then, citizenship is defined by factors accessible to all. Moreover, since the civic conception of citizenship is a liberal conception, commitment to principles of political morality does not require the endorsement of a particular set of lifestyle or cultural preferences, or to a way of life in the communitarian sense. Political communities that imagine themselves in civic terms thus aspire to be open, pluralistic, and inclusive. The civic conception is also democratic, and implies the possibility for citizens to deliberate about, commit to, and reinterpret the principles of political justice that are the basis of social unity. More moderate formulations of the civic conception of citizenship embrace and celebrate the particular way in which universal principles of political morality are embodied in and articulated by a political community's particular institutions and political culture.[12] However, even here, the celebration of the particular is careful to remain open, tolerant, and inclusive, and thus draws a sharp distinction between the affirmation of the public or institutional aspects of a particular political community and the normative communities of the private sphere. Howse's 'community of association', Elizabeth Meehan's 'principled bonds', and Habermas's

[9] Jürgen Habermas, *Between Facts and Norms* (Cambridge: MIT Press, 1996), 491–515; R. Howse, 'Searching for Plan A: National Unity and the Chretien Government's New Federalism', in Harvey Lazar (ed.), *Non-Constitutional Renewal* (Kingston: Institute of Intergovernmental Relations, 1998), at 313–17.

[10] Michael Walzer, 'Comment', in Charles Taylor, *Multiculturalism and the Politics of Recognition*, 2nd edn (Princeton: Princeton University Press, 1994).

[11] Ernest Renan, 'What is a Nation', in Geoff Eley and Ronald Grigor Suny (eds), *Becoming National: A Reader* (New York and Oxford: Oxford University Press, 1996).

[12] For example, Jeremy Webber, 'Just How Civic is Civic Nationalism in Quebec?', in A. C. Cairns *et al.* (eds), *Citizenship, Diversity and Pluralism: Canadian and Comparative Perspectives* (Montreal and Kingston: McGill-Queen's University Press, 1999).

Verfassungspatriotismus—constitutional patriotism—are versions of this conception of political community.

Finally, citizenship can be conceived of in *economic* terms.[13] On this conception, individuals are imagined as principally concerned with pursuing their private economic interests, and therefore view their relationships with each other, and with institutions, in strictly instrumental terms. Political institutions and political communities are valuable in as much as they serve personal or private ends. The primary vehicle for satisfying private preferences is the market. In economists' terms, political institutions exist to remedy market failures: externalities, information asymmetries, monopoly and monopsony power, public goods, and so on. Embedded in this conception of citizenship is a view of politics as continuous with the isolated and private expression of preferences that occurs in the marketplace; the role of political institutions is to register those preferences accurately and to aggregate them correctly. Meehan implicitly refers to this idea when she claims that the EU possesses 'social legitimacy in the delivery of policies that meet peoples' private interests'. Marc Landy and Steven Teles gesture to the same understanding of citizenship when they analogize the provision of private goods in the market to the provision of public goods by federal sub-units.

Set against the background of these different conceptions of citizenship, political theorists working within a liberal democratic framework have raised two sorts of questions or, more precisely, have stipulated that a conception of citizenship must satisfy two constraints in order to be suitable for liberal democracies. The first is the normative question of whether a particular conception of citizenship can serve as the basis of political legitimacy in societies that aspire to be liberal democracies. I term this the *legitimacy constraint*. The legitimacy constraint emerges from the centrality of individual freedom to the liberal conception of political community, both in intimate or associational and in public life. As Jeremy Waldron has explained, liberalism expresses a view on the appropriate relationship between individual freedom and social order.[14] The problem that political community poses for liberals is that individuals are subject to laws which restrain their freedom and which are enforced by the coercive institutions of the state. Coercive impositions *per se* are not objectionable; indeed, had those constraints been consented to, the enforcement of a coercive regime of laws would honour, not detract from, freedom. The problem is that

[13] This account is inspired by Jon Elster, 'The Market and the Forum: Three Varieties of Political Theory', in J. Elster and A. Aanun (eds), *The Foundations of Social Choice Theory* (Cambridge: Cambridge University Press, 1986).

[14] Jeremy Waldron, 'Theoretical Foundations of Liberalism' (1987) 37 *Philosophical Quarterly* 127–50.

coercive laws have, for the most part, not been consented to by the individuals subject to them. Liberal democrats have grappled with the non-consensual nature of public power by proposing what Frank Michelman usefully terms a constitutional contractarian justification.[15] In the place of consent, liberals invoke the second-best of hypothetical consent, and ask whether the coercive exercise of political power could be reasonably accepted by citizens considered free and equal and who possess both a capacity for and a desire to enter into fair terms of cooperation. The argument from hypothetical consent, though, has limited legitimizing force, because it cannot plausibly be used to justify each and every exercise of public power within a political community. Accordingly, liberal democrats argue that the legitimacy constraint is satisfied if citizens would have consented to a system of law-making; the legitimacy of that *system* secures the legitimacy of whatever particular decisions emerge from it. In the liberal political imagination, the constitutional scheme that emerges from this exercise is the familiar package of civil and political liberties, along with the institutions of democratic decision-making: electoral systems, legislatures, and perhaps even written constitutions and judicial review.

Additionally, for a conception of citizenship to be appropriate for liberal democracies, it must comply with what I term the *stability* constraint. Here, the question is whether a conception of citizenship provides a sufficiently strong basis for social unity to ensure the survival of a political community. Thus, in contrast to the legitimacy constraint, the stability constraint is a sociological criterion. The stability constraint emerges from what can be called the social peace purpose of liberal political theory, as reflected most recently in the political liberalism of Rawls.[16] Rawls's starting point in his most recent work is a pair of sociological facts. The first is the fact of reasonable pluralism, that is, the claim that the existence of a diversity of comprehensive religious, philosophical, and moral doctrines found in modern democratic societies is not a mere historical condition, but is rather a permanent feature of the public culture of modern democracies, and is in part a function of the political and social conditions secured by institutions of liberal democracy. The second is the fact of oppression: that is, the claim that, given the fact of reasonable pluralism, the construction and maintenance of a political community around a single moral, religious, or philosophical doctrine would require the oppressive use of state power. The challenge for liberal democrats is to fashion terms of social cooperation that would permit such a deeply divided

[15] Frank Michelman, 'W(h)ither the Constitution?', (2000) 21 *Cardozo Law Review* 1063–83.

[16] John Rawls, *Political Liberalism* (New York, Columbia University Press, 1993). I am indebted to Rob Howse for pressing this point on me.

citizenry to live together in a single political community without recourse to oppression.

As William Galston reminds us, the social-peace purpose of liberal political theory originated in Europe during the Reformation, where the issue at hand was how to fashion political communities for societies deeply and profoundly divided along religious lines.[17] The religious differences of the Reformation gave rise to the doctrine of toleration as a central strategy for managing diversity. In this light, the Rawlsian project is to extend the notion of toleration from religion to cultural, moral, and philosophical differences. The image of political community which is demanded by the social-peace purpose of liberalism has a variety of characteristics; for the purposes of this brief discussion, it is broadly similar to the one that emerges from the legitimacy constraint. In particular, liberal democrats posit that political communities which are open, tolerant, and pluralistic—that is, which do not conflate membership in cultural, religious or ethnic communities and citizenship in political communities, and allow agreement on common terms of political cooperation, without demanding in addition agreement on a common normative framework for intimate and associational life—are *for that reason* stable.

To be sure, the legitimacy and stability constraints are distinct. Thus, societies can be stable while lacking legitimacy. I have in mind here authoritarian regimes, or traditional, hierarchical societies based on personalized systems of authority. Conversely, societies can meet the test of legitimacy, while lacking stability; the Weimar Republic is a well known example. The distinct feature of the civic conception of citizenship is that it ties together these two conditions, such that the criteria that lead a political community to satisfy the former simultaneously lead it to satisfy the latter. This is no coincidence; the convergence of the legitimacy and stability constraints is a core feature of the civic conception of citizenship. To put the point another way, the very same principles of political morality that legitimize the constitutional framework of liberal democracies also perform the sociological function of serving as the cement of social unity. Moreover, I would argue that it is the aspiration of the civic conception of citizenship that the legitimacy and stability constraints be satisfied simultaneously, because it is based on an image of political community held together only to the extent that there is sufficient reason or justification for it to exist.

The civic conception of citizenship has come under trenchant criticism, though, from those who doubt that the bond of social unity created by the civic conception of citizenship is sufficiently strong for a liberal political community to achieve some of its central goals. There are a number of

[17] William Galston, 'Two Concepts of Liberalism' (1995) 105 *Ethics* 516–34.

variations to this criticism.[18] Habermas suggests, for example, that the civic conception of citizenship alone is insufficient to ensure the stability or endurance of the institutions of liberal democracy, and must be supplemented by a supportive political culture.[19] In a similar vein, Taylor argues that the civic conception of citizenship cannot nurture in sufficient numbers of citizens the capacity for outrage required for citizens to be able to guard against violations of the norm of self-rule and to protect liberal democracies from descending into tyranny.[20] David Miller claims that the civic conception of citizenship on its own is insufficient to generate the sort of social trust that is required for democratic decision-making: for example, the sort of trust that makes compromise possible in the face of conflicting interests and scarce resources on the understanding that in future circumstances, parties that benefit from those compromises will make concessions.[21] Miller also claims that something more than the civic conception is necessary for schemes of redistribution that are based on grounds of social justice or need, as opposed to self-interest: that is, as a form of social insurance. Finally, it has also been argued that in moments of political crisis, the civic conception of citizenship provides insufficient resources for a political community to respond to threats to its survival.

Taken together, these criticisms suggest that the civic conception of citizenship fails to satisfy the stability constraint, because it is incapable, sociologically speaking, of generating a sufficient degree of social unity for liberal democracies to realize many of their most important objectives. What are the reasons for this inadequacy? The civic conception of citizenship, since it imagines political communities as voluntary associations, depends on the will of its members to exist. But it is far from clear what the source of this willed commitment is. One answer, pressed most recently by Habermas, is that the universalistic principles of political morality that underlie the civic conception of citizenship itself can generate this sort of associational impulse, a sort of belonging or identification historically associated with the ethnocultural conception of citizenship, that at once generates a willed commitment that avoids the exclusionary and discriminatory tendencies of the latter. However, critics have argued that constitutional patriotism is incapable of this task, because universalistic principles of political morality are too general and abstract. Patchen Markell, for

[18] For a partial taxonomy of these criticisms, see Andrew Mason, 'Political Community, Liberal-Nationalism, and the Ethics of Assimilation' (1999) 109 *Ethics* 261–86. For an interesting discussion of this issue, see Christopher H. Wellman, 'Relational Facts in Liberal Political Theory: Is There Magic in the Pronoun "My"?' (2000) 110 *Ethics* 537–62.

[19] Habermas, *Between Facts and Norms*.

[20] Charles Taylor, 'Cross-Purposes: The Liberal-Communitarian Debate', in *Philosophical Arguments* (Cambridge, MA: Harvard University Press, 1995), 181–203.

[21] David Miller, *On Nationality* (Oxford: Oxford University Press, 1995).

example, claims that an important motivation for complying with the terms of political cooperation—apart from the principles of political morality upon which those terms of cooperation are based, and self-interest—is that those terms of political cooperation generate an image of a visibly identifiable group of citizens in which citizens can see themselves.[22] In other words, citizens must be able to *identify* with a political community as their own—they must be able to claim ownership in the institutions of a political community, in the issues dealt with by those institutions, in the manner in which those issues are debated, and in the decisions of those institutions.[23] Markell's point could be put another way: that the universalistic principles of political morality that underlie the civic conception of citizenship cannot serve as a source of associational motives for *particular* political communities because they are framed in *universal* terms, that is, in terms that seem to forbid the invocation of these particular relationships as justifications for political action. Accordingly, they must be supplemented with reasons that explain why individuals should meet the obligations of citizenship of the political communities of which they are a part.

One response to the challenge of social unity, then, is to embrace and celebrate the particularity of political communities. Thus, as Jeremy Webber argues, for example, alongside universalistic principles of political morality, political discourse in liberal democracies should cherish a political community's specific institutions, its particular political history, its particular culture and perhaps its language.[24] There is an important ambiguity here, though, over the manner in which these particular characteristics are connected to universal principles of political morality. I shall return to this issue below. At this point, though, let us assume that nationality is being harnessed in the service of liberal state, whereas by contrast, in the ethnocultural conception of citizenship, the state is harnessed in the service of nationality. National identity, for liberal democrats, possess instrumental as opposed to intrinsic value.

For liberal democrats, though, the problem that this strategy poses is that the social unity achieved through the affirmation of particularity may conflict with both the legitimacy and the stability constraints. The conflict with the legitimacy constraint is clearest, and has been voiced most frequently. The central fear is that public policies which valorize or affirm the particularity of a political community may clash with the commitment of the civic conception of citizenship to a tolerant, pluralistic, and inclusive

[22] Patchen Markell, 'Making Affect Safe for Democracy? On "Constitutional Patriotism"' (2000) 28 *Political Theory* 38–63.

[23] Kymlicka, *Multicultural Citizenship*, 188–91.

[24] Webber, 'Just How Civic is Civic Nationalism'.

political community. These sorts of conflicts, for example, have arisen in Quebec with respect to language and educational policy, where the protection and promotion of the use of French as the principal language of public discourse has been relied upon to restrict the protected rights of the English-language minority and recently arrived ethnic immigrants. And the same sorts of policies may conflict with the stability constraint, because the construction of a political community in particular terms creates the danger of exclusion. As Andrew Mason argues, when people cannot identify with the institutions and public policies of a polity, they are less likely to have a stake in the stability or survival of that political community.[25] Indeed, the reason for the shift to civic nationalism in the first place was the search for principles of social integration that could provide the cement of social solidarity within a heterogeneous polity. The search for identity may accordingly have a perverse effect, and undermine rather than strengthen the stability of a liberal political order.

Most of the authors in this section engage with this debate, either implicitly (Meehan, Landy, and Teles) or explicitly (Lacorne). However, they reframe both the stability and legitimacy questions in the context of the EU, and ask what conception of citizenship should operate at the Union, or federal, level. As this brief discussion suggests, citizenship is hardly a new question to political theory. But it is worth noting that while the intellectual terrain has been well-trodden within the context of unitary states, the unique challenges posed to citizenship by federal arrangements, *at the federal level*, have not received the same degree of attention.

The Problem of Divided or Multiple Allegiances

Federal systems raise an additional complication for theories of citizenship, which I term the problem of divided or multiple allegiances. It is often asserted that the existence of divided or multiple allegiances is one of the defining features of federalism, and that this trait somehow creates difficulties for traditional understandings of citizenship. Unfortunately, it is not at all clear what the problem of divided or multiple allegiances is, and accordingly, what complications it creates. Three plausible interpretations present themselves.

First, federalism may create multiple loyalties because it demands that individuals be citizens of more than one political community simultaneously. A citizen of Spain, for example, is also a citizen of the EU; a citizen of Quebec is also a citizen of Canada. On this interpretation, multiple membership is problematic because it is the potential source of political

[25] Mason, 'Political Community'.

instability. The implicit hypothetical here is a situation where the sub-federal and federal political communities impose conflicting obligations on citizens, such that the good citizen cannot satisfy both. For example, Europe demanded that *as good Europeans*, Austrians not include the Freedom Party in a coalition government, whereas the Austrian state demanded that its citizens, *as good Austrians*, abide by the results of a free and fair electoral process. Individuals who wish to satisfy the obligations of citizenship of both political communities will be torn. Granted, the conflicts may not be as fundamental as this one; the European Union and a Member State, for example, may disagree over labour or environmental standards; or, in the Canadian context, the federal and provincial governments may differ over the best way to structure and deliver social policy. Nevertheless, the possibility that the obligations of citizenship at the federal and sub-federal level may conflict remains.

The problem of *conflicting obligations* should be distinguished from the political instability created when individuals understand their membership in a federal entity as conditioned on their prior membership in a federal sub-unit. Call this the problem of *conditional membership*. For example, as a matter of law, citizens of the United Kingdom are citizens of the EU *because* they are citizens of the United Kingdom; moreover, they may understand their European citizenship in a parasitic or secondary way. As Will Kymlicka has explained, the problem here is that the authority of the federal political community is sometimes derivative upon the powers ceded to it by pre-existing sub-federal political communities.[26] Implicit in this arrangement is the understanding that the cession of powers is conditional upon respecting the terms of federation. The derivative and conditional nature of certain federal arrangements, it is thought, manifests itself in a form of derivative and conditional citizenship which is weaker than membership in a sub-federal community, which is primary and unconditional.[27] Moreover, in cases of conflict—particularly when the terms of federation are breached—sub-federal allegiances prevail. Indeed, should the terms of federation not be respected, secession by a federal sub-unit remains an option.

The third interpretation of the problem of divided or multiple allegiances refers to the reliance on differing conceptions of citizenship at the federal and sub-federal level. Call this the problem of *normative disso-*

[26] Kymlicka, *Multicultural Citizenship*, 182. The obvious exception is the United States, where it is thought that the federal government derives its constitutional authority from the American people, not from the States. For a recent statement of this view, see Bruce Ackerman, *We The People: Foundations* (Cambridge, MA: Harvard University Press, 1991).

[27] One could argue that the derivative and conditional nature of federal citizenship is more a feature of confederal than of federal systems.

nance. To again use the example of Europe, imagine that the EU invokes a civic or economic conception of citizenship, or some combination thereof, whereas Italy relies on an ethnocultural understanding of membership in its national political community. The complication raised by federalism is that these conceptions of citizenship might be in tension, leading to the political version of cognitive dissonance. Is it coherent, for example, for an individual to understand her membership in the Italian political community in ethnocultural terms and at the same time understand her membership in the political community of Europe in civic terms? Would the adoption of a civic notion of citizenship at the European level not pose a challenge to national communities to redefine themselves in civic terms? Many authors answer this question in the negative, arguing that federalism promotes political stability precisely because of the potential to define citizenship at the federal and sub-federal level in dramatically different terms.[28, 29]

How do these interpretations of the problem of divided or multiple allegiances relate to our earlier discussion? I would argue that they implicate the stability constraint, because each of them provides a different reason why federal political communities may face challenges to social unity. In this respect, though, it is important to be very clear about the *way* in which federalism may contribute to instability, because it is so often misunderstood. In this volume, for example, Lacorne appears to analogize between the threats to social unity posed by social heterogeneity and those posed by federal arrangements, suggesting that the former holds important lessons for the latter. It is understandable that Lacorne should make this link. As I argued above, theorists working within the social peace tradition of liberalism have been preoccupied with the threat that social heterogeneity poses to the stability of political communities. The concern appears to be that the various collective identities possessed by citizens in liberal democracies characterized by the fact of reasonable pluralism—gender, ethnicity, race, religion, and so on—might weaken the attachment or identification of individuals with their political communities. Federal arrangements, on this view, generate another set of collective identities that pose the same sort of problem.

However, it is important not to conflate the manner in which collective identities and federalism implicate the stability constraint. As Joseph

28 For example, Raymond Breton, 'Identification in Transnational Political Communities', in Karen Knop *et al.* (eds), *Rethinking Federalism: Citizens, Markets, and Governments in a Changing World* (Vancouver: University of British Columbia Press, 1995), at 55.

29 My intuition is that the three senses of multiple or conflicting allegiances can have a synergistic effect. Thus, the problems for political stability inherent in a federal system can be compounded by the conditional and derivative nature of federal citizenship, and the adoption of different conceptions of citizenship at the federal and sub-federal level.

Carens is right to point out, the liberal tradition does not claim that citizens lack forms of collective identity other than membership in political communities, or even that those forms of collective identity are not politically significant.[30] Indeed, the creation of a space for the flourishing of communities of identity, and the political salience of those identities, is a central part of the liberal settlement. Carens's point is that these sorts of identity groups are not typically experienced by the persons who possess them as political communities. Rather, members of those identity groups, despite their differences, still understand their primary political identity as citizens of the state.

The key difference is that membership in a federal sub-unit or federal entity *is* experienced as a sort of political membership. Federal entities are therefore characterized by multiple political communities. The key point is that political diversity of this sort is qualitatively different from cultural diversity. The difference lies in the fact that each of these political communities requires the same sort of identification on the part of its citizens in order to possess the degree of social unity that political communities in unitary states require. In fact, we can say that political communities make identification claims on their citizens, and these claims compete in the same political space with one another. The manner in which these identification claims conflict can vary, and in essence, the differing interpretations of the problem of divided or multiple allegiances specify different ways in which they can conflict.

3. Conceptions of Citizenship in the European Union

Despite their practical importance and theoretical interest, the issue of conflicting or divided loyalties, and its connection to the problem of stability in liberal democracies, is one which the chapters in this section do not squarely address. In the course of my discussion, though, I will draw out the implications of what the authors *do* say for these issues. So what do these chapters add to the discussion on citizenship? They make two contributions. First, the difference between the ethnocultural and civic conceptions of citizenship, although important in theory, may be somewhat less so in practice in the context of federal states. Second, the trade-off in federations that allow for the mobility of factors of production is not between local democracy and economic efficiency, but is rather between the promotion of political community at the level of federal sub-units and

[30] Joseph Carens, *Culture, Citizenship, and Community: A Contextual Exploration of Justice as Evenhandedness* (Oxford: Oxford University Press, 2000), 166–7.

at the level of the federation as a whole. I make the first point against the background of a discussion of Lacorne with an essay by Howse addressing similar problems in the Canadian context, and the second through a comparison of Howse's reflections on the Canadian context with Landy and Teles.

Beyond Civic vs Ethnic Citizenship: Toward the Community of Fate

Lacorne's contribution occurs against the background of a widespread debate over the possibilities for, and the shape of, European citizenship. In some quarters, there has been a great deal of scepticism about the prospects for a European citizenship, largely because citizenship has been imagined strictly in ethnocultural terms. The model here is the European nation-state. Since there is no European people or nation to speak of, who share a common race, religion, language, or history, the idea of a European political community, and hence a European citizenship, are logical non-sequiturs. Joseph Weiler, who himself does not hold this position, describes this view well:

> Turning to Europe, it is argued as a matter of empirical observation, based on these organic cultural-national criteria, that there is not European demos—not a people not a nation. Neither the subjective element (the sense of shared collective identity and loyalty) nor the objective conditions which could produce these (the kind of homogeneity of the organic national-cultural conditions on which peoplehood depend exist).[31]

In the opposite camp lie constitutional patriots like Habermas, who imagine a European political community liberated from the ties of ethnocultural identity, and united instead by a shared commitment to liberal democracy. As Habermas writes, 'The nation of citizens finds its identity not in ethnic and cultural commonalities but in the practice of citizens who actively exercise their rights to participation and communication.'[32] This is Habermas' ideal of a nation-state; however, he would also apply to 'a future Federal Republic of European States'.[33]

At first glance, Lacorne and Howse would appear to have aligned themselves with the opposing camps in this debate. Thus, Lacorne is deeply sceptical of the prospect of a civic conception of citizenship being sufficient for the emerging European federal entity. As he puts it, 'abstract "postnational citizenship"' or 'pure constitutional patriotism' will not

[31] Joseph H. H. Weiler, *The State 'über alles': Demos, Telos and the German Maastricht Decision*, Jean Monnet Working Paper Series 6/95 (Cambridge: Harvard Law School, 1995), 5.

[32] Habermas, *Between Facts and Norms*, 495.

[33] Ibid., 499 and 500.

suffice, because citizenship requires a thicker set of commitments, a 'substantial citizenship'. By contrast, Howse is critical of fashioning federal citizenship around a community of identity, asserting that it will likely produce forceful and highly destabilizing counteractions from the pre-existing communities of identity; in the Canadian case, the example is Quebec. By contrast, a federal entity organized as a community of association—Howse's version of the civic conception—can exist as a genuine and original democratic community, and is therefore normatively preferable.

But, upon closer inspection, Lacorne and Howse are not as far apart as they originally seem. First consider Lacorne. Although an enthusiast of a citizenship based on a shared identity, Lacorne cannot argue for a European citizenship based on a shared *ethnocultural* identity, because there is none. Instead, he grounds European citizenship on 'common and concrete political experiences'. He then argues that the value of these shared experiences is that they give rise to 'a new European ethics of responsibility'. In other words, the European identity should be centred on a culture of democracy and public accountability, and, after the EU's response to Haider, non-discrimination. But these values, of course, would be regarded by constitutional patriots as universal values.

Lacorne might respond that his position is different from that of constitutional patriots like Habermas, because the salience of these values is illustrated and reinforced by their use in historical and political narratives that grow out of and rely on concrete political events. But even here, the distinction is not as sharp as it initially seems. Faced with the criticism that the civic conception of citizenship cannot serve as the cement of social solidarity, Habermas's response is, at first blush, to accept it. In a passage suggestive of Montesquieu, Habermas argues that 'constitutionally protected institutions of freedom are worth only what a population *accustomed* to political freedom and settled in the "we" perspective of active self-determination makes of them'.[34] Indeed, in a later passage, Habermas makes the point rather more explicitly:

> Constitutional principles can neither take shape in social practices nor become the driving force for the dynamic project of creating an association of free and equal persons until they are situated in the historical context of a nation of citizens in a way that they link up with those citizens' motives and attitudes.[35]

So wherein lies the difference between Lacorne and Habermas? Earlier on, I mentioned that the celebration of particularity necessitated by political communities that understand themselves in civic terms in order for citizens to identify with them is ambiguous on the relationship between

[34] Ibid. [35] Ibid.

those particular features and universalistic principles of political morality. The central case here is the American identity, and students of European integration would do well to examine it carefully. Taylor, for example, discusses the patriotic identification of Americans with 'the American way of life', which he describes as a

> common identity and history defined by a commitment to certain ideals, articulated famously in the Declaration of Independence, the Gettysburg Address, and such documents, which in turn derive their importance from their connection to certain climactic transitions of shared history.[36]

This passage from Taylor is ambiguous with respect to two different accounts of the relationship between universal values and the particularity of political communities. On the one hand, these particular features can possess *intrinsic* value, such that the mere existence of historical events or particular political institutions counts as reasons in an account of national identity and as sources of political argument. In the American context, for example, the constitution is often invoked in this way in political discourse, so that the fact that the constitution speaks to an issue carries normative force. Likewise, in American political culture, history is invoked as a distinct source of obligation. The crime of slavery, for example, is thought to give rise to a special obligation on the part of the American political community to combat racial discrimination. In the same way, one could argue that the Holocaust creates a special responsibility on the part of Germany toward combating religious bigotry. All of this is not to say that universal values do not matter. Rather, the claim is that the particular features of political communities count as additional sources of political obligation above and beyond principles of political morality. Indeed, some would go further and argue that those values acquire their significance only because of their role in the history of the polity, and their embodiment in its institutions. Those particular features have a kind of enacting force.

On the other hand, the particular features of a political community can have merely *instrumental* value. They are valuable not in themselves, but because they embody or implement general principles of a universal nature. The particular features of a political community serve a functional role, because universal principles cannot serve as the cement of political integration unless they are situated in a historically informed and concrete way so that they can count as reasons for participating in schemes of political cooperation. As Kymlicka argues, history furnishes the symbols, precedents, and reference points for political discourse.[37] On this account, the American constitution is valued because it creates an effective

[36] Taylor, 'Cross-Purposes', 196.

[37] Kymlicka, *Finding Our Way*, 174.

institutional mechanism for realizing the universal values of freedom and equality. Likewise, the civil war and the Holocaust are concrete narratives that illustrate the importance of the universal value of non-discrimination. At the end of day, though, what counts are not the particular features of a political community per se, but the possibility of deriving the values embedded in that particularity from the universal values upon which liberal democracies are founded.

I suspect Lacorne—and Taylor—prefer the intrinsic value of particular political communities, whereas Habermas clearly views their value in instrumental terms. Thus, Habermas does not take his concession to the importance of history and context to require an abandonment of the universalist ideals that underlie the civic conception of citizenship. On the contrary, he points to the example of the United States as a political community in which shared principles of political justice are woven into historical narratives and have served as a basis for social unity without the need to resort to pre-political traits of the American political community. He concludes, then, by reasserting that 'democratic citizenship need not be rooted in the national identity of a people', but while at the same time, acknowledging the need for 'a common political culture'.[38]

But how far can the construction of political communities around particularity take us beyond a strictly instrumental account? Howse is illuminating in this regard. Howse defines a civic identity not only in terms of a commitment to universal values, but also by a commitment to 'shared or overlapping goals and common projects' that are quite specific: for example, saving the environment or eliminating child poverty.[39] Given that, on the civic conception of citizenship, it is the shared principles of political justice that lie at the foundation of political community, how can Howse also justify the reliance on specific projects or ends as part of the civic bond? Howse is not explicit on this point. I suspect that he would argue that these specific projects are interpretations or applications of shared political values, in light of a political community's concrete experiences. However, there are limitations to this rationale. Although some specific public policies can be understood as the implementation of basic principles of political justice—for example, rights to basic income support and health care—many others cannot. It is not entirely clear, for example, why basic principles of political justice would demand the protection of important public spaces, both urban and natural, for their aesthetic value, or a massive public investment in basic scientific research for its own sake, or the arts, or even the promotion and protection of particular industries—for example, agriculture—of long-standing importance.

[38] Habermas, *Between Facts and Norms*, 500.

[39] Howse, 'Searching for Plan A', 315.

Alternatively, it could be that these shared projects arise out of the shared experiences of a political community. Thus, shared experiences or history, on Howse's version of the civic conception of citizenship, *can* count as reasons in political discourse. But how can political communities avoid the danger that the history that is relied on is exclusionary, fraught with controversy, and hence of dubious legitimacy and a threat to stability? Again, Howse does not address this issue, but, if we are working from within the civic conception, a crucial point must be that those experiences *cannot* be traced to some pre-political bond of identity or ethnicity. Rather, they arise out of the shared political history of a community that understands itself in civic terms. As well, in order to maintain fidelity to the civic conception of citizenship, two constraints must be complied with. First, shared experiences or history can count as reasons in a civic political community as long as they do not contravene the basic principles of political justice. For example, appeals to traditions that are discriminatory or exclusionary—for example, strictly heterosexual notions of the family, or the gendered division of labour—are inadmissible. Second, shared experiences and history can count as reasons in a political community so long as they are not immune from critical reflection and reassessment, for at the very core of the liberal democratic tradition lies a desire to challenge the conventional wisdom and received dogma as the basis for political order.

There are two lessons to be drawn from this discussion. The first is that an ethnocultural conception of identity is, sociologically speaking, not an option for federations that incorporate more than one ethnocultural group. And the second is that the option that falls out of Howse's discussion—a shared set of political projects that arises out of common and concrete political experiences—can have a place in a political community that understands itself in civic terms, as long as those shared projects do not contravene basic principles of political justice, and are open to reassessment. In very practical terms, in the European context, and I suspect in the Canadian context, there is a convergence between the two radically different ways of understanding political community that are on the table. Following Raymond Breton, I would tentatively term this conception of citizenship the *community of fate*. As a matter of political sociology, Breton suggests that this conception of community could arise in a transnational political entity through 'the experience of interdependence', which leads to people perceiving their economic well-being and prospects for survival as being tied to members of other federal sub-units.[40] As he writes, 'identification with the system of organized interdependence is

[40] Breton, 'Identification in Transnational Political Communities', 42.

based on reciprocity, on joint investments and participation in collective achievements, and on the perceived fairness of the distribution of costs and benefits'.[41] This conception of political community has affinities with the economic conception of citizenship—'organized interdependence based on reciprocity'—but it goes well beyond it. Thus, Breton speaks of a sense of political community that grows out of politics, instead of preceding it, and that combines questions of justice—'the perceived fairness of the distribution of costs and benefits'—with a commitment to specific ends—'joint investments and participation in collective achievements'. At first impression, the community of fate likely meets both the sociological constraint of a durable social bond, and the normative constraint of compliance with the basic principle of liberal legitimacy.

Moreover, my initial intuition is that it is particularly well-suited for Europe. The project of European integration was not premised on any pre-political identification among the citizens of Member States, but has instead generated a nascent political identity that has grown out of the concrete political experiences surrounding the creation and regulation of the European economic space. The European political ethos is clearly concerned with the distributive implications of economic integration, through the various components of the EU Structural Funds programme—the European Regional Development Fund, the European Social Fund, and the European Agricultural Guidance and Guarantee Fund. It would be fair to say that Europeans consider economic integration to be an enormous collective achievement, to a considerable extent because it has institutionalized peaceful relations of interdependence governed by law among Member States that a half-century ago were engulfed in continent-wide armed conflict. For all these reasons, the European political identity appears to fit the community of fate. However, I leave the elaboration of this model, including its implications for the problem of divided or multiple allegiances, for another day.[42]

Political Community Trade-Offs arising from Economic Integration

What of the economic theory of citizenship? This understanding of citizenship would appear to be central to any account of the European Union, given that the 'fundamental freedoms' enshrined in the EC Treaty

[41] Breton, 'Identification in Transnational Political Communities', 42.

[42] My instinct as that the community of fate may have the potential to justify the inter-regional redistribution of wealth that is one of the defining features of the Canadian federation. However, I leave the difficult question of the source and scope of obligations of distributive justice in federations for another occasion. I begin to explore some of these issues in a project tentatively titled 'Recasting Social Canada: A Reconsideration of Federal Jurisdiction over Social Policy'.

are not the traditional package of civil and political liberties, but rather a set of economic rights relating to the mobility of goods, services, and labour that speak to the economic, rather than to the civic or ethnic, dimensions of persons' lives. The economic conception of citizenship views these rights as securing the means whereby citizens can satisfy their preferences in the European marketplace. However, from another perspective, that of economic integration, these rights, which protect the mobility of factors of production, can be considered to be instruments for securing the efficiency-enhancing benefits of trade.

There are two ways of characterizing the relationship between the economic citizenship and efficiency-enhancing functions of economic rights in federations. According to the traditional account, the prospect of inter-jurisdictional economic mobility either invites federal sub-units to differentiate themselves with respect to the package of public policies that they provide citizens—and hence increase the satisfaction of citizens' preferences—or encourages regulatory harmonization by creating the need for positive integration. Moreover, inasmuch as the satisfaction of citizens' preferences for public policies is a democratic ideal, the obvious tension between these two end-states—diversity and uniformity—is often framed as a tension between the promotion of democracy in federal sub-units and economic efficiency across a federation. I want to argue that the traditional way of framing the problem, which exists in all federal entities, misstates the trade-off at hand. The real trade-off is not between democracy at the level of a federal sub-unit and efficiency across the federation, but between the promotion of political community at the level of a federal sub-unit and at that of the federation as a whole.

I begin with the traditional account. I take as a given the relationship between the mobility of factors of production—a *sine qua non* of economic integration—and the efficiency-enhancing aspects of trade. The arguments for economic integration between political entities come out of the international trade literature, and focus on the economic gains to be derived if trading partners focus on activities where they enjoy a comparative advantage, as well as the gains to be derived from economies of scale.[43] The key point for this discussion is that economic integration can be described in both negative and positive terms. Negatively, it demands that factors of production from outside a jurisdiction be accorded 'national treatment', that is, that they be treated on the same terms as domestic factors. The principle of national treatment clearly prohibits a variety of familiar tariff and non-tariff barriers—customs duties, quotas,

[43] For a useful account of these arguments, see Michael J. Trebilcock and Robert Howse, *The Regulation of International Trade* (London: Routledge, 1995), ch. 1.

and so forth—that facially discriminate against imported factors of production. The criticism of negative integration is that it adopts too narrow a view of impediments to economic mobility, because the mere existence of regulatory diversity among jurisdictions can act as a barrier to trade. The solution here is to expand the definition of discrimination from facial or direct discrimination to encompass instances when compliance with 'national standards' might have a disparate impact upon factors of production from jurisdictions whose policies—product standards, professional licensing requirements, and so forth—are different. The concern here, though, is that a reciprocal set of challenges to regulatory regimes on the grounds of indirect discrimination would allow the trading partner with the lowest standards to set the standard across the entire trading regime. The solution, then, is to allow for joint standard-setting at a level potentially much higher than the lowest common denominator—so-called positive integration. The logic of economic integration, then, tends to uniformity across jurisdictions, which presumably reduces the margin for choice among trading partners. Since the mobility of factors of production among federal sub-units is a standard goal of federations, although imperfectly realized in practice, the dynamic of uniformity is thought to operate in federations as well.

The economic conception of citizenship offers a rather different perspective on federalism in the work of Charles Tiebout and Wallace Oates.[44] In the economic theory of citizenship, the satisfaction of citizens' preferences is of principal importance. Tiebout and Oates focus on citizens preferences for public policies. Federalism, it is argued, can produce a higher degree of fit between citizens' preferences and public policies than would a unitary state, in the following fashion. Suppose that each federal sub-unit offers a package of public policies that can vary along a number of different dimensions. As a simplifying device, assume that the two dimensions which matter most are equity and efficiency. Each jurisdiction can balance these two goals in a unique way. One federal sub-unit, for example, may offer better public services but impose higher taxes. Others may offer less generous public services but impose lower taxes. Also assume also that citizens are mobile, so that they can migrate to the jurisdiction which offers the basket of policies that suits them best. Some may prefer jurisdictions that give priority to questions of equity, while others

[44] Charles Tiebout, 'A Pure Theory of Local Expenditures', (1956) 64 *Journal of Political Economy* 416; Wallace Oates, *Fiscal Federalism* (New York: Harcourt Brace, 1972). Also see Robert P. Inman and Daniel L. Rubinfeld, 'Rethinking Federalism' (1997) 11 *Journal of Economic Perspectives* 43–64, and John D. Donahue, 'Tiebout? Or Not Tiebout? The Market Metaphor and America's Devolution Debate', (1997) 11 *Journal of Economic Perspectives* 73–82.

would prefer jurisdictions that redistribute less, and would migrate accordingly.

Federalism, then, creates a market for mobile citizens, where federal sub-units compete with one another through the mechanism of public policy. Those who justify federalism in these terms posit that such an arrangement would increase the degree of fit between citizens' preference and public policy, for two reasons. First, the mere existence of federal arrangements allows a territorially concentrated minority to become a local majority, allowing it to vote for policies with respect to which it would be out-voted at the federal level. Second, citizens will sort themselves through migration into sub-populations that are much more homogeneous than the population as a whole. By contrast, unitary states are less sensitive to varying preferences for public policies. Though individuals' preferences for public policies may vary, unitary states would offer only a single set of policies, a 'one size fits all' solution.

For the market analogy to hold, there must be a means for citizens to communicate their preferences. The economists who first proposed this model of federalism thought the primary mechanism for the communication of preferences was exit. The constant threat of exit would keep the governments of federal sub-units honest, as it were. As a result, in concrete constitutional terms, this model requires guarantees of personal mobility rights. In this connection, it is worth noting that both the Treaty of Rome and the American constitution, through judicial interpretation, enshrine mobility rights.[45] However, it is important to contrast the existence of these formal legal guarantees with the actual propensity or ability to migrate inter-jurisdictionally. It has long been recognized that rates of labour mobility among Member States of the European Union are much lower than among States in the United States. The general consensus is that the lower rates of labour mobility in Europe can be attributed to cultural and linguistic differences between Members States that are absent within the United States. What this suggests is that this model of federalism should also give an important role to mechanisms of voice as a mechanism for the communication of preferences. Voice would be particularly important for those citizens whose prospects for mobility were limited because of the high transaction costs associated with that option, as they appear to be in Europe. Thus, along with mobility rights, this model would appear to require the familiar package of civil and political liberties.

The key point to note is that although this model of federalism focuses on the satisfaction of citizens' preferences, and analogizes between politics and the market, as Landy and Teles imply, it has important *democratic*

[45] Article 39 of the EC Treaty; *Shapiro v. Thompson*, 394 U.S. 618 (1969).

overtones. It is democratic in two senses. First, it is democratic because voice can be an important mechanism for citizens to communicate their preferences to the governments of federal sub-units; civil and political liberties have a central place in the scheme. Second, it is democratic because it creates the space for local populations to choose public policies in a manner they could not in unitary states, because a local majority might be a federal minority. To be sure, federalism can frustrate the will of federal majorities by conferring on local majorities a right to veto important public policies. But the point remains that federalism is also democracy-enhancing, by redistributing political sovereignty from the federal polity to sub-federal political communities. Framed in this way, then, Landy and Teles see a fundamental tension between economic integration and democracy. Federations must strike a balance between these two competing values, which are diametrically opposed to one another.[46]

One of the most interesting aspects of Howse's account is that it challenges this view of the conflict at hand. According to Howse, economic mobility, of both persons and capital, is valuable because it facilitates the economic and social intercourse that serve as the cement of solidarity in democratic federations. Discussing the Canadian context, Howse argues that 'When Canadians trade across the country, move for reasons of work or study, maintain friendships that cross provincial, regional and linguistic boundaries, they affirm the reality of this way of belonging to a Canadian community'.[47] This is certainly seems to be Weiler's conception of the source of political community in the EU, when he describes as to 'long term peaceful relations with thickening economic and social intercourse'.[48] Understood in this way, the economic mobility of citizens is not

[46] Indeed, aside from the trend toward harmonization created by trade law, harmonization can occur through the operation of the market for citizens. The model relies on citizen—or labour—mobility, but also on the other factors of production, such as capital. The difficulty in any market is that the direction of that market is driven by those with market power, so that high-income wage earners and capital will migrate in search of the regulatory mix that produces the lowest costs of business and tax burdens, exerting a pressure on jurisdictions to harmonize downward. This is the familiar story of the 'race to the bottom', whereby inter-jurisdictional competition produces lax labour laws, weak environmental standards, and limits the ability of jurisdictions to engage in redistribution—through the tax system, direct social assistance, or otherwise. Mobile capital and labour operate to limit the scope for jurisdictions to differentiate themselves from each other. Some, like Barry Weingast, argue that this is a strength, not a weakness, of economic mobility, because it limits the ability of the governments of federal sub-units to engage in rent-seeking activity; Barry R. Weingast, 'The Economic Role of Political Institutions: Market-Preserving Federalism and Economic Development' (1995) 11 *Journal of Law, Economics, and Organization* 1–31; Yingyi Qian and Barry R. Weingast, 'Federalism as a Commitment to Preserving Market Incentives' (1997) 11 *Journal of Economic Perspectives* 83–92. However, democrats usually lament the loss of the margin for local choice.

[47] Howse, 'Searching for Plan A'. 315.

[48] Weiler, *The State 'über alles'*, 5.

at odds with the idea of democratic community per se. On the contrary, economic mobility is not only a component of citizenship in democratic federal communities but actually can give rise to and sustain that democratic federal community.

What light does this insight shed on Landy and Teles? Although Howse does not speak to this issue, what his analysis suggests is that the trade-off at hand is not between economic efficiency and local democracy, as Landy and Teles would tell us. Rather, the trade-off is between democracy and democracy—between the fostering of political community at the level of the federation and at the sub-federal level. The character of *this* trade-off is rather different because it brings to the fore the problem of divided or multiple allegiances. Why is this the case? As I argued earlier, political communities, even those that understand themselves in liberal democratic terms, make identity claims upon their citizens, and in federal entities those claims compete in the same political space. The fostering of federal political community gives rise to this sort of political dynamic, in which a nascent federal political community inevitably challenges and perhaps destabilizes—or forces the contraction or recasting of—the pre-existing political communities of sub-federal units. What is really at stake, then, in debates over economic mobility within federations is some version of the conflict or tension between membership in sub-federal and federal political communities that I outlined earlier.

4. Conclusion

This way of framing the issue invokes the first interpretation of the problem of divided or multiple allegiances that I described at the outset. But it also raises the question of why membership in one political community—most likely a federal political community—should be fostered at the expense of membership in another, sub-federal, political community. Unfortunately, neither Howse nor Landy and Teles suggest how we might begin to address this question. And they are silent with good reason. Although there are good reasons why political communities might want to organize themselves on a federal basis, at first blush there seem to be few compelling reasons why political communities hitherto separate *must* federate, or alternatively why federations *must* continue to survive as opposed to dissolve. Indeed, on the civic conception, the existence of a political community ultimately depends on a willed commitment either to constitute a new political entity or to continue an existing one.

Alternatively, though, the community of fate might yield a justification for the creation of federal political community, although I cannot develop the point here. Where significant policy interdependencies—for example, arising out of trading relationships or the regulation of international finance—and inter-jurisdictional policy externalities—for example, with respect to the environment—create circumstances that create conflict and necessitate cooperation among political communities, those politics must come together to deal with problems that affect their common fate. David Held's observation, that 'some of the most fundamental forces and processes which determine the nature of life-chances within and across political communities are now beyond the reach of nation states' rings true at the dawn of the new millennium.[49] At first, inter-state relations might suffice, but, as both the problems and solutions grow in complexity and scope, the creation of institutions with independent decision-making authority might be required. But in order for those institutions to be both legitimate and stable from the perspective of liberal democracy, they must become the objects of the sort of identification that lies at the heart of political communities. As Kymlicka writes, 'People belong to the same community of fate of they feel some sense of responsibility for one another's fate, and so want to deliberate together about how to respond collectively to the challenges facing the community'.[50] To be sure, Kymlicka claims that this sense of common fate does not and cannot exist in supranational arrangements such as the European Union, in contrast to federal entities such as the United States which possess the requisite degree of linguistic unity that he claims to be necessary for deliberation in democratic politics. However, notwithstanding the hurdles posed by linguistic diversity, the relative success and stability of multilingual democracies such as Canada, Switzerland, and Belgium suggests that communities fate can emerge and endure in situations not dissimilar to that facing Europe.

[49] David Held, 'The Transformation of Political Community: Rethinking Democracy in the Context of Globalization', in Ian Shapiro and Casiano Hacker-Cordón (eds), *Democracy's Edges* (Cambridge: Cambridge University Press, 1999), at 103.

[50] Will Kymlicka, 'Citizenship in an Era of Globalization: Commentary on Held', in Ian Shapiro and Casiano Hacker-Cordón (eds), *Democracy's Edges* (Cambridge: Cambridge University Press, 1999), at 115.

15

The Constitution of Institutions

ELIZABETH MEEHAN

1. Introduction

This chapter begins with a brief reference to the constitutional and institutional frameworks of allegiances, identification, and citizenship rights. It then argues that there are grounds for questioning the customary conceptual and political overlap between nationality and citizenship. Some decoupling has taken place in the European Union (EU), opening, according to some commentators, the possibility of a new paradigm in citizenship praxis. Thus, the chapter explores Carlos Closa's idea that supranational citizenship has more potential than national citizenship to be democratic. It also draws on Joseph Weiler's ideas, which in some respects are similar to those of Closa but which differ in respect of the significance of nationality and national identity. Weiler's acknowledgement of national forces is, however, consistent with Closa's suggestion that civil society in the EU is too weak to take advantage of the more democratic potential of supranational citizenship. Both can be used to infer that difficulties in European citizenship may be reinforced by enlargement. This is not because of the introduction of a further set of nationalities per se into a supranational citizenship system but because of a new complexity in the principled norms which Closa says have to be present in a site of democratic citizenship. In view of this, there are lessons to be learned from American theories of republican federalism which, as expounded by S. H. Beer (1993), have much in common with a modern interest among radical democrats in deliberative or dialogic democracy. In this respect, Weiler's ideas about a European public space must be taken seriously.

2. The Constitution of Institutions

In this respect, the EU experience is considerably different from that of the United States (US). First, the authority of states that formed or joined the

EU was incomparably more entrenched than that of the young ex-colonies which came together to make the constitution of the US (Meehan 1996). Thus, the EU states had the power and legitimacy to do what the anti-federalists argued for in the debate about the American Constitution. They created a system in which the apex of the 'government' of the EU and the governments of the Member States are not separated. The European Council, which discusses intergovernmental strategy, is composed of heads of government; the Council of Ministers, which makes the final decisions about common policies, is made up of relevant ministers from Member State cabinets. Thus, the EU is regulated by its own members, notwithstanding the fact that the Commission has more powers than national bureaucracies. This confederal characteristic of the EU is bolstered by a state-based system of elections to the European Parliament and by the absence of union-wide parties—though there are increasingly coherent transnational groupings of 'party families'.

However, the free choice of states to found or join the EU becomes more constrained when it comes to determining its development. As Closa (1998*a*, *b*) points out, Member States do not remain 'the masters of the contract' because of a vigorous EU legal doctrine that 'the Treaties are a kind of constitution'. These have led to 'a body of legislation and principles' whose future cannot be predicted and from which Member States cannot exit. They cannot exit because they all subscribe to the principle of the rule of law and, hence, to the obligation of compliance—though, according to Weiler (1997*a*, *b*), a means could be introduced to underscore the boundaries between state and EU competences.

Closa argues that political decisions taken by the Member States themselves have similar consequences to effects of jurisprudence. Member States do control explicit 'constitutional' reform of the EU through the procedure of unanimous decision-making in the Council of Ministers—though this does not mean much for control by national citizens, given the difficulties of parliamentary scrutiny. This is the same for some 'ordinary' policy decisions. But other 'ordinary' policy decisions are made by qualified or simple majority voting which are binding on all, whether or not national democratic procedures have resulted in a government with a contrary conception of its interests.

But, as Closa also argues, there is a further twist to this problem. This is that, if the EU lacks popular democratic legitimacy in an institutional or procedural sense, it has a social legitimacy in its delivery of policies that meet peoples' private interests in a European market economy. The stagnation induced by a long period up to 1985 of insistence on unanimity about everything put integration at risk sufficiently for Member States to agree to more frequent use of majority voting so that policies could be delivered more effectively and efficiently. Paradoxically, then, weak national control is functional to the maintenance of the EU's social legitimacy.

The question arises, therefore, as to whether supranational democratic citizenship can grow in a context in which current national conceptions of it seem inconsistent with what is apparently needed for EU legitimacy. By definition, the growth of supranational citizenship implies a breach in the conventional overlap between nationality and citizenship and consideration of whether the elements of decoupling that have begun to take place in the EU have any prospects of being more than 'titlting at windmills'.

3. Citizenship and Nationality

Though it is a matter of controversy, there are grounds for treating the overlap of citizenship and nationality as a matter of historical contingency and not as an analytically necessary connection. In short, nationality is a legal identity from which no rights need arise, though obligations might—as is obvious when nationals are called 'subjects'. Conversely, citizenship is a practice, or a form of belonging, resting on a set of legal, social, and participatory entitlements which may be conferred, and sometimes are, irrespective of nationality—or denied, as in the case of women, regardless of nationality.

The idea and practice of an overlap developed with the growth of the modern state (Leca 1990). While borders had been porous in the middle and late-middle ages and migration normal, the strategic interests of new states lay in impregnability and control of persons with or without leave to cross frontiers. Nationality was an obvious criterion and proof of nationality a simple method of verification. The process of modernization in the new states went hand in hand with the construction of the nation. This served external and internal purposes. It created a sense of the 'otherness' of those who were a threat to the strategic interests of political elites. And it fostered the loyalty or allegiance that induced willingness to be taxed to fund the defence of the state and to be enlisted into military service. Since 1945, allegiance is relevant less to military purposes than to the legitimacy of redistribution and the funding of welfare systems (Miller 1993).

The construction of the nation was promoted through the dismantling of feudal bonds and their replacement by a gradual extension of legal and political rights. So complete became the overlap between national identity and citizenship status that, in many political systems, the words 'citizenship' and 'nationality' became almost interchangeable. At the same time, it was held that only a state, or a nation-state, was capable of guaranteeing the legal and political rights. Thus, when invited to speculate about the then European Communities, Raymond Aron (1974) argued that it was a contradiction in terms to see citizenship rights as capable of being guaranteed by a regime that was not a state and, more particularly, a nation-state. Weiler (1997*a*: 507) also points out that nationality is 'inextricably' linked to citizenship, even though, unlike Aron, he does accept the possibility of European citizenship based on different nationalities.

While it can be acknowledged that, in practice, there has been an 'inextricable' link between the two concepts, it is easy to slip thereafter into using them synonymously; and this can result in peculiar distortions of meaning. In late nineteenth-century America, the Supreme Court ruled that a woman was, indeed, an American citizen but that being a citizen did not necessarily carry the right to vote. This empties the classical conception of 'citizen' of part of its core meaning and the ruling makes conceptual sense only if we substitute 'national' for 'citizen': that is, a woman might be an American national but that being a national did not necessarily carry the core citizens' right. In other systems, both terms are employed in legislation but as though 'nationality and citizenship' were all one word in which the first and last components were interchangeable. For example, except for one article of the 1922 Constitution, it was not until 1962 that Irish official documents began to be clear that there was a difference between citizenship as nationality and citizenship as the capacity to exercise rights. The current British passport still says 'Nationality: British citizen'.

Moreover, from a longer historical perspective, such as that by Heater (1990), we can see that citizenship is not the same as nationality but is about enabling people to participate in creating, maintaining, and enjoying the good society, whether the people belonging to a society inhabited a citadel, a city-state, a locality, an empire, the world—and even, since John Stuart Mill and especially in Germany, the work-place. In respect of the work-place, the tendency to compare the relationship between capital and labour in the US and the EU, and to ask whether the United Kingdom (UK) is pulling the EU away from the Rhenish model to the American, in terms simply of conditions of employment is to overlook another dimension altogether (Meehan 2000). In social-democratic conceptions of citizenship in the UK, social and workers rights sit alongside and buttress political citizenship. In Germany, industrial citizenship is itself a form of political citizenship or an element of the good society.

In the young US, a century before the aforementioned ruling and at the time of the making of the Constitution, there was no overarching American national identity. And, as Lacorne (this volume) points out, *ante-bellum* conceptions of citizenship focused considerably upon the

States, being civic republican and based on the virtues of small republics—at least, when not serving to justify the preservation of slavery. The proper level for the protection of citizens' rights was a passionate bone of contention between the Federalists and Anti-Federalists, the latter believing that they were best protected through foci of allegiance and channels of accountability that already existed. The benign conception of state-centred citizenship appears similar to what exists in the EU now and in either of the two versions of subsidiarity in the Maastricht Treaty. It was superseded in the US as a result of federal powers of naturalization. Such powers were not 'communitarized' by the EU Member States, though it should be noted that there are the first signs of 'spill-overs' into their competence over nationality in some recent cases in the European Court of Justice.

In contrasting the modern US with the EU, Lacorne notes that EU 'citizenship' derives from 'citizenship' of a Member State. In fact, it derives from 'nationality' of a Member State and EU Member States differ from one another in how far any overlap between citizenship and nationality is complete. A survey of eleven European countries shows no wholly systematic pattern of attaching nationality restrictions to legal and social entitlements and rights to participate in politics (Gardner 1997). For example, the British are aliens under Irish law but British nationals resident in Ireland now have most of the rights of citizenship. The Irish are neither alien nor British under UK law but, like resident Commonwealth nationals, have always been able to exercise all the rights of citizenship.

For those who have been defined as nationals of Member States, and, hence, EU citizens, their European citizenship is about participation and the enjoyment of 'the good society' in the Union as a whole. As noted in conclusion, the European 'good society' is criticized as libertarian: offering private rights to individuals. But it may be worth noting that the preambles to its directives on social policy often echo, if dimly, the classical conception of the 'good society' as a collective moral order of justice and conviviality. This invites consideration of how well the promise of supranational citizenship has been met in the EU.

4. EU Citizenship

Assessments of EU citizenship are contradictory, possibly being determined by divergent general ideological and epistemological outlooks. Sometimes they seem guided by whether the commentator favours or opposes European integration (Meehan 1996). Sometimes they seem to depend on whether the analyst is a positivist who examines only what exists concretely and compares its slightness to national provisions—but overlooking the contrast between decades and centuries of evolution in the EU and national systems respectively (Meehan 1993). Conversely, other analysts suggest that what is important is not the size but the dynamics of change: that is, the fact that established norms have been breached at all opens the possibility, though not the inevitability, of new paradigms. For example, while specific EU rights are often argued to be little more than a cosmetic addition to national forms of citizenship, Wiener's (1995; 1999) broader approach comes to different conclusions.

She identifies in the history of integration confluences of policy imperatives and the interests of key political actors which have created breaches in nation-state experiences of citizenship and opportunities for new paradigms and practices. In her account, the regulation of social rights and relations between Community institutions and the 'social', local and regional 'partners'—pre-dating Maastricht—are part of 'access' and 'belonging'. The period of acceleration towards union is, she argues, a time of discernible movement in the paradigm of citizenship, containing the seeds of new practice in the activation of rights. In particular, markets and migration make 'place', as well as nationality, the conceptual and practical pre-condition for activating legal, political, and social entitlements.

Wiener's account is consistent with O'Keefe's summing up of the Maastricht Treaty; that '[t]he importance of the TEU citizenship provisions lie not in their content but rather in the promise they hold out for the future. The concept is a dynamic one, capable of being added to or strengthened but not diminished' (cited in Chryssochoou 1996: 30). The same can be said about Amsterdam. As is well known from American history, however, all stories of rights depend on what people make of them. This requires some consideration of the state of civil society.

5. Civil Society, National Ties, and Supranational Bonds

If rights are to be more than empty symbols and result in real redistribution of power or influence, much depends on the ability of civil society 'to seize the day'. Closa (1998*a*, *b*) sees more potential, in principle, in supranational than national arenas for democratic citizenship. In practice, he suggests, however, European civil society may be too fragile to transform EU citizenship into an arena for democratic self-determination from what he calls an enhanced set of private rights to make the most of new market opportunities—or be sheltered a little from its threats.

His argument rests on a critique of the case that a shared national identity is a pre-condition for citizenship. For, by insisting that citizenship can be built only on such bonds, such theories propose that a democratic practice be based on a commonality that was formed under pre-democratic conditions. In contrast, a site of democratic citizenship is one in which people live together under a set of principled bonds, such as those identified by Robert Dahl as voting equality, effective participation, enlightened understanding, control of agendas, and inclusiveness. In drawing this contrast, Closa suggests that supranational citizenship is less vulnerable than national citizenship to charges of exclusion and discrimination because, being unable to draw on comparable non-principled bonds, its success must depend on democratic and human rights norms.

To some extent, Weiler (1997*a*: 508–9) shares Closa's view that such norms are necessary to a successful EU citizenship based on shared values. However, these shared values necessarily inhere in people of different nationalities; and this remains important not only legally and conceptually but also psychologically. Thus, Weiler's equivalent of Closa's principled bonds include not only mechanisms to democratize the EU—for example, a legislative ballot, a public space, some direct taxation, and more extensive horizontal human rights such as those adumbrated in the Amsterdam Treaty—but a measure to reassure people about state-based competences: a European Constitutional Council to adjudicate on allegations that boundaries have been overstepped. This would go some way to enable the EU to sustain its dual claim of being 'for its citizens' while also 'respect[ing] the national identities of its Member States' (European Commission 1997: 5; Duff 1997: 3).

Dahl, of course, is a citizen of the US where, as mentioned earlier, democratic norms and ties, albeit defective, preceded national bonding. In contrast, Britishness was forged by elites, prior to democracy, to make bonds between peoples who had been enemies of one another. It worked for some centuries, in the context of different sub-state national identities, while principled bonds were grafted on to the pre-democratic unifications. But the fragility of the origins is re-emerging and there are claims, at least in Scotland, and to some extent Wales, which support Closa's case: that is, that, from a democratic basis, a new union of principled norms can be negotiated at the supranational level—the EU.

The idea that a multi-state supranational union may be preferable to unification with a single neighbour arises from experience among the component peoples of the UK in trying to make what Closa calls their private EU rights have public consequences. That is, people—not only nationalists but also advocates for their regions—whose material interests are enhanced by learning to use EU partnership opportunities are trying to redefine their relationship to the domestic state in a European context, to bring about new forms of mobilization and interaction, and to influence agendas. But, again in line with Closa's theoretical case, unification into the British state left pre-British civil society institutions intact, especially in Scotland and Northern Ireland and, hence, in a position to try either to improve the principled bonds of the British state or to negotiate new ones in a different arena.

Closa (1998*b*) is guarded about whether there is a strong enough civil society in the EU as a whole to transcend the defects of national citizenship in order to bring about the benefits of a regime based on principled bonds, without a willingness on the part of states themselves to agree to stop trying to maintain the impression that anxieties about national identities are well attended to in EU provisions. The changes which he suggests are necessary include the avoidance of derogations and exemptions which 'offer shelter to communitarian understandings of the relationship between individuals and the state premised on nationality' (Closa 1998*b*: 431–2); 'the full constitutionalization of a European political status' (Closa 1998*b*: 431); greater opportunities for direct citizenship participation in EU affairs; stronger commonality and reciprocity of rights in different Member States; and willingness by states to respond to 'spill-over' pressures from EU citizenship status on to varying nationality laws, including greater willingness to acknowledge dual or multi-nationality. As noted something of the last is beginning to happen in the European Court of Justice. And, although the German government was forced by opponents to abandon a plan to make dual citizenship legal, it is going ahead in allowing German citizenship to be acquired, not only as before by ancestry and discretion, but also, as of right, through residence and naturalization.

If Closa is right about the weakness of European civil society in combating a privatized, liberal, or libertarian conception of citizenship, then enlargement may reinforce the challenge. The prospective Member States, while having to subscribe to principles of liberty, democracy, and human rights as a condition of entry are not well placed to do so in practice, emerging as they are from totalitarianism which suppressed civil society or bent it to the will of the state.

Moreover, the links between national identity—through, for example, shared religion—nationality, and citizenship rights are far less open to a secular supranationalism based on Enlightenment values than even the least amenable in western Europe—with adverse consequences for minorities. If emerging concepts of citizenship seem to hark back to the old right, the concept of liberty—perhaps necessitated by dire economic conditions—is even more libertarian than that which Closa sees in the EU. It is the negative one of 'freedom from' restraint, not the 'freedom to' which is implicit in Christian- and social-democracy and still has some place in the link in the EU model between social inclusion and economic progress.

The point to be drawn here is not about the addition of more nationalities, either per se or in their further reduction of the overlap between nationality and citizenship. It is that growing mismatches amongst sets of principled bonds, not a more complex collection of pre-democratic identifications, may inhibit the transformation of EU citizenship along the lines aspired to by Closa. If this is so, there is a heavy burden on the political realm to democratize the public space so that the various associations of people can come face to face with their different interests and agendas (Tassin 1992) and, through a process of dialogue, try to achieve outcomes that are, if not satisfactory to all, at least reasonable. Here, Weiler's (1997*a*, 514–6) *Lexcalibur* becomes crucial.

References

Aron, Raymond (1974). 'Is multinational citizenship possible?'. *Social Research*, 41/4: 638–56.

Beer, S. H. (1993). *To Make a Nation: The Rediscovery of American Federalism*. Cambridge, MA: The Belknap Press of Harvard University.

Closa, Carlos (1998*a*). 'Some Foundations for the Normative Discussion on Supranational Citizenship and Democracy', in Ulrich K. Preuss and Ferran Requejo (eds), *European Citizenship, Multiculturalism, and the State*. Baden-Baden: Nomos Verlagsgessellschaft.

——(1998*b*). 'Supranational Citizenship and Democracy: Normative and Empirical Dimensions', in M. Torre (ed.), *European Citizenship: An International Challenge*. Deventer: Kluver Law International.

Chryssochoou, Dimitris (1996). 'Democratic Theory and European Integration: The Challenge to Conceptual Innovation', in Hazel Smith (ed.), *New Thinking in Politics and International Relations*. Kent Papers in Politics and International Relations, Series 5, No. S2. Canterbury: University of Kent.

Duff, Andrew (ed.) (1997). *The Treaty of Amsterdam: Text and Commentary*. London: Federal Trust and Sweet and Maxwell.European Commission (1997). *A New Treaty for Europe: Citizens' Guide*. Luxembourg: Office for Official Publications of the European Communities.

Gardner, J. P. (ed.) (1997). *Citizenship: The White Paper*. London: The Institute for Citizenship Studies and The British Institute of International and Comparative Law.

Heater, Derek (1990). *Citizenship. The Civic Ideal in World History, Politics and Education*. London: Longman.

Leca, Jean (1990). 'Nationalita é Cittadinanza nell'Europa delle Immiagrazione', in various authors, *Italia, Europa é Nuove immagrazioni*. Torino: Edizione della Fondazione Giovanni Agnelli.

Meehan, Elizabeth (1993). *Citizenship and the European Community*. London: Sage.

Meehan, Elizabeth (1996). 'European Integration and Citizens' Rights: A Comparative Perspective'. *Publius: The Journal of Federalism*, 26/4: 99–121.

——(2000). 'British and German Approaches to EU Social Policy: Industrial Citizenship', in Klaus Larres and Elizabeth Meehan (eds), *Uneasy Partners: British German Relations and European Integration Since 1945*. Oxford: Oxford University Press.

Miller, David (1993). 'In Defence of Nationality'. *Journal of Applied Philosophy*, 10: 3–16.

Tassin, Etienne (1992). 'Europe: A Political Community', in Chantal Mouffe (ed.), *Dimensions of Radical Democracy: Pluralism, Citizenship, Community*. London: Verso Press.

Weiler, J. H. H (1997*a*). 'To be a European Citizen—Eros and Civilization'. *Journal of European Public Policy*, 4: 495–519.

——(1997*b*). 'The European Union Belongs to its Citizens: Three Immodest Proposals'. *European Law Review*, 22/April: 150–6.

Wiener, Antje (1995). Building Institutions: The Developing Practice of European Citizenship. Ottawa: Ph.D. thesis, Department of Political Science, Carleton University.

——(1999). *'European' Citizenship Practice: Building Institutions of a Non-State*. Boulder, CO: Westview.

16

Beyond Devolution: From Subsidiarily to Mutuality

MARC LANDY AND STEVEN M. TELES

The European Union, it is said, suffers from a democratic deficit. Unfortunately, reform of EU voting or administrative procedures will go only a small way toward closing this deficit, since a degree of bureaucratic insularity is an inherent quality of supra-national government. No amount of tinkering can make Brussels 'close' to those who live far away. 'Europe' is simply too large and disembodied to provide ordinary people with sufficient opportunity to hone their democratic skills, and thereby to move beyond a purely procedural democracy.

Paradoxically, the best way to strengthen the democratic legitimacy of the EU is by using it's available policy tools and subsidies to strengthen democracy at the grass roots. The EU can help resuscitate local government, the true seed-bed of democracy, and thus provide citizens with the political skills and self-reliance necessary to live in a vast multi-layered confederal system. The EU needs democratic legitimacy, but that legitimacy should derive from its ability to protect the possibility for democratic government in its Member States, not from the largely fruitless mission of democratizing itself.

1. Unpacking Subsidiarity

Coming into office due to the malfeasance of its predecessors, the European Commission of Romano Prodi will be judged primarily by its success in rebuilding confidence in the EU's institutions. Putting the financial affairs of the Commission in good order, establishing clearer lines of responsibility, and eating away at the national fiefdoms which have prevented the Commission from acting as a unitary executive will be at the top of Mr Prodi's list for some time to come. But rearranging the deck chairs on the ship of state will prove insufficient. Sooner or later the Commission will have to return to the question of how some modicum of self-government is to be retained within an ever larger and more centralized Union.

The increasingly popular concept of subsidiarity is inadequate for addressing this problem. In its typical formulation, it states that political decisions should be made at the lowest feasible level. But this formulation is hopelessly vague. If emphasis is put on 'lowest' then it sounds like a decentralizing principle. But if emphasis is put on 'feasible' then the concept can be used to justify the most thoroughgoing centralization, since it could be claimed that large number of functions currently exercised by lesser governments could be more effectively administered by the Union itself. Thus the language of subsidiarity merely restates the basic question of the proper geographic distribution of power.

Subsidiarity assumes that establishing appropriate relations between different levels of governments is essentially a matter of line-drawing: figuring out which functions should be placed at what level of government. As if one were carving a turkey, one finds the joints that link different public problems and splits them there. Unfortunately governments are more complex than carcasses; real policy questions have no joints. Therefore the problem of intergovernmental relations is not one of discovering what questions are intrinsically local, national, or super-national but rather one of coordinating the overlapping involvement of different governmental actors in matters of common interest.

In place of subsidiarity we suggest the principle of mutuality. It should be the obligation of each level of government as it participates in joint decision-making to foster the legitimacy and capacity of the other. Local government contributes to central government by taking the brunt of the burden of citizen-demands and of providing a coherent and properly constrained voice for citizen grievances. To do so adequately it must be both responsive and capable. Central government has the responsibility to facilitate and encourage the ability of lower-level governments to act as sites for deliberation and administration.

Mutuality is not the same as devolution. Devolution is a technique that may or may not foster local government, depending on the circumstances. If the specific context in which devolution occurs is likely to foster destructive competition between localities, or if local governments lack administrative and/or deliberative capacity, devolution may well prove counterproductive. Competent and spirited local government does not necessarily emerge spontaneously: it is dependent upon the prior creation of a regulatory, social and economic framework that only higher levels of government can provide. This responsibility provides supra-national governments such as the EU with a substantial positive agenda, but also with a serious challenge. Rather than asking 'is this an intrinsically local or supra-national issue?', the EU would ask 'what conditions are necessary to enable local government to effectively contribute to the effective overall management of this task? And how can the EU foster those conditions?'

Like subsidiarity, the principle of mutuality makes a territorial assumption. It defines citizen involvement in terms of governmentally constituted physical spaces: cities, towns, regions, and so forth. But, many might counter, in the age of the Internet and other electronic communication, the most important source of community identification for many is not a locality, but a community of interest that defies physical boundaries. For many it is indeed easier to find kindred souls in an AOL chatroom than in ones own hometown. But emotional solidarity is not at the core of our defence of local government and politics. What differentiates localism from other forms of association is not that the bonds of spatial community are more emotionally rich, nor that the interests within them are so much more homogenous, than non-spatial communities. In fact, in many cases, non-spatial communities, such as those on the Internet, win on both counts.

The difference is that local communities possess common public goods, such as safety, education, and public space. Local community is characterized not so much by affection as by conjoined self-interest. Whatever their differences or dislikes, citizens within local communities must work together if the things they hold in common are to be conserved and improved. Local community is different from virtual community because it is inherently political, meaning that it combines responsibility—public goods—with heterogeneous interests—conflict. Non-spatial communities do not combine these two elements, and therefore lack the capacity to inculcate the political skills and outlooks upon which democratic government depends.

In the modern world, technological and economic changes press on localism at every turn. As a consequence, decentralization cannot be achieved simply by 'laissez faire'. Instead, decentralization must be an active project: it requires affirmative action by central government to maintain the conditions under which localism can flourish. National and supra-national government need not be the enemy of local government. Indeed, helping local democracy to flourish can and should be a great unifying purpose of European Union.

2. The Sources of Legitimacy

Within the European Union, this is a time in which fundamental institutional issues are once more at stake: we have reached a 'constitutional moment'. This is music to the ears of the political scientist, since his art consists, at its highest level, in constitution-making, in making suggestions as to the basic architecture of political things. Constitutions may be written or implicit, long or short, but their core is the distribution of power among institutions and between levels of government. On such questions, political science has at least some interesting and useful things to say.

Much of what we have to say in this short chapter will be general in nature, for two reasons. First of all, neither of us is an expert in European politics, although both of us have done some work on individual European nations—Ireland and Britain. What expertise we have is on the 'politics of scale': the precise relevance of what we think we know is better left to European specialists. Second, constitution-making is properly a combination of the general and the particular: the general because constitutions need to be made for varying conditions and durable across long periods of time; specific because they must account for the diversity of human nature and the burden of institutional and cultural legacies. Even the finest general principles are only as good as their application to concrete circumstances. That said, let us suggest some general principles.

At the core of all constitutional thinking is the question of legitimacy, for a very simple reason: ultimately, what determines the fate of constitutional designs is consent. This is not to argue that consent is the only measure of the goodness of a political regime. Clearly, there should be room to question the goodness of what people are willing to consent to, to question its intrinsic worth. Also, we must be able to ask if the consent which the public invests in government is informed and aware. But investigating the constitutional question through the lens of consent is not an enterprise without its dignity. Constitutions, unlike almost all other human contrivances, are simultaneously means and ends: means because they seek to provide a framework within which individual flourishing is possible; ends because the sense of being rightly governed is itself a necessary component of human happiness. This approach takes ends as given. Whether the public *should* consent to a constitutional regime is a less pressing question to the political scientist than whether they *do* consent and *why*. If the essentially constitutional project of reforming the European Union is to succeed, it is difficult to imagine how questions of legitimacy could not be at the forefront.

To observe that constitutional reform should be judged by its capacity to increase the legitimacy of political institutions is merely to state the problem. The difficult questions concern from whence legitimacy is derived. This chapter, in a preliminary way, will try to pursue this question through a series of smaller questions. What are the foundations of political legitimacy? How might federal political institutions enhance political legitimacy? What sort of federal arrangements can best achieve this goal? Finally, what do these conjectures suggest for the project of shaping European institutions?

For our purposes, we shall define legitimacy as that attribute of political institutions which generates ongoing, active consent for a pattern of rule. Defined this way, legitimacy is primarily an empirical rather than a normative concept, a simple observation that a constitutional arrangement is maintaining its stability through political means rather than through violence.[1] However, by adding the term 'active' we want to separate out consent that comes through the 'breaking of the spirit' or from a condition of servility, from that which emerges from an at least minimally independent spirit.

So where does legitimacy come from? The first source is what Hamilton referred to as the 'reverence that time bestows upon all things'. Simple stability of constitutional arrangements is itself an important part of the legitimacy equation, since one purpose of a constitution is to give its members a groundwork they can count on, a form of 'credible commitment' as to the stability of a set of rules. Once a constitution starts to change with excessive rapidity, it becomes not a context in which a conflict of interests may be waged, but part of the conflict itself. Constitutional stability gives people a sense that the rules won't be changed in the middle of the game. In doing so, it gives citizens a rational basis for their expectations of the future, and through this a strong justification for giving active consent to a particular constitutional arrangement.

The second source of legitimacy is efficiency. It was the genius of the framers of the American Constitution to observe that competence is itself a critical source of popular legitimacy, and that maladministration is as often a source of the withdrawal of consent as is a positive violation of liberty. A republic must not only be fitted with the proper restraints on its ability to violate the rights of the people, nor merely with the most elegant democratic forms of accountability: it must be able to effectively dispatch those duties which are within government's responsibility. Remember that Mussolini's claim against the Italian government was that it failed to 'make the trains run on time': that is, democracy was incompetent, it could not perform those services that the people required. One could multiply the cases in which inefficiency has led to the collapse of democracy, which makes Hamilton's words in Federalist No. 30 all the more relevant: 'How is it possible that a government half-supplied and always necessitous, can fulfil the purposes of its institution . . . How can it ever possess either

[1] We use the term 'political' in the manner of Bernard Crick (1972) to mean non-coercive mechanisms for the conciliation of interests.

energy or stability, dignity or credit, confidence at home or respectability abroad?' (Rossiter 1961: 191). All else equal, people consent to governments they find useful and resist those that are persistently incapable of satisfying basic civic needs. It may even be that competence can provide a degree of legitimacy even when other sources of it are absent.

The third source is responsiveness. A constitutional regime capable of generating legitimacy needs to be capable of responding to the persistent preferences of the people, while on the one hand respecting minorities and on the other not becoming captured by the loudest or best-organized voices. If any of these elements is absent, the legitimacy of the government is likely to come into question. If in attempting to be responsive the government simply becomes the plaything of organized interests, the pretense of democratic openness becomes little more than a cover for well-mannered corruption. If the attempt to respond to majorities leads to the violation of individual rights, democracy devolves into majoritarian tyranny. And if in avoiding either of these dangers, government becomes excessively insular, it threatens to lose legitimacy and become an easy target for populist demagogues. This element of the legitimacy equation is the most necessary but also the most difficult to achieve. This becomes even more complicated when the responsiveness principle is combined with the other elements.[2]

The next element is the most problematic: common nationalism or participation in the same 'people'. The quality of government, as important as it is, will never be the sole standard by which people judge the legitimacy of government. Government is perceived to be illegitimate if its image or reality suggests that one 'people' is ruling over another. The original understanding of 'republicanism' was that it was the inversion of empire—being ruled over by another people—rather than monarchy—being ruled by one rather than the many. It focused on how the collectivity related to other, usually distant, collectivities. This old idea of republican government is still tenacious—and probably explains much of the resistance to 'being ruled from Brussels'—and may put strict limits on the size and centralization of any political institution. Compound republics of various sorts may be able to tame or temper this old republican principle, but can never eliminate it.[3]

There are other considerations which should concern the constitution-maker, but which are somewhat distant from the essentially empirical, subjective, and relativistic—and therefore Weberian—understanding of

[2] An excellent discussion of responsiveness can be found in Key (1961), especially chapters 4 and 9.

[3] The best discussion of nationalism in this particular context is by Sam Beer (1993), especially chapters 1 and 2.

legitimacy. It is worth at least pointing to one which we consider especially important, the 'non-servility' constraint: a government which generates voluntary consent only by so debasing the character of its citizens that they will consent to anything has emptied the concept of consent of any substance. Citizens must have sufficient character that they are not willing to accept a government unworthy of their consent, one which were they more spirited and autonomous they would reject. Clearly, the non-servility constraint, if taken to an extreme, would collapse into a wholly normative conception of legitimacy. It should therefore be understood pragmatically, which in practical terms means minimally.

Given this understanding of the sources of legitimacy, how might political decentralization help ameliorate the problems of liberal democratic rule in the new political institutions of Europe? What are the opportunities—and shortcomings—of political decentralization as a legitimacy-producing strategy?

The arguments we make for decentralization are of two sorts: those intrinsically connected to legitimacy and those based on claims of beneficial effects regarding legitimacy. These arguments are not equally compelling and should therefore be subject to different types of scrutiny and evaluation. The intrinsic arguments make claims about how decentralization affects the character and quality of public life. Assuming those arguments are true, they are worthy of the deepest respect because they speak to fundamental questions about the character and quality of human existence. Borrowing from the language of American constitutional theory, one would want to apply a 'strict scrutiny' test to policies and programmes that derive their justification from them. Such policies and programmes could be still be countermanded, but only for the most compelling reasons. Our other arguments seek to make government and administration more effective and efficient. In any particular instance, they serve as, at best, a rebuttable presumption, and should be accepted only if the political and/or economic benefits they provide exceed the costs they impose.

3. The Contribution of Decentralization to Civic Liberal Principles

The arguments from principle are rooted in a version of liberalism that we term 'civic liberalism'. We associate it most closely with Alexis de Tocqueville but it also resonates with other seminal French and English liberal thinkers like Benjamin Constant and John Stuart Mill. Civic liberalism treats political institutions and their legitimacy as intrinsically valuable. 'Do people feel that the regime that rules them is just and deserving of its authority?' is one of the basic questions by which civic liberalism judges itself. It is liberal in that it cherishes the existence of a plural society: one that secures fundamental political and civil rights for its citizens and which operates on the basis of limited, constitutional government. It is civic in that its liberal commitments are best realized in a polity capable of: enforcing minimal civilities and civic attitudes, such as self-reliance, obedience to the law, and respect for the rights of others; providing sufficient opportunity for political participation to foster civic education and discourage servility; and drawing upon certain non-, but not anti-, liberal aspects of the human personality. For purposes of this analysis, the central non-liberal value is attachment to place. In our conception of civic liberalism, we posit that human beings have a need to attach themselves to some grouping larger than themselves and their family. Place, as opposed to race or religion, is particularly valuable as an identity in a liberal society, since membership is non-essentialist in nature: that is, one can choose it.

Decentralization is an important means for restraining the pressures towards homogenization that threaten to engulf Europe and America as well. The greater diversity of lifestyle promoted by a decentralized political system is of intrinsic value. In such a context, if one does not like the way a community is governed, one can move elsewhere and, in all likelihood, find a community operating under governing principles, that, within limits, promote a very different conception of the good. Just as allowing different individuals to match their preferences to different packages of private goods maximizes individual utility, decentralization allows for a closer fit between collective preferences and public goods (Rivlin 1992). In addition, political decentralization can act as a shield against the tendency of centralized government and free markets to make all places alike. Local governments, with enough constitutional protection, can defend the peculiarities of place upon which people construct geographic identity.

Engagement in local politics is an indispensable form of civic education. It enlarges peoples' outlooks, encourages responsibility, and develops greater sobriety about the limits of politics. It extends people beyond their narrowly private concerns while still enabling them to operate within a sphere that is tangible and comprehensible. It inculcates the idea that government is in fact a difficult enterprise, dependent upon difficult trade-offs, sticky administrative questions, and inevitable conflict. By limiting both the costs and benefits of certain policy areas to smaller jurisdictions, decentralization forces mature political choice, the recognition that the cost and benefit sides of the ledger have to balance out. It also provides a bulwark against both despotism and cynicism. The development of a comparatively large group of citizens who have had a taste of administering the law is a civic resource, both for calling government to account and for defending it against unreasonable expectations.

Finally, decentralization provides a political focus for civic spirit. Civic spirit is an impulse characterized by increasing returns: the more is asked of it, the more it comes into being. But it needs a visible outlet to become manifest. Good local government can serve as a mechanism for mobilizing, organizing, and focusing this love of place.

4. Decentralization's Contribution to Policy Efficiency and Effectiveness

In addition to questions of principle, decentralization may, under the right conditions, serve other, less elevated purposes. Decentralization can lead to more efficient policy outcomes, but only to the extent that it provides information about facts and preferences that is more accurate and richer than that to which the centre has access. In all large, centralized bureaucracies decisions must be made on the basis of abstractions, ideas about generalized humanity and typical conditions (Scott 1998). This need to abstract and to homogenize may be a necessary part of statecraft, but it is also a dangerous one. Variations in local practices often exist for very good reasons, as adaptations to localized circumstances or unsystematic resolutions of conflicts between groups or individuals.

Diversity of jurisdiction permits experimentation. In a decentralized governmental system policy change does not have to squeeze through a single pipe. Policy can be improved through trial and error. As Louis Brandeis proposed, local governments can serve as 'laboratories of democracy'.[4] They can provide each other with practical lessons in what works and what fails, reducing the need to rely on abstract reason in order to anticipate failure or success.

Local control may also enhance the legitimacy of onerous governmental activity. For example, the police, in the everyday conduct of their job, rely on dozens of instances of voluntary cooperation. People either do or do not voluntarily provide them with evidence, leads and tips. Potential witnesses are either forthright or guarded in sharing information. Those who interact with the police communicate to others the image of the police either as protectors or as an occupying force harassing their community. Meaningful political control increases public trust in an institution such as the police and is therefore likely to raise levels of voluntary cooperation.

[4] *New York State Ice Co. v. Liebman*, 285 U.S. 262 (1932).

Local government permits policy coordination to be achieved on a more tangible basis than the abstract formalizations available at the centre. Consider the case of environmental protection, which encompasses: transportation, urban planning, waste disposal, economic development, and myriad other policy areas. It is almost impossible to create policies at the national level that will anticipate and account for the ways these various policy areas interact at the point of implementation. To make them make sense together, there needs to be an executive authority at the local level to coordinate these various policies and ensure that the multiple and often contradictory guidelines established at the national level attain some coherence as they are administered. A polity with a single tier of executive authority at the national level is likely to be less efficient at the point of implementation than one with two tiers, one which sets broad goals and the other which integrates those goals into administerable plans.

Local government is valuable as a training ground for higher office. Politicians trained in centralized legislatures depend heavily on abstract reason and ideology, and thereby overlook the formidable obstacles to attaining any social goal through government action. Local government provides an alternative proving ground, and one that has an executive component. Local executives are forced to deal with tangible problems and trade-offs and therefore bring a useful admixture of sobriety and pragmatism when they advance up the political ladder to the central government. And place is relatively heterodox. One's townsmen are likely to be a more diverse lot than one's professional peers or the members of one's religious denomination or ideological sect. Under most conditions, place lends itself better to the development of tolerance and moderation than do its essentialist or creedal competitors.

5. Devolution versus Localism/Decentralization

Concluding that political decentralization is critical to the perpetuation of democratic institutions and civic capacity does not imply a blanket preference for devolving public policy and public administration to the local level, nor does it require the emasculation of national and supra-national government. Far from it. Devolution, we will argue, is a substantially different thing from decentralization. The former is a method—sometimes valuable, but often dangerous and counterproductive—while the latter is an end, the methods towards whose attainment will vary according to policy, place, and institution.

Diversity and localism do not emerge merely from the forbearance of national or supra-national governments. There are many cases where the exercise of effective local control requires the existence of strong national rules of inter-State competition, protection against forces which spill over local and State borders, and in some cases full national control of public policy. Conversely, there are cases where devolution would actually weaken local governments by giving them functions that they are ill-suited to; would require that they organize in a techno-bureaucratic form; or would open them up to damaging forms of competition.

Possibly the strongest argument against devolution as a method for encouraging greater local control over politics is the danger of a 'race to the bottom'.[5] The theory behind this is quite clear. Competition between jurisdictions forces them to engage in strategic action, to adapt their policies, not to the preferences of the public for different levels of public goods or regulation, but to the bargaining power of mobile actors, such as multi-State corporations. Giving local jurisdictions the power to enter this kind of competition could be seen as devolving power, but it would clearly have the effect of creating a less decentralized outcome, one that could be understood to be a stable equilibrium, but which reflected a very different set of policies from those an equally stable equilibrium that was closer to local policy preferences would reflect. The outcome of such competition is often the impression that local government is in the hands of large mobile corporations rather than local citizens.

Devolution could also run contrary to the dictates of legitimacy if it involved powers which created temptations to solve problems by violating rights or by 'purging undesirables', a concern for which the ongoing conflict in the Balkans should be a powerful reminder. Devolution, if not properly designed and fitted with the appropriate safeguards, might encourage localities into 'exclusionary spirals', attempts to solve problems by: stripping some citizens of their rights; subjecting some citizens to harsher treatment or less protection than others; or encouraging the 'bad risks' to leave the community. These concerns all suggest the necessity of accompanying any devolutionary processes with strong constitutional rules of equal protection and procedural rights.

The final case where devolution may not lead to political decentralization is where the devolved function is incapable of being effectively administered by the jurisdiction, or where it is of sufficient technological complexity that effective public deliberation is not feasible, and where local knowledge is unhelpful. In the first case, devolving the function would lead to poor service, which would lead to popular animosity toward local government and quite possibly withdrawal of attachment. In the second case, devolution would create a similar level of technocracy as at the

[5] The best discussion of this is in Peterson (1995).

national or supra-national level, but without, in all likelihood, the checks on technocratic government that would exist at higher levels—closer judicial scrutiny, competing sources of expertise, multiple interest groups, competing agencies, and so forth. In both of these cases, creating a true sense of localism and the nationalization of important policy functions do not work at cross-purposes: you can harm localities as much by giving them burdens they cannot handle as you can by stripping them of things they can and do manage tolerably well.

The ultimate criterion for judging these questions is simple, at least in principle: devolution should be attempted when it would lead to genuinely improved deliberation. This is likely to occur where issues are of a moral/political dimension rather than based on forms of professionalized expertise (McWilliams 1995). There is no reason to think local technocrats are better than national or supra-national technocrats—probably worse—while there is equally no reason to think experts are better than average citizens or local politicians at grappling with moral/political questions.

6. A Direction for Constitution-Making

To return to the central argument of this chapter, devolution is a necessary but not sufficient condition for political decentralization. In addition to devolving power, the EU must actively work to sustain and support political decentralization. Although the policy tools available to the EU for this endeavour are limited, it should take pains to ensure that the marginal means at its disposal are used effectively to foster the goal of enhanced local government.

At a minimum, the EU should refrain from undermining local democracy by subsidizing entrenched, insular local government. The American Constitution guarantees to every State a republican form of government. Obviously, the EU cannot make such a guarantee. But the EU does possess a powerful lever over depressed regions through its dispensation of equalization funds. It should at least ensure that its schemes do not enrich corrupt and incompetent local governments. If the EU is presented with impressive evidence of corruption and/or effective disenfranchisement, it should investigate those charges and deny its funds to those local authorities that are wilfully anti-republican.

The EU can also establish rules that discourage destructive competition between local governments. Because they face great pressure to lure new business, localities, especially poor ones, feel compelled to offer increasingly generous tax breaks and other forms of costly incentives. The economic equivalent of an arms race ensues as each is compelled to increase its arsenal of subsidies merely to keep up with what the others are offering. The 'subsidies race' saps the resources of local governments and provides no net increase in business investment as a whole.

The most effective way of discouraging such counterproductive forms of locational gamesmanship would be an EU-wide agreement on permissible forms of tax subsidy. Far from taking away power from national and local governments, this would effectively empower them, by giving them the instruments with which to defend their own spending priorities against the equivalent of political blackmail. Given the increasing globalization of capital, this 'economic non-aggression pact' would be an effective instrument for defending national and local political autonomy.

The EU has already done a great deal to subsidize local infrastructure improvement. But development is not just bricks and mortar, it is also the building up of the capacity for effective collective decision-making and implementation. Without the political preconditions for development, EU funds will do nothing to change the long-run ability of depressed areas to solve problems on their own.

The EU needs to contribute to the technical and administrative support systems required to sustain local public deliberation. Such deliberation can take place only when supported by a rich knowledge base regarding local needs and problems. Many places are simply too poor to engage in sufficient expertise and data gathering on their own. The EU should generously fund local and regional think tanks and research institutions whose mission it is to provide the intellectual and empirical underpinning for public deliberation. In addition, it should provide seed money to local governments that wish to professionalize and democratize their operations.

Local public deliberation depends upon active and inquisitive media. Locally focused newspapers, radio stations, and television not only serve as the major disseminators of information; they are also indispensable as scrutinizers of the behaviour of local government. The survival of such forms of media is threatened by the increasing consolidation and globalization of all forms of mass communications. Obviously it is not the EU's role to dictate what forms of media the public reads, watches, and listens to. But it can make the encouragement and celebration of local media a priority. In the United States, the prestige that attends winning a Pulitzer prize serves as a very powerful stimulus for local newspapers to strive for excellence. The EU could sponsor a similar prize programme that rewarded local media for outstanding investigative reporting and other forms of local civic education. Perhaps even more important, the EU can take a very hard line against further media consolidation in its enforcement of anti-trust standards, and provide start-up funds for new locally-oriented media.

The EU cannot create civic spirit and commitment where it does not already exist. But where localities are endeavouring to revive and mobilize such spirit, the EU can indeed make a meaningful contribution. The EU has attempted a number of initiatives to foster a 'European identity', without much evident success. In the long run, subsidizing efforts to reinforce existing civic attachments is likely to be more successful. The EU can help local governments and civic associations to foster such spirit by subsidizing the sort of projects which provide localities an example of civic grandeur and beauty, such as great urban parks, libraries, museums, and city halls.

In the modern age, politics has two ineradicable goals. It undertakes vast, ambitious projects for human betterment and it seeks to satisfy the craving of citizens to exercise meaningful control over the lives. Seen in this light, federalism is not simply an organizational scheme but rather a principle by which these two ambitions can be pursued simultaneously. It weds powerful central governments capable of great undertakings to strong local governments capable of nourishing and sustaining democratic decision-making. By building local civic capacity, the Europe Union has the potential to foster both of these great objectives simultaneously. It can build a stronger foundation upon which to base its great undertakings, while transforming the democratic deficit into a healthy surplus of civic talent and energy.

References

Beer, S. (1993). *To Make A Nation: The Rediscovery of American Federalism*. Cambridge, MA: Harvard University Press.

Crick, B. (1972). *In Defence of Politics* (2nd edn). Chicago: Chicago University Press.

Key, V. O. (1961). *Public Opinion and American Democracy*. New York: Alfred Knopf.

McWilliams, Carey (1995). 'Two Tiered Politics and the Problem of Public Policy', in Marc Landy and Martin Levin, *The New Politics of Public Policy*. Baltimore: Johns Hopkins University Press.

Peterson, Paul (1995). *The Price of Federalism*. Washington, D.C.: Brookings Institution.

Rivlin, Alice (1992). *Reviving the American Dream: The Economy, the States and the Federal Government*. Washington, D.C.: Brookings Institution.

Rossiter, C. (ed.) (1961). *The Federalist Papers*. New York: Mentor.

Scott, James (1998). *Seeing Like A State*. New Haven: Yale University Press.

17

European Citizenship: The Relevance of the American Model

DENIS LACORNE

1. The Irrelevance of the American Model of Federal Citizenship

I find it ironic that one of the most enthusiastic articles ever written about European citizenship was signed by Joseph Weiler, a professor at Harvard Law School, in the weekly magazine, *Le Nouvel Observateur*.[1] There is, in France, much less excitement: we still struggle with our own definitions of citizenship and the nation-state remains as strong as ever, despite the globalization of world economies and the universal melange of cultures. Here is a typical statement by the leader of French conservatives, President Jacques Chirac: 'Far from being incompatible with the concept of nation, Europe is the spiritual and political site which allows this idea to breathe and develop to the utmost.'[2] Chirac's statement was designed to reconcile Eurosceptics with Europartisans. For the most stubborn Eurosceptics, however, there is no salvation in a Europe of strong nations. Chirac's Europe, according to another prominent French conservative, Charles Pasqua, is a myth which, if it were accepted, could lead only to the 'dissolution of nations' into some vague 'federal machinery'.[3] The dissolution of nations, according to Pasqua, will in fact accompany the fragmentation of peoples through well-meaning but ill-defined and irresponsible measures, such as the recent European Charter on regional and minority languages.[4]

[1] Joseph Weiler, 'L'Europe, c'est Babel réussie . . .', *Le Nouvel Observateur* (28 May 1999).

[2] Jacques Chirac, Speech to the French National Assembly [2 March 1999], *Le Monde* (4 March 1999).

[3] Charles Pasqua, 'Réponse au président', *Le Monde* (4 March 1999).

[4] This Charter was signed by the French government in May 1999. Several articles of the Charter were later declared 'contrary to the Constitution' by the French Constitutional Council on the ground that, 'in giving specific rights to 'groups' of regional language speakers . . . the Charter violated the constitutional principles of the indivisibility of the Republic, of equality before the law and of the oneness of the French people'. Conseil Constitutionnel, 99-412 DC (15 June 1999).

The Charter, concluded Pasqua, is the clearest sign that 'European peoples' will lose their respective common languages and therefore their identities.[5]

The attempt to define a meaningful post-national European citizenship is recent, and it is always tempting to discover the image of our future in looking at more advanced forms of federal citizenship. The United States is often referred to as the model of a successful federal experience. How relevant is the American model for a Europe in the process of being built? Comparisons can be disappointing: a careful examination of the American federal model, as it exists today, suggests that it cannot be transposed to the European continent. This is particularly clear with respect to citizenship.

The modern American definition of citizenship is the opposite of the European definition. In the American case, State citizenship is derived from federal citizenship; in Europe, citizenship in the Union derives exclusively from citizenship in a Member State. The Amsterdam Treaty is quite explicit about this: 'citizenship of the Union shall complement and not replace national citizenship.'[6] While State citizenship matters a great deal in Europe, in the United States it has become a non-issue, as well demonstrated by Gerald Neuman in a paper presented at a French conference on 'American Federalism and its Implications for Europe':

> Ordinary people don't think about [State citizenship], and lawyers and academics rarely write about it. It has legal consequences but little intellectual interest. That does not mean, however that people never identify with their states. For many people, being a Texan, being a New Yorker, or being a Georgian are matters of identity and pride. But being a Texan in that sense only correlates, and does not coincide with, being a citizen of Texas.[7]

But this was not always the case. State citizenship, before the civil war, mattered a great deal. But it had an ambivalent meaning: it meant 'citizenship' in the civic-republican sense of the term, and implied virtues traditionally associated with the 'small republics' so well described by Montesquieu in *L'Esprit des lois*. But it was also used to defend the south's 'peculiar institution'. The primacy of State citizenship, in *ante bellum*

[5] Pasqua, 'Réponse au président'.

[6] European citizenship was introduced in the Maastricht Treaty in those terms: 'Citizenship of the Union is hereby established. Every person holding the nationality of a Member State shall be a citizen of the Union' (Art. 8, §1). For further details, see Catherine Wihtol de Wenden, *La Citoyenneté européenne* (Paris: Presses de Sciences Po, 1997).

[7] Gerald L. Neuman, 'European Citizenship and Modern U.S. Federal Citizenship', paper presented at the Conference on 'U.S. Federalism and its Implications for Europe', Centre d'Études et de Recherches Internationales (CERI-Sciences-Po, Paris, 10–11 December 1998), 1. CERI and Editions KARTHALA, Paris, 2002.

America, was justified by the doctrine of 'dual federalism'. This doctrine was initially construed by Chief Justice Marshall and his disciple Joseph Story to mean that 'federal and state governments should be as separate and distinct as the governments of the states'[8] and it had a specific purpose: that of protecting a weak national government against the 'intrusion' of powerful States. This was the defensible aspect of the doctrine. But it also had a less defensible side, for it was often invoked to justify slavery and white supremacy.[9]

In the most infamous decision of the Supreme Court, the Dred Scott decision of 1857, Chief Justice Taney offered the following defence of States' rights:

> We must not confound the rights of citizenship which a State may confer within its own limits, and the rights of citizenship as a member of the Union. [The] Constitution has conferred on Congress the right to establish an uniform rule of naturalization, and this right is evidently exclusive, and has always been held by this court to be so. Consequently, no State, since the adoption of the Constitution, can by naturalizing an alien invest him with the rights and privileges secured to a citizen of a State under the Federal Government . . .[10]

This meant that a former slave, recognized as a free person in a given State, could not remain free in another State if the latter had not abolished slavery. Contrary to a naturalized foreigner, he could not be a citizen of the United States, or the citizen of a State 'under the Federal Government', because he belonged to 'that class of people' who had been slaves at the end of the eighteenth century. A free person of African descent was at best the 'citizen' of a particular State. But that form of citizenship was purely local. It did not provide his or her inclusion within 'what we familiarly call the 'Sovereign People', as Taney put it. For instance, former slaves, born free in a northern State, were indeed citizens of that State, but they were not 'a portion of [the] people' of the United States, since their ancestors, according to Taney, had not been 'acknowledged as part of the people' at the time of the writing of the Declaration of Independence and the Constitution. Dual sovereignty, as construed by Chief Justice Taney, inevitably led to dual citizenship: a *federal citizenship* reserved for white Americans whose ancestors had been free 'at the creation' of the United States, and *state citizenship* for persons born in a given State. But the latter form of citizenship, so far as former slaves were concerned, was not binding on the other States. It was, according to Gerald Neuman, 'a lesser

[8] Jeffrey Rosen, 'Dual Sovereigns', *The New Republic* (28 July 1997), 16–19.

[9] See Rogers M. Smith, 'Participation and Subordination: The Double-Edged Sword of State Citizenship', paper presented at the Conference on 'U.S. Federalism and its Implications for Europe'.

[10] *Dred Scott v. Sandford*, 60 U.S. (19 How.) 393 (1857).

form of state citizenship conferred for local purposes, valid within the state but not binding on the other states, and not resulting in inclusion within the sovereign people'.[11]

In the end, as argued by Jeffrey Rosen, 'the question of who was sovereign, the people of each State or the people of the United States was settled at Appomattox'.[12] It is only with the ratification of the Fourteenth Amendment in 1868 that national citizenship became the 'primary legal category, and state citizenship a derivative one'.[13] The Amendment does not specify the rights and duties conferred by State citizenship. It simply provides that 'no State shall make or enforce any law which shall abridge the privileges or immunities of citizens of the United States', and it specifically overrules Dred Scott when it states that 'All *persons* born or naturalized in the United States . . . are *citizens of the United States and of the State wherein they reside*'. As a consequence, 'a citizen of any State [could] acquire citizenship in any other State simply by changing residence. There are no interstate naturalization procedures and no eligibility criteria, other than the change of residence itself'.[14] State citizenship no longer confers exclusive political rights, with two exceptions: the right to vote in local elections, and the right to run for an elective office. With regard to national elections, it is the federal Constitution alone which defines the qualifications for candidates to the House of Representatives, the Senate, and the presidency.

Should we conclude, given the derivative nature of State citizenship in the United States, that the American model has lost all relevance for a 'Europe of strong nations' where Union citizenship can only 'complement' State citizenship? The answer is 'yes' if one considers modern, post-civil war America. But ante-bellum America, particularly at the time of the writing of the federal Constitution, may still provide a useful example of federalism in the making. Consider Tocqueville's reflexions on the difficulties of constructing a federal system of sovereignty:

> In examining the Constitution of the United States, which is the most perfect federal constitution that ever existed, one is startled at the variety of information and the amount of discernment that it presupposes in the people whom it is meant to govern. *The government of the Union depends almost entirely upon legal fictions; the Union is an ideal nation, which exists, so to speak, only in the mind, and whose limits and extent can only be discerned by the understanding.* After the general theory is comprehended, many difficulties remain to be solved in its application; for the sovereignty of the Union is so involved in that of the states that it is impossible to distinguish its boundaries at the first glance. The whole structure of the gov-

11 Neuman, 'European Citizenship and Modern U.S. Federal Citizenship', 2.
12 Rosen, 'Dual Sovereigns'.
13 Neuman, 'European Citizenship and Modern U.S. Federal Citizenship', 2.
14 Ibid., 4.

ernment is artificial and conventional, and it would be ill adapted to a people which has not been long accustomed to conduct its own affairs, or to one in which the science of politics has not descended to the humbler classes of society.[15]

Applying Tocqueville's argument to Europe, one could argue that the success of the European Union depends on the progress of 'the science of politics' among the different peoples of Europe, that is, a public spirit enlightened enough to grasp the 'complicated theory' of a federal system which mixes local and national allegiances and 'bends the traditional rules of logic' in attempting to reconcile a multitude of national sovereigns with a single, supranational sovereign.[16] The low turnout rate in European elections, the strength of Euroscepticism in France and England, and the exceptionally high level of absenteeism among European parliamentarians, particularly French, suggest that much remains to be done to achieve the 'ideal nation' contemplated by Tocqueville. In addition, the lack of a common European language and unified European media suggest that common perceptions and attitudes have not yet reached the degree of cohesion which already existed in the United States at the end of the eighteenth century.[17]

2. The Relevance of the American Multicultural Model

Multiculturalism is difficult to define. It can refer to an outright rejection of the melting pot, to claims for the recognition of group rights and identities, to a 'democracy of nationalities' or a 'federation of national cultures', once defended by Horace Kallen, the founding father of modern cultural pluralism.[18] It can be used, as I have argued elsewhere, to express conservative, moderate, and radical ideologies.[19] But, for the sake of

[15] Alexis de Tocqueville, *Democracy in America*, i (New York: Vintage Books, 1945), 172–3, emphasis added.

[16] Ibid., 172, 122.

[17] See Dominique Wolton, 'La communication et l'Europe: du multiculturalisme à la cohabitation culturelle' and Yves Hersant, 'Critique de l'euroculture', in Riva Kastoryano (ed.), *Quelle identité pour l'Europe?* (Paris: Presses de Sciences Po, 1998).

[18] 'Democratism and the federal principle have worked together with economic greed and ethnic snobbishness to people the land with all the nationalities of Europe, and to convert the early American nationality into the present American *nation*. For in effect the United States are in the process of becoming a federal state not merely as a union of geographical and administrative unities, but also as a cooperation of cultural diversities, as a federation or commonwealth of national cultures.' H. Kallen, 'Democracy versus the Melting-Pot', in H. Kallen, *Culture and Democracy in the United States: Studies in the Group Psychology of the American Peoples* (New York: Boni and Liveright, 1924), 116.

[19] See Denis Lacorne, *La Crise de l'identité américaine: Du melting-pot au multiculturalisme* (Paris: Fayard, 1997). See also Denis Lacorne, 'Pour un multiculturalisme modéré', *Le Débat*, 97 (1997), 158–67.

argument, I shall retain only one working definition. By multiculturalism I mean the extraordinary capacity Americans have to feel and express several identities and allegiances at the same time. One can be an Irish-American, who strongly supports the IRA and at the same time is a good American patriot; a Latino, proud of his Mexican or Cuban origins and a dedicated citizen of the United States; a Zionist and an American patriot. What is remarkable about such dual or multiple allegiances is that they can be expressed at the same time, without the perception of contradictions. This is the 'ethno-civic' quality of American citizenship, which the philosopher John Dewey well described 83 years ago:

> Such terms as Irish-American or Hebrew-American or German-American are false terms because they seem to assume something which is already in existence called America, to which the other factors may be externally hitched on. The fact is, the genuine American, the typical American, is himself a hyphenated character. It does not mean that he is part American and that some foreign ingredient is then added. It means that . . . he is international and interracial in his make-up. He is not American plus Pole or German. But the American is himself Pole-German-English-French-Spanish-Italian-Greek-Irish-Scandinavian-Bohemian-Jew—and so on.[20]

Transposed to the European scene, one could conceive of a comparable set of multiple allegiances: to a local territory—Bavaria or Corsica, for instance; to a nation-state—Germany or France; and to Europe—as when voting for candidates to the European Parliament. Such multiple allegiances already exist, but they have not been legitimized the way they are in the United States. European citizenship lacks 'substance' because so little is expected from European citizens. There is no direct European taxation system, no European army, few European symbols, no European civic culture, and no common language.

Yet, if European citizenship is to be the 'complement' to national citizenship mentioned in the Amsterdam Treaty, it can make sense only if it is more than just a marginal addition to national citizenship. A mere, abstract 'postnational citizenship' will not do. The French, German, and American political experiences demonstrate that there is no such thing as an abstract citizenship or a pure 'constitutional patriotism', to refer to Habermas's definition of modern national identity.[21] It is naive to bracket off elements of shared history and national culture.[22] European citizenship, as I see it, can only be 'substantial citizenship', grounded on common

[20] John Dewey, as cited in Kallen, *Culture and Democracy*, 131–2.

[21] Jurgen Habermas, 'Struggle for Recognition in the Democratic Constitutional State', in Amy Gutman (ed.), *Multiculturalism: Examining the Politics of Recognition* (Princeton: Princeton University Press, 1994), 134–5.

[22] See Dominique Schnapper, *La Relation à l'autre* (Paris: Gallimard, 1998), 466–92.

and concrete political experiences. It should include numerous references to a shared past and shared group experiences, to shared memories and dreams, and also to the 'burden' of the past, that is, a critical capacity to re-examine our often conflicting national histories. Citizenship, in other words, cannot be separated from identity building. This identity, given the primacy of the nation in the European system, will necessarily be plural. Hence the relevance of the American multicultural experience.

America has often been defined as 'a nation of nationalities', a 'nation of many peoples', a 'federation of national cultures', an 'unfinished experiment', a 'salad bowl', a 'mosaic', a 'kaleidoscope'. All these expressions point to the 'post-national' nature of the American identity. They could help us understand the nature and complexities of a European identity in the process of being built.

Of course, a 'multicultural Europe' would bear little resemblance to multicultural America. Frenchmen, for instance, who remain strongly attached to their centralized, statist, Jacobin tradition are not particularly receptive to multicultural ideas. They do not understand multiple allegiances, so contrary to the Rousseauist notion of the General Will. And yet the French statist tradition is not just a thing of the past. It has recently been reaffirmed in a key decision of the French Conseil Constitutionnel on the 'statut de la Corse'. The decision invalidated a law which recognized, in passing, the existence of a 'people of Corsica' as 'an element—*une composante*—of the people of France'. There was the crime: 'a *people* of Corsica', a foreign concept in the French political vocabulary. There is, according to the Conseil's reading of the French Constitution, only one people: the people of France and a single republic, 'one and indivisible'. As stated by Art. 2 of the Constitution, the republic 'shall ensure the equality of all citizens before the law, *without distinction of origin, race or religion*'. Corsicans, Basques, and Bretons have no political legitimacy, even though they have cultural rights. Thus, concluded the Conseil Constitutionnel, 'Corsican culture' and 'Corsican language' can be taught in school, but only as optional topics. They cannot be part of the general educational requirement.[23]

Transposed to Europe, the American multicultural experience is not relevant if it gives an exaggerated weight to ethnic variables, or questions of gender and cultural identities.[24] A Europe of nations is not and should not

[23] Conseil Constitutionnel, *Statut de la Corse*, 91-290 DC (9 May 1991).

[24] It would be difficult to transpose to Europe Iris Young's concept of a 'just' post-national citizenship, which she defines in the following terms: 'A just policy must embrace the ideal of a heterogeneous public. Group differences of gender, age and sexuality should not be ignored, but publicly acknowledged and accepted. Even more so should group differences of nation and ethnicity be accepted. In the Twentieth century the ideal state is

be a Europe of ethnics. But the American model is relevant in as much as it helps us think in terms of multi-layered cultures and identities. An ideal European citizen could thus be thought of as a pluri-lingual individual, fluent in at least three distinct 'languages':

(1) the 'language of national citizenship', which, as Jonathan Sacks, the chief rabbi of England, once put it, 'we have to learn if we are to live together';
(2) the language of tradition which, still according to Sacks, 'connects us to our local framework of relationships: to family, group and the traditions that underlies them'[25]—and this could include a particular minority language; and
(3) the 'language of Europe'.

The problem is that the 'language of Europe' remains remarkably empty and unimaginative. In the United States, as noted by Michael Walzer, immigrants could easily accept trans-ethnic symbols which did not threaten their cultural identity: the flag, the Statue of Liberty, the Declaration of Independence, the Constitution, the Pledge of Allegiance, Washington's farewell speech, Lincoln's Gettysburg address.[26] Those symbols did not just build a 'thin identity', for they often refer to deeply felt historical events and crises, such as the civil war, the Depression and the New Deal, the Vietnam war, the civil rights movement of the mid-1960s.

The problem with Europe is the extreme poverty of its symbolic identity. No one knows exactly how to teach European history. Symbols are few and uninspiring: there is a flag, a currency—the euro—a few visible European institutions, and an army of 'faceless bureaucrats' in Brussels.

The 'language of Europe' lacks substance and it is afflicted with the perception of a 'democratic deficit': European decisions are indeed excessively removed from the citizen's daily concerns, and they are perceived as undemocratic.

Reflecting on the nature of this deficit, Joseph Weiler, in a dense and provocative article, has proposed five ways of developing a more democratic 'supranational citizenship'. This new citizenship could be thought of as *multicultural* in the following sense: it would not eliminate state nationality; it would, instead, encourage individuals 'to see themselves as belonging to two *demoi*'—one based on existing national cultures, the

composed of a plurality of nations and cultural groups.' Iris M. Young, *Justice and the Politics of Difference* (Princeton: Princeton University Press, 1990), as cited in David Miller, *On Nationality* (Oxford: Oxford University Press, 1995), 133.

[25] Cited in Miller, *On Nationality*, 138. I am adding a third language to Sacks' concept of a bilingual citizenship: the 'language of Europe'.

[26] See Michael Walzer, *What it Means to be an American* (New York: Marsilio, 1992).

other designed to enhance transnational values and affinities. To illustrate this point, Joseph Weiler offers a set of political artefacts that would literally 'tame the national interest' with new supranational republican remedies:[27]

(1) allow European citizens to initiate and vote in European referendums, modelled on US State ballot initiatives;
(2) create a 'European public square', based on the systematic use of Internet to allow 'widespread participation in policy-making processes . . . through the posting of comments and the opening of a dialogue between the Community institutions and interested private actors';
(3) create a European constitutional council modelled on the French Constitutional Council, which could be 'seized by any commission, council, any member state or by the European Parliament acting on a majority of its members';
(4) introduce a limited system of direct European taxation in order to 'instill accountability'and to 'provoke citizen interest'; and
(5) develop 'horizontal human rights', that is, measures designed to combat racism, xenophobia and various acts of discrimination that originate in the private sector.[28]

Such measures would, no doubt, provoke citizen interest and give more content to the idea of a European citizenship. But they would have to be used with caution. As the American example suggests, direct ballot initiatives can be manipulated by powerful interest groups and populist politicians.[29] Direct taxation, on the other hand, if it is suddenly introduced, could only strengthen the position of the Eurosceptics and weaken the commitment to an integrated federal Europe. As for the systematic use of Internet to discuss major European issues, it is highly doubtful that such high-tech gadgetry would have, in the words of Joseph Weiler, 'the most dramatic impact on European governance'. More convincing is the idea of developing 'horizontal human rights'. This could, indeed, constitute the core of a European civic culture in the making, and it is, in fact, consistent with the new anti-discrimination provisions of the Amsterdam Treaty.

[27] Joseph Weiler, 'To Be a European Citizen—Eros and Civilization', *Journal of European Public Policy*, 4/4 (1997), 507–8. For further discussion of these issues, see Percy B. Lehning and Albert Weale (eds), *Citizenship, Democracy and Justice in the New Europe* (London: Routledge, 1997), and Jean L. Cohen, 'Changing Paradigms of Citizenship and the Exclusiveness of the Demos', *International Sociology*, 14/3 (1999), 245–68.

[28] Weiler, 'To be a European Citizen', 511–18.

[29] A good example is California's 'Proposition 187'—nicknamed SOS, 'Save Our State'—which sought to deny the children of illegal aliens access to school and medical services. See Lacorne, *La Crise de l'identité américaine*, 176–90.

Here again, the American experience is relevant. Its experience with affirmative action could serve as a useful model for European policy makers. But it would have to be adapted to the European context. For reasons that are easy to understand—the Third Reich's and Vichy's politics of race—we cannot measure discrimination exactly as it is done in the United States.[30] In France, for instance, the law prohibits the use of ethno-racial categories in census and survey research, and the fight against discrimination would require the use of non-ethnic categories based on the collection of territorial and socio-economic data.[31]

And yet a specifically European democratic identity is being built before our eyes, and it is quite remarkably political. It has been unexpectedly produced by two recent events : a 'crisis of accountability' which led to the collective resignation of the European Commission in March 1999, and the decision in January 2000 to isolate Austria diplomatically, after the constitution of a governing coalition which includes Haider's xenophobic Freedom Party.

The first crisis signalled the birth of a new European ethics of responsibility. Pernicious bureaucratic practices—fraud, mismanagement, nepotism, and so forth—are no longer tolerated in Brussels, even if they remain the norm in other parts of Europe. The old 'democratic deficit', often alluded to and blamed on the European bureaucracy, is in the process of being erased: it can no longer be found in the central institutions of a federal Europe. But we all know that such pernicious practices remain widespread in France, in Spain, in Belgium, and elsewhere. It is now Brussels and Strasbourg that set the tone for the rest of Europe. This could be the stuff of a positive identity in the making; it is what gives substance to a nascent European citizenship. If Europe is more democratic than my own nation, shouldn't I feel European first, and French/German/Italian second? Commenting on the commissioners' resignation for mismanagement and nepotism, Serge July, the editor-in-chief of the French daily *Libération*, could only deplore the 'prehistorical mores' of the French political class which has not yet understood that 'France is changing', like

[30] On the problems raised by the American reliance on ethnic variables, see David A. Hollinger, *Postethnic America* (New York: Basic Books, 1995) and Lacorne, *La Crise de l'identité américaine*, 283–334.

[31] Michèle Tribalat broke the French taboo in realizing the first French survey of French immigrants, based on the explicit use of ethnic variables. See her *Faire France* (Paris, La Découverte, 1995). Her controversial approach has been severely criticized by other French demographers. The most radical denunciation of the 'ethnic approach' can be found in Hervé Le Bras, *Le démon des origines: Démographie et extrême droite* (Paris: L'Aube, 1998). For a good description of affirmative action 'à la française', see Gwénaële Calvès, 'Affirmative Action in French Law', *The Tocqueville Review*, 2 (1998), 167–77.

the rest of Europe, and that a new 'European democratic culture is now spreading all over the continent'.[32]

The second crisis emerged with the European Union's decision to suspend bilateral diplomatic contacts with the Austrian government, by its refusal to support Austrian candidates for international agencies, by the reduction of all ambassadorial relations with Austria to the strict minimum, and by the more ominous threat of further sanctions, should the Austrian Government attempt to violate the fundamental rights listed in Art. 6 of the Amsterdam Treaty.[33] This decision, announced on 31 January 2000 by the president of the Union and supported by 14 Member States—all but Austria—is a first in the history of the Union. Remarkably, it was reached after only 48 hours of consultation among the leaders of the 14 states. It has been denounced by Austrian commentators as a pernicious decision which can only strengthen the Freedom Party in making its populist leader into a hero or a martyr. This could very well be the case. But, I would argue, this decision is a blessing in disguise: it demonstrates, however clumsily, that there are European political values that cannot be compromised and that Europe's political unity cannot be built on any kind of democratically-elected political coalition. In sanctioning Austria, the European authorities demonstrate that there is such a thing as a European conception of good government. Crises, in Europe as in the United States, are identity-building.

To conclude: the development of a new European ethics of responsibility is at the core of a European citizenship in the process of being formed. It has been made possible by a more assertive European Parliament, by the 'quiet work of integration'[34] of the European Court of Justice, and the progressive incorporation of European legal norms into each of the Member States' legislation and court system, particularly in the areas of human rights. The decision to sanction Austria represents a new step in the construction of a European civic culture. It suggests that European authorities have the right to interfere in a Member State's national politics, should that national politics challenge widely agreed European political norms.

[32] Serge July, 'Le pithécanthrope', *Libération* (24 March 1999). July was, of course, alluding to the curious behavior of M. Roland Dumas, the Chief Justice of the French Constitutional Council, who, although indicted for corruption, refused to resign from his position and continued to behave with the 'arrogance of an Ancien Régime noble', as if Europe was not imposing on France, new and more demanding democratic norms. Roland Dumas has, since then, taken a 'leave of absence' from the Conseil Constitutionnel.

[33] This crisis is well described in Anson Rabinbach, 'EU Says the Right Stops Here', *Los Angeles Times* (6 February 2000). See also Claire Tréan, 'Le rôle moteur de la France dans la démarche des Quatorze', *Le Monde* (11 February 2000).

[34] Greg Steinmetz, 'Quiet Force. European Court of Justice keeps Integration on Course', *The Wall Street Journal* (18 March 1999).

Conclusion: The Federal Vision Beyond the Federal State

KALYPSO NICOLAIDIS

Federal rhythms and federal safeguards, democratic deficits and democratized networks, constitutional tolerance and constitutional constraints, mutuality and multiple loyalties. We have travelled a varied landscape, often familiar, but hopefully with a renewed sense of excitement. Excitement from the creation of new transatlantic bonds of collaboration without guarantees of mutual relevance, excitement from prescriptive relevance without concerns for sects and labels, excitement from transdisciplinary scope without pretensions of multidisciplinary theorizing. The road has been travelled before us and the most we can hope is to be read as a renewed *invitation au voyage*. We will never, like the poet, see the land of order and beauty, but we continue to be fascinated with ours, the lands of compromises, cross-purposes, and contradictions.

Taking the contributions in this volume as a whole, then, can one discern the broad outlines of what we have boldly labelled 'the federal vision'? Not if what is meant by 'vision' is a collective blueprint: a set of recommendations about specific lessons the EU and US must learn from each other. We did not seek to create an artificial scholarly consensus, when we believe in fact that the main contribution of this volume is to demonstrate once again the kaleidoscopic nature of the federal lens and the multiple ways in which it throws light on the question of legitimacy. Nevertheless, there has emerged from this collective enquiry a number of cross-cutting themes from the thinking together of the EU and US experiences with federal governance and, perhaps surprisingly, a degree of normative consistency. We have not sought to agree on a definition of legitimate governance beyond the common-sense notion that 'it' is whatever it takes for individuals in a polity to consent to being ruled in a certain way. But these cross-cutting themes reflect a widely shared belief among us about the types of institutional designs and practices that are most likely to lead to sustained legitimacy.

The 'federal vision' is part analysis, part prediction, and part utopia. The features that we highlight are sometimes incipient, sometimes dominant, sometimes yet to come in either or both polities. When they exist, they can be harnessed or subverted. Although they are often variations on features of federalism that have long been identified and debated by scholars and political figures in the historical development of federalism, we did not seek to revisit the perennial debate on the essence of federalism in the US and around the world. Nevertheless, the contested nature of what 'federalism' actually means both as an ideal type and as a reality provides the backdrop for our analysis.

Of course, the federal ideal-type is itself but one solution to the dilemma, inherent in most forms of social organizations, of reaching an equilibrium between, 'on the one hand, a respect for the autonomy of the individual unit, freedom of choice, pluralism, and diversity of action, and, on the other hand, the societal need for cooperation, integration, harmony, and, at times, unity' (Cappeletti, Seccombe, and Weiler 1986: 4). But should it not have pride of place? Some sociologists would argue that federalism is such a resilient and universal structure that it characterized the organization of human life in clans and hordes for a hundred thousand years before the advent of empires (Baechler 1994). That is perhaps because its distinguishing feature lies precisely in *not* resolving the tensions which exist between the two poles: the One and the Many. In a federation, each part is itself a whole, not a part of a whole, and the whole itself is more than its parts. Neither is the One a simple expression of the Many—collaboration—nor are the Many simply components of the One—hierarchy. Instead, like fractals in our mental and material maps,[1] each exhibits in its own scale its own version of a familiar pattern; each level operates as a whole albeit with multiple and subtle connections with other levels. Federalism in its essence does not mean bringing together different polities as one—however decentralized—polity. It means instead retaining what is separate *in spite of* all that is common.

Not surprisingly, the practice of federal or quasi-federal polities in the modern epoch has greatly diverged from this ideal type. As Daniel Elazar has been at pains to remind us, Johannes Althusius developed his model of republican federalism *against* Jean Bodin's vision of the state. In doing so, he was advocating a much more radical departure from the authoritarian rule of kings in favour of power sharing in communities of different composition and function to accommodate a European reality of four or five arenas of territorial governance, not all territorially defined. The

[1] Fractals are defined in chaos theory as the separate constitutive elements of universal patterns repeated on different scales.

history of federalism is that of the progressive demise of the Althusian vision of federalism and its subversion by Bodin's paradigm of the state; the latter became so dominant that when it did not prevail outright it turned would-be federations into 'federal states'. In the United States, the essence of 'the federal principle' has been the subject of countless accounts and debates since the foundation. To be sure, none of the pre-civil war American thinkers on federalism—not even Daniel Webster—saw the United States as a 'federal state'. For them the word 'state' still denoted not the whole but the parts of the union (Forsyth 1981). They did disagreed—and debates continue to this day—on whether the Constitution established a consolidated government, simply a compact or federation of sovereign states or, as James Madison suggested, 'a compound of both' (Goldwin and Schambra 1986). But to the extent that the seeds of 'statehood' had been planted in the American construct, it is precisely because the Founding Fathers, like all other men at the time, and perhaps all other men up to that time, regarded federalism not as a kind of government but as a voluntary association of states which sought certain advantages from that association. And it is for this reason that, in their majority behind Madison, they considered their construct as a combination of both 'federal' and 'national' government (Grodzins 1966). Calhoun's attempt to rescue the vision of a 'genuine' American federation, half a century after its foundation, was doomed to fail posthumously under the combined assaults of the civil war, the New Deal, the anti-progressive bent of 'State rights' advocacy of the 1950s and 1960s and managerial approaches to governing in the twentieth century. Already, as of 1870, war had imposed the supremacy of the 'whole' over the 'parts' in the US but also in Switzerland and, most significantly, in the new German empire. European, and above all German, writers at the nineteenth century's end gave the final momentum to the shift to a statist paradigm of federalism. Witness Max von Seydel, founding father of European federalism, quoting a French contemporary in 1872: '*il ne peut y avoir deux unités, car l'essence de l'unité c'est d'être une*'. A far cry from the fractal mental map of federalism.

In short, the 'federal' emerged prior to or in contrast with the 'state' before the two converged; only by questioning the attributes of nation-state that federalism inherited in the course of its history can we recover the federal vision. This does not mean seeking to retrieve the federal ideal type from the vagaries of history. It simply means, in Europe, that our vision is of a federation *of* nation-states, not a federal state; and, in the United States, that the federal state is only one contemporary element of a more lasting federal vision. This also means that such a federal vision is relevant to governance at the world level, albeit in a muted form. This is, in other words, a federal vision beyond the state.

When we come to selling our ideas beyond academia in Europe, we may, however, have to be shamefully inconsistent, disloyal to our scholarly premise. Perhaps Jacques Delors and Joseph Nye are right to say in their Foreword to this volume that 'federalism is no longer taboo in Europe'. Still, whether *for* or *against* many in Europe do not view the notion of a federal state as an oxymoron. Let us hope of course that, in time, the federal vision may be reframed and reconstructed *beyond the state*. In the meanwhile, we may need to refer to our vision as a 'post-federal' vision, one that builds on the insights of comparative federalism and on the concerns of 'federalists', but 'post' nevertheless. If 'federalism' has irrevocably been subverted by its nation-state era incarnation, then perhaps a 'post-federal vision' is called for.

In this conclusion, I will present what I take to be the broad elements of our federal vision. As summarized in Table C.1, such a vision calls for five concurrent shifts in focus in our understanding of what matters about federal contracts. Each is central to fashioning a 'federal' response to the challenge of legitimacy. In each case, we have revisited old themes with fresh insights in light of what we see as some of the most significant recent developments in the worlds that we investigate. In particular, I suggest how the notion of 'subsidiarity' as commonly understood—that political decisions should be made and policies conducted at the lowest, or most appropriate, level—needs to be fined-tuned, reinterpreted and even relabelled. Needless to say, in doing so we raise more questions than we can start to answer.

1. From Allocative Outcomes to the Process of Change: Legitimacy and Flexibility

I start, echoing many of the chapters in this volume, with 'the conventional view'. In a formal legal understanding of federalism, we need to distinguish between three types of enquiry: *where* or at which level should competences lie; to the extent that competences are indeed possessed by one or several levels, *whether* they should be exercised at all and what principles should help in deciding this; and to the extent that competences are exercised, *how* should they be exercised. While these ought in principle to refer to (1) constitutional or quasi-constitutional decisions, (2) the principles of subsidiarity or devolution 'formulas', and (3) the principle of proportionality, 'better lawmaking', and 'better policy-making', in practice these three dimensions are very much intertwined (see Bermann and Nicolaidis in this volume; see also De Búrca, 1999). Nevertheless, for many constituencies, from German *Länder* to British Tories, advocates of

TABLE C.1. *Paradigm shift and the Federal Vision*

Shift	Keywords
From allocative outcomes to the process of change	Flexibility, open-ended dynamics
From distributed to shared competences	Networked cooperation, proportionality, forms of governance
From separation of powers to power checks	*Procedural subsidiarity*, structures of governance, mutual control, constitutional constraint, federalism safeguards, agency ties, forbidden interfaces, asymmetric federalism
From power containment to empowerment	Proactive subsidiarity, mutuality, capacity building, positive sum allocation, managed competition
From muti-level to multi-centred governance	*Horizontal subsidiarity*, transnational federalism, non-hierarchical models of governance, constitutional tolerance, mutual recognition, mutual inclusiveness, shared projects, shared identities

'State rights' in the US, as well as much of public opinion on both sides, legitimacy follows from a clear and transparent allocation of competences across levels of governance. The corollary belief is that legitimacy calls for mechanisms for accountability at each of those levels commensurate with its respective task. As the Appendix to this volume amply demonstrates, even in its own terms, allocating competences among levels of governance is a much more complex legal and political exercise that merely drawing 'lists' that can be posted on walls and webs for the good people of the agora.

But what if, beyond this, there is no general principle out there for allocating competences in a legitimate way, even at any given time? What if, on substantive grounds, the issue of competence is fundamentally indeterminate? What if most responsibilities are shared anyway? And what if, therefore, it is impossible clearly to determine targets of accountability? If legitimacy is bound up with the collective achievement of widely shared objectives that may change over time, why should the focus be on fixing competences? Should we not ask instead how to make it more likely that our governance systems will deliver on the many expectations that people project upon it?

Recognizing the fundamental indeterminacy of competences, legal scholars have struggled with the first-order legal-normative question of who decides 'who decides', and who *ought to* decide, between courts and States or between States collectively and individually, courts at the national or Union level, or indeed electorates through referendums and elections. Our interwoven stories certainly illustrate how different actors have played, and will at different times play, a key role in framing the debate over change as well as managing change. In particular, like many before us, we take on board the complex interaction between the judicial and political spheres in driving competence upward or downwards. But our key interest here has been one step removed, namely, to suggest that what matters is to allow for multiple avenues for change, and to ask how change is negotiated, how it ought to be managed, and how different instruments can be used as alternatives to one another over time in regulating the relationship between the State and the Union. In other words legitimacy requires a certain type of flexibility.

Thus, the first set of lessons we draw in this book is that our quest for legitimacy should focus less on places or loci of governance and more on processes of governance. This is true first and foremost for the process of change in levels of governance itself. The real question before us is *how can changes in levels of governance be conducted so as to enhance the legitimacy of the system?* We are not alone in calling for the need to reassert the importance of process over substance, the need to move beyond comparative statics, in the study of competence and federalism.[2] Yet many scholars or politicians still frame the question as one of optimal allocation of powers between levels of government—if only we could agree on how to define such an 'optimum' and do away with the imperfections in our political system that lead to the gap between such optimal and actual allocations of tasks!

In contrast, the federal vision *does not describe an end-state, or even a series of equilibria, but a process*. There is no *teleology* of federalism, a centralizing or decentralizing trend, or even the possibility of finding a stable status quo for a significant period of time. Instead, political communities will oscillate endlessly between the poles of unity and autonomy as they search for the appropriate scale of their collective endeavour. For one, it is a fact that numerous exogenous and dynamic factors such as crisis situations, social demands, internationalization, and changing technology lead to shifts in the exercise of policy responsibilities either suddenly or over time. A rigid delineation of competences is simply counterproductive in this context. And, as is the claim of most theories of integration, endogenous dynamics also drive the wheels of change, which create new reasons and incentives to shift the exercise of competence. Obviously, part of

[2] This shift in emphasis is palatable on both sides of the Atlantic. A simple overview of the content of *Publius*, the foremost journal in the field, is exemplary in this vein.

the question here is to what extent these endogenous dynamics and the responses to exogenous ones ought to be constrained by the design of our federal systems. The first order answer is: not very much *ex ante*. Since 'the natural starting point for that search [for an appropriate scale] is in the opposite direction from the most recent round of reform' (Donahue and Pollack, p. xx) a well-functioning federal system is one which is always to be a candidate for change, a system in continuous disequilibrium, where the challenge is to smooth out and 'legitimize' the cycles of changes in levels of governance. This is a view inspired by a cyclical account of the history of US federalism. It may be at odds with traditional integration theories developed in the European context to the extent that they point to cumulative sources of centralization over time, albeit with institutional fits and starts. Yet, in Braudelian terms, these few decades 'at the beginning' may not be the relevant time frame. Most importantly, the kind of changes that we discuss and call for, reflecting as they do shifting notions of subsidiarity and legitimacy, can happen against a backdrop of continued integration—if by 'integration' we mean the creation of increasingly dense ties between societies and individuals across borders. Allowing for such cyclical shifts would seem the best way to preserve and even take to its ultimate logic the project-based approach to European integration which consists in mobilizing competences around specific goals.

In spite of these arguments, the debate over governance and subsidiarity in the EU has come to feed into, and been partially overtaken by, the constitutional debate over competences and their formal allocation. Has the EU reached a critical juncture when it needs to behave like a 'mature' polity? Or is there greater value in an ongoing process of legitimization of policy processes and practices? Some would argue that precisely in order to allow for sustainable change, a federal vision calls for embedding flexible adjustment within a context of 'constitutional' stability, whether or not this implies a formal constitution—whether one values constitutional stability like Hamilton because of the 'reverence that time bestows upon all things' or because it provides for credible pre-commitments to sustain societal bargains. Meaning borrows from both the mystery and the reliability of time. If constitutional rules change too quickly, the context they provide in which a conflict of interests could be waged disappears and the constitutional rules instead become part of the conflict itself. At the same time, successful federal arrangements develop forms of flexible governance exactly to allow the federal balance to shift with various social, technological, economic, or ideological trends over time, without the need to remake formal constitutional rules. A constitution is not in and of itself anathema to flexibility: it may even be possible to imagine such a document that would enhance the way the Union orchestrates changes in governing allocations. The real question, as Joseph Weiler argues in his chapter, is whether the EU's existing quasi-constitution is not only sufficient but also a normatively superior approach to traditional constitution making. I will revisit the issue at the end of this chapter.

As an alternative or intermediary step to a full-blown constitution, one option put forward is that of a formal *Kompetenzkatolog*, or 'charter of competence', both as a means of providing greater clarity for citizens and as a break on expanding Union competence. Would a non-binding non-justiciable indicative list describing in clear language the overlapping spheres of competence of EU actors and why and how they may change do the trick? In any event, even while embodying a commitment to flexibility, such a charter could not in any way be considered as a panacea. In the EU as in the US, the spirit of federalism and subsidiarity lies elsewhere. Concern about over-zealous action on the part of the federal level must be addressed in other ways. What then are the alternatives to formal assignment or reassignment of competences?

2. From Distributed to Shared Competences: Networked Cooperation, Proportionality, and Changing Forms of Governance

Consideration of these alternatives needs to be predicated on a second shift that has long been at play both in the workings and in the understanding of federalism, namely, that federal dynamics are increasingly about the management of shared rather than distributed competences between levels of governance. This is not new. It is a little disputed fact—illustrated by many of the authors in this volume—that in the US as in most other federations, and indeed in the EU, 'dual federalism', in which most powers and competences tend to be divided neatly between federal and local governments, has given way to 'cooperative federalism', in which most powers and competences are treated as, in principle, shared by the various levels of government. This on the assumption not just that only on an ad hoc basis is it possible to know whether a particular topic or area in a given time and place is more properly regulated at one level of governance (Cappeletti, Seccombe, and Weiler 1986); but, furthermore, that even then most tasks will need to be undertaken jointly, through an increasingly fine-tuned division of labour between levels of governance. In other words, the sharing is not only of the competences themselves but also of their *exercise*, even in instances of so-called exclusive competences. Thus, in practice, considerations of subsidiarity blend into considerations of proportionality and governance, in the EU but also in the US is best described as a multilevel process (Hooghe and Marks, 2001).

A first, obvious legitimacy problem arises from concurrency. How is it possible, in this context, to draw up meaningful lists of competences? Of course, historically, shared competences have been spelled out in federal constitutions either directly or *by default* as those competences not exclusively attributed or reserved—and then been inferred further from the texts through expansive interpretations of market integration clauses and ad hoc encroachment on States' residual power (Hesse and Wright 1996; Bermann and Nicolaidis, this volume). But codifying such practices in the EU would be akin to political reverse engineering. Would a competence list in the EU need to recognize and present the existing gradation from reserved State competences, to conditionally reserved competences, to national but coordinated competences, to partially or mostly transferred competences? Or could it simply indicate the kind of issues which might a priori be addressed predominantly at the European level, at the state level or at the substate level? At a minimum, an accurate listing of competences would require statements as to when various components of 'shared competence' are activated and under what conditions—for example, in the EU: welfare provision at the state level except for regulation related to trans-boundary movement of workers. But this approach in turn would, if anything, risk exacerbating popular perception of centralization. Thus, if we refer to the issue-areas listed by Moravcsik where the EU is generally *not* involved—such as taxation, social welfare provision, defence, foreign policy, policing, education, cultural policy, human rights, and small business policy—most of these nevertheless appear one way or another to have been partially, albeit marginally, 'federated' as shared competence. We need to develop a public language of shared competence.

More broadly, coming to grips with the implications of shared competences implies a normative commitment to shared authority in the broadest sense and an acceptance that powers held by different levels of government are often implied, tacit, or contested, and not plainly granted by explicit contracts—constitution or treaty. This may of course have different implications as to how levels of government relate to one another. There are those like Albert Breton who extol the virtues of competitive government and prefer to see 'levels' compete in the exercise of these shared competences as to who can best serve the citizen in a given policy field, with a set of background rules to manage spillovers and externalities between their respective actions. In practice however, the sharing of competences has usually led to active cooperation between levels of governance. As Peterson and O'Toole, remark 'legislation at any level is unlikely to achieve its stated goals unless it is shaped, moulded, and scrutinized by actors interacting across different levels. Accordingly, 'federalism usually gives rise to less formal and intricate structures within which a large number of actors, each wielding a small slice of power, interact'. Network modes of governance arise when policy-making depends fundamentally on the concerted action of multiple layers of governance and when policy outcomes need to be the products of negotiation and mutual adjustment between different levels of government.

But such an 'organic' fusion of power can be perceived as much a threat to democratic legitimacy as unwarranted transfers of power to the centre (Wessels, 1997). Citizens face a system of governance where lines of accountability are blurred and available channels for expressing voice unclear. How is one accountable for what one jointly does? If it is true that networks are most powerful 'during the least visible, transparent, and rules-based stages of the policy process [for example, agenda setting and implementation]' (Peterson and O'Toole,), the stakeholders who are not direct participants in network deliberation have little way of knowing when and by whom important decisions are made. When considering the implication of shared competences on democratic legitimacy, therefore, the state versus union dichotomy gives way to the more fundamental dichotomy—between the sovereign 'peoples' and the various loci of governance 'sharing' competence—and to how the former may control the latter.

So when we ask what subsidiarity means under shared competences we must not only ask how lower levels may protect themselves from overreach by higher levels but we must also explore ways in which to guard against potential collusion of diverse levels of government and the dilution of accountability this implies. I will come back to this twin concern in the next section.

Finally, I argued above that the 'federal' legitimacy challenge is first and foremost to establish political arrangements to better manage change in the locus of power and policy-making. But isn't there a tension between this emphasis on change and cycles and the assumption that federal dynamics are increasingly about the minutiae of dividing tasks? How can we argue both that legitimacy in such systems is bound up with finding ways for allowing the periodic reassertion of State or federal primacy and, at the same time, that federalism is above all about the implementation of an ever finer institutional division of competence? Indeed, Grodzins (1966) introduced his famous analogy of the federal form of government as a marble cake whose layers interpenetrate rather than dominate one another in part as a reaction to the understanding of federalism as a cyclical phenomenon; if the 'marble cake' was a better reflection of the nature of the beast than the simplistic 'layer cake' metaphor, then it was also plausible to predict a gradual evolution towards a unitary state, albeit with complex sets of interactions and modes of division of labour within it. Can one accept the premise without endorsing the conclusion? Isn't this reasoning bound up with interpretations through statist lenses, where a trend to concerted action gets immediately interpreted as the creation of some kind of new—statist—centre? If indeed polities develop increasingly subtle and finely tuned allocation of tasks among various levels of governance, does this mean that the degree of 'separatedness' between these levels itself is fading away?—in which cases we may speak of centralization or decentralization along the French meaning of '*déconcentration*': delegation to the periphery, diffusion of responsibility but under a single political authority. Indeed, Donahue and Pollack conclude their analysis of federal rhythms by positing that 'the rhythm tends to slow and cycles to lengthen as a polity matures; first-order ambiguities are settled, and a degree of institutional inertia dampens the effect of discontent with both centralization and decentralization'. With time, there are bound to be less revolutionary swings in respective roles.

This does not make change less relevant, however: only that the object of change may itself change and that what may come to matter most is the way in which collective *forms of shared governance* evolve over time. In this light, subsidiarity concerns variations along dimensions such as the degree of discretion left to the States or lower levels of governance in the interpretation of common policies, the extent to which Union objectives are binding to lower levels, or the relationship between who formulates and who implements policies. Moreover, given that competences are not just about the power to legislate but rather the power to act in general, through framing policies, statements of objectives, financial decision, the delivery of services, various kinds of regulations, judicial rulings, norm creation as well as publicity and communication, then subsidiarity is also about making the appropriate choice between different instruments of action rather than whether or how much to act. Different areas of competences—market liberalization, monetary policy, migration, environment—warrant different types of instruments over time, more or less intrusive depending on the federal claim to relevance, with different functions exercised by different actors. In the end, if most competences are shared, the principle of proportionality is the operational core of subsidiarity. And proportionality can be a powerful source of legitimacy if it can be translated in straightforward notions. Be it under shared or exclusive competence, the question is: are policy means proportional to the ends pursued? To what extent is power to act and make policy exercised? How extensively? Proportionality brings with it an in-built open-endedness and opens up spaces, margins where the democratic process can take place. When, in the name of proportionality, the European Court of Justice (ECJ) requires the states to restrict their market intervention to labelling requirements, it is effectively handing back responsibility to the consumer and consumer associations.

The question is whether and how citizens realize that these spaces have been opened. Schmidt and Peterson and O'Toole discuss how this possibility to 'enter' the policy process varies with stages of policy-making—agenda setting, decision, implementation—as well as across states.

It is through these lenses that we need to interpret recent developments in the US and the EU invoking subsidiarity and devolution, from the rediscovery of the original spirit of the 'directive' in the EU—rebaptized 'framework directive'—to the 'open method of coordination' (OMC) to deal with European labour market reform and unemployment to the reliance on state innovation under broad federal guidelines for welfare reform in the US. As explored further in sections 4 and 5, taking subsidiarity seriously in these contexts means rethinking the role of the Union as enabling rather than constraining for all levels of governance.

In the end, there may be an inescapable paradox in promoting subsidiarity in a context of reigning shared competences both in the US and in the EU. On one hand, in the current political climate, subsidiarity and devolution are generally interpreted as the Union level 'doing less better' to the extent that if and when it acts it should do so in ways deferential to lower levels of government, whether early at the policy formulation stage or late at the implementation stage. At the same time, however, it could be argued that 'softer' methods of intervention are precisely ways of 'doing more better', 'buying' less painful central intervention, extending the scope of Union competences—albeit softly exercised—under 'false' pretences. It matters therefore to ask how the forms of governance associated with *new* Union competences tend to 'harden', and whether methods such as the EU's OMC are introduced only in the context of expanding EU competences or whether they are applied to decentralize the exercise of existing competences in other areas.

3. From Separation of Powers to Power Checks: Governance Structures, Procedural Subsidiarity, and the Safeguards of Federalism

If both the need for flexible governance and the reality of shared competences render the exercise of competence delineation largely pointless, if at the same time subsidiarity is to be found in developing new forms of shared governance, then we need to ask how a system can best be designed to safeguard the interests of all levels of governance. This question brings us back to the very foundation of federalist thinking: that, however powers are allocated between levels and branches of government, the real issue is whether these powers are checked, how to prevent their perennial abuse, and, in doing so, how to ensure accountability in their use. The constitutions of all polities consist to a great extent in setting out limits to the exercise of public and private power. But neither the US nor the EU has been impervious to the Jacobin's impatience with self-restraint, including through the exclusive resort to short-term majorities.

The broad principle espoused here is that, in a world of cooperative or competitive partnership between levels of governance, modes of interaction and institutional design rather than allocation of powers between levels are the key to the legitimization of the power exercised. The sharing of competence renders checks on respective powers both more necessary and more difficult. This was Elazar's insight when he pointed out that a rigid dual federalism never existed in the United States and that cooperation has been the hallmark of national-State relations since the early days (Elazar 1962). What mattered was not the fact of cooperation but the degree of coercion involved in the relationship, one which changed significantly in the US in the 1960s. Normatively, the question raised ever since in the US has been how to constrain such coercive tendencies. In spite of the relatively much greater weakness of the Union, the EU is no longer immune to this fundamental question.

Thus, a federal vision calls for further revisiting the role of 'power checks', constitutional constraints or 'mechanisms of control' in limiting the import of transfers in competence, vertically or horizontally. Here the shift is from examining change simply in the locus of power to assessing how such various modes of control may themselves be the markers and measures of change and how they can and have been refined over time; or, as Coglianese and I ask in this volume, rather than being simply curbed, how can allocational shifts be designed in such a way to ensure that the transfer of authority from one unit to another will be used in the way it was intended?

The safeguards embedded in federal designs exist precisely in order to prevent any level of governance from being absolutely empowered or disempowered over time. We could invoke yet again Calhoun's sophisticated defence of his federal vision almost two centuries ago as one which ruled out allowing any level of government to be the judge of its own competence. Instead, what was needed for Calhoun was a 'mutual negative power' consisting of a right both to nullify the acts of the other and to interpose one's power to arrest such acts. In Calhoun's view, nothing short of this would possibly preserve the division of power on which rested the equilibrium of the whole system (Forsyth 1981). Is it not worth asking whether such balanced deterrence obtains in our respective polities? To be sure, if there has been not only a real divergence between the legal and the political planes of integration but also a constructive tension between them—above all in the EU but also in the US—it is because judges, political leaders, and lawmakers hold conflicting views—and change their views over time—of what it is that most needs to be held in check: discretionary State power or expansive Union jurisdiction (Cappeletti, Seccombe, and Weiler 1986; Weiler 1999).

What one may find fascinating here is that lessons continuously need to be relearned. We need continuously to relearn to think our way from subsidiarity to proportionality, from the 'where' of power to the 'how', from first-order rights, responsibilities, or functions to the safeguards that are crafted on to them. Most importantly, beyond the issue of 'State rights' per se, power checks include all forms of democratic control, including on the States themselves. The challenge here is to think together the checks exercised on each other among levels of governance per se and the checks exercised by 'the people' *on* governments acting individually or collectively: the democratic imperative. In short, the question is not just who is to police the boundary between State and Union but whether the boundary itself is the relevant place to look.

This is not the place to provide an exhaustive catalogue of the safeguards of federalism—what Bermann and Nicolaidis in this volume call 'the core "guarantee" of the values of federalism'—but rather to suggest our bias and our method through some examples picked in this volume. The bias shared by most authors in this volume is to ask critically how the prerogatives of *lower* levels of governance can be, and have been, safeguarded. The method is functionalist: to systematically analyze how these safeguards can act as substitutes for one another. In asking how principals retain some degree of control over agents to which they delegate authority, Coglianese and Nicolaidis seek to highlight the functional equivalence between various sorts of 'agency ties', and the chapters by Bermann, Halberstam, Moravcsik, Majone, and Schmidt all analyze alternative power checks and institutional constraints, suggesting in particular how the potential for substitution between them is key to the adaptability of the systems. We can recognize such tradeoffs in the original institutional designs or in the way they have evolved over time. We can also recognize such tradeoffs by contrasting the US and the EU and assessing whether apparently different power checks actually have similar functions.

If we combine the responses provided throughout this volume, we find that although the US and the EU have leaned towards a very different balance between mutual oversight and autonomy across levels of governance, both have used changing combinations of safeguards in doing so over time. In both sides, the delineation of competences per se and the judicial policing of general principles of allocation—for example, enumerated and residual powers, supremacy, pre-emption—could simply not suffice in establishing operational rules of the game.

Do we need to recall, echoing the US Supreme Court, that in both polities the principal means chosen by the framers to uphold the authority of the States was the structure of federal/Union governance itself? The form and intensity of representation at the centre surely serves as the starting point for debates over legitimacy across a whole range of institutional contexts—from the United Nations to the United Kingdom. And it can certainly serve as a crude test of a polity's federal credentials. The US presidential election in the autumn of 2000 has dramatically reminded us that even there State delegates to the electoral college—or for that matter members of the House of Representatives—are still, to some extent, delegates *of* the States in their sovereign character, not delegates *from* the States considered as mere electoral districts. It is striking that at the very same time, at the Nice Summit in December 2000, EU leaders endorsed for the first time the validity of EU-wide popular majorities as a democratic criterion. Not withstanding this interesting contrast, the distance between the two polities on this count is vast.

As Bermann points out, in the US, as in most mature federations, the constraints on the exercise of power at the federal level itself—structural and to a lesser extent procedural safeguards—have considerably weakened over time. Governors usually need to change hat to be heard in Washington. There may be interesting trends to watch, such as the emerging State representation in external trade negotiations covering areas where they continue to be the primary regulators of standards and services. Nevertheless, in the US legitimacy through safeguards must be found elsewhere.

This is of course in marked contrast with the EU, where state representation *is*, to a great extent, the centre. This fact is familiar terrain but the authors in this volume disagree on its implications for legitimacy. Indeed, Moravcsik believes that it is precisely the EU's stringent 'constitutional constraints' that are responsible for what he sees as a normatively desirable outcome: the limited scope of EU action. Member State veto or the requirement of super-majorities in the Council of Ministers combine with the states' quasi-fiscal monopoly and various kinds of opt-out options in curbing expansionary impulses. The ways in which the extent and forms of such constraints vary according to issue-areas testifies to the EU's sophisticated 'evolutionary pragmatism' (Moravcsik and Nicolaidis 1998) or the organic development in Europe of a hybrid form of customized federalism. On the other hand, Pollack and Donahue highlight the importance of other centralizing or decentralizing factors which in turn will determine how constraining these various constraints might be across issues.

In the pure federal logic, then, one could contend that sustained legitimacy in the EU crucially depends on a 'principled defence' of the national veto in issue areas still seen as 'belonging' to the states even while the Union intervenes—taxation, immigration, welfare state provisions. In these areas, the method of consensual bargaining helps curb centralizing tendencies by ensuring that European new initiatives are Pareto-improving over the status quo, or, as Neil Komesar (1994) puts it, that the 'fear of the few' voters should not always prevail over 'the fear of the many' (majorities). Legitimacy in this context crucially depends on adequate indirect accountability. Alternatively, the resort to 'enhanced cooperation' can serve to provide a political safety valve in cases where states can only agree to disagree. Provided ways are found to minimize its union-wide impact, asymmetric federalism, as testified by the US experience is the safeguard of last resort.

And yet 'sharing' in central power as a mode of control by the states themselves seems inevitably on the decline with the maturing of the EU and with the need for effective decision-making. At a minimum, states in the EU will increasingly need to exercise their control at the centre through coalitions rather than individually; and relative control will increasingly reflect population weights. Yet the bare basics of democratic theory tell us that formal or informal state vetos will not disappear without prejudice to legitimacy before citizens can be reassured either that they will most likely belong to cross-states majorities or that citizens and decision-makers of other Member States will have sufficiently 'internalized' their concerns. It seems misguided in this light to oppose European 'intergovernmentalism' to the 'federal' aspirations of the Union when the former is an inherent part of a genuine federal vision. The real issue is not that intergovernmentalism is *not necessary* in a federal EU but rather that it is *not sufficient*. Other actors than states and other mechanisms of control must be entrusted with upholding the values of federalism.

For one, the Union level needs to design and sustain institutional mechanisms to ensure the participation at the centre of levels of governance lower than the states. And although the call for participation at the centre of the regions, municipalities, and other local or functional authorities has now become the hallmark of EU politics, this is a theme the US needed to revisit as it embarked into decentralized welfare reform. If devolution or subsidiarity means emphasizing decentralized implementation, then participation at the centre of the lower levels of governance is itself a means of increasing efficiency as these levels can indicate what can or cannot properly be implemented. This is where input and output legitimacy converge. If the implementers participate in the central decision making process they are likely to indicate the boundary of the possible—what is sustainable on the ground. As a quid pro quo and in order to alleviate fears of cheating, the Union has the responsibility of ensuring transparency among the actors involved on their respective implementation approaches. In short, there is little doubt that the multiplication of 'veto-points' is the price to pay for shifting from diplomatic politics to politics *tout court*.

Perhaps the most fundamental alternative focus to representation at the centre is to emphasize the procedural dimension of subsidiarity, the question of 'how' powers are exercised beyond the formal structures through which they are exercised. This theme is developed by Kinkaid, Lazer and Mayer-Shoenberger, Bermann, Halberstam, Majone, and Peterson and O'Toole. Procedural safeguards imply that the checks on the actor concerned—the federal government, agencies, states—consist not only in limiting its sphere of action but, within this sphere of action, limiting its freedom of action. Rules of due process, transparency, and openness require neither cumbersome oversight on the part of the principals nor rigid delineation of competence *ex ante*. Instead, they require that whatever takes place in the exercise of competence, and change thereof, does so through procedures that ensure that all stakeholders' viewpoints be considered and extant principles be respected. And crucially it means requiring decision-makers to 'give reasons' for their action and to reflect publicly on the intensity of the actions needed (De Búrca 1999).

The drafting of devolution or subsidiarity 'criteria' in the US and in the EU has raised once again the question of what the explicit benchmarks for giving such reasons ought to be. It may be argued that as they exist, or as they are read, these criteria exhibit a centralizing bias as a result of their economistic inspiration—federal intervention is justified by economies of scale, the existence of 'public goods' or generic efficiency criteria. But there is little explicit basis for considering the more fundamental issue of whether the inherent democratic value of lower-level decision-making may in and of itself justify losses of efficiency. Be that as it may, similar 'federalism' or 'subsidiarity' criteria can in any case lead to radically different allocation decisions. If the prescriptive implications of the relevant texts cannot but be under-determined, stress must be put beyond the formulas on the evaluation procedures themselves. What matters is that the political sphere be pledged to ground decisions about levels of governance in rational argumentation rather than political expediency—and to demonstrate this through public debate.

One may ask whether legitimacy on this count rests with technical or political credentials, whether assessments need to be made *ex post* as well as *ex ante* or whether such exercises need to be conducted in dedicated institutions or not. At a minimum all options need to be considered and weighted. In the US, the emphasis—under the executive orders on federalism—on assessing the cost and benefits of regulation rather than on the federal question per se may reflect the lack of strictly *political* input in the process. In the EU, there may be some scope for enhancing *ex ante* political control over the subsidiarity question, including through the direct involvement of national parliamentarians—beyond those belonging to 'European committees' as in the existing parliamentary network. At a minimum, the EU needs to take the 1997 Amsterdam protocol on subsidiarity and proportionality seriously. The exercise of giving reasons should become an iterated exercise in collective governance instead of the current issuance by the Commission of perfunctory explanatory memoranda. More ambitiously, to supplement the vetting role of the subsidiarity Committee, the EU could follow the US example and grant its own accounting office or a network of national accounting offices the task of evaluating efficiency claims related to subsidiarity through US-style 'regulatory impact analysis'. More research needs to be done on how to adapt to the EU some of the technocratic review procedures in the US legislative processes, as conducted in particular through the Office of Management and Budget (OMB) and the General Accounting Office (GAO).

Ultimately, however, procedural subsidiarity concerns the modes of involvement of societal and public interests at large, especially in the regulatory sphere. In the US, as Majone demonstrates in his chapter, the norms of transparency, inclusiveness, public justification, and judicial review have become the instrument of choice of regulatory agencies through a long learning process of federal governance in regulatory matters. Why not design a European version of the Administrative Procedures Act (APA), which in the last decade has fostered countless procedural innovations simply through elaborating on the general and apparently innocuous imperative of giving-reasons? Experimentation along these lines in the US has been sustained by the belief that procedural safeguards obviously contribute not only to 'input legitimacy' or democratic legitimacy in the classic sense but to the effectiveness of governance 'services', thus promoting 'output legitimacy'.

The apparent success of the APA testifies to the fact that the agents of governance themselves cannot always reliably enforce upon each other such procedural safeguards. We are led once again to the ultimate enforcers of the rule of law: the courts, standing in particular for all affected non-governmental interests. Of course, the rule of law as a source of legitimacy is not self-sustaining if it is not embedded in institutions of governance that are a direct expression of democratic self-determination (Habermas 1996). But the enforcement of the law itself can contribute to creating more optimal conditions for such self-determination. Indeed, US courts have increasingly reasoned that if structural constraints are insufficient to uphold the core values of federalism then they, the courts, must police the boundary between the Union and the States by protecting core sovereign competences or scrutinizing the use of the 'necessary and proper' clause for congressional action. And while the ECJ has been reluctant to directly pronounce on competence issues, some of its recent 'proportionality' judgements come very close. In this regard, the *Tobacco Advertising* judgement of September 2000 will likely be considered as a landmark—ruling as it did against the opinion of a majority of Member States that the Union cannot give itself the right to ban all tobacco advertizing in the name of the single market.

The US Supreme Court has gone a step further by crafting what Bermann refers to as relational safeguards, that is, principles which identify certain 'forbidden interfaces' between levels of governance, such as granting States immunity to suit or prohibiting the federal level from telling the States what to do or what to spend—that is, anti-commandeering. Here, the contrast between the two polities may be most enlightening; but we should not overlook common concerns . Why is anti-commandeering or the prohibition of unfunded mandates considered an important 'safeguard' in the US but not in the EU? As Halberstam makes amply clear, there are two sides to the commandeering coin. On the one hand, ruling it out reduces the margin of manoeuvre of the centre: it must put its money behind its edits. On the other hand, requiring it—as opposed to direct action—allows for appropriation or customization on the part of the commandeered. In the EU this mediation reflects states' capacity to retain control over policies applied on their territory and ultimately to retain the monopoly of 'legitimate governance': no representative of the EU—policemen, judges, custom officers, or ministers—exists in the lives of EU citizens. In other words, the EU's version of a relational safeguard is precisely to require, as Halberstam puts it, that 'the central government work through component States rather than around them'; this is true both for the implementation of norms or laws—directives and now increasingly 'soft law'—and for the provision of resources—human, financial, and administrative—necessary to enforce EU actions and policies. Thus in the US commandeering takes away the resources jealously guarded by the States. In the EU, on the other hand, it is a reflection of state's dominant endowment: as the French would say, their *incontournabilité*. Control is asserted in one case by disallowing, in the other case by requiring, that one's own resources be used on behalf of another level of governance.

While these alternative views reflect different assumptions about preferred channels of accountability in federal systems, it is worth asking how they overlap. The EU's reliance on structural safeguards has led it to underplay relational safeguards. Could this change? It may be, for instance, that EMU's 'stability and growth pact' could be amended to allow states to better control expenditure cycles and the 'broad economic guidelines' read as not to impinge on the social tradeoffs made through fiscal decisions at the domestic level. As important in the current European climate of domestic decentralization, 'unfunded mandates' are the object of increased concerns on the part of those actors of governance who are neither as well endowed nor as 'plugged in' as the Member States: regional and municipal authorities. Procedural subsidiarity for them would require systematic 'financial impact assessment' of EU laws, regulations' and policies perhaps accompanied by corresponding redistribution of resources. Here, better representation at the centre is considered more as a means to strengthen 'relational safeguard' than as an end in itself, whereby consultation at the top can be systematically related to such impact assessments.

In the US, the prohibition of unfunded mandates is certainly considered as one of the main trophies of the devolution camp. But, as Kinkaid sceptically underscores, this has little significance in and of itself in a system of widely shared competences. In some areas, it may be desirable to increase the 'viscosity' of the system and let States be asked to do the work, provided lines of accountability are fine-tuned and proportionality is applied. Moreover, it may be that in the US, too, a greater say could be given to sub-State level authorities in the formulation of policies affecting their own mandate. Education policy may increasingly evolve in this direction.

The ultimate relational safeguards is the clear assignment of responsibility. Could we not envisage the adoption in either systems of formal or informal codes of conduct regarding standards of accountability in order to prevent agents from 'passing the buck' in multi-level governance system? Citizens are concerned with assignment of responsibilities rather that authority per se. They need to see contracts between the different actors involved about who is publicly *responsible* for what result irrespective of who does what. Responsibility here means that certain actors be accountable for outcomes as well as for certain procedural obligations, and motivated therefore to mobilize others towards the task. It is facilitated by diffuse reciprocity *within* governance systems and the existence of political parties responsible across issues and levels of governance. It also rests on broad-based societal involvement in governance. Thus, when we are told of the participatory processes in US or EU policy networks, we need to ask whether such participation succeeds in creating a sense of ownership among non-governmental participants; and we must ask whether there are 'participatory externalities', that is, whether such participation changes the debate externally in the broader polity rather than simply within the networks themselves. In the end, if shared competence means shared responsibility, the ultimate responsibility must also rest with citizens. For legitimacy to be sustained, people must 'own' policy failures as well as success—*in sickness and in health*.

4. From Power Transfers to Empowerment: Proactive Subsidiarity, Managed Competition, and Mutuality

The fourth shift emerging from this volume constitutes as it were the positive counterpart of federal safeguards, namely, towards a more proactive understanding of subsidiarity which implies enhancing the scope not only for mutual containment but also for mutual empowerment between levels of governance. In other words, if we are to reinterpret subsidiarity and devolution in light of the reality of shared competence and therefore shared governance, we need to move away from a zero-sum approach to power distribution. How? Through the presumption, to start with, that if the centre or higher level of governance is to act, it need not be as a result of a wholesale transfer of competence but in order to contribute to the better exercise of their own competences by the States and local levels. This presumption would be in keeping with the broader principle of mutuality, defined here by Landy and Teles as 'the obligation of each level of government as it participates in joint decision-making to foster the legitimacy and capacity of the other' (p. xx). If legitimacy is indeed enhanced by the sense that governance takes place as close to the people as possible, then we need to probe into the conditions that make such 'closeness' more likely (Howse 1995).

Subsidiarity takes these conditions as exogenous: levels of governance are determined by the scale and boundaries of the problems. Mutuality endogenizes them: governance is about making it possible to deal with problems at the level commensurate with people's expectations. Rather than asking 'Is this an intrinsically local or supra-national issue', we need to ask 'What conditions are necessary to enable state or local government to effectively contribute to the effective overall management of this task?' and 'How can the "Union" foster those conditions?': a kind of qualitative interpretation of the principle of proportionality.

Here again, we draw on a core extant insight of most theories of political and economic integration. Institutions of all sorts have always be understood to be potentially both constraining and enabling. Functional theories of state-building, whether of the liberal state as the agent of individual liberty or of the capitalist state as the instrument of capital accumulation, do not view centralization through the state as an end in itself. And beyond the debate over what has historically fuelled the creation of federations lies the firm belief that with the *tous pour un* comes the *un pour tous*: we are *each* more powerful, more wealthy, and so forth, when we pool our resources than by standing alone (Hesse and Wright 1996).

The question remains, however, as always, at what (democratic) price? How much agency needs to be given up to the whole in order to strive from taking part in it? Genuine empowerment is not mainly about distributed benefits: it is about distributing means of action. And in doing so, the question is not only 'to do what?' but 'against whom'? If empowerment applies both to lower levels of governance, including the state, and to people or societal groups *within* the state a coherent strategy of 'proactive subsidiarity' needs to take into account the many connections, synergies, and contradictions between these two dimensions.

The need for empowerment of the first kind arises in the EU context from the general *malaise* felt in consequence of the challenge to the democratic welfare state from economic integration at the regional and global levels. Here, the positive argument that the EU has 'strengthened the state' or parts thereof (Milward 1992; Moravcsik 1998) even if *historically* correct need to be expanded into a *normative* argument as to how it can continue to do so *across the board*, especially in the context of monetary union. Analysts may disagree over the extent to which national problem-solving capacities have been affected by the economic and legal constraints of economic integration and by conflict between states with regards to precisely those instruments of market correcting policy that have been of critical importance for the legitimization of the welfare state, such as social policy. Whatever its magnitude, the fact is that effective loss of control of economic outcomes at the national level has not been compensated by a concurrent shift of resources to the federal level. As Sharpf argues in his chapter, this means that other compensating mechanisms need to be found. Since Europe is part of the problem, European policies can also help to alleviate it—provided that measures can be identified that will not be blocked by massive conflicts of interest among the member governments. But the challenge to the democratic welfare state cannot be simply addressed by some kind of assignment of greater power to the level of the federal sub-unit, much less the local community; limits on beggar-thy-neighbour competition at the federal level may be needed to (re)-empower these democratic communities to respond to demands for social justice. In the spirit of mutuality, the Union should only provide a space within which states can chose to adopt their own idiosyncratic tradeoffs between social and economic values. And indeed, there are ways in Europe to address such problem-solving gaps, albeit imperfectly: from co-ordinated policy reform and 'shaming' methods to the monitoring by the Commission of 'unfair regulatory competition', to the policing of competitive subsidies. But as Vivien Schmidt shows persuasively, it is the very characteristics of different Member States that will determine the extent to which they can be strengthened or empowered by the federal level. Here, studies of federal systems may do well to borrow from some of the nascent insights of globalization scholarship regarding the 'mutual constitution' of the global system and those 'globalized states' which are agents rather than object of global transformations (Clark 1999).

While this last point is also applicable to the US context, the US has of course had a very different trajectory from Europe in this regard. As Kinkaid points out, 'After World War II . . . the federal government engaged in many capacity-building exercises to help State and local governments become stronger intergovernmental partners'. To this day, fiscal redistribution plays a crucial role in capacity-building across States in the US. And the welfare-state devolution experiment reflects in part a broad commitment to 'mutuality' as the federal level distributes resources accordingly. In the field of health and safety regulation, States with approved Implementation Plans retain primary regulatory responsibilities, while the Union's main task is to assist and supplement their action. In all these dimensions, empowerment from the top is all the more prevalent that the power, authority, and resources in the US have been vested at the centre before being channelled back down.

When it comes to empowerment 'of the people' the contrast between the two polities may be less stark. One of the foremost values of federalism on both sides is to provide individuals with rights, claims, and opportunities at least partially lacking within the confines of their own polities. There is no greater symbol of citizen empowerment by the federation in the US than the subjugation of an Alabama school in 1963. And while the EU has no federal guards to send, its has empowered unions, women, gays, and children through its rights and programmes—under the general rule that the higher level of protection applies. In empowering individuals, the role of 'standards beyond' as empowerment is a basic feature of international relations, not just federal unions; and there is of course a thin line between empowerment and co-optation. The question here is whether 'proactive subsidiarity' can mean more than that, whether it also ought to mean that the centre of gravity where claims are aired and resolved and action taken should not itself be kept at as low a level as possible. In this sense, perhaps the need for empowerment also stems from a rather pessimistic assessment of the capacity of societal agents for spontaneous organization and the possibility to rely on a bottom-up solving of democratic deficits. If subsidiarity is defined in terms of 'closeness to the people', then the question should be raised not just as to the role of civil society in EU governance—as 'participative constraints'—but to the role of EU governance in fostering vibrant civil societies in Member States.

In this light, a focus on the empowerment imperative can lead to more radical brands of devolution advocacy. This is definitely the line taken by Landy and Teles when they argue that local communities may actually need to draw from the centre to build or rebuild the social capital and public infrastructure needed to fulfil the ideal of grass-roots public empowerment. 'Local government', they argue, 'contributes to central government by taking the brunt of the burden of citizen-demands and of providing a coherent and properly constrained voice for citizen grievances. To do so adequately it must be both responsive and capable. Central government has the responsibility to facilitate and encourage the ability of lower-level governments to act as sites for deliberation and administration'. The implication for the US is radical devolution with support from the centre: not even 'funded mandates' but 'funded self-mandating capacity'. Local authorities should be able to experiment freely, and to do so with federal moneys. The implication for the EU is perhaps even more radical but also more sobering. Here, support for local democracy is not just a necessary supplement to but the only option for pursuing legitimacy-enhancing strategies. The legitimacy that the EU so much covets 'should derive from its ability to protect the possibility for democratic government in its Member States, not from the largely fruitless mission of democratizing itself'. Therefore, the best way to strengthen the democratic legitimacy of the EU is through 'indirection', using the policy tools and subsidies available to the EU to strengthen democracy at the grass roots and help resuscitate local government, 'the true seed-bed of democracy'. In this sense, the argument by Moravcsik and Majone that democratic outcomes may result from non-democratic processes, by empowering the median voter, fails to take into account the *intrinsic* value of fostering democratic cultures.

Localism is the reading of mutuality which is the closest to what people understand subsidiarity to mean. But top-down empowerment should not necessarily imply that those thus empowered are meant to limit the scope of their action to a given bounded space. Landy and Teles may be right that many public goods and infrastructures are local, but others—the environment, transnational railway networks, or the ability to control crime—are definitely of a greater scale. Different communities are characterized by different configurations of 'conjoined self-interest'. Moreover, in order to provide citizens with the political skills and understanding necessary to fully take part in complex multi-layered polities like the US and the EU, it is not clear that the purely local space is the only relevant one. There are, for instance, democratic gains from centralization as groups with dispersed interests benefit from economies of scale or groups previously disenfranchised are given access previously denied to them. These gains can in turn trickle down at the local level. If it is seen as a virtue for the existence of the wider community to empower certain groups or interests that have hitherto been marginalized at the local level, then strategies of empowerment may call for creating channels of access to the centre rather than simply protecting local political space. Negotiations over the Convention on Human Rights, Commission transparency programmes, entrepreneurship projects supporting the unemployed, proactive moves from the EU Commission and Parliament to empower consumers against business all fall in this category.

There is no denying, of course, the tensions that do or may arise from these different targets of proactive subsidiarity. 'Multi-tier empowerment' of states, executives within states, regions, cities, citizens, and NGOs may be another way of enhancing checks and balance in a federal system. In some cases, state actors are likely to be empowered at the expense of civil society and vice versa. The suggestion here is that such tensions be mitigated by thinking more systematically of ways in which citizens and groups within the state can be empowered to better engage with rather than bypass the state. In this light, proactive subsidiarity should consist above in creating process obligations at the national and sub-national levels that ultimately empower both states and citizens at the expense of the Union. This implies for instance that the federal level creates duties and responsibilities on the states themselves to inform, involve, and negotiate with those that lay claims upon it. Rather than encourage labour unions, minority protection associations, or consumer associations to bypass the state, invoke federal laws, or negotiate directly at the union level, the Union should lay emphasis on the state's duty to negotiate with its citizens. In the end, such an approach is certainly not less intrusive upon state sovereignty than substantive obligations but it is certainly more likely to foster a participatory culture at all levels of governance.

There are undoubtedly powerful counter-forces to the self-limiting commitment of empowerment. They converge in what we may call the demand for 'integrated governance': the need for any political community to generate the institutional underpinning for making inter-issue tradeoffs at the centre—the balancing of priorities, and thus investment and policy choices, interests groups, beliefs, and arguments—and its capacity to deliver on compensatory mechanisms: if obligations are undertaken by parties that might stand to lose from such implementation, costs are born by the whole community. It is this more than anything that distinguished a federation-in-the-making like the EU from issue-specific international regimes like the World Trade Organization (WTO). And yet EU decision-making structures and processes are themselves still highly fragmented in comparison with the US. Perhaps this will continue to be the price to pay for adopting a strict 'empowerment' approach to EU competence. But if integrated governance continues over time to exercise its centripetal force, there may be a need for an even more radical re-writing of the federal game.

5. Beyond Hierarchy: The Shift to Horizontal Subsidiarity and Multi-centred Governance

In the end, the most fundamental challenge that we face is to engage with Joseph Weiler's call for thinking federalism outside the state-centric paradigm which informs all constitutional enterprises and with Daniel Elazar's vision of a 'post-modern' version of federalism that would somehow come back to its origins and eschew hierarchical models of federalism altogether. Rethinking federalism means thinking beyond the traditional Weberian hierarchy of the state. Accordingly, the federal project must shed its image as a device for vertical division of labour, focusing instead on horizontal division of labour, cooperation and competition among states, regions, and peoples—and so recover a concept of horizontal rather than vertical subsidiarity. In doing so, the EU needs to take on board the notion that permeates the US system that government is perceived to be illegitimate if its image or reality suggests that one 'people' is ruling over another; and the US needs to take on board the notion of mutual recognition that permeates the European Union.

The fifth and last shift underpinning our federal vision is therefore from a vertical paradigm of *multi-level governance* to a horizontal one of *multi-centred* governance. In this vision, no sphere of competence dominates another and the Union becomes the warrant of coherence, the benign arbiter, the facilitator of horizontal transfers of sovereignty rather than the apex of a pyramid. This is not to say, of course, that notions of vertically ordered jurisdictions and the hierarchy of norms that follows—Weiler's 'legal' federation—are irrelevant to the reconstruction of the federal vision. When it comes to the fundamental constitutive question of pronouncing about competences, however, only a polycentric understanding of the EU—and, we would argue, the US—can allow for the sustained legitimacy of the system. If such legal pluralism implies that the issue of 'who decides who decides' should be left open (MacCormick 1993), then 'the constitutional discourse in Europe must be conceived as a conversation of many actors in a constitutional interpretative community, rather than a hierarchical structure with the ECJ at the top' (Weiler 1999: 322). Of course, such a conversation must be punctuated with resolutions of potentially conflicting viewpoints. But why necessarily fear cacophony if law can acquire the 'counterpunctual' character that allows melodies to be heard at the same time in a harmonic manner (Maduro 2001)? In fact, the conversation needs to extend beyond judicial networks to the many political communities that constitute *multi-centred* governance systems.

Paradoxically, this is perhaps where the US of today may have most to learn from the evolving EU. Paradoxically, of course, because, as we stressed in the introduction to this volume, historically and ideologically the defining feature of the US has been a collective aversion for strong centralized power. Non-centralization is the very essence of American federalism. At the foundation, to the extent that the power of both the States and the union was seen to be delegated by the peoples of the various States—the *only* holders of sovereignty as an indivisible attribute—the putting in trust *jointly* by all of the member States of certain powers had precisely the same quality as the putting in trust *separately*, by each member State, of its own powers: each sovereign people created two equal governance structures (Forsyth 1981). Up to the 1960s, 'political leaders and federal administrators alike viewed the role of the federal government as one of assistor to the states not as their superior . . . they understood the federal system to be a matrix of larger and smaller arenas instead of being a pyramid of lower and higher levels' (Elazar 1984). The choice was not between one centre and none but between one and many, with different ones taking precedence in different situations. And the notion of partnership implied the distribution of real power among several centres needing to negotiate cooperative arrangements with one another in order to achieve common goals. For Elazar, in such a non-centralized system power was so diffused that it could not legitimately be centralized or concentrated without breaking the structure and spirit of the constitution. But as States increasingly came to serve as administrative arms of Washington, US federalism turned from the traditional *non-centralized* system to a *decentralized* regime. And the devolution era of the 1980s and 1990s, if not entirely rhetoric, has been but a very partial attempt to recover the former spirit of federalism: 'federalism without Washington'.

'Thinking federal' certainly comes less naturally to Europeans with their history of centralized national governments, unmediated state-society relationships, and strong entrenched social hierarchies. And yet the EU has evolved organically, as it were, towards a federal model that is much less state-centric than that of the US at the end of the twentieth century. Most recently, the new forms of governance mentioned earlier in this chapter have come to resemble a new 'federalism without Brussels', or at least federalism without Brussels' supranational institutions, *à la US*, albeit institutionalized *à la Europe*. The 'open method of coordination' refined from the Luxemburg to the Lisbon Summits may flagship of this proclaimed new era is pervading other than areas of social-economic policy, culture, or education. The new credo of policy experimentation, national action plans, mutual learning processes, benchmarking, and transfer of best practices is reminiscent of the 'states as laboratories' so familiar to the US policy landscape. Today, Europeans might like to think that the US could borrow a leaf from its own books on how to orchestrate such non-centralized processes of governance . . . with little danger of being heeded!

The question remains: is it the narrower character of European ends that saves the EU from its statist demons, as Elazar would have it? Or is it simply that a federal 'state' is less likely to emerge from a federation of nation-states than from a federation of States *tout court*?

In both polities, nevertheless, 'non-centralization' has both micro-foundations and macro-manifestations. At the micro-level, analysts concern themselves with the lack of hierarchy within the policy structures themselves. For Peterson and O'Toole, 'what most distinguishes networks from more traditional forms of governance is their lack of hierarchy across nodes' (p. xx). Nevertheless, networks are not neutral horizontal structures within which interests simply converge through generalized mutual accommodation. Instead, they are constituted by hubs and spokes, where the hubs serve as temporary repositories of information and focal points of authority. There are indeed centres in a multi-centred governance system, but many centres with no pre-ordained hierarchical ordering among them. It is worth noting that the term 'horizontal subsidiarity' is sometimes used to refer to the transfer of competence from public to private actors or from governmental actors to independent para-statal agencies. While I use the notion here to refer mainly to horizontal transfers between states or equivalent levels of governance, it is also true that in a world of networks the two are often intertwined.

These micro-foundations make possible and to some extent require the macro-level shift, that is, the understanding that what ought to ultimately matter in a federal construct is the mutual relationship between the constituent units, between the states themselves, as well as that between other actors forming horizontal bonds across borders; and that increasingly this mutual relationship is one of mutual transformation and penetration. This is what Keohane and Hoffmann (1991) were pointing out when they observed that the EU itself was constructed as a kind of network. The shift can be seen as part of a broader change taking place in the international system, which has been described as the emergence of a 'post-modern state' where transnationalism trumps both nationalism and supranationalism (Cooper 1996; Slaughter 1997). It echoes the notion that has been around for some time of a Europe at the forefront of a world-wide trend towards a 'new medievalism'—the prevalence of increasingly complex and fluid systems of overlapping jurisdictions and multiple loyalties (Bull 1977; Ruggie 1993)—and in many ways harks back to Deutsch's early functionalist understanding of the European project. But the federal vision precisely also seeks to draw out what makes certain kinds of political communities special in this global trend towards transnationalism. It stresses that the trend is embedded in a state system of great resilience and that the constituent units are strongly *territorially* bounded communities. In this light, what is relevant is not just common transnational structures and rules but, perhaps more importantly, *extraterritorial* governance patterns, which constitute a much greater challenge to traditional notions of sovereignty. In short, our vision is one of *transnational federalism*.

This vision is a far cry from the teleological view of the European Union as the 'Universal and Homogenous State' *en herbe* heralded by prophets of the end of history (Kojève 2000). At the same time it is predicated upon a similar assumption, namely, that those that join in such a union have come to a tacit or explicit agreement over what constitutes acceptable differences among themselves and have developed enough mutual trust to believe that they will all continue to act within these parameters (see Robert Howse's introduction to Kojève 2000). But how far then can we stretch the notion of acceptable differences? Isn't subsidiarity also about being able to renegotiate the scope of such allowance? More radically, does it not imply that different parties to the federal covenant might interpret such allowance differently? Europe's version of asymmetric federalism under the label of 'enhanced cooperation' simply follows from this presumption. Such flexibility in turn implies that, in different areas of actions and at different times, the 'centre' of Union action will change location. In the US, interestingly, external pressure to negotiate agreements pertaining to the domains of individual States—for example, financial or professional standards—might revive the virtue of 'flexibility' there.

'Mutuality' Revisited: Mutual Tolerance, Recognition, Inclusiveness, and Empowerment

If we are to explore the normative implications of such a focus on horizontal subsidiarity, I believe that we need to revisit the principle of mutuality as a horizontal commitment between states or peoples rather than primarily between levels of governance. I will do so primarily in the EU context.

First, and at the foundation, is what Joseph Weiler refers to as 'constitutional tolerance'. Weiler celebrates the unique brand of European constitutional federalism—or Europe's federalism without a constitution—as embodying Europe's deepest set of values, namely, that kind of tolerance which leads one to embrace the other without trying to change him, which leads European political systems to interact without necessarily converging. The fact that Europeans, through their institutions, practices, and habits, need to continually re-elect to submit themselves to their mutual obligation without questioning the legitimacy of these obligations is a testimony to the profoundly pluralistic nature of their Union's covenant. National constitutions in Europe may be far from paragons of virtue but they have become the symbolic signposts of the continued survival of the peoples of Europe. Most importantly, European constitutionalization has profoundly contributed to the reformulation of national constititutionalism. Not only is there no need for an overarching legitimizing framework—a European constitution—but if such a framework aimed at the emergence of one people of Europe it would be normatively flawed. In effect, Weiler bypasses the intense but often fruitless debate as to whether European law and regulation is sufficiently direct an expression of democratic will to possess a legitimately constitutional status. Instead he calls for a deeper engagement with the real philosophical meaning of the constitutional status quo.

To be sure, we may disagree with the prescriptive implications drawn by Weiler. In the early days in the US, many followed Calhoun's vision in which the Constitution did not stand *over* the States but was a compact *between* them, which meant that a State, in its sovereign capacity, could be guilty of violating it as a compact but not as a fundamental law. Can we not recover a *minimalist* version of a European constitution against *maximalist* versions anathema to constitutional tolerance? I will come back to this point below. In any event, the premise, and the basic precept of mutual tolerance, I would argue, matters more than the prescription. The European Union cannot but continue to be one of 'peoples' and its constitutional order must continue to reflect this imperative.

Second, if mutual tolerance is the ontological feature of multi-centred governance, mutual recognition is its constitutive principle. Mutual recognition has not only been the hallmark of the EU single market since the early 1980s but has arguably become the modus operandi in the EU as a whole (Nicolaidis 1993, 1997). It calls for participating states or jurisdictions to recognize their respective norms, rules, and standards as valid in each other's territory. In this vein the prevalence of shared competences discussed earlier is as much about sharing competence horizontally across states as it is across levels of governance. What is, in effect, mutual recognition if not the search for a more effective division of labour between regulators and lawmakers across countries through optimal combinations of home- and host-country control? We need to be better able to account for the fact that the US brand of federalism is much less prone than the EU to implement mutual recognition between its Member States' regulations or to engage into a mutual recognition logic externally (Nicolaidis and Egan 2001). Perhaps the tolerance for extraterritoriality is greatest in places which have a long tradition of mutual invasion and takeover—mutual recognition as the reciprocal and peaceful version of conquest.

Overall, mutual recognition is the legal and political impetus for and the expression of extraterritorialization. It reflects not a force outside states to which they have become subject but a proactive political choice to institutionalize and 'mutualize' extraterritoriality. When applied to the recognition of education, skills, and professional qualifications it means that we are no longer prisoners of our original polity and can choose to live among a variety of polities. While relying on the passport of our home laws and regulations, we are also granted a new form of social contract that includes the—still limited—right to choose among those different national polities in the European space. Mutual recognition ultimately means being at home abroad.

Third, mutuality implies an injunction of mutual inclusiveness. In the spirit of power checks the key corollary to mutual recognition is horizontal mutual control, or 'horizontal' federalism safeguards. This means setting up a system of reciprocal *droit de regard*, mutual control between the states themselves. If states increasingly become each other's agents—agreeing to yield jurisdiction over their nationals by virtue of their consumption patterns—then it follows that states are increasingly in the business of monitoring each other, mutually spying on one another to ensure residual control over extraterritorial dynamics. Héritier (1999) refers to these as processes for 'managing distrust', the underpinning of the EU's governance structure. Yet constitutional tolerance and mutual recognition are not sustainable without some degree of trust, as lack of trust eventually leads to pressures for harmonization joint enforcement.

It is against this backdrop that emphasizing the need for mutual inclusiveness is key to the sustainability of a non-hierarchical system. Mutual inclusiveness implies not just a *droit de regard* but a *right of voice* in each other's polities so as to legitimize the different decision-making processes that affect our lives. A horizontal approach to subsidiarity calls for obligations of inclusiveness in political processes, not simply of citizens or groups at the centre but, perhaps more radically, of citizens and groups in each other's polities. Such obligations need to rest on express rights of multiple membership horizontally *across* communities—I am Italian and British or Welsh and Catalan—as well as the more classical vertical multiple membership—I am a Parisian, French, European. Already, as Maduro (1998) has argued, EU economic law can be conceived as providing the European citizen not only with economic rights but with political rights to have their interests taken into account in non-domestic national political processes. The EU needs to build on this legacy. In this volume, Weiler foresees that in the kind of Europe that he calls for 'every norm will be subject to an unofficial European impact study' (p. xx). The interests and practices of the other *as other* become part of the decision-making matrix in all arenas of power. While the traditional hallmark of functioning federal systems is to provide opportunities for access at each level of governance, we need to reframe this question of access in horizontal terms. To what extent do citizens benefit from 'horizontal' access, upheld by obligations of transparency and participation, in order to hold accountable loci of governance in which even their own governments do not partake? Hence, obligations of inclusiveness could be applied in certain areas to earlier stages of law and regulation making, whereby calls for input would have to be issued in areas of extraterritorial effect. The EU has pioneered this to some extent in the field of environmental law. This process can be onerous and unwieldy but can be revolutionized through the Internet.

In this context, we need to think more systematically about the connection between the 'outside-in' and the 'inside-out' dimensions of inclusiveness. The demand that one takes into account the other when acting at home—outside-in—and the incorporation of such acts into the common body of reference—inside-out—are mutually reinforcing. The same logic applies to the legal as well as the political sphere. Under a non-hierarchical vision of legal pluralism, national deviations from Community law can be sustainable only if argued in universal terms, destined to become themselves part of the Community's legal corpus. Henceforth, national courts will be more prone to internalize the views developed beyond their jurisdiction. Similarly, if a group of states decides to 'deviate' from common EU or federal practice or action through enhanced cooperation, it is more likely to internalize the interests of the 'outs' if its own initiatives are likely to become building blocks of future Union-wide action.

Fourth, mutuality ultimately calls for mutual empowerment between states and citizens of these states while minimizing mediation by the centre. To be sure, if there is to be horizontal empowerment it is often through the role played by the centre. When asked 'what is Europe for' politicians ought to respond 'to help us help each other'. In this light, Choudhry's final point opens up a critical debate for our volume as a whole by relating the economic conception of federal citizenship to the type of democracy citizens may expect from different levels of governance. The traditional view that federalism can produce a higher fit between citizens' preferences and public policy by creating a market for mobile citizens shopping around for their preferred jurisdiction clearly fits the US much better than the EU. But it becomes relevant in the EU if we stress the role of voice, and not only exit, as a mechanism for expressing preferences at the state level: in that sense, mutual inclusiveness and mutual empowerment feed on each other. This is true if we consider that not only output legitimacy but also input legitimacy has to do with the role of 'managed' policy competition in enhancing the legitimacy of governance by allowing voters of each constituent unit to witness and take part in the contestation of their national approach to policy-making through demonstration effects and the institutionalization of such demonstration effect, negatively—naming and shaming approaches—or positively—policy transfers. Accountability and thus legitimacy are enhanced as it becomes easier for citizens to 'vote in a comparative mode' rather than 'vote with their feet'. But it must be clear that legitimacy is not necessarily enhanced by regulatory or policy competition if the feedback mechanism from policy competition to policy reform itself is not mediated through some sort of democratic process. As Scharpf's essay vividly demonstrates, policy competition can act as a *constraint* on democracy. In that sense, mutual empowerment must be conceived as an antidote to the notion of a 'federal state' where local democratic processes are bypassed and subsumed under unified democratic and market dynamics.

Shared Projects, Shared Identities

Ultimately, legitimacy in a federal systems depends on the possibility of citizens' allegiance to several political communities. The federal management of power needs to reflect extant democratic support-based notions of citizenship which has not only economic but also political and social dimensions. Unquestionably, we must relate the relevant conception of community allegiance or belonging to the kind of legitimate power that the community in question seeks to exercise. This is not the place to adjudicate between the many competing claims as to whether this is possible and, if so, how—see Choudhry as well as Meehan and Lacorne in this volume. Simply, I would like to suggest that the principle of mutuality can help us imagine a federal citizenship compatible with multiple extant loyalties by opening up not only the possibility but also indeed the desirability of moving away from polities based on a single common identity without denying the importance of the link between identity and community altogether.

There are those who believe that the building of political communities demands such high levels of solidarity and allegiance that such communities can be rooted only in a common identity, be it civic or ethnic in nature. In the US, they question the sustainability of the nineteenth century melting-pot ideal and prefer to rely on radical versions of multiculturalism. In

Europe, and in response to the need for democratic legitimacy, they confront us with an impossible dilemma: limiting our ambitions to those compatible with the scale of national *demoi*—the 'no *demos*' thesis articulated by the German Constitutional Court in its 1994 Maastricht judgement, or pursuing the chimera of a 'European identity' predicated on the progressive emergence of a European *demos*. The first school encompasses pure nationalists from the *Sun* to Haider as well as the sophisticated French nationalist left or *nationaux républicains*—Regis Debray, Paul Thibaut—the European version of US communitarians (Lacroix 2000). Its exponents view the federation a merely a composite of communities of identity, be it *l'Europe des patries* or the hyphenated American type (Howse 1998). Consequently, the federal project must be reduced to its bare bones of functional cooperation. The second school of so-called Euro-federalists, supranationalists or cosmopolitans, believes that it is possible to construct a community of identity at the federal level, competing or coexisting with national or other local identities. New constructed identities can be layered on top of older, equally constructed ones through the crafting of new symbols and histories of common identity in school curricula and the media, and henceforth the projection in the past of a 'common destiny'.

It should be no surprise that the federal vision we have sketched in this book should chime with neither of these 'nation-state'-centric views but rather with an alternative conception of what a polity is about, that is, the 'post-national' view of political community most famously expounded in Habermas's theory of 'constitutional patriotism' (Habermas 1996). In a post-national view, federalist principles of community create an alternative to, not a replica of, the nation-state; citizenship needs to be conceptually severed from nationality; a common citizenship can be grounded in shared principles of justice and morality rather than territorially defined histories; and a political community should *result from* rather than *precede* the constitution of common political institutions. Accordingly, the question of whether a *demos* is possible at all beyond the confines of a community defined in terms of sub-political ties such as race, language, or cultural heritage depends on what we mean by *demos*. If a *demos* is understood to be a group of people or peoples sharing a common political space and modes of political communication, then it need not be reduced to the territorial confines of the nation. Political communities at the federal level can be 'communities of association' rather than 'communities of identity' (Howse 1998). Moreover, if the power of the federal community does not involve political supremacy, then the federal level of community need not necessarily have to draw on a strong sense of allegiance that can compete with the kind of identity-based allegiance that many nation-states can draw on. To be sure, polls have shown that variation in support for policy integration depends on the personal salience of the policies in questions—identity issues and welfare state issues—and cost-benefit analysis rather than overarching notions of commonness and shared identity. If the federal community can rely on the sharing of common projects and goals—from a clean environment to eradication of world poverty—this will provide the necessary bind. In this vein, it is worth reminding ourselves that, while the goal of market integration may not in and of itself be enough to legitimize the profound reach of EU law in national legal orders, it is still the most legitimate shared project, as polls show in both the US and the EU. In short, the Europeanization of national citizenship through the instrumental benefits or opportunities for empowerment that the Union creates does not necessary require or lead to Europeanness. Deutsch was half right. The Union can draw enough support from the functional logic without significant shifts of loyalty upward at least before generations (Deutsch 1953).

Replacing a common identity with common projects developed in a common or emerging public sphere is not all there is, however, to a post-national agenda. The liberal post-national response to the 'identity focus' needs to be understood more broadly to encompass the deep implication of the principle of mutuality as calling for a mutual involvement in fashioning not only each other's structures and actions but also each other's identities. The European project, just like a truly multicultural American project, requires first and foremost the mutual recognition of the various political sub-cultures that constitute it, leading in time to a progressive opening up of national public opinions to one another through political debate and confrontation. In the process, belonging to a federal community cannot but transform the way in which individuals understand themselves as members of their identity-based polities, precisely because, at a deep theoretical level and perhaps emotional level as well, the possibility of voluntaristic and plural affiliation puts in doubt some of the foundational principles of strong identity politics (Howse 1998). By sharing in a community of project, individuals identify with their social counterparts in other polities and start to acquire the capacity to renegotiate their relative attachment for and endorsement of parts of their own national or state history. After all, constitutional patriotism was first developed to provide a grounding for a self-critical appraisal of German *national* identity; a post-national *federal* community requires that states and the peoples of these states move away from their self-centred national memory in a self-critical stance which consists in recognizing the other by recognizing the crimes committed against him (Ferry 2000). It may not be the sole privilege of a union to be founded on the memory of crimes committed *within* it—civil wars are often part of national founding myths—but its distinguishing feature may be that such a memory can function as a radical empowering mechanism (Nicolaidis 1996). Thus, 'Europeanization' might lead in time to a greater capacity on the part of the nationals of each European country to distance themselves, to enter, as it were, into a dialogue with their separate national pasts by integrating the viewpoint of those 'others' that have become part of their family. The very existence of the intermittently common project may empower individuals or communities within Europe to renegotiate the contours of their own 'group' or 'national' histories, to select and weed out elements of their national identity as well as to appropriate elements of the other's histories with the blessing of Europe, as it were. Perhaps the most radical sign of becoming European is to allow or even promote such mutual appropriation. After all, as Siedentop rightly points out, the complexity of a federal or federation-like system can be sustained only if it is matched by a new complexity of personal identity (Siedentop 2000: 51).

The sharing of identities within a federal community can then serve as the communitarian input into an eminently liberal outcome. Beyond a certain degree of integration, mutual tolerance leads to mutual identification; and mutual identification makes it possible to reconcile diversity with deep integration. We do not need to develop a 'common' identity if we become utterly comfortable borrowing each others'. In that sense, American multiculturalism can serve as a starting point for the rethinking of 'European citizenship', short of its perversion in hyphenated ghettos. Think of the European travelling abroad who now has access to the services of consulates from any of the member countries—not to some 'European consulate'—and who is literally invited to 'identify' himself as Greek when he is Swede or as Dane when he is Portuguese. Mutual tolerance demands that I neither ask you to be me nor demand to be you; our Greek or Dane does not have to stay the 'other' European for ever. At the same time, the kind of mutual tolerance that we mean here, the reaching out and mutual engagement, involves, in the end, being part of each other, being at home abroad. My 'European citizenship' means that I am a bit British and a bit Italian—or whatever I wish to be. I have little to gain in spinning the rainbow white. The sharing of separate identities transcends a common identity.

Let us be inspired by Frank Thompson's enthusiastic acclaim of the prospect of a union of western Europe just before his death in 1944: 'How wonderful it would be to call Europe one's fatherland and think of Krakow, Munich, Rome, Arles, Madrid *as one's own cities* . . . Differences between European peoples, though great, are not fundamental. What differences there are serve only to make the peoples mutually attractive' (quoted in Passerini 1999: 348, emphasis added). A half-century of peace later, let us celebrate with him the pleasure that can be drawn from the multiplicity of Europe, its nations, folklores, languages, and cities, and from the mutual attraction between its utterly separate peoples.

Towards a New European Contract? Exploring Proactive Constitutional Tolerance

Perhaps then is it possible to explore a more proactive notion of constitutional tolerance for the EU inspired by the overarching framework of polycentric federalism. That I would call *the constitution of shared identities*. Could there not be a genuinely pluralist constitution in Europe that would embody the spirit of constitutional tolerance, divesting sovereignty from nation-states without thereby falling into the trap of having to relocate 'it'? Surely, 'true partisans of liberty' since the beginning of the modern epoch have consistently emphasized federal liberty, that is to say, the liberty to enter into covenants and to live by them: a European constitution's ultimate goal can be to limit power and protect individual freedom (Maduro 2001). The habits of tolerance heralded by Weiler have had to be 'artificially' constructed in Europe, except perhaps for the peoples of the frontiers. Could such a contract not contribute to this continued construction?

In this vision one starts from Weiler's premise that there ought not to be in Europe an overarching and explicit constitutional framework denying the EU's paradoxically greater ambition to pursue deep integration *without* a hierarchy of authority. Instead, a non-statal logic could lead us to a post-modern constitution—a new 'European Contract' that would explicitly be aimed at managing differences, not engineering convergence. It would have at least two distinguishing features. First, this contract would be primarily about fostering other-regarding practices within the nation-states, radical obligations of mutual inclusiveness, and entrenched rights of multiple political belongings across polities. Second, this contract would need to capture the open-ended experimental nature of the European construct and thus would need to be much more deeply contestable than what we have ever known constitutions to be. It would self-reflectively be the signpost of a contractual process, the frame for a never-ending constitutional moment rather than a final say than ought to be sparingly revisited. It could include the flagging of agreements to disagree between constitutive states, the facilitation and encouragement of amendment processes, the explicit acknowledgement of the legitimacy of contestation, the institutionalization of opt-outs, and the spelling out of conditions for reversibility. In the end, this is after all the essence of 'Unions': a union is a contract, not a structure; a process, not an end point. It connotes equality between its participants—in principle at least—and at least some reciprocity in their commitments. And not all participants in a Union need to be of the same type: that is, here, not all states.

Perhaps one day, perhaps a century from now, there will be a need in the US itself to revisit its constitutional contract. Perhaps if such a day was to come, Europe may provide an inspiration.

6. Conclusion: Towards a Model of Global Subsidiarity?

At its core this book has been about the complex and changing relationship and tensions between levels of governance within the United States and in the European Union. We started our journey by asking a simple question: how can subsidiarity and devolution contribute to more legitimate governance on both sides of the Atlantic? We have no coherent answer to offer, but rather, perhaps, a different way of formulating the question: what could be the core elements of a federal vision beyond the nation-state at the beginning of the twenty-first century?

The federal vision around which many of our insights converge calls for recovering some of the early historical views on federalism and on traditional sources of legitimacy in multi-level governance systems while recasting them in terms of today's understanding of what democratic processes and legitimate authority entail. Instead of concentrating on boundaries between spheres of power, the federal vision concentrates on their relationship. This implies *inter alia* a shift in focus in the competence debate away from allocation of competences per se towards granting centre stage to the processes of change themselves and the mechanisms that make them sustainable, including governance structures and the many mechanisms of control among the actors involved at different levels, democratic input in the joint management of shared competences, and strategies of mutual empowerment between levels and actors involved in governance. In the end, it calls for a move 'beyond hierarchy' from vertical paradigms of multi-layered governance to more horizontal ones of multi-centred governance where the legitimacy of the system as a whole is grounded in mutual tolerance, mutual recognition, and mutual empowerment rather than in the design of common structures and the pursuit of homogenous practices.

Under such a vision, it makes less sense to speak of 'pro-' or 'anti-Europeans' or 'pro-' and 'anti-federalists'. *Integration* can be more about sustainable decentralization than centralization, horizontal mutual inclusiveness rather than vertical delegation of authority, and managing differences rather than engineering convergence; and *federalism* about exploring the boundaries of sustainable differences between individuals, communities, polities under a profound commitment to living together.

We hope to see future research investigate further the implications of these shifts and their relevance. It will be worth exploring, for instance, the connection between the ways in which authorities and identities interact internally and the ways in which the federation as a whole interacts with the rest of the world.

It will also be worth exploring further whether the features of the federal vision that we espouse can be transposed to the level of global governance. Certainly one of the crucial question faced by policy-makers in the post-Seattle era is how to inject legitimacy into global economic governance. This question will likely be at the forefront of many debates to come and deserves to be explored through dedicated projects. This book can inspire some starting points.

To some extent, the legitimacy problem faced at the global level is more acute than in the US and the EU context. The autonomy of the constituent parts is arguably more threatened by global forces than by federal or quasi-federal encroachments, if only because they have more say over the latter than the former. Globalization may have an unequal impact around the world but it is leading everywhere to the end of the illusion of a symmetric relationship between national political decision-makers and the recipients of political decisions (Held 1995). The worldwide crisis of 'embedded liberalism' has led some to argue that global institutions such as the international financial institutions, the WTO, or United Nations agencies now need to occupy this 'governance gap', but that doing so requires that they recover or establish anew their legitimacy by democratizing their procedures while endorsing and enforcing cosmopolitan norms.

In assessing these claims, we need to be acutely aware of the limits of the analogy and incommensurability between, for instance, the EU and WTO governance debates (Howse and Nicolaidis 2001). The conditions for constitutional legitimacy in the EU accepted even by those on the pro-European constitutionalist side of this debate, to say nothing of those on the intergovernmentalist or nationalist sides, include integrative institutions that can be accountable for the policy and value tradeoffs that they make; a commitment to flexible structures and procedures that can respond to ideological, technological, or economic shifts by allowing reallocation of power through bargaining or other agreed procedures short of constitutional 'revolution;' and mechanisms for co-opting and compensating potential losers. None of these conditions is likely to be present at the global level any time soon.

Nevertheless, the federal vision is relevant, if not applicable, to the global level; the principles discussed in this book in the US and EU contexts can inspire a 'global subsidiarity' model adapted to the more limited and functional nature of international institutions (Howse and Nicolaidis 2001). Such a model would rest on three core principles. The first stems from the fact that power checks are weak at the international level and certainly lack the symmetry that we find in federal contexts. US or Western hegemony is also greater in some institutions then others. And governance is institutionally fragmented among a host of functional international regimes. Global subsidiarity thus requires, first and foremost, radical *institutional sensitivity* both vertically—state and local governance—and horizontally—other international institutions. This means systematic deference to other, more legitimate institutions—say, the WTO or Multilateral Environmental Agreements—and/or superior norms, such as human rights, rather than letting institutions with the greatest hegemonic influence assess for themselves the necessary tradeoffs between competing values.

Second, traditional concepts of territoriality need to be unbundled not only with regard to issues of jurisdiction but also with regard to political processes. At the global level as with the federal level, requirements of mutual *political inclusiveness* are the necessary counterpart to requirements of deference. Within international institutions, however, inclusiveness does not mean the systematic granting of representational rights to NGOs, which belong to the realm of deliberative, not representative, democracy. Nor should all the onus of inclusiveness be put on the supranational level. Procedural obligations need to include more systematically obligations of domestic participation and indirect accountability. And they can include requirements of mutual transnational inclusiveness in domestic legal or regulatory processes.

Finally, global subsidiarity need not be interpreted as shifting functions away from the centre but instead as conceiving of those functions as means of *empowerment* of the sub-units including, but not exclusively, the state. The long-held *permissive* interpretation of embedded liberalism needs to be progressively supplemented by a *proactive* interpretation that lays some of the responsibility on the global community not only to help states fulfil their functions but to help individuals and groups within these states exercise their voice option before considering exit.

* *

Whether in the US or in the EU, whether for polities known as federations, quasi-federations, or confederations, we need a federal vision beyond the state, a vision of transnational federalism compatable with the continued preeminence of individual nation-states in the forseeable future. Its mission? To provide a space for genuine democracy in an era when politics risks becoming at once too global and too local; a space whose scale is compatible both with good economic management and with people's desire to 'do politics' together; a space, in short, reconciling unity of purpose and diversity of belongings. Its mission is also about means: to offer a political form eschewing hierarchical, state-centric modes of governance that have characterized the modern epoch, turning instead to horizontal, multi-centred models based on the principles of mutuality and tolerance. And to offer a political form amenable to multiple permutations at a time when changes in ideas, norms, and technologies have never been so fluid and unpredictable. The 'federal vision' has been in the making since the beginning of modernity. At the beginning of the twenty-first century, we need to reassert its currency and imagine anew its potential.

References

Baechler, J. (1994). 'Fédération et démocratie', in Martine Meheut (ed.), *Le fédéralisme est-il pensable pour une Europe prochaine?* Paris: Kime.

Bull, H. (1977). *The Anarchical Society: A Study of Order in World Politics*. New York: Columbia University Press.

Cappeletti, M., Seccombe, Monica, and Weiler, Joseph (eds) (1986). *Integration Through Law: Europe and the American Federal Experience, Volume 1*. Berlin and New York: Walter de Gruyter.

Clark, I. (1999). *Globalization and International Relations Theory*. Oxford: Oxford University Press.

Cooper, R. (1996). *The Postmodern State and the World Order*. London: Demos.

De Búrca, G. (1999). *Reappraising Subsidiarity's Significance after Amsterdam* (Jean Monnet Working Paper Series, WP N7/99). Cambridge, MA: Harvard University Law School.

Deutsch, K. (1953 [1966]). *Nationalism and Social Communication*. Cambridge, MA: MIT Press.

Elazar, D. (1962). *The American Partnership*. Chicago: University of Chicago Press.

Elazar, D. (1984), *American Federalism* (3rd edn). New York: Harper and Row.

Ferry, J. M. (2000). *La question de l'État européen*. Paris: Gallimard.

Forsyth, M. (1981). *Unions of States: The Theory and Practice of Confederation*. New York: Holmes and Meier Publishers, Inc. and Leicester University Press.

Goldwin, R. and Schambra, W. A. (eds) (1986). *How Federal Is the Constitution?* Washington, DC: American Enterprise Institute for Public Policy Research.

Grodzins, M. (1966). *The American System: A New View of Government in the United States*. Chicago: Rand McNally.

Habermas, J. (1996). *Between Facts and Norms: Contributions to a Discourse Theory of Law and Democracy*. Cambridge: Polity Press.

Held, D. (1995). *Democracy and the Global Order*. Cambridge: Polity Press.

Héritier, A. (1999). 'Elements of Democratic Legitimation in Europe: An Alternative Perspective'. *Journal of European Public Policy*, 6/2: 269–82.

Hesse, J. and Wright, V. (1996). *Federalizing Europe*. Oxford: Oxford University Press.

Hooghe, Liesbet, and Marks, G. (2001). *European Integration and Multi-level Governance*. Boulder: Rowman & Littlefield.

Howse, R. (1995). 'Federalism, Democracy and Regulatory Reform: A Sceptical View of the Case for Decentralization', in K. Knop, S. Ostry, R. Simeon, and K. Swinton (eds), *Rethinking Federalism: Citizens, Markets and Governments in a Changing World*. Vancouver: University of British Columbia Press.

——(1998). 'Searching for a Plan A: National Unity and the Chrétien Government's New Federalism', in H. Lazar (ed.), *Canada and the State of the Federation 1998 Constitutional Renewal*. Toronto: Queen's Institute for Intergovernmental Relations.

——(2001). 'Transatlantic Regulatory Cooperation and the Problem of Democracy', in G. Bermann *et al.* (eds), *Transatlantic Regulatory Cooperation*. Oxford: Oxford University Press.

——and Nicolaidis, K. (2001). 'Legitimacy and Global Governance: Why Constitutionalizing the WTO Is a Step Too Far', in Roger Porter, Pierre Sauve, Arvind Subramanian, and Americo Zampetti (eds), *Equity, Efficiency and Legitimacy: The Multilateral System at the Millennium*. Washington, DC: Brookings Institution.

Keohane, R. and Hoffmann, S. (1991). 'Institutional Change in Europe in the 1980s', in R. Keohane and S. Hoffmann (eds), *The New European Community: Decisionmaking and Institutional Change*. Boulder, CO: Westview Press.

Kojève, A. (2000). *Outline of a Phenomenology of Right*. Oxford: Rowman and Littlefield.

Komesar, N. (1994). *Imperfect Alternatives: Choosing Institutions in Law, Economics and Public Policy*. Chicago: Chicago University Press.

Lacroix, J. (2000). 'Les nationaux-républicains de gauche et la construction européenne'. *Le Banquet*, 15/November: 157–68.

MacCormick, R. Neil (1993). 'Beyond the Sovereign State', 56, *MLR*, 1993, 1.

Maduro, M. P (1998). *We The Court: The European Court of Justice and the European Economic Constitution*. Oxford: Hart Publishing.

——(2001). 'Europe and the Constitution: What if this is As Good As It Gets?', in J. Weiler and J. Wind (eds), *Rethinking European Constitutionalism*. Cambridge : Cambridge University Press.

Milward, A (1992). *The European Rescue of the Nation-State*. Oxford: Oxford University Press.

Moravcsik, A (1998). *The Choice for Europe*. Ithaca, NY: Cornell University Press.

——and Nicolaidis, K. (1998). 'Federal Ideals vs Constitutional Realities in the Amsterdam Treaty'. *Journal of Common Market Studies*, 36 (Annual Review): 13–38.

Nicolaidis, D. (1996). *Oublier nos crimes: mémoire et identité nationale*. Paris: Autrement.

Nicolaidis, K. (1993) 'Mutual Recognition Among Nations: The European, Community and Trade in Services,' doctoral dissertation, Harvard University.

——(1997). *Mutual Recognition of Regulatory Regimes: Some Lessons and Prospects* (Jean Monnet Working Paper Series, WP N7/99). Cambridge, MA: Harvard University Law School.

——and Egan, M. (2001). ' Regional Policy Externality and Market Governance: Why Recognize Foreign Standards?'. *Journal of European Public Policy*, 8/3: 454–73.

Passerini, L. (1999). *Europe in Love, Love in Europe: Imagination and Politics in Britain between the Wars*. London: I. B. Tauris.

Ruggie, J. (1993). 'Territoriality and Beyond: Problematizing Modernity in International Relations'. *International Organization*, 47/1: 139–74

Siedentop, L. (2000), *Democracy in Europe*. London: Allen Lane, The Penguin Press.

Slaughter, A. M. (1997). 'The Real New World Order'. *Foreign Affairs*, 76/5: 183–97.

Weiler, J. (1999). *The Constitution of Europe*. Cambridge: Cambridge University Press.

Wessels, W. 'An Ever Closer Fusion? A Dynamic Macropolitical View of an Integration Process.' *Journal of Common Market Studies*, 35/2: 267–99.

Appendix

Basic Principles for the Allocation of Competence in the United States and the European Union

GEORGE A. BERMANN AND KALYPSO NICOLAIDIS

'Who does what', 'who decides', and 'on what grounds' are surely fundamental questions for all political systems of a federal nature. Under what kind of safeguards did American States choose to part with some of their competences? Is the allocation of competence that we witness today in the US consistent with the principles adopted two centuries ago? To what extent are the same basic principles at play in the European construct? And what kind of explicit choices would a 'charter of competences' for the EU actually entail? Although the answers to these questions will inevitably reflect variation across time and space, a few basic principles of federal allocation of competence can offer a point of departure.

While the chapters in this volume inevitably draw attention to broader issues of legitimacy and levels of governance, this appendix is meant to provide a rough overview of the legal basis for allocating competences between the States and the Union in the two systems. This exercise should better enable us to appreciate the nature of the choices that have been made, and are being made, in Europe and the United States—or indeed in any other regional grouping in which federalism or aspects of federalism are present.

In our discussion we adopt two assumptions. First, we assume that, to qualify as legal principles, the lines of federalism *should be* drawn in some more or less regular fashion rather than haphazardly or through the sheer exercise of power. This is an assumption that, in legal traditions based on the rule of law, we should be prepared to make. Second, we assume that, whatever the lines of federalism may be—for example, whether power is allocated by subject matter or function—certain legal mechanisms *will in fact* be put into place in order to ensure that these lines are respected. In

This appendix is heavily drawn from George Bermann, *Regulatory Federalism: European Union and United States* (The Hague: A. Martinus Nijhoff, 1997).

reality, there is a much broader range of legal instruments and controls available for these purposes than is commonly supposed; and both the European Union and the United States have made, and are still in the process of making, their selections. Thus, deciding that the lines of federalism *should* be drawn in a regular fashion and that legal mechanisms *will in fact* be put in place in order to secure them is only the beginning, not the end, of the enquiry.

In a nutshell, federalism principles can be organized around three broad sets of legal criteria, namely, allocative, structural, and procedural. First, the *substantive allocation* of subject matters or functions to different levels of government would seem to be the most basic approach to the relationship and balance of power between the States and the Union—at least for the general public. Second, the *structures* or *institutions* at the federal level may be designed to promote indirectly the interests of the constituent States and their separate populations. Third, those institutions can be required to employ certain *decision-making procedures* or *decisional processes* aimed at promoting the values of federalism and the respective interests of the various levels of government.[1] We focus in the first section mainly on the *allocative* principles of federalism and, in the second section, merely signal other considerations that may be relevant to the distribution of competences. While this is by no means an exhaustive account, we review a number of simple questions, each constituting one part of the puzzle and ultimately one element of the legal framework of federalism.

1. Allocative Principles of Federalism

Locus of Sovereignty

The first question that arises is: *what, and how many, are the levels of government within a federal system that possess lawmaking authority?*

Crudely, the answer could be 'one or more'. In reality, even this very foundational question is a contested and complex one in the European Union much more than in the United States.

Some scholars, like Daniel Elazar in this volume, would argue that the most fundamental difference between the US and the EU is that in the former sovereignty is seen to lie with the people, while in the latter it is still

[1] These various principles are discussed throughout this volume although often under different labels. For a formal discussion, see in particular the chapters by George Bermann and Daniel Halberstam in this volume, as well as, in a more stylized fashion, Cary Coglianese and Kalypso Nicolaidis and John Peterson and Laurence O'Toole. On structural principles, see in particular Vivien Schmidt.

largely attributed to the state, at one level or the other. While this is certainly a fundamental consideration in political philosophy, formal legal understandings relate to the secondary question of levels of governance. On this count, the prevailing view in the United States is that both the States and the federal government have an original sovereignty. The people of the United States have directly constituted themselves both in States and in the United States.[2] This initial choice is reflected in the direct bonds between the people and each level of governance. Consequently, government at both levels—each in its own sphere, of course—is assumed to exercise that sovereignty *vis-à-vis* the people directly. This is what is known as 'dual sovereignty'.[3]

In the European Union, however, the very relationship of the individual States to the Union is much less clearly defined. On the one hand, the EU could have been described at its inception as a system of 'single sovereignty'. The European Union itself, not to mention its institutions, is essentially the product of international treaties entered into by the individual Member States acting in a sovereign capacity. On the other hand, the constitutive treaties are traditionally distinguished from other international agreements by virtue of the fact that they are deemed to have made limited 'transfers of sovereignty' to the European Union, acting through its institutions.

The result is that, while the European Union is undoubtedly 'constituted' by and of its Member States, and while those States are in that sense its 'constituent' parts, the Member States are not necessarily *federated.* Their sovereignty has not been absorbed and subsumed in the sovereignty of the European Union.[4] Another way to put the matter is to note that the EU Treaty, however 'constitutive' a document—'a constitution in the making'—is still as much an international treaty as it is a constitution as such,[5] and the fact that it is amended only through

[2] The preamble to the United States Constitution thus reads: 'We the people of the United States, in Order to form a more perfect Union . . . do ordain and establish this Constitution for the United States of America.'

[3] W. G. Vause, 'The Subsidiarity Principle in European Union Law: American Federalism Compared', *Case Western Journal of International Law*, 27 (1995), at 70.

[4] See J.-C. Piris, 'After Maastricht, Are the Community Institutions More Efficacious, More Democratic and More Transparent?', *European Law Review*, 19 (1994), 449; W. Wallace, 'Europe as a Confederation: The Community and the Nation-State', *Journal of Common Market Studies*, 21 (1982), 57.

[5] S. J. Boom, 'The European Union after the Maastricht Decision: Will Germany Be the "Virginia of Europe"?', *American Journal of Comparative Law*, 43 (1995), 177; D. Grinim, 'Does Europe Need a Constitution?', *European Law Journal*, 1 (1995), 282; T. C. Hartley, 'The European Court, Judicial Objectivity and the Constitution of the European Union', *The Law Quarterly Review*, 112 (1996), 95. Alan Dashwood calls the European Community 'a constitutional order of States'. A. Dashwood, 'The Limits of European Community Powers', *European Law Review*, 21 (1996), 113.

intergovernmental conferences and unanimity vote is a forceful reminder of that fact.[6]

Accordingly, while the European Union, like the United States, contemplates government at *both* the State *and* the Union—or federal—levels, the relationship between the peoples of Europe and the European Union is still not the direct and immediate one that characterizes the relationship between Americans and the United States. The European Union institutions, particularly the European Court of Justice, have undoubtedly done a great deal to close this 'gap', but a fundamental difference remains.

Finally, we need to remember that some of the EU Member States are themselves organized along federal lines, in some cases as strictly federal entities, in others in terms of regionalism and local autonomy. This is true both of some original Member States, such as Germany, Belgium and Italy, and of later entrants like Spain or the United Kingdom. The existence of federal structures, and the recognition of federal principles, within the Member States themselves have obvious implications for federalism at the European Union level, and vice versa.[7] The participation of these Member States in the European Union makes it difficult for them to preserve fully intact the institutions of their own 'internal' federalism and the specific internal balance of power that those institutions are supposed to secure. Conversely, the integrity of European Community law may itself suffer to the extent that authority for implementing that law rests, not in the hands of *national* officials, but in the hands of state, regional, or local officials whose governments are not themselves parties to the constitutive treaties or to the transfers of sovereignty that those treaties embody. However, the latest amendments to the Treaties whereby Member States can be represented by their constitutive units in some Councils of Minister represent an important step in the formalization of this relationship.

In this respect, too, American federalism presents a somewhat neater picture. First, in the United States, the States are unequivocally part of a federal nation-state. While the United States Constitution—which, again, is presumed to have been entered into by the American people and not by the States—reserves important powers to the States, it is unquestionably the organs of the *federal* government, and most notably the *federal* courts, that ultimately determine where the limits of federal power actually lie. As a corollary, no American State is even conceivably permitted to invoke its internal constitutional allocations of power in order to avoid respecting decisions that have been otherwise properly taken by federal authorities. This does not mean that the States are not themselves subdivided, or that

[6] See D. Curtin, 'The Constitutional Structure of the Union: A Europe of Bits and Pieces', *Common Market Law Review*, 30 (1993), 66.

[7] For a discussion, see Vivien Schmidt in this volume.

their subdivisions are without power, but any such power is enjoyed by delegation under State law. Although every State has a system of local government and gives local governmental units a measure of political autonomy, commonly known as 'home rule', it has never been suggested that such arrangements can operate as a legal restraint on the ways in which the institutions of the federal government are organized or on the extent to which they may exercise powers otherwise falling within the federal sphere.

Mode of Allocation of Powers

When regulatory authority is attributed to a level of government, in what terms is it attributed? For example, is it attributed in terms of subject matter or governmental function or still some other characteristic? If it is attributed according to subject matter, is the attribution expressed in terms of substantive rubrics, or rather in terms of more general criteria, or some combination of the two?

Whatever may be the 'ultimate' locus of sovereignty in a federal system, a question necessarily arises as to modes of attribution of competence to the different levels of governance. In this regard, one tends naturally to think, first and foremost, of allocation by subject matter. To a very large extent, this is the case for both the European Union and the United States. But while this approach may be the clearest one both descriptively and prescriptively for citizens to grasp when asking 'who does—or should do—what?', both the US and the EU systems have evolved towards a more complex, less transparent approach. This is true for both regulatory and fiscal competences, although we focus here on the former.[8]

In the US, the Constitution confers on Congress—and, through the practice of broad statutory delegation, on federal regulatory agencies—the power to 'regulate' certain fields. These expressly include such specific subjects as currency, maritime law, the law governing intellectual and artistic property, and foreign affairs. At the same time, the Constitution gives Congress the more general power to regulate interstate and international commerce.[9] Not surprisingly, the latter provision, the so-called

[8] In his classical study, Musgrave offered a three fold categories of policy-making functions, namely, allocation, stabilization, and distribution. Broadly, allocation covers mainly regulatory policies while stabilization and distribution are carried through fiscal instruments. See R. Musgrave and P. Musgrave, *Public Finance: Theory and Practice*, 3rd edn (New York: McGraw-Hill, 1980). Musgrave's functional classification was developed for the US context but is widely used in the EC context. See for instance the Padoa Schopa Report, *Commission of the European Communities* (Luxembourg: EU Publication Office, 1987).

[9] 'The Congress shall have the power to . . . regulate commerce with foreign nations, and among the several states.' US Constitution, Art. 1, Sec. 8.

'interstate commerce clause', has been the source of some of the most important and far-reaching federal regulation.

Similarly, both in the objectives that the original EC Treaty assigns to the Community and in the means that it authorizes for achieving those objectives, the EC Treaty's primary reference is likewise to subject matter. Thus, Art. 2, introducing the 'tasks' of the EC refers to 'a common market', 'an economic and monetary union', and 'the raising of the standard of living and quality of life'. While these references sound much more like objectives than policies, particularly in comparison with how national constitutions typically couch their enumeration of competences, they nevertheless correspond to sectors of governmental action,[10] and they are certainly references to specific rather than general objectives, with such 'specificity' coming close to traditional subject matters.[11]

Art. 3 of the EC Treaty also designates certain narrower 'policies' as constituting Community spheres of action. These 'policies' include commercial policy, agriculture and fisheries policy, transport policy, competition policy, social policy, environmental policy, industrial policy, research and development policy, health protection policy, education and training policy, overseas development cooperation policy, consumer protection policy, and 'energy, civil protection and tourism'. These sound especially like subject matters.

However, in the EU context, the meaning of 'allocation to the federal level' requires even further clarification. The Treaty does not stop at designating certain subject matters as 'European'. Rather, it enters into considerable substantive and procedural detail, specifying for each subject matter, or 'chapter', the institutions that are competent, the particular procedures that those institutions must follow, and the substantive conditions that any such action must satisfy. This subject-based differentiation became still more visible with the 'pillar' structure adopted under the 1992 Maastricht Treaty, although the 1997 Amsterdam Treaty went on to blur the distinctions between the pillars, introducing subtle differences among the instruments applicable to different subject areas.[12] The combined EU

[10] For a discussion of harmonization in the interest of the internal market as a 'subject matter' for Community legislation, see P. J. Slot, 'Harmonisation', *European Law Review*, 21 (1996), 378.

[11] For a discussion, see Daniel Elazar in this volume.

[12] This was done, for instance, by transferring some areas of action—migration and asylum—from the third to the first pillar, thus granting a greater role to supranational institutions while retaining the practice of unanimity voting. This practice of institutional differentiation stems from the fact that the 'federal' level in the EU is a complex mix between intergovernmental and supranational decision-making and that the relative weight to be given to each dimension is a function in part of the sensitivity and 'newness' of the policy being centralized. For a discussion of the 'evolutionary pragmatism' characterizing the Treaty of Amsterdam, see Andrew Moravcsik and Kalypso Nicolaidis, 'Federal Ideals

treaties accordingly constitute a complex blueprint spelling out not only the actions that one or more named 'federal', or EU, institution may take, but also the form in which and the procedure by which it may take them.

How do both systems then move beyond allocation by subject matter? In both settings, regulatory competences are exercised primarily through legislative acts. Yet neither in the EU nor in the US is federal regulatory power exclusively *legislative* by nature. While EU interventions typically take one of the principal legislative forms—regulations or directives—they may also take the form of individual decisions by EU institutions. Practically speaking, regulatory policy in the areas of competition law and State aids, for instance, is very largely the product of a long series of individual decisions taken by the Commission. Similarly, the treaties authorize the institutions to affect public policy by making expenditures from various funds that they themselves establish or authorize the Union institutions to establish. Through the power to issue binding individual decisions and the power to make expenditures of European Union resources, the institutions can enhance their basic powers to prescribe the Union's regulatory policy.

The same is undoubtedly true in the United States. While the Constitution refers chiefly to Congress's 'legislative' power, Congress has used that power very extensively to create federal 'agencies' that enjoy either a delegated power to issue secondary legislation or a power to issue individual 'administrative' decisions, or both. It is well established that, within the limits of the existing statutory framework, individual agency decisions are themselves a source of regulatory policy and regulatory law. The EU itself has most recently moved in the same direction, by creating a series of regulatory agencies, albeit with a lesser degree of autonomous decision-making powers.[13]

As to spending *per se*, the Constitution actually expressly authorizes Congress 'to pay the Debts and provide for the . . . general Welfare of the United States'.[14] According to Supreme Court precedent, Congress is permitted to 'spend' federal money for *any* public purpose, including one that is not in itself among the enumerated federal legislative subjects. This undoubtedly has served to expand the scope of federal regulatory authority beyond those subjects listed as such in the Constitution.

vs Constitutional Realities in the Amsterdam Treaty', *Journal of Common Market Studies*, 36, (1998) 13–38 ; see also Andrew Moravcsik and Kalypso Nicolaidis, 'Explaining the Treaty of Amsterdam: Interests, Influence and Institutions', *Journal of Common Market Studies*, 31 (1999), 59–85.

[13] See Giandomenico Majone in this volume.

[14] US Constitution, Art. 1, Sec. 8, clause 1.

In practical terms, Congress has further enhanced the effectiveness of its spending power by making its grant of funds to the States or private parties 'conditional' on the recipient's fulfilment of certain policy requirements specified in the legislation establishing the programme of grants. If States, local governments, or other recipients of grants need or want the federal funds in question badly enough, they will naturally agree to comply with those requirements. The Supreme Court has ruled that Congress can impose virtually any condition it wishes, provided the condition bears some relationship to the purpose for which the money is being given, and is otherwise constitutional. And even though these conditions must relate to the purpose for which the moneys will be used, they do not have to relate to one of the enumerated subject matters over which Congress has the independent constitutional power to legislate; the purpose, as the wording of the spending clause itself suggests, may be anything having to do with the 'general welfare'. The spending power thus represents a vast expansion of de facto federal regulatory authority.

A spending power is of course useful to a level of government only in so far as that level has revenue-raising powers or otherwise has access to funds. This is where the difference between the US and the EU is certainly the greatest.[15] Contrary to the US, in the EU the common budget was never seen as having a redistributive function across States.[16] Thus, while the United States federal level has the express power under its Constitution to 'levy taxes', that is, to raise the revenue that will support its 'spending' activities, the European Union's own revenues are meagre in comparison, drawn above all from customs duties. Today, taxes raised by the US federal government constitute 25 per cent of GDP, while the EU budget is capped at 1.27 per cent of GDP, part of which is a transfer by the Member States. There is little doubt that differences in the allocation of power have an enormously important fiscal dimension.

Residual Authority

As between the levels of government exercising authority, which, if any, has residual authority: that is to say, which enjoys regulatory and policy competence in the absence of a specific indication otherwise?

Despite their differences, both American and European federalism subscribe to the theory that central authorities enjoy only those regulatory powers that have been accorded to them by the basic constitutive docu-

[15] See T. C. Fischer, '"Federalism" in the European Community and the United States: A Rose by Any Other Name', *Fordham International Law Journal*, 17 (1994), 389.

[16] See Loukas Tsoukalis, *The New European Economy Revisited* (Oxford: Oxford University Press, 1997).

ments, that is, the United States Constitution and the treaties establishing the European Communities, respectively. Residual authority belongs to the States.

In the United States, the principle of 'reserved powers' was made explicit at an early date by the Tenth Amendment, adopted as the last of the original Bill of Rights in 1791:

> The powers not delegated to the United States by the Constitution, nor prohibited to it by the States, are reserved to the States respectively, or to the people.

Although this same notion had been assumed from the very beginning to apply in the European Communities, it was introduced formally only through the 1992 Treaty on European Union, or Maastricht Treaty. Art. 5 [ex Art. 3b] reads: 'The Community shall act within the limits of the powers conferred upon it by this Treaty and of the objectives assigned to it therein.'

Of course, it goes nearly without saying that the real effect of a principle of residual or reserved powers depends upon the breadth of the terms in which powers are conferred on the central authorities, and the breadth with which those powers are construed.[17] Here, the parallels between the United States and European experiences are actually quite striking.

Historically, the interstate commerce clause of the United States Constitution enabled Congress to enact legislation bearing on subject matters that, as such, would ordinarily fall within the States' residual or 'reserved' powers. The same is demonstrably so in the European Union, whose central institutions are authorized to adopt, and have adopted, 'measures for the approximation of the provisions laid down by law, regulation or administrative action in Member States which have as their object the establishment and functioning of the internal market'.[18] Moreover, in the absence of legislative action at the federal level both the US Supreme Court and the European Court of Justice have interpreted extensively the obligations of the interstate commerce clause and of the 'common market', embedded in Arts 28 and 49 [ex Arts 30 and 59] of the EU/EC Treaty, so as to constrain the freedom of action of individual states.[19]

Such expansive judicial interpretations of the US interstate commerce clause and the EC's internal market provisions have lessened the need for

[17] G. Falkner and M. Nentwich, *European Union: Democratic Perspectives after 1996* (Vienna: Service Fachverlag, 1995).

[18] EC Treaty, Art. 95 [ex 100a], para. 1.

[19] There has been ample discussion on the similarities and differences between the jurisprudence of the two courts. The classical study is still Mauro Cappelletti, Monica Seccombe, and Joseph H. H. Weiler (eds.), *Integration Through Law: Europe and the American Federal Experience* (Berlin and New York: de Gruyter, 1986).

the legislative institutions on both sides to resort to other general 'federal' legislative based in the constitutive documents. While it is true that European institutions commonly include Art. 308 [ex Art. 235]—a broad-ranging basis for increasing federal competences without resort to Treaty amendment[20]—among the recited 'legal bases' of Community legislation, this is virtually always in conjunction with one or another more specific basis that might alone justify the measure—for example, Art. 95 [ex Art. 100a] on the internal market. In the United States, where there is not understood to be any formal obligation to recite a 'basis' in the Constitution for a given federal legislative measure, references to what is 'necessary and proper', within the meaning of the United States' implied powers equivalent, are even more scarce.

Thus, both the European Union and the United States subscribe to a constitutional principle of enumerated powers under which, in order for powers to belong properly to the federal level, they need to have been enumerated as such. Moreover, those powers that are not enumerated are 'reserved' to the States. They are reserved to the States within the European Union because it is the States that initially 'transferred' the powers. They are reserved to the States within the United States, not because the States originally transferred them, but because the people of the United States so provided in the Constitution.

Exclusive or Concurrent Authority?

Is regulatory authority distributed in such a way as to give different levels exclusive or merely concurrent authority? And, if concurrent, are there any established criteria for determining how that authority will be shared or what the relationship between exercises of power at different levels of government shall be?

In both the United States and the European Union relatively few subject matters are denominated as exclusively 'federal'. At the same time, very few subjects have remained under exclusive 'State' competence. This state of affairs is often described as 'cooperative federalism'. The US Constitution entrusts the federal government above all with foreign relations: that is, trade on one hand, foreign affairs on the other. Other exclusively federal matters include maritime law, bankruptcy, and industrial and intellectual property rights. However, most of the subjects that have

[20] Art. 308 [ex Art. 235] of the Treaty of Rome reads: 'If action by the Community should prove necessary to attain, in the course of the operation of the common market, one of the objectives of the Community and this Treaty has not provided the necessary powers, the Council shall, acting unanimously on a proposal from the Commission and after consulting the European Parliament, take the appropriate measures.'

come to be governed by federal law, be it legislation or regulation, fall within the federal government's concurrent competences. States are bound to respect all such federal laws, but they are not precluded as such from otherwise continuing to regulate those subjects.

The EU presents a basically similar picture with one major caveat. Exclusive federal competences in the Treaties include external economic relations but not foreign policy, the latter even not becoming a concurrent subject until the 1970s. Other European competences, including agriculture, fisheries, and transport, became exclusively federal only to the extent that they had actually been exercised at the Community legislative level. But most subject matters on which the European institutions regulate or legislate lie within the Community's concurrent, not its exclusive, competence, including the power to enact and apply rules of competition policy. Even the crucial Community power to harmonize Member State laws in the interest of facilitating or completing the internal market cannot properly be described as exclusive. While the legislative power to harmonize national law may, as such, be exclusively Community since no Member State can 'harmonize' the laws of other Member States, the Member States nevertheless retain the power to regulate at least some aspects of the fields that have been the subject of harmonization measures at the Community level, provided, of course, that they do respect the conditions laid down in those measures.

Concurrent powers can be allocated in countless different proportions among those government units that share them. Accordingly, to the extent that federal authority is concurrent rather than exclusive, general principles are needed for determining the relationship between federal and State bodies of law. We highlight two: one fundamentally political, the other legal.

A first principle addresses the mainly political question of whether the federal government should exercise its concurrent authority at all, in view of the fact that the States are also in a position to act. More generally, how is each level of governance to know, before acting, when and to what extent it is best to act, and when and to what extent it is best to leave it to the other holder of concurrent powers to do so? This is the core 'subsidiarity question', analyzed in great detail in other contributions to this volume, including that by David Lazer and Viktor Mayer-Shoenberger.

A second set of principles reflects the more traditional way of analyzing the relationship between federal and State law in areas of concurrent competence, namely, by asking what the priority is between federal and State laws *once* those laws have been adopted. It is useful in this connection to distinguish between the notions of the 'supremacy' of federal over State law on the one hand, and 'pre-emption' of State law by federal law on the other.

Supremacy is the easier of the two terms to grasp, and it is recognized in both the United States and the European Union, albeit with nuances of difference. The supremacy of federal over State law as such is expressly inscribed in Art. 8 of the US Constitution, and there is no significant dissent from this principle in any State quarters. It is precisely because the *legal* principle of supremacy is so fully accepted in the United States that advocates of greater State autonomy direct their efforts primarily to the *political* process—linked to the first principle discussed above—urging that overly expansive or intrusive federal legislation and regulations not be adopted in the first place.

While the EC Treaty is not explicit on the subject of supremacy, the Court of Justice, and indeed all the Union institutions, act on the conviction that, *to the extent of any conflict or inconsistency between them*, Community law takes precedence over Member State law.[21] In such situations, according to the Court's case law, Member State authorities are duty-bound *not* to apply Member State law.

The notion of unqualified supremacy of Community law over national law has not been accepted in every Member State. The most notable example is, of course, Germany, whose Constitutional Court ruled in its 1993 Maastricht Treaty decision that national authorities are not bound to respect and apply Community law to the extent that it exceeds the outer boundaries of Germany's transfer of sovereignty to the European institutions.[22] In a similar vein, the German Constitutional Court has ruled that no transfer of sovereignty is valid to the extent that it results in the violation of the fundamental individual rights guaranteed in the German Constitution.[23] Like views have been expressed, albeit in less clear terms, by courts in certain other Member States, including Ireland and Italy.

The term 'pre-emption' is commonly used, in both the United States and the European Union, to indicate that federal law both displaces any inconsistent State law and precludes the adoption of any State law on that subject, whether consistent or inconsistent, from then on.[24] Under this notion of pre-emption, federal law bars the adoption or application of *any*

[21] *The Queen v. Secretary of State for Transport ex parte Factortame Ltd.*, Case C-213/89, [1990] ECR 1-2433, [1990] 3 CMLR 1. The principle of supremacy was originally established by the Court in *Van Gend en Loos v. Nederlandse Administratie der Belastingen*, Case 26/62, [1963] ECR 1, [1963] CMLR 105.

[22] Judgment of 12 October 1993 (*Brunner v. The European Union Treaty*), Cases 2 BvR 2134/92, 2159/92, [1994] 1 CMLR 57 (Ger. Const'l Ct.).

[23] Although the Court's latest ruling on that particular subject indicated that it was willing to rely on the European Court of Justice for the vindication of those fundamental rights. Judgment of 22 October 1986 (*In re Application of Wunsche Handelsgeselischaft (Solange 11)*), Case 2 BvR 197/83, 73 B. Verf. GE 339, [1987] 1 3 CMLR 225 (Ger. Const'l Ct.).

[24] See Slot, 'Harmonisation', 388–9.

State law on a subject; it 'occupies the entire field', no matter how consonant with federal policy such State law may appear to—or even actually—be.

Pre-emption may be 'constitutional' in the sense that the Constitution, or constitutive treaties, themselves provide that federal law in a given area shall be exclusive of all State law. This, in a sense, is the import of *exclusive* federal legislative competences, as discussed above. More interesting and problematic is the question of 'legislative' or 'regulatory' pre-emption, under which a matter does not fall under exclusive federal competence until it is actually addressed federally. Thus, the exercise of federal legislative authority turns concurrent competences into exclusive ones. 'Legislative' pre-emption arises when the legislature declares that federal policy on a given subject shall be exclusive of all State law, whether consistent with it or not; State authorities may not even supplement it. In principle, whether federal legislation is pre-emptive in this sense is purely a matter of legislative intention.[25]

Unfortunately, Congress does not always clearly indicate whether or not it has the intention to pre-empt. Recognizing this fact, courts are willing to accept the possibility of *implied*, as well as express, federal pre-emption. Implied pre-emption arises when, despite the legislature's failure to make its intention to pre-empt State law explicit, the circumstances of the legislation, including its legislative history, make this intention sufficiently clear. Systems which more or less readily accept the notion of implied federal legislative pre-emption—treating such pre-emption as basically a question of statutory interpretation—almost invariably vest *federal* courts with the power to determine whether there is federal legislative pre-emption or not.

The situation in the EU appears to be evolving in much the same general direction. Thus, even if the Community's Treaty-based legislative authority on a certain subject is concurrent only, this will not in itself prevent the EU legislature from legislating pre-emptively on that subject; and whether it has done so is basically a matter of legislative intent and statutory interpretation. The Community's internal market harmonization is widely considered to be pre-emptive in that, once a relevant measure is enacted, the Member States are deemed to lose the right to legislate any further on that subject, pre-emption being in effect the default mode. The Council and Parliament may have to state expressly, as by setting *minimum* standards, that the measure does not prevent the introduction by Member States of more stringent protective standards, if that possibility is to be

[25] See S. A. Gardbaum, 'The Nature of Preemption', *Cornell Law Review*, 79 (1994), 767.

left open. Conversely, they may decide that Community-wide standards should be fully uniform and thus legislate comprehensively by indicating that the standards adopted are both minimum *and maximum* standards. In some subject matter areas, the intent to pre-empt may be very strongly presumed. Such is the case, for example, with EU legislation in the areas of agriculture and fisheries. It is simply assumed that, once the Community institutions establish a 'common' organization of a particular agricultural market, that regime becomes a fully exclusive one. As a consequence, the Member States' competence is limited to implementing that policy; they may not add to it.

Since the correct interpretation of EU legislation is ultimately a matter of EU law itself, pre-emption is an appropriate and indeed a common subject of preliminary references from national courts to the Court of Justice under Art. 234 [ex Art. 177] of the EC Treaty. The question may be posed whether, even if the Constitution—or a constitutive treaty—treats federal legislative authority over a certain subject matter as concurrent, the federal legislature may in its discretion choose to adopt a pre-emptive federal policy over that subject matter. This means that we can ordinarily anticipate controversy in both the political and the judicial arenas: controversy within the legislature over whether to adopt pre-emptive federal legislation in the first place, and controversy before the courts over whether the federal legislature did in fact do so.

Doubts over the legitimacy of pre-emption become heightened when pre-emption is neither 'constitutional' nor 'legislative' but simply 'regulatory' or 'administrative'. In a system like the United States, in which federal legislative power is broadly delegated to federal administrative agencies, it may become necessary to decide whether the regulatory or administrative agency to which the federal legislature has delegated legislative authority may itself adopt pre-emptive federal rules. Basically, the question whether an agency is empowered to adopt pre-emptive federal rules depends upon the intention of the legislature in creating and empowering that agency: that is to say, on the scope of the delegation. On this question, we are likely to be even less well guided by statutory language. Indeed, we may not even be certain that the agency *intended* to adopt pre-emptive rules in the first place. If the federal legislature does not always express itself clearly on the question whether its policies are pre-emptive of State law, it should not be surprising that it also does not always express itself clearly on whether it, in turn, has authorized a federal agency to adopt policies that are pre-emptive of State law. The determination of that question can be made only on the basis of a close examination, not only of the statutory language, but also of the precise policy purposes for which the statute was adopted. Legislative history will play a large role in this determinations.[26] Given the widespread practice of delegating legislative powers to federal administrative agencies, the question of regulatory or administrative pre-emption arises with great frequency in the United States, and ultimately ends up in the federal courts.

As Giandomenico Majone discusses in this volume, the European Union is at a different stage of evolution in this regard. Community regulatory authority still remains largely concentrated in the hands of the Community legislature—the Council and the European Parliament—and of the European Commission, even in areas where regulatory agencies have been created, as with food standards or pharmaceuticals. Even so, the pre-emptive or non-pre-emptive effect of legislation adopted by the Council and the Parliament depends largely on their implicit or explicit intention in adopting that legislation. Thus, the only remaining issues are (1) whether the Commission had legislative authority under the delegation from the Council and the Parliament to adopt a pre-emptive Community policy and (2) whether the Commission actually exercised that authority by in fact adopting a pre-emptive Community policy.

Fortunately, legislative drafting and legislative history in EU practice up to now have been such as normally to enable us to know fairly clearly what the intentions of both the Council and the Parliament were, and, where relevant, also the Commission's intentions, as to the pre-emption question. But there is always a danger that the Community institutions will become less attentive, or in any event less legislatively explicit, in this regard.[27]

The likelihood of this happening may well increase with enlargement of the Community and with the resulting political necessity of leaving matters such as pre-emption unresolved, or unclearly resolved, in the legislative process. To the extent that this occurs, the solution to pre-emption questions may become every bit as obscure in the European Union as it has come to be in the United States, with difficult pre-emption cases increasingly surfacing before the courts. And the diffuse fear of 'creeping competences' as both an invisible and an irreversible process is likely to increase as a result. It may be advisable for the EU to draw lessons from this aspect of the US experience.

[26] R. J. Pierce, Jr., 'Regulation, Deregulation, Federalism, and Administrative Law: Agency Power to Preempt State Regulation', *University of Pittsburgh Law Review*, 46 (1985), 636–41.

[27] For a very useful discussion of the different usages of the term 'pre-emption' in the European Union, and a call for greater clarity, see E. D. Cross, 'Pre-emption of Member State Law in the European Economic Community: A Framework for Analysis', *Common Market Law Review*, 29 (1992), 447. Cross distinguishes four attitudes towards pre-emption: (1) express saving; (2) express pre-emption; (3) 'occupation of the field'—as used here; and (4) 'conflict pre-emption', which in turn has two subcategories: direct conflict and 'interference' or 'obstacle' conflict.

Overriding Principles of Division of Labour under Concurrent Competences

Are there any general principles of allocation of competences which might serve as overriding constitutional limitations on federal powers—operating either in conjunction with or in the absence of more specific criteria? Do these general principles take priority over specific allocations that may have been made, or do they merely bear upon our understanding and interpretation of those allocations?

This question naturally arises only in connection with the exercise of concurrent competences. Where federal powers are exclusive, the limits, if any, on their exercise will by definition have nothing to do with the reservation of powers to the States, for none have been reserved. On the other hand, the exercise of exclusive federal legislative competences may of course be limited by other constitutional considerations, such as fundamental individual rights or general principles of law including, for example, principles of proportionality, equal treatment, and protection of legitimate expectations.

To some extent, this may be only a matter of *defining* the competences attributed to federal authorities or qualifying existing definitions. Thus, in its *Lopez* decision,[28] the US Supreme Court explained that Congress could not constitutionally exercise legislative power predicated on the interstate commerce clause unless it could—and did—rationally consider the legislation to be a response to a problem of interstate commerce and rationally demonstrate that this is the case. Similarly, in its path-breaking decision in *New York v. United States*,[29] the Supreme Court declared that Congress may not use its power to legislate over interstate commerce, or any other subject within its constitutional scope of authority, in such a way as to coerce or compel the States to use their own legislative powers in implementation of policies made at the federal level. The Court determined that such federal 'commandeering' of the States' apparatus to carry out federally imposed policies constitutes a violation of the Tenth Amendment; if Congress empowers federal agencies to 'commandeer' State resources, it goes *too far* in the exercise of its subject matter competences.[30]

Within the European Union, the principle of subsidiarity is unquestionably the pre-eminent general principle of this sort, as incorporated in Art. 5 [ex Art. 3b] of the Maastricht Treaty as follows:

[28] 514 U.S. 549 (1995). See, more recently, United States v. Morrison, __U.S.__, 120 S. Ct. 1740 (2000).

[29] 505 U.S. 144 (1992). See, more recently, Printz v. United States, 521 U.S. 98 (1997).

[30] For further discussion of commandeering, see the chapters by George Bermann and Daniel Halberstam in this volume.

The Community shall act within the limits of the powers conferred upon it by this Treaty and of the objectives assigned to it therein.

In areas which do not fall within its exclusive competence, the Community shall take action, in accordance with the principle of subsidiarity, only if and in so far as the objectives of the proposed action cannot be sufficiently achieved by the Member States and can therefore, by reason of the scale or effects of the proposed action, be better achieved by the Community.

Any action by the Community shall not go beyond what is necessary to achieve the objectives of this Treaty. (emphasis added)

The principle of subsidiarity thus requires that the Community institutions refrain from taking action, even when admittedly acting within the scope of their competences, where the objectives to be met by such action could be effectively achieved by action taken at the Member State level or below, and where action at the Community level would not be markedly more efficient; and the complementary principle of proportionality as stated in the last paragraph of the Article calls for acting with restraint even when it does take action.

The subsidiarity principle has many presumed origins and as many presumed sins. It is said to have been inspired by the Catholic Church, the German *Länder*, and the Founding Fathers themselves. It has been accused of being too vague and of generating undue expectations. It is in any case a contested principle, whether it is examined primarily as an analytic matter, as a political issue, or as a matter of practical implementation. While more detailed operational criteria were included in a 'Subsidiarity Protocol' to the Amsterdam Treaty, these criteria remained to be tested in Court or even through a high-profile case at the political level.[31]

While the anti-commandeering principle of *New York v. United States* in the US and the principle of subsidiarity in the EU are quite different in the precise kind of limitations that they place on the exercise of concurrent competences, they are alike in that they both operate as an additional constitutional constraint.[32] It is not enough for federal or Community institutions to remain within their proper subject-matter fields; it is also necessary that, in exercising their powers within those fields, they do so in a fashion that is compatible with the Tenth Amendment and the principle of subsidiarity, respectively.

[31] For a discussion, see David Lazer and Viktor Mayer-Shoenberger in this volume. To some extent, the *Tobacco* case where the Court supported Germany's position that the EC acted beyond its remit in banning all tobacco advertising constitute a first step in this direction.

[32] For a more nuanced assessment see Halberstam in this volume.

2. Supplementary Mechanisms to Safeguard Basic Allocation of Competences

The set of basic principles outlined above is meant to provide agreed-upon limitations on the exercise of central powers in a federal system. Assuming that the rules of the game are set in this way, how sustainable are they? Are they the sole guarantee of appropriate division of labour between levels of governance? And if not, what other safeguards are there of federalism principles? We will quickly review two sets of additional considerations below.

Alternatives to Legal Allocative Principles: Structures and Processes

To what extent is federalism organized through the structures of the federal institutions or through any particular decisional processes that those institutions are required to employ, instead of, or in addition to, particular allocations of competences?

It is important to recognize that constitutional protections of federalism do not necessarily take the form of legal principles. They may also take the form of legal structures and processes. For example, a constitution may structure 'federal' institutions or their workings so as indirectly to promote respect for the interests of the constituent States and their separate populations. This point is explored more systematically in the contributions to this volume by George Bermann, Daniel Halberstam, and Cary Coglianese and Kalypso Nicolaidis.

The view that the structure of federal institutions can itself operate as the core 'guarantee' of the values of federalism has long been associated in the United States with the writings of Herbert Wechsler.[33] According to Wechsler, the architects of the US Constitution anticipated the needs and interests of the States by providing that the Congress and the President would be selected in ways that cause them to give due regard to those needs and interests. Therefore, rather than review directly whether a given federal measure respects the Constitution's limitations on the exercise of federal powers *vis-à-vis* the States, the courts should simply enforce the rules that govern the structure and procedures of the federal institutions themselves.

[33] Herbert Wechsler, 'The Political Safeguards of Federalism: The Role of the States in the Composition and Selection of the National Government', *Columbia Law Review*, 54 (1954), 543. For a contemporary endorsement of the theory, see H. Hovenkamp, 'Judicial Restraint and Constitutional Federalism', *Columbia Law Review*, 96 (1996), 2213.

The Wechslerian theory was attractive in large part not simply because it affirmed the importance of respecting the institutional ground rules of federalism—which in itself is presumably a good thing—but also because it called for avoiding 'judicial second-guessing' of fundamentally *political* judgements about the appropriateness of federal legislative interventions. In other words, the theory operates openly in support of the principle of the separation of powers, notably, the separation of judicial power from legislative and executive powers.

Critics of the theory have disputed the empirical basis for the claim that the way the federal government is structured or functions offers any serious guarantee that the prerogatives and interests of the States will be safeguarded, and that the balance of power between the federal and State governments will thereby be maintained.[34] The theory is widely considered today as being unduly optimistic about the capacity of the prevailing structural and functional rules at the federal level, and therefore of the federal political process, to guarantee respect for federalism.

The Wechslerian theory has had a particularly uneven fortune in the US Supreme Court over recent decades. At the present time, the Court remains quite divided over the notion that maintaining the balance between federal and State regulatory power is primarily a political and not a judicial function. In fact, Supreme Court developments in this respect are more in flux than ever. Ironically, one could argue that the Wechslerian theory applies much more straightforwardly to the European Union than to the United States. The institutional structure of the EU rests on the representation of the Member States at the centre, in the European Council and the Councils of Ministers, the bodies that to this day ultimately control the legislative process and provide political oversight of the Commission's exercise of executive functions. Albeit less overtly, Member States are also represented in the appointment of the Commission itself. The Treaty of Nice signed in December 2000 constituted a forceful reminder of the import of structural safeguards of federalism in the EU as Member States finally agreed to a new bargain over new voting weights, the scope of national veto powers, and the numbers of Commissioners to be nominated by each Member State—a bargain that had been in the making for at least five years.[35]

[34] See, for example, L. B. Kaden, 'Politics, Money, and State Sovereignty: The Judicial Role', *Columbia Law Review*, 79 (1979), 847; D. B. La Pierre, 'The ism Redux: Intergovernmental Immunity and the on', *Washington University Law Quarterly*, 60 (1982), 779; D. J. Meritt, 'The Guarantee Clause and State Autonomy: Federalism for a Third Century', *Columbia Law Review*, 88 (1988), 1.

[35] See Moravcsik and Nicolaidis, 'Explaining the Treaty of Amsterdam'.

At the same time, however, the asymmetric character of the EU calls for a more differentiated understanding of State representation at the centre than that prevailing in the early history of the United States. In a Union where differences in size and power of the constitutive units are extremely wide, we need to ask further how such differences are reflected in relative influence at the Union level. This question becomes all the more delicate with the increased resort to variable geometry configurations in the Union, now institutionalized under the procedures of 'enhanced cooperation'. Increasingly, it seems, with the enlargement of the Union, the dilution of individual State influence will be compensated by greater allowance for institutional configurations giving bigger States a leadership role in specific areas of integration.

Principles of Federalism and Constitutive Texts

Through what kinds of instruments are all of these ground rules of federalism laid down? And what difference does that make?

Due to their perceived fundamental importance in federal and federal-type systems, rules on the allocation of power between States and federal or Union institutions are typically expected to figure directly in the federal constitutive documents. In a 'true' federal system like the United States, this document can only be the federal constitution. In the European Union, absent a true constitution, such principles are expected to be laid down in the constitutive treaties, namely, the Treaty of Rome, as revised by successive intergovernmental conferences. To a considerable extent they are.

But it is one thing for constitutional documents to purport to articulate basic federalism principles; it is another thing for them to express those principles faithfully and accurately in accordance with prevailing political understandings. As Jack Donahue and Mark Pollack demonstrate vividly in this volume, the real balance of federalism within any vertically divided power system is subject to change over time, with or without formal constitutional amendments. Thus, whether a written constitution or constitutive document fairly reflects prevailing legal and political principles of federalism may depend on the frequency with which such foundational texts are amended in the light of considerations such as these.

The United States and the European Union offer a lively contrast from this point of view. As far as express principles of federalism are concerned, the US Constitution has rarely been fundamentally altered. The first time was in 1791 with the Tenth Amendment, previously mentioned, which reserved residual powers to the States—and the people. American federalism was affected less overtly, but no less fundamentally, by the adoption of the Fourteenth Amendment following the Civil War, which extended to the States the federal constitutional principles of due process and equal protection, thus empowering the federal courts to impose on the States far-reaching substantive and procedural requirements derived from *federal* constitutional law.

The fact remains that, on its face, the United States Constitution does not reflect the strong and sometimes bitter disputes that have been waged over the question of the proper balance between federal and State competences. Nor does it necessarily reflect the principles or practices of federalism that prevail at any given point in time. It is no exaggeration to say that the United States constitutional text, as it reads, is a poor guide to the political, and even the legal, realities of US federalism. This is perhaps truer now than ever. Ground rules for the allocation of power between State and federal authorities in the United States may at present be undergoing as fundamental a change as at any time over the past 60 years. However, virtually all such change is taking place without the benefit of any formal change to the constitutional text.

For obvious reasons, the architects of the European Union have been much less willing to leave the issue of the balance between Member State and Community powers to the 'federal' political process. The States that came together to form the Communities, and that are now acceding to the EU, were and are mature and fully developed nation-states. They are not likely to let the process of European legal and political integration simply take its course. Not only does the Treaty speak with relative specificity to the scope of federal legislative power, but the terms in which it speaks have been modified at strikingly short intervals, precisely because the Member States as such continue to want to be heard on all the issues. When the time comes to amend the constitutive treaties, the procedure of choice is an intergovernmental conference, in which the Member States negotiate among themselves as independent states and take no action except upon a full consensus. Intergovernmental conferences have been convened for this purpose with increased frequency, becoming almost a constant fixture of EU politics. And it is telling that the constitutive treaties have been amended, following these intergovernmental conferences, not only in their descriptions of particular EU competences, but even in their broad statements about federalism, including of course the variations on subsidiarity. But while the subsidiarity protocol clearly seeks to shift the burden of proof that EU action is necessary on to the Union institutions, it does not constitute a clear-cut principle like the Tenth Amendment. As discussed in this volume by Lazer and Mayer-Shoenberger, its functional equivalent in the US is the executive orders which would be considered far too detailed to qualify for constitutional status.

Thus, the European Union treaties have tended to confront the problems of federalism more regularly than the United States Constitution. Whether this causes the treaties to give a truer picture of the federalism balance within the Union than would otherwise be the case, or than is characteristic of the United States constitutional text, remains to be seen. Echoing an increasingly widespread call for greater clarity of the EU federal bargain, the British Prime Minister, Tony Blair, in September 2000 called for the adoption of a 'charter of competences' that would presumably spell out the EU's answer to the various questions laid out in this appendix. Could this be done in a clearer and simpler way than the current statement on subsidiarity? The other heads of state responded at the December 2000 Nice Summit by committing to an open debate on the EU's architecture culminating in 2004.

The ultimate question for the EU in the next few years will be whether such constitutive texts ought eventually to be turned into a traditional constitution covering a wider array of topics than subsidiarity. In his contribution to this volume, Joseph Weiler argues that the United States cannot constitute a model for the EU in this regard, as its constitution reflects the existence of a single constitutional *demos*—a 'singleness' that is neither likely nor desirable in the EU context. More prosaically, our discussion suggests that the one of the keys to a sustainable federal contract between States and Union lies in being able to combine clarity of basic principles with flexibility in their application. The United States has succeeded in doing so in spite of its relatively immutable constitution. The European Union may well continue to chose a more political and flexible approach. In both cases, however, citizens will increasingly hold politicians accountable for their answer to the 'who does what?' question. Understanding the basic principles for federal allocation of competence ought to be a starting point in addressing this question. But as the chapters in this book demonstrate, we also need to move beyond this basic legal approach if we are to tackle the challenge of legitimacy head-on.

ABOUT THE CONTRIBUTORS

KALYPSO NICOLAIDIS is University Lecturer at the University of Oxford, a Fellow at St Antony's College where she teaches in International Relations, and a member of the faculty of the World Trade Institute, Bern, Switzerland. Previously she was Associate Professor at Harvard University's Kennedy School of Government, where she served as the faculty chair for the Socrates Kokkalis Program on Southeastern Europe. She also taught at the École Nationale d'Administration in Paris. She has published on the European Union, eastern and central Europe, international trade, the WTO, conflict resolution, and negotiation theory. She is the co-editor of *The Greek Paradox: Promise vs Performance* (1997), translated into Greek and Turkish, and *Strategic Trends in Services: An Enquiry into the World Services Economy* (1989). Her upcoming book is titled *Mutual Recognition Among Nations: Global Lessons from the European Experience.* Nicolaidis holds a Ph.D. in Political Economy and Government from Harvard, a Masters in Public Administration from the Kennedy School, and a Masters in International Economics from the Institut d'Études Politiques in Paris.

ROBERT HOWSE is Professor of Law at the University of Michigan and a member of the faculty of the World Trade Institute, Bern, Switzerland. He has also taught at the University of Toronto, as a Visiting Professor at Harvard Law School, and in the Academy of European Law, Florence. He is author of *Economic Union, Social Justice, and Constitutional Reform* (1991), co-author of *Trade and Transitions* (1990) and *The Regulation of International Trade* (1996; 2nd edn 1999), contributing editor to *Yugoslavia the Former and Future* (1995), editor of *The World Trading System: Critical Perspectives on the Global Economy* (1998), and co-translator and first author of the introductory essay in Alexandre Kojève, *Outline of a Phenomenology of Right* (2000). Howse has been active in the policy and politics of federalism in Canada, co-founding a leading 'NO' committee in the 1992 constitutional referendum on decentralization, and during 1996–9 a consultant to the current Canadian government on social policy and federal-provincial relations. He is an international fellow of the C. D. Howe Institute in Toronto. He has published one book and over 25 essays and articles, scholarly as well as journalistic, on issues in Canadian and comparative federalism. He is a member of the editorial advisory board of the European Journal of International Law.

GEORGE A. BERMANN is the Charles Keller Beekman Professor of Law at Columbia University, and Director of the European Legal Studies Center. He obtained a B.A. from Yale in 1967, J.D. in 1971, and an LL.M. from Columbia in 1975. He is editor of the *Yale Law Journal*, an associate with Davis, Polk, and Wardwell in New York, and Jervey Fellow of the Parker School of Foreign and Comparative Law, 1973–5. He took advanced legal studies at the University of Paris II, 1974–5, the Conseil d'État of France, 1975, the universities of Munich and Heidelberg and the Max Planck Institut für ausländisches öffentliches Recht und Völkerrecht, Heidelberg, Germany, 1975–6. He has been a member of the Columbia faculty since 1975. He was visiting professor at the Universities of Paris II, France and Fribourg, Switzerland, 1997; the universities of Paris I and Rouen, France, 1981–2; Tulane Law School, 1988; and University of Bordeaux, 1994. He was a visiting scholar at the Legal Service of the Commission of the European Communities, 1994; executive director, Leyden-Amsterdam-Columbia Summer Program, 1979–82; and is currently a member of the program's board of directors. He is an editorial board member of the *American Journal of Comparative Law*; a director of the American Society of Comparative Law; a member of Académie Internationale de Droit Comparé (Paris); and Chair of the Executive Editorial Board of the *Columbia Journal of European Law.* He is founder and former member of the board of directors, German American Law Association (New York), and consultant to the New York State Bar Association, the National Center for Administrative Justice, the Ford Foundation, and the National People's Congress of the People's Republic of China. He was public member of the Administrative Conference of the United States, 1985–9. He is a member of the Deutsch-Amerikanische Juristen Vereinigung (DAJV) (Bonn); the American Arbitration Association panel of international commercial arbitrators; and the ICC and ad hoc international arbitral tribunals. He is vice president and former director of the American Foreign Law Association. His principal interests are in comparative law and civil law, the international practice of law, European Community law, European law, transnational litigation and arbitration, international trade, administrative law, contracts, and government liability.

SUJIT CHOUDHRY is an Assistant Professor at the Faculty of Law, University of Toronto. He holds law degrees from the University of Oxford, the University of Toronto, and the Harvard Law School. Prior to joining the University of Toronto, he served as Law Clerk to Chief Justice Antonio Lamer of the Supreme Court of Canada. During the 1998–9 academic year he was a Graduate Fellow at the Harvard University Center for Ethics and the Professions, and a Visiting Researcher at the Harvard Law

School. Choudhry was a Rhodes Scholar, and held a Frank Knox Memorial Fellowship from Harvard, and the William E. Taylor Memorial Fellowship from the Social Sciences and Humanities Research Council of Canada. His principal research interests are constitutional law and theory (with particular interests in federalism and comparative constitutional law) and health law and policy. He has also written on the law's response to ethnocultural difference.

CARY COGLIANESE is Associate Professor of Public Policy at Harvard University's John F. Kennedy School of Government and Chair of the Regulatory Policy Program at the School's Center for Business and Government. His interdisciplinary research focuses on issues of regulation and administrative law. He has published research on alternative means of designing regulatory processes and the role of disputing in regulatory policy-making, including: 'Litigating Within Relationships: Disputes and Disturbance in the Regulatory Process', *Law and Society Review* (1996); 'Assessing Consensus: The Promise and Performance of Negotiated Rulemaking', *Duke Law Journal* (1997); 'The Limits of Consensus', *Environment* (1999); and 'Assessing the Advocacy of Negotiated Rulemaking', *New York University Environmental Law Journal* (2001). His book, *Regulating from the Inside: Can Environmental Management Systems Achieve Policy Goals?*, (2001) examines the public policy implications of new developments in environmental management. He has also published on international regulation, federalism, interest groups, and regulatory politics. He is currently engaged in an empirical study of trends in federal regulation that challenges the widely accepted view among American administrative law scholars that judicial oversight has 'ossified', or delayed, the development of agency rule-making. An affiliated scholar at the Harvard Law School and the director of the Kennedy School's Politics Research Group, Coglianese teaches public law, environmental policy, and professional ethics. He is a member of the editorial advisory board of the *Law and Society Review*, an organizer of the Law and Society Association's international collaborative research network on regulation, and a recipient of the American Political Science Association's Edward S. Corwin Award. Coglianese received his J.D., M.P.P. (public policy), and Ph.D. in political science from the University of Michigan.

JOHN D. DONAHUE is the Raymond Vernon Lecturer in Public Policy at the John F. Kennedy School of Government. His teaching, writing, and research deal with public sector reform and with the allocation of responsibilities across levels of government and between public and private sectors. His most recent books include *Governance in a Globalizing World* (co-edited with Joseph Nye, Jr) and *Making Washington Work: Tales of*

Innovation in the Federal Government. Donahue is also the author of *Hazardous Crosscurrents: Confronting Inequality as Government Shifts Toward the States* (1999), *Disunited States* (1997), and *The Privatization Decision* (1989, with four translations 1990–2), and co-author (with Robert B. Reich) of *New Deals: The Chrysler Revival and the American System* (1985). At Harvard, Donahue directs the Visions of Governance in the 21st Century research project and is faculty chair of the David T. Kearns Program in Business, Government, and Education. He served in the first Clinton Administration as an Assistant Secretary and as Counsellor to the Secretary of Labor, where he helped to frame Administration positions on job training reform and education tax preferences. Donahue has been a consultant to the World Bank, the National Economic Council, and several other business and governmental organizations, and also serves as an adviser or trustee for several non-profits. He holds a B.A. from Indiana University and an M.P.P. and Ph.D. from Harvard.

DANIEL J. ELAZAR (1934–1999) was Professor of Political Science and Director of the Center for the Study of Federalism at Temple University, Philadelphia, Pennsylvania; President of the Jerusalem Center for Public Affairs; and Senator N. M. Paterson Professor of Intergovernmental Relations in the Department of Political Studies at Bar-Ilan University, Israel, where he also headed the Institute for Local Government. Among his last books were *Federalism and the Way to Peace* (1994), *Federal Systems of the World: A Handbook* (1994), a four-volume work titled *The Covenant Tradition in Politics* (1995–98), and *The Covenant Connection: From Federal Theology to Modern Federalism* (2000), co-edited with John Kincaid.

DANIEL HALBERSTAM is Assistant Professor of Law at the University of Michigan Law School, specializing in US constitutional law, institutional issues of European Union law, and the law of federalism. He earned his undergraduate degree from Columbia and his law degree from Yale, clerked for Justice David H. Souter of the US Supreme Court and Judge Patricia M. Wald of the Court of Appeals for the DC Circuit, and served as judicial fellow to Judge Peter Jann of the European Court of Justice. He also served as Attorney Advisor to the Chairman of the US Federal Trade Commission and Attorney Advisor in the Office of Legal Counsel at the U.S. Department of Justice.

JOHN KINCAID is the Robert B. and Helen S. Meyner Professor of Government and Public Service and Director of the Meyner Center for the Study of State and Local Government at Lafayette College, Easton,

Pennsylvania. He has also served as Executive Director (1988–94) of the US Advisory Commission on Intergovernmental Relations, Washington, DC. He is editor of *Publius: The Journal of Federalism*, President of the International Association of Centers for Federal Studies, editor of a 50-book series on the Governments and Politics of the American States being published by the University of Nebraska Press, an elected fellow of the National Academy of Public Administration, and a member of the editorial board of the *State Constitutional Law Bulletin*. His most recent book is *The Covenant Connection: From Federal Theology to Modern Federalism* (2000), co-edited with Daniel J. Elazar. He earned a Ph.D. in Political Science at Temple University, Philadelphia, Pennsylvania, in 1981 and an M.A. in Urban Affairs at the University of Wisconsin, Milwaukee, in 1968.

DENIS LACORNE is Senior Research Fellow at the Centre d'Études et de Recherches Internationales (CERI). He lectures at the Institut d'Études Politiques de Paris (Sciences-Po) and is in charge of the American Studies Program. He is the author of *La Crise de l'identité américaine. Du Melting-pot au multiculturalisme* (1997) and *L'Invention de la République. Le modèle américain* (1991). His recent articles include: 'Sur l'élection présidentielle américaine, Vestiges d'un âge prédémocratique et anti-monarchique', *Le Débat*, Javier 2001; 'The Barbaric Americans', *The Wilson Quarterly*, Spring 2001; 'Corsica: Multiculturalism and the Jacobin Republic', *Correspondence* 7, 2001.

MARC LANDY is a Professor of Political Science at Boston College. He has a B.A from Oberlin College and a Ph.D. in Government from Harvard University. He and Sidney Milkis wrote *Presidential Greatness* (2000). He is an author of the *Environmental Protection Agency from Nixon to Clinton: Asking the Wrong Questions* (1994) and an editor of *The New Politics of Public Policy* (1995). His recent articles include: 'Local Government and Environmental Policy', in Martha Derthick (ed.), *Dilemmas of Scale in American Federal Democracy* (1999) and 'The Politics of Risk Reform', co-authored with Kyle Dell, *Duke Environmental Law and Policy Forum* (1999). During the 2000 presidential campaign his opinion editorials appeared in the *Boston Globe* and *New York Newsday* and he appeared on a wide variety of radio and television news programs.

DAVID LAZER, Assistant Professor of Public Policy at the Kennedy School of Government, Harvard University, teaches courses on management and executive branch politics. He is currently writing a book on the network of interactions within the executive branch with respect to regulatory policy, and how the president can and does use those networks to exercise control. He is also conducting research on the diffusion of information among interest groups and between interest groups and the government. In a different area of research, he is examining how change in the international system may emerge from the purely local interactions of political actors. His research in this area includes a paper on the spread of preferential trade agreements in the 1860s, and current work on the interdependence of regulatory policies of states. Finally, he has a general interest in examining the importance and process by which connections emerge among political actors. He holds a Ph.D. in political science from the University of Michigan.

GIANDOMENICO MAJONE is currently Visiting Distinguished Professor at the Graduate School of Public and International Affairs and at the European Union Center, University of Pittsburgh, and Visiting Scholar at the Sony and Toyota Research Centre, London School of Economics. He was Professor of Public Policy at the European University Institute in Florence. His recent publications include *Regulating Europe* (1996) and *Lo Stato Regolatore* (2000). He is currently writing a book on the role of non-majoritarian institutions in democratic governance.

VIKTOR MAYER-SCHOENBERGER is Assistant Professor of Public Policy at the John F. Kennedy School of Government at Harvard. In his teaching and research he focuses on comparative regulatory policies in the US and Europe, especially in the telecommunication and information infrastructure area. Before moving to Harvard, Mayer-Schönberger was with the Faculty of Law, University of Vienna. He has published numerous books and authored many articles on the legal and policy aspects of modern information and communication technologies. After successes in the International Physics Olympics and the Austrian Young Programmers Contest, Mayer-Schoenberger studied law in Salzburg (Mag.iur, '88, Dr.iur '91), Cambridge (UK) and Harvard (LL.M. '89). In 1992 he received a M.Sc. (Econ) from the London School of Economics. In 2001 he received his *venia docendi* in telecommunications and information law. He advises governments and international organizations on telecommunications and e-commerce issues.

ELIZABETH MEEHAN is Professor of Politics and Jean Monnet Professor of European Social Policy in the School of Politics at the Queen's University of Belfast. Her research lies in the fields of women's rights at work, citizenship, and British-Irish relations in the context of the EU. Publications include *Women's Rights at Work* (1985), *Citizenship and the European Communities* (1993), 'The Europeanization of the Irish Question', in M. Cox, A. Guelke and F. Stephens (eds), *A Farewell to Arms? From War to Peace in Northern Ireland* (2000) and, with Klaus Larres, *Uneasy Allies: British-German Relations and European Integration since 1945* (2000).

ANDREW MORAVCSIK is Professor of Government and Director of the European Union Center, Harvard University. He has published *The Choice for Europe: Social Purpose and State Power from Messina to Maastricht (1998)* and *Fragmentation or Centralization? Europe facing the Challenges of Deepening, Diversity, and Democracy (1998)*, as well as numerous articles and chapters.

LAURENCE J. O'TOOLE, JR is Margaret Hughes and Robert T. Golembiewski Professor of Public Administration in the Department of Political Science at the University of Georgia (US). He is also Senior Research Associate in the Carl Vinson Institute of Government at Georgia. He has published several books and numerous articles on policy implementation and public management, particularly in network settings, as well as on intergovernmental relations. *His American Intergovernmental Relations* (2000) has recently been published in its third edition.

JOHN PETERSON is Jean Monnet Professor of European politics at the University of Glasgow and Visiting Professor at the College of Europe, Bruges. He edits, with Iain Begg, the *Journal of Common Market Studies* and, with Helen Wallace, the 'New European Union' series for Oxford University Press. His publications include *Europe and America: Partners and Rivals in International Relations* (2002), *The Institutions of the European Union* (co-edited with Michael Shackleton, 2002), *Decision-Making in the European Union* (co-authored with Elizabeth Bomberg, 1999), and *Technology Policy in the European Union* (co-authored with Margaret Sharp, 1998). He has held posts at the Universities of York, Essex, Oxford, California (Berkeley and Santa Barbara), and the London School of Economics.

MARK A. POLLACK is an Assistant Professor of Political Science and European Studies at the University of Wisconsin, Madison, where he teaches in international relations and comparative European politics, and is currently serving (September 2000–August 2002) as Senior Research Fellow in the newly created Transatlantic Relations Chair at the European University Institute in Florence. He received his B.A. in political science from Rutgers University in 1988 and his Ph.D. from Harvard University in 1995. His research agenda focuses on the role of international institutions in the processes of international governance, with specific projects examining the role of the supranational organizations in the European Union, the creation of new mechanisms for governance of the transatlantic relationship, and the 'mainstreaming' of gender issues in international organizations. His articles have appeared in journals such as *International Organization*, *Governance*, *Journal of Public Policy*, *Journal of European Public Policy*, *Journal of Common Market Studies*, and *Washington Quarterly*. He received a research fellowship for the year 2000 from the German Marshall Fund for his work on European institutions. He also serves on the Executive Committee of the University of Wisconsin European Union Center and on the Executive Committee of the European Community Studies Association.

FRITZ W. SCHARPF teaches the study of Law and Political Science at the Universität Tübingen, Universität Freiburg, and Yale University (LL.M.). During 1964–6 he was an Assistant Professor of Law, Yale Law School, and in 1968 a Professor of Political Science, Universität Konstanz. During 1973–84 he served as Director of the International Institute of Management, Wissenschaftszentrum Berlin. He served as a Senior Research Fellow at Wissenschaftszentrum Berlin during 1984–6. In 1986 he was named Director at the Max-Planck Institut für Gesellschaftsforschung, Köln. During January–June 1987 he was a Fellow at the Center for Advanced Study in Behavioral Sciences, Stanford, California. His research interests include organization and decision processes in the ministerial bureaucracy, joint federal-state decision making, implementation research, federalism and European integration, game-theoretical applications in empirical research, comparative political economy, and comparative welfare state research.

VIVIEN SCHMIDT, Professor of International Relations at Boston University, has written extensively on European political economy and public policy, including *Welfare and Work in the Open Economy* (co-edited with F. W. Scharpf, 2000), *From State to Market?* (1996), *Democratizing France* (1990) and over 50 articles and chapters in books. Recent articles have appeared in *Comparative Politics*, *Critique Internationale*, *Current Politics and Economics in Europe*, *Daedalus*, *European Law Journal*, *Governance*, *Journal of Common Market Studies*, *Journal of European Public Policy*, *Publius*, *Revue Française de Science Politique*, and *West European Politics*. Currently, Professor Schmidt is working on a two-volume project on the impact of European integration on national economies, institutions, and discourse in France, Britain, and Germany.

STEVEN M. TELES is Assistant Professor of Politics at Brandeis University, having held previous positions at Hamilton College, Harvard University, the University of London, Holy Cross College, and Boston University. He is the author of *Whose Welfare? AFDC and Elite Politics* and of numerous articles and book chapters on such subjects as affirmative action in Great

Britain, US-China relations, and American drug policy. He is currently writing a book on the politics of social security policy in the US and UK, and directing a major project on the social mobility of ethnic minorities in the US and UK.

JOSEPH H. H. WEILER is Manley Hudson Professor of Law and Jean Monnet Chair at Harvard University. He is also Professor at the College of Europe in Bruges, Honorary Professor at University College London, and Honorary Professor at the Department of Political Science, University of Copenhagen. He is a Fellow of the American Academy of Arts and Sciences. He served as a Member of the Committee of Jurists of the Institutional Affairs Committee of the European Parliament co-drafting the European Parliament's Declaration of Human Rights and Freedoms and the Parliament's input to the Maastricht Inter-Governmental Conference. He was a member of the *Groupe des Sages* advising the Commission of the European Union on the 1996–7 Amsterdam Treaty. His recent publications include *The EU, the WTO and the NAFTA* (2000), *The Constitution of Europe—Do the New Clothes have an Emperor?* (1998), *Kompetenzen und Grundrecht* (with Bruno Simma and Markus C. Zöckler, 1999) and a novella, *Der Fall Steinmann* (2000).

INDEX

abortion 152, 153
absenteeism 431
accessibility 321, 323
accountability 154, 156, 180, 181, 208, 264, 340, 364
 crisis of 436
 determining targets of 443
 dilution of 448
 direct, international institutions have much less 299
 effective problem solving and 358–65
 electoral 359
 federal states' fewer lasting problems with 344
 greater, need for 267
 guarantee of 339
 immediate 182
 improving, effective way of 266
 independence and 256
 indirect 454
 insufficient 317
 national policy-making processes and 348
 networks 309, 315, 318, 319, 323, 324
 obscured 231
 problems with 341
 public 392
 responsibility and 214
Ackerman, B. A. 259
Adams, John 84
Adenauer, Konrad 97
adjudication 37, 98, 164, 170, 183, 214
 agency 265
 delegation of 262
administration 37, 68, 69, 77, 323, 414
 apolitical 258
 decentralized 269
 delegating 90
 democracy as largel extraneous to 327
 effective and efficient 419
 IT and 303
 politics and 319
 reason-giving 266
 technical 164
 incapacity 170–1
Advisory Commission on Intergovernmental Relations (US) 145, 150, 195
advisory committees 346
affirmative action 167
Agency for Health and Safety at Work 270
Agenda 2000 112
agriculture 98, 116, 165, 347, 394
 policy 112, 171, 173
 quotas 260
 subsidies 185, 186
 see also CAP
Alabama 461
Alien Act (US, 1798) 84
alienation 66, 76
allegiances 64, 76, 405, 471
 divided or multiple 380, 387–90, 396, 401, 432
 identity-based 472
 local and national 431
Allen, David 167
alliances 59
allocation of powers 56, 191, 193, 209, 487–90
 precise, regulatory policy-making and 255
allocational shifts/mechanisms 279–80, 285, 296, 297
Althusius, Johannes 33–4, 42, 44, 440, 441
Amenta, E. 357
American Constitution 56, 76, 108, 174, 199, 202, 235, 288–9, 441
 Amendments: (10th) 83, 85, 146, 155, 203, 208, 499, 503; (11th) 155, 204, 205; (13th) 85; (14th) 85, 205–7, 430, 503; (16th) 238; (17th) 237, 292
 anti-federalists and debate about 404
 Articles of Confederation (1781) 49, 51, 52, 53, 80–3 *passim*, 108, 220, 247, 248
 compact between States 468
 Congress and 487, 489, 490
 Framers 82, 83–4, 216, 292, 417
 important powers to States 486
 liberal interpretations of 147
 mobility rights 399
 `necessary and proper' clause 98, 200, 239
 shift of authority from States 283
 Supremacy Clause 83, 221, 222, 223, 224
 values of 393–4
Amsterdam Summit/Treaty (1997) 111, 140, 177, 261, 295, 356, 368, 370, 408, 409, 488
 anti-discrimination provisions 435
 fundamental rights 437
 subsidiarity protocol 201, 456, 499
anarchists 152

Anglo-Saxon countries 357, 369
Ansell, C. K. 313
anti-commandeering principle 207–9, 217, 245
anti-competitive agreements 255
anti-discrimination 136, 435
anti-federalists 156, 404, 407
anti-trust 162, 179, 371, 425
Anton, T. J. 321
APA (Federal Administrative Procedure Act, US 1946) 265–7, 456
Appleby, P. 305
Appomattox 430
arenas 44, 47, 465, 470
Aristotle 62
Aron, Raymond 406
Arvidson, E. 145
ASEAN (Association of Southeast Asian Nations) 47
Aspinwall, M. 317
associations 157
asymmetric federalism 454, 467
Australia 35, 367, 377
Austria 41, 65–6, 180, 349, 350
  EU suspension of diplomatic contacts 437
  federal arrangements 377
  Freedom Party 388, 436
  see also Haider
authoritativeness 315, 321, 323, 324, 326
authority 61, 68, 258, 288, 358–9, 420
  allocation of 132–3, 198, 277, 280, 285, 294
  bottom-to-top hierarchy 57
  centralization of 108, 277
  constitutional 60, 238
  constrained 80
  decentralization of 277
  decision-making 153, 402
  delegation of 279, 280–1, 283, 290, 295, 297
  entrenched 403–4
  exclusive or concurrent 492–7
  executive 422
  explicit 262
  federal 87
  focal points of 466
  formal 64, 91
  fragmentation of 76
  institutional 99, 165
  jurisdictional 297
  legislative 192, 199
  local 86
  national 85, 255, 256, 340
  normative 55, 64
  overlapping 303
  personalized systems of 384
  policy 278, 296
  regulatory 255, 291, 487, 490
  residual 490–2
  rule-making 192, 270
  supranational 96
  transferred 280
  ultimate 60, 62, 63
autonomy 54, 74, 150–1, 162, 174, 229, 316, 349
  constitutionally-guaranteed 342
  deletion of 73
  diminished by pluralism 348
  executive 338, 340, 342, 343
  Länder 234
  local 320, 425, 486
  national 425
  officials and legislators 214
  political 487
  reducing 284, 354
  respect for 194, 440
  societal 352
  sub-national 341, 342
  threat to 351
  virtues and defects of 79

Bache, I. 306
Baechler, J. 440
balance of power 150, 155, 156, 339, 342, 344, 484
'balkanization' 150
Balkans 66, 179, 423
Balladur, Edouard 104
Bangemann Group 313
bargaining 156, 247, 308
  backroom 318
  informal 326
barriers to trade 361, 397–8
Bavaria 248, 432
Beam, D. R. 308
Beer, S. H. 319, 323, 403
beggar-thy-neighbour strategies 370, 460
Begg, I. 312
Belgium 42, 45, 47, 111, 364, 367
  consociational democracy 365
  pernicious bureaucratic practices 436
  relative success and stability 402
Benelux countries 97
Berlin Wall 154
Bermann, G. 233, 447, 452, 453, 455, 457, 500
Beveridge, William, Lord 357
'bicycle theory' 162, 163
bigotry 393
Blair, Tony 181–2, 343, 504
Blank, K. 325
Bodin, Jean 33, 34, 42, 440, 441
Bomberg, E. 301, 306, 312, 313, 314, 318
border controls 172
Börzel, T. 302
Bosnia 364
boundaries 67, 70, 127, 359, 459

coping with loss of control 365–7
economic 366
judicial policing of 197–8
jurisdictional 79
permanently fixing 48
removing 66
Brandeis, Louis 86
Braudel, F. 445
Breton, Albert 447
Breton, Raymond 395–6
Bretton Woods 36
Breyer, Stephen G. 215–16, 216–17
Britain, *see* United Kingdom
British empire 35
Brussels 45, 63, 99, 164, 171, 208
faceless bureaucrats 434
Länder missions 243
'superstate' 162, 180
BSE crisis 264
budgetary review 37
Bull, H. 467
Bundesbank 104, 355
bureaucracy 37, 38, 77, 122, 171, 180
central(ized) 154, 241
executive function 339
fledgling 238
large 241
pernicious practices 436
regulatory 258
statist 40
street-level 157
'bureaucratic despotism' 162
Bush, George 90, 131, 151, 269

Calhoun, J. C. 441, 451, 468
Canada 35, 57, 168, 174, 286, 364, 388, 391, 395
affirmation of belonging 400
consociational democracy 365
federal arrangements 377, 378
relative success and stability 402
separation of powers 338
see also Quebec
cantons 35, 44
CAP (Common Agricultural Policy) 116, 169, 173, 177, 262, 263, 315
capital 359, 362, 364, 368, 369
globalization of 425
mobility of 360, 366
capital markets 366
Cappeleti, M. 440, 452
Carens, Joseph 389–90
Caribbean Community 47
cartels 360
Carter, Jimmy 121
case law 63, 367, 370
Castells, M. 300
categorical imperative 67, 371
Catholicism 33, 42, 44–6, 155
CBO (US Congressional Budget Office) 119–20, 290
central banking 164, 184
see also Bundesbank; European Central Bank; Federal Reserve Bank
Central Europe 158, 169
central government 86, 90, 240
authority constrained 80
dependence 238–44
large, reliance on 152
local government contributes to 462
policy-making responsibilities 232
centralization 50, 73–117, 145, 151, 154, 168, 248
concept used to justfy 414
cumulative sources of 445
decentralization and/or 277, 278–9, 280, 285, 296, 299, 420, 449
democratic gains from 462
executive autonomy 338
federalism often associated with 156
limits on 418
looming, alarm about 157
moderate voters tend to prefer 152
open-ended criteria for 286
seen as less of a threat 242
strong 465
varied among policy fields 158
Charter of Human Rights 58
checks and balances 164, 182, 359
Chirac, Jacques 427
choice(s) 42, 44, 77, 79, 404
action 358
allocational 294
consequence and 74, 78
legitimacy-enhancing 366
policy 309, 310, 360, 365, 366, 463
political 420
value 259
Choudhry, S. 470, 471
Chryssochoou, D. 408
Churchill, Winston 96
citizenship 269, 377–402, 427–37
nationality and 405–7, 408, 410, 411, 472, 473
civil rights 94, 152, 167, 178, 248, 322, 434
applying 306
fundamental 420
civil war 364, 473
clarity 309
Clark, I. 460
Clean Water Act Amendments (US, 1972) 269
cleavages 365
Clinton, Bill 90, 123–6 *passim*, 131, 145, 148, 149, 153, 155
Closa, Carlos 403, 404, 409, 410, 411

Cockfield, Lord 102, 103
`co-decision procedure' 105, 339, 361
coercion 41, 51, 164, 171, 178, 382–3, 451
Coglianese, C. 239, 451, 452, 500
cognitive dissonance 389
cohesion 306
Cold War 36, 87, 96
Cole, R. 145, 150
collective action 79, 318
collectivities 418
Cologne Summit (1999) 356
comitology system 157, 264, 292
commandeering issue 213–51, 457
  see also anti-commandeering
commerce 85, 86, 199, 240, 287
  interstate 269, 289, 487–8, 491, 498
Committee of the Regions 195, 202
common fate/destiny 365, 472
common market 98, 106, 233, 298–9
  distortion of competition within 370
Commonwealth of Independent States 47
commonwealths 76, 83
Communists 97
communitarianism 151, 152
communities:
  of association 381
  of fate 395–6
  of identity 381, 390, 472
  of interest 415
Community law 132, 133, 136, 223, 224, 266
  integrity of 486
  internal market and 199–200
  primary 268
comparative advantage 397
competence 37, 50, 109, 110, 112, 203, 267, 314
  allocation of 483–504
  attribution of 283
  boundaries between 404
  charter of 446, 504
  core sovereign 457
  enforcing `catalogues' of 198–200
  exclusive 111, 446
  growth in 261
  increase of 293
  legitimacy and 417
  policing 208
  shared 447, 448, 450, 468
  strict empowerment approach to 464
competition 151, 165, 171, 253, 357
  beggar-thy-neighbour 460
  damaging forms of 423
  distortion of 370
  free 361, 368
  interjurisdictional 154
  international 168, 360, 362, 366
  regulatory 357–8, 359, 379, 367–71
  rules for 97
  undistorted 368
  unfair 257, 370–1, 460
competitiveness 102
compliance 225, 226, 305, 358
compromise 173, 219, 271
  see also Luxembourg Compromise
concurrency 447, 492–7
confederation/confederalism 31, 32, 46–51, 80–4, 158, 221
  democratic government and 51
  development of 48
  EU as 38–42, 165–76
  limited ends 52
  modern 34, 35
  new style 37
  obsolete 36
  old style 49
  ward republics 151–2
confidence 94–5, 150, 367
conflicts of interest 362, 364, 365
  massive 367, 460
conformity 291
confrontation 349, 350, 352, 473
`confusion of powers' 335, 337, 339
Congress (US) 81, 90, 119–23 *passim*, 146, 202, 218–21 *passim*, 230, 247
  abrogation of 11th Amendment 204, 205–7
  commandeering by NAFTA 227
  Commerce Clause powers 240, 368
  Constitution and 487, 489, 491
  enumerated powers 239, 240
  inter-State commerce clause 199, 204
  legal constraints imposed on States 368
  necessary and proper' clause 200
  pre-emption 126, 147
  resistance of waivers 149
  spending power 490
  State protection from over-reaching by 292
  Supreme Court and 490
  unfunded mandates 194
Congressional Review Act (US, 1996) 120
Conlan, T. 144, 308
Connecticut 82
consensus 173, 174, 244–9, 309, 349, 369, 383
  building 157, 314, 315, 323, 325
  inter-institutional 315
  lack of 180
  national moral 248
consent 33, 383, 417, 419
consequence 74, 78
consistency 309, 439
consociationalism 34, 365
consolidation 167, 425
Constant, Benjamin 419
constitution-making 424–6
constitutionalism 34, 378

federalism without 54–70
national, reformulation of 468
constraints 297, 298, 362, 380–7, 395
budgetary 253
constitutional 165, 169–70, 453
economic 356–7, 359, 367
legal 173, 357, 359–60, 366, 367–8
legitimacy 382, 383, 384, 386
negative integration 367–8
non-servility 419
regulatory 253
stability 383, 384, 386, 387, 389
structural 456
substantive 165–8
Consultative Assembly 100
contractarian justification 383
convergence criteria 105
`cooperation procedure' 103
Cooper, R. 466
coordination 349, 369–70
exchange-rate 101
international 163
negative and positive 302
network types of 306
open method of 450, 465
policy 173, 422
COREPER (Committe of Permanent Representatives) 171
corporations 75
corporatism 348–53 *passim*
meso- 318
corruption 64, 149, 174, 180, 340, 424
Corsica 432, 433
Council of Europe 55, 96, 101, 115, 132, 167, 175, 178, 194, 236, 243, 245, 292, 316
composition 404
Eastern enlargement 356
Hanover (1988) 104
Milan (1985) 103
political judgements 368
strategic priorities 260
Council of Ministers 38, 98, 100, 105, 171, 173, 175–6, 186, 292, 31
closeness to people 182
Comitology Decision (1987) 263–4
consolidated 364
dynamic confusion of powers' between institutions 335, 337, 339
EP the primary interlocutor of 181
internal delegation 260
Member State powers 340
national executives 341
politics 346, 368
powers to Commission from 260, 262, 263, 264
super-majorities 453
unanimous agreement on decisions 361, 367–8, 404
upper-level governance 287
courts 162, 193, 198–203, 218, 259, 341
constitutional 37, 38, 58
lower 342
national 101, 255, 342
new procedural rules 265
state immunity 204–5
see also ECJ; Supreme Court (US)
covenants 45, 50
CPMP (Committee for Propietary Medicinal Products) 270–1
Cram, L. 312
creative accounting 169
credit 366
Crémer, J. 152
Cresson, Edith 174
crime 162, 166, 473
Croly, Herbert 85–6
cronyism 340, 346
Cuba 432
culture(s) 31, 48, 50, 75, 157, 167, 172, 466
civic 435
decision-making 352–3
differences 399
fostering, intrinsic value of 462
homogeneity of 40
multi-layered 434
national 432, 434
regulatory, different 347
shared 297, 380
currency 38, 80–1, 104, 105, 112, 434
common/single 161, 173, 177, 369
customs checks 173
customs duties 397
CVMP (Committee for Veterinary Medicinal Products) 270–1
Czechoslovakia (former) 364, 378

Dahl, Robert 409
Damrosch, Lori 218
Debray, Regis 472
debt 81, 105, 112
De Búrca, G. 133, 138, 140, 442, 455
decentralization 43, 50, 74–80, 146, 151, 152, 168, 281, 297, 414
centralization and/or 277, 278–9, 280, 285, 296, 299, 420, 449
civic liberal principles and 419–21
decision-making 78, 229
devolution versus 422–4
domestic 458
extremist voters tend to prefer 152
federalism now usually associated with 155
greater 267
implementation and enforcement tasks 297
policy efficency/effectiveness and 421–2
public life and 419

substantial support for 319
decision-making 153, 175, 180, 239, 263, 270, 337, 352–3, 426
access, in policy formulation 352
agency 265, 267
backroom 313
central structures 244
collective 325
consensual 173–4
decentralized 78, 229
effective, need for 454
important 309
independent authority 402
intergovernmental aspects 249
joint 246, 247, 404
legitimizing 469
lower levels of 455
majoritarian 164, 173, 174, 180, 181, 183, 185
non-governmental actors' access to 341
non-majoritarian 184
peculiarly obscure process of 317–18
procedure which could paralyze 264
regulatory 266, 267
rules 174, 292
shared 344
social trust and 385
super-majoritarian 185
technical 345
unanimous 404
upper-level 292
decolonization 46
Deelen, B. 154
defence 36, 82, 97, 163, 168, 172
industrial rationalization 166
policy 100, 161, 166, 170, 173
Defense of Marriage Act (US, 1996) 151
Dehejia, V. H. 368
Dehousse, R. 261
Delaware 82
delegation 90, 123, 146, 185, 235–6, 279, 281, 283, 290, 297
ability to revoke/change 295, 298
allocational 294
commitment and 260–2
delineated 284, 286–9
doctrine against 258
horizontal and vertical 287
internal 262–4
regulatory authority 291
statutory 487
voting procedures 293
delineation 239, 241, 283, 284, 286–9, 452
narrowness in 296
Delors, Jacques 37, 102–3, 104, 110, 316, 355, 442
democratic deficit 179, 180, 261, 303, 339, 434
alleged, political silence of 356
being erased 436
demos 56–7, 60, 65, 178, 391, 434, 472
'we-identity' of 364
denationalization of economies 326
Denmark 105, 111, 362, 367, 368
Depression (1920s) 4
deregulation 123, 146, 360, 371
derogation 349, 410
Derthick, Martha 324
despotic rule 181
Deutsch, K. 467, 473
devaluation 179
devolution 113, 118–43, 144–60, 307, 320, 321, 326, 343
decentralization versus 422–4
local government and 414–15
radical 462
unfunded mandates and 458
welfare state 461
Dewey, John 432
DiIulio, J. J. 145
Dilger, R. J. 145
diplomacy 184
direct effect 56, 361
directives 110, 113, 136, 139, 140, 157, 235, 306–7
adapting to technical progress 263
framework 262, 287–8
implementation of 242–3, 291
limited tool of commandeering 230–4
Member States prefer 229
social policy 407
translating into national law 341
dirigisme 155
discipline 70
constitutional 57, 59, 60, 68–9
discretion 234, 256, 258, 259, 263
administrative 348, 349, 350
agency 265–6
discrimination 136, 167, 168, 395, 435
direct 398
racial 322, 393
disenfranchisement 424, 462
distributive policies 109, 256
diversity 67, 73, 74–5, 397, 474
cultural 390
lifestyle 420
linguistic 402
localism and 422
political 390
division of labour 317, 448, 468, 498–9
gendered 394
vertical 464
division of power 244, 335, 337, 338, 451
Donahoe, J. D. 144, 150, 319, 445, 449, 453, 502
due process 455

Duff, A. 409
duties 430, 463
Dyson, K. 355

Eastern Europe 104, 158, 169, 356
Easton, D. 153
EC (European Community) 36, 37, 38, 41, 48, 105, 201, 267
  budgetary resources 100, 103–4
  competition law 254
  decisions 361
  directives 110
  founders 40, 355
  law 132
  legal prohibitions 359–60
  legislation 98
  national sovereignty within 103
  policy-making 253, 259
  relaunching of 102
ECJ (European Court of Justice) 56, 59, 65, 98, 132, 175, 264, 287, 292
  advisory opinions 170–1
  authoritative guidance 342
  case law 367, 370
  Community law measures and internal market 199–200
  constitutionalization groundwork 223
  core sovereignty interests 203
  decisions 174, 233, 368
  development of 342
  direct effect and supremacy 224
  discretion 262–3
  dynamic confusion of powers between institutions 335, 337, 339
  excluded from areas of cooperation 105
  harmonizaton provisions 199
  important constitutional principles 178
  integration 361, 437
  interpretation of term 'implementation' 262
  judges 181
  legal architecture 228
  obligation of giving reasons 266
  powers 162, 171, 175, 264, 294
  proportionality 449
  role in constitutionalizing treaties 154
  rules devised by 209
  shifting role 289
  subsidiarity inquiry 201–2
  supranational actions 355
  US Supreme Court and 252
ECOFIN ministers 371
economic issues 326
  constraints 359
  development 154, 362
  growth 169
  well-being 395
economic union 36
*Economist 1*03
ECSC (European Coal and Steel Community) 95, 96–7, 263, 266
EDC (European Defence Community) 97
education 163, 168, 172, 182, 184, 466
  policy 167, 170, 387, 458
  recognition of qualifications 469
EEC (European Economic Community) 98–9
effective action 358
efficency 79, 132, 153–4, 184, 185, 302, 323
  allocative 78
  economic 77, 360, 390, 397
  generic 455
  governing 358
  losses of 455
  political 421–2
Egypt 43
Eichener, V. 362
Eisenhower, Dwight D. 87, 149
Elazar, Daniel J. 54, 148, 176, 440, 451, 465, 466, 484
elderly people 168
elections 246
  general/national 359, 430
  primary 152
Elling, R. C. 148
Else, B. A. 305, 310
emancipation 61–2
EMEA (Agency for the Evaluation of Medicinal Products) 270, 271
Emergency Highway Energy Conservation Act (US, 1973) 144
employment 102, 359, 360, 362
  legitimacy-enhancing choices 366
empowerment 149, 154, 242, 259, 314, 370, 425
  co-optation and 461
  focus on 462
  genuine 460
  horizontal 470
  multi-tier 463
  mutual 470–1
  opportunities for 473
  strict 464
  top-down 462
EMS (European Monetary System) 101, 104, 177
EMU (economic and monetary union) 58, 104, 105, 113, 170
enforcement 171, 175, 192, 226, 241, 255, 282
  anti-trust standards 425
  bureaucratic 'tackle' in 305
  decentralized 297
  delegation of 262
  joint 469
  national agencies 291
England 33, 43–4, 370
  Euroscepticism 431

'enhanced cooperation' 111, 173
enumerated powers 239, 240, 241
Environment Agency 270
environmental issues 320, 346
  degradation 168, 184
  policy 161, 164, 168, 171, 172, 312, 314
  protection 154, 309, 422
EOs (US Executive Orders) 121, 123–31
EP (European Parliament) 55, 98, 105, 137–8, 156, 175, 176, 292, 361, 437
  advisory committees 264
  co-decision rights 361
  Committee of Independent Experts (1999) 313, 340
  competencies 356
  democratic controls 181, 182
  dynamic confusion of powers between institutions 335, 337, 339
  election campaigns 365
  European government politically accountable to 364
  lack of control of Council of Ministers from 339–40
  Member State interests 194
  plenary sessions 315
  politics 346
  powers 162, 171, 261, 339
  proactive moves to empower consumers 463
EPA (US Environment Protection Agency) 119
equality 360, 366, 394
  gender 167
  socioeconomic 183
equilibrium 79
equity 320, 398
escape clauses 312
Esping-Andersen, G. 357, 369
ESPRIT programme 109
ESTA (European Science and Technology Assembly) 313
Ethiopia 46–7
ethnic groupings/ethnicity 48, 76, 380, 384, 387, 389, 433–4
ethnoculturalism 380, 389, 390, 391, 392, 395
ethnoi 56
ethno-racial categories 436
EU (European Union) 31–53
  allocational debates 285, 299
  budget 109, 112
  Catholic cultural origins 44–6
  citizenship 390–401, 407–8
  commandeering 214, 217, 220, 225, 227, 228, 241
  competences 108, 111, 112
  confederal structure 165–76
  constitutional issues: development 255; discipline 59, 60; precepts 60; settlement 176–9
  development of policies 106–10
  devolution 155–8
  Enlargement project 58
  'faithfulness' to the common enterprise 242
  federalism 95–116, 161–87; asymmetric 467; regulatory 254–6
  foundation 95–9, 105–6
  institutional structures 165–76, 336–44
  introducing subsidiarity to 132–5
  judiciary 238
  key differences between US and 109
  legitimacy and regulatory competition 355–74
  lessons from US to 413–26
  Member State legislatures 248
  networks 306, 346; comparing US and 306, 307, 324–7; governance and 311–18
  normative consequences of structure 179–86
  policy-making processes 345–53
  regulation 110, 113–15, 167, 252, 253; 'where' and 'how' of 132–41
  see also under various headings, e.g. common market; Council of Europe; Council of Ministers; directives; EC; ECJ; ECSC; EDC; EEC; EMU; EP; MEPs; OEEC; SEA; Single Market; United Europe Movement; *also under following headings prefixed* 'European'
Euro (currency) 38, 434
Euro-federalists 472
European Agriculture Guidance and Guarantee Fund 396
European Atomic Energy Community 98
European Central Bank 351, 355
European Charter on regional and minority languages 427–8
European Commission 55, 98, 101, 134–9 *passim*, 176, 180, 185, 270, 292, 338, 361
  accountability problems 340
  appointment of 261
  assigned tasks, insufficient resources to carry out 326
  autonomy 162
  case law 367
  collective resignation (1999) 436
  decisions 488
  democratic legitimacy 262
  Directorates-General 314–15
  dynamic confusion of powers between institutions 335, 337, 339
  emphasis on inspection 291
  enforcement powers 171, 175
  EP usurping role of 181
  excluded from areas of cooperation 105
  formal rules of procedure 315
  harmonization of laws and regulations 267

influence 292–3
integration 361
Member State interests 194
monitoring of unfair regulatory competition 460
monopoly right of initiative 316
national identities 409
officials 345–6
organizational resources 370
perfunctory explanatory memoranda 456
policing functions 370
powers 260, 262, 263, 264, 294, 361, 404
proposals for withdrawal of legislation 196
report into allegations of fraud (1999) 313
scrutiny of 325
supranational actions 355
transformation into European government 364
transparency programmes 463
White Papers: (1985) 268; (1999) 255
European Constitutional Council 409
European Convention on Human Rights 167, 463
European Regional Development Fund 396
Europeanization 473, 474
Europeanness 473
Europessism 100–2
Euro-sceptics 162, 163, 180, 427, 431, 435
Eurosclerosis 101, 103
Eurostrikes 347
exchange rates 101, 105, 360
exclusion 395, 423
executives 94, 121–31, 194, 338, 339, 341
all-powerful 343
local 422
relative strength and weakness of 342
traditionally strong 343
expectations 39, 259, 443
stability of 357
unreasonable 421
experimentation 75, 456
expertise 258, 259, 265, 271, 311, 317, 425
accountability, transparency and 319
competing sources of 424
experts 346
externalities 78–80, 165, 382, 447
economic 168
environmental 168
negative 321
policy 74, 402
regulation of 179
trans-border 163, 168
extraterritoriality 467, 469, 470
extremists 151, 152, 180

factors of production 359, 360, 397
imported 398
Fainsod, M. 258
favouritism 346
Featherstone, K. 355
Federal Administrative Procedure Act (US), *see* APA
Federal Cartel Office (Germany) 254
Federal Reserve Bank 153
federalism 33, 35, 39, 51, 73–117, 161–87, 335–54, 439–81
allocational legitimacy and 295–9
allocative principles 484–99
Catholic 45
caveat on 8–10
comparative 213–51
constitutional 61, 70, 467
cooperative 40–1, 446
covenant-based principles 42
creates a market for mobile citizens 399
defining features of 387
democratic government and 51
dual 429, 451
economic theories of 277
failure of 46
federalism breeds 44
institutional design 277–99
law and 192–203
political theory and 377–80
power-sharing part of the essence of 157
pre-emptive 268
principles of 502–4
procedural reinforcements 195–7
regulatory 254–6
reinvented 34
'relational' problem 203–9
statism and 32, 36, 49, 441
without constitutionalism 54–70
see also EOs
federation(s) 35, 52, 58, 163, 181
citizenship and 377–402
creation of 459
divergence from 54–5
early phase of 298
emerging 285
federalism and 36, 46
invention of 49
modern 34, 42, 49
move from confederation to 31
national 168, 170, 172, 173
new 46–7
processes of importance in maintaining 40
rejecting 35–8, 49
Ferry, J. M. 473
Financial Perspective 115
financial transfers 170
fiscal constraints 169–70
flexibility 111, 147, 170, 233, 317, 349, 353, 354, 467
legitimacy and 442–6
proscribed 350

flexibility (*cont.*):
  provisions for 173
  reduced 348
Follesdal, A. 132, 133, 134
force 42
Ford, Gerald 121
foreign policy 100, 105, 161, 163, 171, 172
  States' call for inclusion in debate 248
Forsyth, M. 441, 451, 465
Fouchet Plan (1961) 100
France 33, 112, 177, 178, 343, 354, 367
  access to decision-making in policy formulation 352
  allegiance to 432
  *ancien regime 1*62
  citizenship 427
  Constitution 433, 435
  EU foundations 95, 96–7, 98, 100, 103, 104
  Euroscepticism 431
  extreme right 180
  federalist tradition 52
  Jacobinism 50, 52, 433
  nationalist left 472
  pernicious bureaucratic practices 436
  simple notions of representation 344
  state-society interaction 349, 351
  statist pattern 348, 353, 433
  Vichy 436
  see also Chirac; Corsica; Delors; Gaulle
Franck, Thomas 378
Franco, Francisco 40
Frankfurt 161
Frankfurter, Felix 86
free trade 299, 314, 361
  see also NAFTA
Friedrich, Carl J. 155
functionalism 32, 36, 47, 48, 258
fundamental freedoms 396–7
funded mandates 462

Gaebler, T. 302
Gallup organization 94
Galston, William 384
GAO (US General Accounting Office) 119–20, 131, 456
Gardner, J. P. 407
Garrett, G. 355
GATT (General Agreement on Tariffs and Trade) 161, 218–19, 244
Gaulle, Charles de 99–101, 103
GDP (gross domestic product) 89, 109, 112, 116, 161, 169, 369, 490
gender 167, 389, 394, 433
Genschel, P. 368
George, S. 306
Germany 34, 64, 77, 162, 168, 178, 364, 367
  allegiance to 432
  anti-EU backlash 111
  *Bundesrat 1*75, 235–6, 237, 239, 242, 245
  citizenship and nationality 406
  co-determination rights 362
  codification and application of laws 352
  commandeering 213, 214–15, 217, 225, 236, 238, 241
  competition law 253–4
  compounded representation 344
  Constitution/Basic Law 174, 215, 216, 223, 236, 239
  Constitutional Court 65, 234, 236, 260, 356, 472
  corporatism 349, 353
  'donor fatigue' 112
  EU foundations 95, 96–7, 100, 104, 105
  'faithfulness' to the common enterprise 242
  federal government 241, 377
  Holocaust and responsibility 393
  judiciary 350
  modern territorial states 35
  national identity 473
  net distribution 109, 113, 115–16
  policy-making effectiveness 338
  rehabilitation and reintegration 177
  separation of powers 338–9
  support of subsidiarity 138
  Third Reich 436
  see also Länder; Weimar
Gettysburg Address (1863) 358, 362, 393, 434
Gewirtz, Paul 91
Ghana 46
Gingrich, Newt 144, 152, 154
'giving-reasons' obligation 266, 456
globalization 36, 47, 167, 177, 184, 307, 320, 427
  amorphous 1
  capital 425
  economies under pressure from 326
  increased 310
Goldwin, R. 441
government expenditure 170
governmental scale 75–7, 92
Grande, E. 325
Grant, C. 316
grants 88, 89–90, 490
  block 144–5, 148, 150
Great Society 88, 89, 151
Greece 40, 109, 169, 362
Greenwood, J. 313, 317
Grodzins, Morton 88, 320, 441, 448
Grønbech-Jensen, C. 313
*Grundnorm 6*0, 62, 69
Gun-Free School Zone Act (US, 1995) 199, 230

Haas, Ernst 99, 258
Habermas, Jürgen 378, 381–2, 385, 391, 392, 394, 456, 472

habits 62, 69, 468, 475
Haider, Jörg 65–6, 392, 436, 472
Halberstam, D. 452, 455, 457, 500
Hall, T. E. 305
Hamilton, Alexander 83, 220–1, 417–18, 445
Hanf, K. J. 304
harmonization 98–9, 111, 136, 139, 157, 199, 200, 209, 233, 263
  fiscal 293
  integrated market and 270
  joint enforcement 469
  minimal/minimum 255, 268
  optional 255, 268
  pre-emption of 295
  regulatory 397
  safety and environmental standards 362
  social-welfare systems 368
  tax 368
  total 254–5, 267, 268
Hartley, T. C. 263, 266
Hassler W. T. 259
Heater, D. 406
Heclo, H. 309, 316
Heilman, J. G. 323
Heinz, J. P. 307
Held, David 402
Henkin, L. 226
Henning, H. C. A. 304, 307, 317
Héritier, A. 469
Hesse, J. 447, 460
heterogeneity 48, 338, 387, 389
hierarchy 42–4, 45, 55, 152, 253, 288, 440
  bottom-to-top 57
  EU unique in lack of 315–16
  judicial 342
  legal 63
  social 465
  top-to-bottom 57
  Weberian 304
Hills, Roderick 222, 239
Hindmoor, A. 310, 327
Hissong, R. V. 145
history 380, 391, 394, 395, 432
  national 433, 474
Hobbes, Thomas 50
Hoffmann, S. 306, 466
'hollow state' era 323
Holocaust 148, 393, 394
Holy Roman Empire 34
home affairs 105
homogeneity 40, 77, 278, 391, 415, 420
  economic and cultural 338
Hooghe, L. 301, 325
Hoover, Herbert 87
Horwitz, M. J. 258
Howse, Robert 231, 381, 391, 392, 395, 400, 459, 467, 472, 473
Hull, R. 314
human capital 154
human rights 58, 64, 65, 167, 168, 209, 410
  breach of 295
  norms 409

ideals 393, 394
ideas 312
identity 58, 62, 432
  bounded, non-ethnic 66
  building 437
  collective 63, 64, 364, 389, 390
  common 365, 393, 428, 471, 472, 473; absence of 176, 178–9, 338
  communities of 381, 390, 472
  cultural 433, 434
  ethnic 63, 365
  ethnocultural 391, 392, 395
  'European' 426, 433, 472
  gender 433
  moral 65
  multi-layered 434
  national 63, 386, 405, 406, 408, 409, 410, 473
  personal 474
  political 67, 68, 390, 396
  shared 391, 392, 408, 471–5
  symbolic 434
ideology 31, 177, 294, 362, 431
IGCs (intergovernmental conferences) 103, 104, 105, 203, 294, 356, 364
immigration 69, 161, 171
immunities 430
implementation 135–7, 162, 238, 245, 312, 339, 350, 448
  decentralized 297, 454
  delegation of 262, 264, 335, 345
  directives 242–3, 291
  flexible 349, 353, 354
  less accommodation in 352
  monitoring 284
  networks 305, 307, 308, 310
  plans 461
  reduced flexibility in 348
  rule 347
  single market 291
incentives 282, 309, 318, 370
  costly 424
inclusion 429, 430
  social 410
inclusiveness 469, 470, 471, 475
incomes 359, 360, 364, 366, 368
  business 369
incrementalism 309
independence 38, 39, 62, 198, 239, 242, 271
  accountability and 256
  court 341
  judicial 174, 343
  sub-national authorities 342
  unity and 73

India 46, 377
individual freedom 382
individualists 152
inducement 282
industrial relations 362
industry 168
inequality 366
inequities 154
inflation 80, 105
infrastructure 167, 168, 170, 360
central 247–8
local 462
innovation 310, 312, 320, 456
adaptability and capacity for 311, 321
instability 57, 388, 389
institutions 37, 38, 43–4, 49, 75, 132, 179, 248, 335–54
central 99
centralized 285, 296, 319
common 309
competence of 200
`confederal' arrangements 58
consensus forming 325
constitution of 403–12
decentralized 285
decision-making 175, 340
dependence on cooperation of Member States 239
federal 39, 55, 56, 195, 202, 299
formal 35, 306
indirect democratic control 181–2
informal 306
intergovernmental 157
international 161, 299
key 98
law-making 139
many ways to constrain and control 180–1
monitoring 290
non-majoritarian 183, 184, 185, 262
parliamentary 35
political 382, 393, 416, 472
qualified majority voting 103
reforms 103, 104, 163
regulatory 257, 267
stable and powerful 162
supranational 290, 355, 465
tightly constrained 164
transfer of powers to 260
see also under various headings, e.g. courts; Council of Europe; Council of Ministers; ECSC; EDC; EP
integration 32, 48, 49, 57, 60, 163, 178, 342
commitment to pervasive programme of 357
deep 474, 475
defence against 99–100
economic 258–9, 357, 359, 368, 378, 396–401, 459, 460
EP's `quiet work of' 437
guided and controlled by sovereign democratic states 260
integration breeds 162
Länder power eroded as a result of 343
legal 102, 451
market 209, 447, 473
material 58
Monnet method of promoting 312
most important force underlying 177
national 87
negative 359–60, 361, 362, 367–8, 398
policy 345, 473
political 39, 44, 378, 451
political-economic trilemma 356–8
positive 361, 398
project-based approach to 445
relaunching of 102–6
set-back in 295
social 387
subsidiarity and 95–116
interdependence 41, 177, 178, 395, 396
network 304, 307
interest groups 147, 149, 151, 153, 164, 175
access to regulatory process 266
broadly representative 314
multiple 424
openness to 335
particularist 184, 185
powerful 184, 435
satisfying policy demands of 247
societal 347
interest rates 360, 366
intergovernmentalism 41, 70, 101, 109, 171, 177, 228, 260, 280, 306, 307, 323, 325
agreement 355
cooperation 158
costs/mandates 119–20
decision-making 249
legitimacy 339, 340, 356
negotiations 324, 361
opposition to 454
programme negotiations 324
relations 156, 157
shared responsibilities 148
treaties 39
weak 96
see also Advisory Commission; IGCs
interjurisdictional matters 154, 158
internal market 102, 103, 108, 112, 263, 361, 491
American States 356
Community law measures and 199–200
fully integrated 209
regulations needed for completing 264
segmentation of 268
internalization 67
international agreements 219, 227

international law 55, 218–20, 226
international relations 156, 461
internationalism 177, 432
internationalization 367
Internet 415, 435, 470
Interstate Commerce Act (US, 1887) 257
Interstate Highway Act (US, 1956) 87
intervention 287, 450
intervention 200–2
intolerance 66
Ipsen, 259
Ireland 109, 169, 407
  Constitution (1922) 406
Irish-Americans 432
Islam 62
ISTEA (Intermodal Surface Transportation Act, US 1991) 145
IT (information technology) 303
Italy 42, 46, 47, 97, 367
  extreme right 180
  moral corruption 64
  societal interests 348, 349
  see also Mussolini

Jackson, Andrew 84
Japan 102
Jefferson, Thomas 151–2, 317, 321
Jeffery, Charlie 243
Johnson, G. W. 323
Johnson, Lyndon B. 88
Johnson, Samuel 65
'joint-decision trap' 361
Jospin, Lionel 352
Judaism 61–2
judicial function 69, 258, 339
  policing of boundaries 197–8
judicial review 258, 265, 266
judiciary 185, 239, 338, 339, 341, 342
  highly subordinated 350
  independent 343, 350
  miniscule 238
July, Serge 436–7
justice 53, 105, 407
  distributive 379
  political 394, 395
  social 385

Kallen, Horace 431
Kant, Immanuel 64, 67, 371
Kellerman, Carol 150
Kelsen, H. 60, 63
Kenyon, D. A. 154
Keohane, R. 306, 326, 466
Kerwin, C. 121
Kettl, D. F. 305, 320
Kincaid, J. 144, 147, 150, 153, 154, 155, 156, 455, 458, 461
Kingsley, G. 144
Klijn, E.-H. 309
knowledge transfer 313
Kojève, A. 467
Komesar, Neil 454
Korean War (1950–3) 97
Kymlicka, Will 377, 388, 393, 402

labour mobility 399
Lacorne, Denis 387, 389, 391–2, 394, 406–7, 471
Lacroix, J. 472
Laffan, Bridget 170
Länder 44, 111, 215, 223, 242–3, 343
  autonomy 234
  federal issues in elections 246
  fiscal equalization among 239
  hailed as principal safeguard of democracy 248
  horizontal agreements 247
  lawmaking 235–7
  monopoly over implementation 245
  see also Bavaria
Landis, J. L. 258, 270
Landy, Marc 382, 387, 391, 399–400, 401, 459, 462
language(s) 75, 76, 157, 314, 387, 433
  constitutional 379
  differences 399
  minority 427, 434
  multilingual democracies 402
  regional 427
  shared/common 380, 391, 428, 431, 432
  statutory, vague 259
LaPorte, T. R. 309
Laski, Harold 87
Latin America 35
Latinos 432
law(s) 50, 55, 56, 63, 69, 98, 231, 255, 433
  administering 421
  anti-trust 371
  central 242
  coercive 383
  competition 253–4
  constitutional 235, 360
  criminal 91
  discretion in material development of 234
  domestic 168, 218
  enforcement of 208
  environmental 288, 294, 470
  federal 84, 91, 146, 214, 243, 290
  freedom of information 265, 290
  government-in-sunshine 265, 290
  implementation of 242–3
  inconsistencies 75
  international trade 244
  Member State 224
  minimum-wage 360
  national 101, 270, 341

law(s) (*cont.*):
  nationality 410
  regulatory 267
  role in functioning of federal systems 191–212
  State (US) 126–9, 151
  supremacy of 101, 162, 220–4
  supremacy of 162
  unfair regulatory competition 370–1
  welfare 288
  see also case law; Community law; international law; natural law; rule of law
Lazer, D. 122, 123, 124, 125, 455, 493, 503
learning 75
Leca, J. 405
legal arrangements 58
legal systems 157
  viscosity of 224–30
legislatures 248, 338, 339, 341, 342, 422
  traditionally weak 343
legitimacy 93–5, 245, 277, 280–5, 293–4, 343
  allocational 280–99
  basis of 382, 396
  challenge of 2–3
  challenges to 320
  direct 58
  dubious 395
  empirical 56
  enhanced 302, 321, 459, 462
  federal 448
  federal states' fewer lasting problems with 344
  flexibility and 442–6
  input 179, 454, 456, 471
  intergovernmental 339, 340
  locus of 338
  long-term 76
  mechanisms to address concerns 299
  national level problems 344
  national policy-making processes and 348
  networks and 302–3, 305, 309–11, 318, 322, 323, 327
  output 454, 456, 471
  policies detrimental to 351
  popular, lack of 404
  problems of 339, 341, 353
  reduced 302
  regulatory 252–74
  regulatory competition and 355–74
  social 382, 405
  societies can be stable while lacking 384
  sources of 415–19, 449
  sustained 439, 459
Leibowitz, Isaiah 61, 62
liberalism 382, 384, 389, 419–20
liberalization 163, 177, 178, 268, 360, 362, 449
liberty 50, 51, 52, 53, 410
  civil 396, 399
  federal 475
  individual 216, 459
  political 39, 397, 399
  rational 62
  true partisans of 475
  violation of 417
Liebfried, Stefan 186
Lijphart, Arendt 244, 245
Lincoln, Abraham 85, 358, 362, 434
Lisbon Summit (2000) 465–6
litigation 167
lobbying 111
local government(s) 44, 55, 90, 94, 169, 426
  compliance costs 129
  contribution to central government 462
  corrupt and incmpetent 424
  devolution and 414–15
  good 421
  policy coordination and 422
  popular animosity toward 423
  resuscitating 462
  scrutiny of 425
  subsidizing 424
localism 422–4, 462
Lord, C. 313
Low Countries 34
Lowi, Theodore 109, 304
loyalty 69, 94, 326, 391, 405, 471, 473
  multiple 303
  regional 175
Luhmann, N. 264
Luxembourg 164, 369
Luxembourg Compromise (1966) 100, 102, 293, 361

Maastricht Treaty (1992) 38, 58, 104–6, 110, 111, 112, 133, 171, 173, 177, 228, 261, 488
  Social Chapter 351
  subsidiarity provision 277, 407
  see also TEC; TEU
MacCormick, R. Neil 464
McCubbins, M. 308
McNamara, K. R. 312
macroeconomic policy 360
McWilliams, C. 424
Madison, James 76, 155, 221, 319, 441
Maduro, Miguel 63, 465, 469–70, 475
Majone, G. 110, 113, 170, 184, 253, 256, 258, 268, 313, 326, 327, 452, 455, 462, 497
majority rule 364–5
Major, John 106, 343, 351
maladministration 417
Malaysia 377
Markell, Patchen 385–6
market access 167

Marks, G. 301, 325
Marshall, John 84, 429
Marshall Plan (1947) 96
Martens, Wilfrid 37
Marxism 47
Maryland 81
Mason, Andrew 387
Massachusetts 81
Mayer-Schoenberger, V. 455, 493, 503
Mayntz, R. 302, 307
Mazey, S. 314
media 76, 167, 425
  unified 431
MEDIA programme 109
Medicaid 145, 148, 149, 320
medical care 166
Medicare 92
Meehan, Elizabeth 381, 387, 406, 407, 408, 471
MEPs (Members of the European Parliament) 261, 346
Mercosur 48
mergers and acquisitions 103
Meroni doctrine 270
Metlay, D. S. 309
Mexico 377, 432
Michelman, Frank 383
Michigan 148
Migué, J.-L. 298–9
military issues 184
  essential irrelevance of force 176, 177–8
  spending 166
Mill, John Stuart 406, 419
Miller, David 385, 405
Milward, H. B. 305, 310, 460
minorities 154
  federal 400
  linguistic 387, 427
  outvoted 364
  racial and ethnic 168
Miranda rights 148
Mississippi 154
Mitrany, 258
monarchy 35, 44
monetary policy 161, 165, 171, 262
monetary union 360, 460
  see also EMU
money 80–1, 88, 104, 147, 182
  federal 462
  sound 312
  see also EMS; EMU
monitoring 284, 289–91, 292, 296, 469
  policy change 369–70
  unfair regulatory competition 460
Monnet, Jean 96, 97, 98, 99, 312
monopolies 360
Montesquieu, C. L. de Secondat 52, 76, 392, 428
Montjoy, R. S. 308
moral commitment 62
morality 39
  political 385, 386, 393
Moravscik, A. 259, 355, 447, 452, 453, 460, 462
Morris, Gouverneur 83
multiculturalism 66, 167, 365, 378, 431–7, 473
  radical 471
multilateralism 172
multilingual democracies 402
multinationality 410
Mussolini, Benito 417
mutuality 414, 415, 462, 467–71, 473

NAFTA (North Atlantic Free Trade Area) 48, 76, 218, 227, 244
naming and shaming approaches 471
Napoleonic wars 34, 35, 37
nation-states 176, 359, 362, 378, 380
  allegiances to 432
  alternative to 472
  divesting sovereignty from 475
  ethnic groupings 48
  federal 163
  federation of 441
  functions and borders 177
  Habermas' ideal of 391
  strong, prior existence of 179
national democracy 365–7
National Industrial Recovery Act (US, 1933) 258
national interests 325, 362, 435
nationalism 152, 387
nationality 405–7, 408, 410, 411, 472, 473
nationhood 39, 83, 85
NATO (North Atlantic Treaty Organization) 36, 166, 351
natural law 64
naturalization 407
Nazism 35, 162, 248
necessity 200–2
negotiations 338, 363, 448, 463
  characteristics 156
  intergovernmental 324, 361
  trade 164, 171
neo-functionalists 99, 101, 258
Netherlands 34, 45, 97, 100, 349
  successful adjustment 366–7
networks 152, 300–34, 346
  information 291
  multi-state 48
  regulatory, transnational 255, 256, 267, 271
Neuman, Gerald 428, 429
New Deal (US, 1933–39) 80, 86–7, 89, 94, 151, 240, 248, 357, 361, 441
  emphasis on expertise 258, 259, 265

New England 81
New Federalism 89–90, 148
New Jersey 154
New Left 152
New York 81, 220
NGOs (non-governmental organizations) 317, 463
Nice Summit/Treaty (2000) 453, 501, 504
Nicolaidis, D. 468, 469, 474
Nicolaidis, K. 239, 326, 447, 452, 453, 500
Nigeria 46, 377
Nixon, Richard M. 89, 90, 149
Noll, R. G. 308
Nomos 61
non-centralization 45, 50, 465
non-compliance 225, 227, 228
non-discrimination 392, 394
Norman, Wayne 379
normative dissonance 388–9
norms 55, 57, 68, 69, 178, 225, 284
 central 235
 constitutional 56, 59–60
 constraining 288
 cultural 322
 exit from 228
 human rights 409
 informal 304
 legal 218, 437
Northern Ireland 364, 410
not-for-profit entities 322, 323
NPDES (US National Pollutant Discharge Elimination Scheme) 269
NPRMs (US Notices of Proposed Rule Makings) 121
Nugent, N. 315

Oates, Wallace 398
obedience 62, 67, 420
 constitutional 68
observances 61
O'Connor, Sandra Day 214
OEEC (Organization for European Economic Cooperation) 96
officials 68, 69, 345–6
 autonomy 214
OIRA (US Office of Information and Regulatory Affairs) 121, 122, 124
O'Keefe, 408
oligarchies 34, 164
 cantonal 35
Olson, Mancur 78
OMB (Office of Management and Budget (US) 121–3, 124, 129, 131
Omnibus Budget Reconciliation Act (US, 1981) 89
one-person, one-vote election 257
opacity 264
openness 335, 418, 455
opinion polls, *see* polls; public opinion
opportunity costs 246
opposition 59, 179, 316, 366
opt-out provisions/options 105, 453
Osborne, D. 301–2
OSH (Occupational Safety and Health) Act (US, 1970) 269
OSHA (US Occupational Safety and Health Administration) 119
Ostrom, E. 327
Ostrom, V. 319
otherness 67
O'Toole, L. J. 301, 303, 304, 305, 307, 308, 310, 312, 321, 322, 323, 327, 447–8, 450, 455, 466

pacta sunt servanda 226
Pakistan 46
Palfrey, T. R. 152
Pappi, F. U. 304, 307, 317
Pareto-improvement 454
participation 259, 292, 347, 391, 420, 470
 effective 409
 policy-making, widespread 435
particularism 84, 184
partnerships 306
 public-private 302, 317
 social 351
Pasqua, Charles 427–8
Passerini, L. 474
path dependence 179
patriotism 64, 65, 365, 393, 432
 constitutional 76, 382, 391, 392, 472, 473
Paul, St 61, 62
Pennsylvania 81, 83
pensions 166, 168, 184
perfect markets 304
Pescatore, P. 54, 252
Peterson, J. 301, 306, 311, 312, 313, 314, 316, 318, 325, 447–8, 450, 455, 466
PHARE programme 317
Philadelphia 82
Pierson, Paul 186
Pleven, René 97
pluralism 259, 320, 325, 335, 350, 353
 characteristic of 317
 citizen participation 347
 cultural 431
 hyper- 318, 321
 legal 470
 less politicized 346
 quasi- 348
 reasonable 383, 389
 transnational 345
police/policing 148, 168, 171, 370
 judicial 197–8
 national 166
policies 177, 185, 207, 208, 300–34, 398–9

agricultural 112, 171, 173
anti-trust 179
bias in 185–6
budgetary 116
citizens' role in selecting 180
competition 165, 171
consumer 165
core 165
cultural 163, 167
defence 100, 161, 166, 170, 173
development of 106–10
devolution 145
distributive 109, 256
economic development 81
education 167, 170, 387, 458
external trade 244
hermetic 314
immigration 161, 171
implementing 238
infrastructural 167, 170
internal 116
long-term guidelines 37–8
lowest common-denominator 314
market-correcting 361, 362, 460
military 166
monetary 161, 165, 171, 262
national 179
new 170, 173, 174
police/policing 161, 166, 171
positive 167
primary responsibilities for 41
redistributive 109, 256
regulatory 109, 110, 253, 261
setting 37–8, 69
small business 168
statist 39
structural 112
subsidy 172
technical 121
transferred 312
transport 161, 173
variations in 75
welfare 170
workplace 165
see also environmental issues; foreign policy; social policy
political communities 380–402
political order 39, 395
political parties 365
left-of-centre 361, 472
opposition 366
right-wing 152, 180, 388, 436
politics 39, 97, 345, 346, 416
administration and 319
backlash against centralized policies 110–11
clubby 43
defence of 415
devolution 153–5
direct participation, limits on 182–5
federalism and theory 377–80
identity 473
local control over 423
national 338, 437
race 436
reformist imperatives 301–2
regionalization of 326
renationalization of 326
safeguards 193–5
shared 338
small-scale 77
surrogate 259
transnational 164
Pollack, M. 314, 319, 362, 445, 449, 453, 502
polls 94–5, 319, 472–3
pollution 269, 279
poor people 154
populist demagogues 418
populist misunderstandings 366
'pork barrel' benefits 109
Portugal 109, 169, 362
Powell, Jefferson 222
power-sharing 42, 148, 157–8, 244, 289, 291–3, 298
pragmatism 422, 453
prerogatives:
institutional 164, 175
regulatory 291
Pressman, J. 308
princes 34
principal-agent relationship 281–5, 289, 308, 313
Principle of Constitutional Tolerance 65, 66–7, 68, 69
principled bonds 381, 409, 410, 411
private sector 152, 435
privatization 253, 322, 323, 360
problem solving 302, 361–3, 367
Prodi, Romano 413
productive activity 161
profits 359, 360, 364
Progressive Era (US) 319
Progressivism 86
proportionality 175, 287, 446, 449, 456, 457, 459
prosecution 170, 171, 184
protectionism 164
Protestantism 31, 33, 45, 155
Proudhon, P. J. 52
Provan, K. G. 305, 310
provinces 44
provincialism 378
Prussia 35
public interest 258, 259, 325, 326, 359, 456
public opinion 111
public ownership 253

public sector 92, 152
public spending 92
pyramids of power 43, 45

QMV (qualified majority voting) 103, 105, 132, 261, 263
Quebec 57, 68, 387, 392
quotas 260, 397

R&D (research and development) 109, 173, 294, 366
race 380, 389
  common 391
  politics of 436
  segregation 152
racial discrimination 322, 393
racial profiling 148
racism 322, 435
Rapaczynski, A. 240
Rawls, John 378, 383, 384
Reagan, Ronald 80, 89, 90, 92, 121–5 *passim*, 130, 131, 148–52 *passim*, 155, 269
reciprocity 396, 410
red tape 320
redistribution 109, 256, 320, 322, 385, 399
referenda 111, 182, 435
reflection 42, 44, 395
Reformation Europe 384
Reformed Protestantism 31, 33, 45
reforms 370
  constitutional 365, 404, 416
  coordinated 369–70
  decentralizing 342
  institutional 103, 104, 163
  labour market 288, 450
  parliamentary 173
  welfare 144, 320, 450, 454
regional funding 165
regional groupings 47–8
regulations 75, 85, 110, 113–15, 165, 167, 252–74, 361
  agency 290
  considerable responsibilities to implement 162
  cross-cutting 306
  harmonization of 98–9, 111
  highly technical 317
  'how' of 121–5, 130–1, 132–41
  immediately effective 238
  labour 166
  market-correcting 358, 368
  national 164, 368
  productive activity 161
  regulatory competition preventing adoption of 357
  technical 170
  'where' of 125–31, 130–1, 132–41
regulatory agencies 270
Rehnquist, William H. 91
Reich, N. 139, 255
Reinicke, W. H. 327
Reissert, B. 326
religion 167, 168, 384, 389
  bigotry 393
  shared/common 380, 391
religious right 152
Renan, Ernest 381
representation:
  compounded 344
  corporate 235–8, 242–4
  interest 346
  parliamentary 343
  simple notions of 344
  territorial 175–6
representativeness 314, 322, 347
repression 364
republicanism 48
resources 92–3, 208, 269, 326
  authority of territorial state over 358
  budgetary 100
  component states, central government dependence on 238–42
  financial 238
  fiscal 169, 338
  natural 168
  political 338
  scarce, commandeering of 207
retirement benefits 166
reversibility 285, 293–5, 297, 475
Rhine Valley 45
Rhode Island 81
Rhodes, R. A. W. 304, 305, 306
Rhodesia 46
richer countries 369
Rieger, Elmar 185
rights 50, 113, 148, 248, 258, 430
  citizenship 269, 406, 407, 408, 410
  co-decision 361
  co-determination 362
  communication 391
  economic 167, 397, 469
  entrenched 475
  fundamental 437
  legal 405, 406
  mobility 397, 399
  multiple membership 469
  participation 391
  political 167, 178, 405, 406, 420, 469
  procedural 423
  protected 387
  reciprocity of 410
  sovereign 223
  State 443
  violation of 417
  worker 366
  see also civil rights; human rights

Riker, William 281, 322, 366, 377
Rittel, H. W. J. 305
Rivlin, Alice M. 153, 420
Rogers, E. M. 321
Rome, Treaties of (1957 and subsequent) 57, 67, 98–100 *passim*, 103, 167, 170, 177, 253–5 *passim*, 262, 263, 266, 286, 295, 502
  'constitutionalized' 102
  mobility rights 399
  unanimous amendment 173, 179
Roosevelt, Franklin D. 86–7
Roosevelt, Theodore 89
Rosen, Jeffrey 430
Ross, G. 316
Rossiter, C. 418
Rover 370
Ruggie, J. 467
rule-making 260, 262, 265
  control over 269
rule of law 63, 378, 456, 483
rules 61, 97, 121, 122, 193, 245, 253
  background 447
  common 371
  constitutional 423, 445
  decision-making 174, 292
  derogation of 349
  environmental 306
  exceptions to 351–2
  formulated by social partners 350
  free trade 299
  harmonization of 254
  implementation of 347
  industrial-relations 362
  informal 304
  national 157, 268, 423
  'paper' 225
  regional 157
  relational 208
  secrecy 339
Russian Federation 47

Sacks, Jonathan 434
Sale, Kirkpatrick 152
sanctions 358
Sandel, Michael 76
Santer, Jacques 112, 316
scale economies 75, 77, 154, 278, 462
  high 168
Scalia, Antonin 216
scandals 174–5
Scandinavian countries 349, 357, 369
  see also Denmark; Sweden
Schambra, W. A. 441
Scharpf, Fritz 78, 185, 239–40, 246–7, 249, 301, 302, 304, 307, 326, 361–4 *passim*, 366, 367, 369, 460, 471
Schengen Agreement (1985) 173, 261
Schilling, T. 135
Schmidt, S. K. 362
Schmidt, V. A. 367, 450, 452, 460–1
Schmitt, C. 60, 63
Schmitter, Philippe 106, 108
Schnabel, F. 326
Schuman Plan (1950) 96–7
Scotland 45, 410
  Enlightenment 31
Scott, Dred 429, 430
Scott, J. 421
scrutiny 174, 240, 265, 312, 315, 325, 370, 447, 457
  avoidance of 318
  judicial 200, 424
  parliamentary 404
  public 256
SEA (Single European Act, 1992) 38, 58, 103–4, 133, 177, 261, 262, 293, 351
  safeguard clause 295
Seccombe, M. 440, 452
secession 84–5, 364
security 105
  collective 36
Sedition Act (US, 1798) 84
self-aggrandizement 64
self-determination 67, 68, 392, 456
self-interest 349, 385
  conjoined 462
Senate (US) 132, 149, 174, 175, 193, 218, 298, 319
  qualifications for candidates 430
separation of powers 40, 47, 183, 258, 325
  constitutionally-fixed 342
  formally unchanging 338–9
Seydel, Max von 441
Shackleton, Michael 170
Shapiro, M. 265, 266
shared experiences 433
  see also competence; culture(s); decision-making; history; identity; language(s); religion
Sharp, M. 325
Shklar, Judith 378
side-payments 170, 173
Siedentop, L. 474
Single Market 58, 173, 287, 291, 355, 457
  mutual recognition the hallmark of 468
Skocpol, T. 357, 361
Slaughter, A. M. 306, 310, 466
small business 168
small-scale government 76, 77
social contract 357
Social Dialogue 313
social expenditures 369
social-market economies 357
social order 382

social policy 161, 172, 173, 180, 186, 314, 466
ambitious goals 366
arguments over best way to structure and deliver 388
development impeded 357
directives on 407
implementation rates 312
legitimacy-enhancing choices in 366
networks and 313
redistributive 253
Social Protocol 106, 111
Social Security 92
social solidarity 392
socialist dictatorships 358
societal interests 348–9
SOCRATES programme 109
Sonderweg 60
Souter, David H. 214
South Africa 47, 378
South Carolina 82, 84
sovereignty 34, 56, 103, 220, 351, 430
challenge to traditional notions of 467
defence of 99–100
divesting from nation-states 475
dual 429
federal system of 430–1
locus of 39, 90, 484–7
loss of 97
political 400
pooled 318
protecting 63
retained 80
statist approach to 39
subordination to 68
vested in the people 35, 37, 50
violation of 100
see also state sovereignty
Soviet bloc 36
Soviet Union 96, 97, 177
collapse/dissolution of 47, 378
see also Commonwealth of Independent States; Russian Federation
Spain 33, 40, 42, 47, 57, 169, 387
pernicious bureaucratic practices 436
redistribution of funds to 109
specialization 281
spillovers 407, 410, 447
stability 357, 383, 384, 385, 386, 402
constitutional 445
exchange-rate 105
monetary 177
structural 304
threat to 395
stabilization 48, 253
standardization 161, 256, 268, 284, 320
standards 174, 233, 260, 286, 461
anti-trust 425
centralized setting of 287
labour 166
national 268, 291, 322, 362
performance 256
product 398
proportional minimum 367, 368–9
rational-leal 309
regulatory 172, 257
safety and environmental 362
technical 268
Starr-Deelen, D. 154
state sovereignty 86, 205, 463
bolstering 90, 91
debates on 293
identifying 'core' aspects of 208
made untenable 35
protecting the 'core' of 202–3
statism 32–7 *passim*, 40, 43, 348–53 *passim*
emergence of 44
ethnic groupings submerged by 48
expectations 39
federalism and 32, 36, 49, 441
mothers of 39
Stewart, Richard 257, 265
Story, Joseph 429
Strasbourg 164, 178, 307
strategic control 284
Streeck, W. 362
Structural Funds 104, 109, 115, 165, 169, 173, 342, 396
submission 61–2
sub-national authorities 341, 342, 343
subordination 68, 350
subsidiarity 42–4, 111, 155–8 *passim*, 172–3, 196, 198, 200–2 *passim*, 208, 267–71, 407, 442
Catholic Church and 45
efficiency claims relating to 456
global 476–9
horizontal 464–76
implementing 135–7
integration and 95–116
introducing to EU 132–5
proactive 459, 460, 461, 463
procedural 138–41, 450, 457, 458
proportionality and 446, 449
securing 277–99
understanding 462
unpacking 413–15
vertical 464
subsidies 168, 172, 184, 185, 186, 370, 413, 424
subsidies tax 425
superiority 66
supremacy 55, 56, 60, 101, 220–4, 361, 441
Supreme Court (US) 84, 86, 87, 91, 147, 200, 202–7, 230, 234, 292, 377
abortion 152, 153

attempts to curb expansion of federal government 240
commandeering 213, 214, 220, 239
commerce clause 199, 287, 357, 360, 368
Congress and 490
ECJ and 252
jurisdictional limits enforced through review by 289
non-delegation doctrine 258
powers 154–5, 156
recent decisions 277
'relational' aspects of federalism 203–4, 457
sharing of duties fears 231
States' rights 248
Supremacy Clause acceptance 221
women and citizenship 406
Sweden 362, 366, 368
Switzerland 35, 45, 64, 148, 186, 216, 364, 367
federal arrangements 377
fierce national patriotism 365
Helvetic Confederation 34
relative success and stability 402
supremacy 441

Taney, R. B. 429
tariffs 81, 98, 99, 102, 110, 172, 397–8
reductions 260
see also GATT
Tassin, E. 411
taxation/taxes 81–2, 88, 145, 147, 164, 168, 184
business-friendly 359
business profits/incomes 364, 369
concessions 371
direct 248, 409, 435
generous breaks 424
income 368
interest 371
limited 238
mobile factors of production 360
power to impose 239, 241
progressive 154
value-added 169
Taylor, Charles 378, 385, 393, 394
Taylor, Paul 101
TEC (Treaty of the European Community) 133, 139, 199–200, 205
harmonizaton provisions 209
subsidiarity clause 201
technocrats 424
technology 152, 279, 294
telecommunications 152, 313, 360
Teles, Steven 382, 387, 391, 399–400, 401, 459, 462
telos 57
Temporary Assistance for Needy Families (US) 144–5
territorial democracy 39
TEU (Treaty on European Union) 260, 267
Thatcher, Margaret 37, 103, 172, 343, 351
theology 45
Thibaut, Paul 472
third world states 36
Thompson, F. J. 145, 474
Thompson, L. 148
Tiebout, Charles 398
Tocqueville, Alexis de 52, 430–1
tolerance 35, 66–7, 69, 422
civic 67–8
constitutional 467–8, 475–6
mutual 468, 474
toleration doctrine 384
totalitarianism 50, 410
Trachtman, J. 133
trade deficits 179
trades unions 313, 360, 361
trading partners 397, 398
traditions 395
transaction costs 320, 399
transfer of powers 260
'transmission belt' theory 259
transparency 77, 174–5, 264, 321, 455, 470
accountability, expertise and 319
effective way of improving 266
greater, need for 267
insufficient 309, 323
lack of 313, 339
programmes 463
Transport Equity Act (US, 1998) 145
trans-border problems 166
treaties 55, 97, 222, 235
ECJ's role in constitutionalizing 154
intergovernmental 39
negotiation of 338
self-executing 218, 220
see also Amsterdam; Maastricht; Rome; Westphalia
Truman Administration 87
trust 94, 150, 297, 326
mutual 467
reduced 309
social 385
Tsebelis, G. 361
Tullock, Gordon 79
Turkey 158

UMRA (Unfunded Mandates Reform Act (US, 1995) 119, 120, 129 n., 195, 290
UN (United Nations) 36
Security Council 298
unanimity 99, 132, 367–8, 404
unemployment 112, 168, 367
entrepreneurship projects 463
unemployment insurance 166

unfunded mandates 91, 194, 458
  see also UMRA
unification 32, 97, 112
uniformity 157, 347, 397, 398
unilateralism 172, 349
United Europe Movement 96
United Kingdom 42, 47, 82, 104, 111, 132, 169, 354, 369
  challenge to EU 317
  citizenship 388, 406
  devolution 146
  extreme right 180
  judiciary 350
  nationality 406
  opt-out provisions 105
  public benefits 362
  refashioning along federal lines 377
  relationship with US 100
  relative decline 177
  rigidification of public life 352
  simple notions of representation 344
  societal interests 348, 349
  statism 351, 353
  successful adjustment 366–7
  support of subsidiarity 138
  traditionally strong executive 343
  see also Blair; England; Major; Northern Ireland; Scotland; Thatcher
United States 31–53, 100, 102, 243–4
  ad hoc collaborative arrangements 173
  allocational debates 285, 299
  bilateral agreements 172
  bureaucracies 241
  citizenship model 427–37
  commandeering 217, 225, 227
  competences 483
  decentralized functions 168
  decisional structure of bargaining 247
  delegation of powers 262
  Department of Health and Human Services 288
  devolution 119–31, 144–60
  division of policy authority 278
  executive branch 94, 121–31, 194
  federalism 73–95, 117, 129, 155, 197, 216, 232, 356, 377, 378, 440, 441, 468, 486; asymmetric 454; 'marble cake' 108, 148, 320, 448
  fierce national patriotism 365
  general legal authority 238
  House of Representatives 430, 453
  Interstate Commerce Commission 257, 258
  key differences between EU and 109
  legislative branch 119–20, 151, 219
  legitimacy 355, 453
  lessons to EU 413–26
  national identity 406
  networks 152; comparing EU and 306, 307, 324–7; governance and 318–24
  Office of Management and Budget 269, 456
  political justice 394
  Pulitzer prize 425
  radical multiculturalism 471
  regulatory competition 355
  regulatory legitimacy 252
  separation of powers 338–9
  SIPs (State Implementation Plans) 269
  subsidiarity 455
  supremacy 441
  see also Advisory Commission; American Constitution; Congress; New Deal; Senate; Supreme Court
unity:
  federal 37
  independence and 73
  national 84
  political 437
  social 384, 386, 390, 394
  virtues and defects of 79
USSR, *see* Soviet Union

values 63, 64, 77, 151, 195, 311, 360
  assaults on 152
  authoritative allocation of 153
  core 65
  economic 460
  environmental 196
  federalism 196, 197
  normative 61
  social 460
  universal 392, 393, 394
Van Kersbergen, K. 301
Verdun, A. 355
vested interests 147, 148
vetoes 106, 145, 148, 174, 175, 194, 339, 371, 453, 455
  avoidance of 173
  institutionalization of 359
  principled defence of 453–4
Vietnam war (mid-1950s–1975) 47, 92, 94
virtue 62
Volkswagen 370
voluntary agreements 288
voluntary associations/sector 152, 154, 306
voluntary cooperation 421
Vos, Ellen 264
voters' preferences 152
Voting Rights Act (US, 1965) 322

wages 366
  minimum 360
waivers 149, 294
Waldron, Jeremy 382
Walker, D. B. 308

Wallace, H. 315, 317, 318
Wallace, William 101
Walzer, Michael 434
Watergate 94
wealth 369, 460
Weatherill, S. 255
Webber, Jeremy 386
Weber, Max 304, 309, 317, 358, 418
Weber, M. 305
Weber, S. 313
Webster, Daniel 441
Wechsler, Herbert 500–1
Weiler, Joseph 102, 228, 391, 400, 403, 404, 406, 409, 411, 427, 435, 441, 446, 452, 464, 467, 468, 470, 475, 504
Weimar Republic 248
Weingast, B. R. 308
welfare 288, 362
  decentralized 168
  economic 258
  reforms 144, 320, 450, 454
  social 149, 154, 163, 166, 169, 170, 368, 369
welfare states 253, 256, 356, 362, 379
  devolution 461
  differences in structures 368
  Keynesian 252
  legitimization of 460
  retrenchments of 366
  richer/more advanced 369
  Scandinavian 357
well-being 395
West Indies Federation 47
Westphalia, Treaty of (1648) 33
Wheare, K. C. 283
Wiener, A. 408
Wildavsky, A. 300, 308
Williams, Shirley 356
Wilson, Woodrow 84, 319
Winter, G. 259
Winthrop, John 50
women 168, 240
  and citizenship 406
Work Opportunity Act (US, 1996) 144
working groups 346
workplace issues 165, 167
  conditions 366
World Wars:
  First 35
  Second 35, 64, 66, 87, 94
Wright, V. 447, 460
WTO (World Trade Organization) 65, 161, 218–19, 244, 298, 299, 361, 463

xenophobia 435, 436

Young, Ernest 240
Yugoslavia (former) 137, 378

Zionists 432